Neoclassical and

Institutionalist Perspectives

on Economic Behaviour

MICROECONOMICS

Neoclassical and

Institutionalist Perspectives

on Economic Behaviour

MICROECONOMICS

SUSAN HIMMELWEIT

ROBERTO SIMONETTI

ANDREW TRIGG

Australia • Canada • Mexico • Singapore • Spain • United Kingdom • United States

Microeconomics

Copyright © 2001 The Open University

The Thomson logo is a registered trademark used herein under licence.

For more information, contact Thomson, High Holborn House, 50-51 Bedford Row, London, WC1R 4LR or visit us on the World Wide Web at: http://www.thomsonlearning.co.uk

British Library Cataloguing-in-Publication Data
A catalogue record for this book is available from the British Library

ISBN-13: 978-1-86152-539-0

First edition 2001 Thomson Learning
Reprinted 2002, 2005 and 2007 by Thomson Learning

Cover and text designed by Design Deluxe, Bath
Typeset by Saxon Graphics, Derby

Printed in Great Britain by TJI Digital, Padstow, Cornwall

Contents

Firms

Labour

Technology and Finance

 MARKETS

LIST OF CONTRIBUTORS

Jane Wheelock, University of Newcastle

Elizabeth Oughton, University of Durham

John Shorey, Cardiff Business School

Robert McNabb, Cardiff Business School

Keith Whitfield, Cardiff Business School

Andrew Tylecote, Sheffield University

Andrew Trigg, The Open University

Susan Himmelweit, The Open University

Neil Costello, The Open University

Vivienne Brown, The Open University

Maureen Mackintosh, The Open University

Roberto Simonetti, The Open University

Graham Dawson, The Open University

Acknowledgements

Grateful acknowledgement is made to the following sources for permission to reproduce material in this book.

Figures

Figure 1.5: adapted from Hodgson, G.M. (1988) *Economics and Institutions*, Polity Press/Blackwell Publishers, copyright © Geoffrey M. Hodgson, 1988. Also by permission of the University of Pennsylvania Press.

Figure 3.4: reprinted from Rosengren, K.E., 'Substantive theories and formal models - Bourdieu confronted', *European Journal of Communication*, **10**, pp. 7-39, (1995) by permission of Sage Publications Ltd.

Figure 5.1: UNDP (1995) *Human Development Report 1995*, Oxford University Press, Inc., copyright © 1995, by the United Nations Development Programme. Reprinted by permission of Oxford University Press, Inc.

Figures 6.1 and 6.2: Miller, B.D. (1981) *The Endangered Sex*, Cornell University Press. Reprinted by Oxford University Press, India and reproduced with their permission.

Figure 7.1: adapted from United Nations (1992) *World Population Monitoring 1991*, United Nations Publications.

Figure 7.3: adapted from Bettio, F. and Villa, P. (1980) 'A Mediterranean perspective on the breakdown of the relationship between participation and fertility', *Cambridge Journal of Economics*, vol.22, by permission of Oxford University Press.

Figure 12.19: Jackman, R., Layard, R. and Pissarides, C. (1989) 'On vacancies', *Oxford Bulletin of Economics and Statistics*, **51** (4), Blackwell Publishers Ltd.

Figure 12.21: Morgan, J. (1996) 'What do comparisons of the last two economic recoveries tell us about the UK labour market?', *National Institute Economic Review*, **2/96** (156), May 1996 © 1996 National Institute of Economic and Social Research.

Figure 13.4: adapted from Vietorisz, T. and Harrison, B. (1973) 'Labor market segmentation: Positive feedback and divergent development', *American Economic Review*, **63** (2), May 1973, American Economic Association.

Figure 14.2: adapted from Drago, R. and Perlman, R. (1989) *Microeconomic Issues in Labour Economics: New Approaches*, Harvester Wheatsheaf.

Figure 15.12: Schmookler, J. (1966) *Invention and Economic Growth*, Harvard University Press, copyright © 1966 The President and Fellows of Harvard College. All rights reserved.

Tables

Table 2.1: Sippel, R. (1997) 'An experiment on the pure theory of consumers' behaviour', *Economic Journal*, September 1997, Royal Economic Society, Blackwell Publishers.

Table 3.1: 'The luxury goods trade: upmarket philosophy' © *The Economist*, London, 26 December 1992.

Table 4.1: Fry, V. and Pashardes, P. (1986) *The Retail Prices Index and the Cost of Living*, The Institute for Fiscal Studies.

Table 12.1: adapted from Nickell, S. (1996) 'Can unemployment in the UK be reduced?' in Halpern, D., Woods, S., White, S. and Cameron, G. (eds) *Options for Britain: A Strategic Policy Review*, Dartmouth Publishing Company Ltd.

Table 17.1: adapted from Corbett, J. and Mayer, C. (1991) 'Financial reform in Eastern Europe: progress with the wrong model', *Oxford Review of Economic Policy*, **7** (4), by permission of Oxford University Press.

Table 17.2: Berglöf, E. (1988) *Ägarna Och Kontrollen Över Foretaget - En Järnförande Studie Av Finansiella System*, Statens Offentliga Utredningar.

Text

P.48: 'Me and my trolley ... with Paul Bradley' *The People*, 16 June 1996, Mirror Syndication International.

Pp.63-5 : McKendrick, N., Brewer, J. and Plumb, J.H. (1982) *The Commercialization of Eighteenth Century England*, Europa Publications Limited, © McKendrick, N., Brewer, J. and Plumb, J.H., 1982.

Pp. 67-8: 'The luxury goods trade: upmarket philosophy' © *The Economist*, London, 26 December 1992.

P.206: Owen G. (1996) 'Survey – Britain: Transformation in the past 20 years', *Financial Times*, 12 June 1996.

P.382: 'New work order' © *The Economist*, 9 April 1994.

P.504: 'The London Gold Fixing' reproduced by courtesy of N.M. Rothschild & Sons Ltd., London.

Photograph

P.75: Russell Lee, *Hands of Old Homesteader, Iowa* (1936); gelatin-silver print (16.5x24.44cm), The Museum of Modern Art, New York, gift of the Farm Security Administration, © 1996, The Museum of Modern Art, New York, reproduced in Bourdieu, 1979, p.45.

PREFACE TO MICROECONOMICS

This book should be seen as an accessible introduction to intermediate microeconomics. It can be used for both second and third year microeconomics courses, and may also be relevant for joint honours students – for example, in business studies, sociology and social policy – who do not specialise in economics but would like to learn about its fundamentals in an interesting and evaluative way.

The material in *Microeconomics* is drawn from an Open University course, D319 *Understanding Economic Behaviour*, that assumes a basic knowledge of economics such as that provided in a first year introductory economics course. In particular, it follows on from the Open University's introductory economics course, *D216 Economics and Changing Economies*. The text of the D216 course is also available from Thomson Learning as *Economics and Changing Economies* by Mackintosh *et al.*, 1996 (ISBN 0 412 62846 6). Throughout *Microeconomics* the links back to Mackintosh *et al.* are shown as (*Changing Economies*, Chapter number).

We have a number of grateful acknowledgements to make for the help, both official and unofficial, that we received for the writing of this book. First we have received a wealth of incisive comments from our external assessors Paul Auerbach, Ben Fine, Ben Knight and Nancy Folbre, who each commented on many drafts of several chapters of the book. Shaun Hargreaves-Heap, the overall assessor for the project, was also extremely helpful with structural as well as detailed suggestions. Invaluable advice was also provided by John Clarke, Paul Du Gay, Peter Hamilton, Chris Jones, J.S. Metcalfe, Simon Mohun, Ram Mudambi, Bruce Philip, Janette Rutterford, John Sutton, Jeremy Smith, Mike Waterson and Marc Wuyts. Great credit is due to everyone at Thomson Learning for their superb production and design of the book, with particular thanks to Fiona Freel and Maggie Smith. And finally, we would like to thank all the production and teaching staff at the Open University, including Giles Clark for arranging the contract; Avis Lexton, for excellent secretarial support; and our editor Penny Bennett, whose patience and support has been invaluable. The academic editors are responsible for any remaining errors.

INTRODUCTION: NEOCLASSICAL AND INSTITUTIONALIST PERSPECTIVES

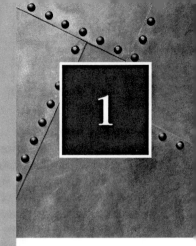

Susan Himmelweit, Roberto Simonetti and Andrew Trigg

1 INTRODUCTION

The standard argument for a market-based economy is that it generates the means of material well-being much more abundantly and reliably than any alternative economic system. In the broad sweep of history, the market-based economies of industrial capitalism have experienced a higher level of material well-being than has been achieved by any alternative economic system. This view of the benefits of a market economy contributed to the collapse of the Soviet bloc in the 1980s, the consequent wholesale privatization of state-owned assets and the adoption of market capitalism by countries in Eastern Europe. In Western economies, market forces have been encouraged to develop in areas where they were previously given less scope; a decline in trade union power has been managed as part of a move to more 'flexible' labour markets, and additional market pressures have been introduced in the provision of government services.

Since the 1990s, however, political debate has also centred on the limits to the market. In Eastern Europe the early optimism about the benefits of unregulated markets has been tempered by the need to examine closely the institutional structures which may best generate growth and prosperity. It has been argued that, despite problems of recent stagnation, Japan and Germany have demonstrated the benefits of government intervention in the market, by successfully co-ordinating relationships between financial institutions and companies; an argument that Eastern European countries have begun to examine in relation to their own institutional relationships. In Western economies, deep unease has been expressed about the inequalities and inefficiencies of market-based capitalism, as evidenced in the UK by the contrast between the huge remuneration packages given to the 'fat cats' running the privatized utilities and the shockingly large number of children living in poverty.

In economics the dominant framework for exploring the structure of market economies is provided by the neoclassical school of thought. Its theories are usually, but not always, used to demonstrate the benefits of markets. These theories show that under certain assumptions, markets provide an efficient allocation of scarce resources in response to the demands of insatiable consumers. One of the aims of this book is to explain how neoclassical theory models the way in which markets work, both particular markets and the market economy as a whole.

Underpinning this neoclassical analysis will be an examination of the key decision-making units of a market economy: households and firms. Households are the final purchasers of the economy's products and suppliers of the resources, including labour, used in production. Firms, on the other hand, are suppliers of goods and services and purchasers of labour services. In analysing these demand and supply activities this book will provide an introduction to the *micro* economics of markets, that is, the behaviour of individual units of economic activity.

The starting point for neoclassical theory is the assumption that these individual units, in circumstances not entirely of their own choosing, independently make rational decisions in their own self-interest. 'Rational' here means choosing the best means to pursue whatever goal a decision-maker has in mind. Households make rational choices of what labour services to sell and which consumer goods to buy to best satisfy their preferences in pursuit of utility maximization; whereas firms pursue profit maximization by choosing what to produce and what inputs to use to do so in the most cost effective way. The results of these choices independently made by individual units throughout the economy are then aggregated by the market to determine what happens in the economy as a whole. Such a method of inquiry that uses independent individuals as its starting point, is known as 'methodological individualism'. It is currently the orthodox approach to microeconomic research and teaching.

However, individuals do *not* behave as independent entities in the economy. Individuals make economic decisions in the context of a variety of institutional structures. The behaviour of other consumers and the marketing strategies of firms influence the consumption decisions of households. As employees, the decisions that individuals make about how much time and energy to invest in education and training are influenced by the traditions and habits of the families and communities in which they live. And individual firms are influenced by the behaviour of other firms both in the working practices they adopt and in their production decisions. Neoclassical economics models only one sort of influence by economic agents on each other, the influence that goes through the market by demand and supply affecting the prices at which individuals can trade. However, there is a wealth of evidence to suggest that many other types of interactions between individuals are prevalent in a market economy. A neoclassical economist does not necessarily deny that this is the case, but considers that methodologically it is preferable to build up a picture of the economy by starting with the behaviour of individuals.

Those economists that are critical of the methodological individualism of neoclassical economics are often asked what is the alternative? In this book the seeds of an alternative are presented by introducing the institutionalist perspective. In this approach social interactions between individuals are placed at the heart of economic theory. Drawing on disciplines outside economics, such as sociology, psychology and politics, the institutionalist perspective explicitly examines the *social* construction of behaviour. The behaviour of consumers, for example, is formed in part by consumption norms that arise out of social interactions between consumers and between consumers and firms. The decisions of workers about how much labour to supply depend, among other factors, on their particular relationships with other members of the household, and thus the labour supply of the economy as a whole depends on the institutional structure of households. Relationships with and between firms are also formed by the norms and other institutional practices that are prevalent in particular markets.

The narrative of this book is structured around developing the core concepts and techniques you need to understand neoclassical economics. In this regard, we follow the same basic structure of any standard microeconomics textbook, though we present neoclassical theory as just one particular approach and discuss alternative theories too.

The book's development of neoclassical economics starts with the derivation of the output demand curve in Chapter 2 of the Consumption block, followed by the labour supply curve in Chapter 5 of the Households block. In Chapter 10, in the Firms block, the output supply curve is considered and in Chapter 12, in the Labour block, the demand curve for labour. These demand and supply curves are put together into the neoclassical general equilibrium framework in Chapter 18 of the Markets block.

Among this material, economic issues are considered from a variety of other perspectives. So, although each block plays a part in building up the neoclassical model, a wide range of other issues are also considered. These include the meaning and measurement of economic well-being, the changing gender division of labour within households, issues relating to monopoly power and market structure, how to explain increasing female participation rates in paid employment, and discrimination in labour markets. There is also a whole block devoted to Technology and Finance, which examines how technological change arises and the impact on it of different types of financial systems and capital markets.

In applying neoclassical techniques to a wide variety of problems, we demonstrate their analytical power and tractability. What makes our approach distinctive, however, is the explicit treatment of the limitations of neoclassical techniques. In this book, neoclassical economics is viewed as one particular school of thought that can be compared with other, perhaps less developed, economic paradigms. The institutionalist approach is one particular alternative paradigm that is considered. However, our aim above all is to help you learn to think critically about economics as a discipline in which there are competing perspectives, rather than a single 'right' approach to solving economic problems. In using this material to teach our own students at the Open University, we encourage them to discuss and evaluate both neoclassical and institutionalist perspectives. Our aim is to help them and you form your own opinions as to which paradigm sheds most light on particular economic issues.

In developing the institutionalist approach we have also designed this textbook for a particular type of student. Since institutionalism is an interdisciplinary approach to economics we hope that this book will be accessible and particularly congenial to students who are not specialists in economics. It is, therefore, partly aimed at students studying business studies, sociology and social policy, for example, who would like to learn the basics of economics in an interdisciplinary context. We hope that the material in the book will also help to enrich the critical understanding of microeconomics for single honours economics students and the economics profession as a whole. We hope that this new and radical approach to the teaching of microeconomics may have some small impact on the way in which economics is taught more generally, so that students can appreciate it as a subject full of lively debate rather than there being a single 'correct' approach.

As a foundation for the six blocks of material covered in the book, the rest of this introductory chapter provides an overview of the main assumptions and differences between the neoclassical and institutionalist perspectives. Section 2 introduces the neoclassical theory of competitive general equilibrium, which specifies the conditions under which an economy composed entirely of competitive markets would be in equilibrium. Section 3 introduces some of the main principles of institutionalist economics. As we have seen, the neoclassical tradition sees individual economic agents as the fundamental building blocks of the economy, in the sense that economic processes and structures can be explained only in terms of the behaviour of individuals. The institutionalist perspective reverses this order of understanding, starting with institutions and then analysing individual behaviour within this broader context. For institutionalists, the behaviour of individuals cannot be understood without analysing the framework of institutions, norms, traditions and customs within which economic agents act. In Section 4 a brief overview is provided of the main assumptions that underlie both the institutionalist and neoclassical perspectives, assumptions that will be critically examined throughout the book.

<h2>2 NEOCLASSICAL ECONOMICS</h2>

2.1 Introduction

Neoclassical economics is a potentially confusing term. One problem is that it is named with respect to something else: 'neo' literally means 'new'. It suggests that neoclassical economics is to be differentiated from the earlier 'classical' approach while also being similar to it in some respects. The main classical economists were Adam Smith (1723-90), David Ricardo (1772-1823) and John Stuart Mill (1806-73). Some would also include Karl Marx (1818-83), although his revolutionary stance differentiates him somewhat from the others. The economists whose work later came to be seen as the first concise statements of neoclassical economics were Léon Walras (1834-1910) and William Stanley Jevons (1835-82), although Vilfredo Pareto (1848-1923) was also an important contributor. These neoclassical economists built on the work of the classical

economists, but they focused on one particular aspect of classical economics: the workings of the price mechanism in a competitive market system. Other aspects of classical economics, such as the connection between economic growth and the distribution of income between classes, are downplayed by neoclassical economists, in favour of models based on the behaviour of individuals.

Another problem is that the boundaries of neoclassical economics are unclear. On a broad interpretation, neoclassical economics represents the mainstream and predominant approach within economics, which takes the individual as its basic unit of analysis and makes certain fundamental assumptions about how individuals behave. In Section 2.2 we shall look at this broad interpretation of neoclassical economics. On a narrower interpretation, however, neoclassical economics comprises a particular model of a competitive economy first formulated by Léon Walras (Walras, 1874). Sections 2.3 to 2.5 concentrate on this particular model of competitive general equilibrium, outlining its key assumptions and examining the way in which it provides the basis for the neoclassical view of the market as the most efficient way to allocate resources.

2.2 The price system as an allocative mechanism

Neoclassical theory focuses on the way markets react to the 'general scarcity' of all resources relative to human desires. Each individual in the economy has a particular set of desires, wants or needs for goods and services. These include the desire for food, clothing, transport, holidays, health care – a vast array of potential items of consumption. The economic problem for the neoclassical economist is that the resources available for providing these items of consumption are limited. The economy is characterized by *scarcity*.

Scarcity

Where time and other resources are limited and not sufficient to meet desired ends.

Scarcity involves an imbalance between two features of the world. On the one hand there are limited resources: these include human time, effort and ingenuity, as well as the earth's physical resources. On the other hand, there are desires for items of consumption arising both from the need to be properly fed, clothed and housed, and from all those aspirations for human flourishing that require resources in order to be satisfied. By assuming scarcity as a fundamental human condition, neoclassical theory presupposes that there is an inevitable imbalance between limited resources and the extent of human desires.

The neoclassical postulate of scarcity implies the centrality of a certain kind of choice for all economic agents: choices have to be made between competing ends which require alternative uses of scarce resources, and between alternative ways of achieving those ends. An influential statement of this position by Lionel Robbins put it like this:

> *'But when time and the means for achieving ends are limited* and *capable of alternative application,* and *the ends are capable of being distinguished in order of importance, then behaviour necessarily assumes the form of choice. Every act which involves time and scarce means for the achievement of one end involves the relinquishment of their use for the achievement of another. It has an economic aspect.*
>
> *Economics is the science which studies human behaviour as a relationship between ends and scarce means which have alternative uses.'*

(ROBBINS, 1935, PP.14 AND 16; ORIGINAL EMPHASIS)

Note again that there are two aspects to this explanation of scarcity. First, the means for achieving ends are both limited and capable of alternative application; resources (including time) are limited and can be used in alternative ways. Second, there are various ends and not all of them can be achieved. In order that a choice can be made, Robbins assumes that the ends can be ranked according to their importance. This implies that people have stable preferences by which alternative economic outcomes can be ranked.

Scarcity, according to neoclassical theory, is the central economic problem and so there has to be some mechanism for allocating goods and services between agents in the economy. One mechanism is that a superior authority could decide by edict who should have what and who should perform the tasks that need to be done to produce the chosen goods. Such a system may be feasible if the society is small and relatively simple, and if economic authority is uncontested. Another method of allocating goods and services might be by reference to tradition and custom. This method of allocation may be possible in systems that are relatively static. Another method may be by forms of consensual or democratic decision making where members of the society can agree on objectives and priorities for the allocation of goods and services. A neoclassical economist would argue that it is hard to conceive of such a system working across large and complex societies.

Even in large and complex societies, however, these methods of allocation are still to be found in certain areas. Health and education services may be allocated by the state or by charities. A mixture of custom, state regulations and consensual norms influence, for example, the conventions regarding the appropriate age for schooling or the availability of health services such as immunization for at-risk groups, which vary from country to country. Similar methods of decision making may also predominate within many organizations, such as firms and households, where custom and practice, democratic decision making and obeying the authority of the boss or head of household are all prevalent methods of allocation (these are discussed in Chapters 6, 8 and 14).

In societies characterized by the private ownership of goods and labour services, however, the overriding method of allocation between owners is the price mechanism of the market. Goods, services and resources flow around the economy by means of an intricate web of market transactions entered into by economic agents. All agents make choices as to what to buy and sell, subject to constraints determined by market prices. Households make choices according to their preferences, subject to the budget constraint provided by the income they can receive from the labour services and other resources that they have to sell, and the prices of the consumer goods and services they wish to buy. Firms choose whatever combination of inputs and outputs is most profitable using available technology, subject to the constraints provided by the prices at which inputs can be bought and outputs sold.

It is through this web of constrained choices that the price mechanism works as a means of allocating scarce resources. The price mechanism exists because choices have to be made and these choices are necessary because of general scarcity. Figure 1.1 summarizes this relationship between scarcity and the price mechanism in a market economy.

2.3 The competitive general equilibrium model

The previous section showed how individual choice as to what to buy and sell is central to the neoclassical view of the price mechanism. There are two main types of individual unit in the neoclassical model of an economy: households and firms.

How do these individual units make their choices? For households, the basic psychological assumption of neoclassical theory is that they, and/or the people in them, are self-interested and *rational*. (Chapter 6, explores the difference it makes whether households or people are taken as the decision-making agents and what effect the assumption of self-interest has.) Households choose between different courses of action according to a set of preferences. They also have a set of resources that they own and could sell;

these are known as their 'initial endowments'. Like a calculating machine, households rank available options according to their preferences, and so decide what goods and services to buy and which of their resources to supply to the market. In making those choices, households have to take account of the prices at which such transactions can be carried out.

Rationality

Where individual economic agents are assumed to have given goals which they pursue in the most efficient way possible.

Firms are rather similar. They do not need preferences because they are assumed only to be interested in profits. So firms choose from the available technological possibilities how to transform inputs (i.e. the resources they can purchase) into outputs (i.e. the goods and services they produce for sale) on the basis of profitability. Again they operate like calculating machines, ranking different production possibilities by

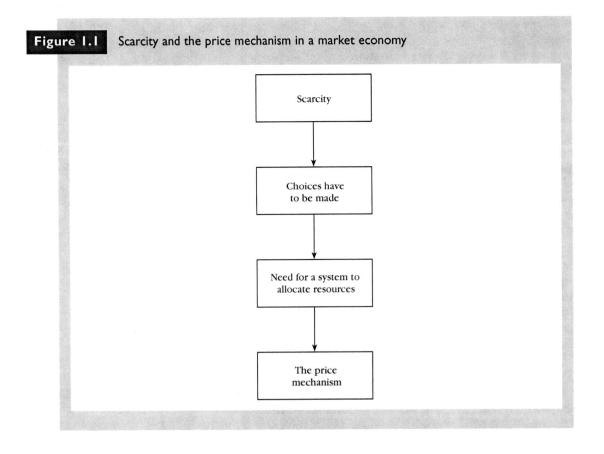

Figure 1.1　Scarcity and the price mechanism in a market economy

their profitability and choosing whatever feasible combination of inputs and outputs is the most profitable. In making this choice, firms have to take account of the prices at which they can purchase their inputs and sell their outputs. (Chapter 8 examines alternative objectives pursued by firms; Chapter 14 examines conflicts of interest between people within firms.)

The basic insight of the general equilibrium model is that putting together all the choices made by households and firms will work only when all markets are in *equilibrium* simultaneously. If this occurs the choices made by all these economic agents are consistent with each other. In equilibrium every individual agent's plans are realized and so no one needs to change their plans.

Equilibrium

In equilibrium the choices made by all agents are consistent with each other, so that everyone's plans can be carried out and there is no need for anyone to change their plans.

Let us examine what has been said here in a bit more detail. First you may need reminding about how the concept of equilibrium applies to a market. A *market equilibrium* occurs when the amount demanded in that market is equal to the amount supplied. It is then that suppliers can sell exactly the amount they planned to sell, and purchasers can buy just the amount they planned to buy. Since both demand and supply depend on price, a market will be in equilibrium only at some prices, usually assumed to be just one.

Market equilibrium

A market is in equilibrium when demand equals supply, so that all agents can sell or buy exactly what they had planned.

Equilibrium in a competitive market for one particular good can be represented using a demand and supply diagram. Figure 1.2 represents the market for a consumer good; the demand curve represents the decisions of households as to how much to purchase at each price, whilst the supply curve represents the supply plans of firms. The conventional assumption has been made in this case that as price falls the quantity demanded by households increases; that is why the demand curve is drawn downward sloping. Similarly, the supply curve has been drawn upward sloping on the assumption of profit maximization, so that as price rises firms are willing to supply more of the good.

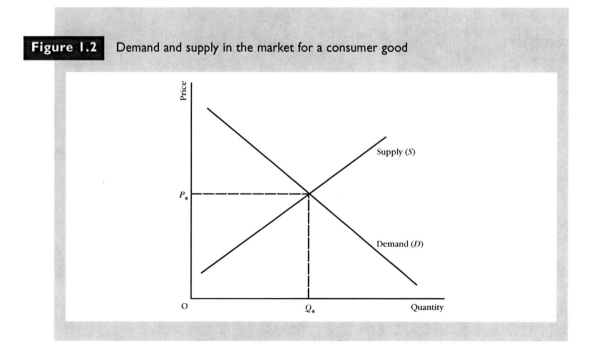

Figure 1.2   Demand and supply in the market for a consumer good

The equilibrium is where the two curves intersect. At the equilibrium price P_* firms want to supply, and households want to buy, the equilibrium quantity Q_* of the good. A market is *competitive* if all firms and households are price takers; that is, agents are not able to influence the price at which they can buy or sell the good.

Competitive market

A market is competitive if agents are price takers, that is, they cannot influence prices.

But our focus here is not on single markets which is the concern of *partial equilibrium analysis*. Here we are concerned with *general equilibrium analysis*, which examines how prices are determined simultaneously in all markets. What happens in one market can affect every other market. To see this, consider what happens if the price of one good rises, say because of production problems. Because of the price rise, households will adjust their purchase plans for that good. In doing so, they will change other aspects of their plans too, deciding either to buy something else instead, thus increasing their demand in some other market(s), or that they need a different amount of income and to adjust their labour supply, for example. In this way, what happens in one market

can have an impact on all others. General equilibrium analysis focuses on all markets simultaneously.

Partial equilibrium analysis

Partial equilibrium analysis studies the conditions for equilibrium in a single market.

General equilibrium analysis

General equilibrium analysis studies the conditions for equilibrium in all markets simultaneously.

Consider, for example, the effect of discovering a new way of making steel. This cuts the cost of steel production thus shifting the supply curve for steel to the right. Figure 1.3 shows that the effect of a shift in the supply curve of steel from S_1 to S_2 is to lower the equilibrium price of steel from P_1 to P_2 and to increase the equilibrium quantity produced and sold from Q_1 to Q_2. But this in turn affects other markets, such as the markets for cars, cutlery and gardening tools. If steel can be bought for less, then all these products can be produced more cheaply and all their supply curves will move to the right, making their equilibrium prices lower too. This in turn may leave consumers with more money to spend on other things, so the demand curves for cardigans, crockery

Figure 1.3   The effect of an increase in the supply of steel

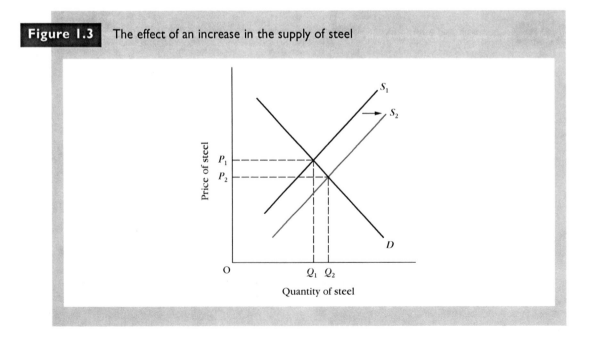

and daffodil bulbs may shift, changing the equilibrium prices in these markets too. Now these price changes may affect other markets, causing further adjustments to take place; for example, the change in the price of crockery may affect the demand for cutlery. Further, these changes may react back on the market in which the original change took place.

General equilibrium analysis recognizes that every market may have an effect on every other one, and thus that all equilibrium prices have to be determined simultaneously.

Exercise 1.1

Draw a supply and demand diagram to illustrate the effects of a fall in the price of steel on the market for cars. What are the possible repercussions in a general equilibrium setting?

In working through these repercussions, we tend to think of them happening as a sequence of events in the same way, for example, as a stone thrown into a pond causes a ripple of waves which follow each other. It seems natural for us to think about equilibrium adjustment in this sequential way, but the competitive equilibrium model looks at only the two general equilibrium outcomes, before and after the price change, where at each time, all prices have settled into equilibrium simultaneously. This implies that competitive equilibrium theory takes the form of *comparative static analysis* where one simultaneous equilibrium in all markets is compared with another simultaneous equilibrium outcome. This takes account of all the mutual interdependencies between markets, but does not analyse them in terms of a sequential series of adjustments.

Comparative static analysis

Comparative static analysis compares two equilibrium outcomes.

When there is a change in demand or supply, this happens because there has been a change in one of the variables that was held constant when the demand and supply curves were drawn. In any model, variables which are held constant in this way are referred to as the *exogenous variables* of the model in that they are determined outside the model

and so are taken as given for the purposes of the model. If there are changes in the exogenous variables they come from the outside the model, as we have seen in the example of the discovery of a new way of making steel. When there is a change in an exogenous variable, this results in changes in those variables which are determined within the model; these variables are known as the *endogenous variables*. In the competitive equilibrium model, the endogenous variables are the equilibrium prices. We have seen how equilibrium prices are determined by demand and supply, and how these prices change if there is a change in any of the factors that are held constant, that is, in any of the exogenous variables. Although equilibrium prices are determined within the model, remember that they are taken as given by each individual agent.

An exogenous variable

A variable whose value is determined outside the model and so is taken as given for the purposes of the model.

An endogenous variable

A variable whose value is determined within the model.

What are the exogenous variables in the competitive general equilibrium model? We have met some already. We have seen that a change in technology (a new way of making a product) will affect equilibrium outcomes by changing the conditions of supply. Technology is therefore an exogenous variable in the model. However, the competitive general equilibrium model does not explain how different technological possibilities arise. We have seen that consumers have preferences and that it is in accordance with these preferences that they make their purchase plans. If those preferences change, then there will be a corresponding change in demand. However, the model does not explain where consumer preferences come from. Preferences are therefore also an exogenous variable in the model. Finally, households have a set of resources – sometimes called their initial endowment of resources – that they own and can sell to firms. These initial endowments include labour services and also all the other inputs available for production. If there is a change in the initial endowment of resources, there will be a change both in the demand for consumer goods and in the supply of inputs to firms. However, the distribution of these endowments across households is taken as given for the purposes of the model in that it is determined by factors lying outside the model. The initial endowment of resources is therefore the third exogenous variable. In summary, the exogenous variables of the competitive equilibrium model are:

● preferences
● technology
● initial endowment of resources.

Figure 1.4 shows how the overall structure of equilibrium prices is determined by demand and supply, which are themselves the result of the particular set of preferences, initial endowments and technology which characterize the system at any point in time.

Since equilibrium prices are determined by demand and supply, which are in turn determined by the exogenous variables of preferences, resources and technology, the equilibrium set of prices will change only if there is a change in one or more of those exogenous variables.

Question

Can you think of examples of changes in each of the three types of exogenous variables that would change the equilibrium prices of a competitive general equilibrium model?

A change in tastes, a catastrophe that wipes out some resources, or a new invention that expands technological possibilities, will shift demand and supply and result in changes in the equilibrium price not only of one good but of many or even all goods simultaneously. It is this simultaneous adjustment of prices that gives the competitive general equilibrium model its flexibility and power, despite the very particular assumptions on which it is built.

Exercise 1.2

Which is the crucial assumption for an equilibrium to be competitive?

The competitive general equilibrium model is a model of a decentralized market system, without any overall plan or sense of direction, in which individual agents make their own choices and pursue their own

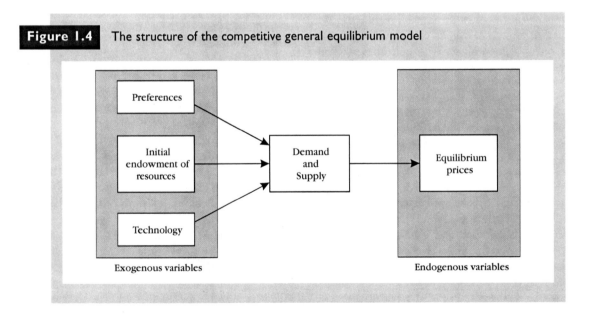

Figure 1.4   The structure of the competitive general equilibrium model

Exogenous variables   Endogenous variables plans in different markets. How is it that such a system can produce a co-ordinated outcome?

We have seen that an equilibrium occurs where agents' plans are consistent with each others'; in a market setting this means that demand equals supply in all markets simultaneously. If agents' plans are not consistent, some agents are not able to implement their plans. For example, if the demand for organic milk is greater than the supply then some consumers are unable to implement their planned purchase of organic milk. Conversely, if supply is greater than demand then suppliers are not able to sell all their output at the prevailing price. Both demand and supply depend on prices. The task for competitive general equilibrium theory, therefore, is to establish whether there is a set of prices that will secure equilibrium, that is, make demand equal to supply, in every market.

If there is such a set of equilibrium prices then a general equilibrium does exist and all agents' plans are mutually consistent. In this case, the system is in a state of balance, as there is no reason for any agent to revise those plans, unless there is an exogenous shock to the system. Here a decentralized system of markets results in an overall equilibrium that is not the intention or plan of any individual agent, but one in which all agents' plans are reconciled. If, however, there is no set of prices that can equilibrate demand and supply in all markets simultaneously, then equilibrium does not exist and agents' plans cannot be reconciled at any set of prices. If such a decentralized general equilibrium exists, it shows that orderly social outcomes do not have to be planned centrally but can be produced as the unintended consequences of individual agents pursuing their own goals.

The appeal of this notion of equilibrium has been enormously powerful within economics. Frank Hahn, a contributor to competitive general equilibrium theory, put it like this:

> '... the notion that a social system moved by independent actions in pursuit of different values is consistent with a final coherent state of balance and one in which the outcomes may be quite different from that intended by the agents is surely the most important intellectual contribution that economic thought has made to the general understanding of social processes.'
>
> (HAHN, 1973, P.33)

Hahn traces the theoretical interest in the decentralized decision making of self-interested individuals to the work of the eighteenth century Scottish philosopher, Adam Smith, who argued that when a person 'intends only his own gain ... [he is] led by an invisible hand to promote an end which was no part of his intention' (Smith, 1776; 1976 edn, p.456). Smith's metaphor of the invisible hand refers to the process by which unintended beneficial consequences for society are the outcome of the decisions of individual economic agents who are simply attending to their own specific interests. The invisible hand ensures that the self-interested actions of individuals serve the public interest better than anything ostensibly designed to do so. The extent to which Adam Smith's economics can be captured by modern neoclassical economics is open to question as his arguments were the product of the concerns of an earlier period (see Brown, 1994). Nevertheless, neoclassical economics regards Adam Smith's *The Wealth of Nations* as a founding statement of the benefits of free market solutions to economic problems.

2.4 Competitive equilibrium analysis and efficiency

Smith's passage on the invisible hand refers to the idea that the public interest is best served by people pursuing their own private interest. This raises the question of the desirable properties of the equilibrium in a competitive general equilibrium model. Overall consistency, by which no person is frustrated in carrying out planned actions, may itself be considered a beneficial property of an equilibrium. However, neoclassical theory considers a competitive general equilibrium to have a second beneficial property: that the allocation of goods and services is efficient.

An economic outcome is regarded as efficient if no single agent can be made better off, in that agent's estimation, without making someone else worse off, in their own estimation. This definition was proposed by Vilfredo Pareto and is now known as *Pareto efficiency*. So, an existing economic allocation is regarded as Pareto efficient when any further improvement for some would have to be at the cost of a deterioration for others. This definition of efficiency has been widely adopted because it involves neither making judgements about an individual's real interests, nor assessing whether benefits to one individual might outweigh losses to another.

Pareto efficiency

An outcome is Pareto efficient if it is not possible to improve the position of any agent (in that agent's own estimation) without at the same time worsening the position of any other agents (in their own estimation).

There is a very close relation between the neoclassical competitive general equilibrium model and Pareto efficiency. Intuitively this can be understood in terms of *opportunity cost*. (Chapter 18 presents a more detailed argument to show this result.) Whenever there is a choice to be made between goods, we can measure the opportunity cost of any one good in terms of the best alternative which has to be foregone (see also *Changing Economies,* Chapters 11 and 13). The notion of opportunity cost involves the idea of trading off one thing against another. For example, a firm may have the choice between using its resource to produce two types of products, racing cars and family saloons, say. The opportunity cost of producing each racing car is not being able to produce a certain number of family saloons instead.

Opportunity cost

The opportunity cost of an economic good or action is measured in terms of the best alternative foregone.

Similarly, consumers will have opportunity costs reflecting the relative prices of the two types of cars. The relative price of two goods is the ratio of their prices. It says how much of the second good could be bought or sold for one unit of the first good. The opportunity cost for a consumer of buying a racing car is the number of family saloons she would have to forego to purchase the racing car. It is equal to the relative price of the racing car to the family saloon.

Relative price

The relative price of one good to another is the amount of the second good that could be bought or sold for one unit of the first good. It is equal to the ratio of the price of the first good to that of the second good.

Finally, consumers make their choices on the basis of their relative preferences. The relative preference of a consumer for one good relative to another is the amount of the second good the consumer would be willing to give up for one unit of the first good.

Consumers and producers are connected in a market economy by the fact that they all face the same relative prices. Both consumers and producers decide what to do on the basis of relative prices that convey the opportunity costs facing producers and the relative preferences of consumers. In a competitive general equilibrium model all markets clear, so all consumers and producers can buy and sell what they choose to at the equilibrium prices. This means that it is impossible to reallocate resources to produce an outcome that better meets the preferences of some consumers without making others less satisfied. In other words, the outcome of a competitive general equilibrium model is Pareto efficient.

Consider a situation where consumers' relative preferences for one good in terms of another are not equal to the relative price of that good. If, say, the relative price is greater than their relative preference for that good for any consumer, then that consumer would satisfy his or her preferences better by buying less of that good and using the money to buy more of the other good. Conversely, if relative price is less than relative preferences, then a consumer would want to purchase more. The same holds for producers. If the relative price of one good is greater (less) than the opportunity cost of producing that good in terms of the other, then it would be profitable to produce more (less) of that good. Only when relative prices throughout the model exactly equal opportunity costs for producers and relative preferences for consumers does it make sense for consumers and producers to stay doing what they are. This is when all consumers and producers are doing the best they can for themselves. In this situation there are no further gains from trade.

The condition that prices accurately reflect all opportunity costs is a very stringent one, however, and it will not hold if there are any market failures. This means, for example, that a competitive equilibrium is not Pareto efficient if there are any externalities. (Externalities are defined in *Changing Economies,* Chapter 10, Sections 2 and 3.) If there are externalities in production or consumption, the private costs and benefits of an activity are not the same as the social costs and benefits of the activity, and relative prices do not reflect opportunity costs and relative preferences. For example, factories that emit harmful effluents for which they do not pay will charge low prices that do not reflect the true opportunity cost of this production, and the allocation that results will not be Pareto efficient.

Further, we need to recognize that any competitive equilibrium outcome depends on the exogenous variables of technology, preferences and initial endowments of resources. This section has shown how, provided relative prices accurately reflect opportunity costs and relative preferences, a competitive general equilibrium makes a Pareto efficient use of resources and available technology in meeting existing preferences. However, the outcome also depends on the distribution of resources across economic agents. In particular, a different distribution of initial endowments would result in a different Pareto efficient outcome. Pareto efficiency says nothing about whether the initial distribution of endowments is desirable. These issues will be examined further in Chapter 18.

2.5 Neoclassical economics and equilibrium

It has been argued in this section that the neoclassical model emphasizes the importance of the role of prices in a world of scarcity. A competitive general equilibrium model results in a Pareto efficient outcome (assuming there are no market failures such as externalities). Each Pareto efficient allocation takes as given a particular initial endowment of resources, and so there is a different Pareto efficient allocation for each conceivable initial distribution. This model assumes rational, self-interested behaviour on the part of all economic agents.

The competitive equilibrium model is a comparative static model in which only equilibrium outcomes can be compared. This means that the competitive equilibrium model does not address the question of the process of adjustment from one equilibrium to another. The comparative static approach may, therefore, be contrasted with an approach which does analyse the process of change during disequilibrium. This contrast may be illustrated using the notion of a journey from one place to another: the competitive equilibrium approach can compare the starting point with the final destination, but it does not analyse the journey. In Section 3 of this chapter you will see that the institutionalist approach regards the issue of the actual journey as the important one.

Neoclassical economics tries to provide some content to what might be happening during the

disequilibrium process by suggesting we imagine a process of adjustment that would be consistent with the competitive equilibrium model. Thinking how prices could change is a problem because the model assumes that all agents are price takers; all agents are so small that no one is able to influence the price. The problem here is how to operationalize the model and describe a disequilibrium process of price adjustment when there is no one who can actually change a price.

One attempt at resolving this is to specify all the conditions under which a real market would approximate to the competitive equilibrium model. This model is known as perfect competition (see *Changing Economies*, Chapter 7). It assumes that all agents are small relative to the market so that no one agent can have an influence on the price. All goods must be homogeneous (rather than differentiated) otherwise firms would have some control over the market. This model also assumes that all agents are perfectly mobile and can respond costlessly to market signals; there is freedom of entry and exit for firms. It is also assumed that all agents are well informed and that the existing technology is available to all firms. This model of perfect competition is an attempt to operationalize the abstract theoretical notion of a competitive equilibrium by rooting it in the required characteristics of actual markets. As all agents are price takers, the equilibrium outcome in the perfectly competitive model is also Pareto efficient, but there is still the problem of how prices actually change in a model where all agents are price takers. This is sometimes glossed over by saying that 'market forces' make the price adjustments.

The models of competitive general equilibrium and perfect competition have proved to be powerful theoretical tools in providing insights into competitive equilibrium outcomes and in showing the efficiency properties of these outcomes (under certain conditions). A weakness is that they are not easily interpretable as a description of actual markets. Thus, although they present a model of a decentralized market economy that many economists find intellectually rigorous, they have been criticized by other economists who feel that they leave out too many features of actual economies where the assumption of price taking cannot be sustained. Section 3 describes some of these other approaches that have tried to break away from the neoclassical emphasis on equilibrium outcomes.

3   INSTITUTIONAL ECONOMICS

3.1   Introduction

The institutions within which economic agents operate vary substantially even between capitalist economies. It may, therefore, seem strange that the theories of the market we have examined so far in this chapter pay no attention to the institutional forms markets take (except that we have assumed them to fulfil the rather abstract criterion of competitiveness). The model of rational individual choice upon which neoclassical economics is based is presented as independent of any particular institutional context. However, since it implicitly assumes the institution of private property and a legal framework to enforce contracts, it can be argued that neoclassical theory takes these institutions for granted as though they were universal. Most neoclassical economists do not try to explain how these institutions come about.

Institutionalist economists, on the other hand, see an analysis of the institutional context as vital to any study of economics. Rather than individual behaviour being the building block out of which a picture of the economy can be built, the order of determination is turned the other way around. Institutionalists would assert that the behaviour of the individual can only be analysed within an institutional context. This means that they have a different view of what markets do and how to analyse them. Warren Samuels, a prominent institutionalist, puts it like this:

> '... Institutionalist economists assert the primacy of the problem of the organization and control of the economic system, that is, its structure of power. Thus, whereas orthodox (i.e. neoclassical) economists tend strongly to identify the economy solely with the market, institutional economists argue that the market is itself an institution, comprised of a host of subsidiary institutions, and interactive with other institutional complexes in society.'
>
> (SAMUELS, 1987, P.864)

A number of things are worth noticing from this quotation. First, if the market is only one of a number of interacting institutions, its analysis cannot be conducted in isolation from that of other 'non-economic' institutions. Institutionalist economists do not, therefore, base their theories on a single type of economic behaviour, such as maximization, which is assumed by neoclassicists to pertain to all 'economic' decisions. Instead they see the study of markets as requiring an interdisciplinary approach, within which it can be expected that people behave differently in different institutional contexts. In the institutionalist approach, other social science disciplines, such as sociology and political science, are given equal standing alongside economics.

Further, this means that institutionalists focus less on particular issues of price formation and resource allocation, and more on the organization and control of the economy. They are interested in the ways in which different economic systems vary and in the institutional histories of different economies. When compared with the neoclassical approach, institutionalists see more variables as endogenous to their economic system and, moreover, they see this system as not a purely economic one. Unlike the neoclassical system, in which preferences, resource endowments and technology are variables exogenous to the economy, an institutionalist view sees individual preferences, resource endowments and technologies as formed within a *socio-economic* system, and therefore endogenous to it. For example, within institutionalist theories individual preferences depend on the interactions between individuals in society; people define their social standing and differentiate themselves from others by their consumption behaviour (see Chapter 3). Institutionalists would, therefore, replace the neoclassical order of determination of Figure 1.4 with a more complex picture of interactions in a socio-economic system as shown in Figure 1.5.

A particular example of how this institutionalist perspective works is in providing a way of explaining technological change. Unlike the neoclassical perspective in which technology is exogenous, for institutionalists technology is explained by interactions with other institutions. In Chapter 17 the role of financial institutions in relation to firm innovation is examined. There we ask why the boom in new technology industries in the US has been so pronounced compared to the UK and the rest of Europe? This may have something to do with the prominence in the US of venture capitalists, organizations and individuals prepared to invest in long-term risk finance for new start-up firms. This form of finance in itself is an innovation which both drives and responds to firm innovation. One of the strengths of the institutionalist approach is its flexibility in allowing for feedback loops between technologies and institutions.

In providing explanations of rapid change and innovation, a vibrant strand of the institutionalist approach is provided by evolutionary economics. This tradition borrows some of its ideas from evolutionary biology. In addition to being able to offer explanations of change, evolutionary theories also provide suggestive insights into why regularities of behaviour persist. By way of analogy, in evolutionary economics stable units of analysis are defined that are like genes in biology. As part of the culture and social interactions within and between organizations, particular norms and routines of behaviour become established over time. For example, in households the norm is for parents to care for children (see Chapter 7), whereas in firms routines in relation to the keeping of company accounts become established. These norms and routines, once successful, persist over time, in the same way that in biology genes are inherited by successive generations. By identifying these regularities the underlying structure of the economy can be explained.

Norms and routines are not, however, as static as the equilibria in neoclassical economics. Borrowing further from biology, in evolutionary economics the possibility of mutation in the norms and routines is embraced. An innovation in how children are cared for, that came with the rise in female participation in the labour market during the last 40 years, infuses a new norm into the economy: that some women now go out to work and pay other people to look after their children (see Chapter 5). This new social norm, once established, may become the defining feature of the new structure of relationships between women, households and the labour market. The institutionalist approach offers an organizing framework for explaining the evolution of these types of relationships.

3.2   An interdisciplinary approach

Institutionalist economists see markets themselves as institutions and different markets as characterized by different sorts of institutions. As a result, the type of behaviour exhibited by consumers in markets cannot be expected to be all of one type. This has facilitated a more interdisciplinary approach in which economists have drawn on approaches taken in other social sciences. Hirschman's comparison of 'exit' and 'voice' is such an example, where insights from political science have been used to analyse market processes.

Hirschman (1970) defined 'exit' and 'voice' as two methods by which consumers express dissatisfaction and thereby set in motion efforts by firms to adjust their standards of performance, for example, by changing the products they produce. The concept of *exit* is related to one of the defining characteristics of competitive markets, the freedom of consumers and producers to enter and exit the market at will. In Hirschman's analysis, exit is exemplified by the

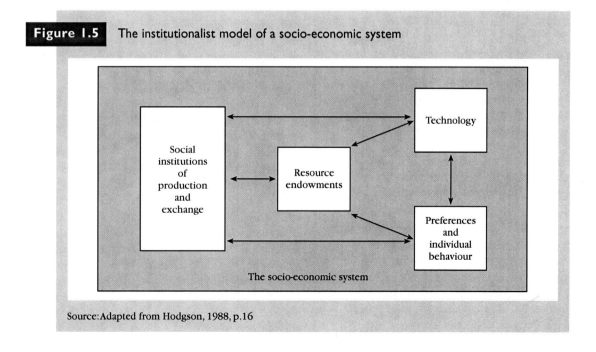

Figure 1.5   The institutionalist model of a socio-economic system

Social institutions of production and exchange

Resource endowments

Technology

Preferences and individual behaviour

The socio-economic system

Source: Adapted from Hodgson, 1988, p.16

'customer who, dissatisfied with the product of one firm, shifts to that of another' (p.15). If, for example, you decide that beef will damage your health, you can simply stop consuming it – you exit the market for beef. In doing so, the customer may set in motion 'market forces which may induce recovery on the part of the firm that has declined in comparative performance' (*ibid.*). To continue the beef example, you may induce beef producers to sell meat from healthy cattle only. Exit is not a 'fuzzy' concept; it is an all or nothing affair; customers either exit or they do not. It is impersonal in not necessitating any direct communication of a customer's decision to switch suppliers. And the recovery or collapse of the firm, whichever occurs, comes about as an unintended consequence of the customer's action 'by courtesy of the Invisible Hand' (*ibid.*).

Exit

An agent exercises exit behaviour by leaving a particular market in response to an unsatisfactory standard of performance by a supplier.

Voice

An economic agent can exercise voice by communicating an opinion to a supplier in a particular market without necessarily leaving that market.

Voice, on the other hand, has its origins in the political or non-market realm. You may, for example, voice your concern for the health risks associated with beef by taking part in a radio phone-in programme or by voting against the government. Voice is a much more ambiguous concept than exit and this fuzziness is exhibited along three dimensions:

1 The exercise of voice is matter of degree, in that the force with which it is exercised varies from 'faint grumbling to violent protest' (*ibid.*).

2 Voice takes a variety of forms, from the ad hoc, unstructured or informal episodes exemplified by grumbling and protest, to institutionalized activities, such as participating in the design of a product or the negotiation of conditions of work.

3 Unlike exit, the process of voice is not an all-or-nothing affair (one either exits or one does not) because it typically involves compromise.

Neither side gets everything it wants (or nothing at all); instead, having sacrificed something of what they wanted at the outset, they both come away with what is left.

Hirschman draws attention to another important characteristic of voice: 'it implies articulation of one's critical opinions rather than a private, "secret" vote in the anonymity of a supermarket' (*ibid.*).

Question

Identify whether the following types of behaviour represent exit or voice:

● buying a can of baked beans from Tesco's rather than Sainsbury's
● picketing lorries carrying veal calves to France
● choosing a personal computer.

Switching supermarkets is straightforward exit behaviour; the picketing of veal calves is a strong case of voice. Buying a personal computer can involve both exit and voice; the enquiries you make about the characteristics of different computers is a form of voice, but, ultimately, when you choose to purchase one brand rather than another, it is exit behaviour with respect to the rejected brand.

The concepts of exit and voice exemplify the interdisciplinary approach favoured by institutional economists, bringing insights and methods of analysis from political science to bear on economic issues. Recognizing that exit and voice may interact in the same market allows one to analyse markets that exhibit elements of both monopoly power and competitive pressure. For example, in some circumstances the threat of exit is one way of making the exercise of voice effective; the supplier is more likely to respond to a customer's complaint if the alternative is the loss of future business. Hirschman also identifies some situations in which the possibility of exit undermines the effectiveness of voice. If exit is possible, the potentially most vociferous may be the first to exit. Competition may, in fact, be collusive, with 'competitors' taking each other's dissatisfied customers rather than adjusting their behaviour. The optimal mix of exit and voice in such a situation is, Hirschman concludes, elusive; but it is that optimal *mix* which constitutes the solution, not just the freedom of exit which is all that perfect competition permits.

The importance of voice in markets is illustrated by Okun's analysis of the 'customer market as an institutional form'. In customer markets, the assumptions of perfect competition, for example that potential purchasers react only to price and that all suppliers are identical, do not hold. The characteristic features of customer markets can be described in these terms:

> *'Customers are valuable to sellers because of their potential for repeat business ... The firm comes to recognize its ability to discourage customers from shopping elsewhere by convincing them of the continuity of the firm's policy on pricing, services, and the like. It can encourage them to return to buy, or at least to shop, by pledging continuity of that offer.'*

(OKUN, 1981, P.141)

The transactions typical of customer markets involve recurrent rather than once-in-a-lifetime purchases, with the consequence that consumers believe that 'the experience of their last shopping expedition conveys relevant information for their next one' (p.140). Shopping around to find the lowest price or the most satisfactory price–quality combination incurs costs. Shoppers, therefore, have an incentive to stay with a previous supplier, provided they can be confident that no lapse in quality or rise in price has occurred. For example, it is inconvenient to keep switching between Tesco's and Sainsbury's, since it is easier to find where things are kept by sticking to one supermarket. For the owners of these supermarkets, such customers are worth retaining on a regular basis. This is why they seek to encourage repeat business by using devices such as loyalty cards, discount vouchers or special offers that are available only to regular customers.

In customer markets, relationships between buyers and sellers typically involve the exercise of voice rather than exit. Such relationships are far from impersonal, involving direct communication of a customer's decision to switch suppliers. Moreover, in an effort to avoid this outcome, sellers try to convince customers that repeat shopping will be worthwhile and they pledge continuity on pricing and services. Repeat business also offers opportunities for customers to be consulted on the range and quality of services provided by sellers. Exit may be used to reinforce such exercises of voice, when customers threaten to end an extended relationship on the grounds of unsatisfactory performance.

3.3   New institutionalism: rational action and institutional context

We have shown that the institutional approach is usually seen as a critique of neoclassical theory. However, there is also a 'new' institutionalism in which it is assumed, as in neoclassical theory, that individuals are self-interested and rational. This approach is institutional, since it examines a variety of institutions beyond the competitive market, but it shares with neoclassical economics the assumption that human behaviour is fundamentally unchanging and characterized by the rational pursuit of self interest. This approach has been used to explain the emergence, existence and performance of particular types of institutions. For example, let us consider what difference it makes whether the institutional context is such that firms can collude with each other and make legally binding agreements on pricing policy. Countries vary in their laws on collusion. In many countries pricing agreements are illegal and therefore unenforceable.

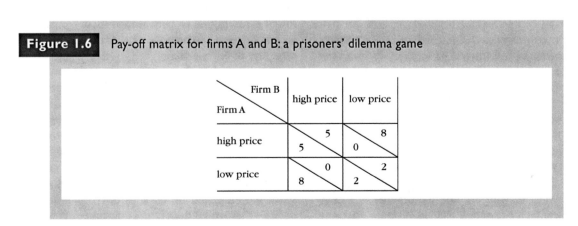

Figure 1.6   Pay-off matrix for firms A and B: a prisoners' dilemma game

	Firm B high price	low price
Firm A high price	5 5	5 8 0
low price	0 8	2 2

The US has particularly stringent, though not always effective, 'anti-trust' legislation.

Let us suppose there are just two oil firms, A and B, in the market who make an 'agreement' to keep their price high. One set of possible outcomes of this situation is given in Figure 1.6. (See *Changing Economies*, Chapter 5 if this type of diagram looks unfamiliar to you.)

If the agreement holds, so that both firms charge a high price, then the firms get a profit of 5 units each – they settle at the top left quadrant of the pay-off matrix.

Question

Faced with the pay-off matrix in Figure 1.6, will firm A charge a high price?

Firm A is not sure what Firm B will do. Will it keep to the agreement? Consider first the scenario in which firm B charges a high price. Firm A will earn 8 units of profit if it charges a low price and only 5 units of profit if it charges a high price; so in this case it is better for firm A to charge a low price. Second, consider the scenario in which firm B charges a low price. Firm A will again prefer to charge a low price since this will result in a profit of 2 units, compared to 0 units if it charges a high price. Regardless of firm B's decisions, firm A makes the higher profit if it charges a low price. This makes charging a low price the *dominant strategy* for A. Check that you can see that, on the same grounds, firm B's dominant strategy is also to charge a low price.

Dominant strategy

A strategy preferred by a player regardless of the strategy of the other players.

If the agreement to charge a high price is not legally enforceable, both firms will be tempted to break the agreement. Whether the other firm's prices are high or low, each will do better from charging the low price. However, if they do so, they will each get a profit of 2 units, which is less than the 5 units they would have made by keeping to the agreement. This situation in which independent self-interested decision making leads to an outcome which is not optimal for either party is an example of a prisoners' dilemma game.

Now let us suppose the agreement is legally enforceable. For example, let us suppose that any

firm that breaks the agreement has to pay 10 units to the other firm. This changes the pay-off matrix.

Exercise 1.3

Draw up the pay-off matrix for the situation where there is a penalty clause so that, if either firm breaks the agreement, it has to pay the other firm 10 units. What now is the dominant strategy for each firm?

The technique used in this section is known as game theory. It can be used in any situation where the best course of action for an individual depends on what others do – situations when strategic planning is necessary. Strategic planning is not necessary in the model of perfect competition since no individual has the power to influence the market on their own. Where markets are not perfectly competitive, however, game theory can be used to explain how the pursuit of self-interested objectives might lead to particular institutional forms being set up.

For example, in the case of the two firms considered above, the benefit to both firms of the strategy of charging a high price can be used to explain why firms try to set up institutions which enable them to follow this strategy: whether through enforceable contracts, or through some other institutional form such as 'gentlemen's agreements' or observed norms of behaviour or strategic alliances (Chapter 11 considers strategic behaviour by firms in more detail). New institutionalism uses its analysis of the best strategy for individuals in particular institutional forms to explain why those individuals might find some institutional forms more to their advantage than others, and therefore have an incentive to set them up. In this way, new institutionalism, although starting from the individualist behavioural assumptions of neoclassical theory, produces an explanation of some aspects of the institutional structure of the economy.

Game theory is also used by new institutionalists considering policy issues to model the effects of different institutional frameworks. For example, firms would prefer to be able to make enforceable pricing agreements with each other. However consumers would prefer the outcome in which such contracts to collude are not enforceable (or are illegal). Game theory provides an analytical framework which could be used to develop industrial policies that would benefit the consumer.

4 DIFFERENCES BETWEEN THE SCHOOLS OF THOUGHT

Economics is unlike other social sciences in that one particular school, neoclassical economics, dominates the discipline, particularly over the microeconomic subject matter of this book. This means that this book, reflecting that influence within the discipline as a whole, may often seem like a conversation between neoclassical economics and its rivals, but with no one particular rival having as prominent and sustained a voice in the conversation as the neoclassical approach. The main alternative approach in this book is the institutionalist perspective. However, as you have seen in the previous section, there are different schools of thought within institutionalism – 'old' institutionalist, evolutionary and new institutionalist – that each differ from neoclassical economics in particular ways. Indeed, the institutionalist approach itself is largely defined in terms of its differences from the neoclassical approach. This means that, whichever approach you end up favouring, it is extremely important for you to understand thoroughly the main characteristics of the neoclassical school of thought. The following is a brief overview of these main characteristics which will be used to structure the comparison between schools of thought throughout the book.

4.1   Core neoclassical assumptions

One reason that neoclassical economics will seem to have something to say about everything is that it is in many ways more a methodological programme than a single theory that can be put up to empirical test. We can pick out three core assumptions which are associated with neoclassical methodology: methodological individualism, rationality, and a focus on equilibrium. In outlining these assumptions, we shall highlight some of the main criticisms that rival schools of thought have made of the neoclassical programme.

Methodological individualism

This is the methodological position which aims to explain all economic phenomena in terms of the behaviour of individuals. Margaret Thatcher's famous claim that there is no such thing as society, just individuals and families, can be seen as a classic statement of the politics which is often seen to lie behind the neoclassical view. And just as she recognized families

as well as individual people, neoclassical individualism embraces other individual units, specifically firms and households.

In contrast to this, institutionalists have traditionally argued that human behaviour is fundamentally shaped by its environment, in particular the social and economic institutions of society, including social norms, so that it does not make sense to talk of a pre-social individual and see society as an aggregate of the behaviour of such individuals. You will meet the views of representatives of the institutionalist approach at a number of places in the book when discussing consumer behaviour (Chapter 3), household allocation of labour (Chapter 5), caring for children (Chapter 7), the behaviour of firms (Chapters 8 and 9), and the labour market (Chapters 13 and 14).

Rationality

Neoclassical theory assumes that all individual behaviour is 'rational' according to a very specific definition of this term. Individuals are assumed to have given goals which they pursue in the most efficient way possible. To do this, they maximize something; usually consumers are assumed to maximize pleasure (utility) subject to what they can afford, and firms are assumed to maximize profits subject to what it is technically possible for them to achieve.

A number of other economic theories, notably evolutionary theory, reject this characterization of individual goals, seeing behaviour as a result more of adaptation in response to previous experience than of conscious effort to maximize. Evolutionary theory is used in this book to develop theories of the firm (Chapter 8) and the development of technology (Chapter 16).

Other institutionalist theories question whether we can see the goals of individuals as given rather than themselves produced by the economy, while more interdisciplinary approaches suggest that values beyond pleasure and profit inform human behaviour; in particular, that people may also act out of habit, a desire for status, a sense of obligation or concern for others. These approaches will be introduced to examine consumer behaviour (Chapter 3), household decision making (Chapter 6), the labour market (Chapter 13) and the allocation of care both within the household and by the market (Chapters 7 and 19).

Equilibrium

Neoclassical theory tends to work by calculating how individuals would react to a particular set of prices.

This information can then be aggregated to establish at what prices individuals would behave in ways in which their different objectives could be reconciled in the marketplace. Prices that lead to such compatible behaviour are known as equilibrium prices, because when they hold no individual has any incentive to change what they are doing. Much of neoclassical theory is concerned with understanding the conditions under which an equilibrium exists and whether those equilibria are unique and/or stable. A frequent next step is the method of comparative statics, which compares the equilibrium that results in two different situations to see the effect a change in external conditions, say a change in the cost of raw materials, has on output and price within a particular market.

Two main criticisms are made within this book of the neoclassical emphasis on equilibrium. First, proponents of evolutionary economics consider the equilibrium state in which nothing changes to be of little practical or theoretical interest. Instead, they focus on the dynamic process of disequilibrium.

Second, the method of comparative statics seems to imply that with an appropriate change in external conditions any equilibrium is achievable. In contrast with this approach, other economic theories see economic processes as path dependent so that past conditions have a lasting and cumulative effect on theory. Path dependence is necessary if we are to explain why there are different economic systems in the world today, both in the whole economy sense of different systems, and in the sense of different ways of organizing particular aspects of the economy. We need a notion of path dependence to explain how those different systems arose and also to investigate different possible future paths.

4.2   Non-core neoclassical assumptions

In addition to the core assumptions of the neoclassical approach, which have provided the main areas of contention between neoclassical theorists and their critics, there are also a number of additional non-core assumptions. Some economists who are neoclassical, in that they accept the core assumptions, have in recent years been extending the theory in order to do without some unrealistic further assumptions commonly made by orthodox neoclassical theory. Three of these non-core assumptions are: the extent of competition, the degree of knowledge economic actors can be assumed to have, and the use of formal modelling.

Competition

A strong assumption of much neoclassical economics is that the power of individual economic actors is sufficiently small that they can take their environment as given, without thinking about the effects of their own actions on it. Specifically, this assumption means that all agents are price takers, reacting to prices which the agents do not believe that they themselves can influence. In practice, of course, many agents have much more power than this and can have significant effects on prices in the markets in which they buy and sell. If an agent is a monopolist or monopsonist, the situation is still fairly simple to analyse (see *Changing Economies*, Chapter 6). However, in more complex cases, where more than one agent has this sort of power, the game theory approach, introduced in Section 3.3, is used to analyse the strategic thinking that is called for when the outcome of one agent's actions depends on what another does. This book uses game theory in a number of places, particularly in the context of inter-firm contracting relations (Chapter 9), strategic thinking by oligopolistic firms (Chapter 11) and professional service provision (Chapter 19).

Agents' knowledge

Traditionally, in neoclassical theory the unrealistic assumption is made that all economic agents have perfect knowledge of anything in the past, present or future that might influence their decisions; in particular, that they know all future prices. There are now modified versions of neoclassical theory that allow for agents being uncertain about the future.

However, when knowledge is asymmetric so that some agents know things which others do not, then a different modification is needed which again frequently uses game theory. This is the basis of the new institutionalist school that retains the methodological individualism of neoclassical theory but uses the analysis of strategic behaviour in the face of asymmetric information to explain the formation of particular institutions. You will meet some examples of new institutionalist theories in the discussion of contracting (Chapter 9), the labour market (Chapter 14) and social markets (Chapter 19), and at various other places in the book.

The use of formal modelling

One of the characteristics of economics as compared with other social sciences is its systematic use of formal models, models which abstract from the complexities of the real world to concentrate on a few variables at a time, and investigating very thoroughly the relationships between these variables, sometimes using mathematical techniques to do so. Neoclassical economics, in particular, uses a highly developed set of formal models.

However, in using such models certain abstractions have to be made and theories often differ in what they see as the significant aspects of an economic problem. Because neoclassical theory uses mathematical modelling a great deal, some of its abstractions are designed to make the mathematics tractable.

For example, neoclassical theory tends to assume that all quantities can be adjusted in infinitesimally small steps, so that they can be represented as continuous rather than discrete variables. Continuity is basically a simplifying assumption, which makes the mathematics easier but is not core to neoclassical theory. Nevertheless, it does have real effects on the predictions of the theory, ensuring that in many situations the model identifies a single rational course of action. In practice, of course, economic agents face choices which are discrete rather than continuous, and there may well be two or more equally rational courses of action.

5   CONCLUSION

The overall aims of the book are twofold. First we wish to give you a stimulating and insightful account of the ways in which economists have tried to understand how economic agents behave and interact in a market economy. Notice the plural in 'ways in which economists have tried to understand'. The most basic message of the book is that economics is not a subject in which there is one single correct answer. We thus adopt a pluralistic approach to economic problems and questions; that is, a range of theoretical approaches is considered, not just one. This makes the book quite distinctive and, we believe, exciting.

Our second overall aim is to let you develop *your* ability to use and evaluate economic theory, and to help you build or improve other academic skills as you progress through the text. In order to equip you as an economist, key microeconomic skills are developed as the book progresses, with a summary of the main concepts and techniques provided at the start of each chapter. The evaluative skills developed as part of this learning process will help

you to begin to form a properly considered view about the merits of the alternative theoretical approaches. In addition, at the start of each chapter a set of links highlight some of the main connections between different parts of the book in terms of the schools of thought.

In this chapter we have introduced some of the questions economists ask about the ways in which markets work, and some of the theoretical frameworks they use in answering them. Our approach has been to discuss markets in general. However, as you work through the rest of this book, you will encounter discussion of different kinds of markets, such as goods markets, labour markets, financial markets and markets in caring. This raises the possibility that a particular theoretical perspective, say, institutionalist economics, might be more helpful in understanding a certain kind of market, perhaps markets in caring services, than other approaches. Similarly, you might find that an institutional approach is particularly illuminating in connection with markets characterized by high rates of innovation (see Chapters 15 and 16). Both within the economics profession and in the wider public debate, there is intense controversy about which economic approaches are relevant to which particular issues.

 FURTHER READING

Neoclassical economics

Henderson, D. (1986) 'Soap opera in high places', Chapter 2 in *Innocence and Design: The Influence of Economic Ideas on Policy,* Oxford and New York, Basil Blackwell, pp.17–35: a brisk and readable exposition of the neoclassical theory of how markets allocate resources efficiently.

Robinson, J. (1963) 'The neo-classics: Utility', Chapter 3 in *Economic Philosophy*, Harmondsworth, Penguin, pp.48–70: a classic polemical piece on the philosophical foundations and ideological significance of neoclassical economics.

Institutional economics

Hodgson, G.M. (1994) 'Institutionalism "old" and "new"', in Hodgson, G.M., Samuels, W.J. and Tool, M.R., *The Elgar Companion to Institutional and Evolutionary Economics*, Aldershot, Edward Elgar, pp.397–403: a brief and authoritative historical survey of institutional economics.

 ANSWERS TO EXERCISES

Exercise 1.1

Figure 1.7 shows the initial equilibrium price and quantity traded of P_1 and Q_1. The fall in the price of steel results in a rightwards shift of the supply curve of cars from S_1 to S_2 as car production costs also fall. There is no shift of the demand curve but there is a movement along it as consumers respond to the fall in price by demanding more cars. In a partial equilibrium setting, the equilibrium price falls from P_1 to P_2 and the equilibrium quantity traded increases from Q_1 to Q_2.

In a general equilibrium setting, it is possible that other markets would now be out of equilibrium as a result of the fall in the (partial) equilibrium price of steel and cars. For example, the fall in the price of cars is likely to result in an increase in the demand for a complementary good such as petrol, and an increase in its price. This increase in the price of petrol may then react back on the car market by reducing the demand for cars. On the supply side, the reduction in the price of steel may lead car producers to switch to a more steel-intensive method of production in order to reduce costs still further. This would lead to a further rightwards shift in the supply curve of cars. It would also lead to an increase in the demand for steel as producers find new uses for it. This in turn would tend to raise the price of steel which would then have a new series of repercussions on the market for cars, and so on. The new general equilibrium outcome would depend on the overall quantitative effect of all these changes taken together.

Exercise 1.2

All firms and households have to be price takers, that is, they have to consider themselves to be unable to influence prices in any market.

Exercise 1.3

The new pay-off matrix is given by Figure 1.8. The transfer of 10 units, if the agreement is broken by one firm but not the other, results in a drop to –2 units for the offender, and a payoff of 10 units for the recipient. Of course, if both firms break the agreement, the transfers balance each other out. Note that for both firms the dominant strategy is now to charge a high price.

Figure 1.7   The effects of a fall in the price of steel on the market for cars

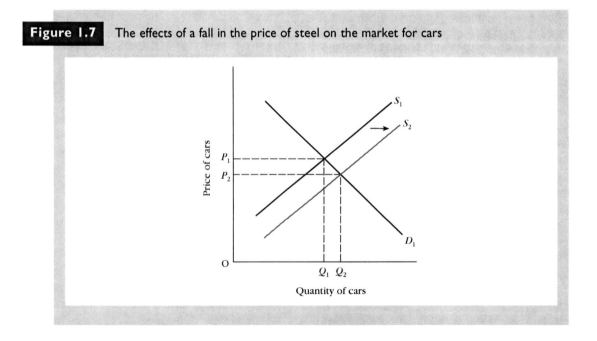

Figure 1.8 New pay-off matrix after introduction of penalty clause

Firm B Firm A	high price	low price
high price	5 5	-2 10
low price	10 -2	2 2

CONSUMPTION

Consumer Sovereignty

Andrew Trigg

Concepts and Techniques

Consistent preferences

Indifference curves

Ordinal preferences; utility maximization

Marginal rate of substitution

Diminishing marginal rate of substitution; convexity

Feasible consumption set; budget constraint

Slope of a line; slope of a curve; tangency

Income and substitution effects

Normal, inferior and Giffen goods

Lexicographic preferences

Slutsky approximation

Revealed preference

Links

- This chapter shows how two of the core assumptions of neoclassical economics, methodological individualism and rationality, explored in Chapter 1, form the basis of the neoclassical theory of consumption.

- The consumer demand curve forms one of the essential building blocks of the general equilibrium model. It was introduced in Chapter 1 and will be explored further in Chapter 18.

- Similar techniques of maximization under constraints will be used in Chapter 5 to derive a household's labour supply curve, and in Chapter 10 to consider how firms choose between competing techniques of production.

- Alternative theories of consumption will be explored in Chapter 3.

- In Chapter 4, demand curves and the Slutsky approximation are used to derive price indices and provide one measure of household welfare.

1 INTRODUCTION

'The free enterprise economy is the true counterpart of democracy: it is the only system which gives everyone a say. Everyone who goes into a shop and chooses one article instead of another is casting a vote in the economic ballot box: with thousands or millions of others that choice is signalled to production and investment and helps to mould the world just a tiny fraction nearer to people's desire. In this great and continuous general election of the free economy nobody, not even the poorest, is disfranchized: we are all voting all the time. Socialism is designed on the opposite pattern: it is designed to prevent people getting their own way, otherwise there would be no point in it.'

(POWELL, 1969, P.33)

In this quotation from the late Enoch Powell's book *Freedom and Reality*, the once prominent UK politician conveys the idea of *consumer sovereignty* – the idea that in a free market economy, individual consumers choose which goods are produced. Instead of a king, dictator or central planner making decisions, sovereignty is vested in the everyday choices of individual consumers. These individual choices lead by an 'invisible hand' to the best possible outcome for the economy as a whole.

Consumer sovereignty

Consumer sovereignty holds when consumers have the power to dictate what is produced in the economy.

This view of the free market became increasingly dominant with the emergence of Thatcherite and Reaganite policies in the early 1980s, and the collapse of the eastern European bloc of centrally planned economies in the late 1980s. Indeed, it has been argued that the inability of the Soviet system to satisfy consumer demand was one of the main reasons for its demise. John Kenneth Galbraith, for example, has pronounced that the Soviet system:

'… could not satisfy the infinitely diverse and unstable demand for the services and products that make up the modern consumers' goods economy. Here socialism, both in planning and administration, proved far too inflexible. One may marvel at the attraction of often frivolous and dispensable consumer artifacts and entertainments in our time, but their ultimately controlling appeal cannot be doubted.'

(GALBRAITH, 1992, P.7–8)

An enduring image of the collapse of communism in eastern Europe was that of East Germans queuing to cross into the west in their patched-together Trabants. These 1950s style vehicles revealed how starved the East Germans had been of western consumption goods during the years of state planning. More than anything, the car has provided the symbol of the triumph of consumerism. For those on the right of the political spectrum, '… the motor car epitomizes the freedom of private consumers to go where they please, without relying on government, business or anyone else to run the buses, coaches or railways on time' (Gabriel and Lang, 1995, p.16). In this view, the triumph of western capitalism can be attributed more to Mercedes Benz and BMW than to Cruise and Trident missiles.

Mirroring this dominance of capitalism in the world economy, the world's economics profession has been dominated by neoclassical economics (Chapter 1 outlined the framework of neoclassical economics and some alternative approaches). Although neoclassical economists vary in their individual political allegiances, their approach has been used to provide a technical demonstration of why free market capitalism offers the best system for organizing an economy. In neoclassical economics, the choices of the individual consumer are shown to determine what is produced: this is what is meant by consumer sovereignty. A defining assumption of neoclassical economics is that all individuals follow their own self-interest, whether as producers deciding which is the most profitable method of production, or as consumers choosing which goods to purchase. To make profits, producers must sell their wares. To do so, they must produce what consumers want. The neoclassical approach shows how consumer sovereignty is achieved by a market economy in which both producers and consumers act according to their self-interest.

The sovereign consumer

This chapter focuses on the individual consumer whose behaviour provides the key building block for the neoclassical theory of consumption. In this theory, the individual's preferences provide the basis for choosing between different goods and services. I may, for example, according to my own particular tastes, prefer to buy a Top 10 CD than a record by Showaddywaddy. It follows, since others obviously feel the same way, that we will be prepared to pay the full price for a Top 10 CD in a Virgin Megastore, but we will only buy Showaddywaddy records when they are discounted for 99p in Woolworths. The point here is that my preferences drive my demand and hence provide the signal in the marketplace as to what prices can be charged. This relationship between preferences, demand and price provides the focus of Section 2 of this chapter which demonstrates how the tastes and preferences of individual consumers are communicated in the marketplace.

The rest of the chapter critically discusses the neoclassical theory of consumer behaviour. Of particular interest is the way in which consumers respond to changes in price. Say the price of bread falls sharply in your supermarket. This can have two effects. It may encourage you to buy more bread instead of, say, potatoes; and it will also mean that you are better off in real terms and can, therefore, afford to buy more bread *and* more potatoes. Section 3 provides an initial analysis of these two impacts of a price change, using the neoclassical theory of consumer behaviour.

In Section 4 I look at this theory's core assumption that consumers act according to their own preferences, like rational calculating machines, and that this gives them a full say in the ballot box of consumer democracy. I shall consider the implications of consumers either being too poor to exercise much choice in this ballot or being irrational in their behaviour.

As part of this discussion, a test of the model is provided by introducing an example from experimental economics. The problem with economics, in comparison with many physical sciences, is that it is very difficult to carry out controlled experiments. A chemist can control the amount of chemicals in his measuring jar and test whether or not they will generate an explosion. Experimental economics tries to carry out its own tests by setting up artificial environments in which economic behaviour can be observed.

2 THE NEOCLASSICAL THEORY OF CONSUMPTION

A schoolboy calling at the corner shop on the way home from school has to decide how to allocate his pocket money on crisps and chocolate; a young executive decides how to spend her month's salary on clothes and jewellery; and Lennox Lewis, surviving yet another challenge to his world heavyweight boxing title, decides whether to spend his earnings on a helicopter or a yacht.

Neoclassical consumer theory is based on the assumption that, in making a comparison between different items of consumption, individuals have preferences which they use to rank the possible alternatives. Assume, for example, that the schoolboy has to choose between two possible combinations of crisps and chocolate. In one shopping basket there are three packets of crisps and three bars of chocolate – this can be referred to as bundle A. In the other shopping basket there are two packets of crisps and two bars of chocolate, referred to as bundle B.

In choosing between these two bundles, the individual, in this case the schoolboy, must decide 'Do I prefer bundle A to bundle B?' We use the symbol > to indicate the direction of preference:

A > B; read this as A is preferred to B.

Since the schoolboy likes both crisps and chocolate, he will prefer bundle A to bundle B, and it follows that he ranks bundle A more highly than bundle B. The bundles are arranged in a particular order, in which A is ranked higher than bundle B. Notice that we are not assuming that the individual places any particular absolute value on either basket, merely that one is valued more, or ranked higher, than the other. Since preferences produce a ranked ordering in this way, they can be said to be *ordinal*.

Ordinal

An individual's preferences are ordinal if they allow different baskets of goods to be ranked in order of preference.

The assumption that individuals use preferences to rank alternatives provides the starting point for the neoclassical theory of consumption.

In addition to assuming that consumers rank alternatives, neoclassical economics also assumes that their rankings are consistent. Consumers must be consistent in their choices: if an individual prefers bundle A to bundle B, he or she cannot also prefer B to A. Consumers must behave like rational individuals who carefully calculate choices and then stick to these choices. Switching from one choice to another would be behaving inconsistently and this would be considered irrational by the neoclassical economist.

The assumption of *consistency* can be represented formally by the statement:

$$\text{If A} > \text{B, then B} \not> \text{A}$$

Consistency

If a consumer prefers A to B then for consistency to hold he or she must never prefer B to A.

Many of the important predictions and policy implications of the neoclassical approach depend on the consistency assumption. Some of these predictions and the evidence for and against them will be dealt with specifically in this chapter, while Chapter 4 will look at the way in which consumer theory is used for measuring the welfare of individuals. For welfare purposes, when someone prefers A to B, the neoclassical assumption is that

we can infer that they are better off with A rather than B, so that a policy which results in that person consuming A is better than a policy that results in them consuming B. If, however, the individual's choices were inconsistent then they would not provide a basis for assessing welfare and making policy choices. It would be impossible to judge whether consuming A or B is the better outcome. As well as examining the theoretical implications of the consistency assumption, the discussion that follows will also examine some empirical evidence as to the viability of that assumption.

2.1 The indifference map

To examine a consumer's preferences between two goods, F and G, a diagram can be drawn in which quantities of good F are measured on the vertical axis and quantities of good G on the horizontal axis. To continue with our schoolboy who likes chocolate (good F) and crisps (good G), assume that he has to choose between bundle A, which contains three of each good, and bundle B which contains two of each good. These bundles are represented by points A and B on Figure 2.1.

Now there is, of course, a reasonable explanation why bundle A will always be preferred to bundle B. If we assume that consumers always prefer more to less then bundle A will be preferred to bundle B and the schoolboy will always prefer a bundle containing more bags of crisps and more bars of chocolate.

Bundle A is, in fact, preferred to all the bundles in the bottom left shaded quadrant of Figure 2.1. Each bundle inside this shaded area contains less of both good F and good G than bundle A. On the top boundary of the shaded area are bundles containing the same amount of chocolate but less crisps than bundle A. On the right boundary are the bundles containing the same amount of crisps but less chocolate than bundle A. All of these are less preferred than A by the schoolboy.

Bundle C in Figure 2.1, however, represents a combination of good F and good G which the consumer will prefer to the bundle at point A. It contains four bags of crisps and four bars of chocolate, compared to only three of each good at point A. If, as before, the consumer prefers more to less, all the bundles in the top right shaded quadrant will be preferred to point A. In this model, it is assumed that the consumer is never completely satisfied, always preferring more to less. However much he or she consumes, the consumer has never had enough of either good. This is the assumption of non-satiation.

This leaves the top left and bottom right quadrants of Figure 2.1. The important point to note about these unshaded areas is that they contain bundles of crisps and chocolate which are not necessarily regarded more highly or less highly than bundle A. There could, in fact, be some bundles which the consumer ranks equally to bundle A. The consumer is *indifferent* between these bundles, not preferring one particular combination of good F and good G to the others.

Assume that in Figure 2.1 our schoolboy is indifferent between the bundles at A and D. He is equally satisfied with a bundle which contains four bars of chocolate and two bags of crisps (bundle D) and a bundle which contains three bags of crisps and three bars of chocolate (bundle A). Assume further that crisps and chocolate can be divided into infinitesimal amounts. This allows us to join up all the bundles between which the individual is indifferent by a line which we call an indifference curve. All the bundles of goods represented by the points on

an *indifference curve* are ranked equally by the consumer.

Indifference curve

An indifference curve represents all bundles of commodities which are ranked equally by the consumer.

Before looking at how such an indifference curve is used, we need to spend some time examining the assumptions underlying its shape. The magnitude of the slope of an indifference curve measures the rate at which a consumer is willing to give up one good in order to consume more of another. This rate is known as the consumer's *marginal rate of substitution* (MRS).

Marginal rate of substitution (MRS)

The marginal rate of substitution (MRS) of good G for good F is the amount of good F the consumer is willing to give up for one additional unit of G, thus remaining on the same indifference curve.

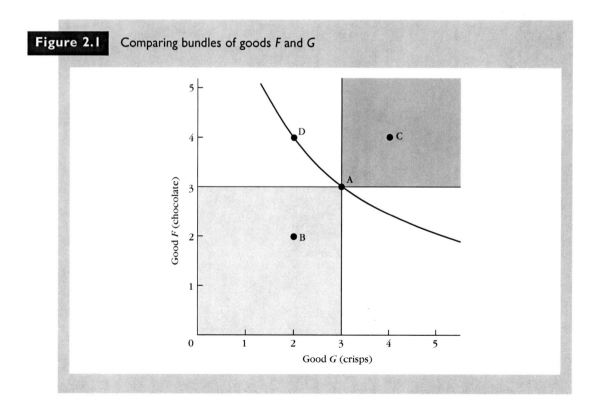

Figure 2.1   Comparing bundles of goods F and G

Consider an indifference curve of an individual choosing between crisps (good F) and chocolate (good G) in Figure 2.2. At each point on the indifference curve, the marginal rate of substitution of good G for good F, MRS_{GF}, is the amount of good F the consumer must give up to remain on the same indifference curve when he or she gets one more unit of good G.

A key assumption in drawing an indifference curve is that its marginal rate of substitution diminishes. The economic reasoning behind this assumption can be explained by first examining the movement from A to B in Figure 2.2. Here the schoolboy willingly gives up two bars of chocolate in return for one additional bag of crisps. This substitution leaves the schoolboy indifferent between the new bundle B and the original bundle A. Consider what he does, however, when moving from C to D. Here he is only willing to give up one bar of chocolate in return for one bag of crisps. Between C and D he is less willing to give up chocolate for crisps than between A and B. As the schoolboy moves along the indifference curve, crisps become progressively less attractive in comparison to chocolate which becomes progressively more attractive. The individual is assumed to have a diminishing marginal rate of substitution – the rate at which chocolate is willingly given up for crisps diminishes.

This means that, in the neoclassical theory of consumer behaviour, each individual is assumed to rank bundles of goods in a particular way. As the individual consumes more of good G he or she is assumed to find good F relatively more attractive. For an individual giving up good F and consuming more of good G there is a diminishing marginal rate of substitution.

Indifference curves with diminishing marginal rates of substitution all have a similar shape to the one drawn in Figure 2.2, that is, they all bow in towards the origin. The indifference curve has a slope which gets flatter as more of good G and less of good F is consumed. This gives the indifference curve that bowed shape. Such a shape is known mathematically as *convex to the origin*. Indifference curves with diminishing marginal rates of substitution are convex to the origin.

Figure 2.2   Diminishing marginal rate of substitution

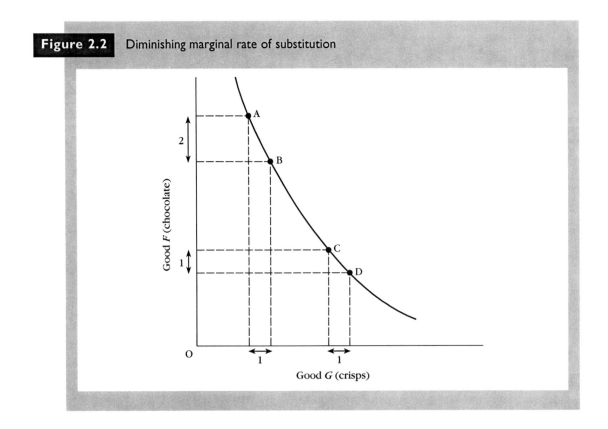

The indifference map in Figure 2.3 shows a number of indifference curves, each of which represents bundles between which the individual is indifferent. Of the three curves in Figure 2.3, the schoolboy will most prefer bundles on indifference curve 3. These bundles include larger amounts of crisps and chocolate than those on indifference curve 2. The least preferred options lie on indifference curve 1.

The traditional way of looking at these comparisons was to say that the individual is maximizing 'utility'. Early neoclassical economists, such as Alfred Marshall (1842–1924), assumed that each individual calculates the amount of pleasure derived from consumption. A bundle anywhere on indifference curve 3, bundle A for example, could yield say five units of utility, and a bundle anywhere on indifference curve 2, such as bundle B, only three units. If the consumer maximizes utility, then it follows that bundle A is preferred to bundle B. The problem with this approach, however, is that utility is impossible to measure. To avoid this problem, modern neoclassical economists have developed the ordinal approach which requires merely the assumption that consumers rank bundles A and B in order of preference.

Once we recognize that it is the *ranking* of preferences that is fundamental to neoclassical economics, we can keep the notion of utility but use it simply as a way of looking at preferences. We can say that an individual obtains a higher level of utility by choosing bundle A instead of bundle B, but all this means is that the consumer prefers A to B without giving any meaning to the amounts of utility associated with each bundle. Throughout this chapter, therefore, I will use the shorthand description of maximizing utility to refer to actions which best satisfy the consumer's preferences.

In terms of the indifference map, the consumer will always maximize utility by trying to get on the highest feasible indifference curve, the indifference curve that is furthest away from the origin. Increasing utility is represented by the broadening smile in Figure 2.3 as the individual moves on to the indifference curves further from the origin. Each trip to the supermarket, each flick through the pages of the Argos catalogue, is geared towards the pleasure-seeking principle, the maximization of utility – that is, the best satisfaction of preferences.

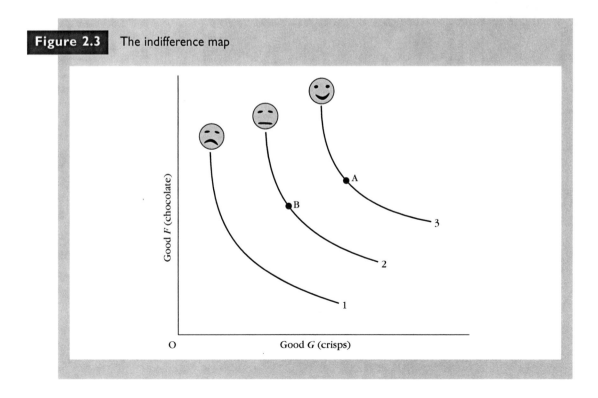

Figure 2.3 The indifference map

2.2 The consumer's feasible set and budget constraint

Of course the consumer cannot buy everything he or she wants; only certain bundles of consumer goods can be afforded. There are two main constraints on the consumer pursuing utility maximization:

- income
- the price of the goods to be purchased.

For example, a consumer receiving income support of £45 a week will be unable to purchase a basket of goods that costs £60 at the supermarket. The restrictions of income and price are embodied in the individual's *feasible consumption set* and *budget constraint*.

Feasible consumption set

A consumer's feasible consumption set is the set of all consumption bundles that can be afforded at current prices with the consumer's income.

Budget constraint

A consumer's budget constraint is the frontier of his or her feasible consumption set. It represents the consumption bundles that can be afforded if all the consumer's income is spent.

Assume that this time our individual chooses between two goods: food (good *F*) and alcohol (good *G*). Each can of food costs £9, as does each bottle of alcohol. With an income of £45, how much of each good will he decide to consume? To model this we need to represent the budget constraint by drawing a straight line, as shown in Figure 2.4.

Each point on the line represents a combination of goods *F* and *G* which our individual can purchase given his income and the price of the goods. At A, he purchases five cans of food which, at a price of £9 each, would use up all his income of £45. In this case he would spend none of his income on alcohol. At B, he would purchase three cans of food (at a total cost of £27) and two bottles of alcohol (a total cost of £18); this also adds up to the full £45 of income. At the other

---

Figure 2.4 The budget constraint

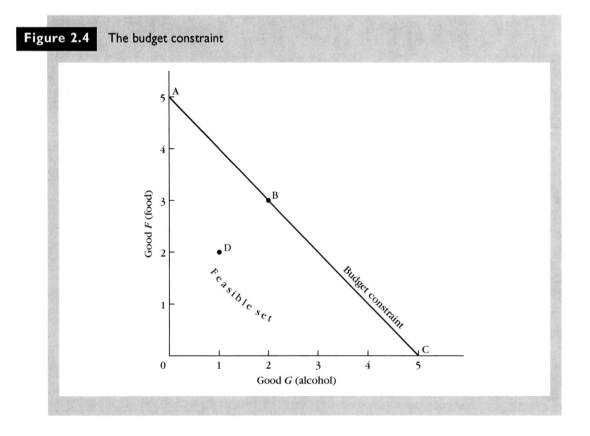

extreme, if he chooses not to buy any food, all of the £45 could be spent on five bottles of alcohol, as shown at C.

Note that the line does not just account for whole bottles of alcohol and cans of food, since it joins up all infinitesimal combinations of the two goods, down to fractions of grammes and millilitres. Note also that the individual could choose point D where only £27 is spent on two cans of food and a bottle of alcohol.

The question which we can now ask is 'Which combination of food and alcohol will the individual choose?' To provide an answer, the consumer's indifference map needs to be brought back into the picture. Our individual will have particular preferences for food and alcohol which are represented by his indifference map. Given these preferences, and given the budget constraint, his objective is to maximize utility by reaching the highest possible indifference curve.

In Figure 2.5 the point of utility maximization is represented by A where the individual consumes three units of good F and two units of good G. At A, the indifference curve is tangential to (just touches) the budget constraint. Indifference curves any further out would not meet the budget constraint and would, therefore, be unattainable; indifference curves further towards the origin represent less preferred options to bundle A.

Bundle L is preferred to bundle A but is not affordable, since it lies beyond the budget constraint. Bundle D, on the other hand, is affordable but gives less satisfaction than A. Bundle T costs as much as A, but gives only as much satisfaction as D. Bundle K is not affordable even though it lies on the same indifference curve as A. The optimum bundle to chose is bundle A, the point of utility maximization, given the constraints of income and price. At this point the consumer's indifference curve just touches the budget constraint and the consumer reaches the highest indifference curve possible, given the budget constraint.

Exercise 2.1

Assume that a schoolgirl has £10 pocket money per week. She spends all of her income on sweets and soft drinks. In her local shop a bag of sweets costs £2 and a can of Coca-Cola costs £1.

1 Draw a diagram showing this schoolgirl's budget constraint.
2 Draw an indifference curve on the same diagram to show which bundle of sweets and chocolate she might choose.

Figure 2.5 Utility maximization with a budget constraint

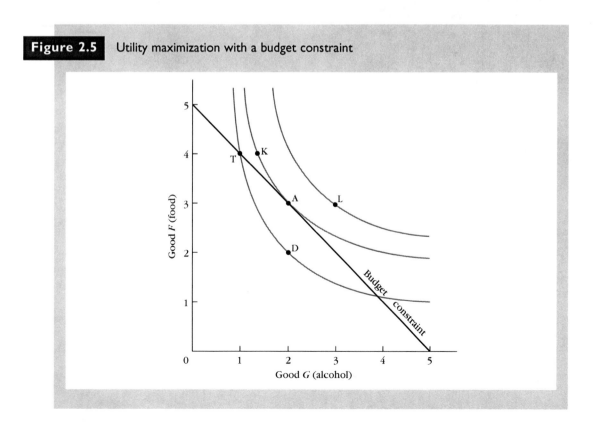

The indifference curve approach has been used for the analysis of a whole range of individual choice decisions. It has not been restricted to choosing between items of consumption from the supermarket but has been applied to many other decisions, from the choice of school for your children to your preferences for the environment and military defence. One particularly important area of choice, which is examined in Chapter 5, is the choice between leisure and income from working.

Utility maximization with a budget constraint

Your understanding of economic theory can often be improved if a little mathematical language is introduced. In the case of neoclassical consumer theory this involves consideration of the mathematical properties of both the indifference curve and the budget constraint.

The indifference curve

The slope of the indifference curve at point A in Figure 2.6a can be calculated by drawing a dashed line which is tangential to the indifference curve at this point. The slope of the indifference curve at A can be calculated in terms of the rise and the run of this dashed line (see Chapter 9, *Changing Economies*).

The rise of this line is represented by ΔF which is negative because the line is downward sloping, that is, there is a fall in the amount of good F as the amount of good G increases. The run of the line is represented by ΔG. It follows that:

$$\text{slope of indifference curve} = \frac{\text{rise}}{\text{run}} = \frac{\Delta F}{\Delta G}$$

Because ΔF is negative, so also is this slope. Not taking account of whether the slope is positive or negative, we find that its magnitude equals the marginal rate of substitution of good G for good F ($\text{MRS}_{G,F}$). It shows the rate at which the individual gives up good F for good G while remaining on the indifference curve. Hence:

$$\text{MRS}_{G,F} = -\frac{\Delta F}{\Delta G}$$

The budget constraint

The mathematical formula for the budget constraint is:

$$Y = P_F F + P_G G$$

where Y represents money income and P_F and P_G are the respective prices of goods F and G. The term F represents the amount of good F the individual consumes, while G is the amount of good G consumed.

Figure 2.6 The mathematical properties of the indifference curve and the budget constraint

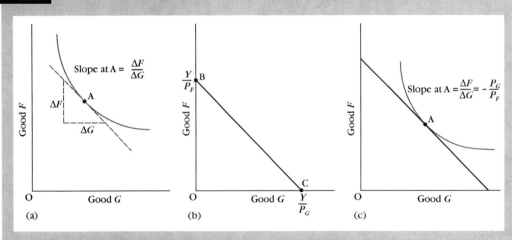

(a)   (b)   (c)

The above formula shows the constraint on the individual's budget if all income is spent on goods F and G.

Using this formula we can establish where the budget constraint cuts the horizontal and vertical axes in Figure 2.6b. It cuts the horizontal axis at point C where the individual allocates all income to good G, so $F = 0$. Inserting $F = 0$ in the formula for the budget constraint gives:

$$Y = P_G G$$

Thus $G = \frac{Y}{P_G}$ at the point C where the budget constraint cuts the horizontal axis.

On the vertical axis, all of the individual's budget is allocated to good F, so $G = 0$. Thus at point B on the vertical axis, inserting $G = 0$ in the budget constraint gives:

$$Y = P_F F$$

So $F = \frac{Y}{P_F}$ at the point B where the budget constraint cuts the vertical axis.

Having found points B and C, we can now examine the slope of the budget constraint in Figure 2.6b. As the amount of good G consumed increases, the amount of good F the consumer can afford decreases so the budget constraint is downward sloping and hence its slope is negative. We can measure this line's rise and run along the axes, so that its slope is given by:

$$\text{slope} = \frac{\text{rise}}{\text{run}} = -\frac{OB}{OC}$$

Now, since the distance OB is equal to $\frac{Y}{P_F}$ and the distance OC is equal to $\frac{Y}{P_G}$ the slope can be written as:

$$\text{slope} = -\frac{\frac{Y}{P_F}}{\frac{Y}{P_G}} = -\frac{P_G}{P_F}$$

Hence the magnitude of the slope of the budget constraint equals the price ratio:

$$\frac{P_G}{P_F}$$

It follows that the original formula for the budget constraint can be re-expressed in terms of its slope and intercept. If, as before:

$$Y = P_F F + P_G G$$

then dividing by P_F gives:

$$\frac{Y}{P_F} = F + \frac{P_G}{P_F} G$$

which by manipulation means that:

$$F = \frac{Y}{P_F} - \frac{P_G}{P_F} G$$

The budget constraint has an intercept $\frac{Y}{P_F}$ (where the budget line cuts the vertical axis) and slope $-\frac{P_G}{P_F}$ (which is negative because the budget constraint is downward sloping). In economic terms this means that the individual's budget constraint can be worked out from:

● real income – the amount of good F that can be purchased for money income Y

● relative prices – the ratio of the price of good G to good F.

The condition for utility maximization

The consumer maximizes utility by choosing the point on the highest possible indifference curve he or she can get to, given the budget constraint. Because indifference curves are convex and so bow in towards the origin, the point of greatest utility on any budget constraint will be not at one of its end points, but somewhere in-between at the point where the budget constraint just touches the highest indifference curve it can reach. This is point A on Figure 2.6c. At this point the indifference curve and the budget constraint have the same slope. So at this point of utility maximization, the slope of the indifference curve $\frac{\Delta F}{\Delta G}$, is equal to the slope of the budget constraint $-\frac{P_G}{P_F}$. Thus $\frac{\Delta F}{\Delta G} = -\frac{P_G}{P_F}$ and so $-\frac{\Delta F}{\Delta G} = \frac{P_G}{P_F}$.

This means that at the point of utility maximization, the marginal rate of substitution between two goods ($\text{MRS}_{G,F}$) is equal to their price ratio:

$$\text{MRS}_{G,F} = \frac{P_G}{P_F}$$

This condition for utility maximization along a budget constraint depends on consumers having diminishing marginal rates of substitution and thus convex indifference curves. The assumption of consumers' diminishing marginal rates of substitution therefore provides a key foundation for neoclassical general equilibrium theory (see Chapter 18).

2.3 Deriving the demand curve

Having introduced the basics of neoclassical consumer theory, it can now be applied to understanding how an individual would react to an event which is of crucial importance to neoclassical economics - a price change. The effect of a price change is to shift the consumer's budget constraint.

Consider the effect of a reduction in the price of good G, as shown in Figure 2.7(a).

At the initial price level, the consumer maximizes utility at A subject to the budget constraint shown by line ZS. A reduction in the price of good G pivots the budget line to the right to ZT. You can see this by considering what happens if the consumer spends all his or her money on good G. When the price of good G falls the consumer can afford to buy more of it than before the price change; T can be reached instead of S. However, point Z on the diagram is unchanged since this shows the amount of good F the consumer could purchase if all income was spent on it; this does not change if neither income nor the price of good F have changed. So ZT is the new budget constraint and, except at Z, the consumer can now afford to buy more of either good F or good G or both, because the price of good G has fallen. The effect of the fall in the price of good

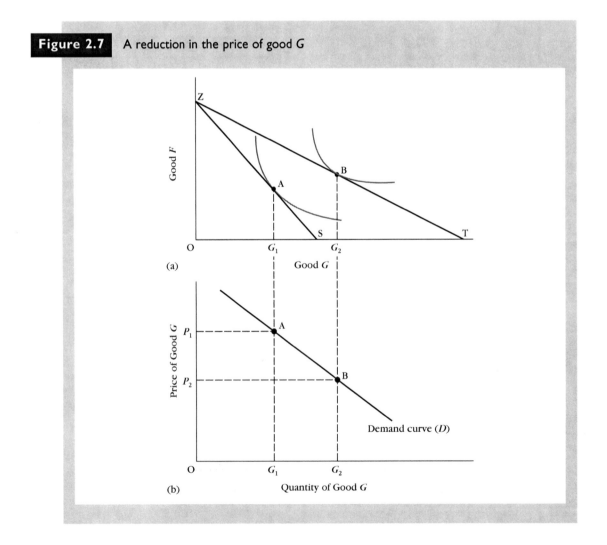

Figure 2.7   A reduction in the price of good G

G is to pivot the budget line around point Z from line ZS to line ZT on the diagram.

The shift in the budget constraint means the consumer can move onto a higher indifference curve. If A was the point of maximum utility on the previous budget constraint, then, on the new budget constraint, a higher indifference curve can be reached by maximizing utility at B. In response to the reduction in price, consumption of good G increases from G_1 to G_2 units.

We can represent the effect of the reduction in price shown in Figure 2.7(a) by drawing the individual's demand curve. When the price of good G falls from P_1 to P_2, the amount of good G the consumer wants to buy increases from G_1 to G_2. This is translated into a demand curve in Figure 2.7(b), showing the relationship between price and demand.

Exercise 2.2

In Figure 2.5 the indifference curve is tangential to the budget constraint at A. Try drawing this diagram on a separate piece of paper. By taking another look at what happened in Figure 2.7, see if you can show on your diagram the effect on the budget constraint of:

1 an increase in the price of good G
2 a reduction in the price of good F.

For each of your answers show a new point of utility maximization after the price change.

2.4 Market demand and consumer sovereignty

The demand curve in Figure 2.7(b) represents the behaviour of an individual consumer. To find the market demand curve we need to add up the demand curves of all the consumers for a particular good.

If there are two consumers in a market, Mr A and Mr B, then the demand curves for the two consumers could be added together, as in Figure 2.8.

At a price of £2, Mr A demands two units of good G and Mr B demands four units; market demand is, therefore, six units. For each price level, the amount demanded by the two consumers is added up to derive the market demand curve. (See *Changing Economies*, Chapter 7, Section 5.1)

The market demand curve can then be used to demonstrate that, under certain conditions, a market economy generates consumer sovereignty. Figure 2.9 shows the market demand curve for good G. Now assume that firms plan to supply 400 units of good G at a price of £2 per unit. This is represented by point A on the diagram. The problem is that consumers want to purchase only 200 units of good G at this price, so there is an excess supply of good G. Firms can only sell what consumers are willing to purchase and as consumers wish to purchase only 200 units at a price of £2, this will be all that firms will be able to sell at that price. How firms react to this situation is considered in Chapter 8. However, it is clear that

---

Figure 2.8   The derivation of a market demand curve

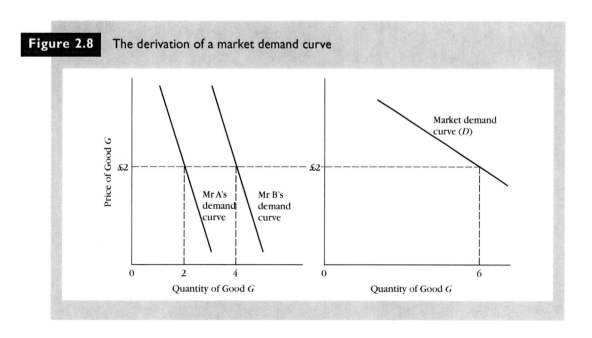

firms will not want to produce more than they can sell, so if firms continue to charge £2 per unit they will be forced to cut their supply of good *G* to 200 units (point B). The point to note is that it is consumers who are dictating how many units of good *G* are produced, not firms, the government nor any other outside body. Sovereignty rests with the decisions of individual consumers.

In demonstrating how consumer sovereignty can be delivered, the market demand curve provides the key building block of the neoclassical approach. We have seen that each consumer has his or her own particular tastes and preferences, and these are reflected in their indifference curves from which their individual demand curves derive. Adding up these individual demand curves to construct a market demand curve is like carrying out a big questionnaire asking how consumers feel about a particular product. In Figure 2.9 firms discover that consumers do not demand the same amount of good *G* that the firms wish to supply at the current price. This power, which consumers communicate to firms through their decisions in the market, is represented by the market demand curve.

In neoclassical theory, the decisions of firms can be represented by a market supply curve. This is shown by the upward sloping market supply curve *S* in Figure 2.9, where output increases as the price increases because production becomes more profitable. If the demand curve slopes downwards, there will be a point of equilibrium at which the demand and supply curves intersect. This is point C on Figure 2.9.

The beauty of this mechanism is that these adjustments between supply and demand take place without any intervention from outside the market. Each consumer and firm acts according to their own self-interest and, as if by an 'invisible hand', the market delivers. This is not to say that there must be a free market economy for consumer sovereignty to hold. From a neoclassical perspective, which judges an economy by its outcome, it is conceivable that the government could carry out a survey and find out from consumers what should be produced. However, the strength of a free market economy is its simplicity. There is no need for social scientists to design complicated questionnaires and conduct surveys of consumer opinion. Individuals communicate their tastes and preferences through their everyday demand decisions in the marketplace.

The market supply curve is derived by assuming competition between a large number of firms, in

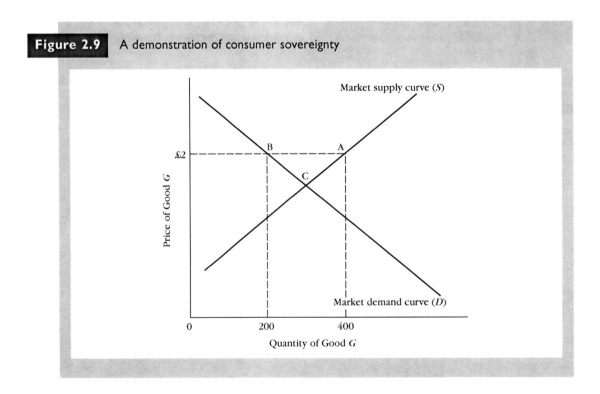

Figure 2.9 A demonstration of consumer sovereignty

which no single firm can influence the price level. If this assumption was relaxed and, say, one firm dominated a particular market, a degree of power would then rest with this particular firm and it could influence the price level; as a result, consumer sovereignty would be compromised. A demonstration of consumer sovereignty, therefore, requires more than just the assumptions about consumer behaviour necessary to derive a downward sloping market demand curve. It requires us to derive an upward sloping supply curve and to make a number of assumptions about the behaviour of firms, in particular, to ensure price taking behaviour in the market in which they operate (see Chapters 1 and 18).

It should also be noted that the scope of this exposition is limited to particular markets for goods. The approach is partial, with each market considered in isolation from others. Unlike general equilibrium theory, in which all markets are interdependent (see Chapter 1), in the partial equilibrium analysis of this chapter there is no feedback between markets.

> ### Reflection
>
> What are the origins of consumer sovereignty? How do consumers communicate their tastes and preferences to firms?

3 THE STRUCTURE OF THE DEMAND CURVE

Since the demand curve is so important to the neoclassical approach, this section examines its structure in more detail and evaluates the assumptions that are necessary to derive a downward sloping individual demand curve. This evaluation will provide the basis for discussing some of the limitations of the neoclassical demonstration of consumer sovereignty.

3.1 Income and substitution effects

Changes in price can have two main impacts on the behaviour of consumers. First, in response to a price change, consumers substitute between commodities. For example, if the price of bread falls and that of potatoes stays the same, consumers will substitute between the two commodities, that is, they will reduce their consumption of potatoes and increase their consumption of bread. This is known as the *substitution effect* of the price change. Second, changes in price have an impact on the income of consumers. A reduction in the price of bread will make consumers better off in real terms and, as a result, they may buy more bread. This is known as the *income effect* of the price change.

> ### Substitution effect
>
> The substitution effect of a price change measures the amount by which a consumer substitutes one good for another, whilst maintaining the same level of utility.

> ### Income effect
>
> The income effect of a price change measures the impact on the amount of the good consumed as a result of the consequent change in real income.

These two effects of a price change are shown in Figure 2.10, which provides a more detailed examination of the price change shown in Figure 2.7(a) above. As before, the price of good G falls and the budget line pivots out from line ZS to ZT. The consumer responds to the price change by increasing consumption of good G from A to B. Notice, however, that a new line, labelled RP, has been drawn on Figure 2.10. This new line enables us to split the price change into two separate steps, from A to A' and from A' to B. The first step, A to A', measures the substitution effect of the price change, while the step from A' to B measures the income effect.

The movement from A to A' is the substitution effect. This is based on the propensity consumers have to substitute between commodities in response to a relative price change. The price of good G falls relative to that of good F and the consumer moves along the indifference curve, replacing good F with good G. This is represented by a rotation of the budget constraint along the indifference curve from line ZS to line RP, so that the individual remains on the same indifference curve but now consumes more of good G and less of good F because of the price change. In defining the substitution effect, we deliberately keep the consumer at the same level of utility so that the effect of the relative price change then can be isolated.

Assume, for example, that good F represents jam and good G marmalade. If the price of marmalade (good G) falls, a typical consumer may substitute out of jam and buy marmalade instead. The substitution effect measures the amount by which the consumer substitutes marmalade for jam in response to a price change while maintaining the same level of utility. Substitution effects always work in the same direction. As a good becomes relatively cheaper, consumers substitute it for other goods and buy more of it.

The second part of the price change is the income effect, the movement from A' to B in Figure 2.10. In the example of marmalade given above, a fall in its absolute price, other things being equal, improves the real income of the consumer as more can be bought than before. The income effect measures the effect of this change in real income on the amount of marmalade consumed. As we shall see, income effects can work in either direction. Sometimes consumers buy more, sometimes they buy less of a good, as income rises.

The effect of such an increase in real income can be represented by shifting the budget constraint to the right, from line RP to ZT. This increase in income does not affect the *slope* of the budget constraint, since this depends on the relative prices of goods F and G and this was taken into account in the shift from ZS to RP. The budget constraint ZT is therefore parallel to the budget constraint RP. It represents the additional amount of both good F and good G the consumer can afford as a consequence of the change in real income.

The total effect of a price change is the combined effect of the income and substitution effects. Substitution, as we have seen, can work in only one direction; as a good becomes relatively cheaper consumers substitute it for other goods. However, income effects can work in either direction. As income rises, people have more to spend, so they may increase their consumption of some goods and not change or even reduce their consumption of other goods.

3.2 Giffen goods

Income effects can be very important, as Robert Giffen (1837-1910), a contemporary of Marshall's, found. Giffen, who examined consumption behaviour during the Irish potato famines, was interested in the effects of a change in the price of a staple food, such as bread or potatoes, on working-class consumption.

The substitution effect suggests that there should be an increase in the demand for bread if its price falls. However, we also have to allow for the income effect and the fact that people will be better off when the price of bread falls. Since bread is a staple part of the working-class diet, a

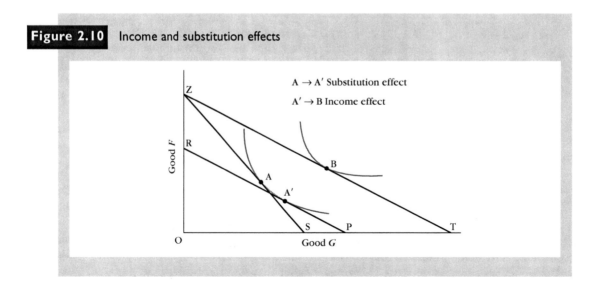

Figure 2.10 Income and substitution effects

reduction in its price will leave more income available for the consumption of other goods. Indeed, since they can now afford other, more expensive items, such as meat, people may consume less bread than before its price fell. Instead of filling up working-class stomachs with bread, a different diet, with less bread and more meat, is made possible. The demand for bread could fall in response to a reduction in price, thereby providing an example of a *Giffen good*.

Giffen good

A good for which demand falls (rises) when its price falls (rises).

A good is described as Giffen-like or Giffenesque in character if its demand increases in response to a price increase or its demand decreases in response to a price decrease. For the case of bread, this could mean that when its price increases, the detrimental effect on income could result in consumers having to buy more bread. If a good is Giffen-like, the effect of the change in price is positive – a price increase leads to an increase in demand; a price decrease leads to a decrease in demand. Although the Giffen good was originally identified as a nineteenth century phenomenon, it is still relevant to the analysis of the consumption of staple foods by consumers living in poverty today.

Looking back at Figure 2.7 you can see how a downward sloping demand curve can be derived from a consumer's indifference map diagram. In this case, in response to the fall in the price of good G, consumer utility maximization results in more of good G being consumed. When the price of good G falls, the budget constraint moves out to the right from ZS to ZT. This reaction to the price fall is shown by the movement from A to B in Figure 2.7(a), which gives a downward sloping demand curve in Figure 2.7(b).

Sometimes, however, the demand for good G will fall when the price of good G falls. In that case, as shown in Figure 2.11(a), instead of moving from A to B, the consumer moves from A to C in response to the fall in the price of good G. This results in a reduction in the quantity demanded of good G from G_1 to G_2 units. This possibility cannot be excluded. Depending on the shape of the indifference map, the consumer could maximize utility at either B or C after the price fall.

Figure 2.11(b) shows that the movement to point C results in an upward sloping demand curve. In this example, good G is a Giffen good: as the price of good G falls, the quantity demanded of good G also falls. The universality of the downward sloping demand curve is contradicted by this example of Giffenesque behaviour. Note that this does not mean that all of the demand curve is upward sloping, only that a part of it may take this shape.

The Giffen good can be examined in more detail by splitting up the effect of a price change on consumer demand into two separate parts. Figure 2.12 provides an illustration of how the income and substitution effects interact to give an upward sloping demand curve.

The effect of the reduction in the price of good G is broken down into a substitution effect, from A to A', and an income effect, from A' to C.

The substitution effect always goes in the same direction (provided the indifference curves are convex). It is the income effect that drives the reduction in the quantity demanded of good G. As a result of the price reduction, when real income increases, the individual in this case reduces consumption of good G and increases consumption of good F.

Income effects can go in one of two directions, and therefore we can distinguish between two types of goods, both of which are illustrated in Figure 2.13. The first, illustrated in Figure 2.13(a), is a *normal* good. The demand for good G increases from G_1 to G_2, when there is a parallel shift of the budget constraint as income increases In calling such a good 'normal', the presumption is that it is normal for the consumption of a good to increase as real income increases and fall as real income falls.

Normal good

A commodity is defined as normal if its consumption increases as income increases and, conversely, its consumption falls when income is reduced.

Figure 2.13(b), on the other hand, shows what happens if good G is an *inferior* good. As income increases, consumption of good G falls from G_1 to G_2 units. This fits the Giffen example in which consumers can afford to buy less bread as real income increases. Conversely, if income falls consumers buy more of a Giffen good since they cannot afford more expensive goods.

Whether or not a good is inferior is crucial to whether its demand curve is upward sloping. If consumption of a good falls as income increases, it is possible that the quantity demanded will also fall if the price of the good is reduced. However, the income effect in this case would have to be strong enough to outweigh the substitution effect, which we know will increase the quantity demanded of a good whose price has fallen.

Figure 2.14 shows three different outcomes of the reduction in the price of good G. If the outcome is to shift consumption from point A to point D, good *G* is *weakly inferior*. The income effect works in the opposite direction to the

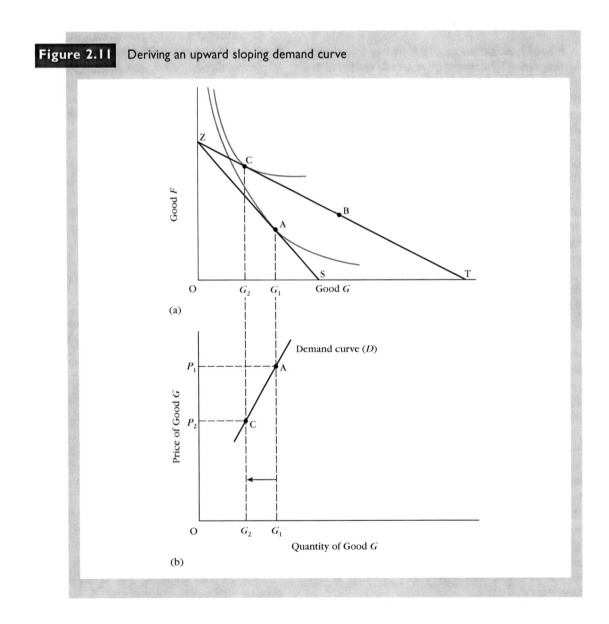

Figure 2.11 Deriving an upward sloping demand curve

substitution effect but is not strong enough to wipe it out. If the outcome is point D, therefore, good *G* is inferior but is *not* a Giffen good, since its demand still increases in response to the reduction in its price.

This contrasts with an outcome at point C which would mean that good *G* is *strongly inferior*. In this case, good G *is* a Giffen good as the income effect works in the opposite direction to the substitution effect and is strong enough to wipe it out. There is a

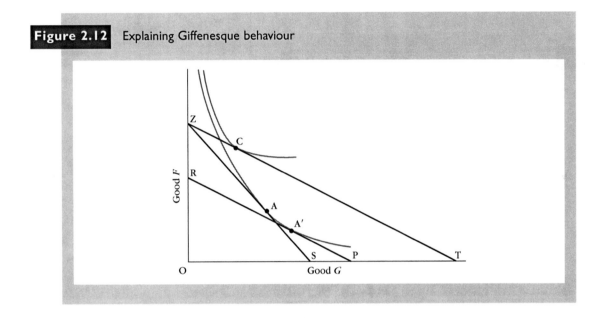

Figure 2.12 Explaining Giffenesque behaviour

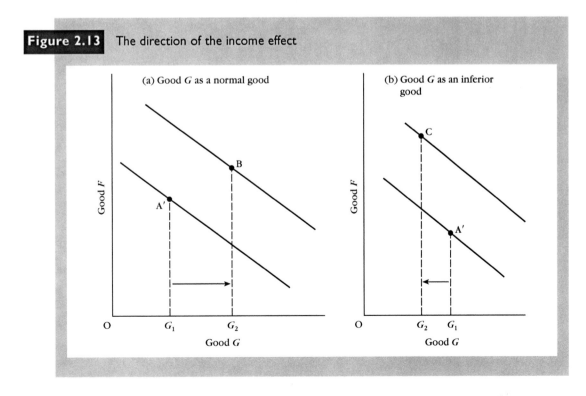

Figure 2.13 The direction of the income effect

(a) Good *G* as a normal good

(b) Good *G* as an inferior good

fall in the consumption of good G in response to its price reduction.

If the outcome is at point B, good G is normal. The income and substitution effects work in the same direction and there is a rise in the consumption of good G in response to the price reduction.

It follows that since strongly inferior goods or Giffen goods are an economic possibility, demand curves cannot automatically be assumed to be downward sloping. Indeed, Zamagni (1987) argues that the general shape for such a demand curve is a backward S-shape. Figure 2.15 shows the shape of a

Figure 2.14 Different outcomes as a result of a price reduction

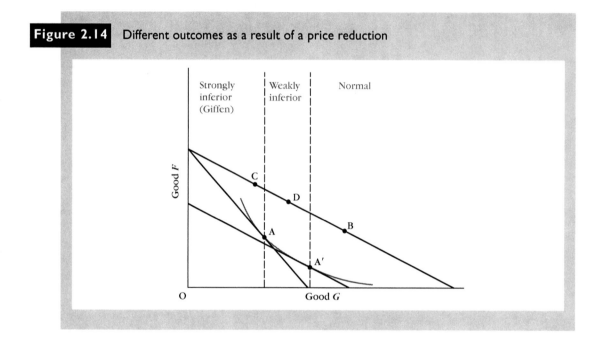

Figure 2.15 The backward S-shaped demand curve

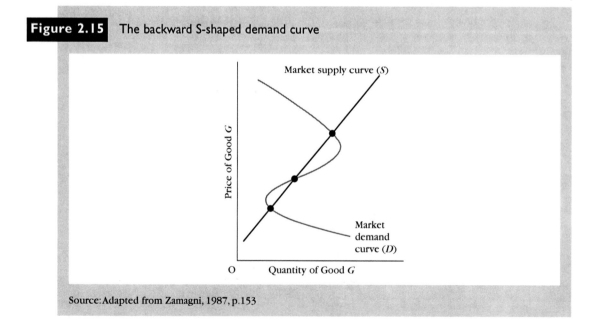

Source: Adapted from Zamagni, 1987, p.153

market demand curve which could conceivably be derived from aggregating individual backward S-shaped demand curves.

Most of the demand curve is downward sloping but there is also an upward sloping part to the curve which derives from Giffenesque behaviour. In general, goods that are Giffenesque behave in this way at some price levels but not at others.

A market supply curve, similar to the one you saw in Figure 2.9, has also been drawn on Figure 2.15. This supply curve is upward sloping because firms increase their supply of a good as the price level increases. If, however, the demand curve is a backward S-shape, a unique equilibrium of demand and supply will not occur. In Figure 2.15 there are three possible equilibria. Giffen goods, with their demand curves that do not consistently slope downwards, therefore create problems for the neoclassical model of demand and supply.

The possibility of multiple equilibria weakens the demonstration of consumer sovereignty which the neoclassical model can provide. If there are several possible equilibria, consumers are not giving a unique answer to the question 'How much of good *G* should be produced?' Consumers are not so much dictating to firms what to produce, as giving them a number of options.

4   QUESTIONING THE ASSUMPTIONS OF CONSUMER THEORY

The derivation of the demand curve and the consideration of the income and substitution effects that give rise to it depend on consumers having indifference maps – a set of indifference curves that join up consumption bundles between which the consumer is indifferent. On the face of things this seems to be quite reasonable. Any schoolgirl with a certain amount of pocket money will have to choose how much to spend on, say, chocolate and crisps. She may prefer chocolate to crisps but if she likes them both there will be some quantity of chocolate that she will give up willingly for an extra bag of crisps. That was how we defined the marginal rate of substitution of crisps for chocolate in Section 2.

But for some consumers the notion of substituting between goods and indifference curves may not be so meaningful.

4.1   *Lexicographic preferences*

Question

Assume that you are unemployed and have £20 available for your weekly shopping bill. Since money is tight you have to draw up a shopping list in advance of your trip to the supermarket. Choose a selection of items on which to spend your £20 from the following alternatives:

Item	£
Toilet rolls	4.25
Tea bags	2.39
Red wine	7.99
Chicken	5.33
Mild Cheddar	3.00
Minced lamb	3.19
Back bacon	4.10
French lager	10.99
Papaya shampoo	2.99
Hair conditioner	3.99
Tomato ketchup	2.30
Chardonnay	5.99

Your choice depends to some extent on your preferences among these goods. You may prefer lamb to chicken, and you may prefer to drink red wine rather than French lager. You are, however, considerably constrained in your choice because you have only £20 to spend. For example, it would not be feasible, within your budget, to buy French lager, red wine, and Chardonnay. By contrast, I can introduce you to a man who could afford all three of these items, and more. Here are the items purchased by the English actor Paul Bradley (who used to play Nigel in EastEnders) during one trip to the supermarket.

Paul is able to spend over £192 during his trip to the supermarket, and the table reveals the host of consumption items he is able to choose. In his case he *is* able to afford French lager, red wine and Chardonnay.

The simple point which this comparison illustrates is that the degree of choice we can exercise in our consumption depends on our level of income. For Paul Bradley, the *People's* psychologist Jane Firbank reports, 'Cooking is obviously a great adventure for Paul and he gets great fun from looking after his family'. This could not generally be said for the unemployed person trying to survive on £20 a

ME AND MY TROLLEY
...with Paul Bradley

EASTENDERS star Paul Bradley was a man with a mission as he shopped at his local Tesco in Edmonton, North London.

"I've just found a new recipe I want to try for lamb with redcurrant jelly," he told *JANE SIMON.*

"I make a mean broccoli pasta too -- but my kids live on pesto sandwiches and bananas."

Here's Paul's list:

Swede	1.05
Toilet rolls	4.25
Watercress	0.85
Mushrooms	1.98
Broccoli	1.50
Spring onions	0.39
Cucumber	0.35
Tomatoes	0.95
Lemon	0.20
Avocados	0.99
Peppers	2.25
Iceberg lettuce	0.49
Mandarins	1.49
Small bananas	0.55
Gala apples	1.69
Grapes	1.85
Cherries	2.97
White loaf	0.49
French bread	0.49
Monkey nuts	0.85
Yoghurt selection	1.59
Apple juice	4.49
Orange juice	3.15
Greek yoghurt	1.79
Variety cereals	1.35
Coffee filters	1.65
Teabags	2.39
Gold Blend	4.25
French lager	10.99
Rice Krispies	1.95
Shreddies	1.96
Milk	1.42
Half-fat milk	0.95
Balsamic vinegar	1.35
Red wine	7.99
Chardonnay	5.99
Sparkling wine	3.99
Redcurrant jelly	1.50
Spaghetti	0.75
Butter x2	1.64
Ice cream cones	1.09
Lamb cutlets	11.52
Emmental	1.50
Feta cheese	1.99
Mild Cheddar	3.00
Spare rib sauce	1.25
Minced lamb	3.19
Camembert	2.09
Pork chops	4.00
Veg stock cubes	0.88
Pistachio nuts	1.39
Conchiglie pasta	0.84
Cheese slices	3.98
Grated cheddar	2.19
Vinegar	0.59
Cheese spread	0.99
Eliche pasta	0.84
Pork sausages	1.69
Back bacon	4.10
Chicken	5.33
Cracker Barrel	1.79
Marmite	0.62
Tomato ketchup	2.30
Long-life cream	0.77
Peanut butter	1.39
Whole nutmeg	1.09
Sesame oil	1.79
Rose essence	0.44
Lemon dressing	0.37
Corn oil	2.49
Mayonnaise	2.25
Free-range eggs	1.59
Orange marmalade	0.71
Strawberries x2	2.38
Olive oil	5.35
Pesto sauce x2	2.98
Strawberry conserve	1.39
Tinned tomatoes	0.24
Trainer pants	3.69
Toothpaste	2.79
Parsnips	2.11
Thread noodles	0.67
Organic carrots	0.99
White bread	0.61
Mustard powder	1.35
Conditioner	3.99
French potatoes	1.99
Toothpaste	0.99
King Edwards	1.98
Papaya shampoo	2.99
Houmous	1.19
Worcester sauce	0.87
Total	**£192.18**

Source: The People, 16 June 1996, p.21

week, where surviving is more likely to be a nightmare than an adventure.

For the individual whose income is restricted, outlay must be directed towards the satisfaction of certain basic needs. He must eat, of course, so food

will be a priority in his consumption basket. He probably has to decide how much food is required before allocating his income to less important items such as hair conditioner. Food obviously satisfies a more basic need, his hunger, than conditioner which helps his appearance. We can now consider the implications of this type of choice for an individual's indifference map.

Consider the consumption of food and hair conditioner by a 30 year old male. According to the Medical Research Council, 'an average 30 year old man needs between 2,500 and 3,500 calorific units a day, whereas a woman will use up only between 1,750 and 2,250' (Cathie, 1976, p.11). Let us say that this man consumes only 2000 calories of food and 20 millilitres of hair conditioner. This bundle is represented by A on Figure 2.16.

At this level of consumption he is still hungry, so bundle A is preferred to any combination of food and conditioner which involves less than 2000 calories a day. If, for example, he consumed 1000 calories a day and 30 millilitres of conditioner, point B, this would give him less utility than his 2000 calories and 20 millilitres of conditioner at A. All bundles which are below the horizontal line in Figure 2.16 are, therefore, worse than A.

Further, because 2000 calories per day leaves him still hungry, all bundles above the horizontal line are better than bundle A. If, for example, the consumer can increase his consumption of food to 3000 calories per day, and only consume 10 millilitres of conditioner, as shown by bundle C, he will prefer C to A.

If, on the other hand, the consumer has to stick to 2000 calories a day, then he will prefer more conditioner to less. All points to the right of point A on the horizontal line are preferred to A, and all points to the left are less preferred than A.

All points on the diagram, therefore, are either preferred to A or less preferred than A. Since there are no points on the diagram which the consumer regards with indifference, as compared to point A, it follows that there is no indifference curve which passes through this point. This example demonstrates the non-existence of indifference curves for some consumers. The individual who prioritizes a certain category of consumption, such as food, displays what are called *lexicographic preferences*. This term is based on the layout of a dictionary, where the letter A is always before the letter B regardless of which letters follow. The word Aztec always comes before Baptist even though the second letter of Aztec (letter z) comes long after the second letter in Baptist (letter a). The same happens with our hungry consumer's consumption of food, which always comes before his consumption of hair conditioner.

Lexicographic preferences

A system for ranking preferences in which the individual gives priority to particular items of consumption.

Admittedly, this is an extreme example in which the individual places absolute priority of food over hair conditioner. In practice there may be some, if only limited, substitution between goods. The point to be made, however, is that to the extent that individuals prioritize their consumption to satisfy particular needs, the indifference map is of limited relevance to understanding their behaviour.

The non-existence of indifference curves when consumers give priority to satisfying a particular need means that there will be no substitution effect in response to a price change. Changes in demand will be driven by the income effect alone. This weakens the notion of consumer sovereignty as some consumers are too poor to have decisions to

make. For example, most of the items on Paul Bradley's shopping list would never be bought by someone with the budget constraint of the unemployed. In communicating to the market whether they prefer, say, red wine to Chardonnay, the poor may not even be consulted. In the quotation at the start of this chapter, Enoch Powell argued that even the poorest members of society are not disfranchised in the great ballot of consumer democracy. The question to be asked, however, is how much weight is given to the votes made by people on different levels of income? It can be argued that for many of the goods which are stacked on supermarket shelves, the poor are excluded from the consumer ballot.

In this view, consumer sovereignty depends on level of income. In the ballot of consumer democracy, those with more money are able to cast votes that have more effect than those with less money.

4.2 Consistency

Thus far we have examined two possible problems with consumer sovereignty. First, Section 3.2 showed that demand curves may not be downward sloping. This means that there may be more than one place where market demand and supply curves intersect,

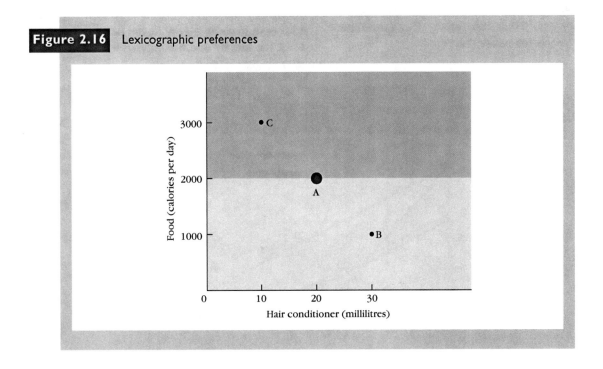

Figure 2.16 Lexicographic preferences

so there may not be a unique equilibrium price and quantity. Consumer demand may be satisfied by a number of different possible equilibrium prices, each corresponding to a different equilibrium quantity, so that how much is produced cannot be determined by consumers alone.

Second, we saw in Section 4.1 that consumers can influence only those markets they enter. In practice we do not buy small quantities of everything. Many consumers, therefore, have no influence in many markets. In particular, the poor, through having less money to spend, will have less influence than the rich. Consumer sovereignty is not egalitarian.

This section will raise a third problem with the neoclassical demonstration of consumer sovereignty. Neoclassical theories of consumer sovereignty depend upon assumptions about the consistency of human behaviour which may not hold. Section 3.2 showed that the effect of a price change could not always be predicted because income effects may work in the opposite direction and outweigh substitution effects, as they do for Giffen goods. However, it is usually assumed that the 'Law of Demand' is met, that is that substitution effects always work in one direction – they are *always* negative. In this section I will show how this assumption of negative substitution effects can be tested by examining the consistency of consumer preferences. To do this I must first introduce you to some additional concepts which are used in consumer theory. These will help to prepare you for a case study in experimental economics at the end of this section.

The Slutsky approximation

In any application of the neoclassical theory of consumption, one of the key problems is that indifference curves, which provide its theoretical core, cannot be observed. We cannot, as it were, peep into the heads of each consumer and find out their preferences among the vast array of consumption goods that are on offer. We cannot plot an individual's indifference curve using real world data.

To overcome this measurement problem, economists make an approximation which was first developed by the Russian economist Eugene Slutsky (1880–1948). This can be illustrated by once again considering a reduction in the price of good G. Figure 2.17, which models the same price change as Figure 2.10 earlier, shows that if the price of good G falls, the consumer moves from the original bundle at A to a new bundle B. The impact of this price reduction is made up of the substitution effect (from A to A') and the income effect (from A' to B).

The substitution effect from A to A' is clearly negative, since the reduction in the price of good G induces the individual to consume more of good G. Indeed, the substitution effect must always be negative if the indifference curve is convex, as shown in Figure 2.17. You can see that in splitting up the impact of the price change into the substitution effect and the income effect, the line RP is drawn parallel to ZT and tangential to the indifference curve that runs through A. If the indifference curve is convex, that is, if it bows in towards the origin, the point of tangency, A', of the line RP and the indifference curve which

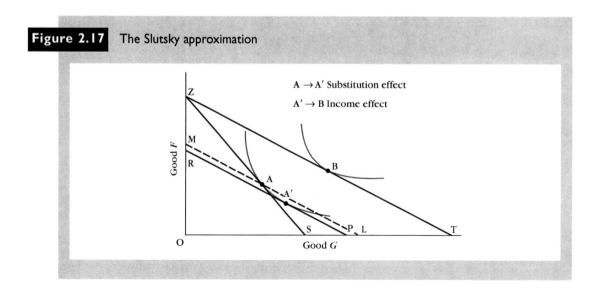

Figure 2.17 The Slutsky approximation

A → A' Substitution effect

A' → B Income effect

runs through A must be to the right of A. There must be a negative substitution effect.

The key thing to notice about Figure 2.17 is that to examine the substitution effect in isolation, we would need to specify an income effect. This income effect compensates for the effect of the price change by keeping the individual on the same indifference curve. It is referred to as a *compensating variation*. (In this case the compensation is negative because the individual gains from the price reduction – the compensation would be positive under a price increase.) The compensating reduction in income is represented by the parallel shift of the budget constraint from ZT to RP.

Compensating variation

Following a change in price, the compensating variation measures the amount of real income that would have to be given to the consumer to ensure the same level of utility.

However, since the indifference curve is not observable we can observe neither the substitution effect nor the income effect. To test whether the substitution effect is negative we must modify the model in some way, using observable data.

Now to make an approximation of the income effect, using information which is at our disposal, a new line ML can be drawn which is close to RP, provided the price change is small, and parallel to it. This new line is drawn through point A. This is because we can observe how much of good *F* and good *G* the individual chooses in the original bundle A. In drawing this new line we make what is known as a Slutsky approximation to the income effect. Instead of trying to find out how much income, after the price change, is needed to keep the individual on the same indifference curve, we can observe how much income is required to enable the individual to afford the original bundle of goods at A. We make a Slutsky approximation of the compensating variation, often referred to as the Slutsky compensating variation.

Revealed preferences

With the Slutsky approximation at our disposal we can devise a simple test of consumer theory. To complete this task I shall now introduce the idea of revealed preference, originally developed by Samuelson (1938). This can be explained by once again considering a reduction in the price of good *G*. Figure 2.18 shows that, as before, the individual moves from bundle A to B after the price change, but

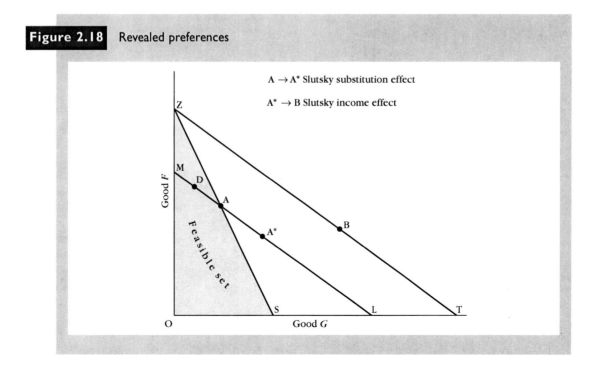

Figure 2.18 Revealed preferences

A → A* Slutsky substitution effect

A* → B Slutsky income effect

the Slutsky approximation to the income effect is established by drawing the line ML through A.

The Slutsky approximation to the substitution effect, more commonly known as the Slutsky substitution effect, is represented by the movement from A to A*. The Slutsky approximation to the income effect, again more commonly known as the Slutsky income effect, is represented by the movement from A* to B.

We saw earlier that if the indifference curve is convex then the substitution effect must be negative. We can also prove that the Slutsky substitution effect must also be negative. Consider the choice the individual made before the price change, when his or her budget constraint was ZS. Bundle A was preferred to all other bundles that could have been afforded within the confines of the budget. Any of the combinations of goods F and G on the budget constraint ZS, and any of the bundles within the feasible set to the left of the budget constraint could have been afforded, for example bundle D in Figure 2.18. The individual could have afforded D but chose bundle A. Indeed, we can say that A is revealed to be preferred to D. By choosing A when D could have been afforded, the individual displays a *revealed preference* for A over D.

Revealed preference

By purchasing a particular bundle of goods, an individual reveals that this bundle is preferred to all other affordable bundles.

Now consider the behaviour of the individual after the price change. If we make a compensating variation of income, in order to isolate the substitution effect, you can see that the individual can now choose a new bundle from the line ML. Will the substitution effect be negative for this consumer?

In asking this question we can establish whether the individual satisfies a basic assumption of neoclassical consumer theory, namely that of consistency, which was defined earlier in Section 2. If an individual prefers A to D then, to be consistent, he or she must never prefer D to A.

Question

On the new line ML in Figure 2.18, to show consistent behaviour which of bundle A* or bundle D should an individual choose?

The individual's behaviour would be consistent only if bundle A* was chosen, since this bundle was not affordable before the price change: choosing bundle D after the price change would be inconsistent behaviour. Before the price change the individual revealed a preference for A compared to D; both were affordable and he or she chose A rather than D.

Consistency requires that after the price change, the individual chooses bundles that fall on the new budget line ML at or to the right of point A. Choosing bundles on the new budget line to the left of point A would be inconsistent. These bundles, since they lie within the original budget constraint ZS, could have been chosen before the price change. Choosing a bundle somewhere between A and L results in an increase in the demand for good G. So consistency requires that a compensated reduction in the price of good G must result in an increase in the demand for good G or perhaps no change in its demand. A reduction in the price of good G cannot consistently result in a fall in its demand. Again this is a negative (or zero) substitution effect, in which the price of good G and its (compensated) demand cannot move in the same direction.

This result enables us to test one of the cornerstones of neoclassical consumer theory, its assumption of consistency. To test consistency by the revealed preference approach and the Slutsky approximation requires only data which are observable, bundles of goods and their prices. We did not need to know anything about indifference curves to draw Figure 2.18; only observable bundles of goods are needed.

In applying this methodology to test for consistency there are two strategies which economists follow. The first is to examine consumers' behaviour over time. A test for analysing time series data has been developed by Varian (1982). The basic approach is to observe consumption patterns at different points of time, and assess whether consumers behave consistently. The problem with this approach, however, is that one cannot be sure that tastes are stable over time. A consumer may appear to behave inconsistently, but it may be instead that his or her tastes have changed and that the observed behaviour is a consistent reflection of the consumer's changed taste.

A second research strategy is to carry out some *experimental economics* by simulating in a laboratory the choices facing consumers. The advantage of this approach is that the economist can, to some extent, control the environment in which individuals make their decisions. An economist using non-experimental data lacks any control over the many factors which influence economic behaviour. However, the experimental economist can ensure in the laboratory situation that choices are effectively simultaneous in order to overcome the problem of changes in tastes over time.

Experimental economics

Where economic theory is tested using laboratory conditions which simulate real-life economic situations.

An experiment to test consistency

In order to test whether consumers made consistent choices, Sippel (1997) invited groups of students to take part in two separate experiments, one in June 1993 and the other in February 1995. In the first experiment, 12 subjects took part and in the second, 30 students were used. Each subject was given a fixed budget within which he or she could purchase a bundle of goods to be consumed over a period of one hour. Table 2.1 shows the goods that were available.

Table 2.1   Goods to be consumed

Goods offered	Description	Range
Video clips	Watching a videotape of rock and pop music video clips	30–60 mins
Computer games	Playing 'Super Blast' (in the first experiment) or 'Pinball' (in the second experiment)	27.5–60 mins
Magazines	Reading a selection of newspapers and magazines	30–60 mins
Coca-Cola	Cold soft drink	400–2000 grammes
Orange juice	Cold drink	750–2000 grammes
Coffee	Prepared when demanded	600–2000 grammes
Haribo	Popular brand of sweets	400–2000 grammes
Snacks	Pretzels, peanuts etc.	600–2000 grammes

To test for consistency, the subjects were confronted with ten different budget constraints, each budget constraint involving a different set of prices for the goods shown in Table 2.1. The subjects were asked to choose their optimum bundle for each of the different budget constraints. However, they were allowed to consume only one of their chosen bundles, selected at random by a computer, at the end of the experiment. By having his subjects make their choices effectively simultaneously, that is, before any consumption took place, Sippel provided a possible way of overcoming the problem of changes in taste, so that he could then check whether the individuals in his experiments made inconsistent choices.

He found that a large proportion of individuals regularly made inconsistent choices. In the first experiment, 11 out of the 12 subjects were inconsistent in some of their choices, and in the second experiment 22 out of 30 subjects were, on occasions, inconsistent.

In assessing the results of his experiment Sippel considers 'how serious these deviations from optimising behaviour really are' (Sippel, 1997, p.1439). Two main points can be made. First, just because an individual occasionally breaks consistency does not mean that this individual is generally inconsistent. Sippel qualifies his results by pointing out that only a small proportion of the possible number of violations took place in the experiments. The individuals behaved consistently more frequently than they behaved inconsistently. Second, on a number of occasions, the breaks in consistency may have occurred because alternative bundles of goods had very similar combinations of goods. For example, could the consumer reasonably be expected to compare a bundle with 30 grammes of Coca-Cola and 30 grammes of coffee with a bundle containing 31 grammes of Coca-Cola and 29 grammes of coffee? As economists we might observe this data as being evidence of consumer inconsistency but, in reality, these bundles are so similar that it may be unreasonable to expect clear rankings between them.

Source: Sippel, 1997

This case study provides an insight into how economists have gone about testing a key assumption of neoclassical economics, but it offers no clear answer as to whether or not reported violations of consistency have serious implications for the neoclassical approach. For most consumers in the experiment, consistency is broken for at least some of their consumption decisions. In defence of the neoclassical approach, however, it can be argued that occasional breaks in consistency do not invalidate consistency as a general assumption of consumer behaviour.

As mentioned earlier, the validity of the consistency assumption has implications for aspects of neoclassical economics beyond the shape of the demand curve and its use in demonstrating consumer sovereignty. The consistency of preferences is central to the application of neoclassical consumer theory to practical policy issues.

4.3 Irrational choices

The main thrust of the argument above is that if consumers behave in a consistent manner, there will be a negative substitution effect. Becker (1962), however, argued that even if human behaviour is inconsistent, the demand curve is still likely to be downward sloping. He considered two extremes of human behaviour. 'On the one hand, households are often said to be impulsive, erratic, and subject to never-ending whim, and on the other hand, inert, habitual, and sluggish' (Becker, 1962, p.5). Consider Impulsive Ian. He doesn't waste his time inspecting the price of items in the supermarket, rather, he races round, throwing all and sundry into his shopping trolley.

We can model the behaviour of Impulsive Ian by assuming that he consumes an initial bundle which represents an average of what is available. So if his budget constraint is the line ZS on Figure 2.19, Impulsive Ian will consume the average bundle A which lies on the midpoint between Z and S. Can we now predict how he would react to a price change?

Becker argues that, when faced with a price change, Impulsive Ian is likely to consume a new

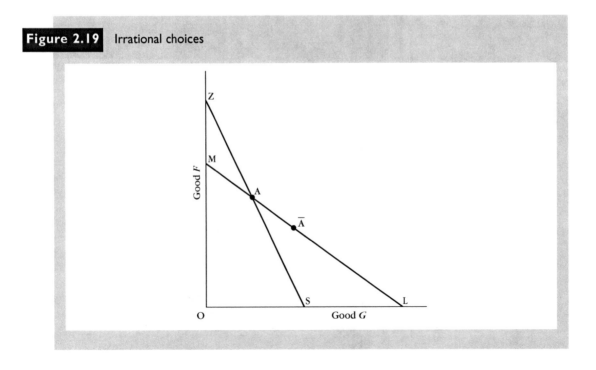

Figure 2.19 Irrational choices

bundle to the right of point A, for the simple reason that most of the new budget constraint ML is to the right of point A. More bundles are available on the segment AL than are available on the segment AM. The average bundle is now $\overline{A}$, the midpoint of the line ML.

In his whiz through the supermarket, Impulsive Ian is more likely to throw combinations of goods into his trolley from line AL than from line AM. Amid the erratic throwing of goods into the trolley, $\overline{A}$, represents the mean combination of goods that he is most likely to purchase. Even though he is erratic, this consumer is likely to increase his demand for good G in response to a reduction in its price. 'The fundamental theorem of rational behaviour, that market demand curves are negatively inclined, is, therefore, also implied by impulsive behaviour ...' (Becker, 1962, p.6).

A similar argument applies to Cautious Colin, the sluggish, habitual consumer. If this consumer starts at point A in Figure 2.19, it might be expected that, out of habit, he will remain at A after the price change. The same follows if he starts anywhere on the segment AS of the budget line. If he chose one of these bundles before the price change he will stick to this choice after the price change. Since these bundles are feasible within his budget after the price change, if he is a creature of habit he will stay on this segment.

However, if Cautious Colin consumes an initial bundle on the segment AZ, the top part of budget line ZS, this is no longer feasible after the price change. Even though Cautious Colin is a bit of a stick-in-the-mud with regards to his consumption, he will reluctantly have to choose a new bundle, since he cannot afford bundles on the segment AZ. In choosing this new bundle he is likely to increase his consumption of good G. This is because his original bundle on line AZ involves less of good G than most of the new line ML. Now that the price of good G has fallen there is more of good G available, so, in being forced to change his consumption, he is likely to consume more of good G.

Becker concludes that for both impulsive and inert consumers, if there is a substitution effect, it is likely to be a negative. The conclusion has implications, however, for the neoclassical idea of consumer sovereignty. The irrational consumer cannot be said to be sovereign in the marketplace. Impulsive Ian, in his whiz around the supermarket, cannot be said to be dictating to the supermarket and its suppliers what goods should be on display. Indeed, modern retailing techniques enable supermarkets to place

and package certain goods such that the erratic consumer is bound to pick them up. Cautious Colin, on the other hand, is so passive that he is oblivious to the array of goods available and he changes his behaviour only when forced to. For consumer sovereignty to hold, he should be forcing suppliers to change their behaviour, not them forcing him to change.

For some economists, it does not matter whether consumers are consistent or inconsistent, as long as the demand curve is downward sloping. Mishan, for example, argues that constructing the apparatus of consumer theory is a waste of time and energy. The economist 'would be no worse off if he remained ignorant of all the theories of consumers' behaviour, accepting the obviously indispensable "Law of Demand" on trust' (Mishan, 1961, p.1). For Mishan, the downward sloping demand curve is a useful device which enables economists to predict the behaviour of consumers in response to price changes. For him it does not matter whether the demand curve derives from the consistent preferences of consumers. All that matters is the practical application of the concept.

This practical interpretation of one of the techniques of neoclassical economics provides an important strand of opinion. Even though the neoclassical approach can be used to show how the free market delivers consumer sovereignty, many neoclassical economists are not concerned with such grandiose political statements. For them, techniques, such as the demand curve, are important for the evaluation of a whole range of economic policy changes. Will a tax on fuel, for example, reduce the demand for fuel? Will an increase in the price of oil reduce the demand for cars? Answering these questions does not necessarily involve drawing indifference curves and budget constraints.

However, the neoclassical theory of consumer behaviour is also used for policy analysis. In policy analysis, the question that is asked is whether a policy change would make people better off. Neoclassical welfare economics assumes that what is meant by people being 'better off' is that they can better satisfy their preferences, and that whether this is the case can be found out by examining the choices they make as consumers. This is because, according to neoclassical theory, consumers choose whatever option will maximize their utility, given their available budget. Therefore, for policy analysis, the assumptions of neoclassical theory *do* matter. This issue is considered in more depth in Chapter 4.

5 CONCLUSION

This chapter has shown how neoclassical consumer theory can be used to demonstrate consumer sovereignty. In a free market economy, consumers dictate their tastes and preferences to firms through their demand decisions. Every expression of a consumer's preferences represents a vote in the ballot box of consumer democracy and provides the mandate for economic activity.

I have shown that neoclassical consumer theory assumes that consumers have preferences by which they rank different bundles of goods. These preferences are represented by indifference curves from which downward sloping individual and market demand curves can be derived. It is through their demand curves that consumers are able to dictate their preferences to the marketplace.

The downward sloping demand curve shows the response of consumer demand to changes in price. This price change can be analysed in terms of two separate effects: the substitution effect and the income effect. Neoclassical economists tend to emphasize the importance of the substitution effect. The more consumers substitute between alternative bundles of commodities in response to price changes, the more able they are to exercise choice in the marketplace. Critics of the neoclassical approach have tended to emphasize the importance of the income effect. In their view, consumers do not have much freedom to choose between commodities as they are constrained by their levels of income. When income changes, the income effect can override the impact of the substitution effect. The importance of this income effect has been considered in relation to the case of the Giffen good, for which the demand curve can be upward sloping.

A number of key assumptions of neoclassical consumer theory have been considered. The assumption that consumers have indifference curves has been examined for individuals with low income. For these individuals, it was shown that lexicographic preferences can mean that indifference curves do not exist. Using an example from experimental economics, the even more basic

assumption that consumers' preferences are consistent was tested. There is some evidence that consumers regularly break consistency, but the consequences of this finding for consumer theory are inconclusive. However, following Becker, it was shown that even if consumers are irrational in their behaviour, their demand curves should still be downward sloping.

In this chapter I have tried to evaluate the neoclassical notion of consumer sovereignty which relies on the assumption that individuals make their choices independently of others in the economy, according to their own particular tastes and preferences. The schoolboy spending his pocket money at the corner shop is not influenced by the proclivity for crisps and chocolate of his schoolmates; the young executive deciding how to spend her salary on clothes and jewellery is not influenced by the consumption decisions of her colleagues; and Lennox Lewis, when deciding whether to buy a helicopter or a yacht, is not influenced by the way in which his opponent spends his purse. He is an individual, his own man, acting independently of other consumers. Here lie the origins of consumer sovereignty, the idea that it is consumers alone who control what goes on in the economy. The next chapter will explore alternative views of consumer behaviour which regard each consumer not as sovereign, but as dependent on the behaviour of other consumers, firms and the wider society in which they are situated.

 FURTHER READING

Donaldson, P. (1973) *The Economics of the Real World*, Harmondsworth, Penguin: includes a brief but very accessible insight into the notion of consumer sovereignty.

Gabriel, Y. and Lang, T. (1995) *The Unmanageable Consumer,* London, Sage: gives an overview of the changes that have taken place in consumer society in recent years.

Mason, R.S. (1989) *Robert Giffen and the Giffen Paradox*, Oxford, Philip Allan: an extensive review of the literature on the Giffen good, with an evaluation of its relevance to the twentieth century.

Lavoie, M. (1992) *Foundations of Post-Keynesian Economic Analysis*, Aldershot, Edward Elgar:

argues that the income effects of price changes are more important than substitution effects; lexicographic preferences are also considered in detail.

Mishan, E.J. (1961) 'Theories of consumer's behaviour: a cynical view', *Economica*: an insight into some of the problems associated with the neoclassical theory of consumption, and its place in the history of economic thought.

Sippel, R. (1997) 'An experiment on the pure theory of consumers' behaviour', *Economic Journal*: shows in more detail how the experiment in Section 4.2 was carried out and provides a good list of references to the wider literature of experimental economics.

 ## ANSWERS TO EXERCISES

Exercise 2.1

1 On Figure 2.20, cans of Coca-Cola are measured along the horizontal axis and bags of sweets along the vertical axis. If the schoolgirl spends all her £10

on sweets, at a price of £2 per bag, she can afford to buy five bags. This establishes the point where the budget constraint meets the vertical axis. If she spent all the £10 on Coca-Cola, at a price of £1, then she could afford ten cans. This establishes the point where the budget line meets the horizontal axis.

2 At the point she chooses, an indifference curve just touches the budget constraint; point A on Figure 2.20 is a possible outcome.

Exercise 2.2

1 Since the price of good *F* is constant, the budget line swivels around point Z: since the price of good *G* has increased, the budget line must move to the left, from ZS to ZT. The price increase means that less of both good *F* and good *G* is available to the consumer within the confines of the new budget constraint. See Figure 2.21a.

2 Since the price of good *G* is constant, the budget line swivels around point Z: since the price of good *F* falls, the budget line shifts upwards, with more of both goods *F* and *G* available to the consumer. See Figure 2.21b.

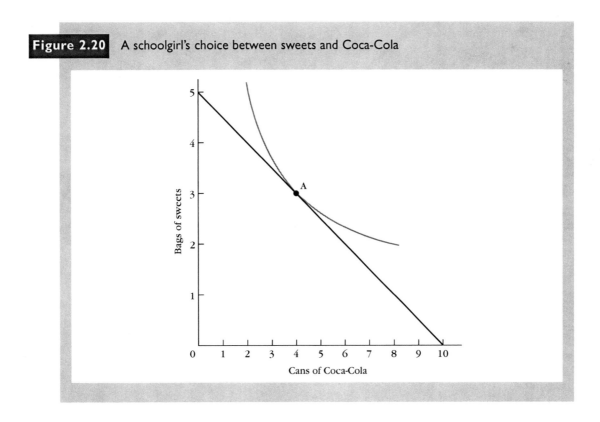

Figure 2.20 A schoolgirl's choice between sweets and Coca-Cola

Figure 2.21a An increase in the price of good *G*

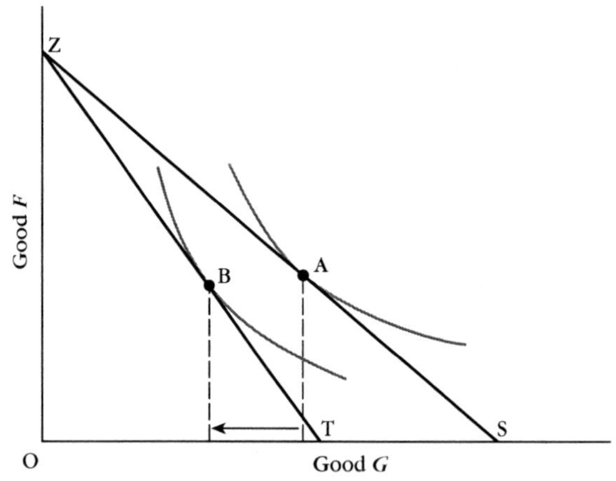

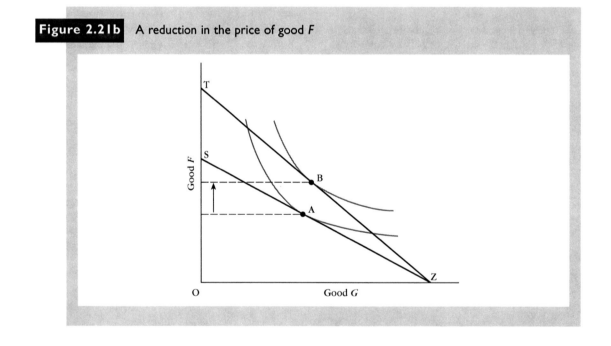

Figure 2.21b A reduction in the price of good *F*

CONSUMER DEPENDENCY

Andrew Trigg

CONCEPTS AND TECHNIQUES

Conspicuous consumption
Luxury goods
Veblen demand curve

Theory of distinction
Cultural capital
Want creation
Latent needs
Consumer dependency

LINKS

- This chapter is a direct response to the discussion in the previous chapter of the neoclassical idea of consumer sovereignty.

- In Chapter 2, it was shown that demand curves could have upwards sloping sections for Giffen goods; in this chapter the Veblen demand curve slopes upwards for a different reason: conspicuous consumption.

- Concepts of personal and social capital, which are loosely related to Bourdieu's concept of cultural capital, are introduced in Chapter 7.

- Chapter 11 considers advertising designed to shape consumers' behaviour from the firm's point of view.

1 INTRODUCTION

'The life of a junior cavalry officer at the end of the nineteenth century was hardly onerous. Leave amounted to five months a year, and officers were encouraged to spend the autumn and winter hunting. Churchill's time in the 4th Hussars was devoted largely to horse-riding, drill, playing polo, eating in the mess, and gambling and drinking in the evenings. Even when on duty at Hounslow, west of London, there was still plenty of time for an active social life in the capital. His fellow officers were rich and well-connected, and determined to maintain the social exclusivity of the regiment. He fitted easily into this world and shared its outlook: he was one of the ringleaders in forcing out of the regiment Alan Bruce (whom he had known at Harrow) because he had a private income of only £500 a year to live on in addition to his pay. As well as his pay and his own small resources Churchill had an allowance of £300 a year from his mother and she also gave him over £400 to help him purchase clothes, saddles and a second horse. Even so his style of life – satin racing jackets, a number of polo ponies and expensive clothes – meant that he was soon in debt. In his first two years in the Army he spent £144 (over £5000 at today's prices) on clothes from just one tailor and the bill was not paid for nearly seven years. In the summer of 1895 the 4th Hussars were told that they would sail to India for a nine year posting in just over twelve months. The result was even more leave and Churchill was able to enjoy to the full the London season.'

(PONTING, 1995, P.18)

Born in 1874 at Blenheim Palace, the family seat of his grandfather the Duke of Marlborough, and destined to be British Prime Minister and a celebrated war leader, Winston Churchill was in many ways the last of the great aristocrats. The quotation from Clive Ponting's biography of Churchill provides a revealing insight, not only into the young Winston's lifestyle, but also into that of the English aristocracy in general at the end of the nineteenth century. For this socially exclusive group, life was devoted to the lavish expenditure of money on items of consumption and of time on leisure activities.

These two characteristics of the aristocracy's behaviour – the intensive pursuit of consumer expenditure and leisure – were the starting point for the work of the American economist and sociologist, Thorstein Veblen. In 1899, four years after Churchill first joined the 4th Hussars, Veblen published his influential book entitled, *The Theory of the Leisure Class*. In the book, Veblen asks why are the aristocracy, and the rich and well-connected in general, driven to devote so much of their time and energy to what he regards as wasteful activities? In attempting to answer this question, Veblen not only develops a theory of the consumption behaviour of the upper classes, he also provides an explanation of the behaviour of people from other social classes who seek to emulate the behaviour of their 'superiors'.

This Veblen-inspired approach, in which consumption is seen as a class phenomenon, provides the main focus of this chapter. This approach provides a critique of the concept of consumer sovereignty developed in the previous chapter. You may recall the quotation from Enoch Powell, at the start of Chapter 2, in which he described the role every individual has to play in the great ballot box of consumer democracy. In this neoclassical approach, consumers have their own independent tastes and preferences and, by maximizing their utility, they have the power to influence what is produced by firms in the economy. In the Veblen approach, however, individuals derive their tastes and preferences from other individuals in the economy – their behaviour is determined *socially*. Rich people seek to emulate the behaviour of other rich people; poor people seek to emulate the behaviour of rich people. The result is a process of 'keeping up with the Joneses' in which the behaviour of consumers is not sovereign to each individual, but *dependent* on outside factors.

In Section 2, Veblen's approach is examined with reference to his own writings where he developed an explanation of how consumption has evolved over time by distinguishing between different stages of history. Section 3 considers two case studies which illustrate some of Veblen's ideas. The first looks at the development of consumer behaviour in the eighteenth century, while the second examines a more modern example of luxury goods in the 1980s.

Section 4 considers the implications of Veblen's approach for the neoclassical theory of consumption, focusing on the relationship between prices and the tastes and preferences of individuals in the neoclassical approach. In Section 5 some problems with Veblen's approach are discussed. In particular, it is argued that often it is the lower classes that shape the development of consumer behaviour.

In view of these problems, a more general model of consumer dependency, based upon the work of the French writer Pierre Bourdieu, is introduced in Section 6. In Bourdieu's model the tastes of consumers are developed through a sophisticated process of cultural learning. The degree to which tastes develop depends directly on how individuals relate to the social hierarchy.

Finally, Section 7 provides a discussion of the role of firms in shaping consumer tastes. Following John Kenneth Galbraith, consumer tastes can be argued to be dependent on the advertising and marketing strategies of firms.

All of these models follow in the tradition of Veblen, the overriding theme being that of consumer dependency. The objective is to provide both a critique of the neoclassical model, since this is the dominant economic model, and to provide an alternative framework in which consumption is viewed from a different perspective.

2 CONSPICUOUS CONSUMPTION

In developing his theory of consumption, Veblen takes as his starting point the way in which a leisure class has evolved over time. For Veblen, the key reason why a leisure class can evolve in any society is that more goods are produced than are required for people to subsist on. This is also the view taken by Karl Marx in *Capital* (1867): that social classes evolve because a proportion of the population does not have to work. Those who do work produce a surplus which is appropriated by the ruling class. Earlier societies, Veblen argues, were only capable of producing enough goods for subsistence purposes. There was no material reason why social classes should exist. The emergence of a leisure class, which is not required to work and consumes the goods produced by members of lower classes, can only happen if the lower classes produce more than their subsistence level of consumption. Each chief, baroness or king, can enjoy their class position in the social hierarchy only by living off the surplus produced by the lower classes.

Once societies start to produce a surplus this entails the introduction of private property. 'It becomes indispensable to accumulate, to acquire property, in order to retain one's good name' (Veblen, 1899, p.19). A hierarchy develops in which some people own property and others do not. To own property is to have status and honour, a position of esteem in this hierarchy: to have no property is to have no status.

Of course, the accumulation of property can indicate that a person has been efficient and productive – it can indicate prowess in financial matters. But Veblen argues that inherited wealth confers even more status than wealth which is gained through efficiency. 'By a further refinement, wealth acquired passively by transmission from ancestors or other antecedents presently becomes even more honorific than wealth acquired by the possessor's own effort' (p.19). It could be argued, for example, that Winston Churchill's family, the Marlboroughs, enjoyed more status in nineteenth-century England than the newly rich industrialists, whose new money was obtained through mining and shipbuilding. By similar reasoning, the Queen may also be accorded more status than, say, Richard Branson, founder of the Virgin empire. One is more likely to curtsey to the Queen than to Richard Branson, even though he has displayed more industry and efficiency in acquiring his position in society than has the Queen, whose position is inherited.

For Veblen, members of the leisure class enjoy their status because they do not have to work. This is the defining feature of being a member of the leisure class. Wealth is produced by those who work and transferred to those who do not work, the leisure class. Unlike Marx, who concentrates on how this transfer takes place, Veblen's interest focuses on the way in which status is established, given that there has been a transfer.

For Veblen, the ownership of property is not enough to give an individual status. If an individual amasses a great fortune but lives as a recluse in a small house, that individual will have no status in society. Status derives from social performance: from the judgements which other people make of an individual's position in society. To gain status an individual must *display* wealth to others.

Veblen identifies two main ways in which an individual can display wealth.

● *Leisure activities*: That the young Winston Churchill was able to spend five months of the year hunting, drinking and gambling, displayed that he was a member of the leisure class.

- *Expenditure on consumption goods*: Churchill's lavish expenditure on clothes, saddles and horses also displayed that he was part of this class.

The common thread that runs through both these methods of displaying wealth is, for Veblen, '... the element of waste that is common to both' (p.53). Being able to afford horses and expensive clothing and being able to spend months on end hunting and gambling, are so divorced from activities that are productive they are characterized by Veblen as wasteful activities. 'In the one case it is a waste of time and effort, in the other it is a waste of goods' (p.53). Being able to engage in such wasteful activities is the key way in which members of the leisure class display their wealth and status.

In principle, people can display their wealth through either method with equal facility – all this requires is an effective network for word to get around about a person's degree of leisure and the objects he or she possesses. Veblen argues, however, that as the population becomes more mobile, communities become less close-knit. In a more mobile society people may be less well informed about the leisure activities in which other people engage, and so the display of wealth through consumption goods becomes more important than the display of leisure. Wealth is easily displayed by driving a particular car or wearing clothes from a particular designer.

Veblen labels this type of behaviour conspicuous consumption. People spend money on artefacts of consumption to display their wealth; to indicate their place in the hierarchy.

Veblen views *conspicuous consumption* as the most important factor in determining consumer behaviour, not just for the rich but for all social classes. 'The result is that the members of each stratum accept as their ideal of decency the scheme of life in vogue in the next higher stratum, and bend their energies to live up to that ideal' (p.52). Each social class tries to emulate the consumption behaviour of the class above it, to such an extent that even the poorest people are subject to pressures to engage in conspicuous consumption. 'Very much of squalor and discomfort will be endured before the last trinket or the last pretence of pecuniary decency is put away' (p.53).

> ### Conspicuous consumption
> People engage in conspicuous consumption in order to give an indication of their wealth to other members of society.

This search for status through consumption is never-ending. What at one time may confer status may later be acquired by all and confer no status. People must always try to acquire new consumption goods in order to distinguish themselves from others. When Veblen was writing in the 1880s, he viewed this drive for conspicuous consumption as the main force behind the consumer boom that was starting to gain pace in the United States.

For Veblen, all sorts of consumption activities were indicative of conspicuous consumption: the fashion tastes of a rich lady; the gambling and drinking of the aristocrat; the smoking behaviour of a journeyman printer. Modern examples include expensive motor cars, holiday cruises, designer clothes, and membership of exclusive leisure clubs. Of course, consumers may not always consider their consumption behaviour to be conspicuous. In some cases, consumption goods may be perceived to be both useful and confer status. In the next section I look in detail at some particular examples of conspicuous consumption.

3   CASE STUDIES IN MARKETING AND CONSUMPTION

As the above exposition shows, Veblen's approach looks at the evolution of consumer behaviour over time. For this reason, therefore, it is necessary to take an in-depth look at some examples of how consumers have behaved in different periods of history. In this section I examine two case studies: the first is taken from the eighteenth century, the second from the late twentieth century.

Although much has been written by historians about the Industrial Revolution which first took place in England during the eighteenth century, an important parallel event was the revolution in consumer behaviour. For the industrial revolution to have taken place, it is argued, there must also have been a consumer revolution. Without new markets for the goods produced by the new methods of factory production, there would be no reason for new factories to be built in the first place. The 'big question' which needs to be addressed is why did this consumer revolution take place?

Champions of this notion of a consumer revolution are the historians McKendrick, Brewer and Plumb, with their book *The Birth of a Consumer Society* (1982). Any recent book on the history of consumer behaviour will take McKendrick *et al.* as its starting point.

The following case study is an extract which looks at the growth in the consumption of pottery in the eighteenth century. In particular, it looks at the success story of one of the great industrial pioneers of this time, Josiah Wedgwood. In reading it you should try to work out how it relates to Veblen's explanation of how consumer behaviour has evolved. After reading it through once, you will be asked some questions at the end. You might like to look at the questions at the end of the case study before you start reading it.

Josiah Wedgwood and the commercialization of the potteries

It is difficult for twentieth-century man to understand the excitement that was generated by pottery and porcelain in the eighteenth century. To a society accustomed to regard crockery as a humble and ubiquitous accompaniment to everyday life, it is not easy to imagine the craving to possess it which gripped so many layers of eighteenth-century society. Most people know of the way in which the Dutch in the seventeenth century were caught in a fever of speculation over the possession and price of tulip bulbs, but very few are familiar with the far more important and far more pervasive china mania of the eighteenth century.

In the face of such ignorance, a consumer boom in pottery may seem an unlikely event. The aristocracy of England blocking the streets outside Wedgwood's London showrooms in their eagerness to buy his latest pottery; 'a violent vase madness breaking out amongst the Irish'; an 'epidemical' sickness to possess his wares amongst the upper and middling ranks; an extension of the market so profound that 'common Wedgwood'

came within the reach of 'common people' – such excitement strikes a surprising note to a society so accustomed to the almost universal possession of ample crockery that a hunger to possess it, a compulsive need to own the latest fashions in it, is difficult to imagine. [...]

When Josiah Wedgwood was born in 1730, the Staffordshire potters sold their wares almost solely in Staffordshire. Their goods found their sale in the local market towns, and occasionally, carried by pedlars and hawkers or on the backs of the wretched packmen of the eighteenth century, they reached further afield – to Leicester, Liverpool and Manchester. To sell in London in any quantity was rare, to sell in Europe virtually unknown. Yet by 1795 Wedgwood had broken through this local trade of fairs and pedlars to an international market based on elegant showrooms and ambassadorial connections; he had become the Queen's potter and sold to every regal house in Europe. [...]

His name was known all over the world. It had become a force in industry, commerce, science and politics. It dominated the potting industry. Men no longer spoke of 'common pewter' but of 'common Wedgwood'. [...]

The reasons why Wedgwood prospered above all others have proved [...] elusive. Most historians have argued that his discoveries – green glaze, creamware, jasper and black basalt – won him technical supremacy over his rivals; and that his factory organization and division of labour – his stated desire 'to make such machines of the Men as cannot err' – confirmed his superior quality. But this alone is not sufficient to explain his supremacy. For his inventions were quickly copied and his quality easily reproduced. They won him immediate attention but they could not keep it unless he could afford to sell his ware more cheaply than his rivals. This historians have cheerfully assumed. The statement by Professor Ashton that 'it was by intensifying the division of labour that Wedgwood brought about the reduction of cost which enabled his pottery to find markets in all parts of Britain, and also of Europe and America' is merely the most recent and most authoritative of a long line of such views – Meteyard, Jewitt, Church, Smiles, Burton and Trevelyan all produce the same argument. They note the efficiency of Wedgwood's factory system, his avoidance of waste, the drop in breakages through the use of canals, the cheapening of transport charges because of canals and turnpike roads, and conclude that Wedgwood's wares were obviously cheaper than his rivals. Unfortunately they were not. His goods were always considerably more expensive than those of his fellow potters: he regularly sold his goods at double the normal prices, not infrequently at three times as high, and he reduced them only when he wished to reap the rewards of bigger sales on a product that he had already made popular and fashionable at a high price, or when he thought the margin between his prices and those of the rest of the pottery had become too great. [...]

Some idea of how this policy developed can be gained from a letter he wrote to his partner, Bentley, in 1771. Faced with a mounting stock he was overjoyed at the prospect of a large order from Russia: 'This Russ.n trade comes very opportunely for the useful ware, may prevent me lower.g the prices here, though it may be expedient to lower the prices of the Tableplates to 4/- Per doz in London, as our people are lowering them to 2/3 or 2/- here. Mr Baddeley who makes the best ware of any of the Potters here, an Ovenfull of it Per Diem has led the way, the rest must follow, unless he can be prevail'd upon to raise it again, which is not at all probable, though we are to see him tomorrow, about a doz.n of us, for that purpose [...] Mr Baddeley has reduc'd the prices of the dishes to the prices of whitestone, [...] In short the *General trade* seems to me to be going to ruin on the gallop – large stocks on hand both in London the country, little demand. The Potters seem sensible of their situation, are quite in a Pannick for their trade, indeed I think with great reason, for *low prices* must beget a *low quality* in the manufacture, which will beget *contempt*, which will beget *neglect*, disuse, and there is an end of the trade. But if any one Warehouse, distinguish'd from the rest, will continue to keep up the quality of the Manufacture, or improve it, that House may perhaps *keep up its prices*, the *general evil*, will work a *particular* good to that house, they may continue to sell *Queens ware at the usual prices*, when the rest of the trade can scarcely give it away. This seems to be all the chance we have, we must double our diligence here to give it effect. [...]'

He did this partly by the capture of the world of fashion. For although Wedgwood had complete confidence in his wares – writing, 'wherever my wares find their way, they will command the first trade' – he also realized that '*Fashion* is infinitely superior to *merit* in many respects, and it is plain from a thousand instances that if you have a favourite child you wish the public to fondle take notice of, you have only to make choice of proper sponcers [sic].' The sponsors he aimed to win for his pottery were the monarchy, the nobility, and the art connoisseurs – in fact, the leaders of fashion. He quickly realized that to make pots for the Queen of England was admirable advertisement. To become the Queen's Potter and to win the right to sell common earthenware as Queen's ware, was even better. As Wedgwood wrote: 'the demand for this s.d *Creamcolour*, alias, *Queensware*, [...] still increases. It is really amazing how rapidly the use of it has spread over the whole Globe, how universally it is liked. How much of this general use, estimation, is owing to the mode of its introduction – how much to its real utility beauty? are questions in which we may be a good deal interested for the government of our future Conduct. The reasons are too obvious to be longer dwelt upon. For instance, if a Royal, or Noble introduction be as necessary to the sale of an Article of Luxury, as real Elegance and beauty, then the Manufacturer, if he consults his own inter.t will bestow as much pains, expense too, in gaining the former of these advantages, as he wo.d in bestowing the latter'. Wedgwood was not a man to fail to consult his own interests. He took immediate action. [...]

By appealing to the fashionable cry for antiquities, by pandering to their requirements, by asking their advice and accepting their smallest orders, by flattery and attention, Wedgwood hoped to monopolize the aristocratic market, and thus win for his wares a special distinction, a social *cachet* which would filter through to all classes of society. Everything was done to attract this aristocratic attention. A special display room was built to beguile the fashionable company which Josiah drew after him to Etruria; steps were taken to make the London showroom attractive 'to the ladies', and to keep the common folk out; he was even prepared to adjust his prices downwards so that they could be paid genteely, writing to his partner 'I think what you charge 34/- should [...] be [...] a Guinea a half, 34 is so odd a sum there is no paying it *Genteely* [...]'. Once attracted everything was done to keep such attention. The good will of Wedgwood patrons never withered from neglect. Sir George Strickland was asked for advice on getting models from Rome; Sir William Hamilton was asked for advice on gilding; they were complimented by the reproduction of their country houses on the great Russian service; and great care was taken to flatter them by giving them first sight of any new discovery. The first Etruscan vases, for instance, were shown before they were put on sale to 'Sir Watkin Williams Wynn, Mrs Chetwynd, Lord Bessborough, Earl of Stamford, Duke of Northumberland, Duke of Marlborough, Lord Percy, Lord Carlisle St James's Place, Earl of Dartmouth, Lord Clanbrazill, Lord Torrington, Mr Harbord Harbord'. These were the nucleus of an aristocratic claque that did Wedgwood untold good. They praised his ware, they advertised it, they bought it, and they took their friends to buy it. Wedgwood had no scruples about exploiting their friendship and their praise. In 1776, for instance, by artful flattery he carefully prepared the ground for his new Bassrelief vases at the next season's sale, writing to Bentley, 'Sir William Hambleton, our very good Friend is in Town – Suppose you shew him some of the Vases, a few other Connoisieurs [sic] not only to have their advice, but to have the advantage of their puffing them off against the next Spring, as they will, by being consulted, and flatter'd agreeably, as you know how, consider themselves as a sort of parties in the affair, act accordingly.' In the small, interconnected, gossip-ridden world of the English aristocracy in the eighteenth century, such introductions were vital, for even a very few sales could have an important effect.

For the lead of the aristocracy was quickly followed by other classes. Fashions spread rapidly and they spread downwards. But they needed a lead. As Wedgwood put it, 'Few ladies, you know, dare venture at anything out of the common stile [sic] 'till authoris'd by their betters – by the Ladies of superior spirit who set the ton'.

Source: McKendrick *et al.*, 1982

Question

- How well does the theory of conspicuous consumption explain Wedgwood's marketing strategy?
- What importance did Wedgwood place on consumers' maximization of utility?
- Explain the relationship between the demand for Wedgwood's pottery and its price.

Much of Wedgwood's energies were devoted to obtaining the support and patronage of the aristocracy. Each lord, earl and duke: each member of the aristocracy were worthy prey for Wedgwood's 'flattery and attention'. Once he had monopolized the attentions of the aristocracy, Wedgwood obtained for his wares the 'social *cachet* which would filter through to all classes of society'. It was not enough for Wedgwood merely to sell a small number of goods to this aristocracy. His great innovation was to use the 'superior spirit' of the aristocracy to unleash the clamour of the lower classes for a small slice of the aristocracy's respectability. This suggests that the revolution in consumer behaviour was driven by conspicuous consumption – by the desire of members of each social strata to display their decency by emulating the behaviour of those in a higher social strata.

The 'real utility and beauty' of Wedgwood's pottery was not central to his marketing strategy. Of equal, if not more, importance was the patronage of the aristocracy. A vase may be made using the latest and most innovative techniques but if it was not fashionable then it would not sell. 'Fashion', states Wedgwood, 'is superior to merit'. At first sight Wedgwood's position may appear directly to contradict the neoclassical theory of utility maximization. Consumers are less interested in the utility of pottery than its fashionability. However, it should be emphasized that Wedgwood is employing the word *utility* in a different way from the definition used in neoclassical economics. In Chapter 2, utility was defined as the pleasure which an individual gains from consumption. Wedgwood, on the other hand, uses the other definition of utility which represents the usefulness of an object.

Under the neoclassical definition, consumers of Wedgwood's pottery could indeed be maximizing utility. All that matters to the neoclassical notion of utility is that they seek as much pleasure as possible. It is not for Wedgwood or Veblen, or anybody else, to judge whether consumers purchase pottery either for its merit or its fashionability – all that matters is that they glean pleasure from its consumption.

Implicit in Wedgwood's approach, however, is a value judgement that his pottery has, on the one hand, a certain degree of *real* merit or usefulness, and, on the other, a groundless fashionability. This fits perfectly well with Veblen's categorization of conspicuous consumption as a wasteful activity, that although individuals gain pleasure from consumption, their pursuit of fashion has no real substance. Instead of being independent, their tastes and preferences are *dependent* upon the behaviour of others. Instead of being exogenous, coming from inside the individual's psyche, tastes are endogenous, dependent upon the rest of society.

The relationship between the demand for Wedgwood's pottery and its price has important implications for the neoclassical theory of consumption. In Chapter 2 a downward sloping demand curve for a typical good G, as shown in Figure 3.1, was derived from the tastes and preferences of individual consumers. For the consumption of a typical good, a reduction in price generates an increase in market demand.

This view of the relationship between price and demand appears to have been held by most of Wedgwood's competitors in the pottery industry. In response to the glut of 1771, Wedgwood's competitors were lowering prices in an attempt to sell their surplus stock of pottery. Wedgwood's main worry, however, was that if he too followed this trend it would lead to the 'contempt' of his customers. They would associate the low price of the pottery with low quality. The price of Wedgwood pottery, therefore, was maintained at a high level. In Wedgwood's view the demand curve for his pottery was not downward sloping: low prices meant less demand, not more.

Reflection

What shape do you think Wedgwood believed the demand curve for his pottery would take?

The next case study looks at a more recent example of the demand for luxury goods in the 1980s. In reading it you should once again try to work out the role of Veblen's theory of the leisure class and the neoclassical theory of utility maximization; and also try to assess the relationship between price and demand.

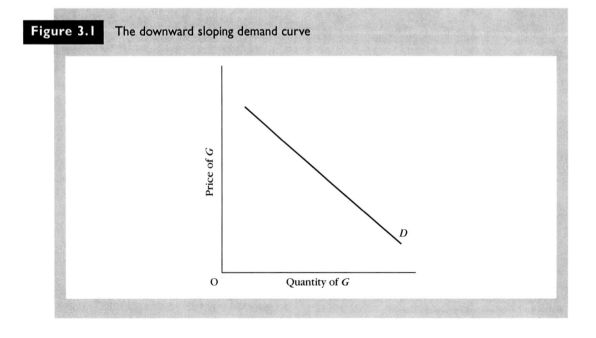

Figure 3.1 The downward sloping demand curve

Price of G

D

O   Quantity of G

The luxury goods trade: upmarket philosophy

At this time of year, the normally sedate scarf-counter of the swish Hermes boutique on the Rue du Faubourg Saint-Honore in Paris looks like the discount aisle in a department store. Though the shoppers are draped in haute couture, they paw over the merchandise as frantically as any blue-jeaned bargain-hunter. Priced at FF1,150 (US$ 215), the Hermes silk scarf, favoured by such upmarket icons as Queen Elizabeth, is no bargain. No matter. In the week before Christmas, one is sold every 24 seconds. Few of those diving into the designer-scarf scrum are likely to have heard of Thorstein Veblen – though some might think they own an evening gown from his autumn collection. Yet if Veblen were alive today he would recognise them instantly. [...]

Veblen's argument was that as wealth spreads, what drives consumers' behaviour is increasingly neither subsistence nor comfort but the attainment of 'the esteem and envy of fellow men'. At the time, academics thought this mildly convincing. By the 1980s it was commonplace. As economies boomed, the nouveaux riches joined the vieux riches in a Veblenian binge. Hermes ties protruded from every striped collar; Rolexes were worn loose on every languid wrist. In the City of London, people watered their plants with Perrier and watered themselves with Dom Perignon. Louis Vuitton became Tokyo's favourite Frenchman.

As this brand-studded description suggests, the beneficiary was the luxury goods trade. [...]

But exactly what sort of goods? The answer is unduly costly ones, which Veblen describes as falling into 'accredited canons of conspicuous consumption, the effect of which is to hold the consumer up to a standard of expensiveness and wastefulness in his consumption of goods and his employment of time and effort' [...] indeed, Veblen argued that since the reasons for buying such goods are pecuniary emulation and invidious comparison, their utility actually rises as their prices go up.

Of course, consumers do not admit it. Instead they say that these products are more beautiful, or of better quality. Veblen replies: consider a hand-wrought spoon of pure silver. Many would find it lovely and pay a hefty premium for it. Now imagine that the spoon is revealed to be a very good fake. Although it would still be the same spoon, Veblen plausibly claims that its 'utility, including the gratification which the user derives from its contemplation as an object of beauty, would immediately decline by some eighty or ninety per cent'.

For evidence that he was right about the relationship between the price and the perceived value of snobby goods, look at the table.

Table 2.1 Luxury good prices

Item and base year	Price		Percentage increase	
	Base year ($)	1992 ($)	nominal	real terms
Russian caviar 2oz (1912)	1.40	129	9 130	535
Jaguar most expensive two-seater (1932)	1 085.00	73 545	6 680	560
Parker Duofold fountain pen (1927)	7.30	236	3 130	300
Purdey shotgun top of the line (1901)	435.00	38 380	8 720	425
Dunhill lighter 'Rollagas' silver plate (1958)	19.00	205	980	122
Louis Vuitton suitcase (1912)	29.00	1 670	5 660	295
Cartier Tank watch (1921)	155.75	4 180	2 580	242
Champagne non-vintage bottle (1912)	1.85	34	1 710	25

Source: *The Economist*, 26 December 1992

Over the past 100 years or so, the real cost of many classic luxury items has soared. As wealth has spread, so rich consumers have been prepared to pay ever larger sums to demonstrate status. This has not been lost on luxury goods firms. As the marketing manager at one such company puts it: 'Our customers do not want to pay less. If we halved the price of all our products, we would double our sales for six months and then we would sell nothing.'

Source: *The Economist*, 26 December 1992

Table 2.1 shows that, for a selection of luxury goods, firms are ever more disposed to charge high prices. The price of a Louis Vuitton suitcase, for example, has increased by just under 300 per cent in real terms over the period 1912–92. Russian caviar has increased in price by 535 per cent during this period. The spread of wealth to the *nouveaux riches*, or newly rich, has meant that to display their wealth through conspicuous consumption, people need to buy even more expensive luxury goods than before. As the marketing manager interviewed by *The Economist* made clear, there is no point, except in the short run, in firms attempting to sell more luxury goods by reducing prices to increase demand – in the long run, the downward sloping demand curve does not apply.

An important insight given by this case study is that the tastes and preferences of individual consumers can actually vary as the price changes. The more expensive a designer good, the more utility an individual may receive from its consumption. The implication of this insight for the neoclassical theory of consumption will be explored in the next section.

Reflection

Consider the implications of the two case studies for the neoclassical theory of consumption. In particular, what will the indifference curves and associated demand curves look like?

 4   IMPLICATIONS FOR NEOCLASSICAL THEORY

In Chapter 2, the typical consumer's demand decision was determined by the nature of his or her tastes and

preferences. If a person has a preference for one particular good over another, then this determines how that person's demand decision might respond to any price change. The consumer is shown to be sovereign in deciding how much to consume of each good. In the neoclassical theory of consumption the preferences of each individual determine what firms should produce in the market place.

A key feature of this neoclassical approach is a separation of the preference sphere from the price sphere. The preference sphere is firmly rooted in each individual's psychology - each individual has his or her own tastes and preferences. The price sphere, on the other hand, is located in the market-place. Firms supply goods and consumers demand goods such that the price is determined as a market outcome. The driving force for this market outcome comes from outside the market - from inside the psyche of individual consumers. In the neoclassical approach, the preference sphere dominates the price sphere.

Veblen's approach represents a direct challenge to this separation of the preference and price spheres. The two case studies above have shown that the preferences and decisions of consumers can be *dependent* upon the price level. Both Wedgwood in the 1700s and the designer goods shops in the 1980s provide examples in which reductions in the price level were looked upon unfavourably by consumers. In such examples, if the price of a good falls, the preference which the individual has for that good is also reduced. This phenomenon is explored in the following example.

Picture this scene. Mrs Connaught-Brown is a wealthy widow living in Berkeley Square, London. Each Thursday she hosts a dinner party to which she invites friends and acquaintances. In treating her guests she likes to purchase a combination of Russian caviar and champagne.

On her trips to Harrods, Mrs Connaught-Brown notices a disturbing trend. The queues at the caviar counter seem to be getting longer and the type of person standing in the queue also appears to be changing. She is increasingly engaged in conversation with ladies with distinctly northern English accents, who are visiting London to see, amongst other things, Andrew Lloyd-Webber musicals. Being of good breeding she is, of course, perfectly civil to these ladies, with whom she enjoys good conversation. She wonders, however, why are they suddenly purchasing caviar? The penny begins to drop that, over a period of time and due to the opening up of trade relations with Russia, the price of caviar has fallen from £40 per ounce to £20 per ounce. The perfectly affable northern ladies can now afford to purchase an ounce of caviar for the price of a Marks and Spencer's cardigan.

Without experiencing any malice towards the ladies in the Marks and Spencer's cardigans, Mrs Connaught-Brown becomes less interested in purchasing caviar. She and her friends find caviar to be less fashionable than before, so that their interest in buying it is reduced. Caviar is now so cheap that it is less suitable for the purposes of conspicuous consumption – it provides a less suitable vehicle for displaying Mrs Connaught-Brown's wealth at her weekly dinner party.

This example can be further explored using the concept of the indifference map, which was introduced in Chapter 2. In Figure 3.2, caviar is represented by good G. Although the price of G has fallen, Mrs Connaught-Brown's demand for G falls from G_1 to G_2 units. This reduction in demand is translated in part (b) of Figure 3.2 into an upward sloping demand curve. Leibenstein (1950) has referred to this as the Veblen demand curve. On this Veblen demand curve (D_v) each reduction in the price level of a good results in a reduction of the amount demanded.

In part (a) of Figure 3.2, the individual chooses a combination of goods F and G at the initial bundle A. The fall in the price of G is represented by a shift of the budget constraint line from ZS to line ZT. Since

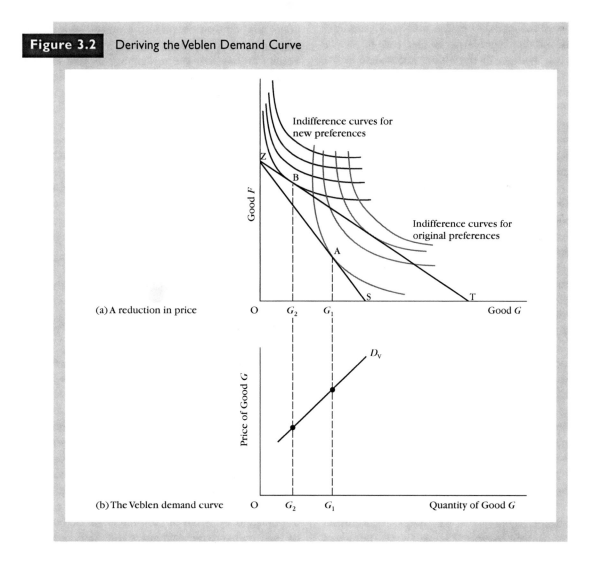

Figure 3.2 Deriving the Veblen Demand Curve

(a) A reduction in price

(b) The Veblen demand curve

the price of *F* remains the same, the line pivots around the fixed point Z on the *F* axis.

For Mrs Connaught-Brown, good *G* becomes a less attractive vehicle for conspicuous consumption. There is a shift in her indifference map. She consumes a new combination of *F* and *G* at bundle B. If there had been no change in preferences, as shown by the original indifference curves, then consumption of *G* would have increased after the price change to *G* at bundle C, but with the indifference curves for new preferences she moves to a new bundle, bundle B. Under conspicuous consumption there is a change of preference in response to the price change.

The ladies from the north of England, in this example, have downward sloping demand curves. Since the price of caviar has fallen, they demand more of it. However, one may wonder whether the ladies from the north of England will continue to be interested in caviar once they realize that Mrs Connaught-Brown and her friends no longer buy it. As the marketing manager of the luxury goods firm in the second case study commented, the drop in price may generate a short run increase in demand, but in the long run, once a good loses its luxury status, market demand may fall. The upward sloping individual demand curves for Mrs Connaught-Brown and her friends, and the tendency of others to emulate them, may translate into an upward sloping market demand curve – a long run market Veblen demand curve.

This derivation has two important implications for the neoclassical theory of consumption. First, it opens up the possibility that consumers are not sovereign in a market economy. Instead of their tastes and preferences determining the price level, causation is in the opposite direction: the price level determines the consumers' tastes and preferences. To recap: following an event in Russia, there is an exogenous change in the price level, which, via the reaction of the northern ladies, leads to a change in the preference for caviar of Mrs Connaught-Brown. Her tastes and preferences are endogenous, dependent on the price level. Consumers no longer tell prices (and thus consumers) what to do. Instead prices tell consumers what they like. In this interpretation, it is the price sphere which dominates the preference sphere. Second, if the market Veblen demand curve is upward sloping, the demand and supply analysis which is central to neoclassical theory becomes problematic. As discussed in Chapter 2, if market demand curves are upward sloping, there may be multiple equilibria - no unique equilibrium between demand and supply is established. The case of

conspicuous consumption provides an additional reason why such problems can occur in the neoclassical approach.

 ## 5 PROBLEMS WITH CONSPICUOUS CONSUMPTION

This chapter has thus far provided an introduction to Veblen's theory of conspicuous consumption using a number of examples. From Josiah Wedgwood's expensive wares, to the scarf counter on the Rue du Faubourg Saint-Honore and Mrs Connaught-Brown's dinner party, each example has the overriding theme of conspicuous consumption in common. In each example it is the behaviour of the rich and aristocratic that consumers seek to emulate, be it in the consumption of pottery, designer scarves or caviar. Veblen argues that the underlying motive for this conspicuous consumption is its wastefulness. To spend such large amounts of money on wasteful products provides a clear message that the money has not been earned through productive activity. If the money had been sweated for in a factory or on a building site, it would not be so readily wasted on obscure fish eggs or garish dinner sets. Conspicuous consumption provides a modern day equivalent to conspicuous leisure.

> **Question**
>
> Consider the consumer goods on which your neighbours, where you live, tend to spend money. To what extent could their consumption be described as conspicuous?

Where they engage in conspicuous consumption, the good in question may be referred to as a luxury good. They may, for example, buy a designer jacket or a motor car, with some inkling that this will impress people as a luxury good. You may have neighbours who spend hundreds of pounds on a personalized number plate, perhaps the ultimate luxury good of no practical use. While neoclassical economists concede that some luxury goods may have Veblen demand curves, they would still hold, however, that in general the demand decisions of consumers are determined by their own independent tastes and preferences.

The argument against the general relevance of conspicuous consumption is not just that many consumers have income levels which are too low for them to afford luxury goods and are, therefore, unable to play the game of conspicuous consumption. Even at quite high levels of income, consumers may still not be interested in emulating the behaviour of the rich. Mason (1981, p.111) argues that working-class people are 'either unwilling or unable to break away' from some peer group pressures.

A simple example of this argument is provided by the wearing of jeans, a garment traditionally worn by manual workers. As the social uniform of youth, there is social pressure to own and wear a pair of jeans. A young British working-class male embarking on a Saturday night out may be doing plenty of overtime, earning good money, and therefore be able to spend a reasonably large amount of money on clothes. However, he may well choose to wear jeans – ostensibly 'work clothing' – for his outing, being 'forced' to wear trousers, and sometimes a jacket and tie, only if he intends to gain entry to a night club. The social norm, if he is only going to a pub, is to wear jeans. There is no aspiration to wear suits, shirts and ties – attire which is typically worn by the upper classes.

Fine and Leopold (1993) view jeans as an example of goods which serve as necessities. As a consumption good, their origin in the United States was as an affordable, strong and long-wearing item of work clothing. The mass production of jeans has meant that the cost of production, and hence the price, is so low that they can be sold to a mass market. The argument here is that, for working-class people, the driving force for consumption is not provided by the emulation of higher social classes, but by the necessities of everyday life.

Thus a possible problem with Veblen's approach is that it plays down the role of working-class values in influencing consumption, emphasizing the *trickle down* of consumption patterns from the rich to the poor when often it is the *trickle up* which may be important. Even Princess Diana wore a pair of jeans, a traditional item of work clothing, so in this case it is not the aristocracy who are setting the trend but the everyday worker.

It is unlikely, however, that Princess Diana bought 'ordinary' jeans. There is a market for designer jeans which are differentiated from ordinary jeans according to their label. It should also be noted that jeans are very much an American product and hence

may be associated with wealth and prosperity. Nevertheless, the point can still be made that the social origin of this product stems from working-class consumption. The original take-off of jeans as a mass produced item of consumption did not take place because of the behaviour of the upper classes.

This argument against Veblen's approach is particularly relevant to the case of Josiah Wedgwood. To recap, the historians McKendrick *et al.* argue that Wedgwood pioneered the revolution in pottery consumption that took place in the eighteenth century. Generalizing from the pottery industry, they argue that the Industrial Revolution in England would not have been possible without a parallel consumer revolution. To have mass production there must also be mass consumption. Wedgwood is argued to have sparked off the consumer revolution in pottery consumption by courting the patronage of the European aristocracy. The scramble to buy pottery that took place is attributed to the need to emulate the behaviour of the aristocracy.

Weatherhill (1986) reports, however, that at the time of its rapid expansion in the eighteenth century, the pottery industry employed only 1 per cent of the total number of industrial workers in Britain. With Wedgwood representing one among many pottery manufacturers, we should be careful not to place too much importance on his role as a pioneer of a consumer/industrial revolution.

Furthermore, Weatherhill argues that even the other pottery manufacturers did not take their lead from Wedgwood. We saw in the McKendrick case study that Wedgwood courted the London aristocracy by inviting them to his exclusive showrooms, which were serviced by London warehouses. McKendrick argues that 'Josiah Spode … and finally Minton followed Wedgwood's lead and established warehouses and showrooms in London' (quoted by Weatherhill, 1986, p.212). For Weatherhill, however, the warehouses used by Wedgwood's competitors were of a different type. Josiah Spode, for example, made use of a warehouse which was run by his son, Josiah Spode II. Yet this was a business independent from Spode's factory in North Staffordshire and dealt with pottery produced by other manufacturers apart from Spode. Indeed, for Weatherhill it was this model that was to provide the lead for all pottery manufacturers as the eighteenth century ran into the nineteenth. 'Producers began to rely on a distribution network, and gradually came to rely less on their own London warehouses' (p.212).

It has even been argued that Wedgwood held back the pace of change in the pottery industry.

Wedgwood's strategy was to court the luxury market by charging a high price, in the hope of eventually reaching a wider market when he subsequently lowered prices. Far from pioneering the opening up of a mass market for pottery, Fine and Leopold argue that this strategy could have *delayed* the increase in demand. If Wedgwood had put all his effort into affordable pottery which everyone could buy – similar to the case of jeans – the pottery revolution may have been more vibrant than it actually proved to be. 'It is at least as plausible to see the luxury market of the eighteenth century as an obstacle to the development of mass production for the lower classes in the nineteenth century, as it is to view it as a stimulus to emulation from below' (Fine and Leopold, 1993, p.79).

For many goods there is not even an opportunity for emulation to take place. Take, for example, the rise in the domestic consumption of coal in the eighteenth century – by at least 3 million tonnes per annum from 1700 to 1800 (Flinn, 1984, p.252). According to Fine and Leopold (1993, p.79), this was made possible by a number of factors, including the cost of production, income levels and rates of population growth. 'Yet it would be far-fetched to view the rise in coal consumption as originating out of the emulative behaviour of the lower classes (with fashion emanating from London as the major domestic market).'

As the neoclassical economist might argue, there is some evidence for saying that conspicuous consumption can take place for certain luxury goods, but there are also many other goods such as coal, jeans and ordinary pottery, for which Veblen's theory breaks down. It can, therefore, be argued that Veblen's theory of conspicuous consumption does not represent a general critique of the neoclassical theory of consumption – it cannot be applied to all goods and to the behaviour of all social classes.

6 THE THEORY OF 'DISTINCTION'

A more general theory of consumption, which to some extent builds upon Veblen's approach, is provided by the French writer Pierre Bourdieu. Campbell (1995, p.103) has described Bourdieu as 'the most important contemporary theorist of consumption proper' and stated that Bourdieu's work, *Distinction: A Social*

Critique of the Judgement of Taste (1979), 'bears comparison, in character and importance, with Veblen's *Theory of the Leisure Class*' (p.103). Like Veblen, Bourdieu looks at consumption as a class phenomenon. The tastes that consumers display in their consumption decisions are inextricably tied up with the position they hold in the social hierarchy.

Following Veblen, Bourdieu also views consumption behaviour as an evolutionary phenomenon (see Trigg, 2001). A consumer's tastes are not a given or fixed entity, as in the indifference curve diagram. Tastes evolve over time; they are cultivated by the individual. In the same way that a farmer may invest energy in developing land in order to cultivate crops, the individual invests in the cultivation of tastes. To become cultured in one's tastes requires the investment of time and energy – the pursuit of *cultural capital*.

Cultural capital

Refers to an individual's accumulated stock of knowledge about the products of artistic and intellectual traditions.

Here is an exercise based on the type of question asked by Bourdieu in a questionnaire he carried out in the mid-1960s on a sample of over 1200 French people.

Exercise 3.1

Name the composers of the following pieces of music.
(Calculate your score out of 15 after checking the answers).

1 The Double Cello Quintet
2 The Apassionata
3 Pictures from an Exhibition
4 The Messiah
5 The Ring Cycle
6 St Matthew Passion
7 Tales from the Vienna Woods
8 The Hebrides Suite
9 Coppelia
10 From the New World
11 The London Symphony
12 Les Sylphides
13 The 1812 Overture
14 Enigma Variations
15 Peer Gynt

The number of correct answers provides a rough guide to your cultural capital. At one end of the scale, if you can name all the composers, this might show that you have maximum cultural capital. If you cannot name any, your cultural capital is zero. Acquired knowledge of culture is viewed as capital, in the same way that a farmer might acquire capital in the form of machinery.

Bourdieu found the score that people achieved in this type of exercise was closely correlated to their educational qualifications. In his sample, 67 per cent of those individuals with only basic education could not identify more than two composers. In contrast, 78 per cent of teachers in higher education could name twelve or more composers. There is a general culture, of which knowledge and appreciation of music is a part, which becomes more developed the more education an individual undergoes. Why should somebody with educational qualifications acquire knowledge of certain types of culture? They may not seek to do so, but may pick up this knowledge through contact with people of similar levels of education. More importantly, however, Bourdieu (1979, p.23) argues that the acquisition of cultural capital is 'inscribed, as an objective demand, in membership of the bourgeoisie and in the qualifications giving access to its rights and duties'. To become accepted as part of the bourgeoisie one must be at ease with the various concerts and exhibitions which make up the cultural social circuit. One must keep up with dinner party conversation which drifts between comparisons of conductors and ballerinas, tenors and sculptors. This is not to say that culture is all the bourgeoisie talks about; only that it is an important entry requirement.

In addition to educational qualifications, a person's social origin is of vital importance to the level of cultural capital which is acquired. While a person of working-class background might bone up on classical music through listening to Radio 3 and Classic FM, for the person of upper-class origin, classical music is part of their upbringing. Bourdieu observes that 'when the child is introduced at an early age to a "noble" instrument – especially the piano – the effect is at least to produce a more familiar relationship to music, which differs from the always somewhat distant, contemplative and often verbose relation of those who have come to music through concerts or even only through records' (p.75).

It should be pointed out, in case you have not realized, that knowledge of the composers asked for in the previous exercise, even if you knew all fifteen, might not be evidence of too much cultural capital. Bourdieu distinguishes between middlebrow and highbrow taste, and I am afraid that the Messiah and the 1812 Overture may relate more to the former: they are more Classic FM than Radio 3. Since Bourdieu's original questions are not fully reported in his book, I have illustrated his approach using a comparable question which, coming from me, is necessarily middlebrow.

For those who do not have the right social background to become accomplished in their knowledge of classical music, the area of film may provide a more convenient outlet. As a form of art, film is not as legitimate as classical music – Bourdieu refers to film as 'not yet fully legitimate' art (p.87). However, despite its limitations, in metropolitan areas such as London and Paris, knowledge of films is central to dinner party conversation.

Exercise 3.2

Name the directors of the following films. (Calculate your score out of 20 after checking your answers).

1 A Clockwork Orange
2 Lawrence of Arabia
3 JFK
4 ET
5 On the Waterfront
6 Pulp Fiction
7 Hannah and Her Sisters
8 Citizen Kane
9 The Maltese Falcon
10 The Third Man
11 North by Northwest
12 Persona
13 Stagecoach
14 Fantasia
15 Malcolm X
16 La Grande Illusion
17 Land and Freedom
18 Little Man Tate
19 Braveheart
20 Gone With The Wind

Bourdieu asked his sample of individuals this type of question. He found that only 5 per cent of those with just elementary education could name at least four directors; of those with higher education, 22 per cent could name at least four directors. In addition, he found that those with just elementary education tended to be more interested in actors than directors. 'Where some only see "a Western starring Burt Lancaster", others "discover an early John Sturges" or "the latest Sam Peckinpah"' (p.28). There is a right way of seeing a film, and a right kind of film to see. It is no big deal if you managed to identify the Spielberg film, since he is well known, but being able to identify the Jean Renoir film shows culture and taste. Culture and taste can depend less on your direct enjoyment from, say, watching a Burt Lancaster film than on your knowledge of who directed it.

According to Bourdieu, therefore, you should not feel at all upset or discouraged even if you could not name any composers or film directors. Moreover, if you could name more of the actors in the films than the directors, this may indicate that your enjoyment of these films was less contrived. Taste is always a negative phenomenon in that it is based on a criticism of that which is popular. The establishment will always try to distinguish their tastes from popular taste. 'It is no accident that, when they have to be justified, they are asserted purely negatively, by the refusal of other tastes' (p.56). In social competition there is no gain from preferring Spielberg to Jean Renoir, since the former is watched by the working classes in droves, whilst the latter is not. Tastes do not come from inside; they are driven by the need for distinction – the need to distinguish one's tastes from that which is popular.

A possible illustration of this drive for distinction is provided by recent developments in the market for classical music. Opera, once the exclusive preserve of the upper classes, has entered into the realm of popular music. The three tenors – Domingo, Carreras and Pavarotti – sang to sell-out open air shows in the early 1990s. By the mid 1990s, however, the *Sunday Times* (21 April 1996) reported that 'classical music has become the latest victim of middle-class "culture fatigue"' and 'the loss of interest by those who regard opera as a ladder for social advancement ... resulted in lower classical record sales and declining concert audiences'. Could this be anything to do with the interest which the working classes have shown in opera since *Nessum Dorma* was used as a theme tune for television coverage of the 1990 World Cup?

In the same way that those higher up the social hierarchy will tend to distinguish themselves from those at the bottom, it also follows for Bourdieu that those at the bottom have their own values and tastes. Take the photograph of an old woman's hands shown in Figure 3.3.

Bourdieu showed this photograph to his sample group and asked them how they felt about it. Working-class respondents tended to respond with distaste: '"Oh, she's got terribly deformed hands!" ... "The old girl must've worked hard. Looks like she's got arthritis"' (Bourdieu, 1979, p.44). For respondents at higher levels of the social hierarchy, however, the responses are much more abstract: ' "The sort of hands you see in early Van Goghs, an old peasant woman or people eating potatoes" ... "I find this a very beautiful photograph. It's the very symbol of toil. It puts me in mind of Flaubert's old servant-woman"' (p.45). The implication is that working-class people see things as they are. They dislike the old lady's hands, because for them hard work is not beautiful or artistic, but an economic necessity. For the holder of cultural capital, the intention is to establish distance from economic necessity. A cultural detachment, which views the old woman's hands as a piece of art 'can only be constituted within an experience of the world freed from urgency and through the practice of activities which are an end in themselves, such as scholastic exercises or the contemplation of works of art' (p.54). Since for working-class people the immediate urgency is to make ends meet, there is little room for cultural endeavours.

This supposed working-class attitude to cultural endeavours extends to the consumption of goods and services in general. A whole series of different questions are asked in Bourdieu's questionnaire. In addition to items of cultural consumption, such as visits to the cinema, Bourdieu also considers more basic items such as food, clothing and furniture. With the consumption of food, for example, Bourdieu argues that working-class households tend to ensure that there is ample available for the satisfaction of hunger. This contrasts with the eating habits of the upper classes who are more interested in treating food as an art form. A working-class household would not tend to be impressed by fashions such as *nouvelle cuisine*, in which the presentation of food is more important than the quantity on offer. With furniture, Bourdieu distinguishes between the fixation the upper classes have for antiques and the more practical requirements of working-class households. And with clothing he argues that working-class households tend to be less influenced by *haute couture* than the upper classes.

In distinguishing between the tastes of individuals, Bourdieu places great emphasis on their level of economic capital. A person of high income, such as a lawyer or industrialist, has a high level of economic capital. An unskilled manual worker has a low level of economic capital. The more economic capital an individual has, the more able they are to develop their consumption patterns; the more able they are to purchase antiques and designer clothes.

It may or may not follow that a person of high economic capital also has high cultural capital. Figure 3.4 lays out four possible combinations of cultural and economic capital. Each block of the diagram is associated with different lifestyles. Block A contains people who have both a high level of income (positive economic capital) and well-developed tastes (positive cultural capital). People such as lawyers and architects can have both the economic resources for expensive tastes in consumption goods, and the know-how to appreciate legitimate culture. At the other extreme is block D – the lifestyles associated with working classes who have neither economic nor cultural capital. As we have seen, for Bourdieu the constraints of economic and cultural capital make it difficult for people to move from block D to block A.

The remaining diagonal blocks, blocks B and C, represent the lifestyles of individuals lacking in one of the two types of capital. In block B individuals have positive economic capital. This could be, say, small business people who make plenty of money but who do not show any interest in the arts. Block C, on the other hand, might include people such as primary school-teachers who do not earn much money (negative economic capital) but who tirelessly visit art galleries and attend the theatre.

Over time, there can be cross-mobility between blocks B and C. A family with a small business, but low cultural capital (block B) may channel its resources into purchasing an education for its children who then develop the lifestyle of block C by moving into teaching. The shape of the social hierarchy, in terms of which people end up where, depends, in part, on the cultural decisions of its participants.

Having considered the consumption behaviour of different social classes in relation to various consumption goods, we can now summarize

Figure 3.3 Photograph of an old woman's hands

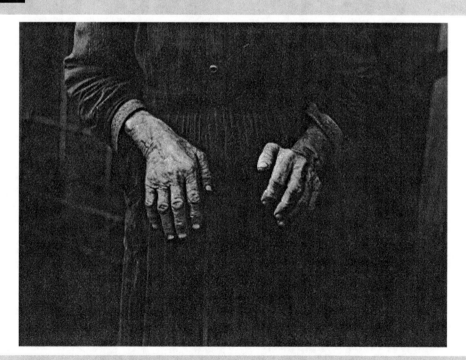

Source: Russell Lee, Hands of Old Homesteader, Iowa (1936); Gelatin-silver print, (16.5 x 24.44 cm). The Museum of Modern Art, New York, Gift of the Farm Security Administration, © 1996, The Museum of Modern Art, New York, reproduced in Bourdieu, 1979, p.45

Bourdieu's theory of distinction. There are two main parts to this theory. The first part, as we have seen, looks at the way in which individuals invest in cultural capital in order to obtain a position in the social hierarchy. Indeed the structure of the social hierarchy itself is shaped by the way in which individuals invest in cultural capital. For Bourdieu, the drive for distinction is a prime mover in the establishment of social classes.

The second part of the theory looks at the way tastes and preferences depend on membership of social classes. A working-class person's preferences may be dominated by functional necessities. This is not to say that the working classes are not influenced by fashion and culture; only that the need to make ends meet is of central importance. Moving up the social hierarchy these necessities have less influence. As a consequence, the tastes of the middle classes tend to imitate those of the upper classes; and the tastes of the upper classes are seen to be the dominant and legitimate tastes of society.

Figure 3.5 summarizes these two ways of seeing the relationship between tastes and the social

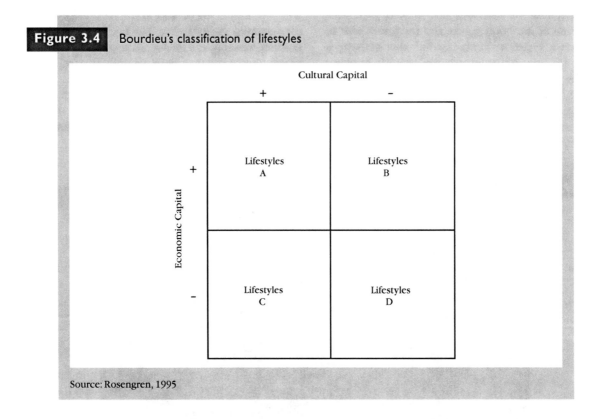

Figure 3.4 Bourdieu's classification of lifestyles

Cultural Capital

Economic Capital

	+	−
+	Lifestyles A	Lifestyles B
−	Lifestyles C	Lifestyles D

Source: Rosengren, 1995

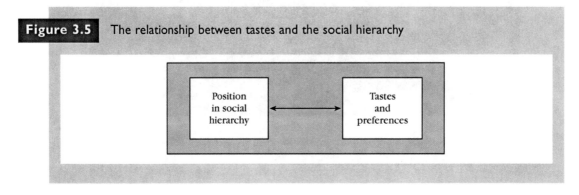

Figure 3.5 The relationship between tastes and the social hierarchy

Position in social hierarchy ⟷ Tastes and preferences

hierarchy. On the one hand, the tastes and preferences of individuals depend on their position in the social hierarchy, as shown by the right-hand arrow. And, on the other hand, the tastes and preferences that individuals cultivate help to determine their position in the social hierarchy (as shown by the left-hand arrow). Whichever direction of causation is dominant, the tastes and preferences of individuals are always *dependent*. They depend either on the position currently held in the social hierarchy or on the target social class that they wish to join. In the neoclassical approach, you simply have your own independent tastes and preferences; nobody else influences these preferences and you, yourself, have no choice or influence over them. For Bourdieu, however, tastes and preferences are determined socially by the way in which each individual relates to their (current or desired) position in the social hierarchy. In short, tastes and preferences are *endogenous*, since they depend on the way in which individuals relate to the social hierarchy.

This theory of distinction provides a more general theory of consumption than Veblen's theory of conspicuous consumption, and hence a more general critique of the neoclassical approach. Set in the context of Bourdieu's approach, conspicuous consumption represents only one particular type of behaviour. Not only are the working classes *not* required to emulate their betters; it is also possible in Bourdieu's system for members of the upper classes to be very inconspicuous in their consumption. Bourdieu emphasizes the subtle nuances and distinctions in which individuals may or may not require conspicuous displays of wealth. This theory is more general than Veblen's theory of conspicuous consumption, since it embraces more different types of behaviour; and, as a consequence, relates to more items of consumption than the luxury goods considered by Veblen.

Bourdieu also improves upon Veblen's system in his more sophisticated treatment of economic necessity. One of the key points of Veblen's approach is that consumer society produces waste products. This involves a value judgement on Veblen's part that some items of consumption satisfy a need – an economic necessity – while others merely satisfy social vanity. By providing a more general theory of consumption than Veblen, Bourdieu provides a more general critique of a consumer society.

6.1 Problems with the theory of 'Distinction'

Although Bourdieu's approach can be argued to be more general than that of Veblen, the question remains whether this is general enough. A number of critics have questioned the general validity of the results from Bordieu's questionnaire. In particular, it has been argued that his case study of a sample of French people in the 1960s may be too specifically French. Jenkins (1992, p.148), for example, is 'less convinced than Bourdieu ... that the use of French data does not undermine the general relevance of the argument'. Similarly, for Lamont and Lareau (1988, p.158) 'Bordieu's model could have been influenced by his context of elaboration, i.e., the small and relatively culturally unified Parisian scene'. The argument here is that in France the intellectualism which surrounds the cultural elite is very specific to France, and does not apply to other countries such as Britain and the United States.

It could be argued that in Britain, Napoleon's 'nation of shopkeepers', and in the US, where even a 'B' movie actor can become president, no such dominant cultural elite exists. In addition, whereas for Americans, film actors are their equivalent of royalty, the French have a particular reverence for intellectuals: Jean Paul Sartre and Simone de Beauvoir are as famous in France as Humphrey Bogart and Lauren Bacall are in the US. Indeed, Bourdieu himself is now something of a celebrity in France; his book, *Distinction*, has sold widely and he is often quoted extensively in French newspapers.

Wacquant (1993), however, has taken particular issue with this viewpoint that Bordieu's work is peculiarly French. Supporters of this position, he argues, 'miss the fact that Bourdieu is uncommonly internationalist in intellectual background, outlook and practice' (p.244). Bourdieu's educational training is in German philosophy and in anthropology of the British and American tradition. Furthermore, the journal which Bourdieu edits and in which applications of his approach are published, *Actes de la Recherche en Sciences Sociales*, is argued to carry more articles by foreign authors than any other social science journal in France.

As for the peculiarly French nature of the data which Bourdieu uses in *Distinction*, Wacquant argues this must be viewed in the context of all of his work. Throughout his career, it is argued, Bourdieu's trademark has been to apply his methodology to a variety of different social settings. From pre-capitalist societies to selection procedures in French grammar schools, Bourdieu has not relied on one type of specific data. Wacquant states that those who make this charge are 'ignoring the extensions, revisions, and corrections he may have made when tackling similar processes and mechanisms in a different social setting' (p.242). Bourdieu's approach is, therefore, defended as a method, as a way of interpreting the behaviour of individuals in different social settings.

For Garnham (1993) however, the general relevance of Bourdieu's method is challenged because it focuses too much on the relationships between individuals. The problem is that individuals may, indeed, differentiate their behaviour from others, depending on how they relate to the social hierarchy, but there are also other powerful influences on their behaviour, namely, the various institutions that make up society.

Garnham argues that one such important institution is television, which people now watch for an average of over twenty hours per week. With this amount of contact with television, Garnham is surprised that it receives so little attention from Bourdieu – there is only one reference to television in the index to *Distinction*. He also tentatively suggests that Bourdieu's methodology may not fit easily with an analysis of television. In particular, Garnham argues that Bourdieu's notion of a dominant class with a dominant culture does not necessarily apply to television. The work of Barwise and Ehrenberg (1988) is cited as showing that 'there is no evidence that members of the dominant faction of the dominant class watch demanding, minority, "cultural programs", whereas the popular classes watch less demanding, lowest-common-denominator pap' (Garnham, 1993, p.188). In Garnham's view, television cuts across social classes in a way which undermines Bourdieu's class-based approach.

There may, however, be specific television programmes to which Bourdieu's approach can be applied. Bonner and du Gay, for example, used Bourdieu to examine the way in which the characters of the American television programme *Thirtysomething* related to the new 'yuppie' class, which emerged in the 1980s. Not only did the programme reflect this new social phenomenon, it also helped to shape it. The Sun Alliance insurance company, for example, urged people in an advertisement to 'celebrate being 30 something' by

starting a savings plan (Bonner and du Gay, 1992, p.168). In contrast to Garnham's approach, Bonner and du Gay argue that 'these are changing times for TV schedulers and advertisers who want access to those with disposable incomes rather than to large audiences dominated by the ageing poor as is the case with the 17 million audience for *Coronation Street*, for example' (p.169). In this view, television is beginning to reinforce the distinctions between social classes which Bourdieu emphasizes.

Whichever view of television is correct, its role in the formation of consumer behaviour needs to be considered. Moreover, once we take an interest in the role of television, the role of other institutions also comes into play. What role, for example, do advertising agencies play in the selling of consumer products, and, indeed, why do firms, such as Sun Alliance, spend so much on advertising their services? Do they actively seek to change tastes? To continue our search for a more general theory of consumption, we now turn our attention to want creation by institutions, especially the role of the firm in this process.

7 WANT CREATION BY INSTITUTIONS

An important insight into how firms influence consumer behaviour is provided by the Harvard professor (and adviser to President John F. Kennedy), John Kenneth Galbraith. The problem for capitalism, as Galbraith sees it, is that we judge its success by production. If the output of the UK economy, for example, fails to grow at its trend rate of 2.2 per cent per annum, a downturn is judged to have taken place; for the economy to be successful, firms must produce more each year.

How, it might be asked, can this additional output be sold each year in the marketplace? The neoclassical theory of consumption assumes that each individual gets less satisfaction as more of each good *G* is consumed. Assume, by way of an example, that good *G* is bread. Galbraith argues that as western economies become more affluent, bread becomes abundant in supply. In Europe there is a grain mountain which suggests that there is no shortage of the main ingredient used to make bread. Indeed, bread can be bought relatively cheaply since it is a lead good which supermarkets tend to price competitively. It follows that there is not much room for increased sales of bread.

So where is the 2.2 per cent increase in sales of goods to come from? Galbraith argues that firms create new wants in consumers by introducing new products to the marketplace. Key to this process are the techniques of marketing and advertising. A good example is provided by brand-name bottles of water, such as Evian and Perrier. It is still every traveller's right in Britain to be given a free glass of water on visiting an inn or public house. The breweries have now managed, however, to sell water in bottles under these brand-names. Consumers now spend money on a product which, at one time, did not exist.

This process of *want creation* is continually at work as firms invent more and more products with which to tempt the consumer. In Galbraith's view the neoclassical theory of consumption breaks down here because it is firms that create wants. 'One cannot defend production as satisfying wants if that production creates wants' (Galbraith, 1958, p.148). Galbraith questions the validity of this consumer bonanza:

> *'Were it so that a man on arising each morning was assailed by demons which instilled in him a passion sometimes for silk shirts, sometimes for kitchenware, sometimes for chamber-pots, and sometimes for orange squash, there would be every reason to applaud the effort to find the goods, however odd, that quenched this flame. But should it be that his passion was the result of his first having cultivated the demons, and should it also be that his effort to allay it stirred the demons to even greater and greater effort, there would be question as to how rational was his solution. Unless restrained by conventional attitudes, he might wonder if the solution lay with more goods or fewer demons.'*
>
> (Galbraith, 1958, p.148)

Want creation

The shaping by firms of new desires for consumer products.

Galbraith views the process of creating wants as analogous to a squirrel on a treadmill. The more the squirrel (or the supposedly sovereign consumer)

propels the wheel, the faster it goes. The squirrel is running faster and faster to stay in the same place.

The dependent consumer

The key problem with this process of want creation is that consumption is divorced from need. It does not matter for the firm whether the consumer needs to buy a product, only that the consumer will buy it. For Galbraith it is difficult to establish that there is an urgent need for a product, if, previously, the consumer never even knew about it. This idea picks up from Veblen's notion that conspicuous consumption is a wasteful activity. Wedgwood saw that people did not buy his pottery for the use they gained from it – consumption did not derive from need. This is a value judgement which Veblen, Bourdieu and Galbraith make about whether or not a product is useful.

By focusing specifically on the role of firms in influencing consumer behaviour, Galbraith's approach can be seen as providing an additional dimension to the other approaches that have been discussed in this chapter. The behaviour of consumers depends not only on the way in which they relate to other individuals, but also on the role of the firm in its advertising and marketing activities.

It should be noted, however, that those who work in the field of marketing do not tend to agree with Galbraith's arguments. In most marketing textbooks, consumption is argued to derive from the needs of consumers. Kotler *et al.* (1996) for example, in their *Principles of Marketing*, state that 'the most basic concept underlying marketing is that of human needs' (p.7). In particular, it is often argued that consumers have *latent needs* – needs of which the consumer is not yet conscious, but which are lurking in the background. Thus it may be the case that new consumer goods satisfy a whole range of latent needs.

Latent needs

Desires not yet exhibited or expressed for consumer products.

Question

Identify any latent needs which the following consumer goods might satisfy:

- refrigerators
- cars
- washing machines.

Refrigerators and washing machines, which are relatively recent consumer goods, may satisfy the latent needs to store food efficiently and to clean clothing more easily. Similarly, cars satisfy the latent need to travel. Although people may not have had a need for these particular consumer goods before they were invented, they could arguably have had a latent need for the attributes of these goods. Sharpe argues that in the past, before these goods were invented:

> '... people needed to eat, wash clothes and move from one place to another. Given the removal of much of the population from farms, the desire of women to be free from the household drudgery of washing clothes by hand, and the increasing sprawl of towns and suburbs, the refrigerator, washing machine and automobile seem natural and logical choices of consumers, requiring an assist from advertising only to familiarize them with the possibilities and jar them out of set patterns of habit.'
>
> (SHARPE, 1973, P.31)

The problem, which Galbraith underestimates, is that launching new products involves great risks. Indeed, Galbraith himself cites the case of a failed motor car, the Edsel, 'as a case in point where a firm made losses because it incorrectly judged the demands (real and potential) of consumers' (Reisman, 1980, p.94). In order to minimize these risks, firms carry out market research to find out whether products relate to consumer needs. Information is gathered about how consumers might react to a new product.

For Reisman, this demonstrates that consumers are sovereign: 'Market research may be seen as no more than an attempt to forecast (in order to satisfy) the future desires of sovereign consumers' (p.96). This contrasts with Galbraith's interpretation of market research, in which market research is seen as discovering what consumers can be cajoled into wanting. Galbraith argues that instead of consumer sovereignty there is producer sovereignty – that it is the producers, not the consumers, who decide what is produced.

Sharpe argues that both the consumer sovereignty and the producer sovereignty positions are perhaps exaggerated, and that there may be some truth in both. It may be the case that consumers desire even the most seemingly frivolous consumer goods according to their latent needs and, at the same time, it may also be the case that firms influence those desires. Firms may carry out market research to find out the needs of consumers; but they spend a great deal of money on advertising campaigns to influence, and to some extent manipulate, the desires of consumers. 'Consumer sovereignty might best be regarded as a doctrine of limited monarchy rather than divine right, with the producer in the role of a very persuasive prime minister' (Sharpe, 1973, p.32).

Taking into account these arguments, the model of consumer behaviour which was developed in the previous section, based on the work of Bourdieu, can be further generalized. Figure 3.6 represents an expanded version of Figure 3.5.

Not only are the interrelationships between tastes and preferences with the social hierarchy taken into account – as developed in Bourdieu's theory of distinction. This more general model also takes into account the relationship between firms and the tastes and preferences of consumers. The direction of causation runs in both directions. Firms can both influence, and be influenced by, these tastes and preferences.

8   CONCLUSIONS

Using the work of Thorstein Veblen as a starting point, this chapter has provided a critique of the neoclassical theory of consumption. In Veblen's view, people engage in conspicuous consumption, their inclination being to buy expensive luxury goods in order to demonstrate wealth and prosperity to others. Unlike the neoclassical approach, in which the preferences of individuals are exogenous to the model and are independent of prices, Veblen argues that preferences *depend* on prices. Instead of consumers being sovereign in the market economy, they are dependent. Preferences are not exogenous to the market – they are endogenous, dependent upon the market. Instead of consumer sovereignty there is consumer dependency.

Two case studies have been considered as illustrations of conspicuous consumption. The first reviewed the argument that Josiah Wedgwood pioneered a consumer revolution in pottery by encouraging consumers to emulate the consumption behaviour of the English aristocracy. In the second, conspicuous consumption was evidenced by the exorbitant prices of luxury goods sold on the Rue du Faubourg Saint-Honore in Paris. As well as illustrating Veblen's critique of neoclassical theory, these case studies also provide the basis for a critique of consumer society. Since luxury goods are only bought for purposes of display their practical usefulness is not important. For Veblen, consumer society is characterized by waste and frivolity.

While both these case studies provide good illustrations of how conspicuous consumption can work, the chapter has also discussed the limitations of the theory. In particular, it could be argued that it is impossible to generalize such examples of conspicuous consumption to the economy as a whole. It would be difficult, for example, to explain the consumption of coal as a vehicle for conspicuous consumption. Some credence has been given to the neoclassical viewpoint that luxury goods may represent exceptions to the general neoclassical story in which preferences are exogenous.

In order to develop a more general alternative to the neoclassical approach, the chapter has also considered the work of Pierre Bourdieu. Instead of emulating the behaviour of others, Bourdieu argues that consumers try to distinguish their tastes from that which is popular. They engage in distinction. This type of behaviour is not restricted to the consumption of luxury goods – Bourdieu relates it to a whole range of goods and services.

The search for distinction provides the driving force behind the evolution of social classes as it provides the entry requirement for membership of the upper classes. At the same time, the structure of the social hierarchy determines the tastes of consumers. Bourdieu develops a two-way model in which structure determines tastes and tastes determine structure. This provides a more general critique of the neoclassical approach in which tastes determine consumption patterns. In Bourdieu's view, tastes are not independent of, nor exogenous to, the model, they are *endogenous*, depending upon how the consumer relates to the social hierarchy. This model also represents a critique of consumer society, since the whole basis of distinction is to differentiate behaviour from that which is necessary and practical. Following Veblen, Bourdieu argues that some consumption is wasteful.

Figure 3.6 A more general model of consumption

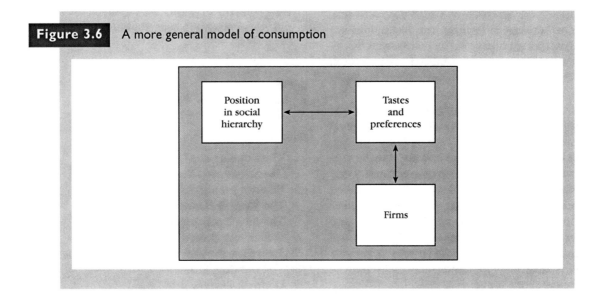

In discussing Bourdieu, two main issues have been considered. First, there is the question of whether Bourdieu's approach is peculiarly French, an issue which has not been fully resolved in the literature. Second, there is the criticism that Bourdieu does not take into account the important role which institutions play in the formation of consumer preferences. This latter deficiency has been addressed by considering the approach taken by John Kenneth Galbraith which also picks up on the notion that consumers are dependent on firms. With their sophisticated advertising and marketing operations, firms are able to shape the tastes of consumers. In keeping with Veblen and Bourdieu, this approach also represents a critique of consumer society in which firms generate wasteful growth which does not relate to the needs of individuals.

By taking Galbraith's approach into consideration, alongside some of the arguments made in the marketing literature, that the goods which firms produce are shaped by the tastes of consumers, an even more general theory of consumption has been suggested. In the same way that Bourdieu develops a two-way relationship between the social hierarchy and consumer tastes, a two-way model of the relationship between firms and consumers' tastes is suggested. In principle this model can be integrated with Bourdieu's framework to provide an even more general theory of consumption.

It should be emphasized that if this more general approach is accepted, then this is not simply a matter of adding other factors to the neoclassical view of consumer theory – it entirely undermines the whole structure and nature of its explanation. By taking an interdisciplinary approach, in which the social relationships between individuals and institutions are considered, an alternative to the neoclassical theory of consumption is developed. Indeed, you may recall from Chapter 1, that these provide some of the ingredients of institutional economics. This chapter has developed both an institutional critique of the neoclassical approach and an alternate conceptual framework for the theory of consumption.

This chapter has focused on only one specific type of social division – that of social class – and mainly one type of institution, the firm. Once consumption is seen as a social relationship there are, of course, many other types of divisions, such as gender and race, and different types of institutions such as schools and households. This chapter should be seen as just one possible starting point for investigating an institutional approach to consumption.

 # FURTHER READING

Bourdieu, P. (1979) *Distinction: a Social Critique of the Judgement of Taste*, London, Routledge (English translation, 1984): this will make you question everything you ever thought about taste and consumption.

Burrows, R. and Marsh, C. (eds) (1992) *Consumption and Class*, London, Macmillan: a collection of articles which contain a good overview of the literature on the relationship between consumption and class.

Calhoun, C., LiPuma, E. and Postone, M. (eds) (1993) *Bourdieu: Critical Perspectives,* Cambridge, Polity Press: a good insight into the literature on Bourdieu's work.

Fine, B. and Leopold, E. (1993) *The World of Consumption*, London, Routledge: a comprehensive survey of the vast literature on consumption; it also contains a critique of conspicuous consumption.

Galbraith, J.K. (1950) *The Affluent Society*, Harmondsworth, Penguin: still stands as a vibrant critique of the theory of consumer society.

Kotler, P., Armstrong, G., Saunders, J. and Wong, V. (1996) *Principles of Marketing*, Hemel Hempstead, Prentice Hall Europe: argues that consumption is based upon the needs of consumers.

Veblen, T. (1889) *The Theory of the Leisure Class*, New York, Dover (1994): the classic on the institutional approach to consumption.

 # ANSWERS TO EXERCISES

Exercise 3.1

1   The Double Cello Quintet *Schubert*
2   The Apassionata *Beethoven*
3   Pictures from an Exhibition *Mussorgsky*
4   The Messiah *Handel*
5   The Ring Cycle *Wagner*
6   St Matthew Passion *J.S. Bach*
7   Tales from the Vienna Woods *Johan Strauss*
8   The Hebrides Suite *Mendelssoh*
9   Coppelia *Delibes*

10 From the New World *Dvorak*

11 The London Symphony *J. Haydn*

12 Les Sylphides *Chopin*

13 The 1812 Overture *Tchaikovsky*

14 Enigma Variations *Elgar*

15 Peer Gynt *Grieg*

Exercise 3.2

1 A Clockwork Orange *Stanley Kubrik*

2 Lawrence of Arabia *David Lean*

3 JFK *Oliver Stone*

4 ET *Steven Spielberg*

5 On the Waterfront *Elia Kazan*

6 Pulp Fiction *Quentin Tarantino*

7 Hannah and Her Sisters *Woody Allen*

8 Citizen Kane *Orson Welles*

9 The Maltese Falcon *John Huston*

10 The Third Man *Carol Reed*

11 North by Northwest *Alfred Hitchcock*

12 Persona *Ingmar Bergman*

13 Stagecoach *John Ford*

14 Fantasia *Walt Disney*

15 Malcolm X *Spike Lee*

16 La Grande Illusion *Jean Renoir*

17 Land and Freedom *Ken Loach*

18 Little Man Tate *Jodie Foster*

19 Braveheart *Mel Gibson*

20 Gone With The Wind *Victor Fleming*

MEASURING WELFARE: ARE PEOPLE BETTER OFF?

Graham Dawson

LINKS

- The discussion of welfare economics in this chapter builds on the notions of utility and Pareto efficiency, which were introduced in Chapter 1. Further discussion of welfare issues is found in Chapter 18, Section 5.

- Like all neoclassical theory, neoclassical welfare economics (both 'old' and 'new') adopts the assumption of methodological individualism. It builds on the neoclassical theory of consumption, first examined in Chapter 2, though in welfare economics the focus is on the implications of that theory for how economic welfare should be understood.

- The Slutsky approximation to the income effect, used in constructing both the Laspeyres and Paasche price indices, was introduced in Chapter 2.

- The Barten scaling technique used in constructing utility-based equivalence scales adopts the assumption that decisions in the households are made by a single decision maker. The implications of this assumption and some alternatives will be discussed in Chapter 6.

- The institutionalist approach, which stresses the importance of social interactions, culture and norms, criticizes the neoclassical welfare economics for ignoring social interactions between individuals. This criticism of the methodological individualism of the neoclassical approach is made in many places in this book, including in Chapter 3, where alternative institutionalist approaches to consumption were suggested.

1   INTRODUCTION

We ask questions about human well-being in a variety of contexts; for example, from the personal – 'Am I better off than I was five years ago?' – through the local – 'Are we better off than our grandparents?' – to the global – 'Is the human race better off as a result of industrial capitalism?' In the 180 years from 1820, average world real income per capita has increased by a factor of 10, from 500 to 5000 US dollars at constant 1992 prices (Maddison, 1995). What else, apart from the level of material well-being, do we need to know in order to answer such questions? How reliable are our answers likely to be? To what extent are they observations, relatively free from theoretical intervention? What are the theories that, to whatever degree, inform our judgements of well-being? The aim of this chapter is to clarify some of the problems involved in constructing a method of measuring whether people are better off and, if so, to what extent.

To make this task manageable, it is necessary to narrow the focus and ask whether some particular group of people is better off than it used to be at a specified earlier date. Looming immediately ahead is a question that looks, at first sight, quite straightforward but can quickly grow to appear too vast to be answerable: what is it about people that we are trying to measure when we set out to discover whether they are better off? A traditional view in moral philosophy is that human beings everywhere have some wants in common. The Greek philosopher Aristotle (384–322 BC) believed that one may 'observe in one's travels to distant countries the feelings of recognition and affiliation that link every human being to every other human being' (*Nicomachean Ethics*, 1155a21–2; quoted in Nussbaum, 1993, p.242). Among the most important spheres of human experience that Aristotle identified were the fear of important damages, especially death; bodily appetites and their pleasures; the distribution of limited resources; attitudes and actions with respect to one's own worth; association and living together and the fellowship of words and actions and the planning of one's life and conduct (Nussbaum, 1993, p.246). So it seems reasonable to say that people are better off when things are going well for them in these spheres of life. This is Aristotle's concept of human flourishing.

It is likely that some components of the list given above are going to be much easier to measure than others. Bodily appetites and the distribution of limited resources seem to be reassuringly close to the economist's concern with the allocation of scarce resources in the production of goods for consumption. Clearly, part of human flourishing is captured by the concept of the standard of living. So we can go some way towards measuring the extent to which people are better off by calculating changes in their real income. But we might want to say that there is more to human flourishing than material considerations of this kind and try to capture the non-material aspects of human flourishing in the phrase 'the quality of life'. At this point, confidence and certainty are likely to leave us. The term 'quality of life' seems to have a less direct connection with the level of the economy's output and is more likely to involve some of Aristotle's spheres of experience, such as matters of one's own worth or self-esteem, social interaction or fellowship and the ability to plan one's life. But how can we measure the extent to which a person can be said to flourish in any of these respects? And how can we reliably compare the quality of one person's life in these respects with that of another? How can we get inside people's minds? And what if, despite Aristotle's belief in global features of humanness underlying local differences, the desires and values of different groups of people seem, in some sense, to be non-comparable?

With these questions in mind, it might be helpful to consider a systematic inquiry into the question whether a particular group of people became better off during a certain period of time. Did the industrial revolution make the people of England, particularly the working class, better off? Here is an economic historian trying to disentangle the issues raised by this question.

> '*The most interesting and inconclusive debate on the industrial revolution in England has been concerned with the standard of living of the workers, particularly the industrial and urban poor, during the first half of the nineteenth century. In the past, those who have argued for deterioration have outnumbered those who believed that conditions of life improved, and the intransigency of both has resulted inevitably in extreme points of view. To a large extent the argument has been, not an objective debate on the interpretation of the facts as known, but a controversy about values,*

about the desirability of social and economic change. Disagreement has stemmed also from the conflicting character of the evidence, which has allowed plausible allegiance to opposed theories; from the fact that there was, for much of the period, no marked trend in living standards, and that the increase in per capita real income still left the majority of workers at a low standard of living, aware more of their unfulfilled wants than of their increasing prosperity... The exact measurement of the standard of living in the years 1800–50 may be impossible, but, eschewing prejudice and preconceived theories, a firm statement about the trend of living standards can be derived from the mass of evidence that has survived, and from an analysis of the likely changes in income distribution during a long period of economic growth. This article argues for an upward trend in living standards during the industrial revolution ... from an examination of national income and other aggregate statistics that have survived ... from wage-price data and from analogy ... from an analysis of consumption figures ... from the evidence of vital statistics, from a comparison with eighteenth-century living standards, and from details of the expansion after 1800 of social and economic opportunities. Briefly, the argument is that, since average per capita income increased, since there was no trend in distribution against the workers, since (after 1815) prices fell while money wages remained constant, since per capita consumption of food and other consumer goods increased, and since government increasingly intervened in economic life to protect or raise living standards, then the real wages of the majority of English workers were rising in the years 1800–50.'

(Hartwell, 1971, pp.313–4)

Questions

1a   What definition of 'standard of living', familiar to economists, is implied in Hartwell's conclusion?

1b   What items are mentioned earlier in the text that seem to have more to do with the quality of life than the standard of living, so defined?

2   Does Hartwell think that it is possible to measure the standard of living, so defined?

3   What do you think Hartwell might mean by suggesting that the controversy over the standard of living is in part 'not an objective debate on the interpretation of the facts as known, but a controversy about values'?

These questions raise the three broad issues of meaning, measurement and values which run through this chapter. First, it is necessary to define as precisely as possible what we mean by 'better off'. Hartwell's conclusion is based on a narrow and, given reliable sources of statistics for the period, a readily quantifiable definition of an increase in the standard of living as a rise in the level of real wages. In economics, well-being has traditionally been thought of in terms of utility, which will be discussed in Section 2. However, earlier in the passage he refers to the 'expansion after 1800 of social and economic opportunities', which seems more closely related to matters of self-esteem, social relationships and the quality of life. The concept of agency has been introduced to recognize this active side of human flourishing and is defined as a person's 'ability to form goals, commitments, values, etc.' (Sen, 1987, p.41).

Second, there is the problem of finding a theoretically robust method of measuring changes in human flourishing, in well-being or agency. As Hartwell recognizes, '*exact* measurement ... may be impossible'. But one aspect of well-being, real income, appears to be capable of quite precise estimation. Some of the techniques used in measuring changes in the real income of households will be explained in Section 3, and the problem of adjusting for differences in household size and composition will be discussed in Section 4.

The use of the agency approach in the construction of the Human Development Index (HDI), which is perhaps the most comprehensive method for the measurement of human flourishing that has yet been devised, will be examined in Section 5.

Third, it is clear that differences in values can lead to conflicting interpretations of the impact on human flourishing of economic change. For example, does industrialization always occur as part of a process of human enlightenment, or may it entail the destruction of intrinsically worthwhile traditional ways of life? Again the observer's focus on the rising trend in real income might be at odds with the experience of working people themselves, who might be more conscious of the low absolute level of living standards. As Hartwell notes, 'rising real income still left the majority of workers at a low standard of living, aware more of their unfulfilled wants than of their increasing prosperity'. Conflicts of perspectives of this kind raise the question whether judgements of well-being are objective or socially generated. This will be discussed very briefly in Section 6.

2 | UTILITY IN THE DEVELOPMENT OF WELFARE ECONOMICS

The fact that neoclassical economic judgements about well-being are grounded in propositions about the utility of individuals has been a source of much controversy. If we are to answer a question such as 'Are we better off than our grandparents?' and assess the impact of industrial capitalism on human well-being, it seems that we must be able to make interpersonal comparisons of well-being or, in the terminology of neoclassical economics, utility. Yet an important tradition in *welfare economics* holds that interpersonal comparisons of utility are deeply problematic.

Welfare economics

Welfare economics studies people's well-being in different economic situations.

In contemporary economic analysis, utility is simply an alternative way of referring to preference satisfaction. For example, to say that consumers maximize their utility means no more than that they satisfy as many of their preferences as possible. It says nothing about how consumers feel, or about whether the satisfaction of their preferences is good for them. However, two other interpretations of utility have been influential in welfare economics. The 'old welfare economics' assumed that the concept of utility had a wide range of application, covering both mental and physical aspects of well-being. For example, the utility from eating ten bananas a day would normally consist both in feeling

better and in performing physical tasks more energetically. So, in principle, I can infer your state of mind from your behaviour and make interpersonal comparisons of utility.

The 'new welfare economics' relied on a narrower, more subjective interpretation of utility as a state of mind, thereby driving a wedge between the mental and physical aspects of well-being. Each economic agent can make judgements only about their own individual utility, and interpersonal comparisons are problematic. This goes some way towards explaining the appeal of Pareto efficiency; if judgements about a person's well-being are always expressed in terms of 'their own estimation', there is no reason to try to make interpersonal comparisons. So a particular interpretation of individual utility contributed to the central position of Pareto efficiency in neoclassical economics, and hence to an identification of well-being with the consumption of goods in perfectly competitive markets.

The contemporary understanding of utility as preference satisfaction also focuses on consumption as the way to achieving well-being. Such a close connection between well-being and consumption, a view shared by the new welfare economics and by contemporary economic analysis, is questionable. As was argued in Chapter 3, the consumer may not be sovereign. In this section I want to make the analogous suggestion that consumption is not the sovereign measure of well-being. I will try to deconstruct the support for Pareto efficiency provided by the 'new' and contemporary interpretations of utility, by defending aspects of the 'old' approach. This will form the foundation for constructing an objective approach to well-being in Section 5.

2.1 The old welfare economics

The term 'the old welfare economics' refers to welfare economics up to the late 1930s (Rothschild, 1993, p.55). Welfare economics emerged towards the end of the nineteenth century as a systematic attempt to formulate judgements about the effects of economic activities and policy measures on the welfare or well-being of people. Economists had always been interested in welfare issues; Adam Smith's metaphor of the invisible hand is an early example of a proposition about the impact of the market on social welfare. However, as the technical apparatus available to economists became more sophisticated, they became more conscious of the need to clarify and justify the propositions and policy recommendations they put forward. In particular, the introduction of the concept of utility into the economist's professional vocabulary gave an impetus to the move to clarify what can, and what cannot, reasonably be said about the implications of economic activity for social well-being. Policy conclusions could be justified only by tracing them back to their ultimate foundations in utility. This early phase of welfare economics is usually regarded as having culminated in Pigou's book, *The Economics of Welfare* (1920). Two assumptions were characteristic of the old welfare economics, both of which concerned the interpretation of the concept of utility.

The first assumption is that utility can be thought of in cardinal terms, that is, in principle, it is measurable. It seemed reasonable to think of putting a figure on the utility a person derives from eating a banana, driving a Ferrari, watching *Brookside*, or growing roses. The utility to be had from these diverse activities could then, in principle, be measured and added up. We might want to know an individual person's total utility from all four of these activities, or the total utility everyone in society derives from them, or we might want to compare the individual or total utility from one particular activity. Total social utility is regarded as the arithmetic sum of the utilities of all the members of society from all of the economic activities in which they engage.

The philosophical foundation for this approach is the 'felicific calculus', literally a calculation of happiness, usually referred to now as the utilitarian calculus. It was originally proposed by the philosopher Jeremy Bentham as a way of aggregating individual utilities (Bentham, 1789; reprinted in Warnock, 1962). In the old welfare economics, the utilitarian calculus depends on utility being regarded interchangeably as a state of mind, the happiness caused by the consumption of a good, and as the material benefits of consuming the good. The metaphor of people as 'utility or pleasure machines, glowing, as it were, more or less brightly as their consumption enables preferences to be more or less satisfied' (*Changing Economies,* Chapter 22, Section 4.1) is certainly a powerful one. No one supposes that utility could be measured literally and directly in 'units of pleasure'. Nevertheless, the old welfare economists seem to have taken it for granted that we can 'read off' a person's utility from some episode of publicly observable behaviour, such as consuming

something or paying a certain amount of money for it. They argued that the price a consumer is willing to pay for a good is a reasonably reliable measure of the utility he or she expects to derive from it.

The second assumption characteristic of the old welfare economics is that interpersonal comparisons of utility are unproblematic. From the perspective of the old welfare economics, it would be reasonable to make judgements such as 'A obtained more utility from driving the Ferrari than B did' or 'I like chocolate more than you do' or 'Holiday-makers will gain more utility from a motorway to speed their route to the coast than owners of houses close to the motorway will lose from the noise and fumes'. This approach was probably a reflection of common-sense attitudes towards interpersonal comparisons of well-being (since utility is not an element of most people's common sense), expressed in statements such as 'This will hurt me more than it will hurt you' or 'Rather you than me'. More seriously, parents choosing which one of two crying children needs their attention first might have nothing more observable to go on than the competing bouts of crying. Mistakes are made; we can be deceived. But it is routine to make interpersonal comparisons of well-being, and the old welfare economists believed that it is reasonable to do the same for its technical counterpart, utility. In summing up the pragmatic attitude of the old welfare economics, Rothschild (1993) comments that it was 'prepared to work with rather simple and robust assumptions about utility and utility effects so as to be able to come to realistic welfare statements' (p.57).

2.2   The new welfare economics

In the late 1930s, the new welfare economics developed as a demand for greater precision and a more comprehensively scientific approach found the two assumptions of the old welfare economics unsatisfactory. The principles of the new welfare economics were formulated by John Hicks, Nicolas Kaldor and Tibor Scitovsky. Rejecting the assumptions of cardinality and interpersonal comparisons of utility, they looked to the principle of Pareto efficiency and the concept of the perfectly competitive market as the basis for a new welfare economics.

The new welfare economics maintained that it is impossible to make scientific statements about our own mental states for two reasons. First, they are not observable, which is taken to imply that a scientific welfare economics must eschew interpersonal comparisons of utility. Second, they are not measurable, which is thought to imply that scientific welfare economics must restrict itself to ordinal utility. The new welfare economists therefore decided to rely on indifference curve analysis, which assumes only ordinal utility, and the principle of Pareto efficiency, which escapes the need to make interpersonal comparisons by conceptualizing a person's utility in terms of his or her own estimation. Let me clarify just what is being denied by the new welfare economics.

One way of approaching their misgivings about the assumptions of cardinality and interpersonal comparisons of utility is to examine Bentham's original definition of utility, which influenced the old welfare economics so deeply: 'By utility is meant that property in any object, whereby it tends to produce benefit, advantage, pleasure, good, or happiness, (all this in the present case comes to the same thing) or (what comes again to the same thing) to prevent the happening of mischief, pain, evil, or unhappiness to the party whose interest is considered' (Bentham, 1789; reprinted in Warnock, 1962, p.34).

Question

Can you think of any reasons for doubting Bentham's assurance that 'all this in the present case comes to the same thing'?

Bentham was careful to add a rider to his claim with the words 'in the present case' and, since he did not expand on the qualification, we should not be quick to accuse him of ambiguity. However, there does seem to be a gap between benefit, advantage and good, on the one hand, and happiness, on the other. That a particular object causes you benefit, advantage or good concerns what goes on in the physical world and we have few qualms about making statements such as 'Eating fresh fruit and vegetables is good for you' or 'You need more vitamin C in your diet'. But even though vegetables are good for you, they will not make you feel happy if you dislike eating them. And when it comes to mischief, pain and evil, there are, for example, long established government campaigns directed against the harm that is done to people by alcohol and tobacco. True, we can all make mistakes and it sometimes turns out

that today's 'clinically proven' fact is tomorrow's discredited fad. But we do not dispute the principle that one person can be in a position to judge the benefit that an object produces for another person.

This does not seem to me to be so unequivocally the case with happiness and unhappiness. One person might enjoy listening to Bela Bartok's *Music for Strings, Percussion and Celeste* but it might be agony for another. We are generally rather reluctant to tell other people what will make them happy. There is a feeling that each person is in a privileged position when it comes to judgements about his or her own happiness. Let us now examine the new welfare economics in the light of these intuitions about language use.

The new welfare economics challenged the accepted interpretation of utility as cardinal and interpersonally comparable, on the basis of the philosophy of the science of the day – logical positivism. It tried, thereby, to claim that welfare economics, properly formulated, could be a science. The central principles of logical positivism are the propositions that only scientific statements are meaningful and that genuinely scientific evidence must be observable and measurable. To see why this caused the new welfare economists such a problem with interpersonal comparisons of utility, let us return to the intuitions about the common usage of terms such as benefit and happiness, mischief and unhappiness.

These facts about language use reflect a distinction which is made by many philosophers between the public and the private worlds. The new welfare economists' rejection of interpersonal comparisons of utility is based on taking this distinction very seriously – perhaps too seriously, as I will suggest later. There is no denying that distinction; the question is the strength and reliability of the connections between publicly observable behaviour and private states of mind. The consumption of goods and the material benefits that consumption brings to people belong to the public world, in the sense that these benefits are common property. You are just as likely to make well-informed and reasoned judgements about your friend's physical fitness, diet and so on as is your friend. We can put such matters to the test: will your athletic friend's prowess on the track decline if he or she stops eating ten bananas every day?

When we turn to the experiences, mental states and feelings of another person, however, they seem, by comparison, to be inaccessible to us. Only you know what your joy or confidence, or your boredom or anxiety, is really like; only you really know how it feels to be you.

For the new welfare economists, imbued with the philosophy of logical positivism, the implication of this line of thought was that interpersonal comparisons of utility were unscientific. They did not deny that we routinely make interpersonal comparisons of welfare, in a general sense. Their point was that since such comparisons could not be tested by means of observations, they could not be admitted to economic science. They were usually analysed either as subjective opinions or as value judgements based on norms and conventions. Either way, they were not scientific statements.

Second, the cardinality of utility was challenged because the new welfare economists thought of utility as a state of mind and, therefore, as something which could not be measured. An economist cannot measure another person's mental states. And there are problems with measuring one's own mental states. Ordinality is unproblematic. For example, for breakfast I prefer marmalade to strawberry jam, so it seems reasonable to imply that the utility I get from eating marmalade is greater than the utility I get from eating strawberry jam. But that seems to be as far as measuring utility goes. If cardinal measurement is to be possible, I need to be able to say something like this: 'I prefer marmalade to strawberry jam more strongly than I prefer muesli to cornflakes'. I would have to be able to compare, on the same scale, the amount by which the utility from eating marmalade exceeds that from eating strawberry jam with the amount by which the utility from eating muesli exceeds that from eating cornflakes. Is the first gain in utility greater than the second? And this is just about eating breakfast. How could we begin to answer the same question about preferring to drive a Ferrari to watching *Brookside* against preferring to run a half marathon to reading *Great Expectations*?

2.3 A re-examination of the concept of utility

In this section I want to review, very briefly, some developments in contemporary philosophical analysis which are much more sympathetic to the interpretation of the concept of utility embodied in the old welfare economics. The logical positivism which informed the new welfare economics has given way in contemporary philosophy to a broad approach originally inspired by the later work of Ludwig Wittgenstein (1889-1951). Logical positivism can, in many ways, be seen as the culmination of a philosophical tradition stretching back to the British Empiricists of the seventeenth and eighteenth centuries (for example John Locke, 1632-1704; George Berkeley, 1685-1753; David Hume, 1711-76) according to which an individual person's mental states or experiences – the contents of that person's 'private' or inaccessible inner world – are the things that a person can be said to know better and more reliably than anything else. For example, I am in the best possible position to know that I am happy (or depressed or thinking about economics or whatever), and in a much better position to know this than to know anything about the external or publicly observable world. These experiences are, therefore, the foundations of all human knowledge, including scientific knowledge.

With this philosophical approach in mind, it is natural for me to believe that I have direct or immediate knowledge of my own utility as a mental state and that other people can do no more than make guesses about it on the basis of my public behaviour in consuming goods of various sorts. This line of thought led the new welfare economists to believe that there was an unbridgeable gap between utility, understood as a state of mind or an experience, and consumers' behaviour.

However, Wittgensteinian philosophers have come to reject the validity of the starting point of this argument for direct knowledge of one's own mental states. To say, for example, that I know I am happy presupposes that I understand how to use the word 'happy'. And this is not something that I could work out all by myself. Understanding the meaning and use of language is, from a Wittgensteinian perspective, a social activity. It depends on rules specifying the circumstances in which it is appropriate to use particular words and expressions: learning to follow rules requires the possibility of an independent check, that is, monitoring by another person. Checking my own use of words like 'happiness' and 'utility' would, in a famous Wittgensteinian aphorism, be like buying a second copy of the same edition of *The Times* in order to confirm a story that had been read in the first copy.

The upshot of this line of thought is that subjective awareness or 'inner' knowledge is only one of the criteria we use in learning and applying such 'mental' terms as happiness. My experiences are interwoven with other people's ascriptions of mental terms to me on the basis of my behaviour. I depend on them for the cues as much as I depend on my own consciousness when learning how to use such words. One formulation of this general approach has been put forward by the distinguished contemporary philosopher Professor Sir Peter Strawson in these words: 'X's depression is something, one and the same thing, which is felt, but not observed, by X, and observed, but not felt, by others than X' (Strawson, 1959). The point Strawson is making here can be understood as a reply to the empiricist (and logical positivist) position that it is possible to drive a 'logical wedge' between feelings which can be felt but not observed, and behaviour which can be observed but not felt. The concept of depression, Strawson suggests, 'spans' both what is felt and what is observed. If it did not do so, we would never have learned how to use the concept.

This argument applies to 'mental' terms in general, including pleasure, happiness and utility. The concept of utility, on this interpretation, spans both the subjective feeling of happiness, pleasure or contentment and the public behaviour of consumption. The implication is that Bentham's comment on 'benefit, advantage, pleasure, good or happiness' – that 'all this in the present case comes to the same thing' – is consistent with an important tradition in contemporary philosophy. The Wittgensteinian argument that identifying subjective states of mind presupposes the social or public activity of following rules, might provide secure philosophical foundations for making the interpersonal comparisons of utility that characterized the old welfare economics.

If this line of thought is justified, two conclusions about welfare economics seem to follow. First, the standard practice among economists of using income or expenditure as proxies for utility is found not to be a rather desperate last resort but more a reasonable procedure which recognizes the way in which experience and behaviour are inextricably intertwined. Second, a welfare economics, capable of making interpersonal comparisons of utility, would be likely to take a more positive stance towards the redistribution of income and government intervention in

markets than the new welfare economics, with its reliance on Pareto efficiency achieved through perfectly competitive markets.

3 THE MEASUREMENT OF HOUSEHOLD WELL-BEING

The aim of this section is to examine the technical meaning which most neoclassical economists give to the idea of being 'better off'. It is traditional in economics to think of the well-being of a household (or of an individual) as its standard of living. There are two approaches to measuring changes in the standard of living, that is, the degrees by which people become better (or worse) off. In macroeconomics, the real income of a country (*Changing Economies*, Chapter 2) is divided by the number of people who live there, to give an estimate of real national income per head of the population. So the standard of living is the value of the goods and services available for consumption by each member of the population. However, this procedure leaves unexamined the microeconomic foundations on which it is based. In neoclassical microeconomics, the standard of living is measured by the utility, or preference satisfaction, consisting in consumption. Since neoclassical consumer theory assumes that utility cannot be measured, this approach is operationalized, or expressed in terms which permit measurement, by estimating the cost of reaching a given standard of living. 'Under changing prices, the true cost-of-living index is the … cost of attaining a reference level standard at each set of prices' (Crawford, 1994, p.1). For an individual what we mean by a 'reference level standard' is a particular level of utility. However, this cannot be observed so instead the effects of a change in prices on consumption can be modelled by considering movements of the budget constraint.

Chapter 2 explained that the impact of any price change on the consumption of an individual can be split into two components: the substitution and income effects. A change in price will induce the individual to substitute between commodities (the substitution effect) and it will also impact upon the income of the individual, inducing a further change in consumption (the income effect). You saw in

Section 4.2 of Chapter 2 how a Slutsky approximation to the income effect using the budget constraint can be estimated.

While we cannot say that a bundle of goods bought by a consumer on a higher indifference curve provides, say, 40 per cent more utility than a bundle bought by a consumer on a lower indifference curve, we can say that the first bundle costs 40 per cent more than the second. This is why we have to use the budget constraint, rather than the indifference curve, to measure changes in the consumer's standard of living.

In this section, two methods of constructing price indices will be discussed. They are used not only in measuring changes in the cost of reaching a specific standard of living, but also have a direct impact on the standard of living of many households, for example through their use in up-rating welfare benefits to keep pace with inflation.

3.1   The compensating variation and the Laspeyres index

If we interpret the standard of living as the ability to consume a specific bundle of goods, we will be confronted by two distinct methods of measuring a change in the cost of doing so, with no compelling reasons to prefer one to the other. Let us suppose that a household can purchase two goods, F and G, and as a result of a fall in the price of good G, the household changes the particular bundle of the two goods it consumes. The decision to be made is whether to define the reference level standard of living as the bundle of goods the household consumed before the fall in the price of good G, or the bundle it consumes after that fall in price. Suppose that we choose the original bundle of goods as the reference level standard of living. We can, in principle, measure the increase in the household's standard of living resulting from the fall in the price of good G by calculating the money income the household would have left over after the price fall if it still consumed the original bundle of goods, that is, by calculating the compensating variation (see Chapter 2, Section 4.2). This approach, using the compensating variation, constructs a base-weighted or (after its inventor) Laspeyres price index.

Consider the choices a household makes between two goods F and G in two particular years. Figure 4.1 shows that in year 1, with budget constraint ZS, the household consumes bundle A, which contains F_1 of good F and G_1 of good G. In year 2 the price of good G falls while that of good F is unchanged, and the budget constraint therefore pivots from ZS to ZT. In response to this price change, the household chooses a new bundle, B, in which F_2 of good F and G_2 of good G are consumed.

Now let us apply this piece of analysis to the measurement of changes in the cost of reaching the reference level standard of living, represented by the bundle of goods, A, consumed in year 1. After

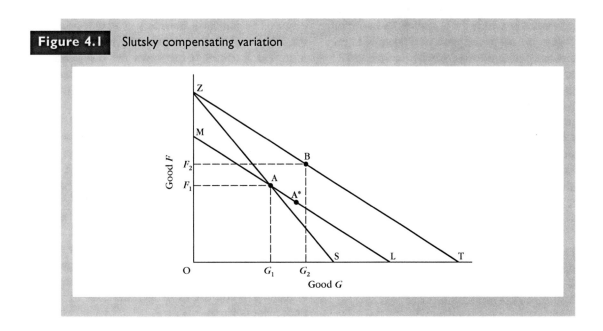

Figure 4.1   Slutsky compensating variation

the fall in the price of G, the household moves to a new equilibrium position at point B. Being able to buy more of both F and G, the household is clearly better off. The question is, how much better off?

In order to answer that question, we need a way of comparing the value of the bundle of goods purchased in year 1 with that purchased in year 2, represented by points A and B respectively on Figure 4.1. The fall in the price of good G results in a substitution and an income effect. It is the income effect that measures how much better off the household is as a result of the price change. Substitution and income effects are, respectively, movements along and movements between indifference curves, but because we do not know where the indifference curves are, we need to work with a Slutsky approximation to the income effect.

We can see this by drawing a new budget constraint ML parallel to ZT but passing through point A. Suppose the intermediate point A* divides the change in consumption into a substitution effect and an income effect, so that the Slutsky approximation to the substitution effect is now shown by the movement from A to A*, and the Slutsky approximation to the income effect by the movement from A* to B.

We now want to assess how large a Slutsky compensating variation is necessary to cancel out the income effect of the price change.

The intuition is that if we take away just enough money income to keep the household at A in Figure 4.1, after the fall in the price of G, then that amount of money income is equal to the increase in the household's standard of living as a result of the price fall. The amount by which the household is better off as a result of the fall in the price of G is equal to the cut in money income that would be needed to restrict the household to buying the same bundle after the price fall. This compensating variation is represented in Figure 4.1 by the gap between the two budget lines ZT and ML.

The budget constraint ML represents the cost to the individual of consuming bundle A at the new set of prices. To measure by how much this cost has changed, ML can be compared with the original budget constraint ZS, which represents the cost of consuming bundle A at the old set of prices.

Question

Looking back at Section 2.2 of Chapter 2, what is the formula for the budget constraint?

Under the assumption that the household's income Y is all spent on goods F and G:

$$Y = P_G G + P_F F$$

where P_F is the price of good F and P_G is the price of good G. Since all income is spent on goods F and G, it follows that this formula represents the cost of consuming goods F and G.

The formula can be used to construct the Laspeyres price index. Let P_{G1} denote the price of good G in year 1 and P_{G2} the price of good G in year 2. Similarly, let P_{F1} denote the price of good F in year 1 and P_{F2} the price of good F in year 2. Then, at year 2 prices, all bundles on line ML cost the same amount, that is, $P_{G2} G_1 + P_{F2} F_1$, the cost of bundle A at year 2 prices. And at year 1 prices, all bundles on line ZS cost the same amount, that is, $P_{G1} G_1 + P_{F1} F_1$, the cost of bundle A at year 1 prices.

If we take the ratio of these two terms, we get the Laspeyres price index:

$$L = \frac{\text{cost of bundle A at year 2 prices}}{\text{cost of bundle A at year 1 prices}}$$

$$L = \frac{P_{G2} G_1 + P_{F2} F_1}{P_{G1} G_1 + P_{F1} F_1}$$

This index divides the amount of income required to purchase bundle A at year 2 prices by the amount of income required to purchase bundle A at year 1 prices. It measures the compensating variation associated with the price change and thereby captures the extent to which real income has changed.

The amount of goods F and G consumed in year 1 (F_1, G_1) provides the key to this formula. The original bundle which the household consumes in year 1 (the base year) is taken as the reference standard of living. It is for this reason that the Laspeyres index is referred to as a base-weighted index. Prices vary between years but the weights, as denoted by F_1 and G_1, are taken from the base year. Note that for simplicity, Figure 4.1 relates to the specific case where only the price of good G changes ($P_{F1} = P_{F2}$). The above formula for the budget constraint is for the more general case in which both prices change.

Exercise 4.1

Consider a household's consumption in two successive years. In year 1, two units of good *G* and three units of good *F* are consumed. Both goods are priced at £2 each. In year 2, however, the price of good *G* falls to £1 per unit, and the price of good *F* increases to £3 per unit. The household responds by increasing consumption of *G* to three units and reducing consumption of *F* to two units.

1 Using the above formula, calculate the Laspeyres index for this change in prices.
2 Has the cost of living increased for this household?

In working through this exercise and checking the answer at the end of this chapter, you will have seen that a value of 1.1 is calculated for the Laspeyres index. By interpreting this index in percentage terms, that is by multiplying by 100, a value of 110 can be derived which means that the index has moved from a base of 100 to 110. The cost of living for this household has increased by 10 per cent. There has been a 10 per cent increase in the cost of maintaining the same standard of living and the household is therefore worse off to this extent.

The Laspeyres base-weighted method provides the basis for calculating the Retail Price Index (RPI) in the UK. There are, of course, many more goods to consider than the two which I have looked at in explaining the Laspeyres index, but the principles are the same. To calculate the RPI the government conducts a survey, known as the Family Expenditure Survey, of the spending patterns of households each year. This is used as the basis for calculating an average consumption bundle for households over the economy as a whole. This is the base year bundle on which the RPI is calculated. When you hear on the news that the RPI has increased by 1 per cent, this means that the cost of this base year bundle has increased by 1 per cent.

The RPI is an important measure of price movements in the economy as it is used to revise state pensions, social security payments and tax allowances, and provides the basis for most wage negotiations. However, the RPI/Laspeyres index is, arguably, not the only index that we should rely upon.

3.2 The equivalent variation and the Paasche index

There is an equally plausible alternative to the Laspeyres approach to constructing price indices. The alternative idea is to choose the bundle of goods the household consumes *after* the fall in the price of good *G* as the reference level standard of living. This approach makes use of the equivalent variation and is known as the current-weighted or, again after its inventor, the Paasche price index. To show how this second price index is derived we need to go back to the simple example of a fall in the price of *G*, with the price of *F* staying fixed. Figure 4.2 shows the same movement of the budget constraint from ZS to ZT, in response to the price change. Once again, the household's consumption moves from bundle A to bundle B.

This same change can be considered from a different viewpoint. Assuming that the household starts off at bundle A, how much extra income would it need to obtain bundle B, without a price change? This hypothetical change in income is known as the *Slutsky equivalent variation* because it can be seen as being equivalent to the price change.

Slutsky equivalent variation

The Slutsky equivalent variation to a price change is the amount by which, before the price change, the household's income would need to be adjusted for it to be just able to purchase the bundle it would have chosen at the new price.

To specify the equivalent variation on Figure 4.2, a line Z'S' parallel to ZS is drawn through the new bundle. The movement from A to B can now be explained in two steps. First, the consumer receives an equivalent variation of income from A to B*, say, and, second, there is a substitution effect from B* to B. The reduction in the price of *G* generates an increase in income (the equivalent variation) which is followed by a substitution out of *F* and into *G*.

Note that the equivalent variation involves a different way of looking at the price change from the compensating variation. Instead of positing that the substitution effect comes before the income effect, the equivalent variation suggests that the substitution effect comes after the income effect. Also, instead of focusing on the original bundle before the price change, for the equivalent variation we focus on the new bundle. If we take this approach, a new price index can be constructed, namely, the Paasche index.

This time the idea is to divide the income needed to buy bundle B in year 2 (that is, the quantities of F and G consumed in year 2 multiplied by their prices in year 2) by the income that would have been needed to consume bundle B at year 1 prices. At year 2 prices, all bundles on line ZT cost the same amount, that is, $P_{G2}G_2 + P_{F2}F_2$, the cost of bundle B at year 2 prices. At year 1 prices, all bundles on line Z'S' cost the same amount, that is, $P_{G1}G_2 + P_{F1}F_2$, the cost of bundle B at year 1 prices.

If we take the ratio of these two terms we get the Paasche price index

$$P = \frac{cost\ of\ bundle\ B\ at\ year\ 2\ prices}{cost\ of\ bundle\ B\ at\ year\ 1\ prices}$$

$$P = \frac{P_{G2}G_2 + P_{F2}F_2}{P_{G1}G_2 + P_{F1}F_2}$$

This is also referred to as the current-weighted price index since the weights provided by bundle B are for year 2, the current year.

Exercise 4.2

Consider the consumption behaviour of the household described to you in Exercise 4.1.

1 Calculate the Paasche index for the change in prices.
2 Has the cost of living increased for this household according to the Paasche index?

By working through this exercise you will have calculated that the Paasche index has a value of 0.9. In percentage terms, the index is 90, which means that there has been a fall of 10 per cent in comparison to a base of 100. This contrasts with a Laspeyres index of 110 for the same example which indicated a 10 per cent increase in the cost of living. Consequently, the Laspeyres index in this example reports a fall in the standard of living, while the Paasche index implies that the household has become better off.

3.3 Comparing Laspeyres and Paasche price indices

This potential disparity between different ways of calculating the cost of living is known as the price

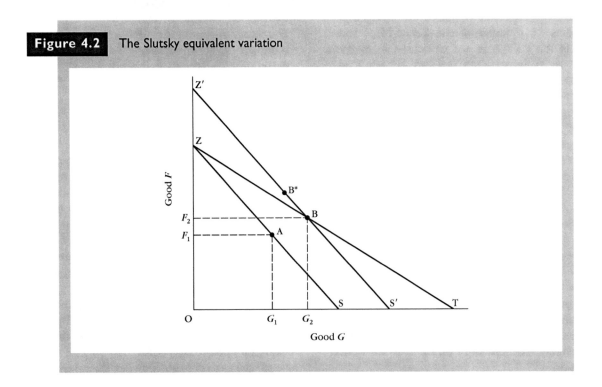

Figure 4.2 The Slutsky equivalent variation

index problem. Its occurrence can be explained by looking at a shift in the budget constraint when both the prices change, as they did in the example considered in Exercises 4.1 and 4.2.

Assume that the price of *G* falls and the price of *F* increases. The budget constraint ZS in Figure 4.3 shifts to PK. In response to the price changes the consumer moves from bundle A to a new bundle B.

Question

Draw in the compensating and equivalent variations on Figure 4.3. Does the cost of living increase?

To specify the compensating variation, a new line P′K′ must be drawn parallel to the new budget constraint PK. This shows how much income is required to compensate the household for the change in relative price. Figure 4.4(a) shows that the household is worse off after the price changes, according to the compensating variation. To get back from B to A there has to be an increase in income. If the household needs to be compensated with more income to get back to the original bundle A, it must be worse off. This increase in the cost of living would be reflected in a Laspeyres index higher than 100, showing that the household has indeed become worse off.

The equivalent variation is shown in Figure 4.4(b) by drawing a new line Z′S′ parallel to ZS. The movement from ZS to Z′S′ shows how much income is required to take the household from A to B without a price change. So by this equivalent variation the consumer is better off at B than at A and the price change is equivalent to an increase in income. This would be reflected in a Paasche cost-of-living index less than 100 since the household has become better off.

For the same change in relative prices, the Laspeyres and Paasche price indices can generate different results about the effect of price changes on the standard of living. The reason for this is that the Laspeyres index is based on the compensating variation and the Paasche index on the equivalent variation. That is to say, they use different bundles of goods as reference standards. The Laspeyres index is base weighted and the Paasche index is current weighted.

In practice, the results will not be so radically different as those provided in this example. Table 4.1 reports some predictions of the two indices.

Both indices report that the cost of living increased over the period 1974–84, with the Laspeyres index reporting a higher increase than the Paasche. The disparities between the two indices could translate into millions of pounds, since so much of government spending is up-rated each year using price indices. It should be noted, however, that with the RPI being based upon the Laspeyres index, the government errs on the side of caution, since, according to Table 4.1, this index has

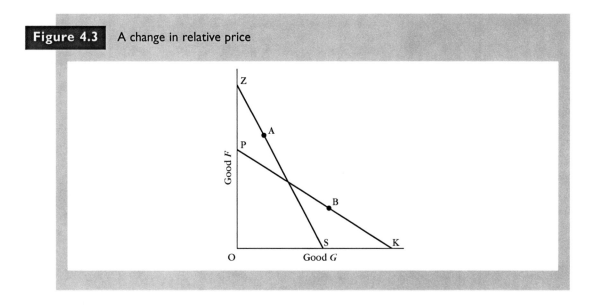

Figure 4.3 A change in relative price

overestimated changes in the cost of living on average over the long term compared to the Paasche index.

It should also be noted that the RPI looks at changes in prices for an average bundle of goods. It does not reflect the change in the cost of each particular household's bundle. The price of a Rolls Royce, for example, may fall, thereby drawing down the price index. But if you do not consume this product it will be irrelevant to your own cost of living. Crawford (1994) has demonstrated that households in receipt of benefits have experienced periods of 2 per cent above-average and 2 per cent below-average increases in living costs lasting up to

Table 4.1   A comparison of the Laspeyres and Paasche price indices

Year (January)	Laspeyres index	Paasche index
1974	100.0	100.0
1975	119.9	119.5
1976	148.0	147.2
1977	173.0	171.5
1978	190.5	187.6
1979	208.0	204.7
1980	246.0	240.4
1981	278.2	268.9
1982	312.5	299.7
1983	329.5	312.4
1984	347.5	326.9

Source: Fry and Pashardes, 1986, p.24

Figure 4.4   Two ways of measuring the cost of living (a) The compensating variation (b) The equivalent variation

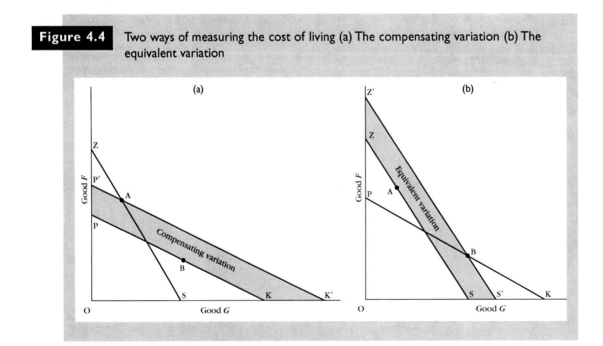

two years. Given that such households are unlikely to be able to reallocate the excess from one period to another in order to smooth their consumption patterns, 'using the "wrong" index imposes costs on poorer households even if the overall increase is more or less right when viewed over a longer period' (Crawford, 1994, p.35).

An additional problem is that the RPI is calculated for a typical household rather than for an individual. In order to establish the spending patterns of the average or typical household, the Family Expenditure Survey is conducted for a sample of several thousand households. The problem is that there is no typical household; they vary in size and composition. The expenditure pattern of a household with children is likely to differ from a household without children, and a household of retired pensioners will differ from one comprising a young professional couple. The next section looks into how these differences can be taken into account.

4 EQUIVALENCE SCALES

In the early 1990s, families with children comprised more than half of the poorest tenth of the UK population (Goodman and Webb, 1994). On what basis can we compare the standard of living of families with different needs? The measurement of poverty relies on the use of equivalence scales, which measure the extra income a particular household would need in order to achieve the same standard of living as a chosen reference or benchmark household. The level of some welfare benefits is calculated on the basis of changes in the cost of living adjusted by equivalence scales for household size and composition. So the actual standard of living of families with children receiving welfare benefits, as well as the measured extent of poverty and inequality, are sensitive to the particular equivalence scales used. The aim of this section is to examine some of the methodological issues surrounding the use of equivalence scales.

4.1 The importance of household equivalence scales

In producing the official low income figures for the UK, known as 'Households Below Average Income' (HBAI), the government has to make adjustments for the size and composition of households. If two households have the same income but one consists of a single adult while the other is made up of two adults and two children, there is clearly a sense in which the single person household is better off. It is better off in that its income is greater than that of the larger household *in relation to its needs*. In assessing the extent and depth of poverty, what matters is the household's income relative to its needs, defined in terms of the number of people the household's income has to support. But it is not simply the number of people that makes a difference. The cost of food and clothing for an adult or a child aged 16 is greater than that for a four-year-old.

How much greater? That is the question which equivalence scales are designed to answer. For example, we might want to know how much more income is needed for a family of two adults and two children aged five and 13 to reach a given level of material welfare, compared with a family of two adults. What difference does it make if there are three children and they are aged two, eight and 11? In order to answer such questions, economists take a single, childless adult or a childless, adult couple as a benchmark or reference household type and then estimate how much more is needed for each additional member of a household if it is to reach the same level of material welfare as the reference household. An equivalence scale therefore expresses 'the extra cost required to restore a household of a particular composition to the same standard of living as that of the reference household' (Banks and Johnson, 1993, p.4).

Let us consider a brief example in which the reference household, which has an equivalence scale of 1.00, is a childless married couple. A married couple with two children (ages unspecified) was given a scale of 1.61 in a pioneering study by Rowntree (quoted in Banks and Johnson, 1993, p.17). This means that the couple with two children needs 1.61 times the income of the childless couple to reach the same standard of living. In order to make their incomes equivalent, we divide the income of the couple with two children by 1.61. The resulting income is equivalent to that required by the childless couple, allowing for the different needs of the two households, to reach the same standard of living.

The equivalence scales used in UK official statistics are the McClements scales, constructed by McClements (1977). According to Coulter, Cowell and Jenkins (1992), they yield a rather low estimate of the extent of poverty and inequality. However, the question whether the McClements scales are biased, in the sense that they produce lower estimates of poverty and inequality than other equivalence scales with more secure methodological foundations, is controversial. Banks and Johnson (1993) for example, are unconvinced by Coulter, Cowell and Jenkins' arguments and conclude that 'the McClements scales appear quite plausible and lie very much in the centre of the range of estimated scales' (p.70). Let us examine the theoretical background of this dispute.

4.2   Objective equivalence scales

The most widely used method of constructing equivalence scales is to put econometric methods to work on observed consumption behaviour in households of different size and composition. Equivalence scales produced in this way are described as objective, in the sense that they are based on observable household behaviour. Two main methodological approaches to objective equivalence scales can be distinguished: welfare proxy techniques and utility-based methods (Banks and Johnson, 1993).

Welfare proxy techniques

On the assumption that the level of household welfare cannot be directly measured, economists have sought a 'welfare proxy', an observable or indeed measurable characteristic of a household which can plausibly be presented as an indicator of its level of welfare. The oldest method of producing equivalence scales uses Engel curves, which plot the relationship between the consumption of food and total household income or expenditure.

The idea is that the share of household income (or expenditure) devoted to food declines as income (expenditure) rises and, other things being equal, the household becomes better off. Thinking back to Chapter 2, for example, it would be interesting to compare the proportion of income that Nigel of EastEnders spends on food with the proportion spent by an unemployed individual. The budget share of food can, therefore, be used as an indirect measure, or proxy, for the household's level of welfare.

The presence of a child leads to an increase in the proportion of the household's total expenditure going on food, from S_0 to S_1 at income Y_0, shown by an upward shift of the Engel curve in Figure 4.5. An equivalence scale for this first child can be estimated by measuring the increase in income, $Y_1 - Y_0$, that is needed to restore the budget share of food to its original level, S_0, on the new Engel curve.

Welfare proxy techniques have been developed in two main ways. First, some studies have replaced the focus on the budget share of food with a wider set of goods such as food, fuel, clothing and housing costs

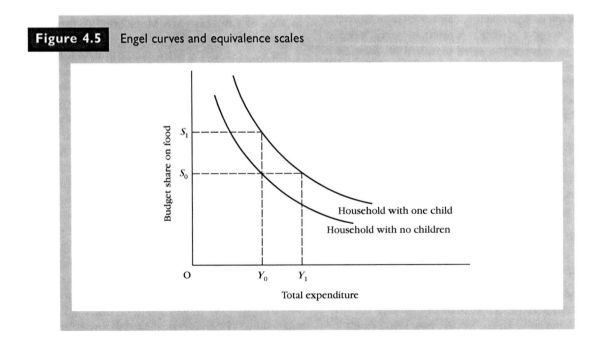

Figure 4.5   Engel curves and equivalence scales

which can be regarded as necessities. Second, the Rothbarth method (Rothbarth, 1943) models the impact of children on household welfare in terms of a fall in the proportion of total expenditure taken by 'adult goods', usually assumed to comprise alcohol, tobacco and adult clothing. Since the share of expenditure on adult goods tends to rise with income, the presence of a child shifts the upward-sloping curve downwards as the share of expenditure on adult goods falls from X_0 to X_1 (Figure 4.6). Once again, an equivalence scale for this first child can be estimated by measuring the increase in income, $Y_1 - Y_0$, that is needed to restore the budget share of expenditure on adult goods to its original level, X_0, on the new, lower curve.

The main weakness of welfare proxy techniques seems to be that they lack an adequate theoretical background. They can be said to be based on 'observation without theory', that is, that certain types of expenditure can be observed to vary with income and with the presence of children. However, these observations are reliable indicators of the effect of children on household welfare only on the assumption of *ceteris paribus*. This assumption is unlikely to be invariably true. In particular, the preferences of adult members of the household may change, perhaps in response to the arrival of children. The only way to incorporate such considerations into the

estimation of equivalence scales is to build them on the notion of utility.

Utility-based equivalence scales

Utility-based estimation of equivalence scales is based on an economic model of household preferences. The foundation of the utility-based approach is the standard neoclassical assumption that any economic agent – in this case, the household – is a rational utility maximizer. The household can, therefore, be modelled as allocating its budget to minimize the cost of achieving a given level of utility. The next step is to analyse data on the household's consumption behaviour, using econometric techniques (see, for example, Curwin and Slater, 2001) in order to estimate, first, demand curves for the different classes of goods consumed by the household and, second, shifts in those curves in response to the presence of children. The result is a complete set of household demand responses to the presence of children, unlike the welfare proxy techniques which just analyse the impact on food or adult goods. In principle, the utility-based approach allows the deduction of a set of household preferences which plausibly explain the demand responses. In this way, household preferences are made dependent on the number of children, thereby avoiding the objection

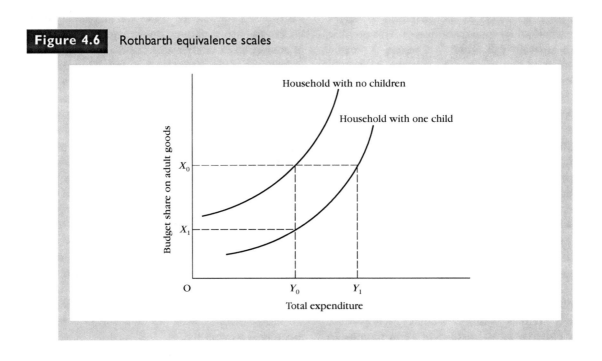

Figure 4.6   Rothbarth equivalence scales

made against the welfare proxy approach that it implausibly assumes that children have no effect on household preferences.

The McClements equivalence scales are utility based. The basic idea is to generalize the Engel approach so that it covers all the goods in the household budget, not just food. The procedure is essentially to measure the increase in income that is needed to restore the budget share of each class of goods to its original level, and then to calculate a weighted average, using the elasticities of demand for each class of goods as the weights. The McClements scale incorporates a method known as Barten scaling (Barten, 1964). If a previously childless household has a child, it becomes more expensive to achieve a given level of utility for the adult(s) or household decision maker(s) from the consumption of food. Instead of buying, say, two ice creams, the adult(s) must now buy three. 'Having children makes ice cream, milk and soft drinks relatively more expensive and makes whiskey or cigarettes relatively cheaper' (Deaton and Muellbauer, 1980; quoted in Nelson, 1996, p.63). This makes it possible to predict that the household, as a rational agent, will switch expenditure away from goods which provide utility for all members of the household and towards goods which provide utility only for the decision maker(s).

The Barten scaling technique has been criticized on feminist grounds. It implicitly assumes that households have a single decision maker, usually male. This single decision maker is also assumed to derive utility only from his own consumption. This premise will be critically examined in Chapter 6. Nelson (1996) argues that assumption that the household will consume more alcohol and cigarettes because the presence of a child makes them relatively cheaper is an example of masculine bias. The problem arises out of the focus on adult, or parental, utility and the assumption that parental preferences do not change with the arrival of children. The Barten technique is based on the factual observation that children eat ice cream but do not smoke and drink – at least, not when they are with their parents – with the result that when a parent buys an ice cream for his or her own consumption, there is pressure to buy one for each child. So ice creams are now bought in multiples, effectively increasing the cost of parental utility from an ice cream. When the parent buys an alcoholic drink, they can still buy for one person. Nelson's point is that this assumes that parents regard children as no more than extra mouths to

feed, and that children have no influence on household preferences. If parents love their children one needs to take account of the utility they will obtain from revising household consumption in the light of the children's expressed preferences.

Nelson concludes that the focus of the Barten scaling technique on unchanging parental utility means that it makes two unwarranted assumptions. First, it assumes that, 'substitution possibilities within the structure of adult preferences will cause children to receive relatively less than they would under a proportional requirements" scheme' (p.86). Second, it assumes that; 'to the extent that children consume goods not consumed by adults, their consumption (and hence welfare) will not rise with household income' (p.86). If equivalence scales are based on this model of self-centred adult utility maximization, they will not adequately represent parental concern for the material welfare of children and thus they will underestimate the extra income parents need to restore their standard of living to that of a childless household.

Nelson's (1996) argument raises some doubts about Banks and Johnson's (1993) endorsement of the McClements scales, which seems to rely heavily on their position in the centre of the range of estimated scales. For the practical purpose of measuring poverty and inequality, Banks and Johnson are probably right in believing that no alternative equivalence scales are indisputably superior. However, to the extent that utility-based equivalence scales are, in general, based on neoclassical economic theory and an assumption of adult-centred utility maximization, the implication of Nelson's argument is that they may all neglect the material welfare of children. The validity of a set of equivalence scales depends on the economic theory on which they are based. From an alternative, institutionalist perspective, for example, we might base equivalence scales on an assumption that parents follow a rule in organizing household consumption according to, say, a requirements scheme under which expenditure on each member of the household would be proportional to their needs. Future research may produce equivalence scales that are informed by a model of the household as such an institution rather than of a utility maximizing head of the household. Only then will it be possible to compare the measurement and policy implications of utility-based equivalence scales grounded in neoclassical economics with those of equivalence scales having an alternative theoretical provenance.

5   AGENCY CONCEPTIONS OF HUMAN FLOURISHING

We have seen that well-being can be interpreted as utility; that an approximation to utility can be quantified to construct real income as a measure of the well-being of a typical household, and that this can be adjusted for the different needs of households varying by size and composition. Now it is time to explore the meaning of a wider conception of human flourishing, its measurement and moral implications.

5.1   Experience, well-being and agency

One way of understanding utilitarianism is to think of utility as preference satisfaction, and to think of preference satisfaction in terms of experiences or felt states of mind, caused by the consumption of the goods we prefer, or are disposed to choose ahead of others. This can be traced back to some of Bentham's statements of the principle of utility, where utility seems to encompass happiness as a state of mind, as a felt experience. In the previous section it was suggested that mental states, including utility in this interpretation, can be both experienced by one person and attributed to that person by someone else on the basis of observable behaviour and shared understandings. So it is reasonable to set aside worries about the impossibility or unscientific character of interpersonal comparisons of utility, and rely on what Aristotle described as 'the feelings of recognition and affiliation that link every human being to every other human being'. This leaves the way open to the next question, which is about the adequacy of a broadly utilitarian account of well-being. Does utility provide a convincing analysis of well-being? Or does it overlook an important dimension of human flourishing? What we need is a way of testing the hypothesis that well-being is nothing more than utility, in the sense of having pleasant experiences.

Nozick's (1974) thought experiment involving an 'experience machine' provides a way of doing this. Suppose that there exists an experience machine which enables neuropsychologists to stimulate your brain so that you think and feel that you are 'writing a great novel, or making a friend, or reading an interesting book' (Nozick, 1974, p. 42) or in general undergoing any experience the neuropsychologist can

program into the machine. In reality you will be 'floating in a tank, with electrodes attached to your brain' (p. 42) but you will not know that; it will feel to you that you are actually doing the things you are experiencing; you will believe that it is all really happening. There could be a 'library or smorgasbord' of the experiences of many other people, from which you could select the experiences that you want to undergo, perhaps for the next couple of years. Then you will be brought back to normal life for an hour or two in order to choose your experiences for the next two years, and so on.

Reflection

Would you plug yourself into the machine? For how long? For a whole lifetime, say, in two year episodes? For a couple of weeks holiday every year? Or not at all?

What about other people? Would you expect a widespread take-up of opportunities to plug into the experience machine?

Nozick's answer is that we 'learn that something matters to us in addition to experience by imagining an experience machine and then realizing that we would not use it' (p. 44). He supports this conclusion with three arguments. First, there are certain things we want to do, rather than just have the experience of doing them. We want to leave our mark on the world, or at least the part of it that immediately concerns us; parents might want to give their children a happy and secure childhood rather than float around in a tank thinking they are doing so. Second, we might want to be a certain kind of person; it is not possible to be generous, brave, honest, caring or witty if all you are doing is floating in a tank. As Nozick puts it, plugging in to the experience machine is a kind of death. Third, we would be limited to a constructed 'reality'; we would be confined to the imagination and design skills of the neuropsychologist.

These arguments are plausible but they do not fully support Nozick's conclusion. I do not find that they make a convincing case for believing that no one would use the experience machine, which is what Nozick seems to suggest by the words 'we would not use it'. People whose lives are severely circumscribed by long-term physical illness, by depression, by long-term unemployment, by drug addiction, by destitution or other forms of hardship and suffering might make a rational decision to plug into the experience machine, perhaps indefinitely in extreme cases. But the recognition that precisely the people who are most likely to make that decision are leading lives that are unfulfilled or unsatisfactory in some other way reinforces the validity of the other part of Nozick's conclusion. In saying that something matters to us 'in addition to experience', Nozick implies that experience itself matters to us. If all or most of our experiences are unpleasant and circumstances limit our opportunities for doing things or being certain kinds of people, our priority will probably be to change them for better ones, even if only by plugging into an experience machine (or, in a more localized and transitory way, by consuming alcohol or other drugs, or by watching television all day).

It seems that utility, in the sense of happiness or pleasant experiences, is a component of human flourishing, but it is far from being the whole story. We can confirm this by asking whether it is better to plug a destitute person into the experience machine or to provide them with the means to do the things they want to do and be the kind of person they want to be. A side effect of the second course of action is that the person may have different and more pleasant experiences; the point at issue is that it matters where the experiences come from. The feeling that human dignity requires that we regard the experience machine as the inferior option suggests that experiences are neither the whole story nor an end in themselves.

Thinking of well-being purely in terms of happiness is also problematic on the grounds that it can distort interpersonal comparisons of utility. The extent to which a person is happy may reflect his or her expectations, and someone may be happy only because a life of hardship or misfortune has left them with very low expectations; 'the hopeless beggar, the precarious landless labourer, the dominated housewife, the hardened unemployed or the over-exhausted coolie may all take pleasure in small mercies, and manage to suppress intense suffering for the necessity of continuing survival' (Sen, 1987, p.45). But it would be wrong to infer that, because they are so easily satisfied, their level of well-being does not count for very much.

5.2 Capabilities and functionings

Let me very briefly review the state of the argument. We have seen that it is, after all, reasonable to measure utility through proxies such as income or expenditure, because of the conceptual connections between feelings and behaviour. However, this 'rehabilitation' of utility is far from complete because it does not seem to offer an entirely satisfactory account of well-being. So the following question now faces us: can we go beyond utility in order to find a more plausible interpretation of well-being without sacrificing measurability?

Indeed it can be argued that non-utilitarian theories of well-being 'should ... be tempting to economists when they make well-being more readily measurable' (Hausman and MacPherson, 1996, p.81). Their reason for making this claim is that non-utilitarian theories are objective in the sense that 'what is good for people is not determined by whether people believe it is good for them' (p.81). Utilitarianism is, by contrast, a subjective view, since utility or happiness or preference satisfaction depend upon 'tastes, attitudes, or interests' (Griffin, 1986, p.53).

I want now to outline an 'objective list' interpretation of human flourishing, which has two main features. First, there is the attempt to set out an objective list of components of human flourishing which do not depend on whether people actually want them or believe them to be good. Second, by drawing on the idea that human flourishing comprises 'doings' and 'beings' as well as experiences, it offers an account of agency as well-being.

Sen (1982, p.367) suggests that utilitarian accounts of well-being omit an important category of 'basic capabilities' – a person being able to do certain basic things. Examples of basic capabilities include being able to move about, meeting one's nutritional requirements, being clothed and sheltered, and the power to take part in the social life of the community. The idea of basic capabilities was introduced in the context of analysing extreme poverty. In later works, such as Sen (1993), the idea of basic capabilities has been elaborated in terms of a distinction between capabilities and functionings. A functioning is something a person does and experiences. Examples of functionings range from the 'very elementary, such as being adequately nourished, being in good health, etc.' to the 'more complex ... such as achieving self-respect or being socially integrated' (Sen, 1993, p.31). Capabilities are abilities to achieve certain sorts of functionings. For example, Hausman and MacPherson (1996) suggest that 'literacy is a capability, while reading is a functioning' (p.82). A measure of well-being could, in principle, be specified by weighting the various capabilities and functionings a person possesses, perhaps according to how basic these capabilities are. The informational and judgmental requirements of such an exercise are formidable.

Nonetheless, the 'capabilities approach' is used by the United Nations Development Programme as a framework for the measurement of the well-being and agency of people all over the world. Instead of focusing on utility, or real income as a proxy for it, the Human Development Index (HDI) is a systematic attempt to measure what the people of a particular country are able to do and to be. This application of the capabilities approach is based on an interpretation of the Aristotelian assumption, discussed in Section 1.1, that there are 'feelings of recognition and affiliation that link every human being to every other human being'. The capabilities interpretation of this assumption is that it is possible to take a stand, and 'indeed an increasingly specific stand, on what functions of human beings are most worth the care and attention of public planning, the world over' (Nussbaum and Glover, 1995, p.5).

The HDI is constructed from data on a number of key indicators of human functionings, including life expectancy at birth, health status, educational opportunities, employment and political rights. These indicators are aggregated for each country and expressed as an index number, which enables countries to be ranked in terms of human development. A number close to one indicates a high level of human development for the population of the country in question.

But there is more to the HDI report than the national ranking of whole populations. The capabilities approach can be used to measure the distribution of resources and opportunities between men and women in each country. In this way it is possible to quantify any disparity in opportunities between the two groups, and to adjust the original HDI value accordingly. The HDI value for women diverges from that for men, indicating inequality in the distribution of resources and opportunities between the genders, and so a Gender-related Development Index (GDI) value can be calculated. Table 4.2 lists countries by their GDI rank. The disparity between a country's HDI ranking and its GDI ranking is shown in the third column.

Table 4.2   HDI and GDI national rankings

GDI rank	HDI rank	HDI ranking– GDI ranking	Country	GDI value	HDI value
1	10	9	Sweden	0.919	0.929
2	5	3	Finland	0.918	0.934
3	7	4	Norway	0.911	0.933
4	16	12	Denmark	0.904	0.920
5	2	–3	USA	0.901	0.938
6	11	5	Australia	0.901	0.927
7	8	1	France	0.898	0.931
8	3	–5	Japan	0.896	0.937
9	1	–8	Canada	0.891	0.950
10	14	4	Austria	0.882	0.925
11	25	14	Barbados	0.878	0.900
12	17	5	New Zealand	0.868	0.919
13	18	5	UK	0.862	0.916
14	19	5	Italy	0.861	0.912
15	38	23	Czech Republic	0.858	0.872
16	40	24	Slovakia	0.855	0.872
17	24	7	Hong Kong	0.854	0.905
18	12	–6	Belgium	0.852	0.926
19	13	–6	Switzerland	0.852	0.925
20	4	–16	Netherlands	0.851	0.936

Source: United Nations Development Programme, 1995

Consider the data in Table 4.2. What are the main differences between the GDI rank and the HDI rank?

The HDI and GDI applications of the capabilities approach to human flourishing perhaps hold out the prospect of a body of work as rigorous and precise as the measurement of real income, but without its adherence to a narrowly materialistic conception of what it is to be 'better off'.

6 ARE JUDGEMENTS OF WELL-BEING OBJECTIVE OR SOCIALLY GENERATED?

In relation to a passage quoted from Hartwell (1971), Section 1 of this chapter discussed the question of whether working people were made better off by the Industrial Revolution. The debate continues about more recent trends in society, as the following quote from Mishan (1982) illustrates.

'In the larger vision of life, what does it avail to smooth the edge of nature, to shut out the draughts and even the temperature? Can there be any true fulfilment without some prior frustration? Can there be any welcome of comfort without prior hardship? Living at the margin of surfeit is hardly better than living at the margin of subsistence. Indeed, humanly speaking, it is worse. For in a world of ample provision, in a world of perfect adjustment, in a world of instant gratification, there can be no self-denial and therefore there can be no romantic love. There can be no conflict, and therefore no drama. There can be no suffering and therefore no tragedy. There can be no passion and therefore no poetry. And there can be no sacrifice and therefore no heroism. The wonderful irony of Aldous Huxley's Brave New World is that in it, in this comically colourless and unheroic society ... have the dreams of countless humanists and reformers been finally and fully realized.

Of course, we have far far to go ere we reach this devoutly desired consummation.

There can be reasonable doubts that – even should we survive the lengthening gauntlet of hazards – we shall ever approach a Brave-New-World civilization. Present trends indicate that life, instead, is becoming increasingly frenzied and frustrating. A high consumption society is also a high tension society ... Tension arises because the proliferation of goods presses harder against the scarcity of time available for their use. Tension arises also because the commercial promotion of hedonic pursuit breeds anxiety and discontent.'

(MISHAN, 1982, PP.235–6).

The neoclassical position, as we saw in Section 3, is that increases in real income, understood as the ability to consume bigger and bigger bundles of goods, are close approximations to increases in utility. But Mishan is clearly a dissident, arguing eloquently that economic growth does not make people happy. This conflict of perspectives raises doubts about the objectivity of the standards used in making judgements about human flourishing. Do the standards neoclassical economists use in measuring human well-being under the capitalist system have any claim to universal validity? Or are those standards themselves the products of the capitalist system? Is the focus on the material standard of living a symptom of a lack of objectivity, indicating, perhaps, an attachment to the political interests of dominant groups? Perhaps judgements about whether people are better off in one situation than in another should be informed by an understanding of how the criteria of assessment have been generated.

If so, we need to raise questions of well-being in the context of society as a whole, in the context of the capitalist system. You might be better off than were your grandparents in terms of a standard generated by the capitalist system (such as real income) but you might also be experiencing some of the costs of success. For example, does the system damage your health; do you experience stress? To answer questions like these, it seems that we need a set of criteria of human flourishing that, in some sense, transcends the capitalist system. Are utilitarian or agency conceptions of being 'better off' able to do this? Let me reflect, albeit very briefly, on the location of the utility-based foundations of the judgements of well-being characteristic of neoclassical economics, and on the possibility that it lends a partiality to such judgements.

The Marxist argument is that moral philosophy, including the utilitarian conception of well-being, is ideological in the sense that it presents capitalism as 'the highest expression of universal ideals' (Reiman, 1991, p.158). The utilitarian conception of well-being is expressed by the principle of utility, which was first introduced in Section 2.1 as a way of calculating happiness. I want to examine two propositions which are implicit in the principle of utility. First, there is the notion of utility itself, which is the property of goods themselves to provide satisfaction or the mental state of happiness associated with the consumption of goods. Utility is a common feature of the consumption of goods and services in general, everything from Ferraris to TV soap operas. Second, economic agents are assumed to be utility-maximizers, each one pursuing his or her own utility. There is no room for collective goals, for the 'community is a fictitious body' whose interest is nothing but 'the sum of the interests of the several members who compose it' (Bentham, 1789; reprinted in Warnock, 1962, p.34).

The Marxist argument that utilitarianism is an ideological product of capitalism is based on a critique of these two central features. First, there is a clear parallel between the assumption that all economic activities can be translated into a common measure, utility, and the way in which money functions in markets. The use of a common standard 'is precisely what occurs in exchange, in which unique and particular human productive endeavours are literally resolved into a common currency: money' (Reiman, 1991, p.164). Second, the belief that individuals pursue only their own utility and that the community is 'fictitious' is the consequence, Reiman suggests, of 'seeing human beings as they function in exchange as one's model of human nature' (p.164). Utilitarianism incorporates a 'fundamentally asocial conception of the self in which the interests of human beings are thought to be naturally in conflict' (p.164).

This critique of the key assumptions underlying the principle of utility is controversial, but it raises the possibility that utilitarianism, and other liberal accounts of well-being, 'arise from capitalism as an idealized version of what is actually there' (p.159). For example, if 'bundles of goods' are a close approximation to utility, industrial capitalism, which has increased the total world production of goods and services by a factor of 60 since 1820 (Maddison, 1995), is a runaway success from a utilitarian perspective. But the utility-based focus on real income growth does not seem to emphasize sufficiently the negative elements of industrial capitalism. These include features such as the persistence of desperate poverty even in its 'heartlands', the unequal distribution of income and wealth, the stress and insecurity that accompanies continual economic change, the emergence of a culture of instant gratification and the increasing scale of environmental damage.

In Chapter 3, Andrew Trigg notes how institutionalist thinkers, rejecting the neoclassical concept of consumer sovereignty, argue that consumer preferences are endogenous to the capitalist system. The Marxist critique of the utilitarian foundations of neoclassical economics suggests that measures of well-being or real income based on utility theory might also be among the products of the system. At the very least, this line of thought highlights the partial and limited scope of neoclassical economists' standard accounts of well-being.

What about the HDI? Can it sustain a more convincing claim to objectivity? Nelson rejects traditional interpretations of objectivity in terms of detachment, or, as she sees it, 'illusions of detachment' (Nelson, 1996, p.48) from social influences, from practical or immediate concerns or from partisan ties. Instead, she suggests that objectivity consists in 'a recognition of one's own various attachments and on the partiality this location lends to one's views' (p.48). There are two reasons for thinking that the HDI is a more objective welfare measure than utility. First, the HDI, by definition, aggregates qualitatively different things – from, for example, life expectancy to political rights – into an index, a single overall numerical value. But this, unlike utility, does not seem to reflect an idealization of the capitalist system so much as the inescapable exigencies of measuring a range of characteristics over large populations. The HDI does not seem to conform to the information requirements of production and exchange for profit. Instead, it seems to be designed to measure the urgency and depth of need in respect to specific cases for remedial action, such as reducing maternal mortality rates or enhancing employment opportunities. Second, in identifying such things as educational opportunities and political rights as key indicators of functionings, the HDI is clearly informed by the assumption that human nature is essentially social and society is a changeable human product. These are indicators of complex functionings such as achieving self-respect and social integration, which belong to the Aristotelian tradition of regarding 'association and living together and the fellowship of words' as an important sphere of human experience (Nussbaum and Sen, 1993, p.246).

There is reason to believe that a focus on real income and utility as measures of human flourishing within the capitalist system risks failing to be objective by not recognizing attachments and consequent partiality. A more comprehensive measure of human flourishing, based on an Aristotelian conception of human nature, seems to offer the prospect of achieving, to some degree, the only kind of objectivity available to us, that of being open to dialogue with thinkers from very different locations.

7 CONCLUSION

Let me conclude by reviewing the three questions I introduced in Section 1. First, what can we say about the meaning of terms such as 'better-off', 'well-being' or 'welfare'? If we start from the Aristotelian concept of human flourishing, we are drawn to the idea of distinguishing well-being and agency. Well-being is about *having* and *experiencing* things, pleasant states of mind or goods and services. Either way, there is a close connection with the key neoclassical concept of utility and the general notion of the material standard of living. Agency is about *doing* and *being*, and can be analysed in terms of capabilities that are necessary for the attainment of human functionings. These range from the elementary, such as being adequately nourished or enjoying a satisfactory health status, to the complex, such as achieving self-respect and social integration.

Second, this chapter has been much concerned with the problems of measurement. The neoclassical assumption is that utility is not measurable and that interpersonal comparisons of utility are problematic. But the cost of buying a bundle of goods is a workable proxy for utility and is measurable, so the Slutsky approximation does bridge the gap between theory and measurement. It is possible, after all, to measure the material standard of living with reasonable precision. However, data on real income per head is of limited usefulness – it tells us nothing about income distribution or the position of the worst-off groups in society. If we are to be able to measure distribution

and poverty, and establish adequate levels for welfare benefits we must turn to equivalence scales. These enable us to assess the different needs of households by size and composition.

Perhaps the most important measurement device is the HDI, which is based on the capabilities approach. There is no doubt that indices of this sort are amenable to almost infinite refinement, but the GDI already draws attention to the depth of gender inequality all over the world. The HDI reinforces the crucial message that there is more to the alleviation of poverty than increasing the supply of material goods; political rights and employment opportunities are important in themselves and a vital means to achieving an adequate command over material goods.

Third, it is likely that judgements about human flourishing reflect the structure of the economic system within which they are made. While it is unrealistic to strive for a complete detachment from economic and political interests, it is possible to temper the historical particularity of some contemporary perspectives on what it is to be better off by drawing on the richness of traditions of thought about human nature.

FURTHER READING

Nussbaum, M. and Glover, J. (eds) (1995) *Women, Culture and Development: a Study of Human Capabilities*, Oxford, Clarendon Press.

Nussbaum, M. and Sen, A. (eds) (1993) *The Quality of Life*, Oxford, Clarendon Press.

These two edited collections provide the best available way of exploring the range of views of philosophers and economists on the issues of (i) defining and measuring the quality of life and (ii) assessing women's quality of life, particularly in less developed countries.

ANSWERS TO EXERCISES

Exercise 4.1

1 You are given the following information:

Year 1		Year 2	
$P_{G1} = 2$	$G_1 = 2$	$P_{G2} = 1$	$G_2 = 3$
$P_{F1} = 2$	$F_1 = 3$	$P_{F2} = 3$	$F_2 = 2$

By plugging this information into the formula,

$$L = \frac{P_{G2}G_1 + P_{F2}F_1}{P_{G1}G_1 + P_{F1}F_1}$$

$$= \frac{(1 \times 2) + (3 \times 3)}{(2 \times 2) + (2 \times 3)}$$

$$= \frac{11}{10}$$

$$= 1.1$$

2 Since the Laspeyres index is more than 1, this means that the cost of living has risen. The cost of consuming F_1 and G_1 at the new set of prices is more than the cost of consuming these amounts at the old set of prices.

Exercise 4.2

1

$$P = \frac{P_{G2}G_2 + P_{F2}F_2}{P_{G1}G_2 + P_{F1}F_2}$$

$$= \frac{(1 \times 3) + (3 \times 2)}{(2 \times 3) + (2 \times 2)}$$

$$= \frac{9}{10}$$

$$= 0.9$$

2 According to the Paasche index, which is less than 1, the cost of living has fallen. The cost of consuming F_2 and G_2 at the new set of prices is less than the cost of consuming these amounts at the old set of prices.

Exercise 4.3

In some countries the degree of gender discrimination is less than in others, with the consequence that the less gender discriminatory countries, such as the Czech Republic, Slovakia, Denmark and Barbados, are much higher in the GDI rank than in the HDI rank. In the sample shown, Netherlands, Canada and Japan are the most gender discriminatory countries.

Households

THE HOUSEHOLD IN THE ECONOMY

Jane Wheelock and Elizabeth Oughton

CONCEPTS AND TECHNIQUES

Different definitions of a household
Market work/non-market work
Labour supply curve
Backward bending supply curves
Z-goods
Comparative advantage/
   opportunity cost
Household production possibility
   frontier
Human capital
Formal and complementary sectors
   of the economy
Formal and substantive rationality

LINKS

- The analysis of a household's labour supply function builds on the neoclassical derivation of consumer demand functions in Chapter 2. A single person who can choose how many hours to work at a given wage has a straight-line budget constraint representing a trade-off between hours of home time and income.

- The institutionalist analysis in the chapter builds on the importance accorded to norms in Veblen's and Bourdieu's theories in Chapter 3. In that chapter norms affected what people consume; here norms affect how people use their time. In both chapters, norms are endogenous to the economic system.

- The human capital argument for gender specialization is an example of positive feedback whereby small initial differences are magnified – there will be other examples of positive feedback having similar effects later in the book, e.g. when considering how tastes for and norms concerning caring for children develop in Chapter 7 and how technologies develop in Chapters 15 and 16.

- The neoclassical analysis of this chapter has assumed that the household can be taken as a single decision-making unit. The next chapter, Chapter 6, will consider whether this is a reasonable assumption to make.

1 INTRODUCTION

'... in recent years economists increasingly recognize that a household is truly a "small factory": it combines capital goods, raw materials and labour to clean, feed, procreate and otherwise produce useful commodities.'

(BECKER, 1965, QUOTED IN AMSDEN, 1980, P.55)

Conventional wisdom has it that the household has moved from being a production unit to becoming almost exclusively concerned with consumption. Indeed, many would say that what is pivotal about industrialization is that the production of goods has ceased to be an activity of the household. We will argue in this chapter that this view ignores the unpaid work done within the household – work which is largely undertaken by women. One of the main issues raised by such unpaid work and the way in which it is gendered is that of how we define and measure 'work'. Quite often, unpaid labour within the household is ignored in official figures. In 13 selected industrial countries, as Figure 5.1 shows, 66 per cent of men's work but only 34 per cent of work done by women is accounted for in the United Nations System of National Accounts (SNA). In nine selected developing countries, the figures are even more unbalanced. This is because the SNA, although it includes some work which does not go through the market, such as agricultural work producing subsistence crops for a household's own consumption, does not include work whose products are not easily given a price. Much of women's domestic work is of that kind. Once non-SNA work is taken into account, women do more work than men in both types of economies (United Nations Development Programme, 1995, p.89).

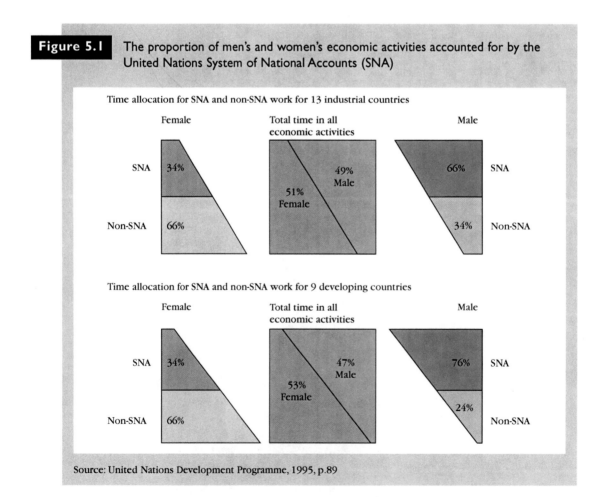

Figure 5.1 The proportion of men's and women's economic activities accounted for by the United Nations System of National Accounts (SNA)

Time allocation for SNA and non-SNA work for 13 industrial countries

Female — SNA 34%, Non-SNA 66%

Total time in all economic activities — 51% Female, 49% Male

Male — SNA 66%, Non-SNA 34%

Time allocation for SNA and non-SNA work for 9 developing countries

Female — SNA 34%, Non-SNA 66%

Total time in all economic activities — 53% Female, 47% Male

Male — SNA 76%, Non-SNA 24%

Source: United Nations Development Programme, 1995, p.89

Exercise 5.1

From Figure 5.1, work out the proportion of the total time allocated to economic activities going to non-SNA work, in:

1   the selected industrial countries;
2   the selected developing countries.

What do these figures suggest about the significance of unpaid work in the world economy?

From your answer to this exercise, it should be clear that non-SNA work is a highly significant part of the work that is done in all economies. Non-SNA work is largely, though not entirely, household work. Figure 5.1 shows that this work is still mainly done by women. This is despite a substantial and continuing change in women's relation to the paid economy in most industrial countries.

In Britain, for example, government policy in 1945 was based on a conception of families with male breadwinners and housewives who, if they were employed at all, earned 'pin-money'. Nevertheless, even in 1951, the economic activity rate for women of working age (16–59 years) stood at 42 per cent. Today, the picture is radically different and the average British household relies on women, not just to do unpaid domestic work, but also to provide a wage which is a substantial part of the household's income. Women working part-time contribute on average one-fifth of family income, while those working full-time contribute two-fifths. Taking half average income as the poverty line, in 1990, one in 12 couple households fell below it; without women's earnings, the proportion would have been 50 per cent higher (Harkness *et al.*, 1996). By 1992, 71 per cent of women were economically active in the labour market. What is surprising is that women's labour market participation rose both in the period of the long post-Second World War boom up until the start of the 1970s, and in the period after it ended, when men's participation rate fell. Since the end of the long boom, escalating levels of unemployment have undermined men's roles as economic providers. There has been a decline in the significance of the male breadwinner, whilst women, in addition to working more outside the home, continue to perform most of the unpaid work inside it (Humphries and Rubery, 1992; Wheelock and McCarthy, 1997).

This chapter examines two routes to understanding these changes: the first based on a neoclassical model of the household, and the second based on an institutional perspective.

The US experience of similarly rising female participation in the labour force fired Jacob Mincer and Gary Becker to use the neoclassical assumptions of scarcity and utility maximization to explain gender divisions within and outside the household, in what became known as the 'New Household Economics' (NHE). Their fundamental insight was to recognize that individuals do not just spend their time either doing paid work or at leisure at home, but that there are also unpaid productive activities which go on at home. The recognition that time has competing uses allowed these economists to investigate non-market activities and see the household as a producing, as well as a consuming, unit of the economy. We shall look at how they did this in Section 2 of this chapter.

Section 3 goes on to examine how Mincer and Becker's neoclassical models explain the connection between changing employment patterns for men and women and changes in the gender division of labour within the household. Using case studies of households in which the man is unemployed, a household in a developing country, and small business households, this chapter will then investigate the changes in working patterns that have occurred. While we shall find that some of the changes are consonant with the neoclassical model, we shall also consider whether they might be better explained in terms of an alternative institutional perspective.

Rather than focusing on the optimal allocation of scarce resources, we shift our concern to how, in particular circumstances, households combine resources to provision people and promote their well-being. An interdisciplinary institutional approach recognizes that economic life is embedded in social and cultural relations which both influence the values that underpin individual choice and in turn are influenced by those values (Polanyi, 1946; Granovetter, 1992). Values and norms vary quite systematically across cultures and individuals, and these variations may be more relevant than a cross-cultural analysis of individual household decisions in explaining economic outcomes. Section 4 of this chapter will examine the claims of interdisciplinary institutionalists to be able to explain some of the complexities of household behaviour that the New Household Economics is not equipped to tackle.

1.1 The household as an economic institution

Households are economic institutions that use material and human resources to provision and support day-to-day existence. A *household* can take many forms; it need not consist of an orthodox nuclear or extended family, but could encompass any unit consisting of people sufficiently closely connected with each other that they jointly organize some aspects of work and consumption together (for example, a group of students living communally, or a couple setting up house together).

> ### Household
>
> A household is a unit consisting of people with a common budget who organize some aspects of work and consumption together.

Here are two definitions of a household that have been proposed:

1 '... the basic units of society in which activities of production, reproduction, consumption and the socialization of children take place' (Roberts, 1991, p.62);

2 '... that group of people, their relationships and activities, who acknowledge a common authority in domestic matters, a budget unit" or a group who have a common fund of material and human resources and rules for practices and exchange within it' (Messer, 1990, p.52).

These two definitions focus on different things. The first concentrates on the activities that go on within the household, and their importance to society as a whole. The second definition focuses on the internal relations of a household – that the people form a bounded unit that makes decisions together, in particular about the use of their budget of human and material resources.

Either of these definitions will produce households of very different types, members and internal relationships, depending on place, culture and history. In some cultures a single type of unit of domestic provisioning, using definition one, is difficult to identify. And in some societies there may be no unit with a sufficiently clear boundary to be identifiable as a household by definition two. Neither the definition of a household by what it does nor its identification as a

budgetary unit can be taken as universal. The coming together of these two definitions has, however, provided the starting-point of most economic analyses of the household, and so it is with that concept of the household in mind that we shall begin.

2 NEOCLASSICAL APPROACHES TO HOUSEHOLD DECISION MAKING

Although economists had for long spoken of the household as an economic agent alongside firms, for many years the inner workings of the household were ignored. Margaret Reid (1934) was an early pioneer investigating the internal workings of the household, but it was not until the 1960s that the New Household Economics (NHE) developed by Jacob Mincer and Gary Becker brought this area of economic research into the mainstream. They were attempting to explain what Mincer saw as 'one of the most striking phenomena in the history of the American labour force ... the continuing secular increase in the participation rates of females, particularly of married women, despite the growth in real income' (1962; quoted in Amsden, 1980, p.42). Mincer and Becker, in their separate work, sought to explain this phenomenon by extending the methods of neoclassical economic analysis to the household, in order to investigate how the household unit made decisions about labour allocation.

The NHE uses the standard principle of neoclassical economics: that rational economic agents exercise choice over the use of scarce resources in order best to satisfy their preferences (maximize utility). In doing this, the NHE extended the neoclassical analysis you have so far encountered by:

1 taking households rather than individual people as the rational decision-making units;

2 analysing labour supply decisions as the result of rational choices made between income and time spent at home;

3 recognizing that time at home has competing uses; it is not all leisure;

4 using the theory of comparative advantage and human capital theory to analyse the division of labour between men and women in the household.

In the remainder of this section, we shall look at the first three of these steps, which examine the issues facing the household as a whole. Then, in Section 3, we shall look at the final step – how those decisions impinge on the individuals within the household – before examining how well the whole NHE approach explains the phenomenon that Mincer was trying to analyse: the rising participation rates of married women.

2.1   *How do households decide what to do?*

One neoclassical approach to household decision making is to treat the whole household as if it were an individual, a single decision-making unit with its own set of preferences. This would at first sight seem a strange thing to do, since, true to its methodologically individualist foundations, neoclassical economics generally seeks to explain all economic behaviour as the result of the choices of individual people, and it is only people who have preferences which can guide their choices.

It is, however, convenient to assume that it is households that have preferences; for then the various results about the expected behaviour of individuals that we have examined earlier in this book apply to the behaviour of households. For example, the neoclassical consumer theory of Chapter 2 assumes that individuals spend only their own income and spend it only on themselves. But if income is shared in households, then the person who does the family shopping is neither spending just her own income, nor buying just for herself. If we want to use that consumer theory unchanged in these circumstances, we would have to say that she is acting just as a representative of the household, implicitly spending *its* income according to *its* preferences.

It would therefore be very convenient to assume that households have preferences, with all the properties of consistency and convexity that were assumed to apply to individuals. If so, neoclassical consumer theory would still apply, except its basic unit would be the household rather than the individual. However, there may be good reasons for doubting whether decisions made by households display the consistency that would be needed for there to be a single preference ordering for the whole household. These doubts, and the justifications that have been given by neoclassical economists for assuming that households have consistent preference orderings, will be examined in

Chapter 6, along with some alternative models of household decision making. In this chapter, we shall assume that households have preferences which can be represented by utility functions, in order to look at how the New Household Economics uses them to examine the choices households make.

2.2   *How do households spend their time?*

Neoclassical theory looks at decisions by a household about how to spend its time in the same way as it looks at consumption decisions. It assumes that a household has a choice of how many hours to spend earning money and how many to spend at home. Prior to the New Household Economics, time spent at home was always called 'leisure'. We have deliberately chosen not to do this because it is inaccurate: much of time at home is spent on productive activities. From now on, we will just call such time 'home time', and look later at what is done with it.

Work carried out in the market is paid a wage. So the choice facing the household is how to combine market work, which brings in desirable income, with home time, which the household sees as desirable in itself. This choice is illustrated for a particular household in Figure 5.2 where time is measured on the horizontal axis and income on the vertical axis.

On the vertical axis, Y_0 represents any unearned income; from property rents, pensions or state benefits, for example. The important point about unearned income is that, unlike income from market work, it is not affected by any decision the household makes as to how to spend its time. Along the horizontal axis, time spent in the home is measured from left to right and so time spent on market work is measured from right to left. The maximum amount of time available for the household is t_{max}. For a one-person household it would be 24 hours. The income this household would receive if all its time were devoted to market work is Y_{max}; it is its 'full' or maximum potential income. However, this income can never be achieved because not all this time can be used for market work. Just to survive, some time must be set aside for eating, sleeping, etc. This time is shown as t_0. Within these limits, the household has a choice as to how many hours to spend on market work and how much to spend at home. Assuming market work of any number of hours is available at the going wage rate, the line ZR shows the possible levels of income which the household can receive at different levels of market work. Because time not spent at market work is time spent at home, this line is also the household's budget constraint; it gives the combinations of the two desirable goods, income and home time, that are feasible for the household.

Figure 5.2 also shows indifference curves connecting combinations of income and home time between which the household is indifferent. As with consumer choice, maximum utility will be achieved at point A, where the budget constraint is tangent to an indifference curve. At this point, the household supplies $t_{max} - t_1$ hours of market labour and receives Y_1 income.

2.3 The household's labour supply curve

By exploring the effect of a change in the wage rate, we can derive the household's labour supply curve.

Figure 5.3(a) shows how an increase in the wage rate increases the slope of the budget constraint. If no market work is done, household income is just the unearned income Y_0 as before. However, in all other circumstances, the household can now earn more money for the same amount of time, so the budget constraint pivots around Z, from ZR to ZS. The household can now achieve a higher level of utility. If it moves from point A to point B, the household increases its supply of labour to the market from $t_{max} - t_1$ to $t_{max} - t_2$, and increases its income from Y_1 to Y_2. Figure 5.3(b) shows the supply curve for labour derived from Figure 5.3(a) in the same way as the demand curve for a consumption good was derived in Chapter 2, Section 2.3, Figure 2.7. Note, however, that hours of market labour supplied are measured in the opposite direction in Figure 5.3(b) from Figure 5.3(a), where they are measured from right to left. The *labour supply curve* shows how, other things being equal, the amount of market work a household will be willing to supply depends on the wage rate; in this case, as the wage rate rises, the supply of labour to the market rises too.

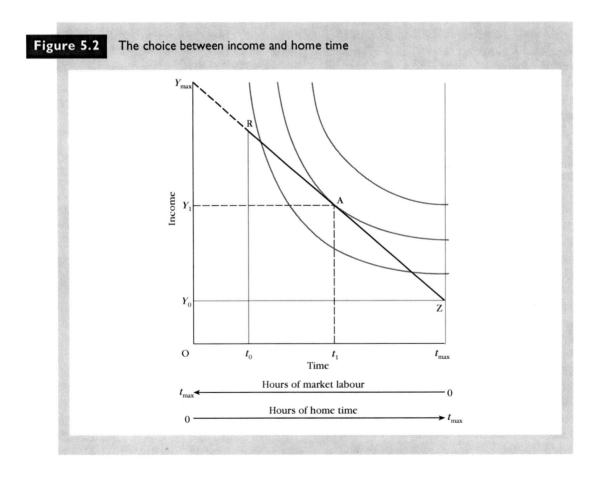

Figure 5.2   The choice between income and home time

Labour supply curve

A household's labour supply curve shows the amount of market work it is willing to supply at various wage rates.

However, there is a lot going on behind the scenes in the claim that as the wage rate rises the supply of market labour increases, which we need to look at in more detail. The wage rate can be seen as the opportunity cost of home time, how much income has to

Figure 5.3   The effect of a rise in the wage rate

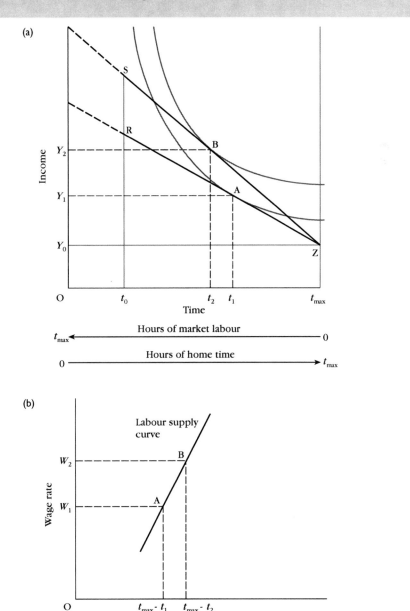

be given up for an extra hour of home time: a rise in the wage rate can be seen as an increase in the opportunity cost of home time. Alternatively, you can think of an increase in the wage rate as a fall in the opportunity cost of income, making income 'cheaper' in terms of the time need to obtain it.

As we saw for consumer choice, the actual effect of a change in a price, in this case a change in the wage rate, will depend on the income and substitution effects of the change. Look back now to Section 3 of Chapter 2 to remind yourself about income and substitution effects. There you will see that substitution effects always work in one direction, to shift consumption away from the good whose price has risen towards the good that has become cheaper. However, income effects for consumer goods may work in either direction, either reinforcing, weakening or even countering the substitution effect, depending on whether a good is normal, weakly inferior or a Giffen good (see Chapter 2, Section 3.2).

The household has a choice between two goods: income and home time. The effect of a rise in the wage rate is to make income cheaper and home time more expensive. The substitution effect therefore results in a shift away from the relatively more expensive good towards the cheaper one, from home time towards income. This is shown in Figure 5.4 as a move from A to A', where less time is being spent at home and therefore more on market work, thus bringing in more money income, while keeping the household on the same indifference curve. A' is the point on the same indifference curve as A that would be chosen by the household at the new wage rate. A' is therefore the point where a line parallel to ZS just touches that indifference curve. The movement from A to A' then gives the substitution effect alone, without considering the income effect of the change in the wage rate.

The other move from A' to B gives the income effect which results from the increase in the wage

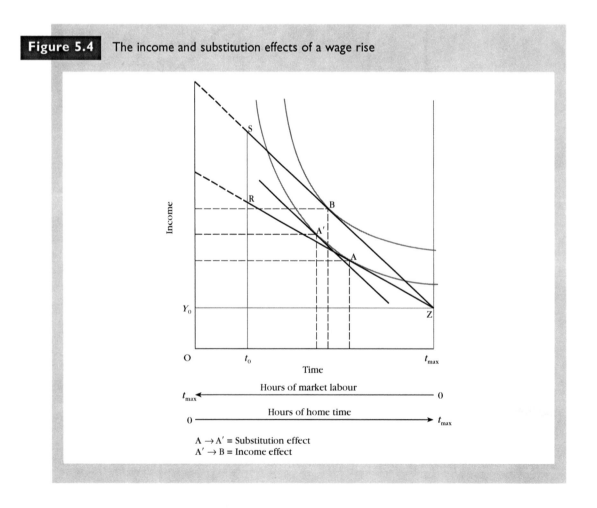

Figure 5.4   The income and substitution effects of a wage rise

A → A' = Substitution effect
A' → B = Income effect

rate enabling the household to shift on to a higher indifference curve, by consuming more of either income or home time. In the case illustrated in Figure 5.4 more of both are being consumed, but that may not always be the case. So, although the substitution effect leads to an inevitable increase in the time spent on market work, the income effect may lead to either an increase in the time spent at home or an increase in the time spent on market work or both. The full effect of the rise in the wage rate is the combination of these two effects.

If home time is a normal good, the income effect of a rise in the wage rate will increase time spent at home. So if the hours spent on market work increase as the wage rate rises, either home time must be an inferior good – that is, the household chooses to spend less time at home as its income increases – or home time is only weakly normal, so that the substitution effect of a rise in the wage rate outweighs the income effect. In these circumstances, the labour supply curve slopes upwards.

However, if home time is a normal good, and the income effect is greater than the substitution effect, the amount of time spent in the market will decrease as the wage rate rises, leading to a labour supply curve with a negatively sloping section as in Figure 5.5(a) and (b) overleaf.

This is not a far-fetched case and backward-bending supply curves have been observed in both developed and developing economies. The following is a plausible example in many parts of Africa. Imagine a woman running a small subsistence farm which she uses to produce food for her household. She also needs to hire out her labour in order to earn a cash income to pay for her children's education and to clothe the family. If her wage rate increases, she would be able to meet those cash needs with fewer hours of labouring work. She could thus increase the number of hours that she works on her own farm, increasing the quality and range of foods available to her household; she might be working just as long hours in total, but she would have a backward-bending supply curve for the labour she sells on the market.

2.4   Competing uses of time

One of the insights of the New Home Economics was that time not used working in the market was not just spent on leisure. Both home time and the goods bought with income can produce utility for the household. However, as Becker pointed out, they do not do this separately. Both home time and goods purchased on the market are used as inputs to produce other goods and services, and it is these other goods and services that produce utility for the household. Becker called such home-produced goods *Z-goods*. The idea of *Z*-goods breaks down the distinction between production and consumption. *Z*-goods cannot be bought; they are sources of utility which are produced and consumed by the household, using its own time together with purchased inputs.

Z-goods

Z-goods are sources of utility which are produced and consumed by a household using its own time together with purchased inputs.

The same Z-good, and therefore the utility that the household gets from it, can be achieved through different combinations of purchased goods and time. For example, the pleasure of sitting in a beautifully decorated room can be achieved in at least two ways. You can redecorate the room yourself,

Figure 5.5   Deriving a backward-bending supply curve for labour

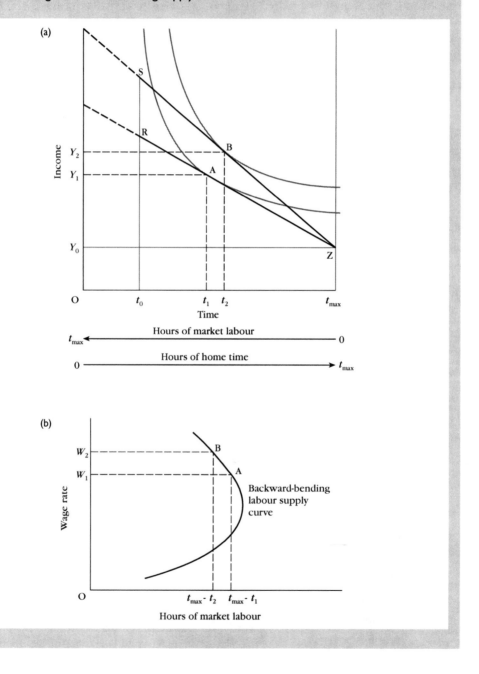

which would use a lot of time and some purchased inputs, or you can pay a decorator to do the work using income generated from your own market work. Let us take, as a second example, the consumption of a good meal. The meal may be obtained in any number of ways: one household may like to garden, will have grown the fresh fruit and vegetables themselves, collected eggs from their hens, shot a rabbit, made their own bread, etc.; another household may rush around Asda, buy frozen vegetables, ready-diced stewing meat and a pie to pop in the oven; a third household may prefer to take their friends to eat in the new fast-food restaurant in the high street. Further, the consumption of the meal takes time, perhaps different amounts of time according to the different ways the meal is served. The varying combinations of purchased inputs and home time that the household uses to create and consume a satisfying meal are innumerable. The actual choice will depend on the time and money available to the household, and its ability to turn them into the Z-good, the meal, from which the household derives its utility.

3   THE DIVISION OF LABOUR WITHIN THE HOUSEHOLD

Having looked at the decisions households make, we now need to consider how those decisions affect what individual household members do. It was Becker who showed how a household can be better off by specialization – by some members specializing in market work and others staying at home. He used the notion of comparative advantage,

which may be familiar to you from the theory of international trade (see *Changing Economies*, Chapter 13), to show how the different household members' time should be allocated to maximize the household's utility.

Imagine a household consisting of two people, Max and Minnie. Both of them use their home time in producing and consuming Z-goods; for simplicity, let us assume that this home time can be split fairly easily into (non-market) work and leisure time. They both work 10 hours a day in all and initially organize their household along fairly traditional lines, with Max in full-time employment and Minnie doing more of the housework alongside a part-time job.

But how should we think about the output they produce? The output of market work to a household is the income it brings in. The output of the work component of home time is harder to measure, but if we suppose we have some measure of it, then we could represent Max and Minnie's allocation of time and their output as in Table 5.2.

> **Question**
>
> ● What does Table 5.2 show about the productivity of Max and Minnie?
> ● Who is more productive in (a) market work and (b) non-market work?

Minnie's output per hour is higher than Max's in both types of work; there is a wage differential by which Minnie earns £12 per hour while Max earns £5 per hour, and she is more productive at non-market work, producing six units to his five units per hour. Minnie therefore has an absolute advantage and is more productive in both types of work. However, it is not absolute advantage but *comparative advantage*

Table 5.2   Max and Minnie's joint output

	Time for market work	Output of market work	Time for non-market work	Output of non-market work
Max	8 hours	£40	2 hours	10 units
Minnie	5 hours	£60	5 hours	30 units
Total	13 hours	£100	7 hours	40 units

that matters in deciding who should specialize in what type of work. (If you need to remind yourself about comparative advantage, you should now read *Changing Economies*, Chapter 13, Section 2.)

Question

- What is the opportunity cost of a unit of non-market production for Minnie, and for Max?
- Who has the comparative advantage in (a) market work and (b) non-market work?

If Minnie were to do an extra hour of non-market work and so work one hour less in her market job, she would earn £12 less but would produce six units more of non-market output. So for her, each unit of non-market output has an opportunity cost of £2 in lost earnings (the concept of opportunity costs was introduced in Chapter 1). By a similar calculation, you can see that, for Max, the opportunity cost of each unit of non-market output is £1, because he could either earn £5 or produce five units of non-market production per hour. This means that Max has a comparative advantage in non-market work and Minnie in market work. Note that this is the case even though Minnie has an absolute advantage in both types of work.

To increase their joint production, it would make sense for them to reorganize their time in the light of their respective comparative advantages: Minnie should do more market work and Max more non-market work. For example, if Minnie were to work all 10 hours at her job, and Max were to work 10 hours in the home, their joint output would look like Table 5.3.

Now the total output of the household has increased in both types of output; the household is better off without doing any more work in total. These are the benefits of specialization when members of the household have different comparative advantages.

3.1 The household's production possibility frontier

In Table 5.3 we looked at just one way in which the household might reorganize its time in order to benefit from specialization. However, Max and Minnie might want a different mix of outputs from this. If, for example, an income of £108 was enough and they would prefer to use any extra time at home, Minnie could work just nine hours in her job and use an extra hour at home in non-market production to create another six units of non-market output. In this case, Max would be completely specialized in non-market production, but Minnie would be splitting her time between the two types of work. In general, the gains from specialization mean that one member of the household should specialize completely and the other should split their time to get whatever balance of output is required by the household.

We can see this by constructing the household's production possibility frontier (PPF), which gives the maximum combinations of non-market output and income that the household can have given the two members' productivities. (*Changing Economies*, Chapter 7, Figure 7.20 introduces production possibility frontiers for whole economies. They are further discussed in Chapter 18, Section 4.3.) First, we need

Table 5.3 Max and Minnie's joint output under specialization

	Time for market work	Output of market work	Time for non-market work	Output of non-market work
Max			10 hours	50 units
Minnie	10 hours	£120		
Total	10 hours	£120	10 hours	50 units

to look at Max's and Minnie's individual PPFs. Max's PPF is shown in Figure 5.6.

If Max spends all 10 hours doing non-market work, he produces 50 units as we have seen. If he takes a job for that time he earns £50. These two points are marked on the two axes. Max's PPF is the straight line joining these two points, showing all the possible output combinations he can achieve by splitting his time between the two types of work.

Exercise 5.3

Draw Minnie's production possibility frontier.

We have drawn the household's PPF in Figure 5.7. To see why it is this shape, we need to consider what is the most effective way for the household to arrive at whatever combination of money income and non-market output they require. Let us suppose first of all that Max and Minnie are only interested in maximizing their money income. They obviously do this by both working the full 10 hours each in market work. This gives them £170 in all: Max earns £50 and Minnie earns £120. They cannot earn more than that and this leaves them no time for non-market work. This is point A on Figure 5.7.

Now consider what it is most efficient for them to do if they want some non-market output: let's suppose just 10 units to start with. We know that the opportunity cost of a unit of non-market output for Minnie in £2 in lost earnings while for Max it is only £1. So Max should be the one to produce the 10 units of non-

market work which means he will need to reduce his time doing market work and so will earn £10 less. This gives point B on the household PPF in Figure 5.7.

At this point the opportunity cost of a unit of non-market output for the household is £1, because this is the income the household has to give up to get one more unit of non-market output.

If the household wants more non-market output, this process can continue, at an opportunity cost of £1 per unit of non-market output with Max shifting his time from market work to non-market work until point C. This is where Max has shifted his time entirely to non-market work and is producing 50 units of non-market output, while Minnie is still specializing in market work, earning £120. If the household wants further non-market output, it will now have to be Minnie who starts shifting from market to non-market work. But for her the opportunity cost of an extra unit of non-market output is £2 and this is what the household now has to give up to gain any more non-market output. In the move from C to D, 10 more units of non-market output require the household to give up £20 of money income. From here onwards, the household's PPF becomes steeper, because it has to be Minnie who shifts from market to non-market work, until both partners are just doing non-market work, producing 110 units in total as at E.

On Figure 5.7, anywhere on line AC, Minnie is specializing in market work completely, while Max is doing a combination of the two types of work. Anywhere on the line CE, Max is specializing completely in non-market work and Minnie is doing a combination of the two types of work. Which

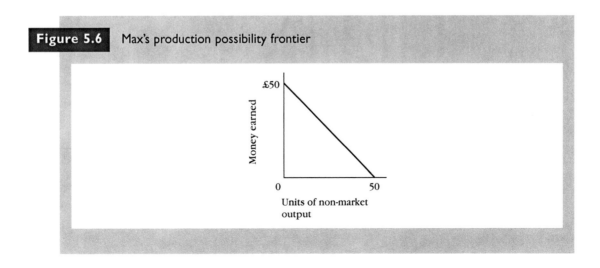

Figure 5.6   Max's production possibility frontier

particular point on their joint PPF represents the work they do depends on the output mix the household chooses, which will depend on its preferences. However, at any point on the production possibility frontier, one or other is specializing completely: either Minnie is specializing in market work, in which she has a comparative advantage, or Max is specializing in non-market work, in which he has a comparative advantage. Since the points on the production possibility frontier are the points of maximum efficiency, this supports the point made earlier that there are benefits to the household from specialization.

Reflection

Using Figure 5.7, tell yourself the story of how Max and Minnie decide who should do which type of work as they move from both wholly specializing in non-market work to wanting increasing amounts of money income.

3.2 Explaining comparative advantages

The previous section showed how specialization within households could be explained by members having different comparative advantages and the household choosing the most efficient use of the collective time. This argument has been used to explain the traditional gender division of labour within households in which men specialize in market work and women specialize in non-market work or do both market and non-market work. But how do such differences in comparative advantage arise?

One possible answer is that these are due to biological differences: that (unlike Minnie) women in general have a comparative advantage in the home because they are biologically more gifted at home-based tasks than men. Alternatively, the argument could focus on men and say that men in general (unlike Max) have a biologically given comparative advantage in market work, because, say, they are

Figure 5.7   Minnie's production possibility frontier added to Max's

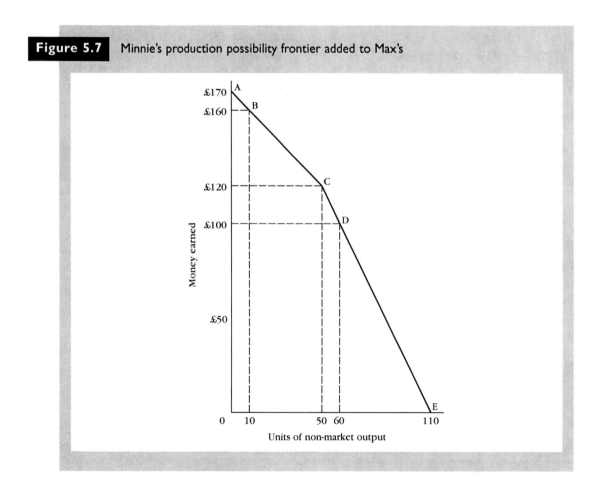

supposed to be more 'aggressive' and therefore more suited to the cut-and-thrust of the market. Note that to base the comparative advantage argument on the fact that men in general earn higher wages than women will do if all one is trying to explain is how a particular household organizes its time, but is not an acceptable explanation at the level of society as a whole, since that wage differential itself has to be explained (Chapter 13 examines some explanations for gender differences in wage rates based on labour-market factors).

However, the New Household Economics does not rely on biological explanations alone to explain why women have a comparative advantage in non-market work and men in market work. The concept of *human capital* is used to explain how small biological differences can make an enormous difference to who does what.

Human capital

Human capital comprises any characteristic of a person which takes time or money to acquire and can increase their productivity later. Unlike physical capital, human capital is embodied in a particular person and cannot be transferred to someone else.

Education, skills and work experience are all forms of human capital. They are *capital* because time or money has to be invested in order to acquire them, and they are acquired in the expectation that they will bring in a return on that investment by rewarding the person for their increased productivity later. In this they are like an investment in a machine that increases a worker's productivity. But they are *human* capital because these characteristics are embodied in a particular person, and unlike a machine cannot be transferred to someone else.

Human capital can be specific to particular types of work. Investing in learning how to sing does not make you a more productive computer programmer. In particular, the New Household Economics argues that the skills used in market work are different from those used in non-market work, so people need to make an investment in different kinds of human capital for each.

The decision on whether to invest in market- or non-market-based human capital will depend on a person's expectations of how much time they will be spending working in each of those sectors. The

more time expected to be spent in a sector, the greater the incentive to invest in developing the human capital appropriate to that sector. Individuals who expect to spend most of their time doing market work will expect to gain a greater return from investment in market-related training than in training for non-market work, and vice versa.

Now if women, for whatever reason, expect to spend somewhat more time doing non-market work than men, it will make sense for them to invest more of their human capital in non-market work than men do. This will give women a comparative advantage in non-market work and men in market work, and it will then make sense for those households that consist of a man and a woman to specialize in the traditional direction. Note that this argument depends on women expecting to spend just *some* more time doing non-market work than men; it does not depend on that difference being large. However small the difference, because it affects people's investment in human capital, their comparative advantage will then be determined.

To explain this initial small difference in expectations, the New Household Economics resorts to the biological difference between men and women in childbearing. Even if the extra time women devote to non-market work because of childbearing is small, it is enough to explain differences in human capital investment and thus differences in comparative advantage and consequent specialization. Indeed, the biological differences do not have to be invoked for all women. Once men and women grow up expecting to find gender differences in comparative advantage, it makes sense to acquire the human capital that one's future partner is most likely to lack.

If women invest less in market-based human capital, the jobs that will be open to them will be less skilled and less well paid than those their male partners can get, and it will make sense for the man to do more of the household's market work. Men's market-based human capital will thus accumulate further through increased work experience. This will further reduce the comparative earning potential of women, who spend more time in the home, making it more likely that it is women who disrupt their market work later if this is needed – to care for elderly relatives, for example. Since women anticipate shorter, more disrupted periods of market work, they will invest less throughout their lives in training for the market and gain less work experience than men. Thus, very small initial differences in comparative advantage can be magnified by differences in investment in human capital to explain and reinforce gender specialization within households.

3.3 Explaining increasing female participation rates

So how does the analysis we have carried out so far help us explain the increased female participation rate of women in market work, the question that first caught Becker and Mincer's imagination?

Figure 5.8 shows how the economic activity rates of women increased in the UK from 1973–92, where economically active means either doing market work or being registered as looking for it. Notice that the existence of children under 10 and the age of the youngest child has a consistent effect on whether women engage in market work. Women with children

under 10, and particularly women with pre-school children, are more likely to specialize entirely in non-market work.

Question

Why, according to the New Household Economics, should women with young children be less likely to do market work than women with no children?

The NHE would explain this in terms of the Z-goods that children require being particularly home-time intensive, so that many households with young children require at least the equivalent of one person's full-time non-market work. In these circumstances, it is more efficient for at least one member to specialize in non-market work. Because of their comparative advantage, women – rather than their husbands, if they

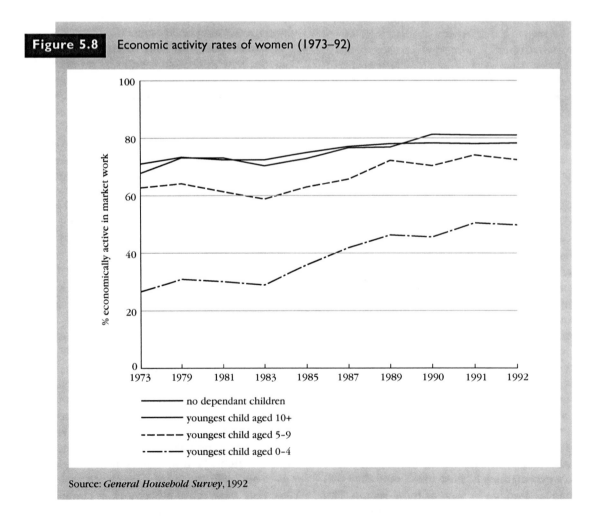

Figure 5.8 Economic activity rates of women (1973–92)

- ——— no dependant children
- ——— youngest child aged 10+
- - - - - youngest child aged 5–9
- -·-·- youngest child aged 0–4

Source: *General Household Survey*, 1992

have them – will do the non-market work. The evidence of relative wage rates from Figure 5.9 supports this conclusion; if women earn less than men they will have a comparative advantage in doing non-market work, quite apart from any greater skills they may have acquired in that area.

But what about the trend displayed in Figure 5.8 towards increasing rates of economic activity for women whatever the age of their youngest child? The NHE would break this question down into two sub-questions:

1 How can the increasing number of total hours put into market work by households be explained?

2 How can the increasing proportion of market work done by women be explained?

The NHE would answer the first question by pointing to either a shift in the productivity of market versus non-market work in producing the same Z-goods, or to a change in the Z-goods that households wish to consume towards those Z-goods that are more market-work intensive (i.e. require more income and less home time).

Question

Why might market work have become relatively more productive for households?

An increase in overall wage rates would increase the relative productivity of market work for households. Rising educational levels might contribute to this, on the assumption that education is more useful in market work than in non-market work. Taxation can affect this too since income tax is only levied on market work, so lowered rates of income tax might encourage more market work. Pension schemes, divorce settlements and national insurance benefits which depend on contributions of earnings from market work would be another factor; if these have become more important, market work would come to be seen as more productive.

Households would also do relatively more market work if they required more of the Z-goods that are market-work intensive and fewer of those that are non-market-work intensive than they had before.

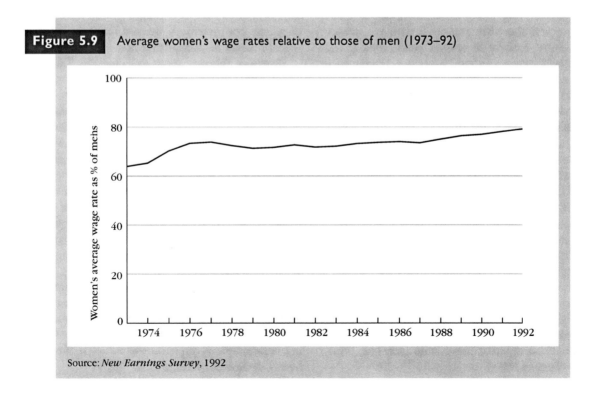

Figure 5.9   Average women's wage rates relative to those of men (1973–92)

Source: *New Earnings Survey*, 1992

Question

What factors might shift the demand by households towards income from market work and away from home time?

Question

Take another look at Figure 5.8. Which group of women has experienced the largest increase in labour market activity?

As we saw, young children are particularly non-market-work intensive, so a falling birth-rate would affect households' requirements for non-market work. Where childcare has become more available than before, households' demand for income over home time may increase. New or better quality products on the market might be another factor increasing the household's demand for income over home time, as would falling prices for existing products that were previously too expensive for many households to afford, such as overseas travel. Increasing productivity in market work, making bought substitutes for non-market work relatively cheaper to buy, would have a similar effect, and so would a shift in cultural norms that diminished the extent to which home products were desired over bought consumption goods.

Now we can turn to the second question about increased female participation rate that the NHE would ask: how can the increasing proportion of market work done by women be explained? The NHE predicts that, in any household, one or other member will specialize entirely. If men are already specializing entirely in market work, then if the household moves towards a greater reliance on market work, it can only be women who shift the proportions of time they spend in that direction.

What the NHE analysis cannot explain, however, is why some households are moving to a less specialized division of labour. This is because it does not incorporate any analysis of shifting institutional factors, such as views on whether traditional gendered roles are desirable in themselves or whether more sharing is beneficial. It assumes that the only issue determining a household's allocation of time is the question of what is the most efficient way of satisfying the household's preferences.

However, such institutional factors are incorporated in the evidence from a large number of qualitative studies showing that women in general, and mothers in particular, are in the labour market and in the family on different terms from men (e.g. West, 1982; Wajcman, 1983).

As Figure 5.8 shows, there has been some modification in the traditional division of household labour, for mothers now increasingly expect to combine their caring role with responsibility for income earning. It is women with pre-school children whose labour market activity increased most in the period 1973–92. Yet it has remained difficult for fathers, or indeed mothers, to accept that men, whether they are employed or unemployed, should give up their breadwinning responsibilities (Wheelock, 1990; Jordan et al., 1991). For low-paid mothers especially, part-time employment is a compromise which, in the absence of childcare that they can afford, enables them to combine an income-earning role with their traditional caring role (Yeandle, 1984; Stubbs and Wheelock, 1990).

Women continue to bear the main responsibilities for work in the home. In three-quarters of the families surveyed for the 1991 study of social attitudes, women did most of the housework (Jowell et al., 1991). In Britain, in two-thirds of the households in which both partners worked full-time, women were primarily responsible for domestic duties.

However, there is some evidence for a limited decline in specialization within the household. Gershuny et al. (1994) show that in Britain, in the decade between 1975 and 1985, the proportion of housework undertaken by husbands has risen for those with full-time working, part-time working and housewife partners, though the increase is greatest for the first of these. Such trends can also be identified in other European countries, and in the USA. Gershuny et al. suggest an institutionally-based model of 'lagged adaptation', where adjustment to roles takes place through extensive processes of household negotiation, or even reconstitution, over many years, and indeed over generations.

Let us illustrate and summarize our arguments with a case study of households with unemployed men and employed women, where there has indeed been a shift in the gender division of domestic labour in a non-traditional direction; that is, where there has been a decline in specialization.

Changes in comparative advantage in households where economic restructuring affects men as providers

Economic change in the peripheral local economy of Wearside in north-east England has brought about substantial levels of male unemployment as traditional manufacturing industries have restructured, cutting back on their labour force or closing down altogether. At the same time, employment for women has remained relatively buoyant, in part because of the continuing expansion of the service sector providing 'women's work', in part because women provide a cheap and flexible labour force. A representative study of 30 households typifying this changing local economy was undertaken in the mid 1980s, a time of peak unemployment. The households consisted of husbands who were no longer in paid work, largely due to redundancy or unemployment, but whose wives were active in the labour market, though not all working full time. The study sought to investigate the changes in the division of domestic labour that took place once men were no longer in paid work.

Four categories of organization of domestic work were distinguished: traditional rigid, traditional flexible, sharing, and exchanged roles. At the traditional extreme, the husband performed almost no domestic tasks apart from some predominantly male-gendered tasks such as mowing the lawn. At the other extreme – exchanged roles – the husband did a substantial range of tasks, either alone, or shared with his wife, whilst she was either the household breadwinner, or had more or less full-time employment. Although this form of organization involved a much looser gender segregation than the others, there were still residual elements of tradition.

When husbands became unemployed, there was some change in the domestic work in nearly half the households (in 8 from a traditional rigid to a traditional flexible form of organization, in 5 from traditional flexible to sharing, and in 1 sharing more extensively) and there was substantial change in a further 6 households (with 3 households moving from traditional flexible to exchanged roles, and 2 from traditional rigid, for example). In other words, 20 households (nearly 70 per cent of the sample) underwent change towards a less rigid division of labour within the household, while only 7 families did not. (Three households could not be assessed, either because they had been unemployed for such a prolonged period, or because they had recently married.) Economic change and male unemployment reduced the comparative advantage of women in domestic work. It was noticeable, however, that whilst there was a relationship between change in the domestic division of labour and hours worked in the labour market by wives, not even when wives were employed full time was there complete role reversal.

There were strong indications that household flourishing could be threatened by the difficulties faced by both men and women through the loss of traditional gender roles. So, for example, women did not wish to give up their roles as mothers, as in the case of Mrs Stirling, a machinist, out at work from 7.30 a.m. to 5 p.m. Although Mr Stirling was responsible for the housework and their three young children while she was out, Mrs Stirling still liked to give the children their supper and see them in to bed. Unemployed men appreciated having more time with their families, and thought it only fair that they should undertake household tasks: 'I cannot expect the wife to come in and do it after a full day's work, and after all, I'm in the house all day and I'm not going to sit on top of muck, I'm not going to neglect me bairns,' said Mr Stirling. However, men accustomed to being the main economic provider in the household found it very difficult to cope with the unaccustomed leisure time, and many discovered themselves understanding why their wives had wished to go back to work even though – in the view of some – 'it should be the bloke out working and the woman in the house' (Mr Stirling again). The strength of traditional gendered values meant that both women and men could be instrumental in the failure to develop the male human capital required to undertake 'bottoming' (pulling out the furniture for a thorough vacuum and clean – 'she'll not let us do that' says Mr Stirling) and ironing in particular, though also the washing.

The compromise solution that preserves household flourishing, but puts limits on the response to changes in comparative advantage, may be to share domestic and child-rearing tasks between husband and wife. Mr and Mrs Kidd provide a good example. Mr Kidd shared three major domestic tasks with his wife (making the main meal, vacuuming and shopping) and did two on his own (decorating and – uniquely for the men in the sample – ironing). Mrs Kidd worked 20 hours a week, and sharing was confirmed by her description of a typical day:

'I go out to work at 8 a.m. and have a bacon sandwich [Mr Kidd has made it] when I get in. Then we tidy up, with a few cups of tea in between and then have dinner. We put the washing in. He washes up and I prepare the tea [i.e. the main meal]. He makes me a cup of tea before I go out to work. He puts the tea on, we have tea at six, and he washes up.'

For this – and other – households, sharing tasks is important but natural. Mr Kidd says of men doing housework: 'It's a good thing now. Times have changed; it was always women's work. They should both share.'

Source: based on Wheelock, 1990, Part II

Question

To what extent does the NHE provide an explanation for the behaviour described?

You will probably have noticed a number of resonances with the NHE model in this case study. Certainly, unemployed men have more time, while their employed partners have less. These changes in the opportunity cost of work in the home for women suggest that falling comparative advantage in market work is part of the explanation of the shift to non-market work by men.

However, the key issue is not so much that some households share tasks, but rather the attitudes they take to sharing and why there is not more role-reversal and specialization as the NHE model would predict. And why are some tasks shared and not others? The meaning given to being a breadwinner versus being a home-maker is something that the NHE model does not recognize, nor does it see that some households might prefer to share tasks. Further, in common with other aspects of neoclassical economics, it fails to take account of how

household preferences are formed. For this we need a broader, more institutionally focused approach.

 4 THE INSTITUTIONAL ECONOMICS OF THE HOUSEHOLD

The institutionalist label can be applied to a range of economists and sociologists whose work amounts to a set of 'variations on a theme' rather than a single coherent body of knowledge. Chapter 1 introduced two types of institutionalist approach in economics: an interdisciplinary approach, which considers a variety of social influences on people's behaviour; and a 'new' institutionalism, which assumes, as neoclassical theory does, that individuals are self-interested and rational. Chapter 6, Section 2, will explore ways in which the New Home Economics can be justified in terms of the rational, self-interested behaviour of individuals. Interdisciplinary institutional economics is generally traced back to the work of Thorstein Veblen in the USA at the turn of the century. Chapter 3 explored his theories of conspicuous consumption, but his wide-ranging enquiries spawned a number of institutional theories.

Here we want to consider what light an interdisciplinary institutionalist approach can throw on household behaviour. This approach regards the preferences, resource endowments and technology of the household as endogenous to, or formed within, the socio-economic system (see Chapter 1, Section 3). So, too, are the social relationships among, and the motivations of, individual household members. The implication is that household behaviour is more varied, and more complex, than it is in the NHE model. This section will explore such interdisciplinary institutionalist perspectives on the household as a production unit, using two case studies.

The first concerns an Indian family, and will be used to illustrate the ways in which social and cultural norms and the particular characteristics of the surrounding economic system shape the behaviour of the household. However, there is a two-way relationship between the household and the socio-economic system of which it is a part. The way in which the household organizes itself as a production unit can also exert an influence on those wider social and economic processes. This aspect of the relation between the household and the wider society is examined in the second case study, which concerns small family business households in the UK.

Institutional economists of this school recognize that the forms of social relationships matter and theorize richer forms of motivation than the utility-maximizing rational choice framework of the neoclassical approach. This makes the institutionalist approach particularly suited to analyse the hybrid nature of the small, family firm in which family relationships and the need to make a profit are intertwined (Wheelock and Mariussen, 1997). We shall see later (in Section 4.2) how a distinction between 'substantive' and 'formal' rationality, first made by the sociologist Max Weber, can be useful in understanding how family firms operate. It can also be used to explain some of the competitive advantages and thus the survival of the small family firm, even in industrial capitalist economies dominated by large firms.

4.1   The institutional context of household production

If it recognizes them at all, the NHE model takes social, cultural and political factors to be incorporated in a household utility function which is exogenously determined, and such factors are therefore not explained within the model. Institutionalists start from a view of households as embedded in a greater social whole. Their research agenda is to investigate how those social, cultural and political contexts shape the preferences, opportunities and constraints that face individuals within their social groups and networks.

We can illustrate the difference between these two approaches with a case study of a small farm household in India. Using this example has a number of advantages. The first is that much of this household's production activities are for the household's own consumption. A large proportion of the immediate subsistence needs of the household are provided for directly by members' unpaid work, rather than through the market. Secondly, because of the strong seasonal pattern of production and consumption, we can begin to appreciate the way in which factors outside the household affect decisions about non-market versus market work. Finally, this example allows us

to identify more easily some of the social and cultural constraints that act upon individuals' choices within the household. Of course, social and cultural factors constrain choice in all societies, but it may be easier to identify them first in a society with which we are less familiar.

Production in an Indian farm household

The household that we are going to describe is that of a family farming in the drought-prone region of southern Maharashtra, in western India. The family is an extended family: a widowed mother lives with her three adult sons and the sons' wives and children. Between them the three grown sons and their wives have 10 children, so in all there are 17 people in the household. The family has 6 hectares of land, of which one-and-a-half hectares are irrigated. The rest is rain-fed and therefore very liable to drought and crop failure. Within this region the family would be considered vulnerable, but not suffering from the extremes of poverty.

The family are Marathas, and it is typical of the Maratha caste in this region that, where there is more than one son, the first will be expected to stay at home and farm, and the second will, if lucky, be accepted into the army. That is just what happened in this family, although the second son has now left the army after serving 15 years and has a lifetime pension. The youngest brother was educated until he finished high school in the hope that he would be able to find a relatively high-status, well-paid job as a clerk in a bank or office. Unfortunately this plan did not work and he has only intermittent and very insecure work.

The eldest son spends all his working day farming. Some of the output from this work is sold in local markets and generates a cash income, but most output is for the direct subsistence use of the household. Immediately prior to the monsoon in June this son will also work in the labour market: he hires himself and his bulls out to plough other farmers' fields. The second and third sons also help on the farm intermittently during the peak seasons: ploughing, sowing and harvest time. The second son has economic kudos within the household because of the small but steady pension he brings in. He has social kudos because he was a soldier, regarded as an important profession by the Marathas. His contribution is to deal and trade. He sells output from the farm to meet any cash needs that they might have, and he buys any goods that the household requires. The third son is in a more difficult position. He does not have any of the status of his army brother, he has no pension income, and he has failed to get the type of job for which he was educated. He does help the family occasionally by acting as a bookkeeper to the village milk co-operative. He is not required to contribute home-time work to the household. As a man he is not expected to do domestic work. Indeed the only domestic-related work that a man within this village society is expected to do is to carry water from the well. He can help on the farm at certain times of the year, but is not needed all the time. During the slack season this youngest son finds paid work on a government-run guarantee scheme which provides a very low but relatively secure income.

The situation of the adult women of the household is very different from that of the men. All three younger women spend the majority of their time on unpaid domestic work within the household. They also collect water, milk the water buffalo and look after the small farm animals – goats and chickens. The wife of the eldest son is regarded as the senior woman of the household – the grandmother no longer has this status. The two youngest women do seasonal agricultural field work on their own farm but none of the women works for cash for other people. To sell their labour power in the market would threaten the status of the household: if women from this family earned money income in the market it would indicate to others in the village that they were very hard up. This could threaten other sources of income: for example, by raising questions about the family's creditworthiness if they tried to obtain a loan. To a certain extent this situation is circumvented by women carrying out exchange labour on other farms, a reciprocal transaction, which still allows them to form the large teams needed for certain types of work but without being stigmatized by cash payments. Women may also be paid in kind for specific jobs, particularly around harvest time when they receive payments in grain rather than in cash.

Although all but the youngest three children are at school, they too carry out unpaid home work by looking after animals and scaring birds from ripening crops. The girls look after the younger children and carry out domestic chores.

Seasonality is obviously a significant feature in the production decision of whether to carry out home- or market-oriented work for all the adult members of the household. Seasonality also affects the consumption needs of the household. In a poor year they may not be able to grow enough grain to feed themselves for the whole year. In the period before the harvest they may be forced to purchase grain from the market. At this time, both the younger sons may work on the employment guarantee scheme to earn cash. In a very bad year the eldest grandsons may also be withdrawn from school to help, and even the wives of the younger brothers may be forced to enter the paid labour market. Cash is also needed at certain festival times. For example, at Diwali in November everyone will receive new clothes, and in the wedding season in April and May cash is needed for new clothes and gifts. In terms of the NHE model, we can say that at different times of the year the relative importance of monetary income and non-market work in creating Z-goods that the household requires will change.

Source: based on Oughton, 1992

Question

- What are the different ways in which this household meets its subsistence needs?
- How do factors outside the household influence its patterns of work and consumption?

Consider how social and cultural constraints enter into your answers to these questions.

This household receives monetary income in a number of different ways, through selling farm output, the direct sale of labour, hiring out bulls, and state support (army pension and employment guarantee scheme). Members of the household also provide directly for much of its subsistence needs by their labour on their own farm and women also do domestic work. Finally, barter and payments in kind provide a third contribution.

This case study highlights how households survive on the basis of inputs from a range of sources in both the monetary *formal sector of the economy* and what we can call the non-monetary *complementary economy* (see *Changing Economies*, Chapter 3). The monetarized, formal, sector includes household purchases of goods and services, paid for by the sale of goods and services produced by the household or its members' labour, or by state contributions. Unpriced goods and services, often produced within the household itself, but possibly resulting from reciprocal exchange of labour and gifts between households, form the complementary sector of the economy. All these forms of production require inputs of labour from the household, but each individual may provide different sorts and amounts of labour input to each of the formal and complementary economies.

Formal and complementary sectors of the economy

The formal monetary sector of the economy comprises all market transactions and those involving the state.

The complementary sector of the economy comprises all other types of economic interaction, including the performance and consumption of unpaid labour, and the reciprocal exchange of labour and gifts.

Being aware that economic activity may be located in the formal or the complementary sector highlights the fact that economic agents within the household are wearing a number of different hats in turn, and that for the household to survive and prosper, both market- and home-based production are necessary. It is also possible that production activities may move between the formal and the complementary sectors. The seasonality that affects the livelihood of the Indian household illustrates both how the household shifts the balance of its activities between the formal and complementary sectors of the economy in different seasons, and how individuals change the distribution of their time between the sectors depending upon the time of year.

There is a considerable difference between what these household members actually do, and what

would appear, from the NHE perspective, to be an economically rational division of labour for this household. The household has very little scope to choose the form of production individuals undertake. As a household this extended family has plenty of non-market labour time available to it, but social norms constrain both men and women in how they may use this time, and limit the opportunities available to them. Across the year, individuals make different forms of contribution to their household's standard of living, which are related to the availability of labour and work opportunities, but also to their different age, gender and status characteristics within their particular society as well as to different seasonal consumption needs which are themselves partly culturally determined.

The way in which time is valued varies considerably throughout the year. While the New Household Economics can model the changing opportunity cost of time, the social and cultural factors in which its variation is embedded remain exogenous and hence unexplained. Similarly, the substitutions and complementaries between work in the formal and complementary sectors of the economy can be analysed within the NHE framework, because the idea of *Z*-goods, created by using time together with purchased goods and services, extends across the usual boundary between production and consumption (see Section 2.4). However, the NHE cannot explain how the production of *Z*-goods depends upon social relationships within and outside the household, and gives expression to the range of values which motivate household members.

The NHE model invokes the neoclassical assumption that economic agents are rational and self-interested. This relatively simple assumption is also made universally, so is taken to hold for all types of economic activity, regardless of whether they are carried out at home or in the market, and in all societies, including those as diverse as the UK and India. The institutionalist approach emphasizes a much greater complexity of motivations and organization to achieve household goals. The motivation for economic activity, in both formal and complementary sectors, is recognized as variable and influenced by the cultural and moral climate. The values incorporated in the ways in which households behave in the market may not mesh with the values expressed in production behaviour within the household; indeed, there may even be a clash between these values. Further, institutionalists do not expect a single model of behaviour, such as the utility-maximizing model, to apply across all societies. In sum, the institutionalist approach regards the norms that affect behaviour as being a part of the subject of study, not exogenous to their concerns.

Exercise 5.4

Refer back to the case study of British households in which the man is unemployed (see Section 3.3). Can you identify the ways in which economic restructuring has affected households' and individuals' participation in the formal and complementary sectors of the economy, and the substitutions and complementarities this involves? To what extent have household preferences, and the values these incorporate, changed in the process?

4.2   An institutional model of household rationality

One of the main differences between the NHE and the institutionalist approach to the economics of the household concerns underlying assumptions about the forms of rationality governing economic behaviour. Institutionalists tend to find a lack of depth in the neoclassical conception of rationality, when applied to non-profit-seeking institutions.

The model behind the neoclassical model of rational choice assumes that indifference curves can be drawn connecting the infinite number of combinations of goods which will yield the same level of utility, representing the infinity of substitutions that will bring about the same level of satisfaction. It assumes that any choice between two alternatives can be modelled in this way. However, institutionalists point out that many of the choices which households actually face are not always amenable to this treatment. How much more productive does a new crop have to seem to be to make it worthwhile to give up ways of feeding one's family that have worked in the past? How much more would you have to pay a woman to persuade her that her husband should be the one to stay at home with the new baby? There may be no sensible answers to such questions. According to institutionalists, the unwarranted assumption of endless substitution possibilities between any two goods simply reflects the presupposition of monetary calculation that everything has a price. We can compare the price of any

good with the price of any other, so it is natural to think that we can choose rationally between any two alternatives. Institutionalists criticize the neoclassical model of rational choice as purely formal, in that it is applied in the same way irrespective of the nature of the choices involved, and does not take account of differences in the institutional settings within which such choices are made.

One of the founders of modern sociology, Max Weber, drew the distinction between *formal rationality* and *substantive rationality* in economic action. He called a system of economic activity 'formally rational' '... according to the degree in which the provision for needs ... is capable of being expressed in numerical, calculable terms'. He contrasted this with substantive rationality, by which he meant 'the degree to which the provisioning of given groups of persons ... with goods is shaped by economically oriented social action under some criterion ... of ultimate values'. Substantive forms of rationality do not restrict themselves to ' goal-oriented" rational calculation with the technically most adequate available methods, but apply certain criteria of ultimate ends, whether they be ethical, political, utilitarian, hedonistic, feudal, egalitarian, or whatever' (Weber, 1922; 1968 edn, p.85).

Formal and substantive rationality

Formal rationality is the calculation of the best way of meeting given needs by quantifiable means.

Substantive rationality is the use of particular values to determine actions.

In these terms, neoclassical theory recognizes only formal rationality in that it considers only how the best way of meeting given ends can be calculated, not how those ends are formed, nor how some ends may preclude the calculated weighing up of alternatives that formal rationality requires. An institutionalist approach, however, recognizes that people are motivated by substantive forms of rationality too, which may make certain values override the calculation of interests, and considers how those substantive ends are determined.

The monetary calculations to maximize profit carried out by firms are the purest examples of formal rationality. The New Household Economics assumes that the same sort of rationality applies within the household, even though its ends are the pleasures of consumption rather than financial profit and its means include unpaid household labour as well as the possibility of selling labour on the market. Institutionalist approaches recognize that households are not the same sorts of institutions as firms (in Weber's terms they constitute a different 'life-order', governed by a different ethos of existence), and therefore that the actions of household members cannot be assumed to follow from the same sort of rationality that governs the conduct of actors in a firm. As we saw in the farm household, values concerning which types of work were appropriate for men and women of particular ages determined the work people did, overriding any rational calculation of the most productive division of labour. Indeed, you could say that such values formed constraints within which any model of formal rationality would have to operate. Put like this, it becomes obvious that investigation of how such constraints are formed is vital to understanding how the household operates.

But does this distinction between formal and substantive rationality help us to explain any economic events or processes that might otherwise be puzzling? In order to answer this question, we shall examine a case study of an organization in which both forms of rationality are said to play a part. This is the family firm, which attracted Weber's attention because of its hybrid or 'in-between' nature. At one end of the scale, the giant firm uses the formal rationality of profit maximization in its accounting. At the other end is the household, whose activities are organized in terms of substantative rationality. Between these extremes, Weber found a number of organizational forms, including the small family firm, whose productive activity is not the preserve of solely formal rationality, but is to some extent guided by a different substantive rationality.

In the late 1970s, many commentators prophesied the extinction of the petty bourgeoisie, represented by the small family firm which was widely regarded as a historical leftover. Since then, however, there has been an upward trend in business start-ups throughout Europe and North America (Mason, 1991). In part, this rise can be put down to post-industrial economies in which the service sector – which has a large proportion of small firms – grows more important. High levels of unemployment are also associated with small-firm growth as a symptom of economic decline. More optimistically, small firms are at the heart of the economic success attributed to the flexible specialization of the industrial districts of northern Italy or of

Silicon Valley in California, for example. For a variety of reasons, then, it looks as though predictions of the demise of the small business have been premature (see the case study below).

The economic character of the small business household

In an in-depth study of small business set up during the 1980s in the peripheral local economy of Wearside, the 'economic character' of the small business household was examined against a national policy background which was promoting small businesses and an enterprise culture as the solution to Britain's regional and national competitive problems. The study sought to investigate the extent to which the household of small business owners contributed to business flexibility and success. The research showed that it was the combination of features of the household and the firm in the small business household that provided the key to business survival in a hostile external environment.

Members of these small business households were motivated by a complex of family- and business-based factors. In the sample of 24 households, the monetary rewards deriving from profit-seeking in the marketplace were modest indeed. Only five families saw themselves as distinctly better off as a result of being in business, with a further six modestly so. Even when looking at this group it is important to realize that some were receiving state benefits (unemployment or sickness) when they started their business, so that income levels were still not high. Seven families were actually worse off than they had been, with four having about the same income levels. The small business owner – and often other household members too – was working long hours to obtain an often meagre financial reward.

It was clear, however, that non-monetary reward also played an important role for these households. Although they were putting in long hours, working in the business could provide husband and wife with more time to be together. It could also allow more time with children; for rather more than a third of those interviewed, husbands had an opportunity to take a role in childcare which they might otherwise not have been able to do. For many, being in business gave the personal satisfaction of being in control of doing a good job or providing a quality service. It could indeed be a product which incorporated domestic values. There were several cases where running a business enabled the household to cope with illness, thanks to controlling hours or workload.

Frank and Fiona provide an illustration of how household-based and market-based behaviour are intermeshed in their bookkeeping and accountancy business. They provide their customers – other small business people working long hours – with the opportunity to discuss their accounts in Frank and Fiona's own home over a cup of tea, bringing their children along if they want. It is a far cry from the daunting formality of a city centre accountancy firm, with services only available in office hours. They are both explicit about the way in which their livelihood has become part and parcel of the values they espouse in their lives.

Frank: It also allows us a particular lifestyle which suits us, basically it's very much a mixture of business and home.

Fiona: Almost indistinguishable.

Frank: And it allows me to take part in a lot of home activities, child-rearing, housework and so on and it also allows me to cope with the illness we were talking about earlier.

Small business households on Wearside want to survive in the market. But they also want to play their part in a social enterprise which has two dimensions to it. The first is that they want to be part of a co-operative household, which, though not by any means free of gender-specific roles, is based on reciprocal values. The second relates to the need people have to undertake purposeful work. Small business can provide for personal dignity and an inherently satisfying way of life.

Source: based on Wheelock, 1994

Question

- In what ways do you think the economic character of the small business household is more complex than a neoclassical model would suggest?
- Can you find any commercial advantages in the economic character of the small business household?

Motivation seems to be the main source of greater complexity. Members of the small business household are not motivated solely by the desire to make, let alone maximize, profits. Some values, such as the desire for partners to spend more time together and to share household activities, are equally important. Other values are related more to the business side of the small family firm; for example, the satisfaction of providing a quality service is valued in a way that the profit-maximizing assumption of the neoclassical model of the firm ignores. Indeed, many of these families were actually worse off in financial terms than they had been before setting up their businesses.

So Weber's different types of rationality seem to have some force here. The family firm does have to make a profit, but it also tries to satisfy other values; it combines substantive rationality with formal rationality. It is motivated by substantive rationality in that it has a range of non-quantifiable values that guide its actions, but it does have to follow a certain formal rationality and calculate the best ways to meet its ends if it is to survive.

What about the commercial advantages that the small business household might enjoy? Flexibility is the key word here. Household members are willing to work long hours when necessary, and they are able to make themselves available for consultation with clients outside normal office hours, away from inconvenient city centre locations.

The personal satisfaction from doing a good job and providing a quality service shared by members of the family reduces the need for monitoring and supervision to ensure that employees work as diligently as they are expected to (see Chapter 14). The accountancy firm in the case study enjoyed a significant competitive advantage in being able to reduce its clients' costs as well as its own; being available outside office hours enabled clients to attend without loss of earnings, and the informality of consultations removed the need for them to incur childcare costs. Where the firm's product incorporated domestic values, discussing it in a domestic setting could have marketing advantages too, allowing a personalized customer market to develop (see Chapter 1, Section 3.2). In a number of ways, the commercial advantages of the family firm derive from its ability to integrate activities with pre-existing, ongoing, significant personal relationships.

An institutionalist approach provides us with a set of tools for examining the behaviour of some households dependent upon small business activities, where lives and livelihoods are intimately entwined. Not all small businesses incorporate a household dimension of course, but a recent study of small businesses in Newcastle and Milton Keynes indicates that, in the business sector, family involvement is high in over 40 per cent of firms employing 10 people or less (Baines *et al.*, 1997).

 5 WHERE NEXT?

This chapter has introduced the New Household Economics (NHE), in which the household is represented as a single decision-making unit that aims to maximize a joint household utility function. The development of the NHE model was a major intellectual achievement recognized by the award of a Nobel prize for economics to Gary Becker. One of the model's main innovations is to recognize the unpaid work that goes on within households, and that utility does not derive exclusively from market goods. However, once we realize that *Z*-goods incorporate non-market oriented activities as a source of human flourishing, then we are likely to ask what are the values and meanings that underpin utility.

This chapter has presented a series of case studies, both to illuminate aspects of the NHE model and to draw attention to some of the merits of the alternative, institutionalist approach.

We found that at most we gain an ambiguous understanding of the real world of the household from the NHE model. Although the changes that the post-war era has brought to women's relationship to the household economy can be explained, the model does not take account of how those very changes have disrupted household utility functions. Insofar as economic life is embedded in social and cultural relations, changing values need to be incorporated into the understanding of women's participation in the labour market. This means that it may be adequate to use the New Household Economics model as a starting-point, but, in order to incorporate an understanding of the changes that structure people's values and motivations, we need to move to a research agenda based on an institutional perspective. The predictive worth of the NHE model remains limited because of the central role played by the unobservable variables incorporated in its assumptions: the values and institutional factors that underlie and determine substantive rationality.

 FURTHER READING

Blau, F. and Ferber, M. (1992) *The Economics of Women, Men and Work*, Englewood Cliffs; NJ, Prentice Hall: acquaints students with the findings of research on women, men, the labour market and the household. It aims to enhance students' knowledge of economic concepts and analysis, but in terms which do not assume advanced theoretical understanding.

England, P. and Farkas, G. (1986) *Households, Employment and Gender*, New York, Aldine de Gruyter: also presents research findings on gender and the household, with a view to assessing the relevance of economic theory.

Smith, J. and Wallerstein, E. (1992) *Creating and Transforming Households*, Paris, Cambridge University Press: analyses the household as an institution in the world economy, presenting historical and comparative material showing changes in household organization and livelihood strategies in times of economic expansion and contraction in First and Third Worlds.

Wheelock, J. and Mariussen, Å (eds) (1997) *Households, Work and Economic Change: A Comparative Institutional Perspective*, Boston; MA, Kluwer Academic Press: develops sociological and economic institutional approaches to explain household responses to economic change in contrasting policy contexts, with case studies of urban and rural households in Britain and Norway.

 ANSWERS TO EXERCISES

Exercise 5.1

1 In the industrial countries women spend 51% of the total time expended on economic activities, 66% of which is on non-SNA activities. Of the

remaining 49% of time spent on economic activities, which is done by men, 34% is on non-SNA activities. So the total proportion of time spent on non-SNA activities is:

$$\left(\frac{66}{100} \times \frac{51}{100}\right) + \left(\frac{34}{100} \times \frac{49}{100}\right) = 0.5032 = 50.32\%$$

2 Similar calculations for the industrial countries give:

$$\left(\frac{66}{100} \times \frac{53}{100}\right) + \left(\frac{24}{100} \times \frac{47}{100}\right) = 0.4626 = 46.26\%$$

Thus, just over half of all work in the industrial countries, and just under half in the developing countries, is spent on unpaid activities which do not figure in the UN system of national accounts.

Exercise 5.2

Our table looked like this:

Table 5.1 (completed)

	Substitution effect of a wage rise	*Income effect of a wage rise*
Household income	Up	Up if income is a normal good; down if income is an inferior good
Hours of home time	Down	Up if home time is a normal good; down if home time is an inferior good
Hours spent on market work	Up	Down if home time is a normal good; up if home time is an inferior good

Exercise 5.3

Minnie's production possibility frontier looks like Figure 5.10.

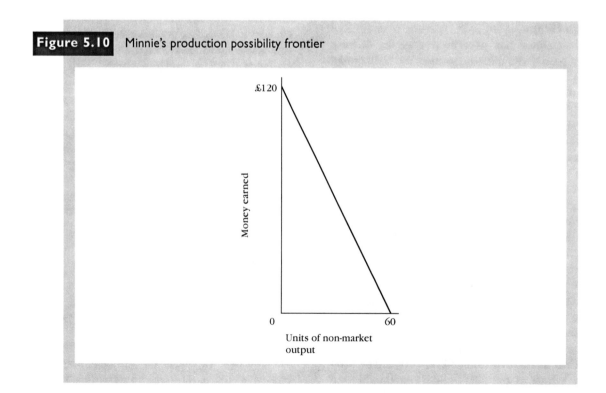

Figure 5.10 Minnie's production possibility frontier

Exercise 5.4

Lower income may lead to household substitution of domestic production (complementary economy) for market purchases (formal economy): men pushed out of paid labour in the formal economy may be drawn into work in the complementary economy within the home; women drawn into employment in the formal economy may undertake less work as home.

There have been some changes in household preferences, best exemplified in the compromise of a 'sharing' form of organization of domestic work. Households preserve preferences for fairness, but both men and women find it difficult to manage the changes to traditional gender values which this involves.

Decision making in households

Susan Himmelweit

Concepts and techniques

Sex ratios

Household's feasible set and consumption possibility frontier

Feasible combination of utility for a household

Altruism

Non co-operative and co-operative outcomes

Threat point or fall-back position

Divorce threat model

Separate spheres model

Measurable utility

Nash bargaining solution

Entitlements

Perceived contributions and interests

Extra-household environmental parameters

Gender-specific environmental parameters

Links

- Whenever economic units are not individual people, a question always arises as to how they make decisions. In the Firms block, issues will arise about how firms make decisions.

- The NHE analysis of an altruistic head of household depends on and extends the neoclassical analysis of consumer choice in Chapter 2. There it was a consumer deciding how to spilt her income between different goods, here it is an individual deciding how to split a household's resources between providing for different members' utility.

- The question of whether we need an objective measure of welfare and Sen's capabilities approach were introduced in Chapter 4.

- The bargaining theories of this chapter could be combined with theories of the division of labour of Chapter 5 to explain how bargaining power might affect who does what in households.

- The bargaining models of this chapter formalize the idea that the outcome of bargaining tends to favour those with the stronger fall-back positions. This idea is influential at various points in the book and used again formally in Chapter 9 in considering contracting.

- Bargaining is an example of the use of game theory. You met a little game theory in Chapter 1. You will meet other examples of game theory at many places in the book including Chapters 10, 11 and 19. The use of game theory is characteristic of new institutionalist explanations.

1 INTRODUCTION

How decisions are made within households is a matter of some importance. It matters to the people within them, and it has profound effects on the way households function as agents in the economy. The last chapter considered one such decision; the choice between market work and home time (including non-market work). To analyse this decision, the New Household Economics model assumed that the household behaved as if it had a single utility function. We are now going to question this rather odd assumption. In the process, this chapter looks at a range of different ways in which households can 'make decisions', from internal bargaining to letting father decide.

This chapter is built around two different types of models of household decision making. Section 2 looks at two explanations of why a collection of people in a household might behave like an individual person with a single utility function, as the New Household Economics model requires. Section 3 – the heart of the chapter – then explores a range of household models which do not see the household as a unified actor. These are bargaining models, which seek to explain household behaviour in terms of contested agreements between household members. Section 4 compares these models along a number of dimensions.

A key assumption in all these models, which is worth emphasizing at the start, is that there are benefits from joint living arrangements which are not available to those living alone. As a result, within the household there are generally gains to be had from co-operation. Models based on a single household utility function see these gains as the reason why people stay in households. The bargaining models all explore how and to what extent such gains from co-operation are achieved and divided within households, given various assumptions about household members' preferences, concerns for others, self-perceptions and chances of life outside the household boundaries.

Throughout, you should bear in mind that households contain people of different sexes and ages and that their power is not equal within the household. Each type of model of household decision making has its own implicit conception of gender, of what it is in economic terms that distinguishes men and women, and what type of power it is that is exercised within the household. Throughout this chapter, I shall be keeping these questions in mind. Section 5 will draw these different concepts of gender and power together, examine their adequacy and consider what else might be needed if economics is to capture the changing yet persistent nature of gender divisions in all economies.

First, however, read the following case study on 'Sex ratios in India' which should give you a feel for the sort of issues which household decision-making models might be required to illuminate. Households have to make decisions concerning the allocation not only of their members' labour but also of consumption goods such as food and medical care.

Sex ratios in India

Although, in most parts of the world, boys have a slightly greater risk than girls of dying before their tenth birthday, in India it has been for many years the other way round, creating a marked imbalance of the sexes among children. This differential seems to be decreasing now, though some of the factors that gave rise to it may still be relevant. Many commentators have suggested that the differential mortality was due to different treatment of boys and girls within the household, in particular unequal access to food and healthcare; boys may be given more and better food than girls, and a girl may have to appear more sick than a boy to receive medical care. In other words, unequal treatment of boys and girls within their households could have been so severe that many more girls than boys died young (Miller, 1981).

However, the sex ratio among children was not, Miller noted, the same throughout India; the 1961 census showed that it varied, not only by class and caste, but also by region (see Figure 6.1).

In the South and East, sex ratios were far more like those of more developed countries, while the highest sex ratios were observed in the North West. (The sex ratio is the number of surviving males divided by the number of surviving females. A high sex ratio therefore means proportionately more female deaths.)

Two other factors showed a similar regional pattern across India. First, the female labour participation rate was very low in the rural areas of the North West, but higher in the centre and moderately high in much of the South, as Figure 6.2 overleaf shows.

A second regional variation in India is in the practice of making substantial transfers of assets between families on their children's' marriages. In the North West, dowries (transfers from the parents of the bride to the groom's family) are prevalent, whereas in the South, bride-wealth (a payment to the parents of the bride) still survives in some castes, although dowries have recently become more common in the South. A significant difference in these practices and in the amounts of money involved remains between North West and South.

Figure 6.1 Sex ratios by district for children under 10 years of age in rural India, 1961 (sex ratio refers to the number of males per 1000 females)

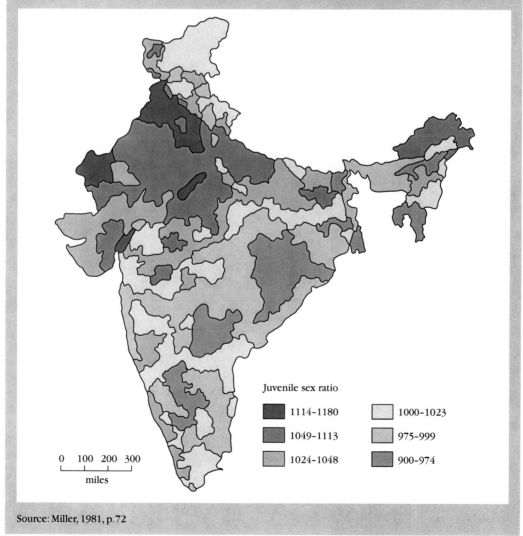

Juvenile sex ratio

1114–1180	1000–1023
1049–1113	975–999
1024–1048	900–974

0 100 200 300
miles

These two factors, female participation in paid employment and marriage payments, have both been suggested as possible causes of the different survival rates of girls and boys. At various points in this chapter we shall return to this case study to examine different explanations for how these factors might affect households' decisions as to how much food and healthcare to allocate to little girls.

2 DECISION MAKING BASED ON HOUSEHOLD UTILITY FUNCTIONS

The New Household Economics examined in Chapter 5, Sections 2 and 3 rested on the assumption that households can be treated as units with single shared preference orderings (and corresponding utility functions) displaying all the properties of consistency and convexity that neoclassical consumer theory assumes

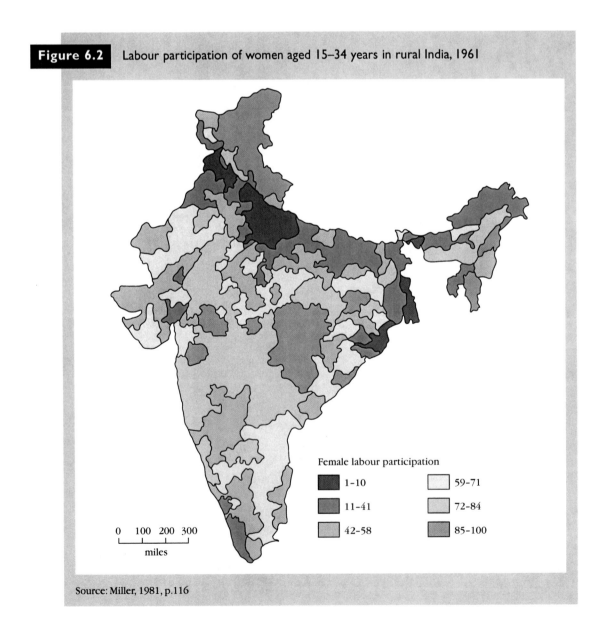

Figure 6.2   Labour participation of women aged 15–34 years in rural India, 1961

Female labour participation

- 1–10
- 11–41
- 42–58
- 59–71
- 72–84
- 85–100

0   100   200   300
miles

Source: Miller, 1981, p.116

for the preferences of individuals. The authors noted that this was a somewhat strange assumption to make, because neoclassical theory is based on individualism: the idea that any theory of the economy should be built up from understanding the behaviour of individuals. Individuals, not groups or institutions, are generally assumed to have preferences which they use to make choices. In this section we shall examine two different justifications offered by neoclassical economists for treating households as if they were individuals. Later sections of this chapter will consider alternative models of household decision making that do not assume a single household utility function.

2.1   Samuelson's family social welfare function

Whether groups of people can be treated as if they were individuals is an issue not only for households but also for any collectivity; for example, a country, a trade union or a business. Paul Samuelson, a highly influential economist who was later to win a Nobel prize for economics, looked at household decision making as only a special case of the general issue of when a collectivity of people with differing individual preference orderings make decisions as if they had a single collective preference ordering. He argued that, because 'blood is thicker than water', families, unlike other collectivities, can be assumed to have the welfare of all their members in mind when making decisions. He saw a household utility function as the result of 'a consistent "family consensus" that represents a meeting of minds or a compromise between them' (Samuelson, 1956, p.9). So, in Samuelson's view, individuals in a household compromise because they care about each other and so, instead of following their own individual preferences, they all act according to an agreed household utility function.

However, this notion that individuals would act according to a utility function different from their own was criticized by Becker, one of the founders of the New Household Economics, for not being consistent with individualism. Becker claimed that if people choose to maximize their household's utility function then this must be what they prefer to do. In other words, their own utility function is the same as the household utility function. So, Samuelson's reasoning behind the existence of a household utility function only works if the household members actually all have the same preferences as to what the

household should do to start with, or change those preferences as a result of reaching a consensus, and does not apply if household members retain their own different preferences. Therefore, Becker argued, the notion of a household consensus does not resolve the problem of how different preferences among household members are in practice reconciled.

2.2   Becker's altruistic head of household and the Rotten Kid Theorem

However, Becker's own analysis also depended on assuming a utility-maximizing household. How did he get over this problem of reconciling different preferences? He did so by showing how, under certain circumstances, all members' actions could be determined by the preferences of just one member of the household, its 'head'. In those circumstances then, the head's preferences effectively became the preferences of the household as whole. But why did the head of household have such power?

Becker assumed that, although people are individual utility maximizers, what gives them utility may include the happiness of others, especially the happiness of others within their family. In support of this departure from the usual assumption of neoclassical economics, that individuals are selfishly interested only in their own welfare, Becker quotes Adam Smith: 'Every man feels his own pleasures and his own pain more sensibly than those of other people ... After himself, the members of his own family, those who live in the same house with him, his parents, his children, his brothers and sisters, are naturally the object of his warmest affections. They are naturally and usually the persons upon whose happiness or misery his conduct must have the greatest influence' (Smith, 1759; 1853 edn, p.321; quoted in Becker, 1991, pp.277–8).

So, recognizing the effects of their conduct on others, men take account of the feelings of those within their households in the decisions they take. Smith and Becker talk of 'men' rather than 'people' here not by chance. I shall explore their reasons for doing so a bit later.

Such a man's utility depends not only on his own consumption but also on that of other members of his household. Thus, for a married couple, U_M, the man's utility, depends on both his own and his wife's consumption. Because U_M is one individual's utility, not the family's, there is not the possibility of disagreement which there could be about a household's utility. U_M reflects the man's preferences alone.

To see this, look first at Figure 6.3, which shows the household's *feasible set*; that is, all the possible combinations of the husband's consumption, measured along the horizontal axis, with the wife's consumption measured along the vertical axis. Strictly, the feasible set consists of allocations of Z-goods to the two partners (see Chapter 5, Section 2.4).

A household's feasible set

A household's feasible set includes all possible allocations of Z-goods to the different members of a household, given the household's resources.

Consumption possibility frontier

A household's consumption possibility frontier is the boundary of its feasible set. It consists of all feasible allocations of Z-goods which use up all the household's resources.

However, to understand why I have drawn the household *consumption possibility frontier* – the boundary of the household's feasible set – with a convex shape, you need to think about two types of goods which households consume. First, there are goods which are consumed individually, such as food, for which more for one partner means less for another. If the household consumed only goods like these, then the consumption possibility frontier would be a

---

Figure 6.3   The maximization of an altruistic husband's utility

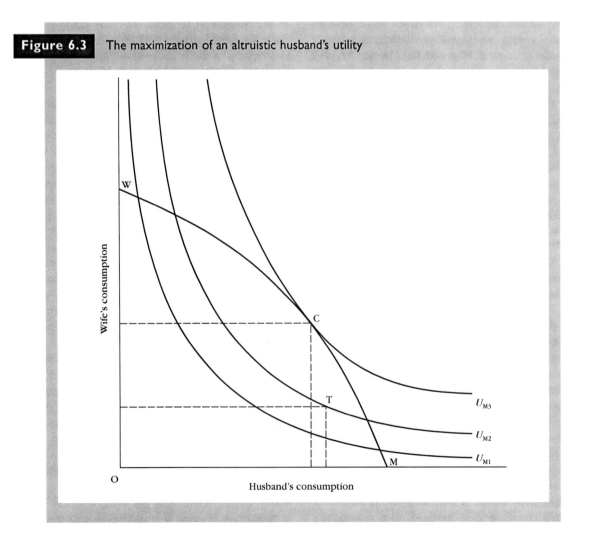

straight line running from W, the point where the woman gets everything and the man nothing, to M, the point where he gets everything and she gets nothing. However, there are also jointly consumed goods, such as housing, which the household consumes; resources spent on these add to both partner's consumption. Provided not all of the household's resources are spent on individually consumed goods, as at M and W, resources spent on jointly consumed goods push the consumption possibility frontier out from the straight line joining M and W, and push it further out the greater the proportion that is spent on jointly consumed goods, giving the consumption possibility frontier the convex shape of Figure 6.3.

I have also drawn on this diagram some of the man's indifference curves, marked U_{M1}, U_{M2}, U_{M3}. Becker would say that this man is *altruistic* towards his wife, because his level of utility depends positively on her consumption as well as his own. If he was not an altruist, his level of utility would depend only on his own consumption and his most preferred point would be M, at which his own consumption level is the

highest possible, without taking any notice of his wife's. But because he is altruistic towards her, he is rather like a consumer who has preferences between bundles of two goods, only in this case the two 'goods' are his own consumption and his wife's. I have drawn his indifference curves so that they never actually meet the axes, like those in Chapter 2, which means that to gain any utility both he and his wife have to consume something. At point W, he consumes nothing and gains no utility, but he also gains no utility at M where his wife consumes nothing. His most preferred point is C.

Altruist

An altruist is someone who gets pleasure from another's well-being.

On Figure 6.4, I have drawn the wife's indifference curves. Because she is not altruistic, her level of utility depends only on her own consumption, so her indifference curves are a series of horizontal lines. Her

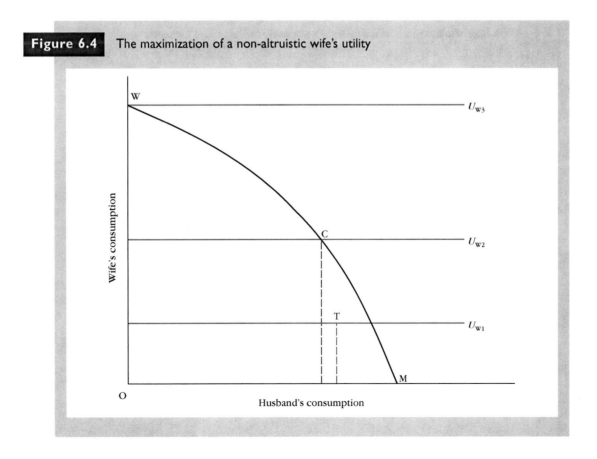

Figure 6.4 The maximization of a non-altruistic wife's utility

most preferred point is therefore W. (I will come back later to why Becker did not need to assume that she was altruistic like her husband.)

From the information on Figures 6.3 and 6.4, we can sketch out all the feasible combinations of utility for the two of them. In Figure 6.5 the utility of each partner is measured along the axes. At W, where the woman consumes the maximum possible, she gets her maximum feasible utility of U_{W3}, and the man gets no utility. As we move down from W, around the consumption possibility frontier of Figures 6.3 and 6.4, redistributing consumption from her to him, her utility falls and his rises until the point C is reached; there he gets his maximum utility of U_{M3} and she gets U_{W2}. After that his utility falls too, because he is concerned about her diminishing consumption, and the pleasure he gets from further increases in his own consumption does not make up for that. By the time we get to M, where he consumes the maximum possible and she is left with no consumption, neither of them gets any utility: she because she does not care about his consumption, and he because he does care about hers and gets no pleasure when she gets nothing.

Exercise 6.1

Think about a household in which neither the man nor the woman is altruistic:

1 On a diagram showing the household's feasible set, draw this husband's indifference curves; identify his most preferred point in the feasible set.
2 Using the diagram you have just drawn and Figure 6.4, draw another diagram, with axes as in Figure 6.5, showing the feasible combinations of utility for this household.

On Figures 6.3 to 6.5 I have marked another point, T, to correspond to how well the husband and wife would each do on their own. T must be inside the consumption possibility frontier because joint consumption and specialization (see Chapter 5, Section 3.1) allows the two of them together access

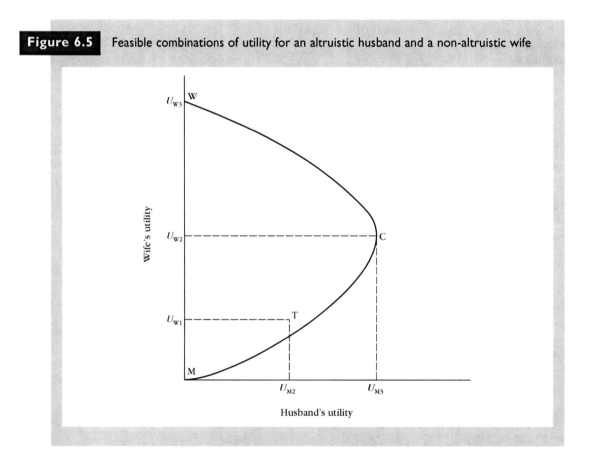

Figure 6.5 Feasible combinations of utility for an altruistic husband and a non-altruistic wife

to greater consumption possibilities than they could manage on their own. In this case, I have put T at a position which implies that the man can consume more on his own than his wife can; perhaps he has a better job. From Figure 6.3, you can see that at C the woman has a higher level of consumption, and thus of utility, than she would have at T. From Figure 6.4, you can see that, although her husband consumes less himself at C than he would have at T, he prefers C because it gives him more utility, through making his wife better off. He chooses to give up some of his own consumption possibilities to enable her to consume more, because that is what gives him most utility.

In the situation represented in Figures 6.3 to 6.5, the wife will benefit from any move which increases her husband's utility (i.e. allows movement on to a higher one of his indifference curves). For example, suppose that the man is offered a better-paid job in another town, but if he takes it his wife will have to take a worse-paid job than she currently has. If his new job brings a sufficient improvement in salary, this is a shift outwards in the household's consumption possibility frontier; the household as a whole has more income to spend, but the distribution of income has changed. As initially put, it implies more income for him and less income for her, but he will redistribute some of the benefits to her so that both of them are made better off. Because he is altruistic, he prefers the situation after redistribution to keeping all the gains for himself. Provided therefore that *he* considers there is some overall gain, his altruism will ensure that they both benefit after redistribution. So the wife can leave the decision as to whether her husband should take the job up to him, because he will decide to take it only if he is better off *after* whatever redistribution between them takes place, and if he still benefits then so will she. More generally, any decision he takes will be on the grounds that it increases his own utility; but because he is an altruist who redistributes some of his gains, this will only happen if her utility increases too.

In this situation, the man's preferences determine the household's choices. Generalizing this to households in which there are more than two people, we can say that when a household has a 'head' who is altruistic and cares about the welfare of others in his family, any decision he takes to increase his own utility will benefit them all. Conversely, anything that decreases his utility will decrease theirs too. In this

situation, it is not in the interests of other members of the household to do anything other than maximize the head's utility.

This result of Becker's, that all members of a household benefit from increasing the utility of its head, has become known as the Rotten Kid Theorem. It says that there is no point being a Rotten Kid, no point doing anything except working for your household's benefit, which is the same thing as doing what Dad tells you, because Dad is altruistic and will redistribute so that you lose out from doing anything else. For example, he may cut your pocket money if you refuse to help with the washing-up. Note that this result depends on Dad being in a position to redistribute towards the other members of his family, otherwise he would not have the power to keep them in line. In these circumstances we can say that the household behaves as if it were a utility-maximizing individual, because what it is maximizing *is* one member's utility. For this to be the case, that member, the 'head of the household', has to be both sufficiently well-resourced and sufficiently altruistic that all the others are recipients of his altruism. Logically, there can only be one such 'head'.

You may feel that this notion of 'altruism' is a rather peculiar one. As Becker says, since this altruist maximizes his own utility, '… he might be called selfish, not altruistic, in terms of utility' (1991, p.279). He acts, as everyone must do in neoclassical theory, to increase his own utility. However, because he is solely concerned about his own utility, he is also not vindictive. When he cuts the Rotten Kid's pocket money, he is not doing so expressly to punish him. Dad is simply following his own preferences, and since these include a concern for the consumption of all members of his family, his utility is maximized by sharing out gains and losses among the whole family.

Neither Becker's nor Samuelson's model really captures the *process* of household decision making. Families rarely sit down together to agree on their set of preferences, nor do fathers spend their time explaining what will happen to members who defy their wishes. Nevertheless, the *outcome* of household decision making may in some ways be as their models would predict. For example, families do redistribute between themselves; members do eat even if they have no income of their own, and not everyone has to do their own washing-up.

Redistribution means that the gains and losses suffered by one member affect all, so that families act as a form of insurance for their members, spreading risk among the whole household. Redistribution reduces both the benefits and the losses of an individual taking a risk, compared to taking all the consequences on their own. Household decision-making models in which a household has a single set of preferences, whether those preferences are those of a household head or are arrived at by a family consensus, do capture this aspect of the household – that it functions in society as an institution which redistributes between its members and so provides some insurance for them; in particular, households redistribute between men and women and between generations. In doing so they form a major plank of society.

2.3 Gender and power in Becker's model

The name of the 'Rotten Kid Theorem' makes one suppose that it is meant to apply to a child, though Becker's own exposition talks of it in terms of the control a man can exercise over his wife. Earlier I said that I believed it was not by chance that Becker talked of the power and altruism of men although, in the model, the 'head of household' does not have to be a man. The model would work as well whatever sex the members of the household were. Nevertheless, it was designed to throw light on the practices of a certain type of household, an 'ideal-type' containing two parents of opposite sex and their children, within which Becker clearly thought of the man as its decision maker. In this sense, his model was built upon an implicit conception of gender relations which it is worth examining here.

In Chapter 5, Section 3.2, you met Becker's explanation of why men were more likely to specialize in market work and thus contribute more income than home time to the household. In calling the man the altruist, Becker seems to assume that the major contribution made to a household is financial. Implicitly then, men are both the breadwinners and – for his model to work – the altruistic main providers for their families; the wives and the children can be altruists too, but the model does not depend upon this.

By implication, for Becker the significant characteristics of men are that they:

1 have a comparative advantage in market work;

2 make the major contribution to households;

3 are altruistic and redistribute towards other members of their families; and so

4 have power over the decisions made by households.

Correspondingly, for Becker, women are those who:

1 have a comparative advantage in non-market work;

2 make a lesser contribution towards their household;

3 are the beneficiaries of men's altruism; and consequently

4 have no decision-making power within their households.

There are a number of criticisms that can be made of these assumptions. First, taking account of time as well as money, it is not clear that men are the major contributors to households; many women have full-time jobs but still do the bulk of domestic work. Nor is it clear that men are particularly altruistic; evidence about the feeding and care of children – that women tend to spend more of their disposable income on their children than men do – would suggest that those with less power may be more altruistic than those with more (Thomas, 1990, 1994). Finally, redistribution between family members is not always the outcome of changes in family circumstances; many studies have found that men hardly increase their hours of domestic work at all when their wives take on employment, although this was not true in many of the Wearside households in which the men were unemployed, examined in the case study in Chapter 5, Section 3.3.

Becker's model depends on the paterfamilias, the altruistic head, behaving quite differently inside and outside the family. In the world outside he is a self-centred individualist, inside the home he is an altruist, concerned about the welfare of others as well as his own; an altruistic Dr Jekyll at home but a self-seeking Mr Hyde outside (Folbre and Hartmann, 1988). Such a view of human nature is held particularly by advocates of free-market economics, because it is hard to justify leaving everything to market forces unless people who cannot look after themselves within the market, such as children, are provided for within their households. The model of an altruistic head of household provides that justification.

However, having an altruistic head does not ensure that the welfare of the other people in the household is adequately maintained. The altruism required of a head of household need only be sufficient to keep other members of his household dependent on him; that is, in a state where what they receive from his 'altruism' is better than they can hope to achieve on their own. That says nothing about fairness within the household, nor the actual level of welfare of its members. All we can say in Becker's model is that the other members of a household, by doing what its head says, are better off than they would be in the next best *currently available* option. But different social arrangements, in which their welfare did not depend on the wishes of their household head, might be much better for them.

2.4   Sex ratios in India revisited

Now is the time to go back to the case study on sex ratios in India and see whether a single household utility function can throw any light on the different treatment of boys and girls within some Indian families (see Section 1). One explanation is that household utility functions may put different weights on the welfare of different members.

> ### Question
>
> What difference would it make to this explanation if the household utility function was:
>
> - following Samuelson, arrived at by a family consensus;
>
> or
>
> - following Becker, that of an altruistic household head?

An altruistic head of household has the power to impose his wishes on the rest of his household. His daughters might well not agree that their welfare is less important than their brothers', but they have no option but to accept whatever his 'altruism' doles out to them. On the other hand, if the household's utility function is reached by consensus, although the daughters may prefer to be treated well rather than badly, they must have sufficiently internalized the idea of their lesser worth to accept that their own level of welfare should have a smaller influence on the family's collective utility than that of their brothers.

Rosenzweig and Schultz (1982), using the idea of a household utility function, have suggested a different explanation that does not rely on any intrinsic preference for the welfare of boys over girls. Rather, they point out that if boys are expected to bring more resources into the household than girls, it would be more efficient for the household to ensure the health and survival of boys than that of girls. As their measure of the resources that children of each sex are likely to bring into the household, they looked at the earning potential of each as adults, effectively therefore ignoring the contribution of unpaid work to the household. The larger the disparity between female and male employment rates, then the larger the difference between their potential contributions to the household and thus, according to this argument, the more utility the household will gain from ensuring the survival of sons over daughters. Rosenzweig and Schultz's predictions are borne out by the evidence in the case study; those regions in which there was a greater disparity between male and female employment are roughly those in which the sex ratio was highest, as Figures 6.1 and 6.2 showed. In Section 3.7 of this chapter we shall examine an alternative explanation of this observation.

> ### Exercise 6.2
>
> Can you think of a similar argument that can be made within this framework about the influence of marriage payments on the different treatment of boys and girls?

 3   CO-OPERATIVE AND NON-CO-OPERATIVE HOUSEHOLD DECISION MAKING

In Becker's model, only the head of the household has any power. The head takes account of what the other members of his household consume, but he does not negotiate with them. He tells everyone what to do and they accept it because they are better off doing so rather than relying on their own resources. But perhaps men do not have such a monolithic sort of power over the lives of all members of their family; other members may have ways of resisting and negotiating patriarchal power. Perhaps all members of a household can influence, to a greater or lesser extent, what the household does.

This section considers how to model situations in which household members are mutually interdependent in this way. In some models, partners make their own decisions without reference to each other, while in other models they bargain. In all the models considered in this section, the behaviour of each member affects the outcome for the others.

3.1 A model of non-co-operative household decision making

Consider, as one extreme, Mr and Mrs Traditional. As their name would suggest, they follow stereotypical gender roles in their household. Each partner specializes in contributing a particular type of resource to the household: Mr T contributes money, earned outside the household, and Mrs T contributes her time directly to the household. They draw on socially sanctioned norms for this division of responsibilities, in which each partner has their own separate sphere of contribution and each makes all the decisions appropriate to that sphere, without negotiating with the other.

Both have a choice as to how much they contribute to the household. Their shared domestic standard of living will therefore depend on the contributions of time and money the two of them make, so both will be affected by the choice the other makes.

The larger the financial contribution Mr T makes, the higher the domestic standard of living of both him and his wife, but the smaller the amount of money he will have available to spend on outside pursuits; if he contributes a smaller amount they will both have a lower domestic standard of living, but he will have more money for his outside pursuits. In choosing how much of his income to contribute to the household, Mr T has to find a balance between enjoying the increased domestic standard of living more money can buy and using the money for other pursuits. He makes this choice according to his own preferences without considering Mrs T's welfare.

Similarly, Mrs T can choose how much time to spend on housework. If she does a lot of housework, she and her husband will have a higher domestic standard of living, but she will have less time for other pursuits; if she does little housework, they will both have a lower domestic standard of living, but she will have more time for the other pursuits she enjoys. Like her husband, she makes her choice by following her own preferences alone.

I shall call the amount Mr T chooses to contribute financially to the household, without reference to his wife's wishes, his 'own choice' quantity of money. Similarly, I shall call the amount of housework Mrs T

chooses to do in these circumstances her 'own choice' quantity of housework. With Mr T and Mrs T making their independent decisions, the household runs on the 'own choice' quantity of housework combined with the 'own choice' quantity of money.

Once adopted, this 'own choice' combination is a stable way of life. Given the financial contribution Mr T is making to the household, Mrs T does not consider it worthwhile to spend any more time on housework. And Mr T is not prepared to contribute any more financially, given the time Mrs T is spending on housework. The opportunity cost of any further improvements in domestic standard of living is too high for either individual to pay on their own. In other words, the 'own choice' combination is an equilibrium outcome: once in it, neither Mrs T nor Mr T has an incentive to move independently away from it. I will call this 'own choice' equilibrium the *non-co-operative outcome*, because it is the outcome reached when each member of the household takes the other's decision as given.

However, other outcomes are possible in Mr and Mrs T's household. As Section 2.1 noted, one household member inevitably gains from the activities of another. One person cleaning a shared living room cleans it for both residents. Money spent by one on redecorating the hallway also benefits both. There are also economies of scale in two people living together. Two meals cooked together are cheaper than two cooked separately. The implication is that, if one person would agree to contribute more than the 'own choice' amount, this changes the opportunity cost calculations of the other. If Mr T would spend more on the house, Mrs T would find it more worth maintaining. If Mrs T would agree to spend more time at home, Mr T would contribute more financially. If both would agree to contribute to a higher domestic standard of living, then the opportunity cost for each would be lower. They would be prepared to contribute more knowing the other was doing so. Think of this like a club, or like the problem of providing public goods: I may be prepared to contribute a certain amount of my money as a donation, but I am likely to be willing to pay more through a subscription or tax when I know everyone is paying too.

Figure 6.6 summarizes the situation facing Mr and Mrs T; check that you understand how the boxes of the matrix represent the joint outcomes of their individual choices.

Let us now consider each of these outcomes. The top right-hand corner will not be an equilibrium.

Mr T will resent contributing a larger amount of money to the household if Mrs T does only her 'own choice' amount of housework, and will revert to his 'own choice' financial contribution. Similarly, the bottom left-hand corner is not an equilibrium because Mrs T will not contribute a larger quantity of housework with only Mr T's 'own choice' financial contribution coming in, and will revert to her 'own choice' housework. So they will be back in the top left-hand outcome.

The bottom right-hand outcome is a different matter. Because of the shared benefits of domesticity, Mr and Mrs T will prefer to contribute more to the household than their 'own choice' quantity so long as the other does too. I shall call this lower right-hand outcome the *co-operative outcome*, because it is an outcome which requires the two parties to co-operate. This outcome is feasible only if they agree to each contribute the higher amount and believe that the other will keep to the agreement. Both parties would prefer this co-operative outcome to the non-co-operative outcome. So there is the basis for co-operation, but neither will make the choice that results in the co-operative outcome on their own. We summarize this discussion in Figure 6.7 overleaf.

There are good reasons for thinking that members of a household probably can arrive at the co-operative outcome, whether by formal agreement or an informal understanding. The affection that members of a household can be hoped to feel for each other may lead to mutual trust. Since households tend to be set up as long-term ventures, once the co-operative outcome is established members will be deterred from cutting back their contributions by the knowledge that their partners may do the same subsequently. However, if attempts to co-operate break down, then each party reverts to the 'own choice' allocation of time and money.

3.2   Different co-operative outcomes

The simple two-outcome matrix just set out made it appear as though there was only one co-operative outcome. But in fact there is a whole range of different possible outcomes of co-operation. Any outcome in which Mrs T does any more than her 'own choice' amount of housework, and Mr T contributes more than his 'own choice' amount of money, will require co-operation. Assuming that the parties co-operate does not determine which particular co-operative solution they will go for.

Figure 6.6 The choices and outcomes facing Mr and Mrs Traditional		
	Mr T spends only his 'own choice' amount of money on the household	*Mr T spends a larger amount of money on the household*
Mrs T spends only her 'own choice' amount of time on the household	Mr and Mrs T have a low domestic standard of living, but have plenty of money and time, respectively, for outside activities.	Mr and Mrs T have a higher domestic standard of living. Mr T has less money for outside activities; whereas Mrs T has plenty of time to enjoy her life outside the home.
Mrs T spends a larger amount of time on the household	Mr and Mrs T have a higher domestic standard of living. Mrs T has less time for outside activities; whereas Mr T has plenty of money to enjoy his life outside the home.	Mr and Mrs T enjoy a much higher domestic standard of living, but have little time or money for outside activities.

Figure 6.8 represents the feasible set of all possible combinations of utility for this household, both Mr T's utility measured along the horizontal axis and Mrs T's utility along the vertical axis. Figure 6.8 looks like the diagram you drew for your answer to Exercise 6.1, rather than Figure 6.5, because neither Mr nor Mrs T is an altruist (we shall consider later what happens if they are). On this feasible set, I have marked some particular outcomes: T is the non-co-operative outcome, and M and W are the outcomes in which Mr T and Mrs T, respectively, receive maximum utility. (Note that T on this figure has a different interpretation from point T on Figures 6.3 to 6.5, where it represented how each partner would do on their own. Here on Figure 6.8, T represents how they each would do in the non-co-operative outcome. I have used the same symbol for both because I want later to compare the two models from which they come.)

Questions

On Figure 6.8:

- To which points on Figure 6.8 might Mr T be prepared to agree?
- To which points might Mrs T be prepared to agree?
- Which outcomes could therefore be the result of co-operation?

Each partner would only be prepared to agree to points that they prefer to the non-co-operative outcome T; Mr T will agree to points to the right of T and Mrs T to points above T. Co-operative solutions must be agreed to by both partners, so they lie in the shaded area to the right and above T.

Pareto efficient outcomes are those from which it is impossible to make one partner better off without making the other worse off. Some of the points on Figure 6.8 are Pareto efficient. (Chapter 1 defines Pareto efficiency and it is discussed further in Chapter 4)

Questions

On Figure 6.8:

- Which points correspond to Pareto efficient outcomes?
- Why are the other points not Pareto efficient?
- Which of these points could be the result of co-operation between the two parties?

The points along the boundary of the feasible set represent outcomes which are Pareto efficient; from these points it is not possible to make one person better off without making the other worse off. From all other points not on the boundary, by moving up and to the right an outcome can be found which makes both

---

Figure 6.7 Evaluating the outcomes facing Mr and Mrs Traditional

	Mr T spends only his 'own choice' amount of money on the household	Mr T spends a larger amount of money on the household
Mrs T spends only her 'own choice' amount of time on the household	The 'non-co-operative' outcome is reached without co-operation between Mr and Mrs T. Both Mr and Mrs T prefer the co-operative outcome to this one.	Not a possible equilibrium; Mr T would go for the 'non-co-operative' outcome instead.
Mrs T spends a larger amount of time on the household	Not a possible equilibrium; Mrs T would go for the 'non-co-operative' outcome instead.	The 'co-operative' outcome, preferred by both to the 'non-co-operative' outcome, requires co-operation to achieve.

parties better off. The range of Pareto efficient points stretches all the way from W, where Mrs T gets her maximum utility and Mr T gets none, to M, where he gets his maximum utility and she gets none. However, only those on the shaded part of the boundary between W* and M* represent Pareto efficient points which could be the result of co-operation.

Successful co-operation should be able to get the parties to somewhere along that boundary; that is, to make use of all the potential gains of co-operation. The range of Pareto efficient outcomes which could be the result of co-operation is decided by the position of the non-co-operative outcome, which rules out certain Pareto efficient points because one partner or the other will refuse to consider them. However, because there are many different co-operative outcomes, there can still be conflict between the partners as to the actual point between W* and M* on which they should settle.

Exercise 6.3

Consider now a household with an altruistic husband and non-altruistic wife whose feasible set is that of Figure 6.5, interpreting T this time as the non-co-operative outcome:

1 To which points might the husband be prepared to agree?
2 To which points might the wife be prepared to agree?
3 Which outcomes could therefore be the result of co-operation?
4 Which points correspond to Pareto efficient outcomes?
5 Why are the other points not Pareto efficient?
6 Which of the Pareto efficient points could be the result of an agreement between the two parties?

Figure 6.8   A household's feasible set

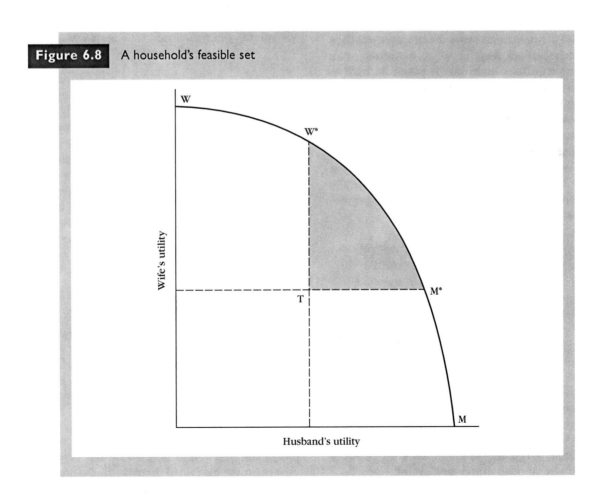

3.3 Two bargaining models of household decision making

If household decision making is a process in which there are gains to be reaped from co-operation but potential conflict as to how those gains should be divided, then there is scope for bargaining between the parties. Bargaining models consider that the main factor affecting the outcome in such a co-operative conflict situation is what would happen if the bargaining process failed.

In any bargaining situation, people are more able to achieve a favourable outcome for themselves when they can walk away if they do not like the outcome. How easily one can walk away depends on what will happen if one does: one's *fall-back position*. Thus, in trade union negotiations, workers have a strong fall-back position when they know, and their employers know, that they can easily get other equally desirable jobs. Workers have a weaker fall-back position in times of high unemployment. Similarly, employers have a stronger fall-back position if it is recognized by all sides that another set of workers could be found to do the work if negotiations broke down. Employers have a weaker fall-back position when bargaining with workers who have skills that it would be hard to replace. The fall-back position of the two sides can also be referred to as the *threat point*, because it is what each side can threaten the other with if negotiations break down. For threats to work they have to be credible. The better the fall-back position of one side, the more credible is their threat of resorting to it; the worse the fall-back position of the other side, the more they will be prepared to concede to prevent negotiations breaking down.

Fall-back position or threat point

The fall-back position or threat point in a bargaining model is how each partner would fare if co-operation broke down.

So, to generalize this idea, we can say that we expect the outcome of a bargaining process to be more favourable to one side, the better that side's fall-back position if co-operation were to break down, and the worse the other side's. The question here is what we mean by the fall-back position in a household bargaining situation. We shall consider two types of bargaining models of household

decision making which differ in what they take to be the relevant fall-back position.

The first bargaining models were *divorce threat models*. These used as their fall-back position, or threat point, how each partner would fare if the marriage broke down and the couple divorced (Manser and Brown, 1980; McElroy and Horney, 1981). Divorce threat models pick up on the idea that the conditions faced by divorced women affect the position of women within marriage. If women fare very badly without a man, this gives men considerable power to set the terms within households. For example, women who previously had nowhere to go to escape violent husbands are helped by the setting up of a refuge for battered women in their area, whether or not they go there, because it improves their fall-back position. The knowledge that their wives have somewhere else to go should make violent husbands realize that to keep their wives they will have to improve their conditions within marriage.

Divorce threat model

Divorce threat models of household decision making are bargaining models whose threat point is divorce.

However, it may be that divorce is not always the appropriate threat point. Even without co-operation, as we saw for Mr and Mrs T, both partners may make contributions to the marriage. So if co-operation broke down, they might nevertheless do better staying in the marriage and settling for non-co-operation. If so, the appropriate fall-back position for bargaining purposes would be the non-co-operative outcome. In the *separate spheres* bargaining model, each partner contributes within their separate spheres determined by traditional gender roles, as Mr and Mrs T did, and the threat point is the non-co-operative outcome (Lundberg and Pollak, 1993).

Separate spheres model

The separate spheres model of household decision making is a bargaining model whose threat point is the non-co-operative outcome in which the partners separately choose how much to contribute from their own gender-specific spheres.

The outcomes of bargaining

Though the outcome is affected by the choice of threat point, the method of determining the outcome in the two models is the same. We can look at this method on Figure 6.9. On this figure, T is the fall-back position or threat point; it could represent the husband's and wife's utilities *either* after divorce *or* in the non-co-operative outcome of a separate spheres marriage, depending on the model. The threat point is inside the feasible set because there are benefits to be reaped from co-operation.

As before, the range of Pareto efficient outcomes runs from M to W, but the existence of the threat point effectively reduces the range of possible outcomes of a bargain to the segment on the frontier from M* to W*. M* is the point at which the man gets all the benefits of co-operation and his wife gets none; W* is the point at which the woman gets all the extra utility arising from co-operation and the man gets none. Allocations outside the segment from M* to W* will not be agreed upon; one or other partner would refuse to agree to an allocation which is worse for him or her than T.

This reduces the range of points, but still does not tell us exactly which one will be chosen. The parties

could come to any decision within this range, depending perhaps on their bargaining strengths or what they both see as the justice of the situation. John Nash (1950), a mathematician and one of the pioneers of game theory, proposed that a particular outcome, which takes account of how much each party gains, would be the rational outcome of such a bargaining situation.

In order to make this claim, Nash had to use some way of measuring how much each partner benefits from any particular outcome. However, when utility functions are simply ways of representing ordinal preferences, there is no immediate method of comparing the amount of utility a person gains from two different changes in their circumstances. There is no way, for example, if Jill likes apples, of measuring how much *more* utility she gains from having two apples than from having one. All we can say is that she prefers two apples to one and one apple to none. However, the Nash solution to bargaining models requires such measurements to be possible. The box called 'On measuring utility' explains how this can be

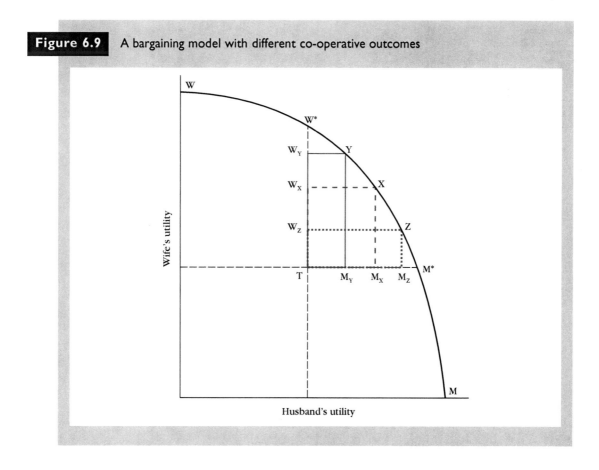

Figure 6.9 A bargaining model with different co-operative outcomes

done in an ingenious way, invented by the mathematician Von Neumann, that is consistent with the ordinal approach to utility introduced in Chapter 2.

On measuring utility

Von Neumann suggested measuring utility gains by considering the utility of bets. He proposed that the utility of a fair bet with an equal chance of any outcome should be taken to be the average utility of its possible outcomes. Using this idea, he would offer Jill the choice of being given one apple or taking part in a fair bet in which she would get two apples if she won, but would get none if she lost. He reasoned that if Jill chose the one apple rather than the bet, then the gain in utility for her from getting one apple must be greater than the gain in utility from the bet. The gain in utility from the bet is the average of the gain in utility of getting two apples if she wins and of no change in her utility if she loses, which works out as half the gain in utility of getting two apples. In other words, if she chooses the apple over the bet, then the gain in utility from one apple is more than half the gain in utility from two apples. If, on the other hand, she preferred the bet over the single apple, then this means that the utility she would gain from one apple is less than half the gain in utility from two apples.

Figure 6.10 shows how this works, with the Von Neumann notion of utility measured on the vertical axis. If we arbitrarily fix U_0 as the amount of utility Jill starts with and U_2 as the amount she would have after getting two apples, then the point A represents getting no apples and B represents getting two apples. The straight line joining A and B represents all possible bets in which she can win either two apples or none; the different points on the line represent bets with different chances of

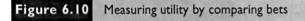

Figure 6.10   Measuring utility by comparing bets

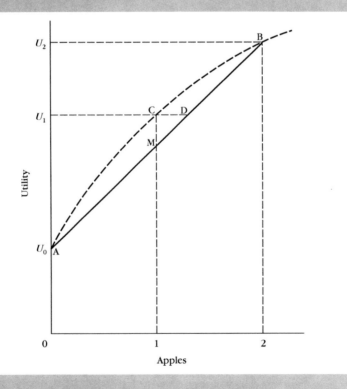

winning. Point A represents a bet with 100 per cent chance of getting no apples and 0 per cent chance of getting two, while point B represents 0 per cent chance of getting no apples and 100 per cent chance of getting two. A fair bet is represented by the midpoint, M, of this line. Bets with a high chance of winning two apples lie near B and have utility near to U_2, but ones with a lower chance of winning lie nearer A and have utility nearer U_0. You can read off the utility Jill gets from any such bet on the vertical axis. Of these bets, there will be just one where Jill is indifferent between taking the bet and being given one apple. Let us suppose that this particular bet is represented by the point D in Figure 6.10. By assumption, taking this bet will give Jill the same utility U_1 as she will derive from receiving one apple, which we can therefore mark as the point C. By this process of comparing bets, we can measure how much Jill's utility increases when she is offered any quantity of apples between zero and two, and so draw the utility function ACB, the dashed curve in Figure 6.10.

Using this procedure of comparing the utility of bets enables us to derive a measurable notion of a person's utility which is consistent with the ordinal concept of utility developed in Chapter 2. Note, however, that although this gives meaning to the measurement of changes in *one* person's utility, we cannot make such comparisons across different people's utility.

Using such a notion of measurable utilities, how much utility does each party gain from a particular outcome? Look back now at Figure 6.9, where a number of different possible outcomes are marked. At point X, the amount the man gains from the bargain is represented by the distance from T to M_X, while the amount the woman gains is represented by the distance from T to W_X. An outcome more favourable to the woman, such as Y, generates the tall thin rectangle TW_YYM_Y of gains, while one less favourable to her, such as Z, generates the low, long rectangle TW_ZZM_Z of gains. The man, on the other hand, prefers Z to Y.

Nash claimed that the outcome which produces the rectangle with the largest area was the one on which a pair of rational bargainers would agree. This solution has a certain intuitive appeal: it is one way

of specifying the best joint gains two bargainers can extract from co-operation. Nash himself argued for his solution by showing that it satisfied certain criteria for rational bargaining behaviour which he thought uncontroversial. Subsequently, his criteria have proved controversial, but the Nash bargaining solution is still used in a number of models, including the classic accounts of the divorce threat and separate spheres household bargaining models (Manser and Brown, 1981; McElroy and Morney, 1981; Lundberg and Pollak, 1993).

On Figure 6.11, I have marked the *Nash bargaining solution* as N. It is the result of maximizing a function, like a household utility function, but with a different interpretation. Instead of maximizing utility, this household reaches a bargain, the outcome of which is the same as if it had collectively decided to maximize a function whose value was found by multiplying its members' gains from co-operation. The Nash bargaining solution, N, is the point which maximizes this function. The important point to note is that what each player gets at the threat point, T, affects this function and therefore the outcome of bargaining, N. The threat point, or fall-back position, first of all rules out all but a particular set of outcomes, and then determines which point is actually chosen. This is quite different from the household utility function which depends only on what household members actually get and does not take account of how people would fare under other conditions.

Nash bargaining solution

The Nash bargaining solution is the outcome of bargaining that maximizes the product of players' gains from co-operation.

Exercise 6.4

Experiment with moving the threat point in order to see its effect on the bargaining solution. On Figure 6.11, mark a different threat point T' at which the woman is better off and the man worse off than at T. What is the range of possible outcomes of bargaining now? And where approximately does the Nash bargaining solution N' now lie? How does the outcome compare with the Nash bargaining solution N when T was the fall-back position?

Figure 6.11 The Nash bargaining solution

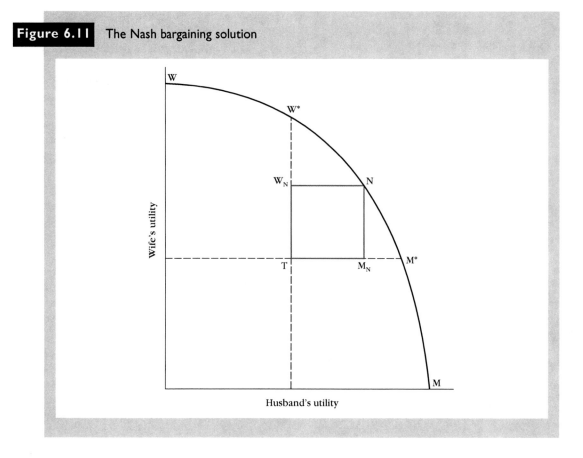

3.4 Dividing resources within a marriage

In bargaining models, who owns and controls household resources matters whenever it affects the threat point, because the threat point influences the outcome of the bargaining process. This is different from models with a single household utility function in which all the resources of the household are allocated together, independently of to which individual they belong. The case study 'Paying for children in the UK' illustrates these differences between the models.

Paying for children in the UK

In 1975, the UK Child Benefit Act abolished the Child Tax Allowance, an allowance against tax that went to the main tax payer of a family (usually the father) and replaced both it and the existing Family Allowance with a roughly equivalent cash allowance, known as Child Benefit, which was paid directly to the person responsible for the child, assumed to be the mother. When parents separated, whichever parent had custody of the child received the Child Benefit; again this was usually the mother.

This was a controversial move, which was phased in carefully so that it would not take full effect until 1979, because politicians were wary of its effects on male wage packets. One MP expressed his reservations as follows: '... far from a new deal for families, it will take money out of the husband's pocket on the Friday and put it into the wife's purse on the following Tuesday. Far from being a child benefit scheme, it looks like being a father disbenefit scheme' (UK, House of Commons, *Hansard*, 13 May, 1975).

The different models we have considered so far predict different results of a switch of resources within the household from the man to the woman.

Question

According to a model with a single household utility function, what would be the likely effect of the changes brought in by the Child Benefit Act on the distribution of household resources?

A single household utility model would predict no change in the distribution of resources, since neither total household resources nor the household utility function has changed.

In the bargaining models, the effect of switching Child Benefit from the father to the mother depends on what happens at the threat point. In the divorce threat model, the threat point or fall-back position reflects what happens if the couple divorces. Both before and after 1975, it was the usually the woman who got custody and therefore any benefits payable in respect of children.

Question

In the divorce threat model:

- What effect do the changes brought in by the Child Benefit Act have on the fall-back position of husbands and wives?
- What would the model predict the outcome of the Act to be on the distribution of household resources?

Again, the Act makes no difference because the total resources available to the household have remained unchanged and the fall-back position is unaltered by the Act, since it did not change the position of parents on divorce. Who actually receives the resources within the marriage does not matter; it is only what would happen on divorce that affects the outcome.

In the separate spheres model, it is not the position after divorce that provides the threat point, but what would happen in the non-co-operative outcome of a separate spheres marriage, in which the partners kept to their gender-specific spheres of contribution to the household. In this case, the woman would not be expected to make any financial contribution to the household, so any Child Benefit she received would be hers alone.

Question

In the separate spheres model:

- What effect do the changes brought in by the Child Benefit Act have on the fall-back position of husbands and wives?
- What would the model predict the outcome of the Act to be on the distribution of household resources?

In the separate spheres model, the fall-back position is the non-co-operative outcome, which *is* affected by who receives the Child Benefit. If the man receives the Child Benefit, he may contribute some of it to the household, but if the woman receives it she will keep it and spend it as she chooses, because she is not expected to contribute financially to the household. This is not, of course, what the separate spheres model actually expects to happen, because the two should be able to reach a Pareto efficient co-operative outcome. But this outcome will be influenced by the fall-back position. The woman's fall-back position in this model is improved by paying her the Child Benefit, which she can then rely on. So the separate spheres model would predict the outcome of household bargaining to be more favourable to women after the Act than before.

So we can see that the different models predict different results from such a transfer of resources from men to women. Lundberg *et al.* (1995) used the UK *General Household Survey* to analyse households' spending on women's clothing relative to men's in the years following the Act. Clothing is a good commodity to observe because, unlike many other items of household expenditure, you can tell whose it is. Holding expenditure on men's clothing constant, it was found that the average household spent £54 more on women's clothing after the Act. It was also found that expenditure on children's clothing rose even more than that on women's, suggesting that women chose to spend much of their Child Benefit on their children. The researchers interpret this both as evidence in support of the separate spheres model and as evidence that the

Child Benefit Act had succeeded in its proposers' intention of redistributing household resources towards women and children.

The rigidity of roles in the separate spheres model provides the rationale for switching the child allowance from the man to the woman. This may explain both the strong support for these measures by feminists and the poverty lobby, who claimed that it would help precisely those women who might most need some cash in their own hands, and the resistance from some men, the most traditional of whom would find their control of household resources eroded by the measure.

Exercise 6.5

Ten years later, in 1985, a social security review recommended a shift in welfare spending away from non-means tested benefits, such as Child Benefit, towards benefits targeted more at poorer households. Consequently, the government froze the level of Child Benefit, so that it no longer would be uprated for inflation and its value fell in real terms.

Using each of the models discussed (i.e. single household utility function and the two bargaining models), assess what the effects of a cut in the real value of Child Benefit would be on the household distribution of resources within the household.

3.5 Perceptions in the co-operative conflict model of the household

Amartya Sen, whose critique of utilitarianism you met in Chapter 4, has also written about households as sites of *co-operative conflict* (1990). He became interested in issues to do with the allocation of resources within households through his work on famines in India and elsewhere. He found that people who starved during famines often did so not because of a general lack of food but because they lacked 'entitlement' to food. He then extended this idea of entitlement to allocations within the household. A person's *entitlement* is defined as the resources to which that person has legitimate access. In the marketplace, it refers to what people initially own or can produce themselves, or what they can achieve by exchange. Within the household, processes of entitlement are less clear-cut; however, people are perceived through custom and practice to have rights to make certain claims on

household resources. When those entitlements are weak, they will get a lesser share of household resources than when they are strong. Though entitlements within the household may have no legal force, they are legitimized through customary norms and practices, and such entitlements may be just as effectively enforced as if they were laid down by law.

Entitlement

A person's entitlement is the resources to which that person has legitimate access.

Sen saw entitlements within a household as the result of a bargaining process in which family members have different interests and different bargaining powers in achieving them. He suggested three factors that might affect the bargaining position of participants and thus their eventual entitlements:

1 how well-off each member would be if the co-operation broke down;

2 the extent to which the different members bargain for their own material welfare;

3 how much each member of the household is perceived to contribute to the household's resources.

In recognizing the first of these factors, Sen was following the same track as that taken by the bargaining models we have considered so far. However, he rejected the Nash bargaining solution because it did not take account of the way in which people's perceptions affect their bargaining strength. He saw people's perceptions, not just their material situation, as affecting the result of bargaining, and thus their entitlements.

Perceptions of the interests of each party

Sen rejected the neoclassical view that welfare is purely subjective and cannot be measured objectively. That, as you may recall from Chapter 4, was why he developed his notion of capabilities, to provide an alternative, more objective, notion of welfare to that of utility. The important aspect of this for discussing household bargaining is that Sen was saying that we require a notion of 'material welfare' that is not necessarily the same as that person's own perception of their own interests. If we keep the term 'utility' for people's perceptions of their interests and counterpose this to their 'material welfare', we can explore his argument further.

People may not see their own material welfare as the most important thing to achieve; they may, for example, put their children's health before their own, or put preserving customary norms of hospitality before getting enough to eat. If this is the case, then individuals within the household will have utility functions and thus bargain for whatever they perceive as their interests, rather than their own material welfare.

Although such a distinction between the interests that drive people's behaviour and their material welfare may be useful in other contexts, it has particular pertinence within the household where people's identification with their family may mean that they do not have a completely separate notion of their own individual welfare. In particular, a sense of obligation to others and of behaviour appropriate to their position in the family may influence people's actions and the goals they pursue. Bargaining behaviour, like other behaviour, is governed by people's perceptions of their interests, their 'utility'. Household members will bargain for their perceived interests, and the outcome will be a compromise between those perceived interests. How much material welfare that gives each partner will depend on how much their own material welfare figures in their perceived interests, in their utility function. Other things being equal, the more their own material welfare figures in their own utility function, the better the outcome will be for them in terms of material welfare.

The argument for separating the notions of utility and material welfare is strengthened by the recognition that habit and social custom are involved in constructing people's perceptions of their interests; for example, women, as a gender, may be brought up to place their husbands' and sons' material welfare above their own. By making a separation between the utility that governs people's actions and their material welfare, a space is opened up in which the construction of people's perceptions and their effects on the actual material welfare of people can be discussed. People bargain in utility terms, for what they perceive as most important, so a woman who perceives her son's health to be more important than her own will bargain for that. If she does not put much importance on her own material welfare, and no-one else does either, it will not figure highly in the outcome. Within the household, Sen argued, the less

importance people put on their own material welfare, the worse the outcome of the household bargain will be for them according to any objective measure of that welfare.

Perceived contributions

Sen also suggested that perceptions affect entitlements in another way, through the contribution that each member of the household is perceived to make. The more a person is perceived as contributing to the household, the greater is their legitimized claim on its resources. It is the *perceived* rather than the *actual* contributions that matter. Perceived contributions of different members of a household may be very different from the number of hours of work done. Indeed, given the close co-operation of household production, it may be impossible to say who is actually producing what. This is not, however, apparently so true of financial contributions. Even if a man can only earn his wages through the indirect support of others in his household, the wages are paid to him and so his contribution to the household is universally recognized. An illustration of this is the finding by Jan Pahl (1995), in her research into the financial management systems of UK households, that men tended to have more personal spending money than their wives, reflecting relative perceptions of financial and domestic contributions to the household.

It is not just whether a contribution is financial or not that determines the perception of it. Maria Mies found, in her study of women who made lace in Narsapur in India, that the location of this activity in the women's homes led to it being seen as just a spare-time activity, weakening the women's bargaining position, not only with respect to their employers but also within their households (1982, p.172). It may be that the perceived contribution depends as much upon the status of the person making the contribution as the nature of the contribution itself, and the lower the status of women, the more difficulty they and others in their household have in recognizing their contribution. Dwyer and Bruce, surveying the literature from many parts of the world, found that gender ideologies commonly 'support the notion that men have a right to personal spending money, which they are perceived to need or deserve, and that women's income is for collective purposes' (1988, pp.5–6).

Given their fall-back positions, perceived contributions may affect the relative power of men and women to bargain for an outcome favourable to their interests. However, the Nash bargaining models we have looked at so far do not accord any significance to the size of each partner's contribution except as it affects the threat point. However, perceived contributions may well affect perceptions of the threat point; if a woman perceives herself to be contributing very little to a household, she will also consider her fall-back position to be weak. Taking account of the fact that the threat point itself is a matter of perception rather than reality could be one way to bring the factor of perceived contributions into this framework.

The divorce threat model captured well the effects of individuals' opportunities outside the household on their bargaining position within it. Provided we take account of the distinction between perceptions and reality, both in terms of people's interests and what they imagine their possibilities are outside the household, such a theoretical model can be modified to capture partially the perceptual factors that Sen saw as affecting people's bargaining power. However, building a model which can be used empirically to take account of those perceptual factors is much more difficult, for by their nature they are hard to measure.

3.6 Gender and power in household bargaining

Bargaining models of household decision making do not have to be interpreted as claiming that husbands and wives openly pit their bargaining strengths against each other. Rather, the habits and customs of a particular society and current ideas of legitimate deserts will play a part in determining the outcomes of such bargains, so that they are not in general seen as the imposition of the wishes of the strong upon the weak, but perceived as legitimate by all the members of the household.

It may well be that a woman secures her longer-term position better by giving less weight to her own material welfare and more to that of other members of her family, and accepting that her share is less for so doing. If the woman has more to lose from marriage failure than her husband, and also has an interest in the long-term prospects of her children, it may be in her interests to accept such inequality in order to keep the household together and for her children to prosper. In this way, we have a self-reinforcing system of inequality, in which her preferences and corresponding actions transmit the inequality she suffers into future generations.

Of course, this can also be put the other way round. Men benefit by giving more weight to their own material welfare. The problem for a woman is not necessarily that she thinks too little of her own material welfare, but that he thinks too much of his. The system of inequality is one which produces the preferences of both genders in ways which perpetuate that system.

It may also be in a woman's longer-term interests to favour her sons' welfare over that of her daughters and herself, because if the sons will eventually be more powerful, it is more important to foster their loyalty to her than that of her daughters. In doing so, she is perpetuating gender inequality into the next generation. Whether you see this as a sensible investment in her own future or a manifestation of the humiliating effects of dependency, this inevitably weakens her and her daughters' current bargaining position. In a society in which there are few ways for a woman to survive except in the household of a man, it is not surprising that women develop strong 'preferences' for their men's material welfare, which men do not need to reciprocate. Women and men learn to internalize the inequalities of their society in the gendered structures of their own preferences (Kabeer, 1994).

The factors that affect bargaining positions within the household were called by Marjorie McElroy, one of the originators of the divorce threat model, *extra-household environmental parameters (EEPs)* because they came from outside the household but affect the bargaining power of people within it. Among the EEPs she lists are the chances for both partners of making another marriage, the material circumstances of the households in which they would live if their marriage broke up, the existence of state support for single parents, any tax changes that would result from divorce, the current law and practice with respect to divorce settlements, and so on.

Extra-household environmental parameters (EEPs)

Extra-household environmental parameters (EEPs) are factors from outside the household that affect members' bargaining power within it.

Nancy Folbre (1997) points out that many of these factors are gender specific at any given time and place; these she suggests we call *gender-specific environmental parameters (GEPs)*. For example, the cost of childcare, the level of child-support payments required of non-custodial parents, and the extent to which they are enforced will have different effects on men and women after divorce, because in most western marriages women are the ones who become single parents should the marriage fail. In other countries, such as Bangladesh, the rule is that women relinquish custody of children on divorce; however, this is frequently enforced only if they remarry (Kabeer, 1995). All these rules, and the extent to which they are enforced, are GEPs that affect women's bargaining power in the divorce threat model.

> ### Gender-specific environmental parameters (GEPs)
>
> Gender-specific environmental parameters (GEPs) are EEPs that affect the position of one gender more than the other.

GEPs can apply in the separate spheres model too. Paying Child Benefit to married women rather than their husbands changed a GEP in the separate spheres model, though not in the divorce threat model. Reducing the amount of Child Benefit, however, changes a GEP in both models. Similarly, setting up the Grameen Bank in Bangladesh, to enable women to get small-scale credit on their own behalf, changed a GEP to the benefit of women according to both models. In this case, women were empowered within their households by a change in the opportunities open to them in the wider economy (Folbre, 1996).

The factors that determine bargaining strength include various aspects of women's and men's lives, and some changes may affect a number of factors simultaneously. Access to outside employment, for example, may not only immediately improve a woman's fall-back position, but also increase the perceived contribution that she is making to the household and, through experience outside the home, give her a clearer sense of her own individuality and the importance of her own material well-being. In the longer term, her bargaining position will be improved through the chance to build up marketable skills, making it less necessary for her to put so much importance on her husband's or her sons' welfare and more likely that she will leave a household in which arrangements are unequal. This may in turn affect men's perceptions.

So, to summarize, in bargaining models, men and women:

1 are affected differently by gender-specific environmental parameters, including social norms;

2 may perceive their own interests differently; in particular, they may differ in the importance they put on their own material welfare;

3 may perceive the size of their respective contributions to the household differently; and so consequently

4 will have different bargaining power within the household.

> ### Reflection
>
> Compare the above list with that of the implicit differences between men and women in Becker's model, in Section 2.3. How would Becker's differences affect bargaining strength? What do you see as the main similarities and differences between Becker's single utility function model and the views of bargaining models on the sources of power differences between men and women in the household?

3.7 Sex ratios in India again

Before moving on to compare the models in general, we can consider whether bargaining models throw any new light on the unequal treatment of boys and girls across India.

> ### Question
>
> How, within Sen's bargaining framework, would one set about trying to explain the unequal treatment of girls in an Indian household? What factors would one need to examine?

To explain the treatment of girls we need to examine:

1 the bargaining power of different members of the household;

2 the weight these members put on the material welfare of girls.

For example, for a girl living in a large family, in a part of the country where women have few employment opportunities outside the home, and for whom a dowry will have to be paid if she marries, we can consider each of the people in her household in turn.

The girl herself probably puts some importance on her own material welfare, but she has very little bargaining power. Even if she does a lot of housework, her perceived contribution may be small and her threat point effectively non-existent. Indeed, the knowledge that a dowry will have to be paid when she is older is rather like a negative threat point for her. If she were to remove herself from the household, the others would not have to contribute to her dowry.

The girl's sisters will, for the same reasons, also have very little power and, if affected by a general devaluation of women in their society, may put little weight on her welfare.

Her brothers may put even less weight on her welfare, and they will, as they get older, have increasing power within the household because their potential for employment improves both their perceived contributions and their threat point. The possibility that their future wives will bring a dowry into the household will also strengthen the sons' bargaining power.

Question

But what about the parents? What factors will affect how much importance they each put on their daughters' material welfare?

If the mother puts relatively little importance on her own material welfare, she may put more on her children's. However, if when she is older she will be dependent on her sons, she may see her own interests as more bound up with their material welfare than that of her daughters. On the other hand, she may value the contributions, and potential contributions, of her daughters more highly than her husband does, since it is her labour that is lightened by their domestic work.

The father may put more importance on his own material welfare and so less on his wife's and children's and, for reasons similar to those we considered for Becker's model, may put particularly little importance on the daughters' material welfare.

Question

Which factors will affect the relative bargaining strength of the girl's parents?

An important factor influencing the parents' relative bargaining strength will be the disparity in their employment opportunities, affecting their threat points and the perceived contributions each makes. Women will have least bargaining power in areas where the disparity between women's and men's employment prospects is greatest.

The bargaining approach comes to a similar conclusion to the single household utility function approach on the causes of the inferior treatment of girls, but for different reasons. Rosenzweig and Schultz (1982) argued that the expansion of employment opportunities for women would lead directly to better treatment of girls, as potential earners. Nancy Folbre (1984), in a critique of their work, points out that we should not assume such automatic causation; in a bargaining model, the causation is more indirect. A shift in relative employment opportunities favouring women will have effect through empowering those members of the household who value the welfare of girls and/or inducing others to do so. Similarly, the payment of dowries affects the position of girls, not only as a cost on the household incurred by raising daughters rather than sons, but also because it gives sons greater bargaining strength than daughters have within the household.

 4 THE MODELS COMPARED

In this section, we shall look again at the different models of household decision making (Becker's household utility function model and the two bargaining models) to compare them by the following criteria:

● how decisions are made;
● the distributional outcomes;
● factors that affect the outcome;
● whether and how control of resources matters.

4.1 The methods of decision making

One major difference between the two types of models is what happens to the less self-centred member of the household. In bargaining models, the woman who puts less importance on her own welfare receives the worse deal; in Becker's model, the altruist man gets everything his own way. How can we explain these different outcomes?

The real difference between the two models lies not in who is the altruist, but in the decision-making rule involved. In Becker's model, the head of the household makes all the decisions for the household according to his own utility function. He chooses the point that gives him the most utility, which is point C on Figure 6.5. His wife can only take it or leave it because, if she thinks about going for any other point, she knows her husband will redistribute in a such a way that she ends up worse off. So the only question for her is whether she is prefers C to T, the point that represents how she would fare on her own. If she prefers C, then she is better off doing what he says, because this household operates on the principle that he gets to decide, or rather that he makes the only offer on the table. If she prefers T, then she is better off on her own. Since she is not given any other choice, if she is worse off at T than at C, she will do what he says and act to maximize his utility. All that the man's altruism does is open up a

space between C and T, so that the allocation he decides on is one that his wife chooses to accept.

Bargaining models assume that the household operates on a different principle in which both partners participate in the decision making. Both partners are able to bargain and the difference between men and women resides in their bargaining power and/or their willingness to bargain for their own interests, rather than in who makes the decisions.

4.2   *The distributional outcomes*

To compare the models' outcomes, we need to represent a household whose members have similar preferences and face similar alternatives in the two frameworks. If we do this we find that, for the same set of preferences, the woman may gain more utility through bargaining than by just accepting what her husband says. To compare the two models, we can interpret T on Figure 6.12, the outcome of the two parties going it alone in the Becker model, as the threat point in a bargaining model. On Figure 6.12,

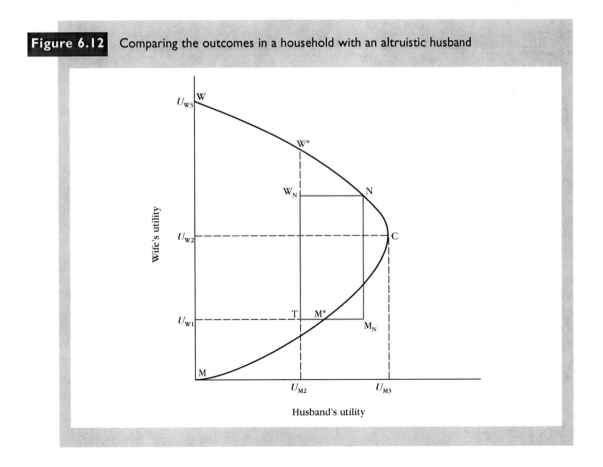

Figure 6.12   Comparing the outcomes in a household with an altruistic husband

the Pareto efficient outcomes run along the boundary from W to C; points below C are not Pareto efficient because for each such point there is always another point above C which the woman prefers and to which the man is indifferent. Of these Pareto efficient points, only those to the right of W* will be agreed to by the man; he would prefer the threat point to those to the left of W*. So the couple bargain about the range from W* to C, and the Nash bargaining solution, N, will be the point between W* and C that maximizes the area of the rectangle $TW_N NM_N$ (although the diagram looks somewhat different this time because one corner of the rectangle happens to lie outside the feasible set). This point N gives the woman at least as much of what she wants as C, the outcome in the Becker model would give her. She can hardly do worse than at C, the point her husband would choose, since it is one end of the range of Pareto efficient points on which the bargaining process focuses. In some cases, the outcome of the two models will be the same, that is, the outcome of bargaining, N, is at C, but in other cases N may lie between W* and C, giving the woman more and the man less than at C.

Question

Try drawing a similar diagram to Figure 6.12 to show what would happen in the two models if the man was not an altruist, assuming the woman remains concerned about only her own welfare.

In Becker's model, if the man is not an altruist, the allocation that he chooses will be M, which will be worse for the woman than T and she will not consider it worthwhile to stay part of the household (see Figure 6.13).

This can also happen if he is an altruist but not altruistic enough to give her more than her threat point, as in Figure 6.14 where C is below T, so that the woman prefers how she can do on her own to what her husband offers her. In these circumstances, even if altruism is insufficient to incline him to do so, he

Figure 6.13 Comparing the outcomes in a household with a non-altruistic husband

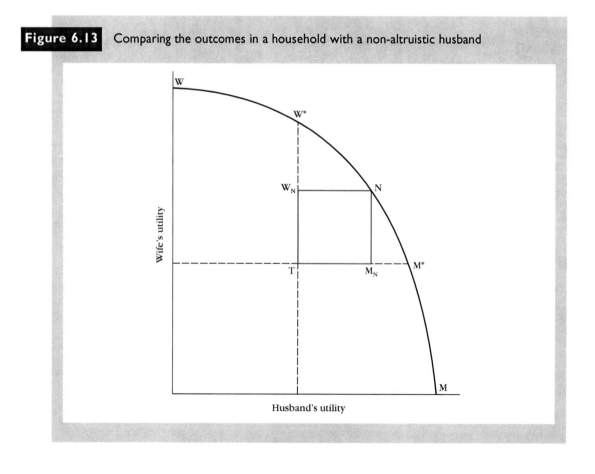

should, if he were sensible, offer her something a bit above M*, which would still be much better for him than T. But this is now moving away from Becker's model into the realm of bargaining. Becker's model only works if one member of the family has the right combination of power and altruism to make it work; that is, to make the other members of his household his beneficiaries.

The woman will not walk out in the bargaining model, because bargaining takes account of threat points. Provided there is some improvement over the threat point of both partners about which to bargain, bargaining models assume that agreement on some co-operative Pareto efficient solution, such as N, will always be reached.

Question

Does the woman always do better from bargaining than from leaving decisions to the man?

The outcome of bargaining will always take at least as much account of what the woman would choose as would be the case if the man only were to make the decision. So the bargaining model will always come up with an outcome at least as close to what the woman would *choose* as the Becker model would. However, this may not be an outcome as favourable in material terms for her; if she puts less weight on her own material welfare than her husband does, she will do worse in terms of material welfare than if she left the decision making up to him.

This is one reason why giving women more power in household decision making may not always work in favour of their material welfare. Bargaining, rather than letting the man decide, will always result in an outcome at least as favourable to whatever the woman thinks is most important – for example, more food for her children – but not necessarily an outcome more favourable in material welfare terms for the woman herself.

4.3 *Factors affecting the outcome*

In Becker's model, external conditions do not change the objectives of the household. Tastes are given, so

---

Figure 6.14 Comparing the outcomes in a household with a not very altruistic husband

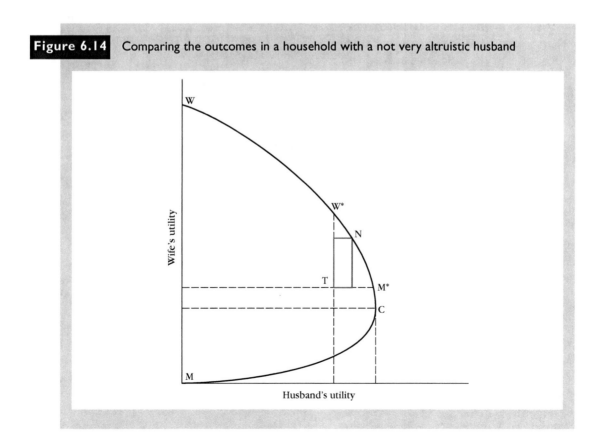

the man's preferences remain fixed and these determine the choices that are made from whatever feasible set is on offer. External conditions, such as the availability of paid work for women, will change the feasible set, but not the preferences that are used to decide what to do within it.

In bargaining models, individual preferences are still fixed, but external conditions can affect the relative bargaining power of the two parties and thus the outcome that is chosen from the feasible set. Thus, for example, the availability of paid work for women not only enlarges the feasible set for their household, but also affects what is chosen from within this feasible set, by improving women's bargaining power within the household.

Bargaining models can be seen as giving the household a sort of utility function, but one which is not fixed, being instead shaped by the bargaining power that individuals have to influence the household's choices. This has a similar effect to the socially dependent consumer preferences considered in Chapter 3, where the utility functions of status conscious consumers depend, among other things, on the price level. As Andrew Trigg pointed out, such dependency of preferences breaks down the separation between a psychologically-based preference sphere and a price sphere located in the market. In the household decision-making case, the separation is between a household utility function and the market which tells the household which choices are open to it. In bargaining models, this separation cannot be maintained because the same external factors that determine the possibilities open to the household often also determine the bargaining power of individuals within it and thus the choices the household makes.

Many of these external factors are the GEPs, the gender-specific environmental parameters that influence men's and women's fall-back positions, inside or outside marriage. These, such as gender-specific employment practices and legislation, the extent and quality of childcare provision, state support for single parents, and laws concerning divorce and remarriage, are the institutional factors that provide the background against which bargaining takes place and influence its outcome. In Becker's model, these GEPs are relevant only in so far as they influence the point at which the model

ceases to apply, the point at which the woman decides that she is better off on her own.

4.4 Control of household resources

The models differ in whether and how the control of resources matters. In Becker's model, all household resources are considered together irrespective of who brought them into the household, income is pooled and the main breadwinner decides how it is spent. It only matters who earns what if some member would be better off on their own earnings, since the household would then break up. In an intact household, increases in the husband's income are spent in exactly the same way as increases in the wife's income.

In the bargaining models, who controls resources matters only when it affects the threat point. So, in the divorce threat model, men who would have greater earning potential than their wives after divorce have greater power during the marriage to determine how their joint resources are used, irrespective of who currently earns what. A house-husband will have more bargaining power than his income-earning spouse, if on divorce he could earn £50,000 to her £20,000. In the separate spheres model, as we saw in the Child Benefit example, exogenous changes in the relative incomes of men and women affect the non-co-operative outcome and thus the balance of bargaining power.

In these bargaining models, the different effects of men's and women's incomes on the spending patterns of households (for example, on the nutrition of children) is not explained by assuming that partners spend their own money. Rather, because women's wages would be their own in the fall-back position, higher potential wages give women greater power within their household to influence the allocation of its joint resources. This is true whether the fall-back position is non-co-operation or divorce. In the latter case, income that women would lose if they left the household gives them no extra bargaining power within it.

There is evidence that women's and men's incomes do have different effects on household expenditures. Increases in wives' income relative to husbands' have been associated with a greater share of expenditure going on restaurant meals, childcare and women's clothing; and a lesser share on alcohol and tobacco (Hoddinott and Haddad, 1995; Phipps and Burton,

1992). The results have been beneficial for children as well as women, with improvements in children's health and nutrition and decreases in their mortality (Hoddinott and Haddad, 1995; Thomas, 1990, 1994).

This might seem like reason to reject the income-pooling hypothesis (that all earnings have the same effect) of Becker's model. However, there is a problem in interpreting the evidence. If a woman's earnings rise, it may be because other factors in her life have changed. It may be these other changes that are influencing the different expenditure effects. For example, she may be earning more because childcare has become available, rather than the other way around. Only extra income that is wholly exogenous to the household decision-making process will really provide a test of the income-pooling hypothesis. That was why the Child Benefit example was a good one to analyse.

5   GENDER AND POWER IN THE HOUSEHOLD

As we have seen, every model of household decision making has its own notion of power. In some cases the power resides in the decision making process involved, as in Becker's model where the main bread-winner makes all the decisions. In bargaining models, the process of decision making is more democratic, but power within that process is unevenly stacked to favour those who have better alternatives if a bargain is not struck. Within Sen's version of that model, power is also exercised through perceptions – the way people perceive the contributions they and others are making, their interests, and the alternatives that make up their fall-back position.

All models showed that power within the household can be seen as a result of an advantageous position in the economy and society beyond the household. In Becker's model, the altruist derives his power from his greater resources. In bargaining models, extra-household environmental parameters, many of which are gender specific, affect the outcome of household bargaining through the threat point.

Furthermore, there is often a dynamic element to power. Those with more power also have the power to recreate for themselves the conditions under which that power is retained. Thus, at an individual

level, bringing in a wage gives more power within the household. Further, those who do paid work are also more likely to develop the skills that will allow them to earn more and be more employable than other members of their family in the future, thus consolidating their power within the household.

This can also occur at a group level. Men as a group have an interest in the perpetuation of the GEPs that give them more bargaining power in their households (Folbre, 1997). We can therefore expect them also to seek to influence public policies and social norms, to tip the GEPs in their favour. Women can be expected to resist this. Public debate over the role of the Child Support Agency in the UK is an example. Men have organized collectively through organizations such as 'Families Need Fathers' to change the rules that determine how much a non-custodial parent must pay in child support. If they are successful, this will improve the bargaining position of all men in all households, in so far as they are the more likely member to become a non-custodial parent if the household breaks down. Feminists, on the other hand, have campaigned against requiring women who fear violence to co-operate with the Child Support Agency. If they succeed, removing the threat of violence over child support will improve the bargaining position of all women in all households. Another less recent example is protective employment legislation. Heidi Hartmann (1981) argues that nineteenth-century male trade unionists fought to restrict women's employment, not only to improve their own wages, but also in order to retain their power in the home. In the language of this chapter, by restricting women's employment opportunities and improving their own, men shifted a GEP in their own favour and thus improved their bargaining power within the home. These examples show how gender-specific environmental parameters may provide a focus for men and women to organize collectively to increase their power within their households.

All the models we have looked at in this chapter were designed to throw light on why women have less power than men in households, whether the intention was then a conservative one, to show how the power imbalance is inevitable, or a reforming one, to suggest ways in which an unequal and unfair situation can be changed. However, the models also differ in what they see as the differences between men and women, and therefore the causes of the inequality between them. For Becker, as we saw in the previous chapter, men and women differ in their natural abilities, reinforced by different investment in human capital; they also, if his model is to work as a method of household decision making, differ in the size of their contributions and their altruism. It is from these differences between men and women that Becker explains why men have more, indeed all, power over household decision making. Since he takes nature and preferences as given, and these determine the division of labour within the household, there is little that can be changed in this model. It is an attempt to explain what is seen as the status quo, rather than to analyse how to set about changing it.

On the other hand, in bargaining models, men and women differ in their threat points, which depend on gender-specific environmental parameters and on people's perceptions, all of which are seen as changeable. Institutions, norms and perceptions in these models can all vary; though knowing *how* to change them may be a different matter. These models are therefore not inherently so conservative. They see gender and power relations within the household as potentially open.

However, all these models do have something in common. They are all methodologically individualist, and share the neoclassical assumption that people's actions, including their bargaining behaviour, are determined by their preferences. This remains the case even if these preferences extend beyond their own material welfare to include a concern for other members of their family. But decision making based on given preferences is not the only way to model behaviour. In Chapter 3 you looked at theories of consumer behaviour in which preferences were endogenous. The next chapter will consider these and other alternative models of how people behave, in the particular context of caring for children.

FURTHER READING

Dasgupta, P. (1993) *An Inquiry into Well-being and Destitution*, Chapter 11, 'Food, care and work', Oxford, Oxford University Press, pp. 305–36: examines a number of issues considered in this chapter, such as regional patterns of household allocation, marriage payments and different allocations between girls and boys.

Dwyer, D. and Bruce, J. (1988) *A Home Divided: Women and Income in the Third World*, Standford; CA, Stanford University Press: is a collection of articles from different perspectives on the division of resources within households in developing countries.

Folbre, N. (1997) 'Gender coalitions: extra family influences on intrafamily inequality' in Alderman, H., Haddad, L. and Hoddinott, J. (eds) *Intrahousehold Allocation in Developing Countries,* Baltimore; MD, Johns Hopkins University Press: shows how the different interests of men and women within the household may lead them to form coalitions based on their gender interests.

McCrate, E. (1992) 'Accounting for the slowdown in the divorce rate in the 1980s: a bargaining perspective', *Review of Social Economy*, Vol. 1, No. 4, Winter, pp. 404–19: uses a household bargaining approach to explain why divorce rates rose sharply and then slowed down in the United States.

McCrate, E. (1987) 'Trade, merger and employment: economic theory on marriage', *Review of Radical Political Economics,* Vol. 19, No. 1, pp. 73–89: is a very interesting survey of some of the different economic models discussed in this chapter.

Pahl, J. (1995) 'His money, her money: recent research on financial organisation in marriage', *Journal of Economic Psychology*, Vol. 16, pp. 361–76: gives, despite the journal in which it is published, a sociologist's view of the division of resources within marriage.

ANSWERS TO EXERCISES

Exercise 6.1

1 Because the husband is not altruistic, his level of utility depends only on his own consumption, so his indifference curves are a series of vertical lines as in Figure 6.15. His most preferred point is M.

2 As Figure 6.16 shows, the man's most preferred point is M, which gives him his maximum utility. Neither he nor his wife cares about the other's consumption, so moving round the household's consumption possibility frontier, as consumption shifts from him to her, his utility falls and hers increases until W, which gives the woman her maximum utility.

Figure 6.15 The maximization of a non-altruistic husband's utility

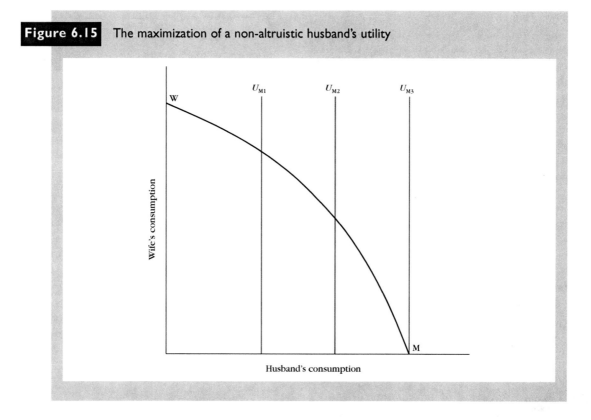

Figure 6.16 The possible combinations of utility for a non-altruistic husband and wife

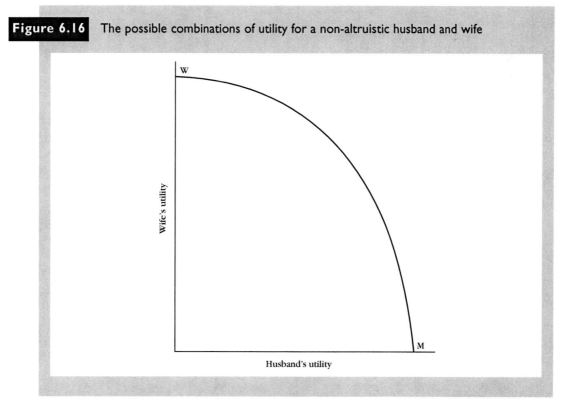

Exercise 6.2

If brides require dowries, then girls will be a cost to their households when they marry, whereas boys, or rather their brides, will bring resources into the household. The larger the dowries that must be paid, the larger the disparity between the cost of daughters' marriages and the benefits from sons', and thus the more utility the household will gain from ensuring the survival of sons over daughters. A bride-wealth system will work the other way around. The evidence from the case study is consistent with this analysis; those regions in which the highest dowries were paid, the North West, were those where the sex ratio was the highest, while the sex ratio was more even in the South, where lower dowries were paid and the system of bride-wealth survived in some cases.

Exercise 6.3

On Figure 6.17, each partner would only be prepared to agree to points that they prefer to the non-co-operative outcome T, so:

1 The husband will agree to points to the right of T.

2 The wife will agree to points above T.

3 Co-operative solutions must be agreed to by both partners, so they lie in the shaded area to the right and above T.

4 The Pareto efficient outcomes are those along the boundary of the feasible set from W to C.

5 From all other outcomes, by moving up and to the right, an outcome can be found which makes both parties better off. This is also true of the outcomes on the boundary from C to M; from these, moving upwards reaches points which make the wife better off without making the husband worse off. This is because he is an altruist, so at these points a transfer of consumption from him to her can increase her utility without decreasing his.

6 Only points on the boundary between W* and C represent Pareto efficient outcomes that could be the result of co-operation between the two parties.

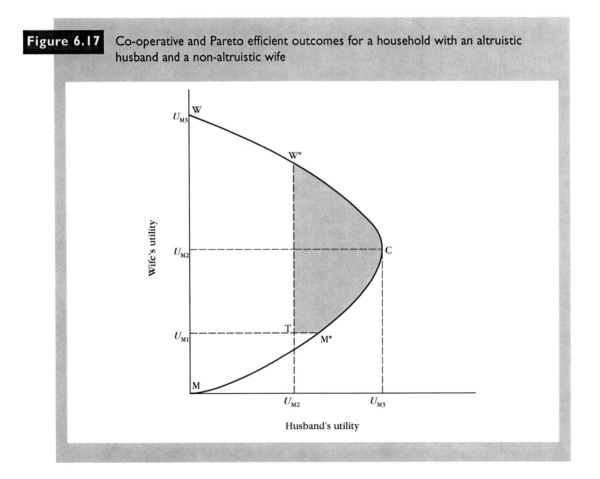

Figure 6.17 Co-operative and Pareto efficient outcomes for a household with an altruistic husband and a non-altruistic wife

The outcomes between C and M* are not Pareto efficient for this household.

Exercise 6.4

Figure 6.18 shows the effect of changing the threat point from T to T′, a threat point which is an improvement for the women and is worse for the man. The range of possible bargaining outcomes shifts in her favour too, ruling out those from M* to M*′, and making those from W* to W*′ possible. The Nash bargaining solution N′ also registers an improvement for her and a setback for him, compared with N.

Exercise 6.5

In all models, total household resources would fall as a result of the cut in the real value of Child Benefit, but the models differ in how that fall would be experienced.

In a single household utility model, the effect of the cut will be spread between all members of the household. The exact proportions in which it is spread will depend on the household utility function, but we have no particular reason to expect the shares of each individual in total household resources to alter in any particular direction. Each party will therefore experience a cut in the resources allocated to them roughly proportionate to the cut in total household resources.

In both bargaining models the woman's fall-back position has worsened; she is both poorer on divorce since the cut in Child Benefit will affect her rather than her husband, and would have less money to keep for herself in the case of non-co-operation. So, not only does the household experience a fall in its resources, but in both models her bargaining position within the household is weakened. She will get a smaller share of a smaller pool of resources; we would therefore expect her share of resources to fall more than proportionately to the fall in total household resources.

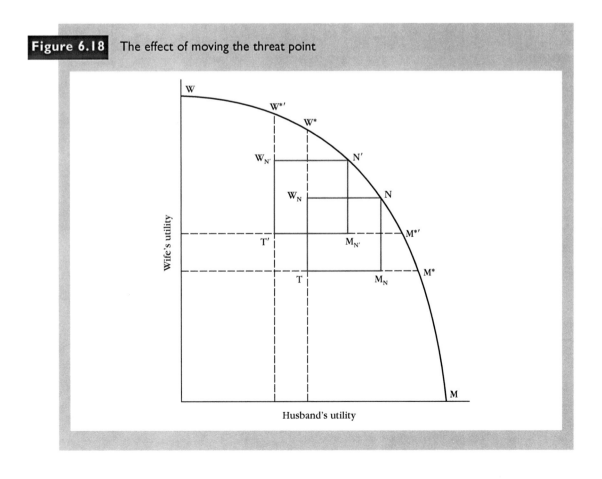

Figure 6.18 The effect of moving the threat point

CARING FOR CHILDREN

Susan Himmelweit

7

LINKS

- The investment model assumes individuals are rational maximizers concerned only for their own welfare. This is the model of why people care for children that corresponds best to the neoclassical consumer theory of Chapter 2.

- The possibility of altruistic preferences was introduced in Chapter 6 to explain why husbands shared resources with their wives.

- The development of personal capital can be used to explain gender differences in caring behaviour in a similar way to the how human capital was used to explain the gender division of labour in household in Chapter 5. Again positive feedback is involved to magnify the effect of small biological differences.

- In Chapter 3, endogenous preferences were seen as part of an institutionalist critique of neoclassical consumer theory. However in this chapter, by using the notions of personal and social capital, endogenous preferences are explained from within a neoclassical framework.

- The notion of social norms affecting people's caring behaviour is much more consistent with the institutionalist approach to consumer behaviour taken in Chapter 3.

- Social norms were important in the institutionalist explanations of the household division of labour in Chapter 5. They will be considered again in Chapter 8, when considering routines in firms' behaviour.

- Other questions about altruism and care are raised in Chapter 19, which considers markets for social goods.

1 INTRODUCTION

Chapter 2 started by laying out the neoclassical model of consumer choice based on an individual with preferences over a range of consumption possibilities. By the time you get to this chapter you will have met a number of criticisms and modifications of this model. In particular, the previous chapter considered neoclassical models which include individuals whose preferences are not entirely self-centred but incorporate concern for the welfare of others, notably those within the individual's family. However, talking about such altruistic preferences immediately raises the question of how such preferences are formed. The standard neoclassical account explicitly rules out consideration of preference formation, treating preferences, whether altruistic or purely self-centred, as exogenous givens.

After Chapter 2's consideration of the neoclassical theory of consumer choice, Chapter 3 examined alternative theories of consumption which focus on how consumer behaviour depends on social factors outside the individual. In these theories, such outside factors either influence people's preferences for particular consumption goods or lead to motivations for consumer behaviour other than the satisfaction of preferences for consuming one good rather than another.

The relation between the theory of this chapter and Chapter 6 is similar to the relation between those two chapters. In this chapter, I want to consider how certain behaviour, that neoclassical theory would see as the result of altruistic individual preferences, can be explained by social factors beyond the individual. As in Chapter 3, we need to consider how social factors might influence preferences, in this case a preference for another's welfare, and also whether all such behaviour can be accounted for as the instrumental satisfaction of preferences, or if quite different types of motivation need to be considered too.

To follow this agenda, we have to work down from society as a whole and its institutions to see how they structure individual behaviour, rather than using assumptions about individuals to build up to a picture of the economy as a whole, as neoclassical theory does. However, like all other chapters, this one has more than just a theoretical agenda; it is also concerned with a particular topic. The topic of this chapter, around which its theoretical agenda will be pursued, is how economies ensure that children are cared for.

Economic theory has always had difficulty dealing with children. If, as previous chapters have shown, adults do not always behave as rational economic agents, children certainly cannot be assumed to do so. All legislative systems have a notion of an age of majority before which children cannot be expected to behave as full citizens. Below such an age (frequently there is a whole series of such ages) children are not considered mature enough to decide to marry, to have the right to vote, or to make a legally binding contract. Somebody else, whether an individual parent, a guardian or the state, has to do it for them. Similarly, in economic theory, children cannot be expected to know what is best for themselves and to act consistently in their own best interests; somebody or something makes those choices for them.

However, despite these difficulties, there is good reason for economists to think about children and the care they need. Any economy has not only to produce goods and services but also to ensure that its population reproduces itself, not just in terms of numbers but as healthy functioning participants in that economy. This requires providing for the needs of children, as well as people currently engaged in the labour force, and preparing those children for their eventual participation in the economy. Children do not only have physical subsistence needs; they also require 'care' in a broader, personal, often more time-consuming sense. Beyond food and shelter, children need to be looked after, prevented from hurting themselves, taught to walk, talk and laugh if they are to stay healthy and sane and learn the skills they need to become full members of their society.

Although all societies, if they are to survive, must manage to turn successive generations of children into adults socialized in ways appropriate to their society, different societies do this differently. They vary in the ways in which responsibilities for children are shared between parents and the wider community: for example, in the extent of publicly provided childcare and state benefits to parents. Societies also vary in the extent to which men and women take responsibilities for children and what those specific responsibilities are, such as whether men are normally involved in childcare or whether women expect to combine earning money to support their family with looking after children.

Section 3 of this chapter will explore a number of theories that could contribute to our understanding of why societies differ in this way, and what makes them change in their attitudes and practices with respect to children. Section 4 will examine one of these theories in more detail to see why in some circumstances behaviour and norms can be quite stable, while in others behaviour and norms change rapidly and irreversibly. Finally, Section 5 will draw on this model, as well as the other theories looked at previously, to consider what characteristics would be likely to make a society care well for its children, and in particular whether more or less specialization by gender is likely to be conducive to good care for children.

However, before moving on to consider any of those theories, the next section will present a case study designed to help you think about the wide range of factors that could be relevant to explaining the different patterns societies adopt with respect to the care of children.

2 CASE STUDY: DECLINING FERTILITY IN THE MEDITERRANEAN COUNTRIES OF EUROPE

Although, in 1975, the Mediterranean countries of Greece, Italy and Spain had higher fertility rates than those of most of the other countries of Europe, by 1993 they had, with Portugal, some of the lowest fertility rates in the world. Figure 7.1 shows how rapidly fertility declined in the 19 years from 1975 to 1993 in these countries compared with the relatively stable fertility rates of some Northern European countries.

The relatively rapid fall in fertility in these countries could just be the result of catching up with their more advanced neighbours. In general, for reasons which will be explored in Section 3 of this chapter, as economies develop their birth-rates tend to drop, and the Mediterranean economies developed later and have recently grown more rapidly than those of Northern Europe. Further, in the case of Spain and Italy, fertility had previously been kept high by restrictions on the use of contraception and abortion which made family size more difficult to plan accurately. It is interesting to note that Ireland, where restrictions on contraception and abortion were only marginally relaxed during this period, displays a similar decline in fertility to the Mediterranean countries though keeping at a much higher level, while Portugal, another predominantly Catholic country, displays a very similar pattern.

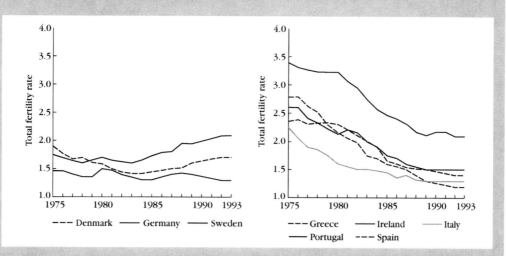

Figure 7.1 Total fertility rates in selected more developed countries, 1975–1993 (the total fertility rate is the average number of children a woman would bear at current fertility rates if she lived to the end of her childbearing years)

Source: based on United Nations, 1992, Figure 23, p.57; additional data from Eurostat, 1992, Table 4, p.52, and International Bank for Reconstruction and Development/The World Bank, 1995, Socio-Economic Time-series Access and Retrieval System

Such a 'catching-up' process may explain the relatively late decline of fertility in these countries, but not why fertility fell so sharply in the Mediterranean countries to rates below those of most of their more developed northern neighbours. Compared with the countries of Northern Europe, the Mediterranean countries have more cohesive families and less developed welfare systems. Far more services are provided by women within families and fewer by private firms or the state. Indeed, a notable feature of the Mediterranean countries, though not Portugal, remains their low rate of female participation in paid employment and a correspondingly small service sector. As Figure 7.2 shows, these two characteristics tend to go together.

Further, as Figure 7.3 shows, the Mediterranean countries, Portugal, and to a slightly lesser extent Ireland, have far more non-wage employment than other European countries. A large amount of non-wage employment is working directly for one's own family, which suggests that families have a particularly significant economic function in these countries. Such patterns of cohesive families, low levels of female participation and high levels of family-based work have traditionally been associated with large families and high levels of fertility.

Two Italian economists, Francesca Bettio and Paola Villa, suggest that this can also work the other way around: that when combined with an uncertain economic climate, a cohesive family structure can result in low levels of fertility. In the Mediterranean countries, with their strong tradition of family support and state welfare systems designed to back-up rather than replace family provision, parents tend to support their children until they can provide for themselves at a similar standard of living to their parents. Increasing insecurity and rising levels of unemployment among young adults have led in the Mediterranean to the phenomenon known as 'prolonged adolescence' whereby children live with and are at least partially supported financially by their parents well into adulthood. In Italy, in 1990, 59 per cent of 18–34-year-olds lived with their parents, a far higher percentage than in Northern Europe; in Denmark, in 1987, less than

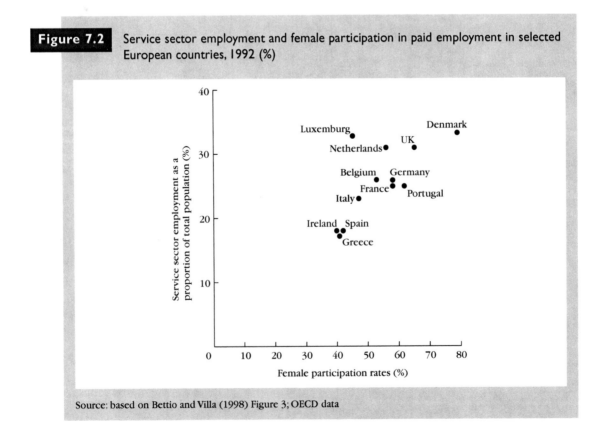

Figure 7.2 Service sector employment and female participation in paid employment in selected European countries, 1992 (%)

Source: based on Bettio and Villa (1998) Figure 3; OECD data half of 15–24-year-olds still lived with their parents (Bettio and Villa, 1998).

This implies that in these Mediterranean countries, parents accept a long period of financial responsibility and care when they have a child. How much support their children will actually need will depend on wider economic circumstances when they reach adulthood. Recent periods of high unemployment may suggest to parents that they need to be prepared for a long period of financial dependence. Bettio and Villa argue that this has changed perceptions of a desirable family size, making large families increasingly uncommon. Although fewer women have no children than in Northern Europe, most women now have only one or two, as the strikingly low fertility rates for the Mediterranean countries attest. Differences in family structure have resulted in markedly different patterns of fertility in these Mediterranean countries from those of Northern Europe.

Questions

From the case study, write down the factors you think might explain why the total fertility rate of the Mediterranean countries:

● fell sharply after 1975;
● fell later than in other countries;
● eventually fell further than in other countries.

Note that the first question is about change within a particular set of countries over a period of time, whereas the second and third questions ask you to make comparisons across different sets of countries. Make sure you separate out clearly the factors that you think are relevant to each of your explanations. Some factors may be relevant to more than one of the questions.

Keep your answers to these questions to refer to later.

Figure 7.3   Non-wage employment as a percentage of total employment in European Community countries, 1993

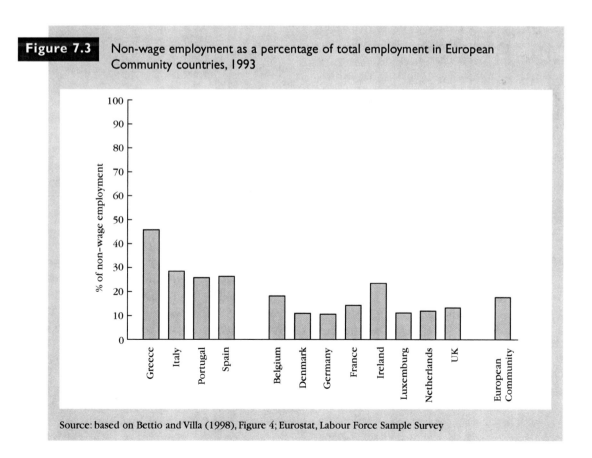

Source: based on Bettio and Villa (1998), Figure 4; Eurostat, Labour Force Sample Survey

3 EXPLAINING CARE

In this section I want to look at four different types of economic explanation of why parents 'care' for children, by which I mean spend time carrying out the activities involved in raising children. By an 'economic explanation' I mean a theoretical account that can be incorporated into an economic model, though the account may well draw upon the insights of other disciplines. I shall not be attempting to provide comprehensive social explanations for the phenomenon of caring.

In keeping with my overall strategy for this chapter, I shall, wherever possible, look at the question of caring in terms of the differences between societies and how these structure behaviour, rather than building up from models of individual behaviour. However, as is often the case in comparing theories, you will find that theories are not all trying to answer the same questions. Some are more focused on societies as a whole; some on particular sets of relations within societies; some on the choices facing individuals. We may find theories that work better for some societies than for others and/or theories that apply to some people's caring behaviour but not to others within the same society. Indeed, the theories we shall be looking at can, in many cases, be seen as different interpretations of the same behaviour, rather than as alternatives to be supported or refuted by empirical evidence.

The four different types of explanation, or interpretation, that I shall examine of parents' caring activities for their children are that:

● care for children is an investment;

● parents get pleasure from caring for their children;

● care for children is part of a system of reciprocal gifts;

● the norms of society make parents responsible for their children.

3.1   Care as an investment

In many economies, the care of children can be seen as an investment by their parents. In economies where children are expected to work from an early age, they can be net contributors to the household in which they are born when they are still quite young. In a village in rural Bangladesh, for example, Cain (1977) estimated that boys produce more than they consume by the time they are 12, and have repaid their families for their cumulative consumption by the age of 15, though this may not take account of the domestic labour that has contributed to their care. Further, the support children are expected to give elderly parents is another critical factor for parents to take into account. Spending more on children's education when they are young may enable them to contribute more to their parents' support when they are older. Money and time spent on the care of children when they are young can be seen as investment in the household's prosperity at a future time, when those children are old enough to contribute to the household themselves and especially when the parents' own abilities to provide for themselves diminishes.

There will, in many societies, be a gender dimension to this. Investment in the care of boys and girls will have different pay-offs. As you saw in Chapter 6, in societies in which women do not take employment and become part of their husbands' families on marriage, the care and education of sons rather than daughters is often seen as the better investment because sons will be able to bring money into the household and will eventually be relied on for the financial support of their parents in their old age. The contribution that daughters make in terms of domestic labour may well be overlooked, will cease when they marry, and is unlikely to be increased by an investment in their education. There may be a class dimension too. If a family owns some land, the parents can use their control over their children's inheritance to ensure that the children fulfil customary expectations and look after their parents as they get older. Such control may not be possible for other parents, such as wage workers with no productive assets of their own, who do not expect to leave any significant inheritance.

So we can see that the plausibility of investment as a motive for caring for children depends to a large extent on the type of society and the social relations within it. In general, as societies have developed, the costs of children to parents have risen. Increased educational demands, resulting in longer periods of economic dependency, imply that children are less likely to be net contributors to households before they leave to form their own. This becomes particularly true as the numbers of households which have no assets from which they can make a living, and are thus dependent on wage labour, increases. In these households, education will make a greater difference to their children's future income. Finally, as inherited property becomes less important to the vast majority of the population, and thus parental control over children declines, children become an unreliable source of support for the elderly, further reducing the investment value to parents of time and money spent on their children.

Question

Look back at the description of the Indian farm household in Chapter 5, Section 4.1. Compare the costs of raising a child in such a household with those likely to be incurred by urban households dependent on wages in a Western European country.

The costs of a child's consumption will probably be lower in the Indian farm household than in Western Europe, though not necessarily as a proportion of total household income. A larger proportion of these costs will be of time rather than money, since much of the farm household's consumption is produced directly by household labour rather than being purchased on the market.

To many households in Western Europe, a very important element of the cost of raising a child is the opportunity cost incurred when a parent, usually the mother, gives up other opportunities, including chances of earning money, in order to care for that child. This may take the form of reduced overtime, part-time working or giving up employment alto-gether for periods when the child is young. Parents who do not incur such opportunity costs will have higher direct costs if they have to pay for childcare. In the Indian farm household case, these opportunity costs will almost certainly be lower, since women do not take employment outside the household. Women work in the household and perform some exchange labour in other households' fields, but this type of work may be more easily combined with childcare. Older girls are also expected to help with looking after younger children, thus lowering the costs to parents of caring for additional children.

Question

Now consider the benefits of raising children in the Indian farm household. Do these apply to many Western European urban households?

Children are expected to work in the Indian farm household. Younger ones carry out unpaid work for

their households by looking after animals and scaring birds. The older girls are expected to help with domestic chores as well as childcare, and the eldest boys may be withdrawn from school to do paid work in a particularly bad year. Furthermore, although the case study does not comment on this, since this family owns its farm we can assume that whoever expects to inherit the farm will also be expected to look after the older members of the household when they can no longer fend for themselves.

Few Western European households can look to any such material benefits from caring for children. Although girls, and less frequently boys, may be expected to help with domestic chores, neither girls nor boys are usually expected to contribute to household finances before they are adults and then are likely to leave home. Nor are children generally relied upon to provide the main financial support to parents in their old age.

For a rural economy based on farm households, such as the Indian one we considered, the investment model does provide a plausible account of how the system works to provide care for children. The model can also be used to explain why such households tend to have large families. Although most of the costs of caring for children in such households can be expected to be low, the costs of education may be particularly high if education has to be paid for and if it prevents children contributing their time to their households. Furthermore, education may not be so economically important for those who expect to inherit their parents' way of life. It may then be a better investment for the Indian household to have more children, rather than spend more on each one's education.

Exercise 7.1

Section 2 referred to a traditional view that a cohesive family structure, low levels of female participation in paid work and high levels of family employment would tend to produce high levels of fertility. What explanation would the investment model give of that tendency?

Question

In the light of your answer to the exercise, consider how the investment model could explain why the birth-rate in the Mediterranean countries:

● fell sharply after 1975;

- fell later than in other countries;
- eventually fell further than in other countries.

When thinking about this, look back at the factors you listed in answer to the questions at the end of Section 2. Does the investment model support and develop the points you listed there?

The investment model would see the fall in the birth-rate in the Mediterranean countries as a result of economic development leading to a declining economic importance of children's work within the family and increasing costs of their education. It would point to the fact that high levels of family employment still exist as evidence that this process occurred later in these countries than in other European countries. It might also suggest some reasons why the birth-rate fell further than in other countries. A less developed welfare state should increase the costs of having children, though this would be counterbalanced by the low level of female participation in paid employment. What seems more significant is the length of time during which parents may continue to bear costs in having children, even well into adulthood in many cases. This might make children appear a particularly poor investment.

However, the snag for the investment model is that in these circumstances children hardly seem to be an investment at all. As their costs rise and the material benefits they can be expected to bring decline, 'returns' on the investment appear to be negative. Yet most families in Mediterranean countries, as the case study noted, continue to have children as they do in other developed economies. The investment model does not therefore offer a very plausible explanation for the care of children in an economy in which most households do not own their own means of production and children tend to require support until they are ready to leave home. To explain why people can be expected to care for their children in such economies, we appear to need a different model of their motivations, based more on emotional than material reasons for caring for children.

3.2 The pleasures of parenthood

Parents might care for children simply because they like the activity of doing so: they enjoy the experience of developing a relationship with their children and

helping them grow and prosper. Demographers who want to extend the use of investment models to explain fertility in countries where children cannot plausibly be argued to bring in a financial return to parents tend to concentrate on the emotional benefits that children bring. With greater economic development lengthening full-time education into adolescence and beyond, children become a negligible source of income when they are young and an unreliable one when they are older, while the length of their financial dependence makes them increasingly expensive. One plausible explanation for why parents continue to care for children in these circumstances is that doing so is enjoyable in itself. Children, such demographers argue, have shifted from being investment goods to becoming consumption goods for parents.

Parents, in this view, have a taste for caring. This is similar though not identical to the neoclassical notion of 'altruism' as a taste for another person's welfare. Either taste can be treated as a preference like any other and can relatively easily be incorporated into individualist models similar to those used in the previous chapter to examine household decision making. Individuals can maximize a utility function that depends on another's welfare in just the same way as one which depends only on their own consumption. Similarly, if they enjoy the process of caring, get pleasure from helping a child take its first steps or enjoy shopping for their children when away on business trips, these will enter into their preferences and so they will make a rational decision to allocate some time to them. Caring in that case is just as self-interestedly rational a choice of activity as consumption.

If preferences are taken as given, as in the strict neoclassical model outlined in Chapter 2, then a taste for another's welfare or for caring activities is just such a given characteristic of an individual's preference ordering. However, it seems more plausible to see such tastes as tastes that can be cultivated, as endogenous tastes affected by previous experience. In particular, the experience of working with children seems frequently to lead people to care for those children and enjoy looking after them. Given that parents, especially mothers, spend a great deal of time with their newborn children, such a learning process may explain why parents care particularly for their own children and usually prefer to spend time caring for them rather than other children. Mother-child bonding would figure in such a model, then, as an example of rapid endogenous preference formation.

Endogenous preferences would also explain why parents often find interest in their children harder to maintain if they see them only infrequently. Further, the experience of paying for children's care may not induce as much altruism or be as enjoyable as that of directly caring for them. This may be why, for example, a significant proportion of non-custodial parents eventually lose touch with their children and fail to support them financially. Caring preferences may also be endogenous in that, if the care that preferences induce is unappreciated, the preferences change. Children who as they get older show no appreciation of the care their parents have given them may find that care diminishes (Folbre and Weisskopf, 1997).

Tastes may also be influenced by wider societal factors. Just like the luxury goods discussed in Chapter 3, whose consumption enabled their owners to hold a particular position in society, so good parenting defines a place in society. To be good parents, people have to develop tastes, for their children's welfare and for child-centred activities, appropriate to that position. If on separation from their children that position is taken away, then the preferences that lead fathers to care for their children may disappear too.

Fathers may not anyway be expected to develop those tastes to the same extent as mothers, since different groups are subject to different influences on the development of their tastes. Although an expectation that women have more concern for the welfare of children and enjoyment of child-centred activities than men must be nearly universal, the extent and form of this gender difference varies markedly across different societies.

Despite the apparent changes in tastes implicit in such considerations, Becker and other neoclassical economists claim that they do not reflect a change in underlying tastes so much as a change in the circumstances of people. To see this, consider the pleasure a mother gets from looking after her child; this is one of Becker's Z-goods, which it takes the mother time and possibly money to acquire. He explains why the experience of looking after a child frequently leads people to enjoy doing so as a process of building up what he calls 'personal capital', the acquisition of which makes looking after that child in the future a more enjoyable experience. Personal capital is similar to human capital (see Chapter 5, Section 3.2). However, instead of making a person more productive of a particular good when doing certain work (as is the case with human capital), personal capital makes that person more productive of a particular Z-good when involved in certain activities. So the time spent in building up a relationship with the child is, in Becker's view, an investment in personal capital – time spent now in order to make time spent in the future more productive of pleasure. By employing this argument, Becker can claim that it is not the mother's tastes that have changed but her ability to generate pleasure for herself through looking after the child. She, like everyone else, always had a taste for such pleasure; it is just that now, through experience, she has got better at producing it for herself.

Similar arguments can be used to explain all cases of apparently endogenous tastes. Where tastes apparently change because of a person's own previous behaviour and experiences, that person is said to have acquired 'personal capital' which makes future actions more or less productive of utility; where tastes apparently change because of a change in the social milieu, such as peer group pressure, it is the actions of others that matter and Becker talks of the acquisition of 'social capital' (Becker, 1996, p.4). Note that this concept of social capital, like Becker's concept of personal capital, is a characteristic of an individual. In this, Becker's social capital differs from a notion of social capital as a characteristic of society, relevant to the discussion of social norms which you will meet in Section 3.4 of this chapter.

The notion that past behaviour by oneself and others may affect the utility that an individual obtains from a current action allowed Becker and Stigler (1977) to make the remarkable claim that economic theory could be best constructed on the assumption that '... tastes neither change capriciously nor differ importantly between people ... one does not argue over tastes for the same reason that one does not argue over the Rocky Mountains – both are there, will be there next year, too, and are the same to all men [*sic*]' (p.76). Becker and Stigler could make that claim because they analysed all cases of apparent differences of tastes between people as being the result of differences in circumstances leading to the acquisition of different types of personal and social capital.

Let us look at how Becker would explain gender differences in parenting behaviour by reference to women's greater enjoyment of child-centred activities than men's, in a way which is consistent with an assumption of similar underlying tastes. Consider a man and a woman with a new baby who have equal earning power and equal productivity in domestic tasks. How might the concept of personal capital be used to explain:

- any differences between the parents' preferences for childcare and for other activities;
- why they might choose to have one of them staying at home to look after the baby full-time, rather than both doing some childcare and some paid work;
- why it would be more likely to be the woman who looked after the baby?

Hint: Think back to the type of argument given in Chapter 5, Section 3, for specialization within the household, but remember that in this case we are assuming no difference in comparative productivities.

Since the parents both have the same underlying tastes, whichever of them looks after the baby will acquire personal capital in doing so, which means that in future they will value looking after the child more. This means the initial carer will have a different trade-off between time spent on childcare and time spent on other activities from that of their partner. Compared with an equal division of time, a switch towards spending more time on childcare by the one with experience of it, and a switch by the other partner towards spending more time on other activities in which they may have acquired personal capital, will satisfy both partners' preferences better. By extension of this argument, there should be complete specialization, so that one does all the childcare (assuming it can all be managed by one person) and acquires the maximum amount of baby-specific personal capital, while the other acquires other forms of personal capital by specializing in other activities. There is a clear parallel here with Becker's argument for specialization within the household based on the acquisition of human capital (see Chapter 5, Section 3.2). And, as in that argument, one only needs a small element of biological difference to explain why women might acquire the

initial bit of personal childcare capital. This is then enough to explain complete gender specialization through the accumulation of capital, whether personal capital affecting the pleasure people get from looking after children, or human capital affecting their productivity in doing so.

Exercise 7.2

Show how each of the following examples of endogenous tastes could be explained in terms of the acquisition or loss of personal or social capital:

1 a father whose altruism towards his children diminishes on divorce;
2 parents who give less care to ungrateful children;
3 women who are keener than their husbands to have children.

Question

Explain how a consideration of the pleasures of parenthood could help the investment model in explaining why the birth-rate in the Mediterranean countries:

- fell sharply after 1975;
- fell later than in other countries;
- eventually fell further than in other countries.

Look back again at the notes you made in answer to the questions at the end of Section 2.

Recognizing the pleasures of parenthood, that parents enjoy having children and care about their welfare, would explain why family size falls with economic development, as children move from being investment goods to being consumption goods. Parents enjoy having children, so they do not stop having them entirely as their costs rise and their investment value falls. But because they care about their children's welfare, parents decide to spend more on each child as the benefits of education increase, in order to give those children better chances in the future. Such a process, this argument would say, emerged in the Mediterranean countries later than in other countries because economic development came later.

The birth-rate fell further than in other countries, it could then be argued, because although people's tastes for the pleasures of looking after children are similar in different parts of the world, people acquire different sorts of social and personal capital. In particular, through their experience of living in cohesive families, people acquire social capital that will lead them to choose to support any children they have until they can achieve a standard of living equal to their parents. Potential parents will take the knowledge that they themselves will make such choices in the future into account when deciding whether to have a child. They will therefore be likely to have fewer children than will parents in those countries where the social and personal capital acquired through having children will not lead to as much expenditure in the future.

A cohesive family structure can therefore lead to fewer rather than more children, especially if rising unemployment among the young leads to longer expected periods of dependency. The difficult step in the argument, however, is explaining how this sort of family structure produces the appropriate sort of social and personal capital to have this effect. The model produces a framework into which such an explanation could be fitted. But a full explanation requires that an account be given of how expectations of appropriate parental behaviour evolve in different societies and different types of families.

3.3   Caring as a gift relationship

In some societies, many goods circulate in the form of gifts rather than as commodities bought and sold on the market. In some of these societies there are no markets, while in others 'gift exchange' continues alongside 'commodity exchange' as a way in which the production, distribution and consumption of goods takes place. Anthropologists such as Chris Gregory (1982) argue that, while there are many variations between societies where gift exchange is extensive, there are also some general rules of gift exchange that seem to apply in most of them.

The first rule is that gifts create debts. If a person gives another a gift, this sets up a debt which the other must repay at some time. Such debts are repayable only by a gift of a similar kind. So if someone makes you a gift of yams, it must be repaid by giving yams or some other food generally considered equivalent to yams. But if they give you a pig, which may be a gift of a quite different type, no quantity of yams will repay it; you will have to find a pig or something equivalent to a pig. You can contrast this classification of gifts into different types with commodity exchange, where,

through the use of prices and money, any two commodities are exchangeable with each other in appropriate quantities.

The second rule, closely related to the first, is that gifts imply relationships. A gift sets up or sustains a continuing relationship between donor and receiver. Again, you can contrast this with commodity exchange which requires no continuing relationship between the two parties to a transaction, who remain independent of each other. By contrast, in a gift-giving society, property is not wholly alienable; even when things are given away they remain connected to their donor. Marcel Mauss, in his classic study of such societies, talks about 'the indissoluble bond of a thing with its original owner' (Mauss, 1925; 1974 edn, p.31). Commodity exchange, however, depends on a notion of alienable property: that owners can do what they like with their property, but have no rights over it once its ownership is transferred to someone else. That notion of alienable property requires a sharp distinction to be made between a thing and its owner (which may be one reason why the sale of some services seems problematic – see Chapter 19, Section 1).

Because gifts imply relationships, in many instances of gift exchange its aim is not the consumption of the thing exchanged, but the building of the relationship entailed by the gift-giving. Further, gifts are not always repaid to the person who made the original gift. Debts may be passed on, so that they are not repaid directly but through a network of gift exchanges, which then is also a network of relationships.

We do not need to see the distinction between gift exchange and commodity exchange in terms of a bipolar opposition; indeed, the same good may exchange within the same society under one system or the other according to social context. In general, commodity exchange is more likely to be used between strangers, while between people who count as kin gift exchange is often seen as more appropriate. For example, among the Baruya tribe of Papua New Guinea, salt was found to exchange as a gift within the tribal community and as a commodity outside it (Godelier, 1973, p.128).

The point of this (I hope interesting) excursion into economic anthropology, is that gift giving may not only apply in societies without developed systems of commodity exchange, but may exist side-by-side with commodity exchange for some goods and services. It could be argued that, even in industrialized capitalist societies, caring is largely organized by a system of gift exchange rather than by commodity exchange. Although paid childcare exists, a large amount of care is done by people not for payment. Indeed, when a neighbour or a relative helps out with childcare, it is often thought inappropriate to pay them. Nevertheless, an obligation is set up which can usually only be discharged by another act of care (or maybe by one of a range of gifts thought appropriate for such occasions: flowers, chocolates, an ornament perhaps, but not five pounds of potatoes, unless they are home-grown).

Care is not the only example of a good whose distribution is organized by networks of gift exchange, even in economies where commodity exchange predominates. Listening to troubles between friends, sharing the driving to work among colleagues, even buying the next round of drinks are all goods that circulate among certain groups of people in a system tantamount to gift exchange. Note that, in all these cases, a prior relationship of some sort exists within the group which is perpetuated by the gift exchange.

The networks of gift exchange through which children may be cared for by a larger group of adults than just their immediate parents are immensely diverse across different societies. In Africa and the Caribbean, networks of female kin may share childcare so that some of their number can work. Grandparents contribute childcare in some societies. In many, older daughters in large families care for younger siblings.

However, to see childcare as gift giving, we also need to analyse parental care for children in this way. In some societies we could see this as a gift exchange in which children are given care, and as a result have an obligation to repay the debt thus set up by caring for their parents (and perhaps other older adults) in old age. However, children in many advanced capitalist economies do not repay much to their parents. Note that such inequality is not unusual in systems of gift exchange, for the terms of a gift exchange are not typically fair or equal; they will depend on the power and status of the people involved. They may allocate small returns for large sacrifices, they may be mutually misunderstood, and they may change within people's lifetimes. All these factors might explain why parents frequently feel let down by their children. A gift-exchange system depends on some expectation that debts will be repaid; if those expectations disappear, the system will cease to work.

The concept of gift exchange may be a more useful one in analysing childcare in industrialized societies, if we take account of the fact that gifts are not always repaid by or to the same individual. A network of gift exchanges set up so that debts are passed on from generation to generation may mean that parents see the care they give their children as a repayment for the care they themselves received as a child. This would explain why parents sometimes feel that their children have a duty to provide them with grandchildren. The loose reciprocity of gift-giving networks does not imply that each child repays directly their own particular debt to their parents, but the debt may be passed on as an obligation on the child to care equally well for his or her own children.

The strengths of the gift-exchange model are that it recognizes the personal nature of the transaction involved between parents and children, and grasps that the motives parents have for looking after their children are not primarily concerned with consumption, but with fostering the relationship between them. Further, much of what parents give their children, in particular most that fits within the more personal meaning of care, is not totally separable from the person who gives it; by its nature it builds a continuing relationship between the care giver and the person they care for. It is this relational aspect of care giving that makes its analysis as part of a system of gift exchange particularly appropriate.

The distinction between gifts and commodities has features in common with the distinction between formal and substantive rationality that you met in Chapter 5, Section 4.2. Formal rationality applies when different quantifiable means of achieving a given end are weighed up against each other. Substantive rationality applies when particular overriding values are allowed to determine actions. Gift exchange does not simply depend upon the quantitative valuation of different goods, just as substantive rationality rejects the weighing up of means. And just as we found that substantive rationality is more appropriate to the analysis of some forms of economic behaviour than formal rationality, so economic theory is enriched by the recognition that some systems of circulation are more appropriately analysed in terms of gift exchange rather than commodity exchange.

Question

Going back again to the very low birth-rate of the Mediterranean countries, consider how modelling parental care for children as a gift relationship could help explain why the birth-rate in these countries:

● fell sharply after 1975;
● fell later than in other countries;
● eventually fell further than in other countries.

Look back once more at your earlier notes.

The gift-relationship model has some difficulty in explaining change, because it is based on describing a relatively stable set of customs in a society. A falling birth-rate as countries develop might therefore have to be explained as a breakdown in the gift relationship of parental care for children brought on by increasing commodification of life. This occurred later in the Mediterranean countries than in Northern Europe, and again the relatively high level of family labour persisting in the Mediterranean countries may be residual evidence of this difference. Alternatively, and more in line with the explanations of the models we looked at earlier, it could be that parental care is being returned in a different form: more expensive care for smaller numbers of children than before.

The gift-relationship model is more successful at explaining differences between societies. If the gift that parents give to a child in Mediterranean societies is care until that child reaches the standard of living of its parents, then this is the gift that has to be returned or passed on, however much the costs of doing so have increased in the meantime as the result of increased unemployment among young people, for example. So the difference between the birth-rates of the Mediterranean and Northern countries of Europe can be explained by different practices in the past and therefore different expectations of what must be passed on to the next generation. Today's adults may not be passing on the parental care they received to as many children as their parents had. Instead, they are ensuring that they are able to pass on as good and as long-term care as they received to those children they can afford to have under changed economic circumstances.

3.4 Norms as reasons for caring

Perhaps the most important reason that most parents would give for caring for their children is a sense of moral responsibility or obligation to care for those particular children. A mother who gets up to see to a crying child at night does so because she sees it as her responsibility, whether or not she feels empathy for the child at that particular moment. Indeed, parents may love one child more than their others, yet still accept an equal responsibility for them all.

Responsibilities are allocated to people according to their positions in society and their relationships; it is as parents, wives, husbands, workers, employers, teachers, school-children and friends that we hold certain specific responsibilities to certain specific others. We also have wider obligations to society more generally: not to cause unnecessary harm to others, to protect the environment, and so on. Some of these are enforced by law, in which case fulfilling them may become a matter of self-interest. However, most caring responsibilities are enforced more by the norms of society than by the threat of any legal sanctions if they are not fulfilled.

But from where do such norms come? Norms form part of the institutions of a society. Norms are institutions that work, not by force, nor by legislation, but by setting up expectations of how particular people should behave in particular circumstances. Together with other institutions, norms form an interlocking system by which society runs. To explain how children are cared for, we should therefore shift attention from the behaviour of individuals to the norms that help form their motivations and the functions these norms have for society as a whole. In some societies and for some periods, the system of norms and other institutions may produce a well-functioning whole; but norms, like all institutions, change and, at other times, the system may work less well, forcing more change or even collapse.

Societies differ in the types of institutions they contain. Different sets of institutions, including norms, distinguish different types of society. Capitalist economies, for example, can be characterized not only by the existence of two classes – a bourgeoisie which owns enough property to use it as capital and a property-less proletariat which needs to take employment – but also by the existence of a norm that makes accumulation the fundamental motivation of the bourgeoisie. Tawney explained the development of capitalism by the growth of this norm, seeing it as specifically bound up with Protestantism. In a similar vein, Morishima has explained the success of the modern Asian tiger economies by the prevalence of certain features of Confucianism, including cohesive family norms (Tawney, 1942; Morishima, 1982).

So norms differ across societies. This includes norms concerning relations between different generations, such as the extent to which children take responsibility for the welfare of their parents. In continental Europe, welfare systems commonly presuppose the so-called *obligation alimentaire* (literally, feeding obligation): the principle that adults have a financial obligation to support elderly parents. Singapore is, at the time of writing, considering introducing such a principle, but with the obligation being legally enforced (Le Grand, 1997). In the UK, debate on the future of social security has started to include the option of such a legal obligation, which would involve the formal means testing of relatives' incomes when an elderly person applied for state financial support. So, as social norms seem to weaken, there may be attempts to use the law to enforce them: a system of so-called 'legal welfare'.

Although a primary obligation imposed by the norms of most societies is that on parents to take responsibility for their children, societies vary in the extent to which that obligation is shared more widely. Some societies are based on a nuclear family norm, some on an extended family, and some on sharing many responsibilities for the next generation between a whole clan. Such different family forms in turn affect the accumulation of capital, the structure of land holdings, the existence of a landless class and so on, and thus the form production relations take in the economy. Responsibilities for children therefore form one part of an interlocking and mutually sustaining set of norms that together make up a society of a particular type.

Some theorists use the term 'social capital' to refer to these kinds of systems of interlocking norms. Robert Putman, in a study of Italian civic organization (Putman, 1993), argues that some areas of Italy find voluntary co-operation among citizens, for economic and social ends, much easier to sustain than others, because the former areas have '… inherited a substantial stock of social capital, in the form of norms of reciprocity and networks of civic engagement' (p.167).

Question

How does this differ from Becker's concept of social capital introduced in Section 3.2?

Becker treats social capital as a characteristic of an individual: it is a stock belonging to an individual, which is social only in that it depends on the actions of others. Putnam uses the term to refer to a characteristic of a society: its system of norms and networks of reciprocity.

Norms form the crucial element of a model of social action in which people's position in society determines their duties and thus their behaviour. This contrasts with the model of the rational individual to whom all feasible actions are open and the chosen course of action is simply the one that maximizes utility. The distinction between the two models is not, however, as watertight as it might seem, for the actions which are 'feasible' to the rational individual are only those which are adjudged so by the rules of that particular society. For example, the feasible consumption set of a consumer, introduced in Chapter 2, Section 2.2, includes all those consumption bundles that can be acquired using only the socially approved method of exchange, rather than the socially proscribed method of stealing. Economic models in general assume that particular norm right from the start.

Analysing norms allows us to recognize how norms apply to particular people in particular circumstances. Norms of parenting are generally different for men and women. In some societies this is highly differentiated and men and women have completely separate spheres of responsibility; such a pattern was assumed in the separate spheres model of household bargaining examined in Chapter 6, Section 3. In other societies, responsibilities may be more shared; this assumption lay behind the neoclassical model of Chapter 5, Section 3, in which it was different comparative advantages that determined men's and women's roles in the household, rather than societal norms. However, in most societies, different norms apply to parents than to other people. And while there may be norms that apply to everyone in a society, such as to help blind people cross roads, these are frequently less stringent than those which apply to people on the basis of their membership of particular groups.

The methodologically individualist neoclassical economist explains all behaviour as the attempts by individuals to act on their own preferences. Such an economist will explain that norms affect behaviour because people do not like to go against the expectations of society: they get disutility from doing so. Norms are therefore a source of preference formation. However, this balancing of the costs and benefits of conforming to a norm against other sources of utility misses the point that norms allow for motivations that cannot be fitted into the logic of utility maximization. Fulfilling norms can be seen as part of the logic of substantive rather than formal rationality, as people let values, responsibilities and obligations override the calculation of the best means to meet given ends. There is room for both types of rationality in explaining behaviour and, when it comes to understanding how particular societies care for their children, a holistic approach based on specifying the norms upon which the society depends can explain much about real connections between different parts of society.

In Becker's neoclassical analysis, by contrast, the particular norms that apply to people are part of what he calls their social capital which they hold as individuals. In this way the neoclassical approach can formally incorporate endogenous and socially constructed preferences. However, unless we have a substantive account of how norms are formed and how they change, they do not affect our analysis, which remains based on how changes in external material circumstances affect the choices individuals make. An approach that focuses on how norms function in a society and consequently why they might change will therefore give different answers as to how and why caring practices change.

Question

What sort of changes in norms could explain why the birth-rate in Mediterranean countries:

● fell sharply after 1975;
● fell later than in other countries;
● eventually fell further than in other countries?

A by now familiar argument can be put into the language of norms: norms concerning parental responsibilities for the education of their children and children's responsibilities to parents change with increasing economic development, affecting desirable family size. An additional factor explaining why birth-rates were previously higher in Mediterranean countries than in Northern Europe was the existence of religious norms and associated legal constraints against the use of contraception and abortion, which made desirable family size difficult to achieve. A shift in norms concerning contraception and a partial legalization of abortion therefore helped cut the birth-rate in Mediterranean countries in the 1970s.

The fall in the birth-rate went further than in other countries because other norms did not shift, despite changing economic circumstances. In particular, parents continued to feel responsible for their adult children's welfare. With increasing unemployment among young people, such norms made the financial responsibilities taken on by parents in having children higher than in other countries.

 ## 4   CHANGING NORMS

So how do norms change? One answer is that they change when they are not fulfilled. If people of a particular group fail to behave according to existing norms, these norms will weaken. Further, norms may conflict with each other. Working mothers, for example, talk about a daily juggling of obligations: to employers, to children, to husbands, to parents, to friends, and so on. Where norms conflict too strongly, people have to choose, consciously or otherwise, between them. This can be another reason for change in both norms and the behaviour norms support.

4.1   A model with changing norms

In this section, I shall develop a simple model of caring based on changing norms, in which the assumption is made that the norm for any group of people is formed by the predominant behaviour of that group. So, for example, if most mothers of children under a certain age are at home before their children return from school, this becomes the norm for that group of mothers, to which most then feel a responsibility to conform (even if not all in fact do so). However, there is also a norm for family expenditure and for some mothers there can be a conflict between these two norms: whether to work long enough hours to ensure their family can live up to current expenditure norms, or to work shorter hours in order be at home before the children return.

If the relative cost of conforming to the two norms changes – let us say there is a rise in women's hourly wages so that the opportunity cost of time at home increases – then some mothers, perhaps those whose children are more responsible or wear out their clothes faster, may increase their hours at work so as to earn more, even though it means coming home later. The fact that more mothers are not now at home when their children come home from school will influence the norm. Similarly, family expenditure norms will change, making other mothers now feel they should do more to augment their family income.

Even if women's wages subsequently fall, reducing the opportunity cost of time at home, the old norm of mothers being at home after school will have weakened and more mothers will be spending their time earning money and may consider themselves to be less needed at home. Rather than re-establishing the norm of being at home before their children, these mothers will now consider whether they should work longer hours to make up for the effect of their wage cut on a level of family income to which they have become accustomed.

Contrast this account, in which norms change, with the basic neoclassical approach that takes preferences as given and exogenously fixed. It too would recognize that a rise in women's wages will, *ceteris paribus*, increase the amount of time a woman works and decrease the amount of time she is at home. (Note that I am assuming, as before, that her supply curve of labour is upward sloping: to examine the conditions under which this is true with unchanging preferences, see Chapter 5, Section 2.3). However, if her wage subsequently falls back to what it was before, the amount of time she spends at home should also return to what it was before, on the assumption that preferences have not changed. The fact that there was a past change is no longer relevant in explaining current behaviour.

This is one important difference between a model that explains norms (or changing preferences to use the neoclassical terminology) and a model that takes preferences as exogenously determined. If preferences are exogenous, then history is irrelevant to them. The same prices in the same circumstances will produce the same behaviour, whatever happens in the meantime. On the other hand, an approach

that models how norms shift (or how preferences change endogenously) can explain why historical shifts may affect current behaviour, even when those historical shifts were caused by changes that have since been reversed. Becker's notion of social capital captures that idea of history too, but, as I have argued above, it lacks an analysis of how norms change.

We can represent the basic distinction between the models diagramatically. Figure 7.4(a) represents the standard neoclassical model. Consider two individuals, X and Y, whose preferences are given. These determine their individual behaviour in the light of external circumstances; that is, the constraints and opportunities they face (which may be different for the two of them). Since preferences do not change, the only way either individual's behaviour changes is if external circumstances change. In the example outlined above, the change in external circumstances was the wage rise, as a consequence of which both X and Y change their behaviour (though not necessarily in the same way, because they have different preferences and individual circumstances). If the wage level falls back again, then, since their preferences have not changed, X and Y go back to their original behaviour.

Now consider Figure 7.4(b); here the notion of group norms affecting preferences is recognized, and now either a change in group norms or a change in external circumstances can affect X and Y's behaviour. Now, if external circumstances *and* norms go back to where they were before the change, behaviour changes back too.

Figure 7.4(c) represents the full norm-based model outlined above. Here there is feedback from the group's behaviour to its norms. Whatever X and Y do affects the norms, which in turn affect preferences and thus subsequent behaviour and so on. You can see the sort of cycle that can be set up on this diagram by following around the arrows from norms to behaviour to preferences and back to norms again. It is this cycle based on feedback mechanisms that makes history matter. Past changes in external circumstances can have lasting effects through starting a cycle of changed behaviour, changed norms, changed preferences, changed behaviour, etc. Further, the preferences and behaviour of X, through their effects on norms, have an influence on Y's preferences and behaviour, and vice versa. One small exogenous change can set up a cycle of changes which, as the case of the wage rise showed, can have substantial, lasting and irreversible effects.

4.2   *Bandwagon effects*

The effects can be lasting because we are assuming that the feedback mechanism of Figure 7.4(c) is one of *positive feedback*, in which, as an initial change works through the system, the further changes that result work in the same direction – that is, they reinforce rather than dampen the initial change. This is quite different from a situation of *negative feedback*, such as occurs when producers cut supply in response to an exogenous fall in demand; then an initial change, a fall in price, is dampened by the subsequent response as producers cut supply and the price rises again.

Positive and negative feedback

Positive feedback occurs when an initial change results in further change in the same direction, reinforcing the initial change.

Negative feedback occurs when an initial change results in further change in the opposite direction, dampening the initial change.

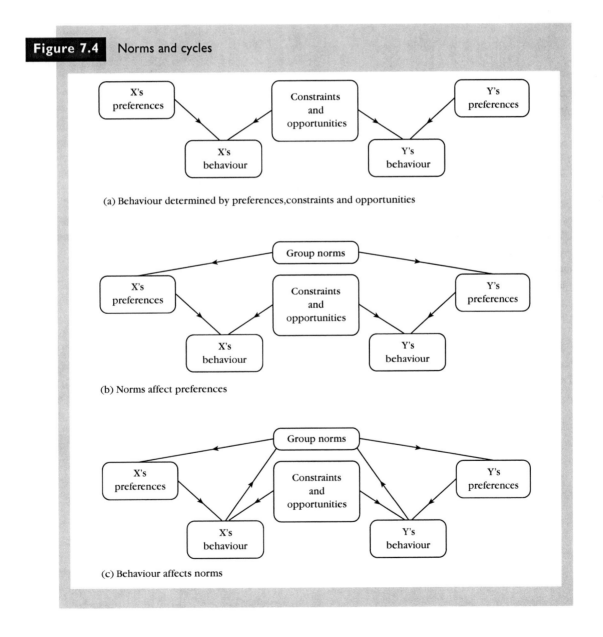

Figure 7.4   Norms and cycles

(a) Behaviour determined by preferences, constraints and opportunities

(b) Norms affect preferences

(c) Behaviour affects norms

Such positive feedback mechanisms can make norms subject to bandwagon effects in which a few individuals changing their behaviour may eventually have a large effect. Whether such a bandwagon rolls will depend on exactly how changes in behaviour affect norms and vice versa. If existing norms are sluggish and do not respond when a few people fail to behave as they prescribe, then bandwagons will be hard to start; a norm that does not easily shift will tend to induce dissidents to conform, rather than their behaviour encouraging others to challenge the norm. Such a norm and the behaviour it induces will be stable. More volatile norms may be unstable and small changes in behaviour may bring them tumbling down. The following account, adapted from Hargreaves-Heap (1992), explains how this works.

What makes a bandwagon roll?

In order to see how norms change behaviour and behaviour changes norms, we have to define what is meant by the strength of a norm. One way to assess the strength of the norm is by the proportion of the relevant population who believe that they ought to act in accordance with it, whether or not they actually do so. Thus, if 70 per cent of mothers feel they ought to be at home when their children get back from school, the strength of the norm will be 70 per cent, even though only 40 per cent of them may in fact be there.

Now, to model how behaviour changes norms and norms change behaviour, we need to make the following two assumptions:

1 The strength of the norm depends positively on the proportion of people conforming to it. As more people conform to the norm, more people feel they should too.

2 Behaviour will tend towards the strength of the norm. This means that, when norms are stronger than the actual proportion of people conforming to them, more people will be induced to behave according to the norm. When the norms are weaker than actual behaviour, conformity will fall.

We can use Figure 7.5 to show the effects of behaviour on norms and vice versa. The horizontal axis measures the percentage of the relevant population behaving according to the norm, and the vertical axis the strength of the norm, the percentage of the population who believe they should behave

according to the norm. The curve traces the strength of the norm as a function of the percentage of people conforming to it; by sloping upwards this curve upholds assumption (1) that the strength of the norm depends positively on the number of people conforming to it. On Figure 7.5, I have also drawn the 45° line, at which co-ordinates on the two axes are the same. Where the curve crosses this line, at B, norms and behaviour coincide: the percentage behaving according to the norm equals the percentage who think they should do so.

B is therefore an equilibrium. Now around B this norm is sluggish; this means that it does not change much in response to changes in behaviour. We can see this on Figure 7.5 because the norm curve around B is flatter than the 45° line, so that any given change in behaviour produces a change in the norm that is less than the initial change in behaviour. So whenever a norm is sluggish the norm curve is flatter than the 45° line, Further, because the norm curve is flatter than the 45° line at B, the norm curve is above the 45° line to the left of B and below the 45° line to the right of B. This means that, to the left of B, the strength of the norm is more than the percentage of people behaving according to it, while to the right of B it is the other way round.

Suppose, then, we begin at point A, where the norm is stronger than the percentage of people behaving according to it. By assumption (2), that behaviour tends towards the strength of the norm, the percentage of people behaving according to the norm will increase from A. This in turn will increase the strength of the norm which, if it remains stronger than behaviour, will prompt a further rise in the percentage of people behaving according to the norm, and so on. This process will only stop at B where the strength of the norm is equal to the percentage of people behaving according to it and there is an equilibrium.

Exercise 7.3

Now consider what happens at point C. What changes will happen to behaviour and the strength of the norm? Will this process come to an end?

Point B is a stable equilibrium. We can see this because, if behaviour and the strength of norms are either above or below B, they will converge towards B. This is because around B this norm is sluggish, the norm curve is flatter than the 45° line, so that any change in behaviour produces a change in the norm that is smaller than the initial change in behaviour. The smaller change in the norm then pulls behaviour back towards B, dampening the initial change. No bandwagons leave from B, because there is a negative feedback to any change in behaviour.

Now consider Figure 7.6, where D is an equilibrium because at D the strength of norm equals the percentage behaving according to it. However, the norm is volatile around D, so that a change in behaviour has a larger than proportional effect on the norm. We can see this because the norm curve at D is steeper than the 45° line, making the norm curve below the 45° line to the left of D and above the 45° line to the right of D. This means that, to the left of D, the strength of the norm is less than the percentage of people conforming to it, while to the right of D it is the other way round.

From points E and F, both behaviour and the norm diverge from D. At E, the norm is weaker than current behaviour, so, as at C on Figure 7.5, this means that the percentage of people acting according to the norms falls, which will in turn reduce the strength of the norm, and so on. This process will only stop when both behaviour and the norm reach 0. At F, the norm is stronger than current behaviour, so, as at A on Figure 7.5, the percentage of people conforming to the norm will rise, which in turn increases the strength of the norm, and so on. This process will only stop when both behaviour and the norm reach I. So the equilibrium E is an unstable one and, through positive feedback, a bandwagon effect can be set off in either direction, through changing norms changing behaviour changing norms, and so on.

Question

On Figure 7.6, what would happen to behaviour and the norm at point E and at point F?

Reflection

Can you think of examples of sluggish or volatile norms? Can you remember any instances of bandwagon effects being set off?

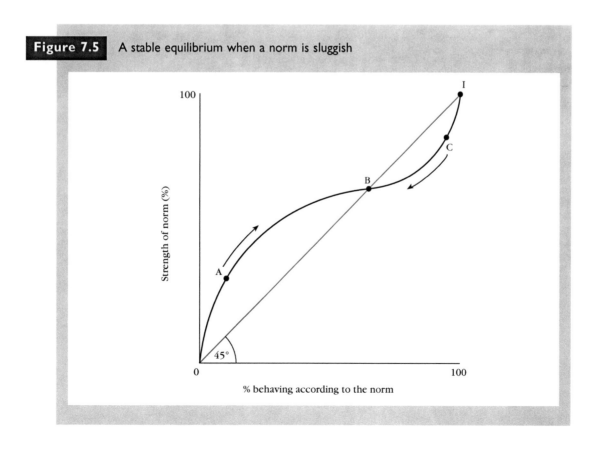

Figure 7.5   A stable equilibrium when a norm is sluggish

Strength of norm (%)

% behaving according to the norm

Bandwagon effects can be found in many areas of life. The example given in Section 4.1 was about mothers staying at home with children. If a change in wage rates makes an increased proportion of mothers think they should go out to work and behaviour then adapts, pushing up norms in a positive feedback bandwagon, this will only stop when ideas and behaviour again converge; for example, at a point where most women without children under school age see themselves as in the labour force. Notice how important perceptions and beliefs are to this model of changing norms. Influencing beliefs can have a powerful effect in starting bandwagons rolling.

A number of practices have also died out or may be dying out through such positive feedback mechanisms; for example, arranged marriages in most Western European countries, or large families in the Mediterranean. Such explanations of how norms work based on positive feedback complement other explanations which focus on the changes in external circumstances that provide the initial impetus to set the process going.

A positive feedback model of how norms and behaviour change in response to changes in external circumstances can explain how ostensibly similar economies, whose economic indicators are at similar levels, can be following different paths because their norms are different. It also explains why it may be difficult for one economy to start to follow the behaviour of other economies. For example, if cohesive family structures are an explanation of the current success of the Asian tiger economies, it does not mean that western economies can easily emulate them, because those norms cannot easily be created; changing norms can be a long and difficult process, involving changes in many other parts of the economy too. In other words, when positive feedback processes affecting norms apply history matters – so that the possibilities of future change are influenced by an economy's prior history.

4.3   Identifying with groups and their norms

The feedback process between norms and behaviour can be particularly strongly positive because the effects on people are interdependent; in Figure 7.4(c) the behaviour of both X and Y feeds into the group

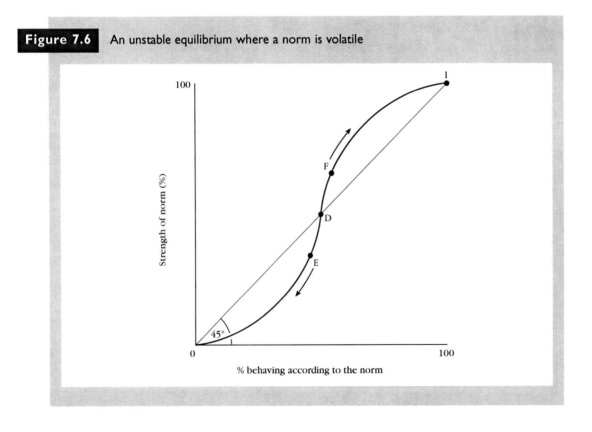

Figure 7.6   An unstable equilibrium where a norm is volatile

norms and this affects both their preferences. The speed at which a norm changes depends, then, not only upon how much each person reacts to a changing norm, but also upon how much the norm changes in response to the behaviour of members of the group. If all members of a group face similar conditions, then there is less chance of some members, because of their particular circumstances, changing their behaviour and thus challenging group norms. We should therefore expect, for example, that if the conditions all women face in a society are similar, the norms governing their behaviour will be relatively strong.

All this points to the importance of the group to which the norm applies. Norms work through groups, through particular people identifying themselves as members of the group to whom the norm applies. The father who defaults on his child support payments may be shifting his identification from the group of fathers to the group of single men. He may be making this shift consciously and hedonistically, or he may feel forced into this position by an ex-wife who denies him access to his children. Either way, by identifying himself with another group, a different set of norms influencing his behaviour comes into play.

If there are rigid gender divisions in society, women and men will be more likely to identify themselves as separate groups with their own separate norms. So a society more rigidly divided by gender may be more successful than a more egalitarian society at enforcing gendered norms of behaviour: that caring is appropriate behaviour for women, for example. This will be especially effective if the range of alternatives for women is small, so that they all face similar conditions and so behave similarly. On the other hand, if women and men begin to identify themselves in less gender-specific ways, so that both see themselves as workers and parents, rather than as mothers and breadwinners respectively, then they will adopt less gender-specific norms.

5 UNDERSTANDING CHANGE

To understand how change happens, we therefore need to consider which factors can increase or decrease people's willingness to care for others according to our different models. Considering the costs and benefits of caring is easiest. Other things being equal, parents will care more for children if the opportunity costs of doing so fall and if the benefits to the parent, financial or emotional, increase. If the opportunity costs of caring increase or the benefits fall, parents will be less inclined to devote their time and energy to caring.

As well as employment and family structures, welfare state benefits affect the opportunity costs of caring for children, and these differ greatly, even among industrialized countries. For example, a comparative European study found that, compared to a woman without children, a mother in the UK or West Germany sacrificed, on average, more than half of her lifetime earnings, while in France and Sweden, with more and better publicly funded childcare facilities, the sacrifice was 12 per cent and 6 per cent respectively (Davies and Joshi, 1990).

In other models too, caring behaviour will change if the conditions that foster it alter. We saw that altruism and pleasure in caring for children are tastes that can be developed. In particular, they can be induced by experience, building up personal capital. A system of gift exchange depends on the recognition of contributions that are made by parents and the existence of stable customs governing how debts are to be repaid by future generations. Caring norms are more likely to be fulfilled when they are in harmony, rather than conflict, with other norms in society.

Putting all the models together, we can list some factors that should work in favour of a society caring well for its children:

1 The costs for individuals of caring are not too high, in terms of both the direct consumption costs of children and the opportunity costs of devoting time to caring.

2 Those who care for children personally benefit from doing so in financial and/or emotional terms.

3 The benefits to society of caring are recognized, so that those who care for children have the chance to develop a taste for doing so, through personal experience and a positive social valuation of caring.

4 There is social recognition of the contribution that those caring for children make to society, and a custom of repaying debts to parents through the care of future generations.

5 A reasonably strong caring norm exists which is not in conflict with other norms of society and places the obligation to care for children upon a sufficiently large group of people.

This list of factors obviously oversimplifies many of the factors involved. Nevertheless, it can be used to analyse two possible ways of improving the care of children. One, the traditional view, is to attempt to get men and women to fulfil their conventional gender-specific responsibilities better. The advocates of such 'family values' may well have realized that the best hope of establishing a breadwinning norm for men and a caring norm for women is through emphasizing gender differences and restricting the choices open to women, decreasing thereby both the opportunity costs of caring, for individual women, and their variation across women.

However, this is not the only way in which children could be better cared for. Another way would be to encourage men and women to identify with each other across gender boundaries by pursuing a greater equality of experience, through developing norms which required both men and women to contribute financially to their children and to care for them. If the above analysis of how norms change is correct, it is equality of experience that matters in fostering group identity and shared norms. Widening the numbers who contribute time to caring would also reduce the individual costs to those who do so and ensure that the opportunity costs are more spread. Greater shared experience of caring could also result in the community at large recognizing better the benefits that it derives from the caring work of parents, and so becoming more willing to contribute institutionally and financially to these costs.

To put this in a contemporary context, consider the anxieties about the care that children receive which have been expressed in many countries where gender norms are changing. Some of these anxieties are about inadequate diets or educational failings, for example. However, some anxieties focus directly on gender norms (Folbre, 1994). The analysis above suggests that, once we start moving away from a gender-divided society, in which each gender is expected to make its own specific contribution to the care of children, towards a more equal one, we have to go the whole way if children are to be sufficiently well cared for. If caring is determined by norms, and norms depend on the group with which people identify, then any contemporary deficit of care may have to do with being in transition between a gender-divided society and a more equal one. Effective norms require a well-defined group for them to apply to. In the current transitional situation, women may no longer sufficiently identify themselves as the only ones who should

provide the care that children need and men may no longer sufficiently identify themselves as the sole breadwinners to provide either enough care or enough money. Traditional norms of breadwinner father and caring mother may have sufficiently broken down that men and women fulfil neither norm adequately on their own, yet a new egalitarian norm based on equality of caring and financial support may not be well enough established. If children are to be cared for while such more egalitarian norms are established, society more widely will surely need to contribute more to the care of its children than it does in most economies.

FURTHER READING

Bettio, F. and Villa, P. (1998) 'A Mediterranean perspective on the breakdown of the relationship between participation and fertility', *Cambridge Journal of Economics*, Vol. 22: this is the article from which the case study on the Mediterranean family was prepared. It includes much fascinating background material and detail.

Davies H.B. and Joshi, H.E. (1994) 'The earnings forgone by Europe's mothers', in Ekert-Jaffé, O. (ed.) *Standards of Living and Families: Observation and Analysis*, Paris, John Libby Eurotext: compares the loss of earnings due to motherhood across Europe.

Folbre, N. (1994) *Who Pays for the Kids? Gender and the Structures of Constraint*, London, Routledge: analyses theoretical issues concerning gender and the care of children and examines how different types of economies (in North-Western Europe, the USA and Latin America) provide, with different levels of success, for the care of children.

Gardiner, J. (1997) *Gender, Care and Economics*, Houndsmills and London, Macmillan: discusses the way different theoretical perspectives have taken account of caring labour and suggest directions in which economics should move to be able to analyse care better.

Hargreaves-Heap, S., Hollis, M., Sugden, R. and Weale, A. (1992) *The Theory of Choice: A Critical Guide*, Oxford, Blackwell: looks at the strengths and limitations of the models of human behaviour used in neoclassical economics and examines criticisms and alternatives from other disciplines. A book to dip into rather than read straight through.

Joshi, H.E. and Davies H.B. (1996) *The Tale of Mrs Typical*, London, Family Policy Studies Centre: an economic analysis of how motherhood and marriage affects the lives of women.

 ## Answers to activities

Exercise 7.1

A cohesive family structure suggests that an investment in the care of children would be likely to be repaid and therefore would be worthwhile. Such an investment could be made either by having a large number of children or by having fewer and spending more on each one's care and education. Low levels of female participation in paid employment would indicate low opportunity costs in caring for large numbers of children at home. High levels of family employment might imply that expensive education and skills learned outside the home could be relatively unimportant to future material welfare. Both these last two factors point to large families being the better investment.

Exercise 7.2

1 A father who sees less of his children after divorce will accumulate personal capital in caring for children much less rapidly than before. Perhaps the personal capital may even depreciate, while personal capital from other activities and experiences increases. So the father may get less enjoyment from caring for his children, and choose to do less of it. This withdrawal may be reinforced by social capital changes. The father may interact more with those who are little involved with children, so peer pressure may increase his enjoyment of other activities relative to childcare.

2 If personal experiences are not fulfilling, then the personal capital generated by those experiences lowers the utility of similar experiences in the future. So caring for ungrateful children can put parents off caring in the future. Social capital might reinforce this. In a society which expected children to show some warmth in return for parental care, the failure of children to live up to these expectations would be a loss of social capital to their parents which could diminish their pleasure and thus result in them giving less care to ungrateful children.

3 Someone who expects to look after a child will expect to build up personal capital through doing so, and thus gain increasing amounts of utility from parenthood. Parents who expect to have less contact with their children will not expect to gain so much personal capital, so do not enjoy parenthood so much. If women expect to spend more time with any children they have than their husbands, they will therefore expect to gain more utility from parenthood and, anticipating this, will be keener to have children.

Exercise 7.3

Figure 7.7 overleaf shows the movement from C. At C, the proportion of the population behaving according to the norm is greater than the strength of the norm. On the same assumption as before, that behaviour tends towards the strength of the norm, the percentage of people behaving according to it will fall, and as a result, the strength of the norm also falls. This interaction of falling conformity with declining strength of the norm continues down to B, where the strength of the norm equals the proportion of people behaving according to it and the system settles down to an equilibrium.

Figure 7.7   A stable equilibrium where a norm is sluggish

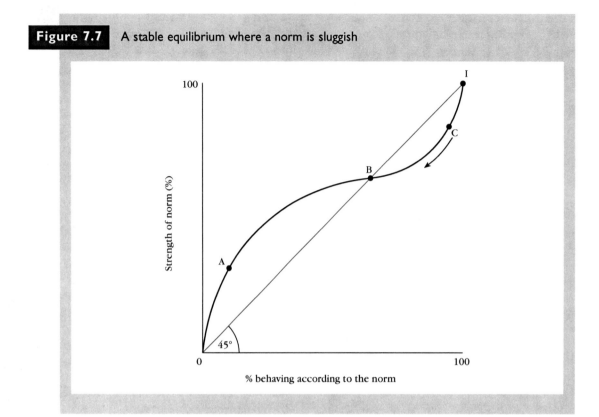

FIRMS

MODELLING THE FIRM

Neil Costello

CONCEPTS AND TECHNIQUES

Limited liability
Monopolistic competition
Risk and uncertainty
Probability
Expected value
Standard deviation and coefficient of variation
Risk-neutral/adverse/seeking
Transaction costs, incentives and opportunism
Specific assets
Instrumental rationality
Bounded rationality, satisficing behaviour and routines in evolutionary theory
Path dependence and irreversibility versus comparative statics
Short and long run in neoclassical theory

LINKS

- This chapter illustrates the basic features of the neoclassical theory of the firm, which has close parallels with the neoclassical theory of consumer choice (see Chapter 2) with the difference that whereas rational consumers maximize utility firms maximize profits. The technical aspects of the theory will be developed in Chapter 10. The theory will also be applied to the theory of labour demand in Chapter 12 and the analysis of technological change in Chapter 15.

- The chapter also introduces the old institutional perspective on firms, which criticizes the neoclassical notion of instrumental rationality. Bounded rationality, routines, path-dependence and irreversibility are explored more in depth in Chapter 16, which illustrates the evolutionary approach to technological and economic change.

- New institutionalism is introduced by relaxing the neoclassical exclusive focus on prices as the main mechanism in markets, and by allowing for imperfect information in the economy. The consequences of the existence of imperfect information are examined in depth in the next chapter.

1 INTRODUCTION

'A striking example [of the change in UK manufacturing] was the transformation of one of Britain's oldest and largest engineering companies, Guest Keen and Nettlefolds (GKN). Formed in Birmingham at the start of the century by three companies making bolts, woodscrews and iron and steel, GKN had expanded, partly by acquisition, into a range of steel-using businesses.

Like many other long-established British companies, it was almost wholly dependent on Britain and the Commonwealth. The nationalization of steel in 1967 removed one of the original props of the group, but it was not until the second half of the 1970s, when its financial position deteriorated, that a drastic change of direction became necessary. As Sir Trevor Holdsworth, who became chairman in 1979, put it: "We were drifting uncertainly into a future without a clear strategy. A new generation of senior executives was emerging and we set about trying to make sense of our inheritance."

In the 1960s GKN had acquired a British engineering company, Birfield, which made components – drive shafts with constant velocity joints – for front-wheel drive cars; its first application was in one of the British motor industry's most famous models, the Mini. As the vogue for front-wheel drive spread throughout the world's car manufacturers, Birfield's unique technology enabled GKN to build an international business in vehicle components, with Continental Europe and the US as two of its principal markets. It was a painful transition, involving divestments, closures and redundancies, but GKN succeeded in reinventing itself in a form which was better suited to the market conditions of the 1980s and 1990s.'

(*Financial Times*, 12 JUNE, 1996)

Industrial firms such as GKN are rather recent economic institutions. Machinery-using factories emerged in Britain in the second half of the eighteenth century (Landes, 1969). Before that time, merchants associated to create trading companies, craft workshops took apprentices, and the early capitalist period saw the development of merchants' 'putting out' work to homeworkers. However, it was the period known as the Industrial Revolution which established industrial firms as we know them today.

For manufacturing firms to grow required innovation in technology, finance and organization. A study of giant firms (Prais, 1976) examined the trend in industrial concentration, in terms of the share of the hundred largest firms in UK manufacturing output, over the period 1909-70 (*Changing Economies*, Chapter 6, explains measures of industrial concentration). Projecting his model backwards, Prais found a hypothetical starting-point for the emergence of industrial concentration – that is, for the rise of some large firms from among small ones – in the 1850s.

That decade has the interesting feature that it saw the principle of limited liability first become easily available in the UK under the Companies Act of 1856. Limited liability limits the financial risk for investors in a firm's shares to the funds they have invested. Without it, shareholders as owners of the company could be liable for the whole of its debts. Pressure for legislation came particularly from railway companies, hungry for capital, and anxious to encourage the burgeoning middle classes to risk their savings in railway investment. The institution of limited liability encouraged new company formation and removed constraints on company growth.

From these beginnings, public limited companies (plcs), such as GKN, have come to dominate the supply of goods and services in industrial capitalism. The GKN story illustrates a number of the themes addressed in this chapter. First, it illustrates the importance of competition and market pressure in forcing firms to change and respond. Section 3 of this chapter considers the neoclassical analysis of firms' behaviour, and the neoclassical framework is developed and applied in subsequent chapters to problems of efficiency, market strategy, industrial regulation, labour demand and technical innovation.

Second, GKN illustrates the importance of mergers and acquisitions in influencing industrial structure. The acquisition of Birfield in the 1960s turned out to have laid the basis for GKN's later survival. Section 4 examines an influential theory of the boundaries of the firm, drawing on the strand of economics known as new institutionalism (see Chapter 1, Section 4.3), and lays a basis for later analysis of inter-firm contracting, industrial regulation and labour relations within firms.

Third, the GKN story demonstrates the importance of a firm's history and its particular set of technical skills and knowledge. Section 5 develops a third perspective on the firm, drawing on a broader tradition of institutional enquiry in economics (see also Chapters 3, 5 and 7). This perspective addresses the evolution of firms' activities in historical time, and their decisions in the face of uncertainty, and has been particularly applied to technical change.

To help to compare the different theories of the firm, I begin in Section 2 with a case study of a decision-making process in a major international corporation. Read the case initially as a story. It is analysed in the sections that follow.

2 THE CASE OF DIGITAL EQUIPMENT CORPORATION

At the end of April 1995, the UK subsidiary of the American computer giant, Digital, made one of its senior managers redundant. Ray Costello (no relation to the author!) was the senior manager responsible for much of the company's work in eastern and central England. He had worked for Digital for 19 years and was regarded as a good, well-motivated staff member. He was the primary architect of new organizational systems which had rescued Digital's operation in eastern England from almost certain closure. Why was this decision taken? To make sense of it we need to examine the history and culture of Digital, and the changing environment in which it found itself in the early 1990s.

Digital Equipment Corporation (DEC) was founded by Ken Olsen, a technologist and a Quaker, in Maynard, Massachusetts, in 1957. The company was a spin-out from the Massachusetts Institute of Technology (MIT), an institution with a worldwide reputation for high quality research, and Olsen established DEC on principles similar to those of other well-known Quaker business families such as Cadbury and Lever. The company took its responsibility for its staff seriously. It believed, and still claims to believe, in core values that made it a great company: integrity, valuing individuals and their diversity, fiscal conservatism, innovation and technical excellence (Digital Equipment Corporation, 1993).

The UK subsidiary is the Digital Equipment Company Ltd. Formed in 1964, it employed just over 4000 people in 1995. Together with the small Irish subsidiary, it accounts for nearly 10 per cent of the company's worldwide revenues (Digital Equipment Corporation, 1995).

DEC was founded upon advanced and innovative technology. It launched the world's first small interactive computer in 1960, and in the late 1990s is still setting world standards with its Alpha system. However, the world of high technology has changed significantly since Olsen had his bright ideas in the 1950s. During the 1960s and 1970s, computing was technical, expensive and the province of experts. Digital was very successful during this period and grew massively. Its VAX range launched in 1977 set an industry standard. By 1983, the company employed over 70,000 people worldwide. This grew to a peak of over 125,000 in 1989.

However, in 1990-91, DEC posted its first ever loss of $617 million. In 1991-92 the company lost $2796 million and losses continued, until 1994-95 showed profits of $121 million. By 1995, total employees had declined to 61,700.

In response to the financial problems of the early 1990s, the parent company appointed in 1992 a new President and Chief Executive Officer who came from a computer manufacturing background. The corporation was reorganized in 1993 into business units and there was a realization that it was over-staffed by industry standards. According to its 1993 *Annual Report*, Digital was transforming itself into 'a leaner, more responsive, more competitive corporation with a new organization, new technology and – most important – a new focus on the customer.' Furthermore, 'This focus wasn't just imposed by management; it bubbled up through the entire company' (Digital Equipment Corporation, 1993, p.4).

It is easy to be cynical about such rhetoric, but discussions with Digital staff in the UK confirm that individuals are given considerable autonomy. Changes can be initiated by staff that make a difference to work patterns and products offered by the company.

Such was the case in the centre managed by Ray Costello. It became clear to Costello and his colleagues in the early 1990s that their long-term security was low. Digital was down-sizing. Furthermore, in recent years, Digital had been moving away from its traditional focus on hardware solutions. During the 1970s and 1980s, the installation of computer systems required support from highly qualified technical staff. Slowly, the nature of this support had shifted so that Digital consultants began to concentrate less on the specific requirements of the hardware, which was becoming predictable and more user-friendly, and more on analysis of the business needs of the customers.

The area of expertise that Ray Costello developed was in 'teleworking'. This is a flexible pattern of work in which the employee works from home or some other remote location using computer networking and co-ordinated support systems. Teleworking makes intensive use of complex computer-driven communication links, but the key features of successful teleworking relate at least as much to the organizational procedures and human networking facilities, which are developed alongside the communication hardware and software, as they do to the computer power itself.

Thus, Ray Costello had been developing a range of customer-focused consultancy skills, relating to teleworking, which reflected the corporation's new objectives. Faced with the threatened closure of Digital's east of England centre, Costello and colleagues proposed instead that it should become a telecentre, adopting teleworking and closing the substantial office block. Costello successfully championed the proposal within DEC, and the telecentre opened in early 1994. It was run from restricted premises containing a small co-ordinating staff, plus a number of 'touch-down offices'. Other staff were provided with advanced communications links in their homes and a structure of group meetings and informal contacts was established to co-ordinate and manage the operation successfully. The telecentre has worked, and its organizational form has been picked up by other Digital offices in the UK.

As a product for sale, however, teleworking practices have been largely abandoned. Digital, who pioneered such flexible working as a business solution, has now turned back to concentrate on what the corporation thinks it does best; that is, selling hardware. Advice on resource management, including flexible working, is bought in.

Ray Costello thus found himself by 1995 in the unenviable position of being an expert with an expertise no longer seen as central to the company's product portfolio, and was made redundant. He had managed successfully significant changes to the company's operation but, even in a company which prided itself on its support for its employees, he no longer fitted the pattern of skills identified as important. (Since then, Costello has set up a business providing flexible working and associated consultancy services.)

That is the case study. It sets out the background to events which were poorly understood by many of the people working in Digital's east of England operation. The next three sections ask you to consider these events in the light of alternative theories of the firm.

3 NEOCLASSICAL THEORIES OF FIRMS' BEHAVIOUR

3.1 The equilibrium of the firm

Different theoretical approaches to analysing firms are designed to answer different questions. Neoclassical models of the firm are, in the words of one economic theorist (Hart, 1989), 'rigorous but rudimentary'. Decision making by the firm is analysed as a procedure of maximization under constraints, a method familiar to you from the analysis of consumer behaviour (see Chapter 2, Section 2). The firm's *objective* is specified as the maximization of profits, defined as the difference between total revenue and total cost. The neoclassical model then identifies the firm's profit-maximizing output, given the demand and cost conditions it faces.

In neoclassical theory, the firm itself becomes an 'unexplored black box'. Inputs are fed into the firm, and the technology that turns inputs into outputs is given exogenously. In the benchmark model of perfect competition (see *Changing Economies*, Chapter 7), the firm is a price taker in markets for its products and for its factors of production. The firm simultaneously chooses the output which maximizes profits and the mix of inputs required to produce the output at lowest cost (see Chapter 10). The equilibrium of the firm in perfectly competitive markets is a building block for the neoclassical model of general equilibrium (see Chapter 18), and indeed neoclassical theory is addressed more to the analysis of markets than to understanding firms.

Despite its pared-down form, however, the neoclassical model of the firm is influential and widely used. It is particularly employed to analyse firms' responses to exogenous changes in market conditions. It also generates predictions about the relation between market structure and firms' behaviour, which is also examined in Chapter 11.

Given its importance, the assumptions of the core neoclassical model are worth exploring in a little more detail. Note first how fundamental is the notion of equilibrium. Historians of economic thought (such as Mirowski, 1989) trace many roots of economic theorizing to the influence of theoretical physics. Economists from the eighteenth century onward drew heavily on metaphors and models from physics and classical mechanics. Economics as a developing discipline took from classical mechanics the idea of equilibrium with equally balanced forces, and applied it to the operation of markets.

The mechanical models adopted by this kind of economics are timeless, in that the irreversibility of historical time is unimportant for them. In these models, a firm's decision can be reversed. If market conditions change – for example, if consumer preferences reverse a previous shift in a demand curve – the firm could move back to the point from which it had just come. Furthermore, whilst neoclassical economists are well aware that firms do not possess perfect knowledge about their costs, revenues and competitive position, full knowledge of this kind has frequently been assumed for analytical purposes. This kind of economics therefore abstracts considerably from the real world to make analysis tractable.

3.2 The monopolistic competition model

The neoclassical theory of the firm makes one further abstraction from the real world: it takes the boundaries of the firm as given. Firms exist, or are created on the model of existing firms when new firms enter a market, to produce an already defined product. The model finds it hard to analyse acquisition and diversification into new product lines. Standard theoretical expositions tend to assume that all the firms in an identifiable product market are themselves identical. Alternatively, a story may be told about market adjustment, in which some firms are less successful than others, with the marginal firm just making normal profits in equilibrium. But why over time do some firms not grow to dominate the market? What limits the size of the firm in neoclassical models?

The problem of reconciling an observed diversity of firms changing over time with models of competitive markets for particular products was one with which Alfred Marshall, one of the most influential founders of modern economics, struggled mightily. Marshall's first edition of *The Principles of Economics* was published in 1890, and was the major work of an economist who immersed himself in real-world phenomena while attempting rigorous formal analysis of competition in individual product markets. He was particularly concerned with the difficulty of reconciling his observation that firms experienced economies of scale with atomistic (or atomic as Marshall called it) competition; that is, competition among many similar firms. (*Changing Economies*, Chapter 4, Section 2 explains economies of scale.)

> ### Question
>
> Why is there a problem of reconciliation between economies of scale and atomistic competition?

A firm that displays economies of scale has a downward-sloping long-run average cost curve. That is, the more the firm expands the more its costs fall, and therefore the more competitive it becomes with other firms. Economies of scale, therefore, are not compatible with competition among many small firms but are likely to lead to monopoly. Furthermore, the evidence available (see Chapter 10) suggests that firms generally do face downward-sloping or horizontal long-run average cost curves.

One attempt to reconcile some degree of market power with atomistic competition was the independent development in the 1930s by the economists Joan Robinson and Edward Chamberlain of the model of monopolistic competition (see *Changing Economies*, Chapter 6, Section 4). Monopolistic competition retains many aspects of perfect competition: large numbers of firms (not the small numbers of interdependent firms characteristic of the oligopoly model to be discussed in Chapter 11), free entry and exit, perfect knowledge, and identical cost curves of firms. But the model allows for some product differentiation between firms, implying that individual firms face downward-sloping demand curves, and it is compatible with 'L'-shaped long-run average cost curves.

Figure 8.1 shows a firm in monopolistic competition. It faces a downward-sloping demand curve, $AR = D$, and is making supernormal profits shown by the shaded area. In the monopolistic competition model such profits are temporary, since new firms are attracted into the industry until only normal profits remain (see *Changing Economies*, Chapter 6, Section 4).

Let us now apply this model to analysing Digital. Suppose that Figure 8.1 shows the situation of Digital when it was making supernormal profits. Digital's innovative products had given it a temporary monopoly position. However, competing hardware producers started to move into the industry, producing increasingly standardized products and differentiating themselves through the service offered with the products.

Exercise 8.1

1 Using Figure 8.1, explain what market changes might result from the entry of new firms, and why this might result in Digital moving from profit to loss.
2 What changes would Digital have to make to regain profitability in this market structure?

This monopolistic competition analysis illustrates two other key features of neoclassical analysis of the firm. The first is the method of comparative statics (see Chapter 1, Section 2), comparing one equilibrium with another after market conditions change. Given the assumption of profit maximization, the model identifies a new equilibrium of the firm when the number of competitors, the tastes of consumers or the nature of competing products change.

Second, the model is an example of partial equilibrium analysis (this concept is also defined in Chapter 1, Section 2). This analysis considers the equilibrium of a single market, treating changes in the other markets as exogenous. A market in this context consists of competing firms producing similar but not identical products.

Question

How well do you think the assumptions of the monopolistic competition model fit the Digital case study?

Figure 8.1   A firm with a temporary monopoly position under monopolistic competition

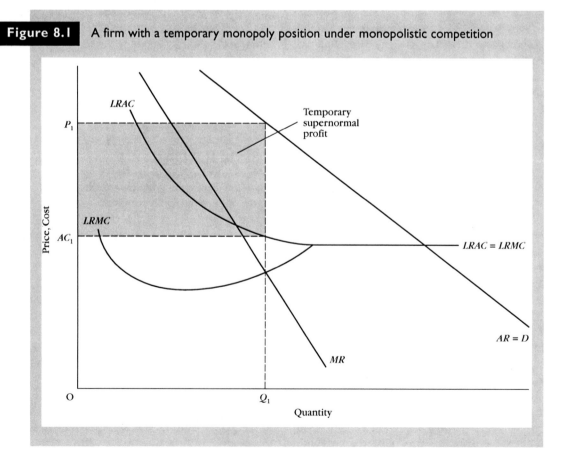

Some aspects of the model seem to fit quite well. Digital's market consisted of increasingly standardized products which were partial but not complete substitutes, limiting but not eroding completely the firm's market power. Since firms retain market power, monopolistic competition allows for competition through advertising, a feature of Digital's market.

However, the case study also points to some common criticisms. The model is hard to apply because it is difficult in practice to identify clear market boundaries containing a set of firms and products. Digital, for example, was making decisions about which products to produce, as well as how to produce them. Another problem is raised by the answer to the second question in Exercise 8.1. The model assumes perfect knowledge, which implies access to the same production technology. But Digital was clearly learning both technically and organizationally from lower-cost competitors entering the market.

3.3 Risk and uncertainty

The assumption of perfect knowledge is an unsatisfactory one in economics and many chapters in this book deal with models of firms and industries which allow for imperfect knowledge. To assume full knowledge of future profit streams seems particularly unsatisfactory. Neoclassical theorists recognize that entrepreneurs cannot know the future with certainty. The risk of loss can be incorporated into neoclassical theory by assuming that the firm considers the probability of all possible future outcomes of its decision making, rather than assuming that it knows what will happen. This section introduces the concepts of probability and risk, and contrasts them with the concept of uncertainty. These are concepts you will need again, so it is worth spending a little time on them now.

Risk

Imagine a firm which has to produce a new component for a product. It can choose between two projects: to build a new plant (project A), or to buy an existing one (project B). Each project costs £10 million. The returns will depend on influences outside the firm's control, but the firm knows quite a lot about the possible outcomes. Neoclassical economists assume that the firm has two important pieces of information: the expected return and the level of

risk attached to each project. This section explains how firms can calculate the risk associated with each project.

Consider project A. The construction of the new plant may proceed as planned, and the return on the investment will be £1 million (planned state of the world). However, there could be delays in the construction, or a new piece of machinery essential to the project might not work properly. In that case (bad state of the world), the return would be zero. Finally, workers and managers may find innovative solutions to the technical problems, and the return would be £2 million (good state of the world). Suppose these three are the only possible outcomes from project A.

This information is not enough to calculate the expected return and the level of risk of project A. If we calculate the simple average of the possible outcomes,

$$\frac{£0 + £1m + £2m}{3} = £1m$$

then we implicitly assume that each outcome is equally likely to happen, and this might not be true. So we make the crucial assumption that firms know exactly how likely is each outcome. In other words, firms attach a *probability* to each outcome. The technical box explains the concept of probability.

Probability

Probability is hard to define and there are (at least) two distinct approaches to its definition. One is that probability captures the notion of chance; the other is that it reflects the degree of confidence with which an individual holds a certain belief. The former approach sees probability as an *objective* phenomenon; the latter sees it as a *subjectively* held belief. One way to look at probability as chance is to understand the probability of outcome X, denoted by $p(X)$, as the relative frequency of X *in the long run*. We can clarify this idea with an example. When we flick a coin, two outcomes can occur: 'heads' or 'tails'. We can discover the probability of heads occurring simply by repeating the experiment (i.e. flicking the coin) many times. For instance, if we flick it 100 times, it is likely that the outcome 'heads' will occur approximately 50 times. The relative frequency f of an outcome is the number of times it occurs (heads occurred about 50 times) divided by the number of times that the experiment is repeated (I flicked the coin 100 times). So the probability of heads is:

$$p(H) = f = \frac{50}{100} = 0.5$$

The phrase 'in the long run' means that the greater the number of times we flick it, the closer the relative frequency gets to the 'true' probability, although this does not happen smoothly. I have repeated the experiment 100 times, and Figure 8.2 shows the results. You can see that the relative frequency of heads converges towards 0.5 when the number of experiments increases.

Probability as degree of belief refers to a subjective assessment of the likelihood of a particular outcome. For example, when planning a construction project, it is hard to see what it would mean to see probability as the outcome of repeating the same project. Instead, probability is seen as the degree of belief investors have in various possible alternative outcomes, based on all the relevant information available on similar projects and on the state of the world.

There are three important features of the definition of probability that you have to keep in mind. First, probability is expressed as a number which has a value between 0 and 1. Second, a probability equal to 1 means that the event is certain. Third, the sum of the probabilities of all possible events is 1. In the case of the coin, heads and tails each have a probability of 0.5. There is no positive probability of another outcome.

Now let us return to our firm. It compares project A with project B, which also has three possible outcomes. The outcome of B in the planned state of the world is the same as for project A (£1m). In the bad state of the world, clashes in corporate culture with the personnel of the acquired plant might create problems, and the return would only be half a million pounds. In the good state of the world, the realization of synergies would give a return of £1.5 million. Suppose that the firm assigns probabilities to

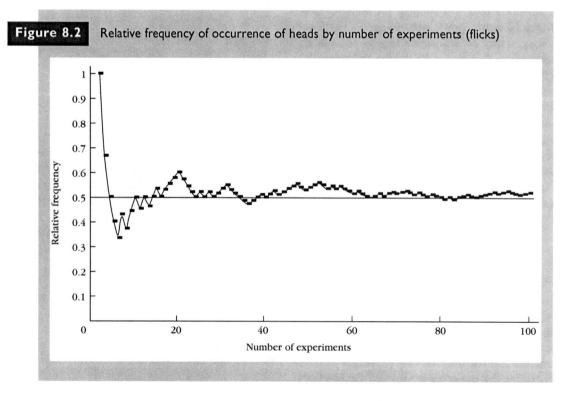

Figure 8.2 Relative frequency of occurrence of heads by number of experiments (flicks)

each outcome for each project through drawing on past experience and the advice of business consultants who have seen many similar projects. For both projects, probability of the planned outcome is 0.5, and the probability of the good and the bad outcomes are each 0.25. Table 8.1 summarizes these data.

We can now calculate the expected value of the returns from each project. This expected return is defined as the weighted mean of the returns, when each return is weighted (that is, multiplied) by its probability (*Changing Economies*, Chapter 9 explains the concept of a weighted mean). The expected return from project A, $E(A)$ is therefore the sum of each outcome multiplied by its probability:

$$E(A) = (0.5) \text{£}1m + (0.25) \text{£}2m + (0.25) \text{£}0 = \text{£}0.5m + \text{£}0.5m + \text{£}0 = \text{£}1m.$$

Question

Calculate the expected value of the returns from project B.

Project B has the same expected return as project A, although the pattern of returns is different:

$$E(B) = (0.5) \text{£}1m + (0.25) \text{£}1.5m + (0.25) \text{£}0.5m = \text{£}0.5m + \text{£}0.375m + \text{£}0.125m = \text{£}1m.$$

So if our firm looks at only expected returns, it will consider the projects to have identical returns. However, looking at Table 8.1, you might feel that project B looks safer than project A, since in the worst case you will still earn £0.5m, whereas with project A you have a 0.25 probability of receiving zero. Figure 8.3 makes the same point graphically. It shows the distribution of the probabilities of all the possible returns from each project.

As Figure 8.3 shows, the returns to project B are less dispersed than the returns to project A. The firm can *measure* the *risk* associated with each project by calculating a measure of the dispersion of the probability distributions shown in Figure 8.3. The standard deviation (*SD*) is a commonly used measure of dispersion (see *Changing Economies*, Chapter 9, Section 3). However, it has the disadvantage that its value is influenced by the value of the mean: the higher the expected return of a project, the larger the standard deviation. Projects with larger returns will therefore tend to appear more risky. This problem can be avoided by using the coefficient of variation (*CV*) (see *Changing Economies*, Chapter 22, Section 5.1) calculated by dividing the standard deviation by the mean.

Risk

The risk attached to an economic action is measured by the dispersion of the probability distribution of its returns in all possible future states of the world.

For projects A and B, the mean, or expected return, has the value 1; therefore the standard deviation and the coefficient of variation measures coincide. The standard deviation of the probability distribution shown in Figure 8.3(a) is calculated as follows. We know that the expected value of the returns, the mean of the probability distribution $E(A) = 1$. The standard deviation is defined as the square root of the average squared distances from the mean. To find the weighted average, each squared distance is multiplied the probability attached to that return. So:

$$SD(A) = \sqrt{(1-1)^2 0.5 + (2-1)^2 0.25 + (0-1)^2 0.25}$$
$$= \sqrt{0 + 0.25 + 0.25} = \sqrt{0.5} = 0.71$$

Table 8.1 Probabilities of all possible outcomes, projects A and B

| State of the world | Project A | | Project B | |
	Return (£m)	Probability	Return (£m)	Probability
Planned	1	0.5	1	0.5
Good	2	0.25	1.5	0.25
Bad	0	0.25	0.5	0.25

The risk attached to project B can be similarly calculated:

$$SD(B) = \sqrt{(1-1)^2 0.5 + (1.5-1)^2 0.25 + (0.5-1)^2 0.25}$$

$$= \sqrt{0 + 0.0625 + 0.0625} = \sqrt{0.125} = 0.35$$

The calculations confirm the visual impression from Figure 8.3 of the riskiness of the projects: project A is more risky than project B.

> **Exercise 8.2**
>
> Suppose our firm has a third option, project C: it can invest its £10 million in research and development (R&D) to develop an innovative solution for the new component. Project C has the same returns as project A: planned return £1 million, good return £2 million, bad return £0. However, the good and bad states, a failure and a very successful innovation respectively, each have a probability of 0.4. The planned outcome, a moderately successful innovation, has therefore a probability of only 0.2.

Figure 8.3 Two projects with the same expected returns, but different probability distributions of returns

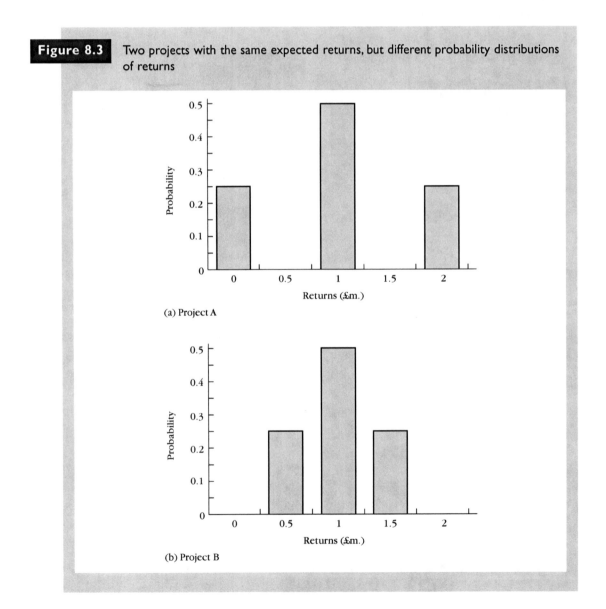

(a) Project A

(b) Project B

Now compare your results for project C (Exercise 8.2) with projects A and B. Each project has the same expected return. If the firm is concerned only to maximize expected returns, and is indifferent to risk, it will be indifferent between the three projects. Such a firm is called *risk-neutral*. If, on the other hand, the firm's decision makers dislike risk, then they will prefer B, which carries the lowest risk. Such a firm is *risk-averse* an assumption quite often made in the economics of managerial decision making, where managers are thought unwilling to make risky decisions for fear of shareholder retribution. Finally, if the firm's decision makers are entrepreneurs – like Digital's Ken Olsen, perhaps, in the early days of the firm – then they may be *risk-seekers* and go for the innovation route C, carrying the highest risk, but also a 40 per cent chance of the highest returns.

Risk-neutrality

An economic agent is risk-neutral if she is indifferent between actions with identical expected returns.

Risk-aversion

An economic agent is risk-averse if, faced with two actions with identical expected returns, she chooses the actions with the lower risk.

Risk-seeking

An economic agent is a risk seeker if, faced with two actions with identical expected returns, she chooses the action with the greater risk.

Uncertainty

The discussion up to this point has assumed that our firm, while it cannot foresee the future, can attach probabilities to states of the world that affect its projects. But this may not of course be true. For some projects (for example, those which are highly innovative, or those which involve moving into geographical areas such as China where the context is changing rapidly) the firm may be unable to assign probabilities to the possible outcomes – may even not know all the possible outcomes. Economists refer to such a situation as one of *uncertainty* rather than risk, a distinction first formulated by Frank Knight in the 1930s.

Uncertainty

An economic agent faces uncertainty if she is unable to attach probabilities to future outcomes from an action.

Uncertainty creates problems for economic analysis, since it appears widespread, and we therefore want to know how decision makers behave under uncertainty. This is an issue that concerned Keynes (Lawson, 1985). He noted that entrepreneurs' investment behaviour is based on expectations about the future, which could be erratic for two reasons. Circumstances may be changing erratically, influencing beliefs. Alternatively, it may be that beliefs are erratic while circumstances are not. Entrepreneurs may be uncertain about the world and, even though the world has not changed, they may believe that it has. These reflections open up the possibility of an influence on firms' behaviour from convention and from the behaviour of other businesses (see Chapter 7, Section 4, for a comparable discussion of the influence of social norms on behaviour). Section 5 of this chapter returns to this theme of behaviour under uncertainty. Before that, we turn in Section 4 to the problem of the size and boundaries of the firm.

 ## 4 NEW INSTITUTIONALISM AND THE BOUNDARIES OF THE FIRM

In theories of the firm, as in other areas of economics, there are two distinct traditions of institutional theorizing. This section introduces the application of new institutional economics to the theory of the firm. New institutional economics retains, as Chapter 1 explains, the individualist assumptions of neoclassical theory. Economic actors are rational and self-interested. New institutional economists apply these assumptions to explain the organization of economic activity, and have generated an influential literature concerning the boundaries of the firm.

This literature, like much other industrial economics, has its origins in the 1930s. In 1937, Ronald Coase, now a Nobel Laureate in Economics, set himself the task of discovering why, if the market is an efficient co-ordinator, some activities are combined together in firms rather than being co-ordinated through markets (Coase, 1937). Coase intended to fill in a gap in economic theory by applying Marshall's concept of decision making at the margin to the problem of defining the boundary between the market and the firm (Coase, 1937, p.386). His analysis has generated an influential body of economic literature called transactions cost economics.

4.1 Transactions cost economics

Much neoclassical theory treats transactions as costless. Market exchange is determined by relative prices, without regard to costs of trading activity. Management costs within the firm are also generally disregarded in neoclassical analysis of productive efficiency. As Coase noted, Marshall was himself aware that this was unrealistic, and indeed suggested that limits on managers' ability to co-ordinate might be an important factor limiting the size of firms. Coase's innovation was to propose that the distinguishing mark of the firm was the replacement of the price mechanism by co-ordination within the firm. Where economic co-ordination could be organized more cheaply within the firm than through the market, he argued that this form of organization would be chosen. The marginal decision to 'make or buy' then determines the size of the firm: 'A firm will tend to expand until the costs of organizing an extra transaction within the firm becomes equal to the costs of carrying out the same transaction by means of an exchange on the open market or the costs of organizing in another firm' (Coase, 1937, p.395).

In the 1930s, these arguments had little resonance. However, since the 1960s, economists have become interested in the impact of the costs of exchange on the pattern and level of economic activity. Oliver Williamson, the most influential industrial theorist to build on Coase's idea, calls transactions costs 'the economic equivalent of friction in physical systems' (Williamson, 1985,

p.19) – so the mechanical metaphor discussed in Section 3.1 is still with us.

'Transactions' are notoriously hard to define. They include all market exchanges, but what are the transactions 'within the firm' that Coase refers to above? These can be defined as those economic relationships that could, in principle, be undertaken through market exchange. Williamson, in *Markets and Hierarchies* (1975), considers transactions across 'technologically separable production stages', which could in principle be undertaken in separate firms. Elsewhere he treats employment relations within a firm as transactions (see Chapter 14, Section 4).

Williamson's starting-point is not a definition of transaction, but a concept of two 'governance structures': markets on the one hand, and hierarchical management on the other. Markets are considered primary: '"in the beginning there were markets"' (Williamson, 1975, p.20; his quotation marks). Firms only emerge where hierarchy economizes on market transactions costs, including search costs, costs of bargaining, and costs of monitoring and enforcing contractual agreements. Firms' internal transactions costs encompass the costs of co-ordinating production, and costs of monitoring and supervising the workforce.

Question

Think back to Digital. What kinds of transactions did it undertake internally which could have been undertaken through the market?

The most striking example in Digital's case is its initial provision of teleworking consultancy services internally. Later, after making Ray Costello redundant, it turned to purchasing these services in the market.

Underlying the concept of transactions costs, as Williamson makes clear, are assumptions which move away from the neoclassical roots of Coase's theory. Transactions are costly because information is incomplete – hence the need for search – and the economic environment is uncertain. Williamson's economic agents display *opportunism*, which he defines as 'self-interest seeking with guile'. He assumes not only that individuals are motivated by narrow self-interest, but also that they will be less than honest in promoting their interests. Since information is limited, opportunism increases the costs and risks of market transactions.

4.2   Markets vs. hierarchies

Vertical integration occurs when a firm takes in-house activities required for final production which could be purchased through the market (see *Changing Economies*, Chapter 12, Section 3.3). Transactions cost theory argues that firms make such decisions by considering each stage in the production process as a separate transaction. In publishing, for example, the production process is broken down into authorship, editing, page design and layout, printing and binding, and other production stages. The author is not normally employed by the publishing house, and editing is frequently carried out on a freelance basis. Printing is usually bought in, often from the Far East. Publishers face uncertainty, but not in the kind of turbulent unsettling way in which the nature of the product changes rapidly, whilst opportunistic behaviour by sellers (authors) is limited, publishers claim, because there are many more people with books to publish than publishing slots available. So market transactions are efficient in this case.

The analysis can also be applied to business services. For example, a small partnership will be likely to buy accountancy services through a market contract. For a major corporation, the accountancy function will probably be carried out by employees with a quite different set of contractual responsibilities: standard employment contracts, various restrictions on employees' opportunities to work for other companies, and open-ended arrangements about the work to be carried out under the direction of a manager. The choice between market contracts and internal employment depends on the scale and type of services required, and on the most effective governance structure to curb opportunistic behaviour in different circumstances.

Transactions cost economics thus allows us to consider systematically the economic factors influencing a firm's decision to buy-in a manufactured input or service, rather than producing it within the firm. In some situations, the difficulty of negotiating and enforcing a market contract – including the search for relevant information – will be reduced by giving one party authority over both 'sides' of the transaction. Williamson suggests that this may particularly be the case where each stage of production requires investments that are tightly adapted to the requirements of the production run; in other words, transactions which require investment in *specific assets*.

Specific assets

Assets are specific to the extent that they have a lower value outside as compared to inside a particular transactional relationship.

As an example of specific assets, consider a car component supplier which invests in equipment to produce components to a precise specification required by a particular assembler. Chapter 9 argues that market contracts can ensure that one firm will make the investment in a specific asset required by another firm. However, such contracting can be costly. Williamson argues that where assets are highly specific, firms will tend to internalize transactions: to make rather than buy.

Investments in human capital can also create specific assets (Chapter 5 defines human capital). Consider the training involved in the installation, design and repair of a particular type of computer system. If a firm buys in these skills from another company, it could be vulnerable to monopoly behaviour by its supplier. If it does its own training, then it may avoid that risk.

Where a firm faces many suppliers of a standardized product, a market transaction is likely to be the cheapest option. Where, however, the quality of a good or service is hard to assess, a supplier will have an incentive to behave opportunistically by reducing the quality. More generally, where a transaction is associated with a good deal of uncertainty, internal supply may improve the information available.

Williamson (1975) also argues that the frequency of a transaction will affect the relative costs of market and hierarchical governance. A repeated market transaction among a small number of participants allows immense scope for opportunistic behaviour. Internalizing the transaction may reduce opportunism: divisions of a company are managed by people who can be sacked if they do not promote the good of the firm as a whole. Furthermore, internal disputes may be more easily and cheaply resolved than disputes over external contracts.

Thus, transactions costs provide us with one type of explanation for the size of firms and their boundaries. The rationale for a firm-like organization becomes clear if we picture a production system in which workers have tightly specified contracts with one another but are all self-employed. Every time a change occurs, contracts need to be rewritten. When circumstances are changing rapidly, it may make more sense to employ staff and managers on loosely specified contracts. The entrepreneur is then free to adapt the firm's behaviour in accordance with long-term policy. The management team, rather than the market, then becomes the co-ordinating device, attempting to prevent employees from taking inconsistent or opportunistic decisions, and defining appropriate responses to changing circumstances. However, a common criticism of Williamson's work is that he is not sufficiently explicit about the costs of hierarchy. Hierarchy also allows scope for opportunism – for example, the opportunistic concealing of information on costs or quality. Chapter 14 explores some of these issues.

Finally, transactions cost economics sees *incentives* as an important influence on transactions costs. Where employees or suppliers have an incentive to act against the interests of the employing or contracting firm, transactions costs of monitoring multiply. Transactions cost economics has therefore stimulated a burgeoning literature on contracting and incentives, the subject of Chapter 9.

4.3 Transactions cost economics and flexible working at Digital

Question

How would a transactions cost theorist explain the decisions around teleworking at Digital?

In Digital's move to teleworking within the firm, the employment transaction was broken down into several components. Staff were Digital employees, but they agreed to use their own homes as work premises, thus saving the company substantial costs, whilst providing time saving and flexibility for staff. The company needed to invest resources in appropriate technology and management to make the system work. The decision separated out the component parts of what had previously been seen as a single transaction, and distributed those parts in a manner which tried to meet the objectives of the company and the staff.

Considering flexible working as a product, the decision by the company to drop flexible working practices from its portfolio, and to make Ray Costello redundant, arose from the judgement that it was cheaper for the company to buy in such expertise from consultants (such as Ray Costello has now become) and therefore move that transaction entirely into the market. Remember that asset specificity can influence the decision to internalize transactions. Flexible working as a product was not thought to require highly specific assets. The technology is readily available and staff can be trained fairly quickly in the use of relevant systems. Consequently, there seemed no reason to maintain in-house expertise, and therefore the company no longer had the ability to supply the product. It was redefining its boundaries in the way Coase and Williamson would suggest.

However, it is possible that the company made a mistake by concentrating on physical assets. It may be that management skills and knowledge of human systems such as Ray Costello possessed are very difficult to replace with outside advice. Certainly, his colleagues believed this to be true. If so, the company might have become a market leader in flexible working practices by building on its skills in human systems (personified by Costello) and its competence in providing sophisticated technological solutions to its clients' problems. These considerations were debated within the company. In developing flexible working the company might have altered the nature of its environment and of itself as a company. But these actions were not taken.

Section 5, which considers models of decision-making processes within firms, offers some explanations of why firms may not seize all the opportunities apparently open to them in conditions of uncertainty.

5 'OLD' INSTITUTIONALISM AND EVOLUTIONARY THEORY

Alongside the rise of new institutional economics, the economics of the firm has seen a revival of an older tradition of institutional thought. The 'old' institutionalism was for many years a particularly American phenomenon (though there was also a German historical school). In the USA it centred on the work of Thorstein Veblen (see Chapter 3) and

John R. Commons who wrote in the late nineteenth and early twentieth centuries. These theorists took an interdisciplinary approach which emphasized social and economic evolution, arguing that institutions are socially constructed and enduring. Like the new institutional economists, broad institutionalists see the market itself as an institution. But their definition of 'institution' emphasizes norms and culture. For example, Richard Nelson, an evolutionary economic theorist, defines an institution as 'a complex of socially learned and shared values, norms, beliefs, meanings, symbols, customs and standards that delineate the range of expected and accepted behaviour in a particular context' (Nelson, 1995, p.80).

An institution in this tradition is thus a well-established way of getting things done. It is not necessarily a legal or physical entity. Customary modes of conduct, for example attending church or participating in lunchtime seminars, are institutions, as are legal agreements such as marriage. Firms count as institutions but so do the cultures and routines within them. To see why this concept of institution has been so productive of new theorizing about the firm, we return to a question raised at the beginning of Section 3 – what are the objectives of the firm? – and consider it in the context of the imperfect information and uncertainty emphasized by the transactions cost theorists.

5.1 Firms' objectives: maximization vs. satisficing

In the 1950s and 1960s, the older tradition of institutionalism influenced a number of economists writing on the nature of the firm. One group, known as 'behavioural' theorists, saw a firm's objectives as arising from compromises among a coalition of key players within the firm. A second set, the 'managerial' theorists, emphasized the role of professional managers in setting firms' objectives, and argued that there was likely to be conflict between managers' objectives and those of shareholders. They held that managers were likely to pursue growth, of sales or assets, and to increase their own incomes, rather than maximize profits. Since shareholders would find monitoring costly, managers would have a considerable margin of discretion to pursue these goals. This theme of conflict between managers and shareholders is developed in the economics of corporate finance (see Chapter 17).

The managerial theorists, however, still drew on the concept of maximization under constraints to analyse firms' objectives. Rationality within this framework is *instrumental rationality* that is, employing the best means to clearly defined ends. An alternative, which has been enjoying a revival, is the concept of *bounded rationality* developed in the work of Herbert Simon from the 1950s onwards. (This concept is also employed by Williamson – there is some overlap between the schools of institutional thought.)

Instrumental rationality

The choice of the best means to specified ends.

Bounded rationality

Bounded rationality exists when decision making is influenced by the limited cognitive capacity of economic actors.

Bounded rationality, in Simon's work, is not simply a recognition of incomplete information, but also of cognitive limitations on rationality. In other words, decisions are made on the basis of partial information, according to Simon, because 'the capacity of the human mind for formulating and solving complex problems is very small compared with the size of the problems whose solution is required for objectively rational behaviour in the real world' (Simon, 1957, p.198).

Question

Which concept of rationality, bounded or instrumental, do you think best fits in the Digital case?

Clearly, Digital was very uncertain about its future and did not appear to be able to compute easily the options facing it. This fits the concept of bounded rationality. We return to the implications of this observation below.

Simon argued that bounded rationality and the implied behaviour meant that firms were unable to maximize. Instead, he proposed (1959) that the decision maker could be modelled as having a pay-off function with two values for outcomes: those which are satisfactory and those which are unsatisfactory. Decision takers would cease the search for new options, according to Simon, once a satisfactory option was discovered. This is not, of course the same process as maximizing, since a more profitable satisfactory option might exist. This decision-making process Simon labelled *satisficing*. It is a way of dealing with uncertainty. The rule-bound behaviour of evolutionary theory, discussed below, can be seen as a form of satisficing.

> ### Satisficing
>
> Satisficing exists when decision takers cease searching for new options once a satisfactory option is discovered.

5.2   Routines in evolutionary theory

The concepts of bounded rationality and satisficing led Simon, as it has led other institutional theorists, to a concern with firms' internal decision-making *processes*, in sharp contrast to neoclassical theorists' emphasis on *outcomes*. The dispute turns on the importance of the descriptive plausibility of models and their assumptions: one of the deepest theoretical divides between neoclassical and institutional economics. Like many economic debates, this one has a long history. Fritz Machlup, an eminent economic theorist, identified the issues in the 1940s. He argued that firms might make the decisions that neoclassical models predict, even though they would not account for their behaviour in a form recognizably similar to the models. He used an example that has been quoted ever since:

> *'What sort of considerations are behind the routine decision of the driver of an automobile to overtake a truck proceeding ahead of him at slower speed? What factors influence his decision? Assume that he is faced with the alternative of either slowing down and staying behind the truck or of passing it before a car, which is approaching from the opposite direction, will have reached the spot. As an experienced driver he somehow takes into account (a) the speed at which the truck is going, (b) the remaining distance between himself and the truck, (c) the speed at which he is proceeding, (d) the possible acceleration of his speed, (e) the distance between him and the car approaching from the opposite direction, (f) the speed at which that car is approaching, and*

probably also the condition of the road (concrete or dirt, wet or dry, straight or winding, level or uphill), the degree of visibility (light or dark, clear or foggy), and the condition of the tyres and brakes of his car and – let us hope – his own condition (fresh or tired, sober or alcoholized) permitting him to judge the enumerated factors. Clearly, the driver of the automobile will not 'measure' the variables; he will not 'calculate' the time needed for the vehicles to cover the estimated distances at the estimated rates of speed; and, of course, none of the 'estimates' will be expressed in numerical values. Even so, without measurements, numerical estimates or calculations, he will in a routine way do the indicated 'sizing-up' of the total situation. He will not break it down into its elements. Yet a 'theory of overtaking' would have to include all these elements (and perhaps others besides) and would have to state how changes in any of the factors were likely to affect the decisions or actions of the driver. The 'extreme difficulty of calculating', the fact that 'it would be utterly impractical' to attempt to work out and ascertain the exact magnitudes of the variables which the theorist alleges to be significant, show merely that the explanation of an action must often include steps of reasoning which the acting individual himself does not consciously perform (because the action has become routine) and which perhaps he would never be able to perform in scientific exactness (because such exactness is not necessary in everyday life).

The businessman who equates marginal net revenue productivity and marginal factor cost when he decides how many to employ need not engage in higher mathematics, geometry, or clairvoyance. Ordinarily he would not even consult with his accountant or efficiency expert in order to arrive at his decision; he would not make any tests or formal calculations; he would simply rely on his sense or his 'feel' of the situation. There is nothing very exact about this sort of estimate. On the basis of hundreds of previous experiences of a similar nature the businessman would 'just know', in a vague and rough way, whether or not it would pay him to hire more men'

(Machlup, 1946, pp.534–5).

The notion that businessmen do not anxiously consult accountants has a pleasantly dated air! Nevertheless, Machlup's key point is a striking one. Business decision making, he is saying, is skilled behaviour, comparable to driving a car. It involves large amounts of learned skill, as well as limited amounts of immediate calculation. Machlup's driver behaves rationally; that is to say he overtakes safely using internalized knowledge and skill. His behaviour will be modified if he learns, through a near-miss perhaps, that his skill and knowledge are inadequate.

The example is interesting because institutional theorists generally *agree* with Machlup's point that management involves internalized skill. The dispute is about how to model it. Machlup argues that internalization of skills implies that the realism of the neoclassical model's assumptions is irrelevant: the business manager can be modelled as if choosing to maximize profits, because that will be the outcome of the 'feel' he has developed. His institutionalist critics argue that this will not do. Skilful behaviour, they argue, is precisely not about choice. It has, as Machlup's example so well demonstrates, become automatic. And just because it is automatic, there is the possibility of serious error. Richard Nelson and Sidney Winter, two influential evolutionary theorists, note that the automatic responses of an American driver in Britain, driving on the 'wrong' side of the road, may be anything but safe (Nelson and Winter, 1982, p.94). Similarly, a firm's manager may display response patterns, drawing on internalized knowledge and skill, after the environment for which they were appropriate has changed. To understand a firm's behaviour, we therefore need to know the sources, in the firm's history, its organizational culture and social milieu, of the response patterns of its staff.

The last twenty years have seen a burst of work on evolutionary approaches to firms' behaviour, drawing on this institutionalist viewpoint (see Chapter 16). There are two key elements of evolutionary models that sharply differentiate them from the neoclassical tradition: their treatment of time and of decision making.

In evolutionary theory, history matters. Time brings with it different cultures, experiences and ways of doing things, so that history constrains the present. In other words, the firm's options are *path dependent*; that is, the path the firm has taken in the past determines what it is capable of, shapes the way it makes decisions, and closes off options. Note that new institutional economists also accept the importance of path dependency. Both schools accept that institutions such as firms and industries may be trapped into inefficient behaviour by long-past influences and decisions: the difference between them lies in the way they analyse the problem.

In evolutionary models, firms operate with bounded rationality in the face of uncertainty. Decisions are therefore taken step-wise and based on rules. A decision taken now is based on previous experience and the current situation. A decision taken tomorrow will be based on the same things plus the effects of today's decision. Firms therefore develop decision procedures. A given stimulus, such as a change in interest rates, will set in motion a particular set of procedures that have worked well in the past.

In a classic text in evolutionary economics (Nelson and Winter, 1982), firms are modelled as having particular capabilities and their own established decision rules. Capabilities are modified both deliberately and randomly, and an economic form of natural selection takes place as less profitable firms are driven out. Predictable patterns of behaviour are called *routines*.

Routine

A routine is a regular and predictable behaviour pattern.

These routines are the building blocks of evolutionary modelling: it is routines, rather than 'choices' which drive decision making. Routines are seen as persistent and heritable, passed on through the operation of the organization. Routines, plus the impact of unpredictable environmental factors, together determine firms' decision making and outcomes in these models.

Nelson and Winter classify routines into three categories. The first are called 'operating characteristics'. These determine what the firm will do in the short run, before it has time to change its capital stock. The second are routines which determine the firm's investment behaviour: its investment rules. And the third are 'search' routines that guide the way in which the firm scrutinizes its own behaviour. They include, for example, the way in which advertising policy is reviewed, the procedures for improving production systems, and the organization of research and development (R&D). This searching responds to external pressures, such as changes in profitability, sales or market share, but Nelson and Winter argue that it too is guided by established procedures within individual firms.

Routines therefore carry the accumulated skill and knowledge of the firm, which would be complex and costly to codify and set down. The firm's managers do not have constantly to consult manuals, because the learned understandings on which the firm works are largely embedded in the firm's routines. Evolutionary theorists agree with Machlup that managers, like skilful drivers, keep the show on the road through internalized skill. But they understand that skill as embedded in routines, limited by past history, and betraying the limitations as well as the strengths of repeated practice.

5.3 Digital once again

> **Question**
>
> How do you think an evolutionary theorist would explain Digital's retreat from selling flexible working processes as part of its product portfolio?

Evolutionary theory can offer an explanation of why that particular activity was chosen for closure. The company had used teleworking effectively, but could not know with any certainty whether it offered a major new market. Nor did the firm's managers know that the new Alpha system would be a potential life-saver. Under uncertainty, evolutionary theorists would look to the firm's history, its culture and its routines to explain the decision. Who, within the staff, was collaborating with whom, and why did they push the company to develop in this particular direction?

The culture of the company was essentially that of a manufacturing organization. When it came to focusing activity to reduce losses, manufacturing was viewed within the company as more important than the softer activity of technical consultancy. Managers' search routines were based in a perception of the firm as a manufacturer of electronic equipment: this was its core capability in their eyes. But the company's cultural roots, from its founding by a Quaker, meant that it should value staff, and made cutting back a difficult activity. It is interesting to note that the process involved the appointment of a new Chief Executive from a manufacturing background.

Major organizational change is frequently associated in this way with new senior appointments.

The uncertainty involved in providing advice and support to the new flexible-working markets was high and, since the company defined itself as a manufacturing operation, those markets were perceived as a distraction.

The *internal* working routines in the company had however been successfully changed during the crisis. Staff were working from their homes using equipment provided by the company. The conventional twentieth-century boundaries of what constituted work space and what constituted domestic space had been questioned by these changes. This was a huge shift in operating characteristics which was sustained as an internal organizational structure after the consultancy product was dropped. The three concepts of routine help to identify the new characteristics of the firm – and its likely behaviour – as it emerged from the crisis.

5.4 Time in models of firms' behaviour

Finally, I want to say a little more about the treatment of time in neoclassical and evolutionary modelling. In many evolutionary models, once a step is taken, it is not possible to go back. This irreversibility of time seems a plausible description of the way institutions change, but it is in sharp contrast to the reversible notion of time in neoclassical comparative statics (see Section 3.1). Comparative static analysis of firms' behaviour compares the characteristics of initial and final equilibria, given a change in the environment and with all other influences held constant (*ceteris paribus*). In this framework, time is in principle reversible – it is theoretical, not historical, time.

Marshall was well aware that there was a problem in incorporating time into formal economic theory. Criticisms of the static analysis in Marshall's *Principles of Economics* brought a response from Marshall in the preface to the fifth edition in which he stated, 'The Mecca of the economist is economic biology rather than economic dynamics' (Marshall, 1907). By 'dynamics' here Marshall was referring to the use of that term in physics; that is, to the mechanical analogies of seesaws and equilibria. He was saying that the most important things for economists to consider relate to growth, change and evolution rather than static equilibrium.

Marshall's wrestling with the problem of time led him to develop a distinction between short and long run. The short run was the period when capital stock was fixed; the long run the period over which a firm could invest. This short/long run distinction has now been taken wholly into neoclassical comparative static analysis (see Chapter 10), but Marshall developed it initially to address the recognition that investment, and increasing returns to scale, happen over time.

Current industrial economics in the neoclassical tradition also recognizes a dynamic element in economies of scale. Falling unit costs can arise from learning – that is to say, from people getting better at doing something over time (see Chapter 11, Section 2). Evolutionary models that treat time as irreversible can incorporate learning as a normal element of a firm's development. In evolutionary theory, therefore, time and sequence of events strongly influence outcomes and there is no assumption of convergence to an equilibrium. So the notion of time that evolutionary models incorporate is closer to historical time than to the formal, reversible 'time' of neoclassical theorizing.

6 CONCLUSION

Neoclassical theory does not really have a theory of the *firm* distinct from its theories of competition. The firm is a black box of technological and managerial relationships, the costs of which are assumed to be minimized in pursuit of the firm's profit-maximizing objective. Coase and Williamson, however, extend the neoclassical starting-point to account for the existence and size of the firm. The focus is on the make-or-buy decision, showing how the firm chooses between hierarchy and market.

Economic theory is also concerned with how firms take decisions. Here there are two different approaches to rationality and routines. Neoclassical theories examine choices at the margin, using the decision rule of maximizing under constraints. Evolutionary theorists argue that processes and routines which allow a firm to cope with uncertainty are more appropriate as a basis for modelling. The broad institutionalism on which the evolutionary theorists draw pays close attention to history and institutional context. Many

institutionalists see detailed case studies as an essential basis for understanding and modelling firms' behaviour.

The different theoretical approaches are asking different questions about firms. In many respects, neoclassical theory is less interested in firms themselves than in the market structures of which they form part. For institutional theorists, however, the culture and internal organization of firms are matters of central concern. The rest of this book draws extensively on the neoclassical and institutional theories of the firm introduced here.

 ## FURTHER READING

Institutional economics

Hodgson G.M. (1994) 'Institutionalism "old and new"', in Hodgson G.M., Samuels, W.J. and Tool, M.R., *The Elgar Companion to Institutional and Evolutionary Economics,* Aldershot, Edward Elgar, pp.397–403: is a good readable historical survey of institutional economics. The *Journal of Economic Issues* is the primary journal in the field.

Transactions costs and new institutionalism

The original article by Coase (1937) is quite readable. Oliver Williamson summarizes his notion of transactions costs in 'What is transaction cost economics?', Chapter 9 of Williamson, O.E. (1986) *Economic Organization: Firms, Markets and Policy Control,* Brighton, Wheatsheaf Books. Williamson's approach is criticized in Ghoshal, S. and Moran, P. (1996) 'Bad for practice: a critique of the transaction cost theory', *Academy of Management Review,* Vol.21, No.1, pp.13–47.

Evolutionary economics

A brief but comprehensive introduction to evolutionary theory is provided by the Introduction in Witt, U. (ed.) *Evolutionary Economics,* The International Library of Critical Writings in Economics, Vol.25, Aldershot, Edward Elgar, pp.xii–xxvii: This collection provides an accessible account of different evolutionary approaches.

ANSWERS TO EXERCISES

Exercise 8.1

1 In Figure 8.1, Digital is making supernormal profits because at Q_1 it can charge prices P_1 substantially above its average cost per unit AC_1. The entry of new competitors will shift the AR curve to the left, since Digital will have to share the market with more competing firms. This change alone could push Digital into loss, if entry was extensive, as Figure 8.4 shows. In Figure 8.4 the shift in AR to AR_2 causes a loss because average cost AC_2 now exceeds price P_2 at the new equilibrium output Q_2. However, this would not be an equilibrium situation. In the long run, enough firms would move out of the industry to allow those left to make normal profits.

Furthermore, the case study suggests that Digital had come to have higher costs than its competitors, through being overstaffed and having high office costs and an expensive organizational structure. This would explain the scale of Digital's losses: since monopolistic competition retains many of the features of perfect competition, Digital would lose all new customers to cheaper competitors unless it reacted fast.

2 Digital therefore had to cut costs sharply to regain profitability, closing offices and making people (including Ray Costello) redundant. Such cost cutting lowers the firm's average cost curve to a position such as $LRAC_2$ on Figure 8.5. At the new price and output combinations P_3 and Q_3, the firm is making normal profits.

Exercise 8.2

1 The expected return to project C is calculated as follows:

$$E(C) = (0.2)\,\£1m + (0.4)\,\£2m + (0.4)\,\£0$$
$$= \£0.2m + \£0.8m + \£0 = \£1m.$$

2 See Figure 8.6.

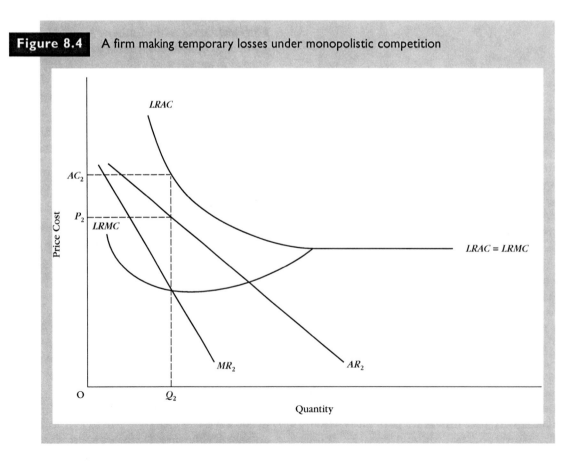

Figure 8.4 A firm making temporary losses under monopolistic competition

Figure 8.5 A decline in costs moves a firm to equilibrium under monopolistic competition

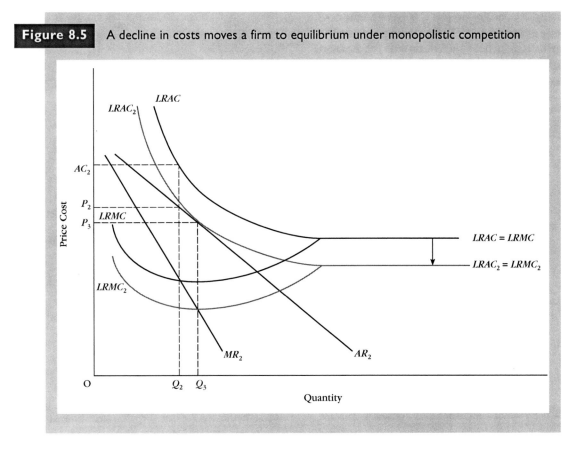

Figure 8.6 Probability distribution of returns from project C

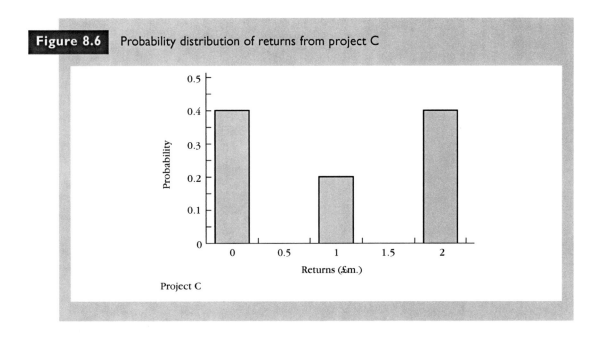

Project C

3 The risk attached to project C is equal to the coefficient of variation of the probability distribution of returns, which is equal in turn to the standard deviation of the distribution, since the expected return = 1:

$$SD(C) = \sqrt{(1-1)^2 0.2 + (2-1)^2 0.4 + (0-1)^2 0.4}$$

$$= \sqrt{0 + 0.4 + 0.4} = \sqrt{0.8} = 0.89$$

CONTRACTS, INFORMATION AND FIRMS' BEHAVIOUR

Maureen Mackintosh

CONCEPTS AND TECHNIQUES

Spot and long-term contracts
Complete and incomplete contracts
Implicit and explicit contracts
Hold-up problem, long-term contracting and the alienation point
Sunk costs
Vertical integration
Asymmetric information, adverse selection and moral hazard
Strategic and extensive form games
Dominant strategies and Nash equilibrium in games
Prisoner's dilemma and reputation games
Discounting
Principal-agent problem, hidden action and incentive contracts
Contract failure and non-profit firms

LINKS

- This chapter introduces many core concepts and techniques of new institutional theory, which are used to analyse various issues in the chapters that follow. The concept of contracting is central to the new institutional approach and represents an important step forward from the neoclassical exclusive focus on spot contracts. Many new institutional theories, such as the principal-agent problem, focus on how various types of contracts can solve problems that arise from the imperfect and uneven distribution of information among economic agents.

- The analysis of social markets in Chapter 19 draws on the concepts of hold-up, adverse selection, principal and agent, and takes the teaching of game theory further. The relationships between employees and employers are also analysed within a new institutional framework that adopts concepts introduced here, including the principal-agent problem, in Chapter 14.

- A key technique developed here is that of game theory. In the absence of full information consumers and firms adopt strategies which are interdependent, that is, dependent on each other's strategies. Chapter 11 further develops game theory to analyse strategic behaviour in oligopolistic industries. Chapter 19 also extends the use and knowledge of game theory.

- The theory of bargaining illustrated in this chapter has a structure similar to the bargaining models already met in Chapter 6. In particular, there is a similarity between the *alienation point* and the *threat point* in the two models

1 INTRODUCTION: CONTRACTS AND MARKETS

British Gas's long-term contracts

In 1995, Clare Spottiswoode, the UK gas industry regulator, gave a downward push to sliding British Gas share prices. She warned that, because of long-term contracts previously signed by the firm, 'It's not obvious that British Gas's long-term financial position is secure.' Before and after privatization in 1986, British Gas had signed £40bn worth of 25- to 30-year contracts to buy gas from large North Sea producers. The contracts included 'take or pay' clauses that required British Gas to pay for the gas even if it could not resell it. At the time the company had been a monopoly purchaser and supplier of gas.

Subsequently, the market for gas supply to industry and commerce was opened up to competition (or 'liberalized'), and the effects were dramatic. British Gas's market share fell below 35 per cent, North Sea gas supplies increased and prices dropped. In mid 1996, British Gas was paying an average of 19p a therm for contracted gas while spot market prices ranged between 9p and 13p a therm; in six months of that year the company lost £180m on reselling gas from the contracts. With the opening of the still-monopolized domestic gas market to competition planned for 1998, the losses were set to grow. Hence the falling share price.

So what should or could be done? The company blamed its troubles on the government's gas industry liberalization – 'The government changed the game on us' – and wanted the contracts renegotiated. In its chief executive's view, 'All the stakeholders in the industry should share the pain of its transformation.' The regulator expected the North Sea gas producers to be unimpressed. After all, she noted, they have legally binding contracts, so why should they renegotiate? She also ruled out suggestions that new entrants to the domestic gas market should be forced also to sign long-term contracts: 'That would be bad for the consumer.'

British Gas responded to the dilemma by a demerger. In February 1997 it split its operations into BG plc, a company including its pipeline arm (TransCo) and its exploration activities, and Centrica, a separately quoted gas trading and domestic supply company which would own one large established gasfield and into which would go all the problematic long-term contracts. The demerger plans focused attention in 1996 on the need for contract renegotiation, since Centrica was thought by some market analysts to have an uncertain future, faced with rising competition and uncertain total liabilities. By January 1998, Centrica had renegotiated all the most problematic contracts. Some contracts were cancelled and others had prices reduced. In exchange, gas producers such as BP and Mobil gained financial compensation, and took over British Gas stakes in gasfields and an offshore pipeline (*Financial Times,* 25–28 September, 1995; 7 February, 26 July, 13 September, 6 December and 24 December, 1996; 13 January, 1997; 8 January 1998).

Contracts and markets

This chapter introduces the analysis of market behaviour understood as diverse forms of contracting. A 'contract' in economics is not necessarily a legal document; it may include the implicit understandings which frame the behaviour of parties to a transaction, as Section 2 explains. We can think of all market transactions as involving contracts. However, in the core neoclassical model, with perfect competition and complete information, defining the instantaneously completed transactions as 'contracts' would add nothing to the model. The economics of contracting has been developed since the 1970s to explore market behaviour in conditions of imperfect information and positive transactions costs: conditions we might regard as the standard market situation. Contract theorists have been particularly interested in the extent to which voluntary contracting can improve efficiency by overcoming market failure.

The British Gas story raises a number of issues which will be explored in this chapter. It illustrates, first, the close interrelationship between market structure and contracting behaviour. The UK industrial and commercial gas market evolved between 1986 and 1997 from domination by a monopoly supplier purchasing gas on long-term contracts, to a much more competitive supply situation where large gas users signed shorter contracts at lower prices directly with a range of competing suppliers. So contracting decisions are a key element of firms' competitive behaviour in markets. An earlier British Gas chairman, Sir Denis Rooke, argued that, without the long-term contracts, the North Sea gasfields could not have been developed (*Financial Times,* 7 February, 1996). In some market contexts, long-term contracts may be both efficient and desirable from the point of view of the consumer; in other contexts they are an anti-competitive device (see Section 2).

The story also illustrates the limits of legally binding contracts: legal rights do not imply certainty. The rights to income established by a contract may turn to dust and ashes if the signatory cannot pay, or if a firm's insistence on its rights frightens off other potential trading partners. Any contract can be renegotiated, and showing the flexibility to negotiate 'a more sensible deal', as a gas industry analyst put it, can at times attract new business and help stabilize a market. Furthermore, the story demonstrates the importance of information: no parties to contracts have complete information, but some are better informed than others. As another gas industry analyst put it at the time, 'most people think that, after the company, the regulator has the most information. And if she thinks the market has not got to the bottom of the problem, the market worries' (*Financial Times*, 29 October, 1995). Section 3 explores the implications of incomplete and uneven information for firms' contracting behaviour and consumers' interests.

Finally, the demerger of British Gas illustrates another theme of the chapter – that the structure of market contracting affects the organization and objectives of firms themselves. The shift to greater competition in gas supply changed the pattern of market contracting to shorter term contracts, and British Gas responded by restructuring. This theme is picked up in Section 4 in a different market context. In sectors where consumers are not in a position to make informed contracting decisions, firms whose explicit objectives exclude profit seeking may have a market advantage. This argument may help to explain the numbers of 'third sector' organizations, encompassing charities and other voluntary bodies, non-profit trading companies, co-operatives and trusts, in industrialized economies.

The chapter begins by explaining some of the key concepts and assumptions of contracting theory. The rest of Section 2 then explores the reasons why firms may tie themselves into long-term contracts even when information is complete. The rest of the chapter considers contracting problems where information is incomplete. Section 3 investigates firms' market behaviour in situations where consumers are poorly informed about their products until they have bought them. Section 4 extends the analysis to cases where users of services can never fully judge their quality.

2 TIME AND CONTRACTS: SHORT- AND LONG-TERM CONTRACTING

2.1 Contract terms

Consider the following contracts.

- A firm sends a purchase order to a supplier of office furniture, based on a catalogue and a price list.
- A firm employs an engineering consultancy firm to design and manage to completion, on its behalf, a large-scale construction project.

Both of these contracts are likely to have been preceded by some market research, and perhaps even by a formal tendering procedure. They are nevertheless quite different kinds of contract.

We can analyse these different types of contract on several dimensions. The most obvious is *time*. The first contract is very short-term: a specific order at an agreed price, completed when the furniture is delivered and the invoice is paid. The second is a long-term contract, perhaps lasting years.

The first contract is an example of a *spot contract*. Spot contracts are very short-term contracts. In the extreme, they are completed instantaneously. The assumption which underlies them is that external conditions will not change during the transaction. So inflation can be assumed away – the prices in the furniture catalogue do not change before delivery.

Spot contract

A spot contract is a contract for a single rapidly completed transaction.

Question

Make a list of examples of spot contracts before reading on.

Spot contracts are extremely common. Your examples might have ranged over shopping for food and clothing, buying a meal in a restaurant, taking a taxi, posting a letter: a whole range of daily purchases and sales. A firm also purchases standard inputs to its production process in this way. When the gas market was liberalized, as described in

Section 1, a spot market in gas emerged. On spot markets for such primary commodities, prices tend to change rapidly, and large buyers can make one-off 'spot' purchases at the market price prevailing at the moment of purchase. Buying and selling financial assets such as stocks and shares is another form of spot contracting.

However, while an industrialized economy operates on huge numbers of spot transactions, the industrial economist John Kay points out that the most important commercial relationships are rarely spot contracts: 'Managers do not raise finance, rent property, hire senior employees or deal with their principal suppliers through spot contracts' (1993, p.51). Such longer term relationships are built on long-term contracts, which therefore need to take account of possible future events, or 'contingencies'. Long-term contracts contain statements in the form 'if x then y', where x is an event and y the response of the contracting parties. If every possible contingency were allowed for, a contract would be *complete*.

> ### Complete contract
>
> A complete contract would be one which specified the actions of the contracting parties in all the circumstances which could arise, including all of each other's possible actions.

Completeness is thus the second dimension on which contract terms can be analysed. Spot contracts may be complete, because they happen fast. But in a long-term contract, it would generally be impossible to specify in advance all the problems which might arise. *Incomplete contracts* are therefore the norm. Long-term contracts vary, however, in the degree of completeness for which they are designed. Some are very detailed: for example, personal insurance contracts or financial agreements. British Gas's long-term contracts seem to have been tightly drawn, but had not provided for the government's changing of the regulatory environment. In other cases, the incompleteness is deliberate. In the construction example considered at the beginning of this section, the engineering consultancy firm is being employed partly for its professional expertise in managing the unforeseen, so the contract will leave quite a lot of issues to be sorted out after the contract is signed.

Where written contracts are incomplete by design, there may be mutual understandings which can be seen as an *implicit contract*. Implicitness is therefore the third dimension on which contract terms can be analysed. British Gas's contracts with its suppliers were wholly explicit. By contrast, custom and practice within an organization can be considered as a set of implicit contracts. Similarly, the explicit element of the 'design and manage' contract of the engineering consultancy firm will have been signed in a context of shared expectations based on experience of similar contracts in the construction industry. Long-term implicit contracts are very common in industry, especially in working relations between firms (Chapter 11) and in employment relations (Chapter 14). Even spot contracts are frequently implicit: taking a taxi involves little paperwork, but the passengers understand that their implicit agreement is to pay the fee on the meter, while the taxi driver is supposed to know the way. Non-compliance on either side causes loud complaint!

> ### Implicit contract
>
> An implicit contract is a set of shared expectations about each other's behaviour which the parties consider binding.

Contract terms can therefore be analysed on three dimensions: length, completeness and implicitness. Contracts in practice are usually incomplete and often partly implicit, relying on working relationships and shared understandings of normal behaviour to oil the wheels of commerce and keep disputes out of the courts. However, complete explicit contracts are a relevant benchmark in economics, because just such complete contracts are assumed in the model of perfect competition, and the general equilibrium model built upon it (see Chapter 18).

2.2 Specific assets and long-term contracts

Given the uncertainties of the future, why should firms enter into long-term contracts? Why not just negotiate each exchange as it comes along? Contracting theory builds upon Williamson's analysis of the make-or-buy decision of a firm (see Chapter 8, Section 4). Williamson noted that investment is a 'lumpy' process, done in discrete chunks, and often creating assets which cannot easily be switched to other uses. He argued that such *asset specificity* can make it worthwhile for a firm to produce an input for itself, rather than buying it in, in order to avoid being subject to opportunistic behaviour by a supplying firm. This approach can be extended to explain some kinds of long-term contracting.

An important set of specific assets are 'relationship-specific' assets: assets which result when one party to a contract agrees to make an investment which is worth much more inside the contract than outside it. Where investments are relationship-specific it may be efficient for contracting firms to 'tie their hands' at the start of a contractual relationship, for reasons to be explained.

Specific investments required by contracts between firms do not have to be in physical plant. For example, a supplier to a large retail chain may make investments in both production systems and training specific to that large contract; a components supplier making specialized components for a car assembler may do likewise. These investments will become worth less if the contractual relationship is not sustained.

The snag here is that, without a long-term contract, the firm making the investment will tend to underinvest. To see why, look back at the British Gas example.

Question

Can you think of a reason why long-term contracts might have been necessary to get North Sea gas produced, as Denis Rooke argued?

Without a guaranteed price over a long period, written into a long-term contract, North Sea gas producers might not have had a high enough expected return to persuade them to invest. British Gas was a monopoly gas wholesaler in the 1980s, and the producers would have been afraid that, once they had invested in developing new gasfields, British Gas would use its monopsony (its market power as sole buyer) to drive down the price. The firms would be in a weak bargaining position because their relationship-specific asset (the gasfield) would only produce a return through sales to British Gas. Foreseeing this problem, the firms would have been unwilling to invest, and gas consumers would have been among the losers.

This type of contracting problem is called by economists the *hold-up* problem, because the circumstances allow one party to 'hold-up' the other, to everyone's detriment. We can think of it as a two-stage decision-making problem, where the bargaining strength of two parties changes at each stage. A project is devised – such as producing and selling North Sea gas – which can benefit both wholesaler and gas producer. In stage one, the producer decides whether or not to make an investment in developing a gasfield, on the basis of its expected returns to the producing firm. In the second stage, there is a joint income stream expected from the investment, to be shared between producer and wholesaler.

Hold up

Hold up occurs when investors in specific assets face less favourable contract terms after the investment is made than the terms agreed beforehand.

Figure 9.1 overleaf illustrates the bargaining problem in a very simplified form. Suppose that joint income will be 100 to be shared between the parties, and suppose that both sides regard those returns as certain. The available shares of the income lie along the line AB on Figure 9.1. At A the producer receives 100 while the wholesaler gets nothing; at B the wholesaler gets the 100 and the producer nothing.

Suppose, further, that over the life of the project – stages one and two – the producer needs a minimum of 60 to cover costs. The wholesaler just needs 10 to make the project worthwhile. Both parties know the other's costs.

If the share-out of returns can be determined before the investment is made, then these assumptions imply that point F is the 'alienation point'; that is, below or to the left of F, the parties will walk away from the deal. (This is similar to the 'threat point' analysed in the household bargaining models in Chapter 6, Section 3.3). The shaded area shows the negotiation set; that is, any share-out within this area will provide a positive return to both parties. Depending on relative bargaining strength and skill, the agreed division of the returns will be somewhere along the line CD where all income is shared out and neither firm makes a loss. Point Z represents a possible outcome, where the producer gets 70 and the wholesaler 30.

Therefore, if the two firms can sign a long-term contract, and both believe the contract will have to be honoured, a share of profits can be agreed (for example, by agreeing in advance the price of the gas to the producer) and the investment will be undertaken.

Figure 9.1 can also be used to analyse the problem that arises if such a long-term contract cannot be signed. Suppose the producing firm invests in stage one. Its investment is then a *sunk cost*; that is, an expenditure on fixed assets which cannot be retrieved. The firm cannot sell the asset, which by assumption is worthless outside the relationship with the wholesaler. Suppose further that, having made the investment, the producer only needs 10 to cover operating costs in stage two. It will then be worthwhile for the producer to sell gas to the wholesaler rather than shut down, so long as the producer's income exceeds 10. The alienation point has moved in stage two to point G. The producer's bargaining position has worsened.

Sunk costs

Sunk costs are a firm's fixed and irrecoverable costs.

The wholesaler thus has an incentive to behave opportunistically, holding up the producer for a higher share of profits once the investment is made. The division of total income in stage two will fall

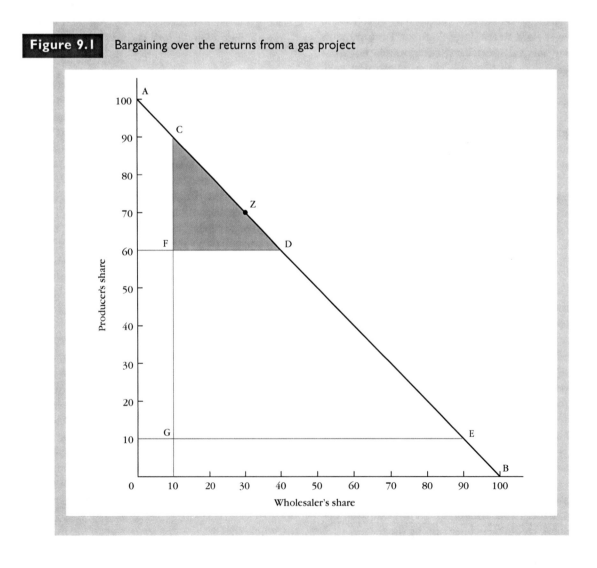

Figure 9.1   Bargaining over the returns from a gas project

Producer's share (vertical axis)
Wholesaler's share (horizontal axis)

between C and E on Figure 9.1, and the producer will fear being forced to accept a lower price from the wholesaler that will move the share-out to between D and E, and thus leave the producer making a loss on its total investment. The implication is that unless the wholesaler signs a long-term contract before the investment to pay a price for gas that will sustain income to the producer of at least 60, and unless the producer believes that the contract is secure, the gas investment will not be made, and its benefits will be lost.

Contracting theorists argue, therefore, that even if – as assumed above – both parties know each other's costs and future returns can be predicted with certainty, the hold-up problem will cause inefficiently low investment when assets are relationship-specific. Since both firms lose out as a result, it can be further predicted that firms will seek an efficient solution through long-term contracting. The widespread use of long-term contracts, often with specified prices, in the energy and minerals extraction industries is consistent with these predictions (Lyons, 1996). This argument implies in turn the need for a legal framework for the operation of markets. If parties do not believe contracts will be honoured, and if necessary enforced in law, then contracts cannot resolve the hold-up problem.

There are, however, other limits to the security offered by such contracts, as illustrated by the British Gas example. The returns from an investment can never be wholly certain. British Gas failed to foresee the changes in its regulatory environment, which in turn changed its bargaining position. When British Gas lost its monopoly of wholesaling, it could no longer set prices for final buyers, and a spot market emerged after all. The amount of income available to be shared fell sharply when the final gas price fell.

Exercise 9.1

Assume that the producer and wholesaler, as represented in Figure 9.1, have negotiated a long-term contract. Out of a joint income of 100, the producer gets 70 and the wholesaler 30 (point Z).

1 Show, on Figure 9.1, what will happen to the line AB if the price of the product falls, reducing joint income to just 30.
2 Assume that after the price change both parties stick to their long-term contract, with the wholesaler being forced to pay the producer 70.

Show the new distribution of income on the diagram.
3 How is the wholesaler likely to react to this situation?

Question

There is one other possible solution to the hold-up problem. What is it?

The alternative was discussed in Chapter 8, Section 4: *vertical integration,* where the two firms become one. There is then in principle no contracting problem. If British Gas does its own production, or the producer sells the gas to final buyers, then the hold-up problem disappears. But that solution may not be costless: firms have their own competencies, and a merger or expansion into a new field of activity may be expensive. Furthermore, in the real world of uncertain returns, vertical integration moves the whole risk associated with the investment inside the integrated firm. British Gas illustrates that point too: the company had pricing agreements within the company, between its North Sea production arm and the distribution division, which transferred gas between the two parts of the company at unsustainably high prices; as part of the demerger, those agreements too had to be changed (*Financial Times*, 6 December, 1996).

In the real world, returns are uncertain and companies must deal with risk. Furthermore, contracting partners may have access to very *different* information about their own and the others' behaviour. Much recent industrial economics has explored the implications of imperfect and uneven information, and the effect of that in turn on the structure of contracting and the organization of firms. This is the subject of the next section.

3 INCOMPLETE INFORMATION AND CONTRACTING BEHAVIOUR

There are two ways in which market information, on which contracts are based, may be incomplete. First, both parties to a contract may share the same incomplete information. Neither may know what technical problems will arise, say, during a big and complex construction project, so they may wish to leave space in the contract for flexibility as conditions change. Second, information may be *asymmetric* as well as incomplete: one party may know more than another, or parties may have different private information or assessments of risk. This section discusses some implications of incomplete and asymmetric information for contracting and for behaviour within contracts.

Asymmetric information

Asymmetric information exists when information relevant to a transaction is known to the one party but not the other.

3.1 Spot contracts, quality doubts and the market for 'lemons'

I shall start with a problem which has become a classic in economics. The story was first told by the US economist George Akerlof (1970) in terms of used cars and their salesmen (a 'lemon' being a poor quality good, such as a bad used car). For a change, I shall tell it in terms of buying a flat (or apartment).

Suppose there is a given number of fairly similar flats on the market in an area. In terms of verifiable features, they are all worth the same. But 20 per cent of the flats have neighbours who keep you awake all night, and only the sellers know which they are. Suppose further, just for the sake of argument, that all buyers and sellers are people who prefer to sleep at night. Suppose, furthermore, that both sellers and buyers agree that quiet flats are worth £50,000 and noisy flats only £30,000. What is the equilibrium price for flats in this market?

Question

Before you read on, try to think about the demand side of the market. If you were a buyer, who, remember, does not know which are the noisy flats, though you do know what proportion are noisy, what price would you offer for one of these flats?

The buyer faces a quantifiable *risk*: an unidentifiable 20 per cent of flats are worth only £30,000. So you would not offer £50,000. How much would you offer?

Exercise 9.2

Start by calculating the expected value of a flat. (Chapter 8, Section 3.3 will help.)

Will you offer the expected value? That depends, as Chapter 8, Section 3 explained, on your attitude to risk. If you are *risk-neutral*, then that means that you make decisions based on expected values in situations of quantifiable risk. If you are *risk-averse*, then you will offer less than the expected value. I will make the assumption that you are risk-neutral, so your offer price for a flat will be the expected value.

So you offer £46,000 (see Exercise 9.2). What happens next? Sellers with quiet flats are not having that, they want £50,000. So they turn you down. Result? All the sellers who accept your offer have noisy flats! Then what? You work that out too, and turn those flats down. The final result is that quiet flats cannot be sold at all; the market collapses into a market for noisy flats at £30,000 – that is, a market for 'lemons'.

If the buyer had been able to evaluate the flats properly, then the market would have produced two equilibrium prices, one for quiet flats and the other for noisy ones. The absence of a market for quiet flats turns on asymmetric information at the time of sale only. If information was symmetric, both buyers and sellers would know about neighbours; with the asymmetry in this example, only the sellers have access to that information at the time of sale.

Later, both buyer and seller will know what was sold, but by then it will be too late for the buyer to back out, since the sale once made is a complete spot contract, not allowing for a change of mind. This situation suggests reasons why estate agents, like car dealers, have trouble establishing reputations for fair dealing and are often the subject of jokes about the unreliability of information they provide.

This 'lemons' story identifies a general market problem. There are many other goods and services, from washing-machines to lawyers' services, for which it is hard to ensure quality before purchase. Buyers also have limits on the cost and effort they can put into trying to find out about quality. (How embarrassed do you get trying to creep around a block of flats at night?) The problem which results is an example of *adverse selection* while buyers would be willing to buy, and sellers willing to sell, quiet flats at high prices, under asymmetric information the market operates in such a way that noisy flats drive out quiet ones, and the market collapses. (*Changing Economies*, Chapter 23, Section 2 also discusses adverse selection.)

Adverse selection

Adverse selection occurs when, in conditions of asymmetric information, all transactions are on similar terms and 'high quality' transactors therefore withdraw from the market.

There are various ways in which sellers may try to get round the well-founded suspicions of consumers in these circumstances. Guarantees of various types are a common method for goods like washing-machines and used cars: for example, a one-year warranty against breakdown. Consumers will understand that sellers will offer a guarantee only if they are reasonably confident about the quality of their product.

Question

In the example above, would it rescue the flats market if sellers were to offer to repay £20,000 if a flat turned out to be noisy during the first six months?

Clearly this would reassure consumers that a flat was quiet. But I can think of a different snag. Suppose you bought a quiet flat? How about agreeing with your neighbours that they would stage a few noisy scenes, and then splitting the profit with them? In other words, the seller now has a different problem. He has given you, the buyer, an incentive to cheat. Such an incentive to cheat is an example of *moral hazard*, and we shall return to it in Section 4.2 below.

Moral hazard

Moral hazard exists when one party to a contract can take advantage of asymmetric information to act in a manner inimical to the interests of the other party.

There are three features of the examples in this section which are relevant to the analysis of contracting behaviour. One is that these are spot contracts which are also one-off deals. These provide an incentive for opportunism: you rarely deal with the same estate agent more than once. (Conversely, an uncle of mine, who knows a great deal about cars, refused a few years ago to help me buy a used car, on the grounds that he had to go on knowing me, so he did not want to risk being blamed for a dud.) The second feature is that eventually in these deals you find out whether you have bought a plum or a lemon: the doubts are temporary. Finally, in the flats example the sellers have no control over quality. Once you relax that last assumption – when we turn from used cars to washing-machine producers, for example – then there are various other ways in which the 'lemons' problem, and other related dilemmas, can be addressed.

3.2   Long-term contracting relationships and asymmetric information

When referring to estate agents above, I mentioned *reputation*. While estate agents may have little control over the state of the flats they advertise, producers of consumer durables have a lot more discretion. They may also have more to worry about. Even if individuals buy washing-machines only rarely, so that the individual deals take the form of one-off spot contracts, sellers may be worried that disgruntled purchasers may later persuade other buyers away. Hence, they may not wish to behave with the opportunism spot contracting in principle allows. Instead, they may seek to persuade purchasers that they can be relied upon to supply a high quality product.

This section uses game theory to model the attempts of firms to establish reputations for quality. Reputations are not gained in a day – they grow over time. If a firm is concerned with its *future* market position, then its *present* behaviour will be influenced by that concern. Game theory can help to explore the impact on firms' current market strategies of calculations about future market advantage. I begin with games in which there is *no* future: games that are played just once. I then go on to consider an example of a game where players interact repeatedly. In the process I introduce some game theory concepts you will use again in Chapter 11.

Consider, first, a washing-machine producer worrying about the 'lemons' problem. We can model the producer as facing a form of the *prisoners' dilemma*. This is a famous game, much cited in economic theory to illustrate the ways in which independent decision making can lead to an outcome which both parties agree is worse than the outcome both would have preferred (see Chapter 1, Section 4.3). The pay-off matrix in Figure 9.2 illustrates the problem facing the producer and a consumer.

Think of the producer as a German maker of washing-machines, considering whether to produce a high quality machine – assumed to be expensive to produce – or a low quality machine. A consumer can choose to pay a high price or a low price for machines on offer, but cannot distinguish high quality from low quality until after purchase. Figure 9.2 shows the game in *strategic form*. The strategic form representation of a game is a matrix that shows the players, the strategies the players can adopt, and the pay-offs to each player from each combination of strategies. A 'strategy' here means a move (or choice) that a player may make. (Further on, you will meet games that require a broader concept of 'strategy'.) In each of the four quadrants in Figure 9.2, the upper right-hand sections show the consumer's pay-offs (ranked from best to worst), and the lower left-hand sections show the returns to the firm (again ranked from best to worst), for the four possible pairs of strategies. The players move simultaneously and we assume that each moves just once: this is sometimes called a 'one-shot' game.

Strategic form game

A representation of a game in the form of a matrix showing the players, the strategies available to them, and the associated pay-offs.

Consider the consumer first. Buyers would like a high quality reliable machine, and they would love to get such a machine cheaply ('best'). Their next preference, as I have set this up, is for a high quality machine at the high price ('good'). Next down their preference list is a low quality/low price machine ('bad'), and the 'worst' outcome is to pay a lot of money for a dud.

Now consider the firm. It is a profit maximizer, so it would be delighted to sell a low quality machine at a high price ('best'). If it had to choose between high quality/high price and low quality/low price, then it would prefer to be known as a high quality producer. The worst-case scenario is to produce high quality machines and find they can only obtain low prices.

Question

What is the *dominant strategy* of each player? (*Changing Economies*, Chapter 5, Section 3 explains this concept.)

Figure 9.2 The market for consumer durables as a prisoners' dilemma game

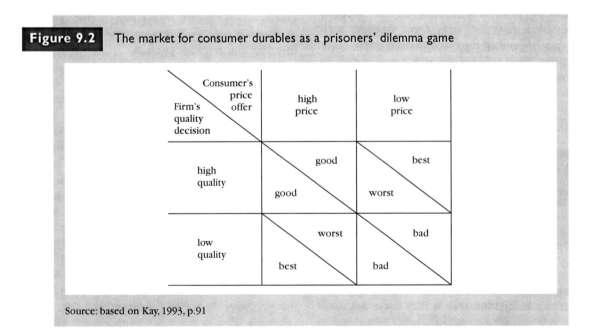

Source: based on Kay, 1993, p.91

Dominant strategy

A strategy preferred by a player regardless of the strategy of the other players.

The consumer, by assumption, does not know if a machine is high or low quality until after purchase. If she thinks the firm will offer high quality, she will prefer to pay a low price; if she thinks quality will be low, she will certainly offer a low price. So the consumer's dominant strategy is low price. The firm does not know what the consumer will pay; if it is a high price, most profit will be made with low quality; if a low price, low quality is the better choice. So the firm's and consumer's dilemma is that the outcome of the one-shot game is the lower right (bad, bad) quadrant, while both would have preferred the top left (good, good) outcome.

The outcome of the one-shot prisoners' dilemma game is an example of a *Nash equilibrium*. The concept of a Nash equilibrium is named after John Nash, a key figure in game theory. A Nash equilibrium exists when each player in a game is choosing their preferred strategy, given the strategy each of the others adopts. Therefore, in a Nash equilibrium, no player has an incentive unilaterally to change her strategy. The outcome of the prisoners' dilemma game is a Nash equilibrium since each player is choosing their dominant strategy. But Nash equilibria also exist in games where players do not have a dominant strategy.

Nash equilibrium

A Nash equilibrium is a set of strategies, one for each player, such that each player is choosing the best strategy given the strategies of the others.

In the game in Figure 9.2, therefore, the market shuts out high quality: consumers who would have paid for it are afraid of being taken for a ride. This is the 'lemons' problem set out in a different format, and suggests that the market for consumer durables should be characterized by indistinguishable, poor quality, cheap machines.

But, in industrialized countries at least, this is not the case. That is why I started with the German producers as my example. Some firms do manage to charge more than others for kitchen equipment, claiming – successfully – to deliver high quality in return. So how has the prisoners' dilemma been overcome? The key strategy has been *branding*: the firms have managed to associate a commitment to high quality, in consumers' minds, with a differentiated brand. But how have the producers succeeded in convincing customers that they will resist the temptations to opportunism?

A reputation game

We can show how producers can successfully establish a reputation for high quality, and hence be able to charge more, by studying a *reputation game*, of which there are many variants. A reputation game assumes that a firm builds up, over repeated interactions with consumers, a reputation for particular behaviour (for example, for producing high or low quality goods), and that its reputation can influence consumers' behaviour (for example, their willingness to pay for the firm's goods). So instead of a one-shot game, reputation games model repeated trading, in which a firm thinks about its actions in the present in terms of their effects on future as well as present pay-offs.

The reputation game that I outline here has another new feature. Players in this game move in sequence rather than simultaneously. We can study such sequential moves by setting out the game in *extensive form*, rather than in the strategic form that you have seen so far.

Extensive form game

A representation of a game in the form of a tree diagram showing the players, sequences of moves available, and the associated pay-offs.

An extensive form representation of a game resembles a tree, as in Figure 9.3, branching out to show players' alternative moves as the game progresses. The dots on Figure 9.3 are 'decision nodes': points at which a player must make a move. Each branch shows an alternative move. Extensive form games are also called dynamic games, and the game theorist David Kreps argues (1990, p.41) that they give us a 'language' for analysing 'specific dynamic competitive interactions' in an economy that are hard to model in other ways.

I am going to build up the reputation game by first considering a two-stage extensive form game in which each player moves just once, so that there is still no future to worry about. Then I go on to look at what happens when there are further moves. Figure 9.3 shows a game played by a firm, F, which is charging a high price for its washing-machine, and a single consumer, C_1, deciding whether to offer to pay that high price or not (by implication, whether to buy some other firm's cheap machine instead). The consumer knows the quality of the machine only after purchase. The pay-offs to the firm are shown at the right hand-side of the diagram, and the consumer knows the firm's pay-offs.

To understand the diagram, start at the left-hand side. The first decision node is drawn as an open circle. Consumer C_1 moves first. If she chooses not to pay the price demanded (no offer), then the firm will receive no profit (0). If the consumer offers the high asking price (high price) then the firm F has two choices at its decision node; it can supply high quality or low quality. The firm earns profits of 20 if it sells low quality at a high price, 5 if it sells high quality at that price. If the game ended here, the firm's best strategy faced with a high price offer would be to sell low quality.

However, suppose now that the firm looks forward to future stages of the game. Now it will worry about the effect on future consumers' decisions of its

decision to sell low quality to C_1. We will assume that each future consumer will know the experience of all previous purchasers.

We can begin to analyse the firm's decision making by adding a second consumer, C_2 to the game. Figure 9.4 extends the tree diagram in Figure 9.3 to three stages: C_1 moves, then F, then C_2. At the third set of nodes, labelled C_2 on Figure 9.4, the second consumer chooses between offering a high price or walking away. C_2 knows what has happened in the previous stages: what offer C_1 made, and what quality F then supplied. Therefore, F will worry that supplying low quality to C_1 may affect the willingness of C_2 to pay the firm's high price. (If C_1 made no offer, C_2 may be the first consumer to interact with the firm, at the bottom decision node.)

Although the consumers' pay-offs are not shown, we assume that consumers prefer to buy a high quality machine rather than make no purchase. Their worst case, as in Figure 9.2, is to pay a high price for a poor quality machine.

I now want to use this framework to think about the strategies firms and consumers might adopt, once they treat this kind of interaction as continuing indefinitely into the future. So think of Figure 9.4 as the first three stages of an indefinite game. After C_2 has moved,

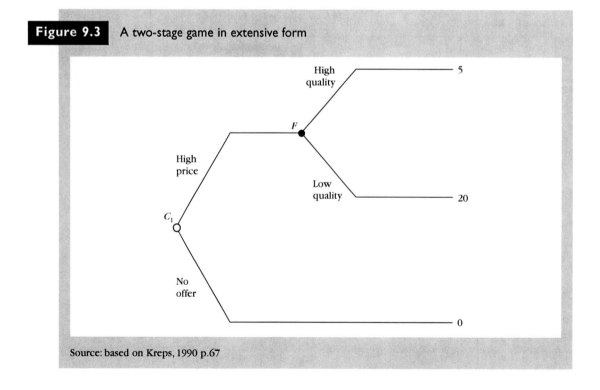

Figure 9.3 A two-stage game in extensive form

Source: based on Kreps, 1990 p.67

F will make another move, and will then be faced with another consumer C_3, and so on. The tree will rapidly spread its branches. In extensive form games with a number of stages, 'strategy' means a player's decision about moves over the game as a whole, stage by stage. So 'always supply low quality' is a possible strategy for the firm. And for each consumer, 'always offer a high price' is one among many possible strategies. Since an indefinite game has a potentially infinite number of consumers, we cannot set out all the possible pairs of strategies, for the firm and for each consumer, but we can identify one (*not* the only) Nash equilibrium pair of strategies for the firm and for the consumers considered as a group.

Suppose the consumers make it clear that they are unwilling to be cheated. They will offer a high price for the washing-machines if and only if no consumer has ever been previously cheated with a low quality machine. If the firm once supplies low quality for a high price it loses its reputation for quality and with it its market. The firm knows that this is the consumers' strategy.

Look again at Figure 9.4 in the light of this strategy. Consumer C_1 will offer a high price. The firm F then has a choice: high or low quality. Suppose it chooses high quality and earns 5. C_2 then has a choice of offering a high price or not, and will choose to do so. Alternatively, the firm may choose to sell C_1 low quality, and earn 20. But it knows that after that C_2 will make no offer, and the firm will lose its market. Given the consumers' strategy, the firm faces a choice: earn 5 and stay in business, or 20 and exit the market.

So what should the firm's strategy be faced with this consumer strategy? To think about this, the firm will look ahead, to the future stages not shown on Figure 9.4. It will work out that, given the consumers' strategy, it will lose its market the moment it sells low quality. In any stage when it is still in business it therefore faces the same choice: earn 20 and exit, or earn 5 and continue. In each stage it will therefore compare a single pay-off of 20 from cheating a consumer to an infinite stream of 5s from maintaining its high quality reputation indefinitely.

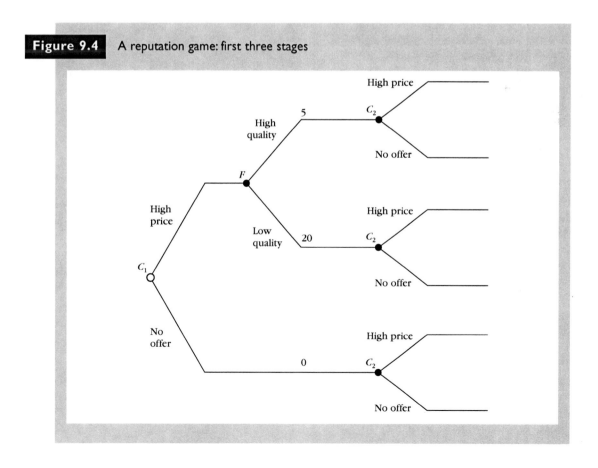

Figure 9.4   A reputation game: first three stages

The firm's best strategy depends on which has the higher value, which in turn depends on the firm's discount rate. The technical box explains how to calculate the present value of an infinite income stream at a given discount rate and, shows that, unless its discount rate is unreasonably high, the firm F in this game will prefer the infinite stream of 5s. So given the consumers' strategy, the firm's best strategy in this game, continued indefinitely, is to supply high quality every time and sustain its reputation and its market.

Once the firm is playing this strategy, is the consumers' chosen strategy their best reply? In other words, is this pair of strategies a Nash equilibrium? The answer is yes. Since consumers by assumption prefer to buy a high quality machine over other options, it is in the consumers' interest to continue to buy so long as the firm never cheats. The key to the continuation of the high price, high quality sequence of moves is that consumers know the value of reputation to the firm in an indefinitely prolonged game. Since firm and consumers are choosing their best strategy, given the strategy of the other, the pair of strategies is a Nash equilibrium.

Clearly, this reputation game is based on very simplified assumptions. But it suggests reasons why firms may find it worthwhile to expend resources establishing reputation. Not only advertising, but also long guarantee periods for goods, and a publicized commitment to investments in high quality production systems, can play a role. Kay (1993) argues that firms producing 'long-term experience goods', which include, for example, accountancy services as well as washing-machines, will be particularly interested in establishing reputation. We can indeed think in terms of the 'reputational capital' of such firms as an important contribution to profitability; as embodied in brands, such capital can form an important element of the market valuation of a firm. This in turn may help firms to raise financial capital.

Exercise 9.3

Here is a problem to think about which foreshadows the analysis of labour contracts later in this book. What does it mean to say that a *firm* has an incentive to maintain high quality? How can a firm ensure that its reputation is sustained by the behaviour of its managers and workforce?

Discounting an infinite stream of returns

A firm is likely to prefer income now to income in the future. The extent of its positive time preference is measured by the rate at which it discounts its future expected income stream (discounting is explained in *Changing Economies*, Chapter 27, Section 2.2). The present value of a future payment is measured by the formula:

$$PV = \frac{payment\ in\ period\ t}{(1 + r)^t}$$

where PV is the present value, r is the discount rate, and t is the time period. For example, if the current time period is year 0, and $r = 10$ per cent (or 0.1), then the present value of an income of £100 in year $t = 1$ is:

$$PV = \frac{£100}{(1+0.1)} = £90.91$$

If the firm expects from some investment an annual return of £100 in each year for the foreseeable future (a most unlikely expectation, I agree), then we can write down the present value of this stream of returns from year $t = 1$ onwards as:

$$PV = \frac{£100}{(1+0.1)} + \frac{£100}{(1+0.1)^2} + \frac{£100}{(1+0.1)^3} + \dots$$

into infinity. Fortunately there is a formula to save us from infinite arithmetic. The present value of an infinite stream of fixed returns (of R per year) is equal to the fixed return divided by the rate of discount:

$$PV = \frac{R}{r}$$

which in this simple example gives us:

$$PV = \frac{£100}{0.1} = £1000$$

You can now calculate the present value of an infinite stream of pay-offs of 5 in the reputation game, at a 10 per cent discount rate:

$$PV = \frac{5}{0.1} = 50$$

The firm will add this present value of future income from high quality to its undiscounted pay-off of 5 from selling high quality in the current round. At a discount rate of 10 per cent, this total of 55 clearly outweighs the single pay-off of 20 from selling low quality

Exercise 9.4

Can you work out how high the discount rate would have to be before the firm would find it worthwhile to cheat in stage two in the reputation game outlined above?

4   INCOMPLETE INFORMATION: INCENTIVES AND FIRMS' OBJECTIVES

4.1   The principal-agent problem and incentive contracts

The consumer durables example discussed in Section 3.2 assumed that sellers know the quality of the goods they are selling, and that after purchase buyers discover the truth too. But there are many market contracts where quality may never be entirely observable or verifiable. This includes many vertical relationships between supplying firms and those who buy their products for further processing or resale, and also many professional relationships between individuals: the relationship between doctor and patient, lecturer and student, lawyer and client.

What these relationships have in common is that the client or customer relies on the supplier to put in effort and/or behave professionally; results may bear an uncertain relation to effort; and the client may never be able wholly to judge whether the suppliers have 'done their best'. For example, suppose that a firm wishes to encourage a supplier, not only to invest in relationship-specific equipment (see Section 2.2), but also to put a great deal of effort into reducing its costs. This might be done through a jointly organized 'just-in-time' supply system, in which the supplier delivers parts just before they are needed, allowing stocks of inputs to be kept very low. Neither party knows in advance just how much increased profit could be extracted from this new investment and joint activity, and, even after the event, the buyer will not know just how much effort the supplier has put in. This is an example of a

widely studied problem in economics called the *principal-agent problem*.

Principal-agent problem

The principal-agent problem arises when one party, the principal, wishes to ensure that another, the agent, acts in accordance with the principal's interests in situations where the agent has information unavailable to the principal.

The 'principal' in the buyer-supplier transaction is the buyer. The buyer's problem is that the 'agent', the supplier, has information that can be withheld from the principal. The agent's actions may not be observed by the principal (this is called '*hidden-action*'), or the suppliers may have information about the conditions for the project unavailable to the principal ('*hidden-knowledge*'). The principal's problem therefore is to devise an incentive scheme to persuade the agent to act in the principal's interests.

In such circumstances, market contracts can be seen as an attempt to solve an incentive problem: how can the supplier be encouraged to put in its best efforts unobserved? The theory of incentive contracting seeks to answer this kind of question, by devising contractual frameworks that give agents incentives to behave in the interests of their principals. This has been a growth area in economics in recent years, and this section is intended to give you a flavour of the results. (You will meet these ideas again in Chapter 14 in analysing employment relationships within the firm.) I shall start by analysing a situation where firms' objectives can be assumed to be wholly self-interested, and then go on to argue that, when quality can never be wholly verifiable, firms may establish market advantage by changing their objectives.

4.2   Incentive contracts in manufacturing

Consider the example of a large multinational car firm, which buys in parts from suppliers for assembly. The assembler (the principal) cannot observe the effort put in by the supplier (the agent); it can only observe the results. So, for example, the principal doesn't know how far costs *might* have been reduced by the supplier, only what was achieved. One way to create incentives for cost reduction is to link payment to a cost reduction target.

For example, some large Japanese automobile and electronics firms pay their suppliers using a formula designed to give suppliers an incentive to reduce costs. The formula shares between buyer and supplier both the benefits of the supplier's effort to reduce costs, and the risk that a supplier may not be able to achieve planned cost reductions. (This example is drawn from Milgrom and Roberts, 1992, p.223, citing Kawaski and Macmillan, 1987 and Anasuma and Kikutani, 1991.)

The buying firm and the supplier agree a target level of costs of production of the parts to be supplied. Payment for the supplied parts then depends both on the target costs and on the actual costs of production shown in the supplying firm's accounts. Payment is therefore determined by a formula such as $x + \beta(\bar{x}-x)$. In this formula, $\bar{x}$ is the agreed target level of costs, and x is actual costs. The incentive term β takes values between zero and one. The supplier is thus paid for actual costs plus a fraction of the difference between target and actual costs.

> ## Question
>
> Suppose that the supplier retrains its staff, and achieves actual costs below the target level. Which firm, buyer or supplier, gains from this extra effort?

The retraining results in x (actual costs) coming in below $\bar{x}$ (target costs). So the element $\beta(\bar{x}-x)$ of the formula is positive, and the buying firm pays to the supplier its actual costs plus an additional sum which is a fraction of the difference between target and actual costs. So some of the benefit of the extra effort goes to the supplier as profit.

The buying firm however also benefits. Since $x < \bar{x}$, and β is a fraction between 0 and 1, the payment $x + \beta(\bar{x}-x)$ is less than $\bar{x}$. The buying firm pays less than target costs as a result of the supplier's cost-reducing efforts. The extent to which each firm benefits depends on the size of β: the larger is β, the more of the benefits of the supplier's extra cost-reducing efforts go to the supplier.

> ## Exercise 9.5
>
> Suppose that the supplier fails to meet the target costs. How does the level of β influence the supplier's receipts.

Since the supplier is the agent, and has a substantial capacity for 'hidden action' – that is, for deciding unilaterally how much effort to put in – it might seem that the principal will always prefer a large β, to give the supplier a large incentive for effort.

Note, however, that there are a variety of reasons, in addition to lack of effort, why the supplier might come in above target costs.

> ## Question
>
> Think of some before you read on.

I thought of rising costs of raw materials; lower than predicted production runs; a fire in the factory store; difficulties in supplies *to* the parts supplier. All of these might be outside the control of the supplier. In making β large, the buyer is shifting most of the *risk* attached to these factors to the supplier. The supplier's reaction to the contract will then depend on the extent of this risk and on how it regards risk.

Suppose the supplier is a small firm, supplying only a single range of parts to a very large Japanese multinational. In these circumstances, the supplier could easily be bankrupted by circumstances outside its control, such as rising raw materials prices, if the contract assigns to it a large part of the risk. Such a bankruptcy could also seriously disrupt a closely organized just-in-time production system in the multinational itself. The large principal is much more able to bear risk than the agent, while the supplier is more likely to be *risk-averse* because of its small size and specialization, including its dependence upon its relationship-specific investments. Conversely, a large multinational is more likely to be *risk-neutral*. Its size allows it to be more concerned with expected income from an activity than with income variability, since it can balance out gains and losses from external factors over time (Chapter 8, Section 3 defined risk-aversion and risk-neutrality).

Incentive contracting theory would therefore predict that the principal would choose to bear a good deal of the risk, and that is indeed what studies of the big Japanese car manufacturing firms show. These firms work with sets of suppliers who are very closely linked to the big manufacturers within industrial groups called *keiretsu*, and also with suppliers external to the group. The 'core' firms – the big manufacturers – absorb a great deal of the risk for their 'satellites' within the *keiretsu*, but not for the more distant firms (Lyons, 1996; Asanuma and Kikutani, 1991). In terms of the formula in this section, the principals (the core firms) keep β low for satellites, but not for other suppliers.

A principal agreeing an incentive contract is therefore faced with a difficult trade-off. The contract needs to balance incentives for effort by the agent against efficient risk-sharing between principal and agent. This is a hard trick to pull off. A contract which provides strong incentives for effort – which is 'high-powered' in the contracting jargon – shifts most of the risk to the supplier. Fixed price contracts are common examples of high powered contracts: the agent bears all the risk and gains all the benefits of reducing costs. In the absence of information on effort, the temptation for the principal is to tie payment closely to something which is observable, such as unit cost. However, the consequences may be perceived by the suppliers as unjust if they result from influences outside of their control. If so, such contracts risk undermining the commitment of and working relationship with the supplier. Even if the monitoring of suppliers' effort could provide more information, that could be very expensive, and might also undermine the working relationship.

The references to working relationships are a key to interpreting the Japanese evidence. The Japanese car manufacturers appear to divide suppliers into those within the industrial group or *keiretsu* – with whom they have a long-term working relationship – and outside suppliers. The willingness of the big manufacturers to bear risk is associated with very close supplier-buyer relationships which provide the core firms with many forms of influence over their suppliers, including involvement in suppliers' investment and production planning. In other words, an explicit supply contract of the sort described by the formula above is surrounded by implicit understandings about future rewards for collaborative cost reduction and innovatory behaviour.

Outside of Japanese manufacturing, however, there is little empirical evidence as yet of this type of risk-sharing contract between manufacturing firms and suppliers (Lyons, 1996). It may be that, given the spread of Japanese manufacturing firms and methods, this will change as other countries' firms adopt closer buyer-supplier relationships. But it may also be that the cultural understandings that underpin the working relationships in the *keiretsu* are deeply rooted, path dependent and hard to reproduce in different manufacturing cultures. The

keiretsu appear to be one among many different ways of trying to deal with the market consequences of incomplete information for supplier effort. I now want to consider another possible response: that of altering the objectives of the firms themselves. For this purpose, I shall turn to another economically important type of production where both effort and quality of provision are hard to monitor: services provided by the professions.

4.3   The non-profit firm as a response to moral hazard

The example I have just been exploring was one where the more powerful party to the relationship was the principal: the Japanese multinational. There are, however, many principal-agent relationships where quite the opposite is true. Consider a patient's relationship with a doctor. We can think of the patient as the principal, needing a service to be provided; the doctor is the agent, the supplier. But most people feel rather powerless faced by doctors: they lack information, and are often frightened and vulnerable at the time of the consultation. A comparable relationship exists between lawyers and individual clients, and between teachers and students. Even after the service has been provided, it is still hard to know whether the professional service provider has done their best.

Lawyers, doctors, and teachers – like the parts suppliers discussed in Section 4.1 above – all have scope for 'hidden action'. The contract (explicit or implicit) creates 'moral hazard' (see Section 3.1): incentives for hard-to-detect actions against the interests of the principal. The hidden action might take the form of over-providing; for example, a doctor who over-treats to increase her income. Or it might take the form of under-providing or negligence; for example, a lawyer who does not prepare a case properly. How in these circumstances can a vulnerable principal (the client) establish an effective incentive contract with the agent?

We only have to put the question in that way to see that individual contractual solutions are problematic. The 'reputation game' will work poorly in this case because quality is hard to judge even after the event. And for the same reason, monitoring of professionals' behaviour is difficult and costly. An alternative approach may be to focus on ways of changing the motivations and hence the behaviour of professionals more directly.

One possible approach is to suppress the profit motive of the agent. If the contracting agent is a *non-profit firm*, then those who work for it may have fewer incentives to exploit the scope for opportunistic behaviour.

Non-profit firm

A non-profit firm can be (narrowly) defined as a firm subject to a 'nondistribution constraint'; that is, one not legally permitted to distribute residual income to those who control it.

Non-profit firms include charities, mutuals and trusts of many kinds, and the economic definition given here hardly captures this diversity. But the narrow definition does allow some economic modelling of the implications of renouncing profit-seeking. Non-profit firms may be able convincingly to pursue objectives concerning the output they produce, as opposed to financial targets. They may be able to attract staff whose motivation is more closely aligned to the needs of the clients (the principals) they serve, lessening the principal-agent problem. Hence, patients may prefer to be treated by a non-profit hospital or clinic, seeing it as more trustworthy than a profit-seeking firm. A similar argument can explain the role of charities in providing emergency aid: the use of funds is hard to observe, and donors reasonably have confidence in non-profit agencies. Arguments along these lines have been used to develop a theory of non-profit firms as a response to 'contract failure'; that is, to the difficulty of setting effective incentive contracts where quality or performance is unobservable (Hansmann, 1987).

Note the form of this argument. The literature in this field is predominantly US-based, and it starts from the premise that non-profit organizations are set up by people who see a market opportunity. Non-profit firms survive in the market against competition from commercial firms because they have a competitive advantage in sectors where there is contract failure: that is, consumers have confidence in them. The earliest work along these lines suggested such confidence is particularly forthcoming when those who run the firm are also using its services (e.g. parent-controlled day care). The argument is supported by some observed association between industries where non-profits predominate in the USA, and industries where these forms of information asymmetry and

incompleteness seem particularly acute. Further supportive evidence is provided by European comparative research, tracing the widespread development of 'stakeholder co-operatives' – controlled by a mix of users, workers and benefactors – providing 'social' services: healthcare, education, training, cultural and environmental services (Borzaga, 1996).

There are other ways too in which professional providers' motives can be shaped, by themselves or by outside bodies. Professional ethics play a role, especially when associated with the threat of being 'struck off' from the professional list – prevented from practising – for unethical behaviour. Such self-policing only works, however, when the bulk of a profession have internalized the professional code, since only then can blatant exceptions be sanctioned. Easier to police – because easier to observe and regulate – are rules which reduce moral hazard and hence help to sustain ethical behaviour. Examples are prohibitions on advertising (on 'touting for business') which reduce the scope for making false claims; rules enforcing referral within professions, which help to reduce information asymmetry; and more broadly rules which reduce the intensity of competition and hence encourage openness (Matthews, 1991). While many professions work along these lines within non-profit organizational forms, this does not – as the economist R.C.O. Matthews goes on to point out – prevent high charges! Indeed, the cost of ethics in some fields may be professional protectionism and some monopolistic pricing.

Businessing the non-profits

The key to mitigating principal-agent problems in professional services, therefore, is to try to change the motivations of agents as well as the incentives they face. However, as Matthews goes on to note in the reflections cited above, the UK in the 1980s and 1990s saw the opposite move, towards 'businessing the professions': encouraging competition, removing restrictions and pushing professionals' objectives in a more commercial direction. At the same time, the UK government sought to push non-profit or 'voluntary' organizations towards more commercial behaviour.

There is evidence that changing incentives do alter the behaviour of non-profit organizations. In Britain, an example of the 'businessing' of non-profit organizations has been the pressures on housing associations to raise commercial funds. The associations are charities or friendly societies set up to provide housing below market rent for those on low income. After 1988, they were required to move away from their traditional reliance on government capital grants towards commercial finance, and were given control of rent setting (Hills, 1991).

The behaviour of associations has changed in response to these new incentives. Like commercial firms facing higher risk, they have sought to diversify. Some have sought out lower risk activities, such as elderly care schemes which attract more generous grant. Some developed commercial property schemes, aiming to cross-subsidize social housing, and therefore faced problems when the property market collapsed in the late 1980s. Most have hired more 'entrepreneurial' staff to put together complex schemes from a variety of funding sources. The associations have expanded their activities, but their main 'principals', low-income tenants, have suffered higher rents because of the cost of servicing commercial loans. There is also a widespread perception that the associations' commitment to a broader social role in poor areas is being eroded. As a manager put it, 'If we are fighting tooth and dagger with someone for a scheme, what is the point of putting money into that area to support a toy library or a youth club?' (*Financial Times,* 20 September, 1996).

Nevertheless, there is also evidence that tenants continue to regard housing associations as more trustworthy landlords and care providers than commercial firms. And the associations continue to be seen as worthy recipients of charitable donations. The housing association movement offers some support both for the argument that the non-profit firm is associated with ethical behaviour, and for the view that such behaviour can be eroded by commercial pressures.

5 CONCLUSION: CONTRACTING AND FIRMS' BEHAVIOUR

This chapter set out to show how economic theory can analyse market behaviour through a 'contracting lens'. In the process, I have aimed to show that voluntary contracting can sometimes overcome market failures and increase efficiency, and to identify some of the limits of such efficient contracting. Section 2 thus showed that long-term contracts can overcome the 'hold-up' problem,

which can cause firms to underinvest in relationship-specific assets, such as a gasfield in a market with a sole gas wholesaler. Once we also allow for incomplete and asymmetric information (Section 3), market contracting can become inefficient, and poor quality can drive out good as in the 'lemons' case. In some industries a commitment to establishing reputation may provide an effective market response. However, in other cases information may be asymmetric even after exchange, and here more drastic remedies may be needed: possible organizational responses are the non-profit supplier and professional associations (Section 4).

The concepts and theories developed in this chapter are used in subsequent chapters of the book. Chapter 11 looks at different types of strategic behaviour by firms in markets, developing further the game theory used here and Chapter 14 explores employment contracts within the firm, again drawing on principal-agent theory.

 ## FURTHER READING

John Kay (1993), in *Foundations of Corporate Success* (Oxford University Press), discusses different types of contract, with industrial examples. If you want to know more about the economics of organizational form, Milgrom and Roberts (1992), *Economics, Organization and Management* (Prentice Hall International) is a comprehensive text, much of which is accessibly written.

 ## ANSWERS TO EXERCISES

Exercise 9.1

1 In response to the reduction in joint income the line AB shifts to the left to A'B' on Figure 9.5. At A' the producer gets all of the 30 joint income; at B' the wholesaler gets it all.

2 Under the long-term contract, even though there has been a reduction in joint income the producer will receive 70 at point Z'. The producer gains all of the joint income of 30 at A', plus an additional 40 from the wholesaler.

3 To find this additional 40 the wholesaler would have to dig into its own funds, just as British Gas faced losses after the fall in gas prices. Rather than fund losses on the contracts indefinitely, British Gas sought to negotiate new contracts. A smaller firm might go out of business.

Exercise 9.2

Chapter 8, Section 3 explained how to calculate expected values.

Expected value of a flat = (proportion of the flats which are quiet × value of those flats) + (proportion of the flats which are noisy × value of those flats)

$$= (80\% \times £50\ 000) + (20\% \times £30\ 000)$$

$$= £40\ 000 + £6\ 000 = £46\ 000$$

Exercise 9.3

Managers and workers may have a stake in the higher salaries and wages payable in a high skill/high quality firm; furthermore, the need to sustain a reputation seems to suggest that a firm in the reputation game may seek a stable, long-term workforce. Some firms may even find appropriate a partnership structure where all employees have an immediate stake in the profits.

Exercise 9.4

If cheating in stage two is to be worthwhile, the present value of the infinite stream of 5s plus the undiscounted profit of 5 in stage two has to be at least equal to the one-off cheating return, 20. We can use that calculation to find the rate of discount r that

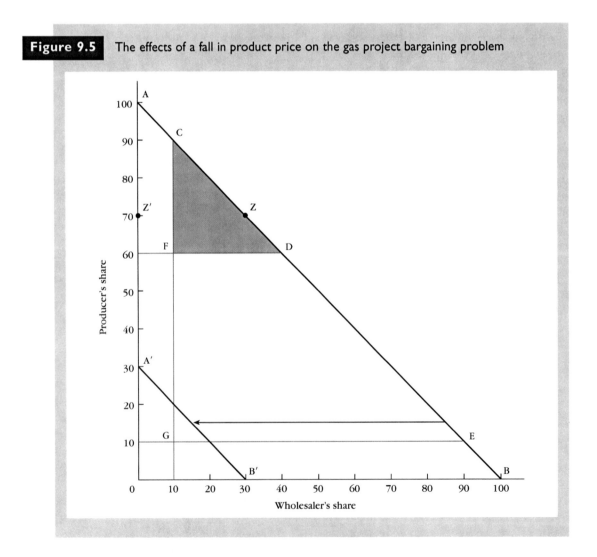

Figure 9.5 The effects of a fall in product price on the gas project bargaining problem

makes cheating just worthwhile. If the present value of the stream of 5s were just equal to the cheating return this implies that:

$$20 = 5 + \frac{5}{r}$$

Rearranging the equation after multiplying both sides by r gives:

$$20r - 5r = 5$$

$$15r = 5$$

$$r = \frac{5}{15} = 0.33$$

Therefore the discount rate would have to be at least 33.3 per cent per period (per stage) to make cheating worthwhile. It requires, in other words, a very short-sighted firm.

Exercise 9.5

If the supplier fails to meet the cost target, this implies that $x > \bar{x}$, and therefore the term $\beta(\bar{x}-x)$ is negative. So the supplier will receive less than actual costs. The larger is β, the larger the size of the cash penalty to the supplier. However, the buying firm also carries some of the costs of missing the target: the lower is β, the more the buying firm carries the additional costs above target costs.

FIRMS AND EFFICIENCY

Neil Costello and Maureen Mackintosh

10

CONCEPTS AND TECHNIQUES

Techniques of production, capital-labour ratio and capital intensity

Constant, increasing and decreasing returns to scale

Isoquants and isoquant maps, isocosts

Marginal rate of technical substitution (MRTS)

Marginal returns to a factor of production

Production function

Economies of scale

Cost curves

Technical, productive and allocative (Pareto) efficiency

Dynamic efficiency

Technical change

Objective and subjective costs

LINKS

- The technical analysis of the production function, using isoquant maps and isocost lines, has close parallels with the neoclassical analysis of consumer choice seen in Chapter 2, in particular with the use of indifference maps and budget lines.

- The analytical strength of neoclassical theory is illustrated by the amount of depth provided here in relation to efficiency. As well as analysing the technical and productive efficiency of individual firms, the notion of allocative (Pareto) efficiency provides the foundation for evaluating markets in general in Chapter 18.

- The distinction between static and dynamic efficiency is central to the evolutionary critique of the neoclassical theory of the firm and is developed in Chapters 15 and 16.

- The technical aspects of the neoclassical theory developed in this chapter, such as the modelling of the impact of a change in factor prices upon the firm's demand for labour, are applied to the theory of labour demand in Chapter 12.

INTRODUCTION: EFFICIENCY,
COMPETITION AND STRATEGY

In an influential management text published in 1993, called *Reengineering the Corporation,* Michael Hammer and James Champy recount the following story. In the early 1980s, the Ford Motor Company in the USA was trying to cut its costs. It estimated that by computerizing its accounts payable section – which paid the invoices from Ford's suppliers – the 500 employees in that section could be reduced by 20 per cent. This seemed from Ford's point of view a desirable saving until, on visiting the Japanese car company Mazda in which Ford had just acquired an equity stake, Ford managers were startled to discover that the smaller Japanese firm employed just *five* people in paying invoices.

Chastened, Ford went away and redesigned its whole procurement process. Its new procurement system eliminated 400 jobs by abolishing invoices, using an on-line, multi-access database of purchase orders to institute payment on arrival of the goods. In one plant, indeed, supplies were paid for only when used: '… every time a truck comes off the line with a set of your brakes on it, we'll mail you a check' (condensed from Hammer and Champy, 1993, pp.39–44).

This short example of a drastic management rethink comes trailing clouds of business history. Behind the comparison with the Japanese competitor lies a history of rapidly increasing competition from Japanese industrial firms with innovative ideas on work organization. Japanese car firms, for example, from the 1950s onwards, took the principle of the production line and rethought the human relations involved in mass production. Firms like Toyota – one of the pioneers – hugely improved quality by making teams of assembly workers responsible for rectifying and preventing mistakes. They cut inventories of supplies to the bone by the now-famous 'just-in-time', tightly scheduled delivery system for parts, which implies much closer working relations with suppliers. They instituted a system of design organization which focused on ease of production. And they integrated dealers into the order system, so cars could be built as orders came in. The ensemble of changed systems – which came to be labelled 'lean production' (Womack *et al.*, 1990) – slashed the unit costs of cars, the classic mass production commodity.

The 'lean production' changes focused initially on the organization of manufacturing processes. By the 1980s, however, the rethinking (or 'reengineering') had moved on to administrative processes. Again, the Japanese were sometimes the pioneers, since cutting administration follows logically from the thinking behind lean production. Firms moved on from 'automating' paperwork using computers to a much more drastic reorganization of administrative work. Information technology has played a key role. A mix of expert systems, telecommunications networks and distributed data processing has allowed administrative processes to be condensed, and decision making to be decentralized – and partly computerized – while increasing centralized monitoring and control. Banks and insurance companies, for example, have seen a huge decline in lower-tier clerical processing work, with data entry shifting to those who deal with customers, though in this sector the Japanese have lagged behind (Bertrand and Noyelle, 1988).

There are several market consequences of these historical trends. In the labour market, low skill jobs are disappearing, bringing rising unemployment costs for the economy as a whole (see Chapter 12). At middle-tier levels, the demand is for more generalist abilities, while greater demand is emerging for highly specialized high-level skills. In the goods and services markets, relations with customers are becoming personalized, and more focused on generating ideas for new products. Supplier-buyer relations are becoming closer. Joint ventures and cross-share-holdings among competitors are becoming more common.

Question

Why should suppliers to the truck plant in the example above have agreed in effect to finance Ford's stocks of their parts, by accepting payment only on use?

No doubt they did so because there were benefits in return. In this case, these included an exclusive deal to supply brakes, plus close access to the truck plant's production schedules. That access allowed efficient scheduling of brake production, keeping down the supplying firm's own stock-holding costs (Hammer and Champy, 1993, pp.43–4). Such close links with suppliers are characteristic of 'lean production'.

The story told so far is all about 'efficiency': about changes in firms driven by the search for cheaper output, or new products, or higher quality output, or all three. This chapter examines some of the ways in which economists analyse efficiency at the level of the firm. Sections 2 and 3 explain the concept of efficiency which is the basis for the neoclassical theory of the firm. Section 4 introduces the analysis of technical change, a topic treated in detail in Chapter 15. The final section also contrasts the static concept of efficiency in the neoclassical model with more dynamic conceptions which allow for learning and an active search for innovation.

2 PRODUCTION TECHNIQUES AND THE PRODUCTION FUNCTION

The neoclassical concept of efficient production focuses on a firm's choice between alternative techniques of production. In this section and the next we shall develop this analysis, moving from a concrete example to a more abstract analysis of the choices facing a firm. Section 2 sets out a framework for comparing techniques of production, then Section 3 considers how a profit-maximizing firm might choose between them.

2.1 A choice of alternative techniques

Imagine a firm which is choosing between methods of producing a given level of output. Suppose, for example, an insurance company is considering methods of processing claims, and has three alternative techniques. To process, say, 10 000 claims a day it can use 110 units of labour services (say, hours), and 55 units of information-processing services. Alternatively, it can invest in computing and push its use of information-processing services up to 70 or 100 units, allowing it to reduce labour use to 70 or 50 hours respectively.

The choice facing such a firm using just two factors of production is illustrated in Figure 10.1, with labour services, L, on the horizontal axis and information-processing services, K, on the vertical axis. Labour and information-processing services are flows which are measured in terms of the service provided per time period.

The firm's alternative methods of processing 10 000 claims are shown by points A_1, B_1 and C_1 on Figure 10.1. Each point corresponds to a different ratio of K to L; that is, it uses the two factors of production in different proportions. This firm's only non-labour factor of production is information processing services, which is therefore its capital input. The flow of capital services is provided by a stock, in this case, a stock of computing capacity, which the firm may or may not own itself. If it does not, it will rent the capacity from another firm.

On Figure 10.1, we have also drawn rays labelled 'Technique A', 'Technique B' and 'Technique C', straight lines from the origin through each of A_1, B_1 and C_1. Each ray therefore represents a particular ratio of the factors of production. For example, all the points on C have the same capital/labour ratio, K/L, of 1/2. Points further from the origin along a ray represent larger amounts of both inputs but the proportions remain the same. If we define a technique of production by its capital/labour ratio, each ray then represents a single technique of production. A technique is more *capital intensive* the higher its capital/labour ratio. Conversely, a technique is more *labour intensive* the higher its ratio of labour to capital.

Capital and labour intensity

A technique is more capital intensive the higher its K/L ratio. It is less capital intensive (more labour intensive) the lower its K/L ratio.

Exercise 10.1

Define the two other techniques of production, A and B, shown on Figure 10.1 in terms of their K/L ratio. Which of A, B and C is the most capital-intensive technique?

As the firm increases its output with any given technique, it moves out along a ray from the origin; output of processed claims per day expands as the firm employs increasing quantities of both factors. Figure 10.1, furthermore, provides some information about how fast output expands along each ray. The points A_2, B_2 and C_2 show how inputs must increase if the firm is to be capable of processing 20 000 claims a day.

Is the firm illustrated in Figure 10.1 producing with *increasing, constant* or *decreasing returns to scale*?

Constant returns to scale

A proportionate increase in each input produces the same proportionate increase in output.

Increasing returns to scale

A proportionate increase in each input produces a larger proportionate increase in output.

Decreasing returns to scale

A proportionate increase in each input produces a smaller proportionate increase in output.

If a firm, by doubling inputs, can more than double output, then it enjoys increasing returns to scale. The firm illustrated is not in this situation; *along each ray* (that is, with each technique), a doubling of inputs produces a doubling of output. Hence the firm faces constant returns to scale. Constant returns to scale means that, along the ray representing any technique, the distance from the origin is proportionate to the output produced. Hence, with constant returns to scale, halving inputs

Figure 10.1 Three discrete techniques of production

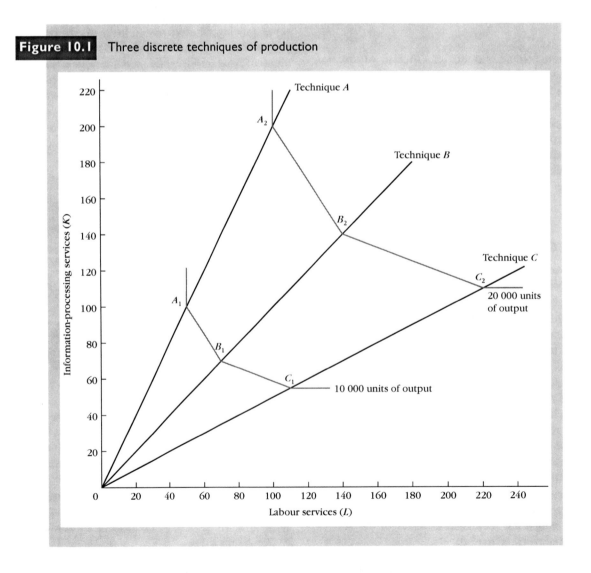

halves output. You can see this on Figure 10.1 by checking that the points A_1, B_1, C_1 are halfway from the origin to the points A_2, B_2 and C_2 along their respective rays.

So to produce 201000 processed claims, the firm's choices are illustrated by points A_2, B_2 and C_2. The line connecting these three points is called an *isoquant*. Meaning 'equal quantities', an isoquant summarizes all the alternative ways of producing a given output. On the assumptions on which Figure 10.1 is drawn, that each technique displays constant returns to scale at any scale of production, the firm could also use combinations of two techniques to produce each level of output; for example, producing 20 000 units with an input combination somewhere along the line $A_2 B_2$. It could also produce them along the line vertically above A_2, by adding more units of K to the 100 labour units, but the extra units of K would be wasted, producing no more output. The isoquant representing an output of 10 000 is drawn in a similar way through the points A_1, B_1 and C_1. By drawing a number of isoquants representing different levels of output, we could construct the firm's isoquant map, which looks similar to the indifference map of a consumer (see Chapter 2, Section 2.1).

Isoquant

An isoquant connects all the different combinations of inputs that can be used to produce a given output and no more.

Question

Stop for a moment before reading on and think about the story so far. Is this a plausible story about the technical choices facing firms?

In some ways it does seem quite realistic. As the example at the beginning of the chapter illustrated, firms may face choices between different methods of producing the same output, using quite different proportions of inputs. And replacing some people by increasing computing power – with associated reorganization – is a familiar trend.

There are, though, some less plausible features of the story. One which may have struck you is the assumption that labour and computing services can each be measured in some physical units. This supposes a level of homogeneity, or sameness, of

each factor of production, which is implausible: computing systems change in type as well as size as complexity increases, and Section 1 noted that the types of skill needed by the labour force also change as techniques alter. Indeed, the definition of a 'technique' used above, as simply a ratio of capital services to labour services, offers too narrow a conception of the differences between techniques and of the process of technical change, as Chapter 15 will explore. For now, however, we will abstract from these problems and continue to talk in terms of homogenous units of factors and of techniques whose characteristics can be defined by their capital/labour ratios alone.

2.2   Substitutability of factors of production

In Figure 10.1, it was possible to *substitute* one factor of production for another: more information-processing capacity per period could reduce the need for labour hours. The scope for such substitution is an important aspect of firms' technical choices.

Exercise 10.2

Draw a diagram of the isoquants of a firm facing constant returns to scale and having only one available technique of production.

If a firm has only one available technique of production, then factors of production cannot be substituted for each other. Hence the shape of the isoquants on Figure 10.20. Figure 10.2 illustrates the opposite extreme, where factors of production are *perfectly substitutable*.

In Figure 10.2, the isoquants are parallel straight lines. Along one isoquant the same output of 10 000 can be produced by 100 units of labour services alone, 150 units of capital services alone or *any* combination in between, such as 60 units of each. For each unit of labour given up, you need to use 1.5 more units of capital to produce the same output. There is no limit to this particular substitution; that is, you can do without one of the factors completely. This is also true of the isoquant representing an output of 20 000 units.

Figure 10.2 still shows constant returns to scale. With given proportions of K and L – that is, along any particular ray through the origin such as A or B

– doubling the output from the 10 000 isoquant to the 20 000 isoquant requires a doubling of both inputs. The rays are drawn as dashed lines, however, to remind you that now you can have any number of different techniques. There is no longer a limited choice of fixed proportions techniques. Instead, there is an infinite number of techniques – or factor mixes – available.

There is, however, an unsatisfactory feel to Figure 10.2. It seems unlikely, even given considerable abstraction from real life, that a firm can manage entirely without one of its main factors of production. Rather, we might expect that, as we try to substitute, say, computing services for labour hours, we reach a limit after a while. We must have some people around to programme, service and monitor the work. Figure 10.3 shows an isoquant which, while still allowing substitutability between labour and capital, takes this insight into account.

In Figure 10.3, the isoquant allows labour to be substituted for capital and vice versa in infinitely small amounts. As in Figure 10.2, there are no fixed proportions and an infinite number of techniques is available. However, unlike the situation in Figure 10.2, in Figure 10.3 the factors of production cannot always be substituted for each other at the same rate. You can see this by observing that L_A, L_B, L_C, etc. are equidistant along the L axis, so that the move from technique A to technique B along the isoquant involves the same absolute increase in L as the move from B to C, from C to D, and so on. But as we move further to the right along the isoquant, each successive increase in L allows a smaller and smaller fall in K. The move from L_A to L_B allows capital services to be reduced from K_A to K_B, but the move from L_B to L_C allows capital services to be reduced only from K_B to K_C, and so on; that is, as the amount of labour increases, further increases in L result in diminishing savings of K if the firm is to produce the same output.

We can state this condition more precisely by saying that the isoquant in Figure 10.3 displays a diminishing *marginal rate of technical substitution (MRTS)* of labour for capital.

Figure 10.2 Perfect substitutability of factors of production with constant returns to scale

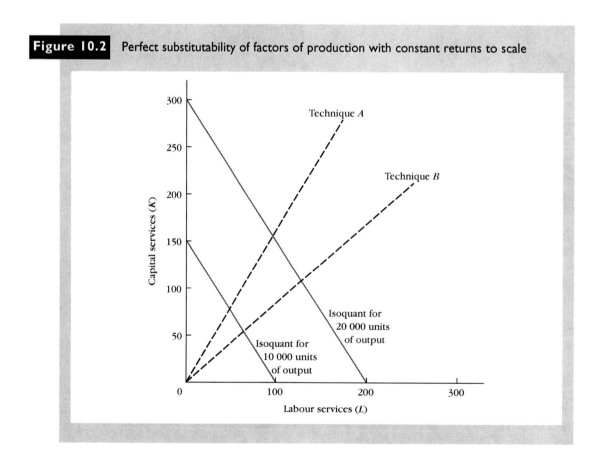

Marginal rate of technical substitution (MRTS)

The marginal rate of technical substitution (MRTS) of labour for capital is the amount of capital the firm can save if it uses one additional unit of labour to produce the same output.

All isoquants with diminishing marginal rates of technical substitution have a similar shape to the one drawn in Figure 10.3; that is, they bow out towards to the origin. Like the indifference curves drawn in Chapter 2, such isoquants are convex to the origin. The isoquant in Figure 10.3 is also drawn as a smooth curve, implying that capital and labour services can be substituted for each other along the isoquant in infinitely small amounts; there is no 'lumpiness' in the sense of a minimum feasible change in the use of a factor.

Now we will drop the assumption of constant returns to scale. Look at the isoquant map in Figure 10.4.

Question

Does Figure 10.4 show decreasing or increasing returns to scale?

Increasing returns to scale means that, as the quantity of output increases, fewer inputs are needed per unit of output. Decreasing returns to scale means that as output rises, so do the inputs per unit of

---

Figure 10.3   Smooth but less than perfect substitutability between factors of production

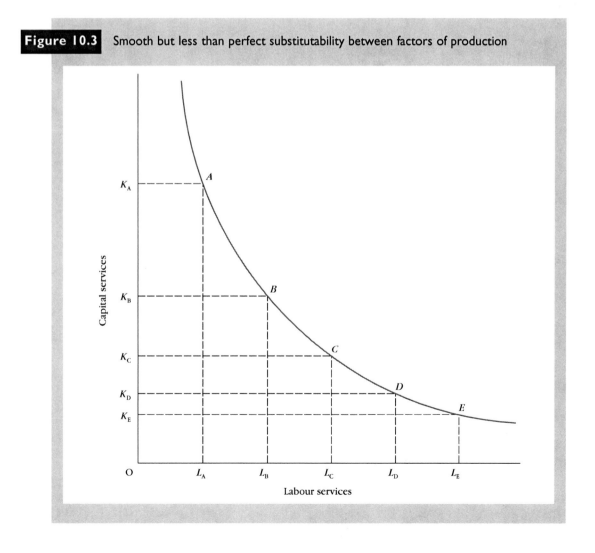

output. Figure 10.4 shows decreasing returns to scale. As the firm increases output - moving, for example, along ray A - then the move from A_1 to A_2 which increases output by 50 per cent requires an increase in inputs of more than 50 per cent; between A_1 and A_3 output doubles, but factor services required to produce it much more than double.

Finally, consider Figure 10.5, which is similar to Figure 10.4 but shows an isoquant map displaying constant returns to scale. An isoquant map such as this, with convex isoquants and constant returns to scale, will also display *diminishing marginal returns to each factor of production*. As additional units of labour are added to a given quantity of capital (and vice versa) the increment to output declines. You need to distinguish carefully the idea of marginal returns to a *factor*, when one factor of production alone is increased, from the concept of returns to *scale* when all factors increase in proportion.

Diminishing marginal returns to a factor

Each additional increment of one factor of production, with the quantities of other factors held constant, produces diminishing increments of output.

On Figure 10.5, each technique shows constant returns to scale. The move from A_1 to A_3, for example, doubles output and requires double the quantity of both inputs. The same is true of the move from B_1 to B_3. Now consider what happens when capital services are held constant while labour services increase. The

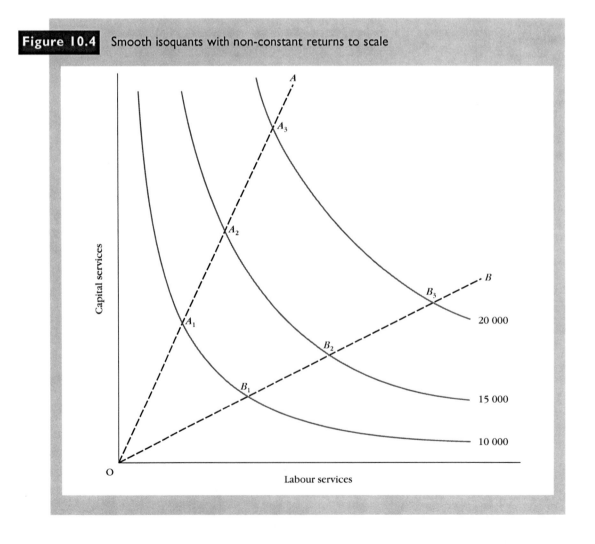

Figure 10.4 Smooth isoquants with non-constant returns to scale

horizontal dashed line at capital input K_1 cuts the isoquants at levels of labour input L_1, L_2 and L_3. The moves from point A_1 to point X, and then from point X to B_3 each represent the same increment in output. But the move from X to B_3 requires a greater increment in labour services ($L_3 - L_2$) than the move from A_1 to X ($L_2 - L_1$). Equal increments in output require successively larger increments in labour services; therefore the additional output from each successive increment of labour services is diminishing.

Reflection

Demonstrate for yourself that the isoquant map in Figure 10.5 displays diminishing returns to capital as well as labour.

2.3 From isoquants to production functions

The isoquant maps drawn so far can be regarded as defining the technological options open to a firm (still accepting for the moment our narrow definition of a technique). These options can be summarized in the form of a *production function*. The phrase 'production function' explains itself: it tells us how production possibilities arise as a (particular) function of the inputs used.

Sticking for the moment to the case of one product and two factors of production, we can write the production function of the firm in its most general form as:

$$Q = f(L, K)$$

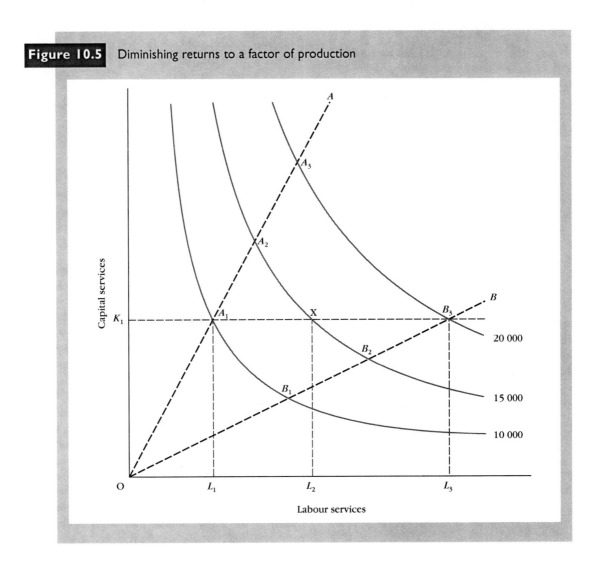

Figure 10.5 Diminishing returns to a factor of production

This is read as, 'Output is a function of labour and capital'. But what sort of function? How does output change as labour and capital inputs are altered?

In order to summarize the characteristics of particular isoquant maps in the form of a production function, we have to specify a particular functional form of the production function. The technical box illustrates how this can be done, by explaining the functional form of the production functions corresponding to the two isoquant maps you have just studied in Section 2.2: zero substitutability and perfect substitutability of two factors of production with constant returns to scale.

Two types of production functions

The shape of a firm's isoquants depends on two key aspects of its technology: the substitutability of labour and capital, and the returns to scale. We can summarize both of these aspects of the technical choices facing the firm using the production function just introduced, of the general form:

$$Q = f(L, K)$$

If there is zero substitutability of factors of production, as shown on Figure 10.20 illustrating the answer to Exercise 10.2, and constant returns to scale, then labour and capital have to be used in fixed and given proportions. Knowing that, we can write out the production function in the following specific form:

$$Q = f(L, K) = \min(aL, bK)$$

This means that the output Q is the minimum of a given multiple, a, of L and a (different) given multiple, b, of K. Q is the minimum of these two because with fixed proportions, as we have seen, excess quantities of either factor have to be wasted if the other is not available in the right proportion. Since we have assumed constant returns to scale, a and b are fixed constants and do not vary with the scale of production.

Exercise 10.3

Suppose that to produce one million units of output a firm needs just 200 labour hours and 100 units of capital services, and that the production function is of the form:

$$Q = \min(aL, bK)$$

Draw the isoquant map for this firm. Can you work out what numbers are represented by a and b?

Conversely, consider the case of perfect substitutability, where K can be freely substituted for L in a given ratio right up to the points where only one factor is used, as shown on Figure 10.2. We can also translate this into a specific form of the production function, assuming constant returns, as:

$$Q = f(L, K) = aL + bK$$

The two factors of production in this case are perfectly substitutable and therefore do not depend on each other for their effect on output. So output can be calculated by multiplying each factor by an appropriate constant and adding the effects of the two factors together. Again, a and b are constants because we have assumed constant returns to scale.

Exercise 10.4

For the production function of the form $Q = aL + bK$ assume that $a = 15$, $b = 10$, and draw the firm's isoquant map.

All the isoquant maps and production functions discussed so far display the same type of returns to scale – constant, increasing or decreasing – at all scales of production. It is not however hard to see that a firm may enjoy increasing returns to scale at lower levels of production, but then find returns to scale levelling out or even decreasing at higher levels of output. Indeed, this pattern of returns to scale is quite a common assumption in neoclassical theories of the firm. Alternatively, a firm may be able to achieve increasing returns to scale with a technique which uses a great deal of capital relative to labour – for example, along ray A in Figure 10.6 – but cannot do better than constant or even decreasing returns if it sticks to highly labour-intensive techniques, such as that along ray B. This latter situation might be true, for example, for a firm which can enjoy increasing returns to scale with a production line system, but not with craft production. An isoquant map with those characteristics can be drawn quite easily, as Figure 10.6 shows, but cannot be summarized in a production function of a simple functional form.

Not all the problems with this type of analysis, however, arise in translating isoquant maps into production functions. The isoquant analysis depends upon some problematic assumptions of its own. We questioned in Section 2.1 the assumption that factors of production such as capital and labour can be measured in homogeneous units that can be physically added up. Clearly, that is not in general true. We can allow in part for non-homogeneous factors of production by separating out different types of inputs – different types of labour, capital and other inputs – but then the analysis becomes much more complicated.

There are also some fundamental suppositions about technology being made in this analysis. The key assumptions are that, at any moment in time, there is a range of possible best-practice techniques, known to the firm, and that the firm is always using a best-practice technique. In this sense the analysis, by drawing an isoquant map, assumes *technical efficiency* in a carefully defined sense: firms never use more inputs than they need to produce a given output. This implies that, on Figure 10.6 for example, the firm will always produce 10 000 output units using a combination of inputs along the 10 000 isoquant, and never a combination of *L* and *K* above and to the right of the isoquant such as at point X.

Technical efficiency

A firm is technically efficient if it is using the minimum quantity of inputs required to produce a given output.

Figure 10.6 Increasing returns to scale available only with capital-intensive methods

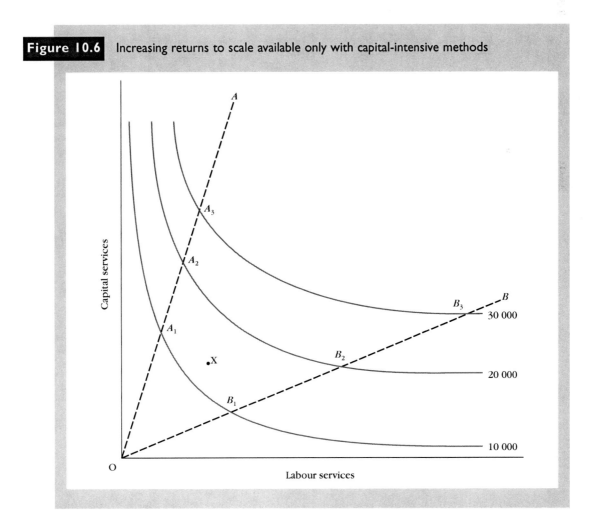

3   CHOICE OF TECHNIQUE AND SCALE BY THE PROFIT-MAXIMIZING FIRM

So much for technical relationships between inputs and outputs. But firms – as you may have been thinking – are not centrally interested in technical efficiency. They are interested in *profits* and hence in costs. As Chapters 8 and 9 noted, firms may have other objectives too, but profits certainly matter. Without at least normal profits the firm cannot continue. We explore here the consequences of the assumption of profit maximization for the analysis of a firm's production decisions.

3.1   From production functions to minimizing costs

Once we recognize that factors of production cost money, we can move from firms' production functions to their cost functions by means of a familiar type of analysis. Neoclassical economics consists of the application of a number of basic techniques of analysis in a wide range of contexts. In particular, there are many parallels between the analysis of households' and of firms' decision making. If you have worked through the standard analysis of household consumption decisions with a budget constraint (Chapter 2), then the diagrams and techniques in this section will look familiar.

The firms we will consider operate in perfectly competitive factor markets; that is, the firm is a price taker when it comes to buying its inputs. It is too small to be able to influence wages, for example, by changing the number of people it employs. So the firm takes the wage, the price of labour, W, and the price of capital services, R, as given.

We need to say a bit more about R – a much less familiar concept than the wage, and sometimes called the rental price of capital. The total K on the vertical axis in Figures 10.1 – 10.6 is not a stock of capital, but the flow of the services employed by a firm per time period, provided by a capital stock. The

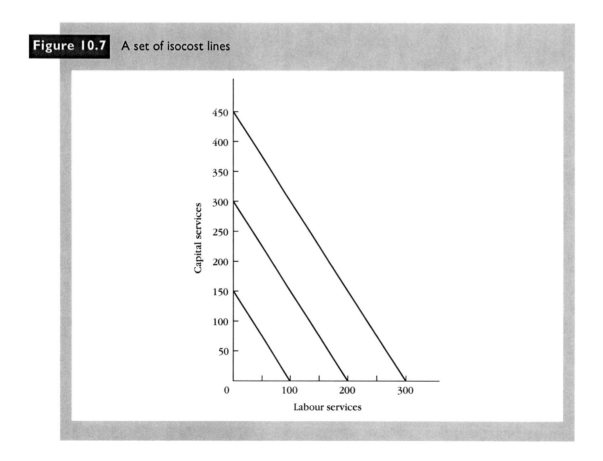

Figure 10.7   A set of isocost lines

information-processing services in Section 2 were an example of such a flow. One way to think about the price of capital services is as the price a firm would have to pay to rent the capacity to produce those services, per time period. When firms own their capital stock, a piece of equipment say, then the rental price is the opportunity cost of owning the equipment, per time period.

Once a firm knows W and R, it can identify the minimum cost method of producing any level of output, given its production function. Figure 10.7 shows a set of *isocost lines*. They are drawn assuming that the factor price ratio – that is, the ratio of W to R – is 3/2. This implies that, for each unit of labour given up, a firm can buy 1.5 units of capital services. For example, if a unit of labour costs £15, and a unit of capital services £10, a firm can spend £1500 on either 100 units of labour or 150 units of capital, or any of the combinations in between along the isocost line nearest

the origin. Each isocost ('equal cost') line therefore shows all the combinations of the two factors which can be purchased by the firm with a given sum of money. All the isocost lines have the same slope because they represent the same factor price ratio. The further to the right the isocost line, the higher the total spending on factors represented by that line.

Isocost line

An isocost line connects all combinations of factors of production that can be purchased for the same total cost, at given factor prices.

Exercise 10.5

If $W = £15$ and $R = £10$, what total cost is represented by the isocost line furthest to the right in Figure 10.7?

Figure 10.8   The minimum cost technique for a given output level

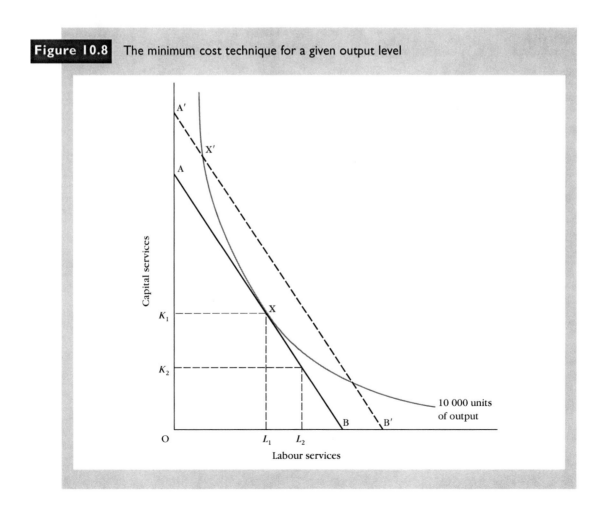

An isocost line is therefore exactly analogous to a consumer's budget constraint (see Chapter 2, Section 2.2): it is drawn as if the firm had a budget to spend on inputs. That analogy between firms and households (or individual consumers) is, however, a bit odd. Firms do not have fixed budgets; what they can spend on factors of production depends upon what they think they can make from sales of the resultant output. However, whatever their output, they will choose to produce at as low a cost as possible. Therefore, if we bring together isocost lines and isoquants, as in Figure 10.8, then we can use a formal analysis very similar to the utility maximization decision of a consumer to consider the firm's rather different decision making-problem.

Suppose the firm represented in Figure 10.8 wishes to produce 10 000 units of output, and faces a factor price ratio, W/R, of 3/2, the same ratio as is illustrated on Figure 10.7. Suppose also that its set of technically efficient techniques lies along the isoquant shown. To produce the required output at lowest cost, the technique at point X with inputs L_1 and K_1 should be chosen. At X, the isoquant for 10 000 units of output is tangent to isocost line AB. At any other point on the isoquant, such as X', 10 000 units would cost more to produce. That is, the isocost line through point X' (the dashed line A'B') lies to the right of the isocost line through X and hence represents higher total spending by the firm. Conversely, any other combination of L and K along the isocost line through X, such as L_2 and K_2, will fall on a lower isoquant, hence produce less than 10 000 units of output.

We can now picture the firm making this decision about a minimum cost technique for each level of output at which it may wish to produce. Figure 10.9 adds an isoquant map to the set of isocost lines on Figure 10.7. With an unchanging factor price ratio,

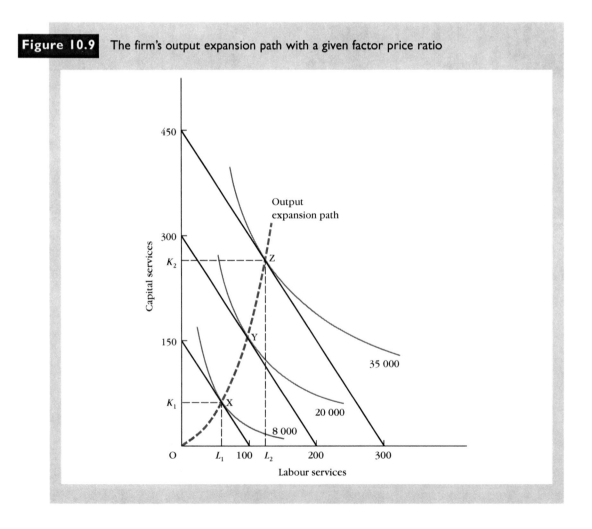

Figure 10.9 The firm's output expansion path with a given factor price ratio

W/R, of 3/2, the firm's choice of technique moves from point X to Y to Z, and the inputs used change from K_1 and L_1 at X, to K_2 and L_2 at Z. The output expansion path, which connects the minimum cost input combinations for different levels of output, is not necessarily a straight line. The path depends on the shape of the isoquants. Looking at costs along the expansion path we can assess whether there are *economies of scale*; that is, whether increasing the scale of production leads to a lower cost per unit of output. As drawn on Figure 10.9, the expansion path brings increasingly capital-intensive techniques of production and economies of scale.

Economies of scale

Cost per unit of output declines as output rises.

Reflection

Satisfy yourself that you can identify those features of Figure 10.9 before reading on.

Cost minimization with a given factor price ratio

The conditions for cost minimization by a firm facing a given factor price ratio can also be stated using algebra. This restatement brings out the parallels with the consumer's utility maximization problem, and working through it will help you to understand the isocost and isoquant analysis more clearly.

First, we can show that the slope of the isocost line is equal to the factor price ratio. For any factor prices W and R, a firm's total costs TC can be written as the sum of its costs of labour and capital:

$$TC = WL + RK$$

Now look at Figure 10.10 overleaf. Figure 10.10(a) shows a single isocost line AB.

Where the isocost line meets the vertical axis at A, purchased labour services are zero. So the equation for total cost reduces to:

$$TC = RK$$

which can be rewritten as an expression for capital services purchased at A:

$$K = \frac{TC}{R}$$

Similarly, at the point B where the isocost line meets the horizontal axis, no capital is purchased, so labour used is:

$$L = \frac{TC}{W}$$

Check that you understand that last step before reading on.

Given these two points, we can derive the general expression for the slope of the isocost line. The slope of a line is given by:

$$slope = \frac{rise}{run}$$

In this case the rise is negative: the line slopes down from left to right. So, on Figure 10.10(a):

$$slope\ of\ the\ isocost\ line = -\frac{OA}{OB} = -\frac{\dfrac{TC}{R}}{\dfrac{TC}{W}} = -\frac{W}{R}$$

That is, the slope of the isocost line AB is equal to minus the factor price ratio,

$$\frac{W}{R}$$

Now look at the isoquant CD drawn on Figure 10.10(b). The slope of a curve at any point can be measured by drawing a line tangent to the curve and measuring the slope of that line. So, on Figure 10.10(b), the slope of the isoquant at point X is:

$$slope = \frac{rise}{run} = \frac{\Delta K}{\Delta L}$$

This slope is negative because ΔK is negative. So its magnitude (that is, not taking account of whether it is positive or negative) is $-\frac{\Delta K}{\Delta L}$. This shows the rate at which the firm can save capital by increasing its use of labour at point X while staying on the isoquant. The magnitude of the slope therefore measures the marginal rate of technical substitution (MRTS) of labour for capital at that point (see the definition in Section 2.2). So:

$$MRTS = -\frac{\Delta K}{\Delta L}$$

Figure 10.10 The algebraic conditions for cost minimization with given factor prices

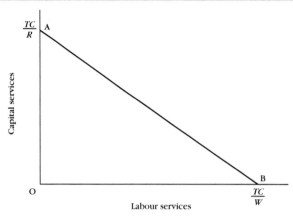

(a) The slope of an isocost line

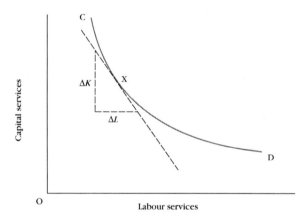

(b) The slope of an isoquant

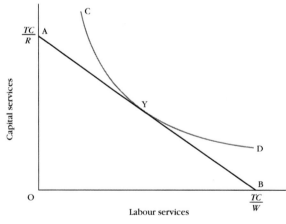

At Y, slope of CD = $\dfrac{\Delta K}{\Delta L}$ = $-\dfrac{W}{R}$ = slope of AB

(c) The condition for cost minimization

The firm minimizes its costs by finding the lowest isocost line consistent with the output it wishes to produce. Assuming convex isoquants, the minimum cost point will be a technique using both labour and capital.

This lowest isocost line will be the one that just touches the isoquant for the desired output. The minimum cost point will be found at the point of tangency, point Y on Figure 10.10(c). At this point, the isoquant and isocost line are tangent and therefore have the same slope. This implies that, at the point of cost minimization:

$$\text{slope of the isoquant} = \frac{\Delta K}{\Delta L}$$

$$= \text{slope of the isocost line} = -\frac{W}{R}$$

But the slope of the isoquant is $-$ MRTS and the slope of the isocost line is $-\frac{W}{R}$. So at the point of cost minimization, the firm is equating the ratio of factor prices to the marginal technical rate of substitution of labour for capital:

$$\text{MRTS} = \frac{W}{R}$$

Reflection

Compare this conclusion with the conditions for utility maximization by a consumer with a budget constraint (see the technical box in Chapter 2, Section 2.2).

So far, we have analysed the firm's choice of technique with a given ratio of factor prices. Now we consider, finally, what happens if factor prices change. We continue to assume that the firm is a price taker in input markets.

Let's return briefly to the example of information processing and labour inputs in Section 2.1. Suppose that the firm finds the price it has to pay to rent computing capacity falling, perhaps because of increasing competition in the computer services industry. What happens to the isocost lines? As a complement to the rather abstract explanation in the technical box above of the slope of isocost lines, Exercise 10.6 provides a numerical example.

Exercise 10.6

Figure 10.11 overleaf shows an isocost line AB and a single isoquant. Suppose that a unit of labour costs £10, and a unit of capital £15, so the firm is spending £4500 at its minimum cost point X. Now assume that the price of information-processing (capital) services falls to £10. If the firm's total spending on inputs remains constant, what happens to the isocost line? Sketch where the firm might now choose to produce.

Exercise 10.6 analysed a fall in the price of one factor of production, on the assumption that the firm continued to spend the same sum of money on inputs. However – as pointed out above – this is unrealistic. Firms do not have fixed budgets: their input spending and output levels depend on anticipated profits. Section 3.2 turns to the profit-maximizing decision of the firm.

The key conclusion however to take away from this section is the importance of the *ratio* of factor prices in determining the technique used by the firm. We have shown that the factor price ratio W/R determines the slope of the isocost lines, and that the most efficient input mix will always be on a point of tangency of an isocost line and an isoquant. It follows therefore that if the factor price ratio changes, but the firm decides to maintain the same output, then *factor substitution* will occur: the firm will substitute the relatively cheapened factor for that which has become relatively more expensive: see Figure 10.12 overleaf.

On Figure 10.12, the firm begins with a particular input price ratio which determines the slope of isocost line AB. Deciding to produce 10 000 units, it therefore chooses the point of tangency between isocost line AB and the isoquant, at point X_1 with inputs K_1 and L_1. Then the factor price ratio changes to that represented by the isocost line EF.

Question

Which factor becomes relatively cheaper?

Capital services become relatively cheaper. Any given sum will now buy more capital *relative* to labour services. The isocost line becomes relatively steeper (more strongly negative). Since, as shown in the technical box in this section:

$$\text{slope of the isocost line} = -\frac{W}{R}$$

Figure 10.11 Cost minimization with a factor price ratio *W/R* = 2/3

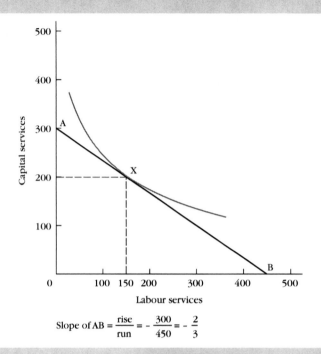

$$\text{Slope of AB} = \frac{\text{rise}}{\text{run}} = -\frac{300}{450} = -\frac{2}{3}$$

Figure 10.12 Factor substitution

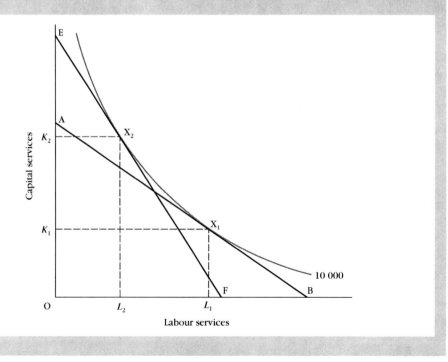

for the slope to become a larger negative number, W must rise relative to R.

When the factor price ratio changes in this way, if the firm continues to produce the same output it will choose a different technique, using more capital and less labour. On Figure 10.12 the new cost minimization point is X_2 using inputs K_2 and L_2. Capital services ($K_2 - K_1$) have been substituted for labour services ($L_1 - L_2$). In general, if output is constant and the isoquants are convex, a relative decline in the price of one factor will raise the firm's use of that factor relative to others. This is analogous to the substitution effect of a price change on the consumption bundle of a consumer who remains on the same indifference curve (see Chapter 2, Section 3.1). However, consumers also experience an income effect when prices change. Similarly, firms find that, when input prices change, their profit-maximizing level of output changes too. The way factor demands change once we allow firms to vary output in response to input price changes is explored further in Chapter 12.

3.2   Cost curves and the profit-maximizing firm

We now turn to the firm's profit-maximizing decision. To analyse this, we need first to translate cost minimization with a given output into *cost functions*; that is, functions which relate minimum costs to output levels. If we assume a perfectly competitive firm, so that the firm is a price taker for its output as well as its inputs, then its market decision is reduced to choosing the quantity of output to produce which will maximize profits.

Question

How does this differ from the market decision of firms in imperfect competition?

Firms in imperfect markets are choosing a price–output combination; they are not price takers. Much of the analysis of cost functions in this section applies equally to firms in imperfect competition; we return in Chapter 11 to the behaviour of firms in imperfect markets.

Look back at Figure 10.9. This shows the firm's output expansion path with a given factor price ratio and its isoquant map which defines its production function. If we specify factor prices, each isocost line defines a total cost for each level of output: the costs at points X, Y and Z give total (minimized) costs for each output level. The expansion path on Figure 10.9 can therefore be expressed as a total cost (*TC*) function of the general form:

$$TC = f(Q)$$

assuming factor prices are constant and all factors can be varied. This total cost function states that total costs are a function of output. Figure 10.13 shows a number of possible shapes for such total cost functions with given factor prices.

In Figure 10.13(a), returns to scale are constant. The total cost function is a straight line, implying that doubling input cost will double output. A firm with a production function displaying constant returns to scale across the whole isoquant map will have a straight line total cost curve and constant unit costs.

Figure 10.13(b) shows a cost curve of a firm facing decreasing returns to scale across the whole isoquant map. The total cost function displays diseconomies of scale.

Question

Explain that to yourself before reading on.

Decreasing returns to scale mean that increases in output require more than proportionate increases in inputs and thus in total costs so the total cost curve bends upwards. Conversely, Figure 10.13(c) shows the total cost curve of a firm with increasing returns to scale: the cost function flattens as output (scale) rises, and the firm enjoys economies of scale. Finally, 10.13(d) looks odd but it is worth considering carefully. In 10.13(d), the firm has economies of scale up to output Q_3. To the right of Q_3 the firm faces diseconomies of scale.

The pattern of economies and then diseconomies of scale shown on Figure 10.13(d) should look familiar to you. It is indeed a key assumption about firms' cost curves in the analysis of perfect competition (see *Changing Economies,* Chapter 7). The onset of diseconomies of scale after a certain output level implies rising *average costs* for the firm, setting a limit on firm size. To see this, you need to translate the total cost functions into their equivalent average and marginal cost functions.

Average costs (*AC*) are calculated by dividing total costs by output:

$$AC = \frac{TC}{Q}$$

Question

So what shape is the average cost curve derived from Figure 10.13(a)?

It will be a horizontal line. As output changes, *TC* changes in proportion, so *AC* remains the same. For Figure 10.13(b), the average cost function will slope upwards because *TC* rises faster than *Q* in the total cost function. Conversely, for 10.13(c), *TC* rises more slowly than *Q*, so the *AC* function slopes downwards. At any point on a total cost curve, the average cost at that point is the slope of a line from the origin to that point. So for example at output Q_2 on Figure 10.13(c), the average cost *AC* will be measured by the slope of the line OA, since:

$$\text{slope of OA} = \frac{TC_2}{Q_2} = AC \text{ at point A}$$

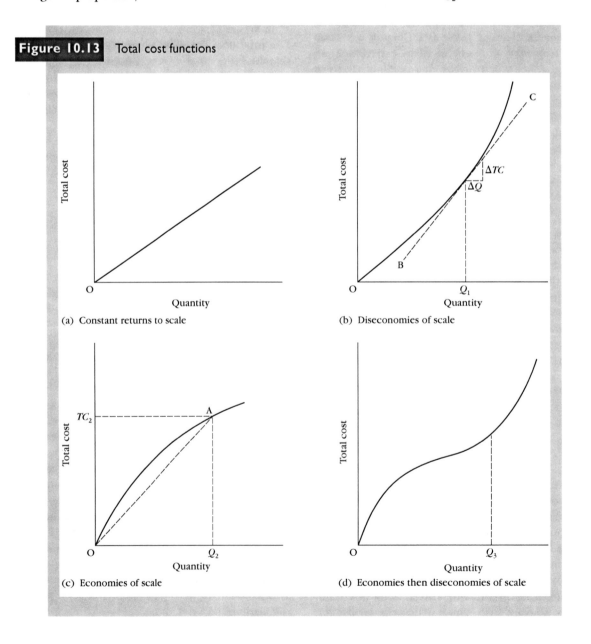

Figure 10.13 Total cost functions

(a) Constant returns to scale

(b) Diseconomies of scale

(c) Economies of scale

(d) Economies then diseconomies of scale

Marginal cost (MC) is a rather more complicated concept. The marginal cost of production at, say, output Q_1 on Figure 10.13(b) is the additional cost incurred by producing one more unit of output at that scale. It is therefore defined as:

$$MC = \frac{\Delta TC}{\Delta Q}$$

You have seen a formula like that above when looking at slopes. The marginal cost of production at a given output level is the *slope* of the total cost function at that output level. So the marginal cost of production at output level Q_1 on Figure 10.13(b) is measured by the slope of the *TC* curve at that point; that is, by the slope of the line BC, the tangent to the curve at that point. That slope is measured as $\frac{\Delta TC}{\Delta Q}$ as shown on Figure 10.13(b).

Now look again at Figure 10.13(d). The *TC* curve is reproduced in Figure 10.14(a). Look first at the line OA, which has been added to the figure. From the discussion above of average costs, you can see that the slope of this line, drawn from the origin to point X measures the average cost at that point. The slope is $\frac{TC_1}{Q_1}$. But line OA is also *tangent* to the total cost function *TC* at point X. This means that the marginal cost at point X is also the slope of OA = $\frac{TC_1}{Q_1}$. So at point X, and only there, on this total cost function, average and marginal cost are equal.

Figure 10.14(b) uses this information to show the shapes of the average and marginal cost curves associated with this total cost function. AC_1 is the average cost at output Q_1, which is the same on both figures. At this point, average and marginal costs are equal, $AC_1 = MC_1$. Below Q_1, average cost falls as output rises.

Reflection

Stop to consider this last statement. As Q rises towards Q_1 on Figure 10.14(a), the slope of a line from the origin to a point on the total cost function $TC = f(Q)$ decreases. Try it for yourself.

Marginal cost falls initially as output rises, and then starts to rise again before Q_1. You can check this for yourself too by drawing in tangents to the *TC* curve in Figure 10.14(a) and looking at how their slope changes. Figure 10.14(b) shows the interrelation between the average and marginal costs for this shape of total cost curve.

The 'U'-shaped average cost curves shown on Figure 10.14(b) may be associated with perfect or imperfect market structures (see *Changing Economies,* Chapter 4). But only where the firm is operating in perfect competition can we make one final move, from the cost curves to the firm's supply curve. Where the firm is an output price taker, the marginal cost curve above the point of minimum average cost, that is, above point Z on Figure 10.14(b), is the firm's *supply curve* (see *Changing Economies,* Chapter 7, Section 3). The firm produces where price equals marginal cost, and the *LRMC* curve traces the output the firm will wish to supply at different output prices. In long-run perfectly competitive equilibrium, the firm will produce at minimum long-run average cost. Figure 10.15 shows a perfectly competitive firm in long-run equilibrium, producing output Q_1 at the point where price P_1 is equal to marginal cost and the firm is making only normal profits.

Long and short run

In that last paragraph we suddenly introduced the notion of long and short run. The isoquant maps, in the form in which we have drawn them, are *long-run* diagrams in the sense defined in Chapter 8, Section 5; that is, they are drawn on the assumption that all factors of production can be varied. There is no fixed factor of production in the time scales implied by these diagrams. As Neil Costello explained in Chapter 8, time in the neoclassical economics of the firm is often defined in terms of the exogenous and endogenous variables in a model. So the 'short run' is defined as the period when capital remains fixed, and only labour inputs can be varied. In that case, the firm is moving out along a line such as $K_1 A_1 X B_3$ on Figure 10.5. With fixed capital services K_1, diminishing returns to labour inputs are more or less inevitable, unless the firm enjoys very sharp increasing returns to scale overall.

The short-run supply curve of the perfectly competitive firm can therefore be expected to be much steeper than the long-run supply curve. Prices need to rise more sharply to make a given level of output worthwhile in the short run than in the long run when capital services can be increased and the benefits of cost minimization over all inputs recaptured. Chapter 12 contains more discussion of the long-run adjustment of the firm to changes in input prices, including the effects on output price at the level of the industry, an issue not addressed in this chapter, which is concentrating on the firm.

While it seems reasonable to suppose that a short-run supply curve of a firm within any market structure may be 'U'-shaped, because of diminishing returns to the variable factor of production, economists are much less certain about the likely empirical shape of firms' long-run average cost

(a)

(b)

curves. Cost functions are hard to estimate in practice for several reasons. Data on costs are time-consuming to collect and hard to interpret. Firms expand over time, and some changes in costs may be the result of learning to use a given input mix more effectively, rather than the result of changing the combination of inputs used. In other ways, too, firms may influence their own costs: for example, they may bid up their own labour costs as they expand if they are large in relation to their own labour markets.

Despite the difficulties, detailed studies of long-run average cost functions produce some rather consistent results. Studies in US manufacturing show that firms tend to reach minimum efficient scale – that is, the point at which average costs reach their minimum – at a rather small plant size relative to the size of their markets, and to then experience rather constant average costs over a large scale range. A minority of firms show diseconomies of scale only at very high outputs (Scherer and Ross, 1990, p.113). The available evidence therefore suggests that long-run average cost curves of manufacturing firms tend to be roughly 'L'-shaped (see Figure 10.16), with economies of scale over an initial range of outputs followed by approximately constant average costs as scale rises beyond minimum efficient scale (Q_1 on Figure 10.16).

4 STATIC AND DYNAMIC EFFICIENCY OF FIRMS

So far, Sections 2 and 3 have considered the neoclassical analysis of firms' behaviour, including the concept of efficient choice of technique when the technical possibilities open to firms are known and stable. This section reviews the concepts of efficiency in the neoclassical framework, and goes on to show how a concept of technical change can be introduced in this type of comparative static analysis. We then introduce a broader concept of dynamic efficiency, which opens up a number of opportunities for strategic behaviour by firms which are explored in later chapters.

4.1 Neoclassical notions of static efficiency

First, we can sum up some notions of *static efficiency* in the neoclassical model of the firm. Considering a single firm, an efficient firm is one that is both technically efficient – that is, does not use more inputs than are required by its production function to produce its output – and cost-minimizing – that is, chooses an input mix that minimizes the cost of producing that output. In

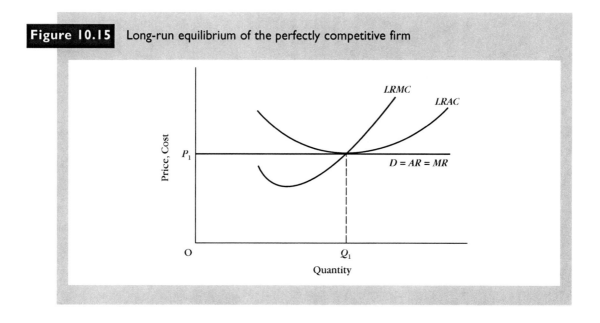

Figure 10.15 Long-run equilibrium of the perfectly competitive firm

other words, it is operating *on* its production and cost functions. Any firm operating *above* its cost function – for example, at point X on Figure 10.16, with output Q_x and average costs AC_x – is exhibiting *X*-inefficiency: that is, it is wasting money. There is, however, another concept of *productive efficiency* requiring firms to be operating at an efficient scale: at the minimum point of a 'U'-shaped *LRAC* curve, and at or beyond the point of minimum efficient scale if the *LRAC* curve is 'L'-shaped. Then the goods in the industry are being produced at the cheapest available cost. The model of perfect competition implies that firms are operating in equilibrium at minimum average cost (see Figure 10.15). Finally, at the level of the economy as a whole, *allocative efficiency* exists when the economy's resources overall are being used to satisfy consumer preferences, in such a way that making one person better off requires making another worse off. (The concept of allocative efficiency or Pareto efficiency, which brings together the behaviour of firms and households, is explored in Chapters 1 and 18.)

Productive efficiency

A firm is productively efficient if it is operating at minimum long-run average cost.

Allocative efficiency (or Pareto efficiency)

An economy is allocatively efficient if it is impossible by reallocating resources to make one consumer better off without making another worse off.

It may be the case that for a firm to operate at minimum average cost implies a scale of production that is large relative to demand. In this case, perfect competition will not be possible. In imperfect markets, in which firms do not operate as pure price takers, firms may choose a scale which is productively inefficient (see Chapter 8, Section 3), and firms with falling average costs over a wide

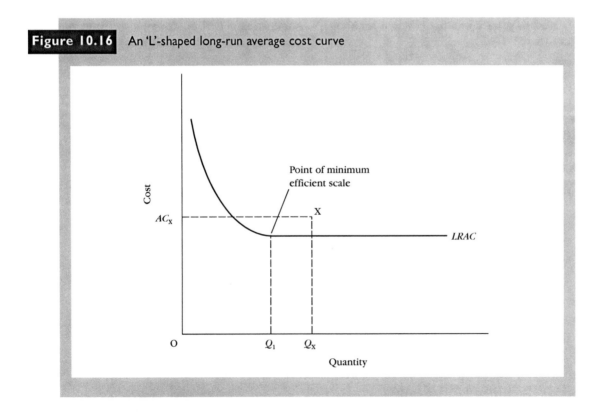

Figure 10.16   An 'L'-shaped long-run average cost curve

output range will tend to develop strong monopoly power. Chapter 11 will explore the strategic behaviour of firms with market power. Leibenstein, who invented the concept of *X*-inefficiency (see *Changing Economies*, Chapter 10, Section 4), argued that firms with market power were also those most likely to display *X*-inefficiency, since they were not subject to the pressures which kept the costs of firms in perfect competition to the minimum, that is, kept firms on their cost functions (Leibenstein, 1966).

The fundamental suppositions about technology underlying all these notions of efficiency are that, at a moment in time, there is a range of possible best-practice techniques, known to all firms, and summarized in the isoquant map. It is not clear, however, that firms *do* know all the possible techniques, especially techniques using factor combinations very different from those the firm is currently employing. Knowledge is expensive to acquire. Changing technique is expensive for firms, it takes time, and is likely to involve learning. In assuming away learning by experiment as scale changes, we end up thinking of a production function as a set of known 'blueprints'. This framework generates a very sharp distinction between technical innovation – which alters the isoquant map – and shifting between known techniques. The artificiality of this distinction is emphasized by those who study technical change, such as Nathan Rosenberg (1982).

4.2   A first look at technical change

Technical change, or innovation, is a major feature of the firm's environment and of its consideration about the most appropriate strategies it should adopt. Chapters 15 and 16 will explore innovation in much more depth. However, to complete the discussion of isoquants and the neoclassical approach to production decisions, we need to reflect on the way in which technical change can be incorporated into the neoclassical model.

Look at the isoquant maps shown in Figure 10.17. They show how an isoquant map will change if the firm is able to take advantage of new and more efficient technical processes. Technical progress will

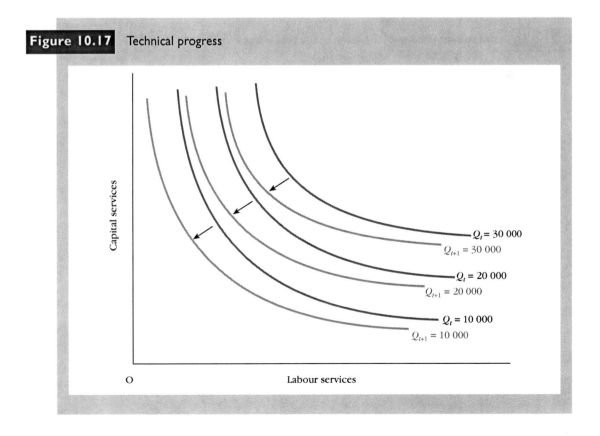

Figure 10.17   Technical progress

$Q_t = 30\ 000$

$Q_{t+1} = 30\ 000$

$Q_t = 20\ 000$

$Q_{t+1} = 20\ 000$

$Q_t = 10\ 000$

$Q_{t+1} = 10\ 000$

Capital services

Labour services

O

enable the firm to produce the same output with fewer inputs, either less capital or less labour, or less of both factors of production. This will move the isoquants for each level of output nearer to the origin. The isoquants labelled Q_t are the firm's isoquants before technical progress. The isoquants labelled Q_{t+1} show the firm's isoquant map after technical progress. The isoquants have all moved towards the origin but more towards the vertical axis than the horizontal axis, implying that the same output can be produced with substantially less labour than before.

The firm's response to technical progress can then be analysed. We draw in isocost lines as before, and look for the point of tangency to give the firm's cost and output decision for the new state of technology.

Figure 10.18 shows this analysis. Point X is the initial point of tangency between the isoquant for 20 000 units of output at time t and the isocost line AB. The firm therefore produces with the input mix K_1 and L_1. After technical progress, at time $t + 1$, the isoquant has moved towards the origin. The firm can now produce the same output at point Y, on isocost line EF, with inputs K_2 and L_2. It has saved some of each input, but has reduced labour use proportionately more than it has been able to reduce capital services employed.

Figure 10.18 therefore shows that, while technical change of this type saves inputs relative to output, the impact on each factor of production may be different. The technical change may affect the technique of production, the ratio of K to L. Economists can therefore differentiate technical change within this comparative static framework into three types (see Figure 10.19).

Figure 10.19 shows three alternative shifts in an isoquant, after technical change. In the initial position, the firm is producing output Q_1 with inputs K_1 and L_1. After technical change, the firm still produces output Q_1. If the isoquant shifts to isoquant Q_{13}, then, with the same factor prices (that is, with isocost lines of the same slope), the firm will produce the same output with the same ratio of K to L, using less of each input. Any technical change that, with given factor prices, moves a firm's cost-minimizing point inwards along a ray such as A through

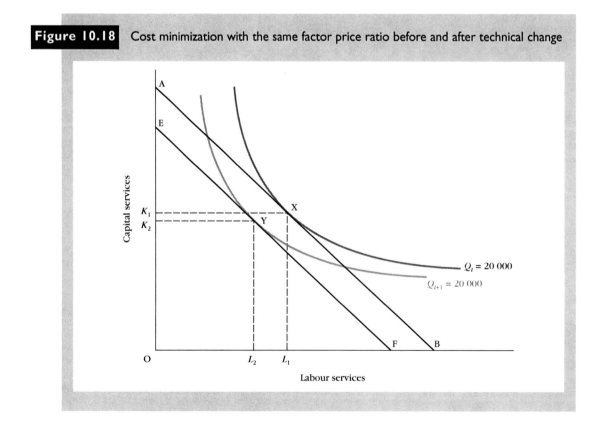

Figure 10.18 Cost minimization with the same factor price ratio before and after technical change

the origin, that is, using the same factor mix, is called *neutral technical change*.

Now consider Q_{12}. Any shift in an isoquant inwards to a new point of tangency above ray A is classified as *labour-saving technical change*, since it will always save proportionately more labour than capital services. On Figure 10.19, the shift of the isoquant to Q_{12} has had the effect that the same output is produced, at constant factor prices, with more capital services, K_2, and much less labour, L_2. Conversely, any shift of the isoquant to a new point of tangency below ray A in Figure 10.19, such as the shift to Q_{14}, displays *capital-saving technical change*.

In practice, it seems likely that factor prices will respond if technical change is persistently biased towards capital- or labour-saving. If capital replaces labour, this may initially at least drive people out of work, but may also raise the productivity of those in work. The net effect on factor prices is hard to predict. Figure 10.19 merely gives us an initial classification of types of technical change with fixed factor prices.

4.3   Objective and subjective costs

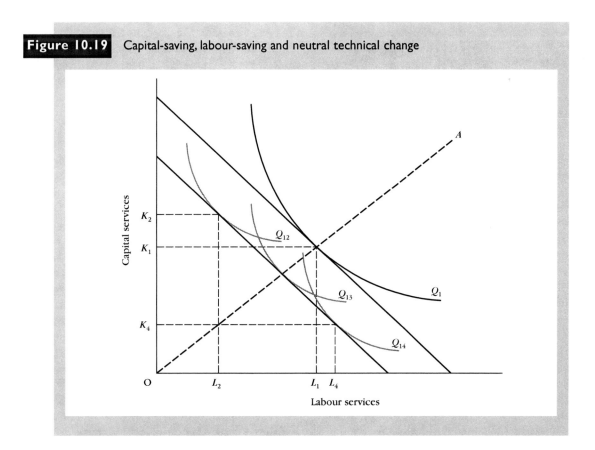

Figure 10.19   Capital-saving, labour-saving and neutral technical change

There is no right answer to these questions, but they raise some interesting issues about the interpretation of the functions you have just been studying. We noted in Section 4.1 that the neoclassical model assumes that a firm is 'on' its production function. But that in turn assumes that best practice at any particular point in time is known and available, which may not be true. There is, too, another complication suggested by the Ford example. The changes which allowed Mazda, and then Ford, to reduce costs required investment in new technology, certainly. But Hammer and Champy note that investment was 'enabling': the big impact on costs came from the rethinking and reorganization of administrative work. This 'reengineering' is in the tradition of Japanese 'lean production'. Toyota's initiatives in the early post-war period involved some new techniques of production which resulted, for example, in being able to speed up set-up times. But much of the cost reduction came from reorganizing the way a production line-based system was *managed*.

This history challenges the common notion that production functions and their associated cost functions can be thought of as 'engineering' concepts. Economists from the 'Austrian' school (see *Changing Economies*, Chapter 6) have emphasized that cost functions have an important *subjective* aspect (Auerbach, 1988). A firm will know its costs at a particular time, given its decisions about scale, organization, input mix and so on. But the whole cost function is a matter of subjective assessment, involving the equally subjective assessment of whether the money could have been spent better another way – that is, of the opportunity costs of the production choices. As Littlechild, an 'Austrian' economist who became the UK electricity industry regulator, put it, 'Two managers with different knowledge about available alternatives, or different views about the future, will associate different costs with the very same output' (Littlechild, 1978, pp.53–4). Peter Earl, a microeconomist with a strong interest in these issues of economic method, draws the following conclusion: 'The moral of all this may be that the theory of costs is at best to be seen as a set of tools for helping potential decision makers to choose, first, which kinds of information they might want to gather, and then between rival courses of action given their perceptions of alternatives' (Earl, 1995, p.157).

Finally, there is one more lesson from the Ford example, also noted by Earl. The story of Ford's cost cutting illustrates the importance, in 'lean production' systems, of reducing transactions costs between suppliers and buyers. So the neat separability implied by the new institutional theory of the firm, between a firm's production costs and its transactions costs, is not nearly as clear in practice.

4.4 Dynamic efficiency

The study of technical change has a way of challenging many of the categories of neoclassical analysis of the firm, because technical change in practice is rooted in learning and in historical time. In the first place, as with objective and subjective costs, we need to recognize that firms make subjective assessments about relevant technical methods in conditions of uncertainty. This was clear in the Mazda case. Firms do not in practice have technical blueprints sitting on the shelf which they can pick up and dust off at the appropriate time. Nor is change so easy to recognize that new procedures will be obvious to the firm's technical staff. If they are following one approach, they may find it difficult to recognize that technical change in a different area has relevance to them.

Second, the neoclassical approach to technical change treats change as exogenous to the model of the firm. This way of modelling technical change is consistent with the framework of static efficiency, since it treats technical change as an exogenous variable, and uses comparative statics to study the equilibria of the firm before and after the event. There is a parallel here with consumer theory: the role of technical change lies outside the model, in the same way as consumer tastes lie outside the analysis of consumer demand in the neoclassical approach. Many analysts of technical change would argue instead that the changes themselves are deeply embedded in the economy, and that technical change should be treated as an (at least partly) endogenous variable. This approach can be described as *dynamic efficiency*; it implies that a firm can, over time, influence its own cost function through innovation; that is, the firm does not take the isoquants as given. As *Changing Economies*, Chapter 12, noted, a concept of dynamic efficiency implies that monopoly power can have beneficial effects on a firm's efficiency, if profits are used to support innovation.

A framework of dynamic efficiency redirects our attention to *how* firms innovate. In other words, it treats efficiency at the firm level as a process rather than as a characteristic of a particular technical relationship. One attraction of evolutionary theory is precisely that it allows us to explore a firm's search for efficiency. The building blocks of evolutionary theory, as Chapter 8, Section 5 explained, include the routines of the organization. Firms follow routine patterns of behaviour, part of which is the search for better routines, and the most efficient survive. In the Ford/Mazda example, this framework would see Ford as engaging in satisficing behaviour initially, using an administrative routine for invoicing that gave adequate results. The visit to Mazda demonstrated that a competitor had found a better routine, and forced Ford to rethink its organization. The example shows that techniques of production and the organization of activity can be hard to separate in practice.

In the evolutionary framework, firms' behaviour is not seen solely as a function of maximizing rules. What works best in meeting a firm's complex objectives may involve apparently inefficient processes. A decision may not achieve maximum returns at a particular moment, but may be efficient for the survival of the firm: for example, it may provide more flexibility in the future. In this context, inefficient routines are those that work against the long-term interests of the firm – as, for example, when previous decisions 'lock-in' the firm to options which later constrain its ability to face competition (see Chapter 16). Evolutionary theory makes clear that, in a dynamic world with path dependency, efficiency requires effective search processes directed to sustain the long-term survival of the firm.

5 CONCLUSION

The core of this chapter has been an introduction to the neoclassical theory of production at the level of the firm. The chapter has developed the theoretical apparatus of isoquants and cost curves which allows us to study the choice of technique of a profit-maximizing firm. These are basic concepts that you will need in working through many subsequent chapters.

At the same time, we hope we have demonstrated that the underlying assumptions of this framework concerning a firm's technology and decision making are both powerful and limited. They provide a narrow but clear definition of techniques of production and of firms' objectives and constraints. This allows us to model firms' decision making and to define distinct concepts of efficiency. It also allows us to model a firm's response to exogenous technical change. But, in a curious way, the firm, as it is discussed in Chapter 8, seems almost absent from the neoclassical framework, becoming a mere machine for optimizing in given conditions.

The introductory story of Ford and Mazda and the discussion in Section 4 suggested that this approach becomes unsatisfactory when we are concerned to understand how technical change occurs. Cutting costs is as much a matter of organizational as of technical change, and through search, reorganization and research and development a firm may influence its own technical options (see Chapter 15). Economists studying industrial and regulatory policy, as well as those analysing the sources of technical change, therefore take a close interest in sources of dynamic efficiency. The next chapter turns to the analysis of strategic behaviour by firms with market power.

FURTHER READING

Earl, P. (1995) *Microeconomics for Business and Marketing*, Cheltenham, Edward Elgar: Chapter 7 provides a fairly accessible discussion of the theory presented here with applications to business examples.

Womack, J.P., Jones, D.T. and Roos, D. (1990) *The Machine that Changed the World*, New York, Rawson Associates and Macmillan Publishing: an immensely readable account of the impact of 'lean production' on the automobile industry.

ANSWERS TO EXERCISES

Exercise 10.1

Technique *B* has a *K/L* ratio of 1/1, and *A* of 2/1. Technique *A* is therefore the most capital intensive of the three; that is, it uses the most capital services with each unit of labour services.

Exercise 10.2

On Figure 10.20, the single technique *A* is shown by the ray *A*. The isoquants are right-angled, because starting from each of points A_1, A_2 and A_3 and adding more of one factor of production does not increase output. Moving from A_1 to A_2 doubles output; from A_1 to A_3 triples it. The factor inputs increase at the same rate as the output.

Exercise 10.3

Figure 10.21 shows the firm's single technique of production, represented by ray A, and the firm's right-angled isoquants. At A_1, the firm needs just 100

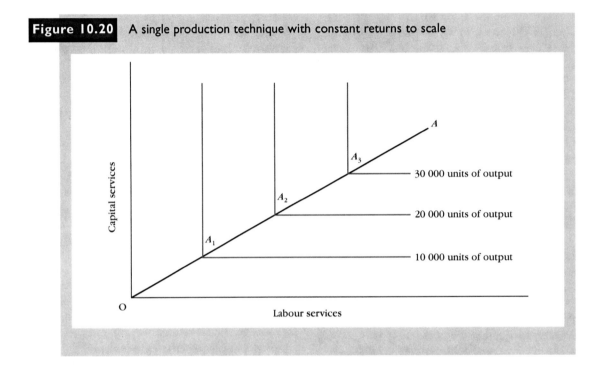

Figure 10.20 A single production technique with constant returns to scale

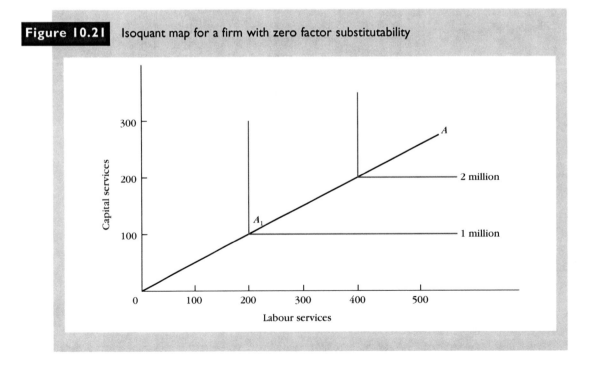

Figure 10.21 Isoquant map for a firm with zero factor substitutability

units of capital and 200 units of labour to produce one million units of output.

As you move along ray A, then given the assumption of constant returns to scale, output is a fixed multiple of labour inputs – so long as sufficient capital services are also employed. This multiple is a in the formula. To calculate it, assume sufficient capital inputs are available. Then, since we know we have enough K:

$$Q = \min(aL, bK) = aL$$

$$1\ 000\ 000 = a \times 200$$

$$a = \frac{1\ 000\ 000}{200} = 5\ 000$$

We can then find b in exactly the same way. Assume sufficient labour inputs are always used. Then:

$$Q = bK$$

$$1\ 000\ 000 = b \times 100$$

$$b = \frac{1\ 000\ 000}{100} = 10\ 000$$

So this firm has a production function of the form:

$$Q = \min(5\ 000L, 10\ 000K)$$

To see how the minimum condition works, assume that the firm tries to use 200 units of capital with 200 units of labour and show that it will still only get one million units of output.

Exercise 10.4

The isoquant map is shown on Figure 10.22. To draw it, choose an output, say $Q = 300$. Then assume input of labour L is zero, and put these figures into the production function. From the question you know that:

$$Q = aL + bK = 15L + 10K$$

Therefore, putting in your chosen figures:

$$300 = 0 + 10K$$

$$\text{hence } K = \frac{300}{10} = 30.$$

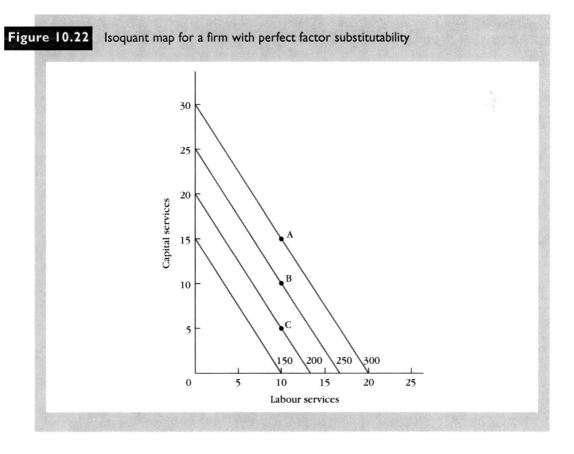

Figure 10.22   Isoquant map for a firm with perfect factor substitutability

That gives you the end-point on one axis. Now, for the same level of output, $Q = 300$, suppose that K is zero. Then:

$$300 = 15L + 0$$

$$\text{hence } L = \frac{300}{15} = 20.$$

You can now draw the 300 isoquant on Figure 10.22. To check that the equation $Q = aL + bK$ gives the same value of output all along the isoquant, put into that equation the factor inputs at say point A ($K = 15; L = 10$):

$$Q = (15 \times 10) + (10 \times 15) = 150 + 150 = 300.$$

You can draw the other isoquants in the same way, and check them at points such as B and C.

Exercise 10.5

The isocost line furthest to the right on Figure 10.7 represents 300 units of labour or 450 units of capital

services or any combination along the line in between. So at £15 per unit of labour and £10 per unit of capital, the firm's spending on inputs is £4 500.

Exercise 10.6

The firm can now buy a maximum of 450 units of capital services, with no labour, or 450 labour units with no capital. So, if the firm continues to spend £4 500 on inputs, the isocost line pivots upwards from AB to EB on Figure 10.23. The factor price ratio W/R has changed from 2/3 to 1/1; a labour unit and a capital unit are now the same price, and the slope of the isocost line EB is -1. If the firm continued to spend £4 500, it could produce a higher output by moving to the highest isoquant touched by the new isocost line. As the isoquant map is drawn in Figure 10.23, the firm chooses to produce at point Y, using more capital and more labour than before: 270 units of capital instead of 200, and 180 units of labour rather than 150.

Figure 10.23   The effect of a decline of one third in the price of capital services

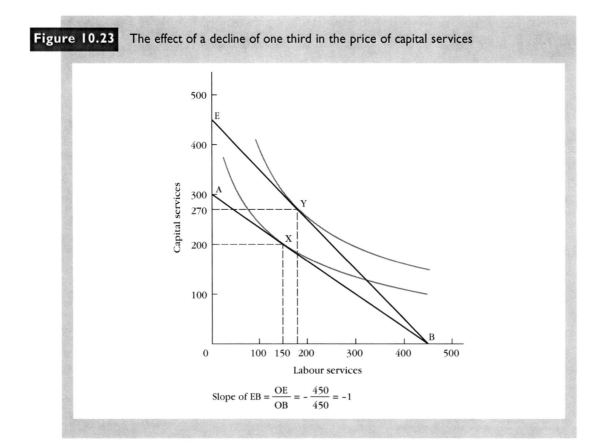

$$\text{Slope of EB} = \frac{\text{OE}}{\text{OB}} = -\frac{450}{450} = -1$$

A STRATEGIC VIEW OF COMPETITION

Vivienne Brown

LINKS

- This chapter shows how the new institutional approach adds to the traditional neoclassical analysis of oligopolistic market structures and market power, which relies on the use of cost curves (as discussed in Chapter 10), by explicitly introducing strategic behaviour into the analysis using game theory.

- The game theory illustrated in the chapter builds on the techniques and concepts introduced in Chapter 9.

- As the assumption of perfect information is relaxed, more institutional material is considered, with particular emphasis on trust and relational contracting, picking up from Chapter 9.

1 INTRODUCTION: THE 'COLA WARS'

In April 1996 at Gatwick airport, UK, amid a razzmatazz of media hype with stars such as Claudia Schiffer, André Agassi and Cindy Crawford in attendance, PepsiCo launched 'Project Blue' by unveiling an Air France Concorde painted blue. Project Blue was a $500 million (£330 million) campaign to relaunch its carbonated cola drink, Pepsi Cola, as a young, hip drink, by changing the colour of its 'livery' to blue in order to differentiate itself more strongly from its arch-rival Coca-Cola's red. 'Blue is cool' was the message that morning as PepsiCo announced that it would drop the red, white and blue of its logo, cans and lorries, and that by the end of 1997, its new blue livery would be in place in 190 countries outside the USA and Canada. Project Blue was, reportedly, the result of two years of design work involving 3000 options. As a result of this, PepsiCo took a calculated risk in opting for blue in the face of market research which had shown that red is a more appealing colour to customers.

The blue Concorde wasn't the only blue offering that morning. The Daily Mirror newspaper in the UK was printed on blue paper for a reported payment by PepsiCo of £1 million. This was part of PepsiCo's extensive international marketing drive to back up Project Blue which also included lavish commercials on peak time TV. PepsiCo's senior vice-president of international sales and marketing, John Swanhaus, was in an ebullient mood and is reported to have said that 'Project Blue represents a quantum leap into the future and redefines how the cola wars will be fought in the 21st century' (*Financial Times*, 3 April 1996).

In spite of all this hype, the Pepsi drink remained the same. Pepsi's new look concerned only its image, not the actual drink to be sold inside the new blue cans. Pepsi's rejuvenation was therefore simply a cosmetic change, aimed at consumers' perceptions of an unchanged product. This example tells us a lot about the power of advertising and the importance of 'image' in firms' competitive strategies, but can the expenditure of a sum as large as $500 million really be justified where the product remains the same? The answer lies in the future performance of PepsiCo. But, whether PepsiCo's Project Blue actually pays off or not, it provides a striking example of some of the moves associated with strategic competition, the subject of this chapter.

Strategic competition takes place where there is a recognition of interdependence between firms. Each realizes that its own actions will have an effect on the behaviour of its rivals which will, in turn, react back on itself. Firms may therefore take certain actions in order to influence other firms' choices and beliefs about possible future reactions. This kind of market structure is sometimes referred to as *oligopoly* or as competition among the few (see *Changing Economies*, Chapter 5). A monopolist who takes strategic decisions to deter potential rivals also engages in strategic competition. Sometimes each firm knows its rivals; PepsiCo, for example, chose blue to differentiate itself more strongly from the red livery of Coca-Cola, its main rival. But this element of personal rivalry may not always be present since firms may be responding strategically to potential as well as actual competition.

Oligopoly

An oligopoly is a market structure containing a small number of firms whose decision making is influenced by recognized mutual interdependence.

The 'cola wars' provide an example of personalized competition, and emphasize the element of conflict – or 'war' – between firms with opposed interests. Indeed, wars and chess games provide one sort of model for strategic thinking in trying to outwit or literally defeat an opponent. As Doug Ivester, Coca-Cola's president, put it: 'I look at the business like a chessboard. You always need to be seeing three, four, five moves ahead. Otherwise, your first move can prove fatal' (Sellers, 1996, p.37). But this warlike analogy is not the only way of thinking about strategic competition, as firms may recognize that they have interests in common. In such cases, firms may find that colluding or forming joint ventures is a better way of coping with rivals. There is thus a range of different strategies that may be available to a firm.

These strategies are the subject of this chapter. In the first part of the chapter, in Sections 2 to 4, I examine different ways in which a firm might deter the entry of new firms or the expansion of existing firms to protect its own position, and the impact of such behaviour on market structure. Then in Section 5 I look at collusion and the ways that firms might try to facilitate collusive behaviour. Section 6 considers the significance of trust among firms and the role of joint ventures. In the course of this chapter I shall be drawing on the insights of game theory, as well as neoclassical theory, since game theory has become a major theoretical tool in industrial economics for studying interdependence between firms. I hope to show how these applications of game theory can provide insights into complex forms of business behaviour such as the cola wars.

2 MARKET STRUCTURE AND BARRIERS TO ENTRY

2.1 Market structure in the cola industry

Worldwide, the market for cola is dominated by the two main rivals, Coca-Cola and Pepsi. Coca-Cola sells about twice as much as Pepsi, although there is considerable variation across countries. Coca-Cola and Pepsi are more equally placed in the USA, but in Western Europe Coca-Cola has been stronger historically, largely as a result of its promise in the 1939–45 war to 'put a Coke in the hand of every US serviceman' for 10 cents. In addition to Coke and Pepsi, there are a number of small brands operating within domestic markets. In the UK, many of these small cheaper brands are own-label cola drinks promoted by supermarkets, for example, Sainsbury's Classic which is sold in Coke look-alike containers.

The market for a product includes those products which are close substitutes for it (Chapter 8). Colas have half the UK carbonated drinks market (Table 11.1), and that share grew in the 1990s.

Table 11.1 shows that the UK market for colas alone is dominated by the two largest firms, Coca-Cola and PepsiCo, selling the 'premium' product. A group of other firms have a small share of cola sales and compete mainly on price.

The cola market can be described as having a dual market structure, with a highly concentrated segment where firms compete by non-price means, and a price-competitive fringe of other firms. By *market structure* I mean the characteristics of markets that influence the nature of competition. Market structure is frequently measured by concentration ratios (see *Changing Economies*, Chapter 6, Section 2). Although cola might appear to be a fairly homogeneous drink to the non-cola drinker, differences in taste are important in differentiating the various brands. In addition, a major factor in differentiation of the premium brands is the product image. The cola war between Coca-Cola and PepsiCo is a struggle for higher shares of the cola market and has included a number of new advertising initiatives over the years. PepsiCo's 1996 initiative was timed at a strategic moment when both brands were poised for expansion in emerging markets such as the Middle East and Eastern Europe. Questions we might want to ask are how have competitive forces in the market for cola led to domination by two firms, and why are other brands marginalized? Is there anything special about the production or marketing of cola that explains why the market is dominated by these two brands which have such a strong image? In Sections 2, 3 and 4, I will examine some possible explanations of this market structure.

Table 11.1 Estimated UK brand shares of colas (% of value of sales for all outlets), 1996

	% of colas	% of all carbonated drinks
Coke, Diet Coke, Tab	65	33
Pepsi, Diet Pepsi, Pepsi Max	23	11
Other packaged brands (e.g. Virgin Cola)	6	3
Grocery own labels	6	3
Total	100	50

Source: Key Note, 1996, p.11

Market Structure

Market structure refers to those characteristics of a market, such as the concentration of sellers, that influence the nature of competition within the market.

2.2 Production economies and market structure

Sometimes market structure can be explained by the relationship between costs of production and size of the market. There are two different versions of this relationship, a static one and a dynamic one. In the static version, the number of firms in a market may be explained by the ratio of market size to the minimum efficient scale of production (MES).

In Figure 11.1, a firm's long-run average cost curve, *LRAC*, shows declining average costs. In markets where there are substantial economies of scale, it may not be possible for more than a small number of firms to survive. At the limit, it is possible that only one firm can produce profitably.

In Figure 11.2, however, the *LRAC* curve is 'L' shaped. Minimum efficient scale is Q_m with minimum average cost C_m (see Chapter 10, Section 3). If the price is set equal to average cost C_m, the quantity demanded will be Q_1, and the number of firms will depend on the ratio $\frac{Q_1}{Q_m}$. If the size of the market is large relative to the MES, then it might be expected that the concentration level would be low, but if the market is small relative to the MES then concentration would be high.

Static economies of scale, given the existing technology, are shown in Figure 11.1. In situations where firms are introducing new technologies, there is scope for dynamic economies of scale. High research and development (R&D) budgets, for example, may create dynamic economies of large-scale production, as new techniques reduce unit costs at high output levels. The semiconductor industry which produces electronic chips provides an example. It has been estimated that plant costs rose from $10 million in 1972 to $800 million by the late 1980s. R&D costs for Intel's first 4-bit microprocessor are thought to have been $10 million in the early 1970s and $250 million in the late 1980s

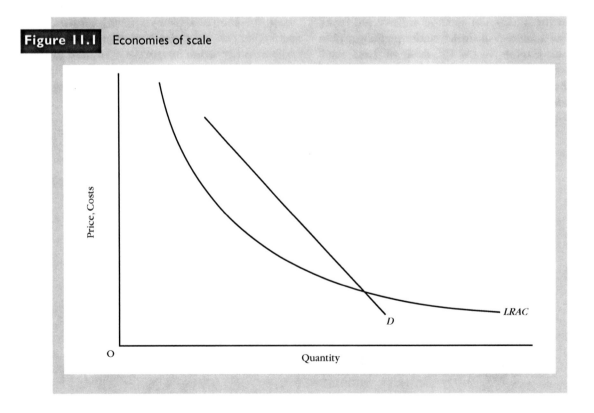

Figure 11.1 Economies of scale

for the 80486 microprocessor family. It has been estimated that the cost of just the R&D investment (ignoring interest charges) in the 80486, introduced in 1989, worked out at $250 per chip if a million chips were sold but only $5 per chip if 50 million were sold (all estimates from Scherer, 1996).

Another type of dynamic economies of scale arises from the process of *learning-by-doing* which takes place when the technology is so new that firms are learning how to implement production systems. Setting up a new production process incorporating leading-edge technology involves much trial and error. As experience of the process of production is acquired, early production difficulties are ironed out and unit costs fall. Thus the cost of each production batch falls along the firm's *learning curve*. The learning curve for the semiconductor industry is shown in Figure 11.3 overleaf. Note that the axes are expressed in log scales. The horizontal axis in Figure 11.3 shows cumulative output and so movements along the learning curve represent movements in real time as the firm's cumulative output rises. The benefits from learning-by-doing accrue as the firm produces more over time. It has been estimated that in the semiconductor industry, unit costs fall by about 28 per cent with each doubling of cumulative output (Scherer, 1996, p.250).

Learning-by-doing

Learning-by-doing implies that unit costs fall as cumulative output increases.

Learning curve

The learning curve traces the decline in unit costs from learning-by-doing as cumulative output increases.

In these circumstances, firms try to race down their learning curve in order to be the first to the bottom and so undercut rivals. Central to this process is the expansion of market demand to accommodate the enormous increases in production that are necessary to exploit the full benefits of learning-by-doing. In order to facilitate this, firms may reduce price even below current production costs in order to increase sales and reduce both price and costs still further in the future. This suggests that the presence of the learning curve may encourage aggressive pricing policies, especially by incumbent firms trying to eliminate other firms which are at an earlier point

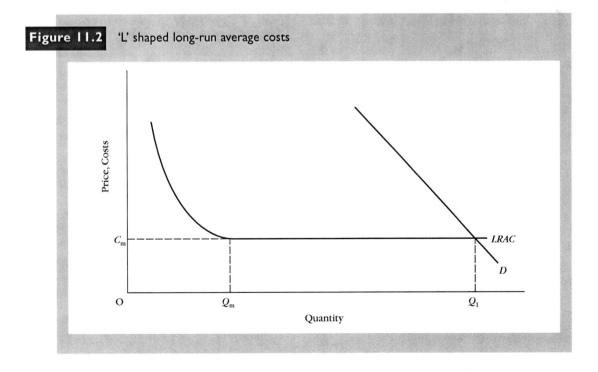

Figure 11.2 'L' shaped long-run average costs

on their learning curves. Knowing that late-comers will be at a disadvantage in this race, existing firms have an added incentive to raise their scale of operations and race down their learning curve to try to eliminate the opposition. If several firms implement aggressive prices in an attempt to be the leader, then a 'bloodbath' may be the result as the surviving firms have to share a market which is too small to repay their investment (Scherer, 1996).

Both static and dynamic economies of scale offer explanations of market structure based on technological factors and underlying costs. Scale economies and learning curves may function as barriers to entry which make it harder for new firms to enter the market because the new firms have higher costs than existing firms, which in turn leads to high concentration levels among suppliers.

Question

Does this approach provide a good explanation of the structure of the cola market? Does it seem plausible to you that the cola market is characterized by substantial economies of scale as in Figure 11.1 or substantial learning-by-doing as in Figure 11.3?

The making of cola is a technologically simple operation of manufacturing the cola syrup, then diluting it and bottling or canning it for consumption. The market for cola drinks is large; in the UK alone in the mid-1990s, the consumption was about 2000 million litres each year. Does the number of dominant firms really seem to be technologically constrained? While economies of scale and learning-by-doing are important features of industries such as the semiconductor industry, they do not look so important for industries such as the cola industry. What other explanations might there be for the dual structure of the cola industry? Some theorists have attempted to answer this by studying the ways in which incumbent firms can deter entry by choosing a particular price or output such that profitable entry by new firms or expansion by existing fringe firms becomes less likely. This is examined in Section 2.3.

2.3 Entry deterrence: neoclassical limit pricing

If supernormal profits are earned by a dominant firm in a market with a downward-sloping demand curve, then new firms would be expected to enter the

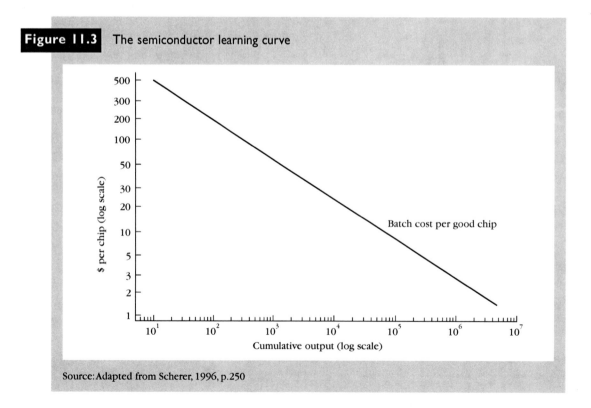

Figure 11.3 The semiconductor learning curve

Source: Adapted from Scherer, 1996, p.250

market spurred on by the prospect of high profits. A dominant firm may therefore face a fringe of small rivals seeking to expand, such as we have seen in the cola example. If the dominant firm has costs below those of other firms, such that its profit-maximizing price is below the unit costs of rival firms, then the dominance of that firm is readily understood. The low unit costs of the dominant firm may be the result of natural monopoly, or dynamic economies of scale, or the result of extraordinarily efficient management. If, however, the dominant firm's profit-maximizing price is greater than the unit costs of its rivals, then it would be profitable for those rivals to enter the market or expand output. Is it possible for the dominant firm to take measures that will make it harder for other firms to challenge its dominant position? This is the question addressed in this section.

Can a dominant firm set price at a level which is low enough to deter entry and so maintain its own dominant position, but yet not so low that its own profits are wiped out? The highest price which entirely deters entry is known as the *limit price*, and this section will now examine how the limit price might be determined. In addition, we shall need to consider whether it is in the dominant firm's interest to deter all entry, and whether there are special conditions required for limit pricing to be successful.

Limit price

The limit price is the maximum price an incumbent firm can set which limits new entry to zero.

We shall find that there are two different situations where the question of entry arises – the situation of small-scale entry where each rival firm's output is too small to have a significant effect on price, and that of large-scale entry where an entrant's output is sufficiently large to affect market price. Following Scherer and Ross (1990) I shall take each in turn.

Small-scale entry

If the firm wishes to preclude entry by small firms, the limit price is equal to the unit costs of the entrants. This would eliminate entrants' supernormal profits and so would take away their incentive to enter the market. This limit price may well be less than the price implied by profit-maximizing behaviour for the dominant firm in the absence of the possibility of entry. Limit pricing is illustrated in

Figure 11.4 (overleaf) for a dominant firm, drawn for simplicity as a monopolist. In the absence of entry, profit maximization takes place where marginal cost equal marginal revenue. This implies a price, P, and output, Q. At Q, average cost is less than average revenue so the dominant firm earns supernormal profits as shown by the rectangle $PABD$.

Suppose that potential entrants' unit cost is shown as C. As P is greater than C, firms have an incentive to enter the market and earn supernormal profit at the existing price. The dominant firm will lose sales and so its market share and profits will decline. Alternatively, if the dominant firm sets price at C, potential entrants have no incentive to enter as they will earn no more than normal profits. The limit price here is therefore equal to the entrants' unit cost, C. Limit pricing safeguards the dominant firm's market share as the sole producer with output Q_L, the limit output, but at the cost of a fall in supernormal profits from $PABD$ to $CXYE$.

Maximizing immediate profits at the expense of a shrinking future market share thus implies higher profits in the current period but falling profits over time. Precluding entry by limit pricing, however, reduces profits in the current period but protects profits in the future. Gaskins (1971) showed that the best pricing policy relative to the limit price for a firm maximizing the net present value of its profit stream over time, is one that balances current profits against future profits. He investigated the optimal time path of prices taking into account the speed at which entrants respond to any given profit level, and the limit price, C. Research building on Gaskins' work has identified three main types of optimal time paths depending on the dominant firm's costs relative to the rivals' costs (Scherer and Ross, 1990, pp. 363–64).

Case I: The declining dominant firm If the dominant firm has no cost or image advantage, its optimal price will initially lie above the limit price (i.e. entrants' costs) since there is no point in losing current profits trying to defend an untenable future market share. As entry takes place or existing fringe firms expand, the optimal price will fall towards the limit price as the firm loses its dominant position and its market share becomes insignificant.

Case II: Exclusionary pricing If the dominant firm has a considerable cost or image advantage over an existing fringe, it can drive them out by pricing below their costs. The optimal price therefore lies

Figure 11.4   Limit pricing and small-scale entry deterrence

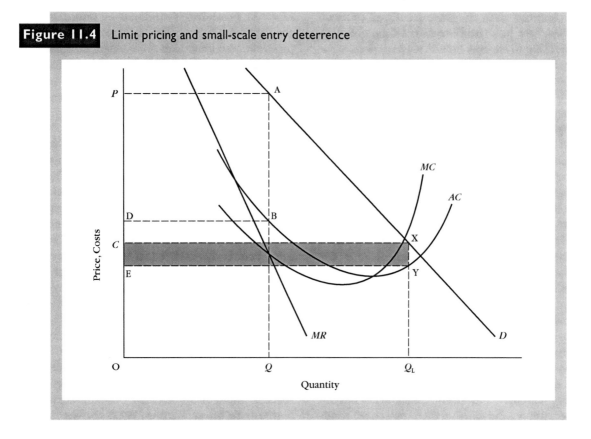

below rivals' costs as long as the lower price and consequent loss of current profit is outweighed by the benefits of a larger market share in the future.

Case III: Eventual limit pricing   A dominant firm with some cost or image advantage over an existing fringe of rival firms may find that the loss of profits implied by further exclusionary pricing is not outweighed by the benefits of larger market share in the future. It will then charge the limit price to prevent further entry or the expansion of existing rivals.

Implementing an optimal pricing policy of this type assumes in each case that the dominant firm has all the relevant information, for example, on the speed of potential entrants' entry given any level of profits, and on the conditions of market demand, and so is able to calculate the profit streams resulting from different pricing policies. A distinguishing feature of this model is that none of the entrants individually is large enough to exert any pressure on market price through its own actions, although collectively such firms will squeeze out a dominant firm which has no cost or image advantage over

them, thus imposing a competitive outcome on the market in spite of the incumbent's initial position of dominance.

Large-scale entry

In the case of large-scale entry, a potential entrant knows that its own output is large enough to have a significant effect on market output and so will depress market price. It therefore needs to take into account the effect of its own entry on the market price in deciding whether to enter. We shall consider whether it is still the case that the limit price equals the entrant's unit cost.

Figure 11.5 shows the current profit-maximizing price, P, and output, Q, of an incumbent firm where there are few significant economies of scale and unit cost is equal to C. Remember that $LRAC = LRMC$ on the horizontal portion of an L-shaped $LRAC$ curve (Chapter 8, Section 3).

Supernormal profits are shown by the rectangle $PABC$. An entrant with unit cost equal to C would therefore know that it could earn supernormal profits, even though entry will drive the price below P.

How can an incumbent firm set a limit price to deter entry, while taking account of the effect of large-scale entry in driving down market price?

In order to analyse this problem, we need to include the entrant's output. This is done in Figure 11.6 by including the entrant's average cost curve $LRAC_N$ as well as the incumbent's $LRAC_I$. In adding the entrant's output to the incumbent's output in Figure 11.6, it is assumed that the incumbent's output is given and does not change in response to entry, and that this is known to the entrant. This is a crucial assumption for limit pricing and large-scale entry, and we shall investigate it critically in a moment. Assuming that the incumbent's output remains constant through the post-entry period implies that the entrant's average cost curve, $LRAC_N$, is drawn with its vertical axis at the vertical line given by the incumbent's chosen output. If the entrant has the same costs as the incumbent, $LRAC_N$ is drawn as a horizontal shift to the right of $LRAC_I$ by a horizontal distance which is equal to the incumbent's output. What we need to find is the incumbent's output – its limit output – that precludes entry.

If the incumbent wishes to deter entry it must increase its output sufficiently above Q on Figure 11.6 so that the entrant has no expectation of profit. The incumbent's output needs to be increased to a level such that the potential entrant's $LRAC_N$ does not lie below the demand curve at any point. By sliding Q and the vertical axis for $LRAC_N$ to the right until $LRAC_N$ just touches the demand curve, the limit output for the incumbent can be found. This is shown in Figure 11.6 as Q_L which is the smallest output for the incumbent at which the entrant would not earn a supernormal profit. The price corresponding to Q_L is the limit price, P_L. The incumbent produces Q_L at price P_L, and so the residual demand curve, shown as XD, is all that is left for the entrant. With this demand curve there is no rate of output at which the entrant can make supernormal profit even though the limit price, P_L, is above its own minimum cost, C.

Figure 11.6 shows that the limit output, Q_L, is greater than the immediate profit-maximizing output, Q, and also the limit price is lower than P at P_L. This is similar to the small-scale entry case. In this large-scale case however, the limit price, P_L, is greater

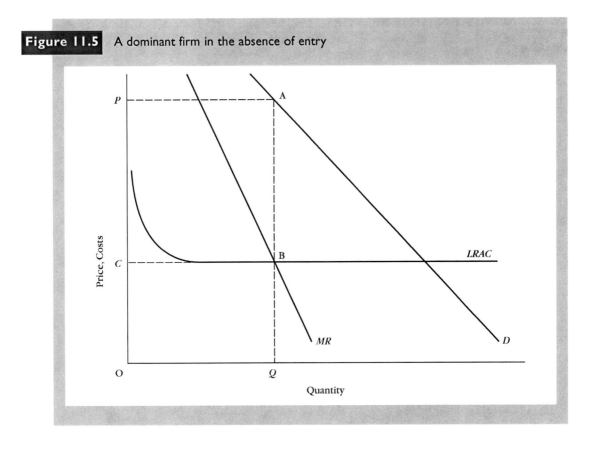

Figure 11.5   A dominant firm in the absence of entry

than the incumbent's cost, C, and so some super-normal profit is still earned by the incumbent as shown by the rectangle $P_L XYC$. Supernormal profit for the incumbent is less than in the absence of entry ($PABC$), but is greater than if price were set at C.

We can see from Figure 11.6 that the excess of the limit price over the minimum unit cost, C, depends on the shape and position of $LRAC_N$ in relation to the demand curve. Basically, any factors that cause the entrant to have higher costs will tend to raise the limit price relative to the minimum unit cost of the incumbent. Thus the limit price will be higher: the greater the entrant's minimum unit cost, the greater the entrant's MES, and the more slowly the entrant's unit costs decline. The steeper the market demand curve, the higher the limit price.

Exercise 11.1

Show on a diagram how an incumbent may be able to set a limit price even where the potential entrant has a lower minimum unit cost than the incumbent.

As in the case of small-scale entry, the limit-pricing model in the large-scale entry case shows how the incumbent may maximize the net present value of its profit stream by overproducing relative to its immediate profit-maximizing output in order to depress price and deter entry, thus protecting future profits. In the large-scale case this may occur even where the incumbent does not have a cost or image advantage over the entrant.

Remember, however, that these results depend crucially on the assumption that the incumbent maintains the pre-entry limit output, Q_L, in the event of entry, and that the prospective entrant knows this. But why should this assumption be valid? Here we come to a crucial difference between the small-scale and large-scale versions of limit pricing. Why should the incumbent maintain the pre-entry output when the fact of large-scale entry changes its optimization calculations? Why should the entrant assume that the incumbent will stick to the pre-entry output in these circumstances? If the incumbent was optimizing when the limit price was set pre-entry, why should it not revise those plans in the event of entry, and if this

Figure 11.6   Limit pricing and large-scale entry deterrence

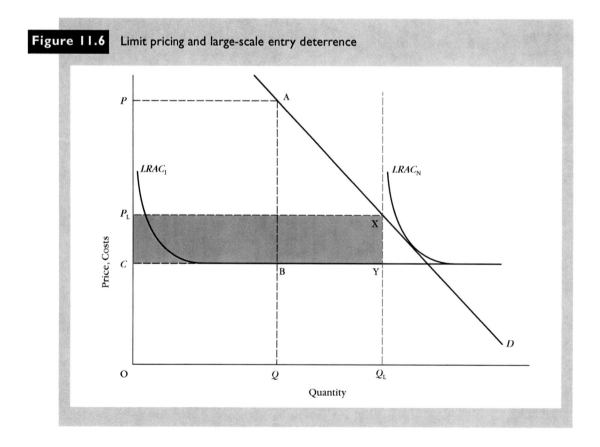

is so, why does the entrant not take this into account when deciding whether to enter?

We therefore have to consider the significance of the assumption needed for the limit pricing results, that the entrant takes the incumbent's pre-entry output as given. For a deeper analysis we need to consider the strategic aspects of entry deterrence, notably the beliefs held by potential entrants about the incumbent's response to entry. In trying to consider this interaction, however, we come up against a fundamental weakness of the neoclassical limit pricing model, in that it is not well suited to considering the mutual interdependence of economic agents' decision making. For this reason, recent research on entry deterrence has drawn on the language and insights of game theory and to this we now turn.

 ## 3   STRATEGIC ENTRY DETERRENCE

3.1   Introduction: a game-theoretic approach

As you learned in Chapter 9, Section 3.2, the basic equilibrium concept in game theory is that of Nash equilibrium, where each agent chooses the best strategy given the strategies of the others. This concept of Nash equilibrium is well suited for analysing situations of strategic interdependence as it incorporates the idea of interdependent maximization. A set of strategies can be a Nash equilibrium only if all agents' strategies and beliefs are consistent.

We saw in the previous section that the success of entry deterrence depends on the assumption that the incumbent will maintain output in the post-entry period. We can now use the concept of Nash equilibrium to examine the conditions under which a strategy of entry deterrence can succeed. We shall find that entry is deterred only if the potential entrant believes that the incumbent would indeed maintain a high output in the event of its own entry into the market. The potential entrant thus 'looks ahead' to the consequences of its own action and then works backwards from that in making a decision about its own behaviour. Its decision about entry is, therefore, made in advance of the incumbent's actual response, but the potential entrant takes account of that response by looking ahead when making the decision.

In order to capture this kind of game-theoretic thinking, I shall present an entry game as an extensive form game (Chapter 9, Section 3, introduced extensive form games). An extensive form game allows us to model the dynamic structure or sequencing of the moves made by the potential entrant and the incumbent, but remember that it is based on the players looking ahead to take into account the consequences of their actions on the other player. In Section 3.2 I present two different entry games where deterrence fails, and then in Section 3.3 I examine the conditions for successful entry deterrence.

3.2   Entry deterrence fails

The first entry game I consider involves two stages; the potential entrant moves first and then the incumbent responds. It is assumed that there is common knowledge of payoffs and the entrant's initial move. The potential entrant, E, can either enter or stay out. The incumbent, I, can respond either by retaliating – playing 'tough' – or by playing soft and accommodating the entrant's presence in the market. How might the incumbent do this? If there is a downward-sloping demand curve, then any increase in output as a result of entry of a new firm reduces the price of the good. If the incumbent plays tough it would produce at a high output, so that price falls so low that the entrant cannot make a profit. Unfortunately for the incumbent, this also drives the price down against itself and so its profit also falls. If the incumbent plays soft it would produce a low output, thus maintaining prices and enabling the entrant to make a profit. The higher price also enables the incumbent to minimize the fall in its own profits.

The extensive form entry game is shown in Figure 11.7. In this game, the entrant moves first – enter or stay out – and the incumbent moves second – soft or tough. There are four pairs of strategies – (enter, soft), (enter, tough), (stay out, soft) and (stay out, tough). The payoffs, here the profits, to the two firms are given on the right hand side next to each of the four strategy pairs, with the entrant's listed first (it is conventional to list the payoffs in the order in which the players make their moves). The entrant's payoffs are zero for staying out, 1 on entry if the incumbent is soft and –1 on entry if the incumbent is tough. The incumbent's payoffs are higher if it goes soft rather than tough, and they are also higher for non-entry than for entry.

To find the equilibrium solution of the game, we do what the players do: we look ahead to the end of the game and work backwards. In game theory this process is known as *backward induction*.

Backward induction

Backward induction is a method of solving games in extensive form which looks ahead to the final payoffs and works backwards.

Looking at the incumbent's two decision nodes at the second stage, we see that it is always in the incumbent's interest to play soft, whether or not entry has taken place. That is, if the entrant enters so that the incumbent is at the top node, the incumbent will choose soft, with a payoff of 2. Alternatively, if the entrant stays out so that the incumbent is at the bottom node, the incumbent will choose soft, with a payoff of 4. At the decision node at the beginning of the game, the entrant looks ahead to see how the incumbent would respond to its own move. The entrant knows that, whatever its own move, the incumbent's payoffs are higher for playing soft, and so the entrant knows that the incumbent will play soft irrespective of entry. In this case, the entrant will choose to enter as it prefers a payoff of 1 to the zero payoff. The equilibrium of the game is therefore (enter, soft)

with payoffs (1, 2). The entrant is not deterred by any fear of the incumbent's reaction.

We have seen by backward induction that the equilibrium of the whole game is found by examining the equilibrium of each *subgame*, where a subgame is any part of a game starting from a decision node and ending at the final payoff (and where players know the payoffs and previous moves). The game shown in Figure 11.7 has three subgames, the two subgames starting with the incumbent's decision node, and also the game as a whole starting with the entrant's decision node. We have seen that the incumbent would play soft in each of the two final subgames, and knowing this, the entrant enters. The equilibrium of the game as a whole is therefore (enter, soft). This concept of equilibrium for an extensive form game is a refinement of the notion of Nash equilibrium as it corresponds to a Nash equilibrium in each of the subgames. This concept of equilibrium is known as *subgame perfect Nash equilibrium (SPNE)*. The SPNE of the extensive form game shown in Figure 11.7 is (enter, soft).

Subgame

A subgame is any part of an extensive form game which starts from a decision node and ends at the final payoffs, where players know the payoffs and any previous moves.

Figure 11.7 A two-stage entry game in extensive form

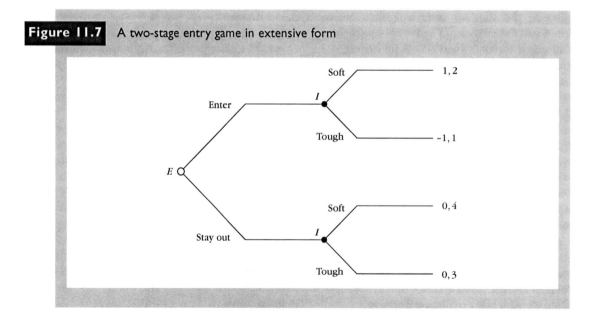

Subgame perfect (Nash) equilibrium (SPNE)

Subgame perfect (Nash) equilibrium is the equilibrium concept of an extensive form game which requires that the equilibrium strategies are Nash equilibria in each subgame.

The reason entry is not deterred in this game is that the incumbent has no incentive to be tough once entry has taken place. Is it possible, however, to deter entry by playing tough pre-entry? We shall examine this by reformulating the game to include an earlier stage where the incumbent can move before the entrant does.

Including an extra stage changes the two-stage game into a three-stage extensive form entry game. This three-stage game is shown in Figure 11.8. The first stage corresponds to the incumbent's move, and is new to this game. The second stage corresponds to the potential entrant's move and the third stage corresponds to the incumbent's move; these were the moves in the two-stage game in Figure 11.7. Again there is common knowledge of payoffs and prior moves. In the first stage, the incumbent chooses whether to play tough or whether to play soft. The issue at stake is whether a tough move here can influence the outcome of the game.

The incumbent's payoffs in the first stage follow directly from the payoffs in Figure 11.7: in the absence of entry, the incumbent's payoff was 3 if it played tough and 4 if it played soft. In the second stage in Figure 11.8 (overleaf), the entrant enters or stays out, and the incumbent responds in the third stage by playing soft or tough. The payoffs in the second and third stages also follow directly from Figure 11.7. Note that the incumbent's payoffs are given first as it now moves first, but there are now two payoffs for the incumbent; the first number refers to the first stage before the entrant moves, and the second number refers to the third stage after the entrant has moved. To keep things simple, the discount rate is assumed to be zero so that payoffs have the same value to the incumbent irrespective of whether they are received in the first stage or third stage. There is one payoff for the potential entrant which is determined by the entrant's second stage move in conjunction with the incumbent's third stage response.

To find the solution of the game, we need to start at the final payoffs and work backwards. We use the same process of backward induction to find the

SPNE of this game as a whole, by finding the Nash equilibrium of each of the subgames. In this game there are seven subgames altogether.

Looking at the four subgames starting with the four final decision nodes, we see that in the third stage, the incumbent's payoffs are always greater for soft than for tough, and this holds true irrespective of the previous move by the entrant (2 is better than 1, and 4 is better than 3). Thus in the final stage, the incumbent plays soft. Looking at the two subgames starting with the entrant's decision nodes in stage two, we see that the entrant knows the incumbent will play soft in the third stage whatever its own move. Enter gives the entrant a higher payoff with soft than stay out does, irrespective of the previous move by the incumbent in the first stage (1 is better than 0). Therefore the entrant chooses enter. The equilibrium of these subgames is therefore (enter, soft). The best move for the incumbent in the first stage is to play soft (4 is better than 3), and so the SPNE of the game as a whole is (soft, enter, soft). The outcome is that the SPNE of the two-stage version of the entry game is unchanged by the inclusion of the first-stage move by the incumbent. Total payoffs for the incumbent are 4 + 2 = 6, and for the entrant the payoff is 1.

Question

Are you surprised by this? How would you explain this result?

The inclusion of the first move by the incumbent does not affect the SPNE of the game because it does not alter the fact that playing soft is the best move in the third stage, irrespective of what happened in the first stage. As the first-stage move has no effect on later moves, there is no point in playing tough at that stage for a lower first-stage payoff. The incumbent therefore maximizes the payoff in the first stage by playing soft, knowing that the entrant will enter in the second stage and that it will respond by playing soft in the third stage. The entrant knows all this as well. The entrant therefore enters, and the incumbent does not forgo the higher first stage payoff by making tough gestures that both it and the entrant know are empty.

3.3   Successful entry deterrence

A crucial point illustrated by the entry game in Figure 11.8 is that tough gestures that do not influence later behaviour are empty threats and are not worth making, and so will not be made by rational players.

What is important for successful deterrence by an incumbent is a *commitment* such that playing tough is the best move for the incumbent, in the event of entry. Commitment binds a player by ensuring that certain moves will not be played. Thus successful commitment is based on the paradox that the player has to bind itself voluntarily to a future course of action (Schelling, 1956). Only when a threat is based on commitment is it a *credible threat*.

Commitment

Commitment binds a firm to make a particular move by changing the structure of payoffs to give that move the best payoff.

Credible threat

A credible threat is a threat based on a commitment.

In the entry game, commitment to deter can be secured only if the payoff for playing tough in the event of entry can be made larger than that for soft. The question then arises whether the incumbent can change the structure of payoffs and make the tough payoff better than the soft one. One way in which the incumbent can change its own payoff structure in advance is by investing in large *sunk capacity* – fixed capacity which is firm-specific and has no resale value.

Sunk capacity

Sunk capacity is fixed capacity, the costs of which are irrecoverable.

Large sunk capacity imposes an irreversible commitment because the high costs cannot be recovered by the firm on leaving the market. It thus

Figure 11.8 A three-stage entry game in extensive form

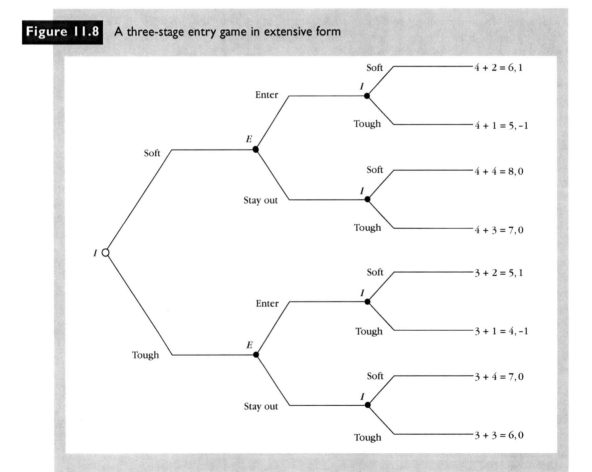

forms a barrier to exit for the incumbent. With a large plant size, the incumbent trades higher fixed costs for lower marginal costs, and this requires larger outputs for profit maximization (Dixit, 1980). Large sunk capacity therefore commits the incumbent to playing tough because large output becomes the profit-maximizing move, irrespective of entry. It thus pre-commits the incumbent to playing tough by making soft have lower payoffs in the third stage. Knowing this, the potential entrant does not enter. The incumbent's decision to produce at the high level in stage one now becomes a credible threat which succeeds in deterring entry because it is based on a commitment to maintain a high output irrespective of entry.

The successful entry-deterring effects of large sunk capacity can be seen by incorporating the new payoffs in the three-stage extensive form game. Figure 11.9 shows a revised version of this game which illustrates the effect of large sunk capacity on the structure of payoffs. Soft moves now have a lower payoff for the incumbent relative to tough moves, and this holds whether or not entry takes place, although it is still the case that the incumbent's payoffs are larger in the absence of entry. In Figure 11.9 the payoffs have been adjusted to take account of the effect of the large sunk capacity: 1 has been subtracted from the incumbent's soft payoffs as given in Figure 11.8 and 1 has been added to the incumbent's tough payoffs.

Question

What is the SPNE of the game shown in Figure 11.9?

The SPNE of the game is (tough, stay out, tough). Looking at the four final decision nodes for the incumbent in the third stage, we see that the

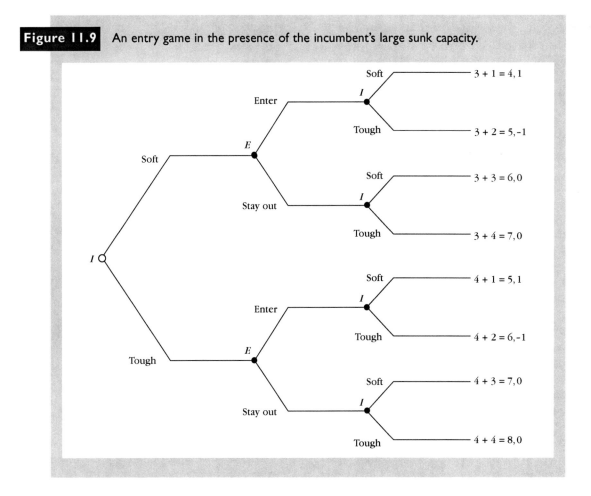

Figure 11.9   An entry game in the presence of the incumbent's large sunk capacity.

incumbent's third-stage payoffs are always greater for tough than for soft moves, and this holds true irrespective of the entrant's previous moves (2 is better than 1, and 4 is better than 3). Thus in the final stage, the incumbent will play tough. At the previous stage where the entrant is facing two decision nodes, the entrant knows that, whatever move it takes, the incumbent will play tough in the third stage. Enter gives the entrant a lower payoff with tough than stay out does, irrespective of the previous move by the incumbent in the first stage (–1 is worse than 0). Therefore the entrant stays out. The best move for the incumbent in the first stage is to play tough (4 is better than 3). The SPNE of the game as a whole is (tough, stay out, tough): the incumbent plays tough in the third stage, so the entrant will stay out, and the incumbent also plays tough in the first stage. The effect of incorporating large sunk capacity and a credible commitment to large-scale output is that the SPNE changes from (soft, enter, soft) to (tough, stay out, tough).

Large sunk capacity provides the incentive, and therefore the commitment, for the incumbent to produce high and hence deter other firms from entering the market or trying to increase market share. The strategy of large sunk capacity – or over-capitalization – works by affecting the structure of payoffs to pre-commit the incumbent to an output which makes entry less profitable for the potential entrant. Knowing this, the potential entrant stays out. Playing tough is now a credible strategy.

The strategic structure of this type of pre-commitment is seen as a paradigm case for a number of different types of strategic commitments by an incumbent that have the common aim of making entry less profitable for a potential entrant. Such commitments work by using large investments in sunk costs to change the payoffs in the post-entry subgame, thus changing the SPNE of the game as a whole. (Sunk costs were introduced in Chapter 9.) Sunk costs include not only sunk capacity but also any fixed and irrecoverable costs such as advertising, R&D and marketing. Sunk capacity itself reduces marginal cost at high outputs by overcapitalizing the production process, as we saw in Figure 11.9. Large sunk costs which include R&D or an exploitation of the advantages of the learning curve may also reduce costs at high outputs. Alternatively, the sunk costs may be directed towards increasing the demand for a particular firm's product. For example, R&D investment may also be seen as a way of improving product quality and hence of increasing demand. High-profile expensive advertising campaigns, such as PepsiCo's Project Blue, are also sunk costs which function as a visible commitment that the firm will defend its market share against rivals. Marketing strategies may also be used to create a base of consumer loyalty. Organizational objectives may be set within the firm which are conducive to acting tough; for example, managers may be instructed to maximize sales as their primary objective.

The game-theoretic analysis in this section explains why the assumption of fixed output in the neoclassical limit pricing model of Section 2 is so important, and what kind of strategic behaviour is needed to sustain it as a credible threat. This analysis also provides a theoretical explanation of the importance of economies of scale from a strategic perspective. This game-theoretic approach has become increasingly influential in industrial economics in recent years, but questions have been raised about its empirical relevance. The following section looks at some attempts to investigate the empirical significance of the game-theory approach to entry deterrence.

 # 4 STRATEGY AND MARKET BEHAVIOUR

Game-theoretic analysis has led to an increased understanding of the strategic implications of interdependence, but a number of economists are sceptical about the insights that such refinements in theory can offer into the messy world of corporate competition. In this section I will briefly explore two different approaches to the question of the empirical significance of game-theoretic analyses of interdependence. The first approach seeks to examine the insights that game theory can contribute to an understanding of market structure, and the other seeks to find out from firms whether they see themselves as following entry-deterring policies.

4.1 Sunk costs and market structure

One implication of the game-theoretic analysis on entry deterrence and pre-commitment is that market structure may be the outcome of firms' competitive strategies. We saw in the previous section that overcapitalization, advertising, R&D and learning-by-doing can be seen as different forms of pre-commitment which can be used strategically to deter entry and so influence the market environment favourably for the incumbent. We have seen this in different ways for silicon chips and the cola market, but research suggests that this is typical of many other markets too, where large-scale advertising and R&D are important (Sutton, 1991; Robinson and Chiang, 1996). Firms respond to their existing market environment, but that environment is the product of past actions by firms, just as the future market environment is the outcome of present strategies. There is, therefore, a two-way relation between market structure and firms' strategies which evolves over time.

In spite of institutional and historical differences across countries, Sutton (1991) has used a game-theoretic framework to search for some relatively stable relationships between market structure and market size. Sutton's analysis hinges on the relation between sunk costs and the extent to which firms can influence consumers' willingness-to-pay for a product. As we have seen, sunk costs include the costs of sunk capacity as well as the costs of other fixed and irrecoverable assets or activities such as advertising, marketing and R&D.

Sutton makes a crucial distinction between *exogenous sunk costs* and *endogenous sunk costs*. Exogenous sunk costs are the setup costs of building a plant of minimum efficient scale and establishing a standard product line, and they are largely given to the firm by the existing technology.

Exogenous sunk costs

Exogenous sunk costs are the sunk costs which are required by existing technology.

Endogenous sunk costs

Endogenous sunk costs are the sunk costs which are incurred to increase consumers' willingness-to-pay.

Endogenous sunk costs are those sunk costs, such as advertising and R&D, which are incurred with a view to enhancing consumers' willingness to pay for the firm's product. Endogenous sunk costs are therefore a choice variable for the firm in raising a product's 'quality', including the product's image, and therefore raising its demand. Such costs are not related to the existing technology in the way that exogenous sunk costs are. We can think of a good's perceived quality as rising with expenditure on advertising and R&D. However, the impact of such expenditure on perceived quality is very much greater for some goods than for others. For differentiated goods, say, computers, cars or cola, the improvement in perceived quality resulting from additional expenditure is sufficiently high to make it worthwhile engaging in such expenditure on a large scale. For homogeneous goods, say, sugar or salt, the improvement in quality from such expenditure is so slight that it is not worth it. The latter goods may be seen as a limiting case where only exogenous sunk costs become relevant.

Sutton uses the distinction between exogenous and endogenous sunk costs to model the relationship between concentration and market size. Sutton's model is shown in Figure 11.10. If the product is relatively homogeneous, then as the scale of the market increases, the number of firms entering the industry increases, causing a decline in the level of concentration, CN. The vertical axis shows the level of concentration, CN, which is measured here by $\frac{1}{n}$ where n is the number of firms in the market. The horizontal axis shows market size. This is the case discussed at the beginning of Section 2.2 and is shown by the downward-sloping line CN_X in Figure 11.10 overleaf.

When the product is differentiated, however, an increase in market size tends to be accompanied by the emergence of a small set of firms with large expenditures on endogenous sunk costs. These firms come to dominate the market while the remaining firms, which spend little, comprise a fringe of minor brands. Such markets therefore have a dual market structure in which a small number of firms with high advertising and R&D expenditures have high market shares, and a fringe of small brands have tiny market shares. In this endogenous sunk cost model, an increase in market size does not lead to a fall in the concentration level. This is indicated by the horizontal line CN_D in Figure 11.10. In these markets, the high-advertising market leaders are often those who were the first, or among the first, to start out, thus showing that historical circumstances often favour the initial firms starting up.

This account of endogenous sunk costs shows how large-scale advertising and R&D make it harder for potential entrants to enter, and for fringe firms to enlarge their market share. This result can be seen as compatible with the game-theoretic model in Section 3.3 where firms chose the level of sunk capacity in order to deter entry. Although Sutton's model is different from the one presented in Section 3.3, it provides an illustration of the way in which the game-theoretic model of sunk capacity has generated a whole class of models that address the various ways in which strategic expenditure on different sunk costs may result in deterring entry.

The cola market may be taken as an illustration of a market where endogenous sunk costs in the form of advertising expenditure are highly important. The cola market is dominated by just two firms and has a dual market structure. In recent years, the development of retailers' own-brands has tried to challenge the supremacy of the high-advertising market leaders since it is thought that consumers associate quality and value for money with the retailers' own-brands, even in the absence of high advertising for the specific product. There is no evidence, however, that the market dominance of Coca-Cola and Pepsi has been dented as their

advertising has kept the fringe brands at bay. Even Virgin Cola, which tried to challenge Coca-Cola and Pepsi as a well-advertised premium brand, has not been successful to date in establishing significant market share.

4.2 Surveys on firms' strategies

Sutton's research uses sophisticated modelling and econometric techniques in order to test the extent to which sunk costs and market structure are associated. A very different approach to finding out just how significant entry-deterring strategies are in practice is that of a questionnaire survey of firms. Smiley (1988) and Singh *et al.* (1997) have pursued this line of inquiry in the USA and the UK respectively. The results that emerge are somewhat mixed and pose problems of interpretation.

In the UK study, three broad industry groupings were investigated – food, electrical engineering and chemicals. Managers in these industries were asked which kinds of strategies they regarded as 'high priority' in deterring the entry of new products. The results are summarized in Table 11.2.

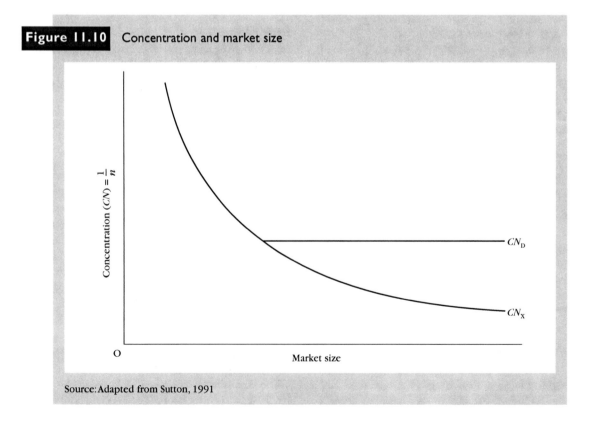

Figure 11.10 Concentration and market size

Source: Adapted from Sutton, 1991

The highest ranked strategic variable in deterring new products is R&D, regarded as high priority by 66 per cent of all respondents, followed by pricing policy at 63 per cent and selling network, a form of sunk capacity, at 62 per cent. Conversely, less than a quarter (23 per cent) regard capacity creation itself as a high priority strategic variable; this result is in accord with Smiley's results. The relatively low priority given to advertising at 33 per cent is commented on in the study. Singh *et al.* contrast their result with the 62 per cent of firms that gave it high priority in Smiley's study. Singh *et al.* point out that there is a greater overall expenditure on advertising in the USA than in the UK, although other parts of their study underline the importance of advertising in the UK for launching new products, as opposed to deterring the entry of products into established markets by other firms.

Interpretation of the importance of sunk costs as a strategic variable in this study is complicated by the fact that firms use a combination of different strategies, so that the significance of any one strategy will partly depend on how it is combined with others. Furthermore, the study shows that the ranking of some of the strategic variables changes considerably when firms are asked about their *own* entry into a market. Capacity creation jumps from seventh in the ranking to second place at 56 per cent when firms are asked about strategic variables relevant to their own entry. Other variables such as pricing and advertising, however, are not much affected by this change of focus. Reflecting on the changes in rankings, Singh *et al.* suggest that 'firms do not see others in the same light as they see themselves' (p.16), a useful reminder in a world of uncertainty and imperfect information that agents are not always symmetrically placed when competing in situations of strategic interdependence.

5   COLLUSION

5.1   Introduction

In the previous section we saw that high advertising by Coca-Cola or PepsiCo makes it harder for new entrants and discourages existing fringe brands from trying to increase market share at the expense of the two dominant firms. Although high-profile advertising by PepsiCo is seen as part of an on-going war with Coca-Cola, it is also the case that each one of them benefits from the other's advertising in keeping the minor brands at bay. In so far as advertising by either one promotes the idea of a 'cola war' between the two brand leaders, it also benefits the other by keeping it too in the public eye as the other protagonist in the war.

As well as being a sign of mutual opposition between Coca-Cola and PepsiCo, the cola war is also therefore a sign of their shared interests. This much was reportedly admitted by John Swanhaus,

Table 11.2 Percentage of manufacturing respondents placing high priority on the use of the strategic variable indicated in order to slow down or dissuade entry of new products

Instrument of rivalry		Industry		
	Food	Electrical engineering	Chemicals	All
Comprehensive patenting	12	25	35	25
R&D	54	69	72	66
Advertising	44	26	29	33
Capacity creation	27	23	20	23
Pricing policy	57	72	61	63
Assured raw materials/intermediate product supply	58	51	56	55
Selling network	61	60	65	62
Agreement with competitors	9	4	7	7

Source: Singh et al., 1997, Table 1, p.7

PepsiCo's senior vice-president of international sales and marketing at the time of the unveiling of Project Blue:

> 'But *Coca-Cola will welcome the publicity. In a private interview Mr Swanhaus admitted that the cola wars are phoney, aimed at keeping both sides in the news. "The cola wars are good for business, they keep up interest in the product," he said.'*
>
> (*The Guardian,* 3 APRIL 1996)

The double function of the cola wars as both contest and collusion illustrates the pervasiveness of shared as well as rival interests in oligopoly markets. This makes collusion difficult to analyse in theory and to detect in practice.

5.2 Failure of collusion

Collusion takes place when firms co-ordinate their output or pricing policies in pursuit of higher profits than could be attained by acting independently. When collusion is modelled using the prisoners' dilemma game, there is a paradox that the collusive outcome is dominated by a non-collusive outcome (Chapter 1 and Chapter 9).

Collusion

Collusion occurs when decision takers co-ordinate their actions in pursuit of common interests.

To see how this happens, consider a 'one-shot' prisoners' dilemma game similar to that in Chapter 1. Each firm's individual interest lies in increasing its market share, but if both firms try to do this, the market is flooded with goods. This will drive down the market price and all firms lose out. Collusion requires firms to recognize this interdependence and each to restrict output, sharing the monopoly profits. For consumers this results in a static loss of welfare similar to that from any monopoly situation, and it is behaviour like this that competition policy is designed to prevent (see *Changing Economies,* Chapter 8). Such a game is illustrated in the payoff matrix or strategic form game in Figure 11.11, which shows two players deciding whether to produce a high or a low output, and their profit payoffs.

An assumption of this game is that the players face a market demand curve which is downward sloping. The (low, low) output combination is the most profitable for the firms taken together, with payoffs (100, 100). The dominant strategy for each firm individually is high output, but if both firms do this they receive the lower payoffs (80, 80). This is a Nash equilibrium because each firm is optimizing given the other firm's strategy, but it is not the optimal outcome for the firms. Here we have, therefore, the classic one-shot prisoners' dilemma result that explains why individual optimization may lead to smaller payoffs than a collusive outcome.

5.3 Sustaining collusion: punishment strategies

Collusion may be made to work, however, if there is a *punishment strategy* that sufficiently reduces the payoffs to firms which default. The non-defaulting firms could increase their output to drive down market price and reduce the profits of defaulting firms.

Figure 11.11   Collusion shown as a prisoner's dilemma game

	B default (high *Q*)	collude (low *Q*)
A default (high *Q*)	80 / 80	20 / 150
collude (low *Q*)	150 / 20	100 / 100

Punishment strategy

A punishment strategy reduces the payoffs to firms that default.

There are different punishment strategies which the firms might operate. One possibility is a *trigger strategy* where a firm colludes until another player defaults, then punishes the defaulting firm, for example by increasing output. There are different versions of a trigger strategy. The punishment could be applied for a given number of periods to give the defaulting firm an incentive to come back into line, or the punishments could be applied indefinitely. What is crucial, however, is that the punishment strategy is both credible and effective as a deterrent. How can these two conditions be met?

Trigger strategy

A trigger strategy is a punishment strategy whereby a player colludes until evidence of another player's default triggers it into administering the punishment.

To be credible, the punishment strategy must be in the interest of the non-defaulting firms, otherwise the defaulter knows that other firms have no incentive to administer the punishment. If there is *explicit collusion*, the terms of the punishment strategy can be agreed upon as part of the collusive agreement, but by itself it does not ensure credibility. If a firm would make lower profits by increasing its own output to punish the defaulting firm, an explicit agreement is unlikely to make it administer such punishment, and the potential defaulter will know that. Thus an explicit agreement does not necessarily make a punishment strategy credible. This suggests that *implicit collusion* may be sufficient for implementing a credible punishment strategy as long as that strategy is in the interest of the punishing firm. What is central is whether collusive behaviour can be maintained by the interests of the individual firms (Shapiro, 1989; Rees, 1993a).

Explicit collusion

Explicit collusion is based on communication and agreement.

Implicit collusion

Implicit collusion takes place without communication and agreement.

Even if the threat of punishment is credible, to be effective as a deterrent the future costs of the punishment for the defaulting firm must be greater than the initial gains from defaulting. This condition explains why collusion breaks down in a one-shot game since there is no future during which the threat of punishment could be realized. Collusion may succeed, however, in a prisoners' dilemma game which is repeated a number of times. As I demonstrate below, a punishment strategy can be effective if the game is repeated indefinitely. On the other hand, if the game is played a known, finite number of times – whether once or many times – a punishment strategy will not work. I will consider this latter case first.

Suppose that the game shown in Figure 11.11 is repeated a finite number of times and this finite number is known to each player. Let's say it is repeated five times. As in Section 3, we use backward induction to work out the solution to the game. I will refer to each repetition of the game as a round, and in each round the players move simultaneously.

Question

Consider the final (fifth) round. What are the dominant strategies in that round for A and B?

In the final round, the dominant strategy for both *A* and *B* is to produce high because there is no longer any fear of punishment in any following round. So even if the punishment threat is credible it will not be effective. So what will happen in the previous round? It has already been established that both firms know both will default in the final round, so there is no incentive not to do the same in the current round. In the penultimate round, too, therefore, both firms produce high. And the round before that? The same reasoning applies here too. As both firms will definitely produce high in the following round, there is no incentive not to do the same in the current round. So in this round too, both firms produce high. The same reasoning proceeds until we have reached the first round where each firm will also produce high. By using backward induction we discover that repeating the prisoners' dilemma game for a known finite number of times does not change anything compared with the one-shot game; there is no real history, just a repetition of what happens in the first round and a failure of the collusive strategy even in the presence of a credible punishment threat. The argument holds no matter how many rounds there are, so long as the number is known.

However, if the game is played indefinitely, a credible threat of punishment can effectively maintain collusion because, in the absence of a known last play, the backward induction argument cannot be used. In indefinitely repeated games, the future is open-ended and so a credible threat of punishment in the future becomes a real threat. In these cases, therefore, the collusive outcome is possible if the future is sufficiently important to the players. If the future is not sufficiently important, firms will discount future punishments so heavily that the punishment is ineffective as a deterrent. Thus, the effectiveness of a punishment strategy partly depends on how firms discount the future; the lower their discount rate, the more likely it is that the punishment strategy will work. (Chapter 9 made a similar argument about the importance of the discount rate to a firm's decision whether to sustain its reputation in a reputation game.)

This can be illustrated by indefinitely repeated play of the game in Figure 11.11. In the first round, B colludes and A has the choice of colluding or defaulting. If A colludes and produces a low output, its payoff is 100, and so is B's. Suppose, however, that firm A defaults and goes for the high output; then it will earn a payoff of 150 and B earns only 20.

Question

What is B likely to do in the next round?

If B does not punish and continues to produce low for the rest of the game, then A will earn 150 per round indefinitely, and B will earn 20 per round indefinitely. If, however, B punishes by producing high indefinitely, A's payoff falls to 80 per round indefinitely and B earns 80 instead of 20. So firm B will go for the punishment strategy, which is a reversion to the Nash equilibrium of the one-shot game. Firm A knows that B will administer the punishment, and so the punishment strategy is credible. Firm B's response here is, therefore, an example of a 'trigger strategy'; B colludes as long as A

does not default, but a default by A triggers B into inflicting punishment.

This punishment strategy is credible, but for A to be deterred from defaulting by it, the present value of the payoffs from defaulting followed by punishment must be less than the present value of the payoffs from colluding. This will depend partly on the structure of payoffs and partly on A's rate of discount. If the rate at which A discounts the future is sufficiently high, then the reduced payoffs in the future following punishment, certain though they may be, will be insufficient to deter A from going for the immediate benefits of defaulting in the current round. The success of any punishment strategy in deterring default depends on the actual values of the alternative payoff streams and the rate of discount for potential defaulters. The technical box illustrates this point using the Figure 11.11 payoffs for a game that is repeated infinitely.

Punishment strategies and discounting future payoffs

A and B are playing an infinitely repeated version of the game outlined in Figure 11.11. A knows that B is following a credible trigger strategy whereby B punishes indefinitely once A defaults. Firm A knows, therefore, that if it colludes throughout all rounds of the infinite game, its payoff is 100 in each round. So in the first, current round ($t = 0$) that payoff is worth 100. If A has a discount rate of r, then the payoff is worth $\frac{100}{(1+r)}$ in the second round ($t = 1$), $\frac{100}{(1+r)^2}$ in the third round ($t = 2$), and so on.

Chapter 9, Section 3.2 gave the formula for the discounted present value of an infinite stream of such fixed payoffs from $t = 1$. If R is the fixed payoff per round, and r the rate of discount, the present value (PV) is:

$$PV = \frac{R}{(1+r)} + \frac{R}{(1+r)^2} + \ldots = \frac{R}{r}$$

To this we have to add the payoff R for $t = 0$.

So the present value to A of an indefinite stream of payoffs of 100 from colluding (PV_{Ac}) is:

$$PV_{Ac} = 100 + \frac{100}{(1+r)} + \frac{100}{(1+r)^2} + \ldots = 100 + \frac{100}{r}$$

If firm A defaults and goes for the high output in the first round, it will earn a payoff of 150 in $t = 0$. If firm B continues to produce a low output, then firm A will continue to earn 150 in each subsequent round and so its discounted stream of payoffs from defaulting (PV_{Ad}) would be:

$$PV_{Ad} = 150 + \frac{150}{(1+r)} + \frac{150}{(1+r)^2} + \ldots = 150 + \frac{150}{r}$$

Defaulting thus allows A to increase payoffs but only on the condition that B does not implement the punishment strategy.

If B does not punish A, however, B's payoff stream from continuing to collude (PV_{Bc}) is 20 in every round:

$$PV_{Bc} = 20 + \frac{20}{(1+r)} + \frac{20}{(1+r)^2} + \ldots = 20 + \frac{20}{r}$$

If B punishes A and produces high once A's default is known in $t = 1$, B's payoffs from punishing (PV_{Bp}) are 20 in the first round ($t = 0$) and 80 thereafter:

$$PV_{Bp} = 20 + \frac{80}{(1+r)} + \frac{80}{(1+r)^2} + \ldots = 20 + \frac{80}{r}$$

B clearly does better by implementing the punishment strategy since:

$$\left(20 + \frac{80}{r}\right) > \left(20 + \frac{20}{r}\right)$$

whatever B's (positive) rate of discount. A therefore knows that B is better off punishing than not punishing; that is, B's punishment strategy is credible.

But will A be deterred? To find this out we need to calculate A's payoffs from defaulting, given that the punishment will be delivered, and then compare this with the collusive payoffs to find out which would be greater. If A defaults in the first round ($t = 0$) and is punished thereafter indefinitely, A receives 150 in the first round and 80 thereafter, so A's payoffs from defaulting and then being punished ($PV_{Ad,p}$) are:

$$PV_{Ad,p} = 150 + \frac{80}{(1+r)} + \frac{80}{(1+r)^2} + \ldots = 150 + \frac{80}{r}$$

So, will A have an incentive to default and then be punished, or will A be better off colluding? The

answer is that A will default only if $PV_{Ad,p} > PV_{Ac}$. This requires that:

$$150 + \frac{80}{r} > 100 + \frac{100}{r}$$

Taking all the expressions containing r to the right-hand-side, we get:

$$150 - 100 > \frac{100}{r} - \frac{80}{r}$$

which implies:

$$50 > \frac{20}{r}$$
$$r > \frac{20}{50}$$
$$r > 0.4$$

Thus A will default only if its discount rate is greater than 0.4, or 40 per cent, since this will ensure that the net present value of the stream of payoffs from defaulting and being punished is greater than from colluding. This is a high discount rate so it is unlikely that A would default. In this case, the trigger strategy would successfully deter A from defaulting.

Exercise 11.2

In an infinitely repeated version of the Figure 11.11 game, suppose that firm A's rate of discount is 0.5 (that is 50 per cent). What is the net present value of its payoffs if it (a) colludes indefinitely, and (b) defaults indefinitely? Explain which strategy A will choose.

5.4   Sustaining collusion: information and business practices

The analysis so far assumes complete information. This is a strong assumption. For collusion to work, firms need to know that other firms share their own beliefs about market demand, that is, about the quantities that can be sold at various prices on the market. They also need information about rivals' output and prices so that they know if a firm has defaulted. Explicit collusion provides a means of sharing this information among firms and so may make the collusion more viable. The distinction between explicit and implicit collusion may, therefore, be significant in so far as explicit collusion provides a means of sharing information rather than of enforcing the agreement on recalcitrant members. For implicit collusion to be successful there must be some other means for an exchange of information.

Consider the detection of defaults. If players have perfect information, then all players know their rivals' previous moves. This is the assumption that has been made so far, and it implies that any default is known to the other players. If a firm increases its output, for example, the other players would know. In an oligopoly market, however, in contrast to a game of chess, there is no presumption that firms know their rivals' moves. If a firm increases its output, we would expect that the price would fall in the presence of a downward-sloping market demand curve. If rival firms observed a fall in the price of the good they might infer that a rival had increased output, but they could not *know* this because the fall in the price might have been caused by other factors. A shift in the market demand curve would cause a change in the price independently of any changes in output. Demand might shift as a result of changes in consumer preferences or the prices of related goods. In addition, market demand for a good might fall as a result of a macroeconomic downswing. Or a period of inflation might cause changes in the price of the good unrelated to changes in its own demand. For firms to be able to infer output changes by their rivals from changes in the product price alone, they would need to be able to differentiate between these various factors.

Anything that gives firms information about rivals' price or output will help them to know whether other firms are defecting. Any practices which help to promote the dissemination of information among potentially collusive firms will help to promote collusive practices. In the case of explicit agreements, firms would exchange this information as part of the process of monitoring the agreement. In the absence of explicit agreements, this information may well be generated by the normal practices of trade and professional associations in forecasting demand, publishing price/fee lists, trade costings, quality standards or haulage rates and, in general, providing a forum for information exchange. Other trade practices also provide information, for example, shared computerized booking services or costing services. Promises to customers to 'meet competition' by matching lower prices of rivals provides an incentive to customers to provide information on rivals' prices when they are undercutting (*Changing Economies,* Chapter 5). There is an irony here. These agreements are seen as evidence of strong competition, yet they also help to facilitate collusion. This is sometimes referred to as the 'topsy-turvy' principle of collusion where the results of game-theoretic analysis give counter-intuitive interpretations on whether activities promote competition or collusion (Shapiro, 1989, p.357).

The frequency with which these business practices occur raises questions about the extent of implicit collusion, especially given the scope for informal business gatherings which blur the line between explicit and implicit collusion. One sign that there may be implicit collusion is price leadership or price parallelism. If all firms face the same costs, then it would be expected that, in a competitive market, prices and price changes would be fairly uniform across firms, but many instances of price parallelism suggest collusive practices to avoid price competition, especially where costs differ between firms.

An example is provided by an inquiry by the UK Monopolies and Merger Commission (MMC) into the UK white salt duopoly. It was found that over a ten-year period, price changes by the two firms, British Salt and ICI Weston Point, were virtually identical, in spite of cost differences between the two firms. The firms regularly informed each other of proposed price changes, defending this practice on the grounds that they sold small quantities to each other. It has been argued by Rees (1993b) that the firms had a clear understanding of the logic of tacit (implicit) collusion on prices and of the role of retaliation in maintaining price discipline, even though they denied collusion. British Salt stated that: 'if it raised prices by a lesser amount than [Weston Point], and [Weston Point] failed to lower its own price to the same level, there would be an immediate transfer of business to itself ... This would lead to a long-term retaliation by [Weston Point] who would seek to take customers from British Salt' (quoted by Rees 1993b, p.842). Rees also argues that the available data on prices, costs and profits supports an interpretation of tacit collusion that is consistent with retaliation as a punishment strategy. Rees agrees with the MMC's conclusion that price competition had been restrained (although the MMC refrained from using the word 'collusion').

Exercise 11.3

The following incident occurred recently in a local stationers shop in the high street in my neighbourhood.

A customer was purchasing some fax facilities and complained that the price was well above the marginal cost of sending and receiving faxes. The shop assistant replied in defence that the shop was not overcharging because that was the going rate in the neighbourhood since all the fax shops charged that rate. The customer accused the shops of acting collusively. It would be better business too, the customer argued, for the stationery shop to undercut the other fax shops in the street and so bring more business in for itself.

What are your comments on this incident?

5.5   Conclusion

Although the one-shot prisoners' dilemma game suggests that collusion is unlikely in practice, this finding does not accord with research in industrial economics which suggests that collusion is not uncommon. A game-theoretic answer to this problem is to model collusion as an indefinitely repeated game where credible and effective punishment strategies can be implemented to enforce the collusive outcome. The crucial issue from the point of view of the competition authorities, seeking to protect the interests of consumers, appears to be not whether an explicit agreement operates, but whether pricing and output outcomes are inefficient in that prices are systematically above costs. The importance of information in supporting collusive outcomes, however, underlines the importance of institutions and mechanisms which may be fostering forms of implicit collusion.

6   TRUST

Section 5 examined co-ordination between firms in pursuit of perceived common interests. The analysis assumed throughout that the firms' common interests took the form of a coincidence of well-specified individual interests in the form of known individual payoffs. There are other important forms

of inter-firm collaboration, however, where the payoffs are not known in any detail in advance, and where the purpose of collaboration is to explore the scope for, and to achieve, future joint payoffs to be shared among the collaborators.

6.1   Relational contracting

Collaboration of the type where joint payoffs are poorly specified in advance, requires a framework of incomplete and implicit contracts within which the parties adapt their behaviour as the project progresses and the environment changes. Contracting of this kind occurs particularly where, as John Kay puts it, 'the returns to the parties to the contract are more sensitive to the size of the cake than to its division' (Kay, 1993, p.57). Such working relationships are often called *relational contracting*, since the need to build and sustain the relationship in order to achieve the joint payoff will influence day-to-day behaviour. Formal (explicit) contracts that frame such relationships are generally brief, and leave a great deal to be developed through custom and practice.

Relational contracts

Relational contracts are long term, incomplete, largely implicit contracts within which behaviour is influenced by the value to the contracting partners of maintaining the relationship.

Classic examples of relational contracts are marriage contracts, and also employment contracts (see Chapter 14). In a corporate context, relational contracting tends to occur where the pursuit of joint payoffs requires flexibility, learning and searching out the best ways of organizing the collaboration. One form of inter-firm relational contracting occurs within buyer/supplier relationships. The implicit understandings framing the Japanese supplier relations described in Chapter 9, Section 4.1, involving collaborative cost reduction and innovation, are an example of such relational contracting.

Another form of inter-firm relational contracting occurs in joint ventures, when firms form an alliance to pursue a specific set of objectives. R&D joint ventures have become especially important in recent years. As the example of the semiconductor industry in Section 2 noted, the budgets that are now necessary for viable R&D are becoming larger, and so in some industries it has become impractical for any one firm to bear R&D costs alone. Furthermore, to turn the results of research into competitive market products, firms may need access to complementary technologies and assets of other firms, such as production, marketing, sales and service facilities. Increasing market size, especially in consumer durables, as a result of falling trade barriers and rising incomes in Pacific Asia, have increased the returns from combining market knowledge between firms (Buckley and Casson, 1996; Jorde and Teece, 1990).

The influence in the west of Japanese business practices and the growth of R&D joint ventures have stimulated debate about the nature of relational contracting and the kinds of situations in which it seems to flourish. In this final section I will first consider a game-theoretic analysis of a situation where the players have an interest in maintaining the relationship, and then I will examine a debate about the kind of 'trust' that is necessary for relational contracting to be successful.

6.2 The 'dating game'

Like marriage, corporate relational contracting involves a mixture of conflicting and common interests, and a commitment to resolving disputes even where it involves concessions. (Indeed, collaborating firms are sometimes said to be 'getting into bed with each other', a process that signals the beginning, not the end, of organizational problems!) The kind of dispute involved can be represented by a game known as the 'dating game' or – anachronistically perhaps – as 'the battle of the sexes'. The game is set up in terms of two players who do not agree how to spend an evening but who would each prefer to spend it in the company of the other player rather than separately. Let's say that one player would prefer to go to the theatre and the other would prefer to watch TV, but that they would both prefer to spend the evening together than apart. The payoffs are shown in Figure 11.12.

Pat would prefer to go to the theatre than stay at home and watch TV, but prefers to watch TV with Chris rather than go to the theatre alone. Chris prefers watching TV to going to the theatre, but prefers the theatre with Pat to lonely TV at home. Each player thus values the relationship more highly than getting their own way on the evening's activity, but each would prefer to have both.

Question

Which quadrants of Figure 11.12 represent Nash equilibria?

There are two Nash equilibria where the players spend the evening together: (theatre, theatre) and (TV, TV). If Pat chooses the theatre, then Chris' optimizing strategy is also the theatre (2, 1), and if Chris chooses the theatre, Pat's optimizing strategy is the theatre too. If Chris chooses TV, then Pat's optimizing strategy is also TV (1, 2), and vice versa. Thus, unlike the prisoners' dilemma game, there is no incentive to cheat; each player attaches a value to spending the evening together and the individual payoffs reflect this. The two pairs of strategies where the players spend the evening alone have lower payoffs. The pair (theatre, TV) where the players pursue their own

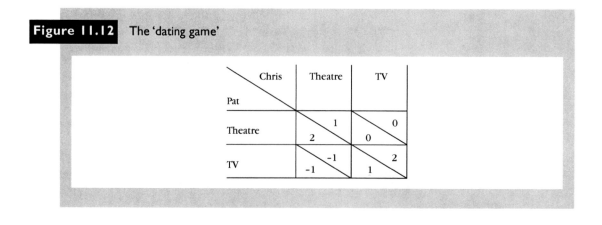

Figure 11.12 The 'dating game'

preferred activity without the other, gives zero payoffs, and the worst outcome is where both players select their least-preferred activity in an act of self-denial in the hope of pleasing the other (–1, –1).

The problem for the players, however, is that there is no way of choosing between the two Nash equilibria. The total payoffs are the same for the two Nash equilibria (2 + 1), but they are distributed differently between the two players. Thus each of the players would prefer a different Nash equilibrium, even though they would both prefer either of them to neither of them. This indeterminacy is a feature of the dating game.

The indeterminacy inherent in the dating game is also a feature of relational contracting (Kay, 1993). For example, joint ventures between firms often generate problems of decision making. It may be the siting of new joint research laboratories, the choice of a joint logo, the technical standards for new products, or even just the day-to-day organization of the joint activities. Neither firm wants to jettison the relationship with the other in order to achieve an immediate individual interest, but each would prefer to have it both ways. A solution may be arrived at by fiat if one player announces a move in advance, knowing that the other one will then follow. Resolution by fiat is sometimes provided by seniority within a corporation, or by external constraints (for example planning permission for a new laboratory), or by reference to independent experts (for example to an artistic designer for a joint logo). But long-term relational contracting between two firms is likely to require perceived give-and-take as such decisions arise, if the working relationship is to last. If Pat is stuck at home watching endless TV, the relationship may eventually appear not worth it!

6.3 Trust and relational contracting

Relational contracting can still founder on behaviour that Oliver Williamson would characterize as 'opportunistic' (see Chapter 8, Section 4.1) – putting immediate individual interests above common interests in building the relationship – though the incentives for opportunism are clearly less strong in the dating game than in prisoners' dilemma situations. Furthermore, unlike the simple dating game, relational contracting arises where payoffs are uncertain and depend upon joint effort.

The need for give-and-take, together with the problems of imperfect information, imply that partners need to have *trust* in each other to behave in the joint interest, even in situations where behaviour may be hard to monitor. Trust can be defined in terms of the degree of belief that one agent has in the beneficial – or at least not detrimental – behaviour of another agent. Trust is important in relational contracting because each firm risks loss from the opportunistic actions of partners. The growing importance of relational contracting has led to questions among economists about the nature and sources of the 'trust' that firms might have in each other. As with many such institutional problems, there are (at least) two economic approaches to an answer.

Trust

One agent, A, has trust in another, B, if A strongly believes that B will behave beneficially – or at least not detrimentally – towards A.

Rational choice and new institutionalist models of the firm suggest that trust can only be based on a recognition that firms are motivated solely by their own individual interests. In game-theoretic terms, trust is a preferred strategy only when it can be sustained as a subgame perfect Nash equilibrium. For example, it might be said of colluding firms that they 'trust' each other to restrict output in the sure knowledge that a credible punishment strategy would be triggered in the event of a default (see Section 5). That is, firms will adhere to the colluding rate of output only when this promotes their individual interest in maximizing the net present value of their own payoffs. Similarly, in a reputation game, firms may decide to provide high quality – not to cheat the consumer in the short run – because of the long-run payoff to sustaining the firm's reputation (Chapter 9, Section 3.2). According to this view, trust between firms is irreducibly self-interested: it is *calculative trust* (Williamson, 1993).

Calculative trust

A has calculative trust in B if A trusts B to behave beneficially towards A so long as it is in B's interest to do so.

Other economists have questioned the notion that firms operate on purely instrumental, calculative rationality. Drawing on the broader tradition of institutional analysis (which Chapter 8 calls 'old' institutionalism) they argue that firms, like people, are enmeshed in institutional contexts which affect norms and expectations. Such institutional norms and expectations come to define what can be regarded as acceptable practice within a given context, and are often summed up by the notion of corporate culture. This approach suggests a concept such as *institutional trust* which reflects the ways in which corporate culture influences relations between firms. Although firms are recognized to be fundamentally self-interested in pursuing their own objectives, it is acknowledged that institutional norms may affect those objectives in practice. In addition, in an uncertain world, it is recognized that expectations about appropriate behaviour emerge within specific institutional frameworks.

> ### Institutional trust
>
> A has institutional trust in B if A trusts B to behave beneficially towards A according to shared norms of appropriate behaviour.

Analyses of institutional trust have explored the differences between corporate cultures, especially between Japan and the West. In a study of Japanese firms, Sako (1992) finds a higher incidence of relational contracting in Japan. She emphasizes the importance in the Japanese corporate sector of personal relations, appeals to the moral responsibilities of stronger partners, and informal resolution of disputes. Other research has explored differences within Europe. Arrighetti *et al.* (1997) examine what they call the 'contractual environment': the combination of legal, social and ethical norms which interact in guiding business behaviour. For example, the importance of the legal concept of 'good faith' in German and Italian contract law doctrine places greater stress on the value of co-operation than is to be found in English law which rejects the notion of a general duty of good faith in commercial contracts. Arrighetti *et al.* argue that in all three countries 'institutional' trust is important in promoting stability and reducing uncertainty in long-term relationships, though it takes varied forms.

6.4 International joint ventures, relational contracting and trust

The above discussion of trust helps us to address some questions of institutional design for international joint ventures (IJVs). In a discussion of the advantages of IJVs, Buckley and Casson (1996) concentrate on the role of uncertainty, including firms' uncertainty about their own technological competence. A joint venture does not specify in advance all the expertise each partner will contribute, but the partners agree to use their best endeavours to achieve the joint objective of a new product or solution to a technical problem. The more uncertain the partners are about their future competencies, the greater the risk of specifying contributions in advance; the joint venture allows flexibility in the face of uncertainty, especially in a period of accelerated technological change. Research co-operation is thus a growing area of relational contracting, within which all the rights and obligations cannot be specified in advance. The generation of trust between the partners will, therefore, be essential, since the willingness to share knowledge is at the core of an R&D joint venture.

Section 6.3 suggests that there are two ways of generating trust in relational contracting, and these may be mutually reinforcing. One is the game-theoretic approach of setting up the joint venture in such a way as to reduce the payoffs to opportunism and increase the payoffs to commitment; this would help to promote calculative trust. Commitment and calculative trust may be promoted by buying shares in each other's firm since this will affect the payoffs: hurting the other will also damage the defaulting firm. Alternatively, sunk capacity investments by both firms in a joint venture can change the payoffs by creating shared interests in a return on the joint investment. And firms' public commitments to the joint venture, by creating a reputational cost to failure, can also enhance each firm's perceived payoff from commitment.

The other method of overcoming opportunism is to create institutional trust between the partners. The discussion of the sources of institutional trust suggests that it is rooted in shared norms and values. As a result, 'cultural distance', as Buckley and Casson note, can be a problem for international joint ventures, as different social norms and business ethics are brought together. Indeed, in severe cases of cultural conflict, a merger may work better, since it gives one party the power to make decisions based on hierarchy. But joint ventures may generate institutional trust over time, as the partners come to understand each other better, and as experience of openness and commitment is mutually reinforcing. Empirically, it is hard to disentangle the role of individual payoffs – which are in any case uncertain – from the operation of cultural assumptions. For example, cross-investments in equity not only change payoffs, but may also lead to closer ties and greater understanding. And the existence of a formal legal framework may reinforce social norms about not breaking contract, and so reduce the likelihood of recourse to legal redress.

R&D joint ventures thus face a complex mixture of conflicting and shared interests. The discussion implies that we would expect to find effective relational contracting in areas where there is a high potential joint payoff that is uncertain and dependent on joint effort. International R&D joint ventures seem to fit this model but we would also expect to find it in contexts where a strong shared culture supports collaboration.

 ## 7 CONCLUSION

In this chapter we have taken a strategic view of competition. We have found that there is no one single model that can be used to encompass the variety of different kinds of strategic competition, or the different combinations of competition, collusion and co-operation that are found in the business world. Many industrial economists have turned from the neoclassical approach to a game-theoretic approach which attempts to model interdependent maximization by corporate players. In addition, issues of corporate culture and norms may also be relevant in some situations, especially where there is relational contracting.

This chapter has also examined aspects of the relation between market structure and firms' behaviour. Analysis of strategic competition suggests ways in which market structure may sometimes emerge as a result of strategic behaviour by firms. The following chapter also explores some determinants of market structure, but it uses empirical data to test a particular model of the relation between market structure and firms' behaviour.

 ## FURTHER READING

The following references have all been helpful in writing this chapter:

John Kay's *Foundations of Corporate Success* (1993) has a very readable discussion of relational contracting written for a general audience.

John Vickers' article 'Strategic competition among the few' in the *Oxford Review of Economic Policy*, 1985, though now quite old, is accessible and still a good survey.

If you would like to learn more about game theory, a good introduction is Hargreaves-Heap and Varoufakis' *Game Theory: A Critical Introduction* (1995).

 ## ANSWERS TO EXERCISES

Exercise 11.1

Figure 11.13 overleaf shows the limit price in a situation where the potential entrant's minimum unit cost, C_N, is lower than the incumbent's, C_I. As in Figure 11.6, the incumbent's limit output is such that the potential entrant's $LRAC_N$ does not lie below the demand curve at any point. This is found in Figure 11.13 by sliding the vertical axis for $LRAC_N$ to the right until $LRAC_N$ just touches the demand curve. This vertical axis now gives the incumbent's limit output, Q_L. This output is sold at the limit price, P_L, which is above C_I, so the incumbent earns supernormal profits of $P_L XYC_I$. A crucial assumption for this result is that the incumbent maintains output at the limit output Q_L in the event of entry, and that the potential entrant knows this.

Exercise 11.2

a) If firm A's rate of discount is 0.5 then the present value of its payoffs if it colludes indefinitely is:

$$PV_{Ac} = 100 + \frac{100}{(1+0.5)} + \frac{100}{(1+0.5)^2} + \dots$$

$$= 100 + \frac{100}{0.5} = 300$$

b) At the same rate of discount, the present value of A's payoffs if it defaults indefinitely is:

$$PV_{Ad} = 150 + \frac{80}{0.5} = 310$$

A will, therefore, choose to default, assuming it knows that B is following a trigger punishment strategy.

Exercise 11.3

The consumer is clearly making a good point in terms of consumer welfare. The going price for sending a fax on local high streets is well above marginal cost, and appears to be sustained by posting prices and exchanging information among local shopkeepers. The situation seems to be one of implicit collusion at least, perhaps having elements of explicit collusion.

However the proposed solution is not likely to be implemented. If the shopkeeper cuts prices and gains more business, in the gossipy network of the high street other shopkeepers will quickly hear of it, and reduce their prices too. The shops will end up in a (high, high) output equilibrium. This will only benefit them collectively if the local market demand curve is very elastic: not a very likely situation in a context where private fax machine ownership is rising, particularly among those who use faxes a lot. The shopkeeper may well know all this, and so will decide to stick to the going rate.

Figure 11.13 Limit pricing with a lower cost entrant

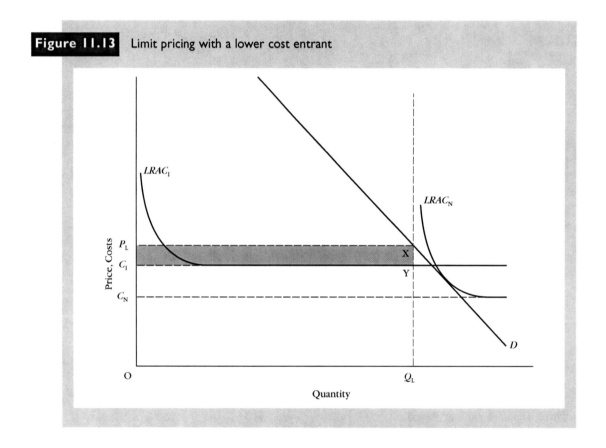

LABOUR

THE FIRM AND THE LABOUR MARKET

John Shorey

CONCEPTS AND TECHNIQUES

Marginal revenue product of labour
Derived demand for labour
Substitution and scale effects
Market demand for labour
Own-wage elasticity of labour
  demand

The UV curve
Dynamic equilibrium
Labour hoarding
Duration-dependent unemployment
Insiders and wage determination
Wage differentials

LINKS

- This chapter applies the neoclassical techniques introduced in Chapter 10 to the firm and the labour market. Of particular importance is the derivation of the labour demand curve using isoquants and isocost lines.

- Note that the derivation of the labour demand curve incorporates the core assumptions of neoclassical theory together with the not-so-core assumption of perfect competition (Chapter 1).

- Later in the chapter the core neoclassical assumption of equilibrium, which is usually used in static terms (Chapter 8), is adapted for the purpose of modelling changing levels of labour demand and supply. The notion of dynamic equilibrium is introduced for this purpose.

1 INTRODUCTION

In modern economies, firms need workers, and households need paid employment. Since we observe a process of exchange taking place based on prices (that is, wages), economists use market models to analyse the demand for and supply of labour. Furthermore, many economic agents are price takers in labour markets, so the competitive market model is widely used. Modelling the labour market as a competitive market suggests that market adjustment, through wage changes and labour mobility, should ensure that demand and supply are broadly in line. Firms will provide the number of jobs at the current wage that matches the amount of labour households want to provide. For the most part, unemployment (the number of workers without jobs willing to work at the current wage) should be small, involving only those in transition between jobs, areas and/or skills. Given adjustment lags, strong cyclical contractions in aggregate demand will to some extent spill over into labour markets, but the impact on unemployment should be tempered and temporary, according to this model, as the market adjusts through price (wage) changes to bring the demand for and supply of labour into line.

However, Figure 12.1 suggests that the behaviour of firms and the workings of the labour market are rather more complex than this model allows.

Figure 12.1 indicates that, until the mid 1960s, firms' employment did indeed grow fairly steadily and in line with the size of the labour force. As a result, the level of unemployment was low and constant. However, severe and prolonged cyclical shocks in the product market, particularly the oil shocks of the mid 1970s and early 1980s, transmitted very strongly into the labour market. The employment line on Figure 12.1 shows the changes in firms' labour requirements and the increased levels of unemployment. In 1981, a trough year of the economic cycle as defined by real GDP, one in ten workers was unemployed. Through the subsequent economic 'upturn', firms continued to restrict their labour demand, so unemployment continued to rise for another two years. And even when unemployment fell, it fell slowly and had reached only just under 7 per cent before the next economic downturn began in 1991.

Unemployment is a good indicator of the effectiveness of the labour market as a mechanism for allocating resources. It would therefore seem that the labour market's sensitivity to economic shocks is very considerable; that adjustment mechanisms are imperfect; and that labour market processes can

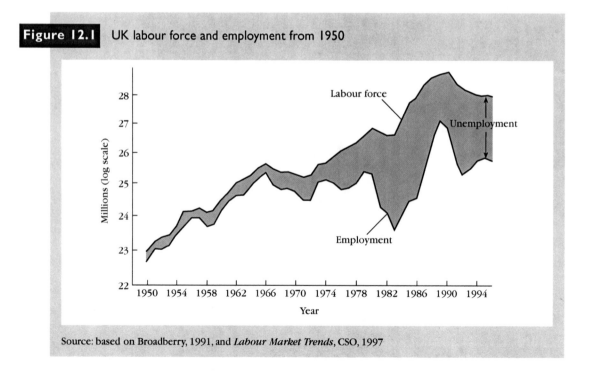

Figure 12.1 UK labour force and employment from 1950

Source: based on Broadberry, 1991, and *Labour Market Trends*, CSO, 1997 generate considerable imbalances between the number of jobs on offer and the number of active workers.

The failings of the labour market prompted a surge in economic theory and empirical work attempting to explain observed behaviour, and renewed debate about policies to improve the functioning of the labour market. The reassessment has covered the whole field of labour economics: wage determination, the activities of unions, internal labour markets within the firm, the employment relationship, segmentation, the search behaviour of workers, and the role of government.

Policies proposed in the UK to stabilize labour demand in the face of shocks have included employment subsidies, expanding government infrastructure investments, encouraging inward foreign investment and stimulating the growth of small firms. Policies to improve labour market adjustment included many designed to increase labour market flexibility: restricting trade union activities; encouraging 'the right to manage', with greater powers for firms to hire and fire, to reorganize production processes and to substitute capital for labour; and deregulating the housing market to facilitate mobility. Policies to reduce imbalances between labour demand and supply included reducing state transfers, removing minimum wages, encouraging local wage bargaining and encouraging training.

This chapter examines certain aspects of these theoretical and policy debates. The starting-point is firms' labour demand. In Section 2, I set out a very basic model, developed from the neoclassical approach to firms introduced in Chapter 10. The model identifies one central cause of the sensitivity of firms' employment to demand shocks, namely the rigidity of wages. Section 3 combines the labour demand model with an equally basic model of labour supply, drawing on the New Household Economics (see Chapter 5), to model the operation of a single labour market. I use this model in Sections 4 and 5 to identify a number of explanations of employment variability, inadequate labour market adjustment, and persistent market imbalances. These include adjustment costs, the effects of long-term unemployment, insider behaviour, and structural change.

Is so much model building necessary? I believe it is, because it provides the basis for designing effective policy. For example, given our concern for the welfare of those out of work, it is important to try to estimate just how employment, and unemployment, would respond to the introduction of an employment subsidy. Modelling gives us an analytical framework through which to derive, interpret and apply empirical estimates, such as estimates of the wage elasticity of the demand for labour.

The neoclassical model used in this chapter is a powerful analytical tool, but it involves considerable abstraction and a very restricted focus. Although I introduce some additional variables and constraints which bear upon employment decisions, such modelling still involves considerable simplification. I would argue that such abstraction is necessary if we are to gain insight into what is after all very complex social behaviour.

THE NEOCLASSICAL APPROACH TO LABOUR DEMAND

The purpose of this section is to develop a model of the firms' employment decision. The neoclassical theory of labour demand proceeds by examining the way in which firms respond to changes in the wage rate. I shall first consider the labour demand of individual firms, before turning to the response of labour demand to wage changes in particular labour markets.

2.1   *Labour demand and the individual firm*

You saw in Chapter 10 of this book that the neoclassical theory of the firm distinguishes between short- and long-run adjustment processes. In the long run the firm can vary the quantities of all factors of production. In the short run, however, at least one factor of production cannot be varied. In the exposition that follows there are two factors of production. I will first consider labour demand in the short run where inputs of capital are held constant, before turning to the long run in which both capital and labour services are variable.

The short run

The isoquant diagram, introduced in Chapter 10, is designed to model long-run substitution between capital and labour. It can, however, also be used to analyse short-run adjustment and therefore to derive the short-run labour demand curve of the firm.

Figure 12.2 Deriving the marginal revenue product of labour (MRP_L) curve

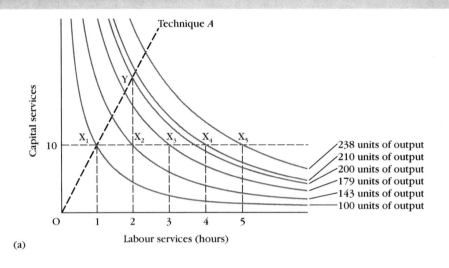

(a)

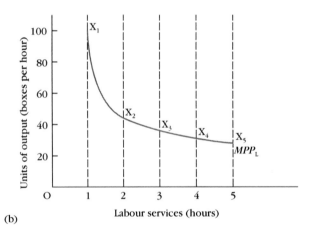

(b)

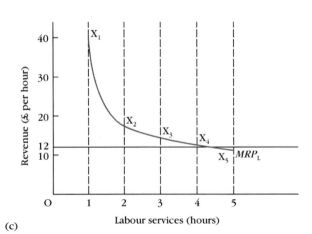

(c)

Figure 12.2(a) shows the isoquant map of a firm that employs capital and labour to make packaging (boxes). This firm employs units of labour services that are all of the same quality – labour is homogenous. The production technology of the firm displays constant returns to scale. So at point X_1 the firm employs one unit of labour services (one hour) and 10 units of capital services to produce 100 boxes. If the quantity of capital and labour services were doubled to take the firm to point Y, this doubles output to 200 boxes. Technique *A* is just one among an infinite number of possible techniques on this isoquant map, each displaying constant returns to scale.

Suppose that in the short run the firm has a fixed stock of capital supplying only 10 units of capital services per hour, but that the firm can vary its inputs of labour services. The firm can therefore increase output by moving rightwards along the horizontal dashed line on Figure 12.2(a). The first unit of labour services, used with the 10 units of capital services, produces 100 boxes at point X_1; an additional unit (hour) of labour produces an additional 43 boxes, or a total of 143 at point X_2. A third labour unit produces an additional 36 boxes, or 179 in total at point X_3. The fourth unit produces 31 extra boxes, or 210 in total at X_4, and the fifth 28, or 238 in total at X_5. The marginal physical product of labour, that is the amount of output produced by each extra unit of labour services diminishes as the firm moves along the horizontal dashed line on Figure 12.2(a) and increasing amounts of labour are employed with the same level of capital input.

Question

Why is there a decrease in marginal product as each additional unit of labour is employed?

There are good reasons why we might expect diminishing marginal returns to a factor of production. As a firm uses more and more labour with a given machine, diminishing marginal benefits in terms of output seem certain to set in eventually. As Figure 12.2(a) shows, a convex technology and constant returns to scale implies diminishing returns to each factor of production (see also Chapter 10, Section 2). If returns to scale are decreasing, this will reinforce diminishing returns to each factor of production, and diminishing returns to a factor can also occur with increasing returns to scale.

Diminishing marginal returns to labour implies that a firm has a downward sloping marginal physical product of labour (MPP_L) curve. This is shown on Figure 12.2(b), which is derived from 12.2(a). Point X_1 on Figure 12.2(b) indicates the 100 boxes produced by the first unit of labour services, and the MPP_L curve shows the extra boxes produced by each successive unit of labour. The MPP_L curve slopes downward because each additional unit of labour produces a smaller addition to output.

To translate the MPP_L curve into a firm's short-run labour demand curve, we need to assume that the firm is a price taker in a perfectly competitive product market. Suppose that the price is £0.40 per box. Figure 12.2(c) then shows the revenue the firm receives for each additional unit of labour employed. This is derived from the MPP_L curve on Figure 12.2(b) by multiplying the marginal physical product of each successive labour unit by £0.40. The first unit of labour earns £40 of revenue for the firm, at point X_1. The second unit of labour earns for the firm an additional £17.20 per hour at X_2, the third unit £14.40 at X_3 and so on. On Figure 12.2(c), the downward sloping marginal revenue product of labour (MRP_L) curve traces these additions to revenue from each successive unit of labour employed.

Finally, we assume that the firm in Figure 12.2 is a price taker in the market for factors of production. Suppose the wage rate is £12 per hour.

Question

How many units of labour services will the firm in Figure 12.2 employ at a wage rate of £12 per hour?

To maximize profits, the firm will employ labour up to but not beyond the point where MRP_L is equal to the wage rate (see *Changing Economies,* Chapter 21, Section 2.1). The firm will therefore employ four units of labour services. This can be seen from Figure 12.2(c), where the horizontal line shows the going wage of £12 per hour. The fourth unit of labour earns £12.40 in marginal revenue. The marginal revenue from the fifth unit is only £11.20, so the MRP_L is less than the wage rate. Hence the firm would reduce its profit by employing the fifth unit of labour. The firm would also reduce its profits if it employed fewer than four units of labour, since the MRP_L of an additional unit would then be greater than the wage rate.

The MRP_L curve is therefore the short-run demand for labour curve of a competitive firm. It shows the amount of labour the firm will demand at each wage rate. As the wage rate falls the demand for labour increases. The demand for labour is a *derived demand*, since a firm's demand for factors of production derives from the demand in the market place for the commodities that the factors produce.

<hr>

Derived demand

The demand for a good or service is a derived demand when it depends upon the demand for another good or service.

<hr>

The long run

Consider a small firm operating in perfectly competitive product and factor markets. Such a firm will face constant or decreasing returns to scale at all levels of output along its supply curve (see Chapter 10, Section 3.2), hence it will experience diminishing marginal returns to labour, and a downward sloping MRP_L curve. Figure 12.3 shows the firm's isoquant map, and in order to examine the firm's labour demand curve in the long run, we now allow the firm to vary both capital and labour inputs. The

isocost line CD shows the factor price ratio initially faced by the firm. The firm is in initial equilibrium at output Q_1, producing at point X where CD is tangential to the isoquant Q_1, using capital services K_1 and labour services L_1. Suppose that there is a reduction in the wage rate which the firm, as a price taker, must pay to its workers. Since the price of capital services does not change, the isocost line pivots around point C from CD to CE on Figure 12.3. The firm can now produce a higher level of output Q_2 at Y, for the same level of total cost. This first impact of the wage reduction on labour demand is known as the *wage effect*.

The shift in the isocost line here is similar to the movement of the budget constraint for consumers in response to a reduction in the price of an item of consumption (see Chapter 2). An important difference, however, is that whilst the individual consumer's budget constraint is fixed by his or her level of income, the firm makes a decision about the level of its costs. Before and after the wage rate change, the firm chooses the output that maximizes its profits, given its input and product prices. The fall in wages reduces the firm's unit costs, and may make it profitable to increase its total costs and move to a higher output than Q_2 such as Q_3. The new equilibrium is then at a point such as Z, where the higher

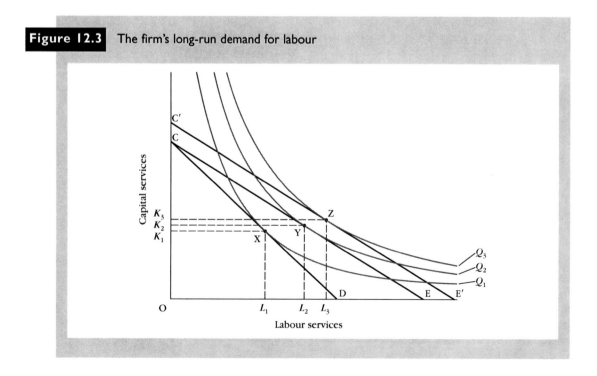

Figure 12.3 The firm's long-run demand for labour

isocost line $C'E'$, parallel to CE, is tangent to isoquant Q_3, with capital input K_3 and labour input L_3. The impact on labour demand of the movement from Y to Z is called the *profit-maximizing effect* of the wage reduction.

The combination of the wage effect and the profit-maximizing effect of a fall in the wage rate creates an increase in labour demand from L_1 to L_3 on Figure 12.3. These effects lie behind the long-run labour demand curve of the firm L_{DF}, shown on Figure 12.4. The curve L_{DF} traces the competitive firm's demand for labour at each wage rate, when the firm can vary its output and its purchases of both capital and labour services, but the prices of output and of capital services are constant. The firm's long-run demand for labour rises as the wage rate falls, giving a downward sloping L_{DF} curve as in Figure 12.4.

Figure 12.4 also shows the relationship between the short-run and long-run labour demand curves. When the wage rate falls from W_1 to W_2 on Figure 12.4, labour demand in long-run equilibrium increases from L_1 to L_2. At the same time the firm changes the amount of capital services it uses. The increase in labour used with each unit of capital services will normally increase the marginal product of each unit of the firm's capital services. Just as in the case of labour services, the firm will then

increase its use of capital services until the marginal revenue product of capital is once more equal to the unchanged price of a unit of capital services. The change in capital input *shifts* the MRP_L curve to MRP_L' in Figure 12.4. The shift to the right in the MRP_L indicates that each unit of labour now has a higher marginal revenue product, as a result of the change in capital input. In the long run the firm still maximizes profit at the point where the wage rate is equal to the MRP_L, but this equilibrium is established on a new MRP_L curve, MRP_L'.

Labour demand curves are relevant for economic policy analysis since they indicate how sensitive employment is to a change in wages. The isoquant diagram, furthermore, shows how a firm's technology influences this employment response. Figure 12.5 breaks down the *wage effect* of a wage reduction shown on Figure 12.3 into two components: the substitution and scale effects. The substitution effect captures the substitution of labour for capital which results when the price of labour falls *relative* to the price of capital but output is unchanged (see Chapter 10, Section 3.1). A new isocost line $C''E''$ is drawn parallel to CE and tangential to the original isoquant at X'. The substitution effect is shown by the impact on labour demand of the movement from X to X'.

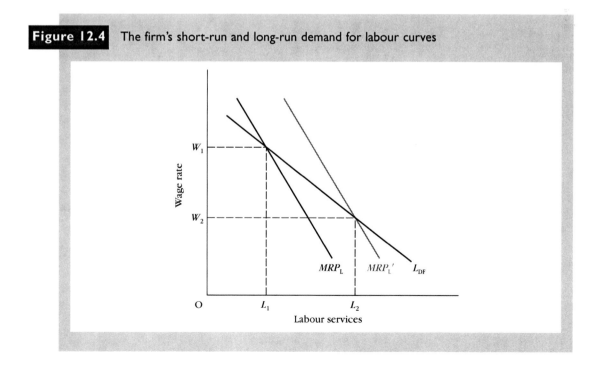

Figure 12.4   The firm's short-run and long-run demand for labour curves

The scale effect captures the firm's increased capacity to produce output for the same total cost because it can now obtain labour more cheaply. This is shown in Figure 12.5 by the effect on labour demand of the movement from X' to Y on the higher isoquant Q_2.

The extent to which labour demand increases in response to a wage reduction depends on the size of the substitution and scale effects which in turn depends on the shape of the isoquants. In particular, a high degree of substitutability between capital and labour will produce a strong substitution effect and boost the impact of a wage change on labour demand.

Exercise 12.1

Show, on a diagram, the wage and profit-maximizing effects of an increase in a competitive firm's wage rate, with constant prices of capital services and of output. Show on a separate diagram the scale and substitution effects that make up the wage effect.

2.2 Market labour demand

We now turn from the behaviour of the individual firm to consider market labour demand. In this section I will continue to assume that labour is homogeneous: there is just one type of labour available. This labour is employed by firms in different industries, including the packaging industry. This assumption allows us to build up the analysis of labour demand in stages, beginning with the industry and market demand for homogeneous labour. Sections 3 and 4 then consider markets for particular types of differentiated labour.

Industry labour demand

I will begin with the labour demand of a single industry. Suppose that there are many small firms in a perfectly competitive packaging industry. Each firm has the same technology, and hence the same long-run labour demand curve. The firms are price takers in the labour and capital services markets.

Question

Suppose that a Wages Council, which previously decided a minimum wage in the packaging industry, is abolished by a newly elected government and wages fall sharply to the market rate paid in other industries. According to neoclassical theory, how will industry output, price and labour use respond?

Figure 12.5 The substitution and scale effects

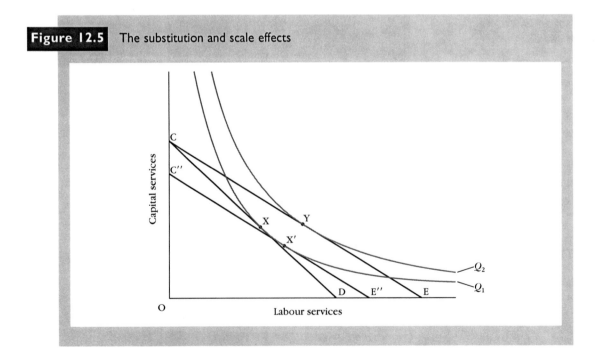

The analysis in Section 2.1 suggests that each firm will increase both employment and output in the short and long run. Labour demand would therefore rise in the industry as a whole. However, we cannot simply add together each firm's long-run labour demand curve to derive the industry long-run labour demand curve. This is because we derived each firm's labour demand curve on the assumption of a constant product price. At the industry level we must drop that assumption, since an increase in output will influence the product price.

To analyse the industry's demand for labour after full market adjustment to a wage change, consider first what happens to each firm's profits. The immediate effect of the reduction in the wage rate is to increase the profits of each firm in the industry. Consider the competitive firm shown in Figure 12.6. Before the wage reduction it maximized profits with product price P_1 by setting marginal costs ($LRMC_1$) equal to marginal revenue (MR) at point A with output Q_1. Point A is also at the minimum point of the average cost curve ($LRAC_1$) (see Chapter 10, Section 3). The reduction in the wage rate shifts the cost curves downwards to $LRAC_2$ and $LRMC_2$. The firm now makes supernormal profits at output Q_1. Furthermore, it can increase these supernormal profits further, and take full advantage of the

reduction in costs by moving to point B where $LRMC_2 = MR$ at output Q_2. The shaded area shows the firm's supernormal profits with output Q_2.

These supernormal profits, however, are temporary. Under perfect competition there is free movement of firms between industries. Therefore, in addition to the increase in output by existing firms, output of the packaging industry will be further boosted by the entry of new firms attracted by the supernormal profits. The additional firms will further increase the demand for labour.

The output decisions of the existing firms and new entrants combined will shift the industry supply curve for packaging to the right from S_1 to S_2 in Figure 12.7, and the product price will fall. Under perfect competition, the new equilibrium price P_2 will eliminate the supernormal profits of the firms, so there will be no further incentive for entry.

This price adjustment now means that it is less profitable to employ labour than at price P_1 because the revenue from output is reduced. Figure 12.8 shows the effect on each firm's labour demand curve. With product price held constant, the decline in wages from W_1 to W_2, resulting from the abolition of the minimum wage, moves the firm along its long-run labour demand curve L_{DF} from A to B. However, once the product price falls, firms find that it is less

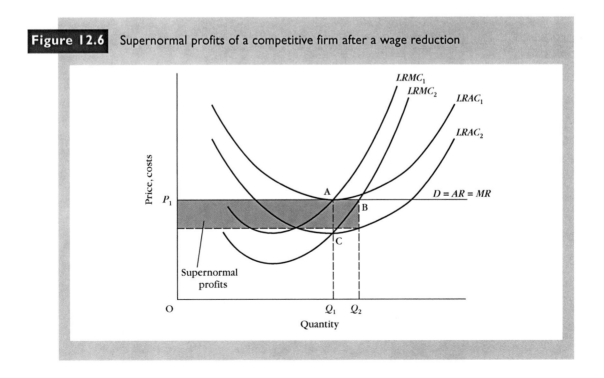

Figure 12.6 Supernormal profits of a competitive firm after a wage reduction

profitable to sell packaging. The firm illustrated in Figure 12.6, facing a declining product price, will move down its new supply curve from B towards C, reducing output below Q_2. The firm's new equilibrium output once prices have fallen far enough to eliminate supernormal profits will depend on the shape of the firm's cost curves: as Figure 12.6 is drawn, output falls right back to Q_1.

As a result of this decline in the firm's profit-maximizing output once product price falls, the firm's

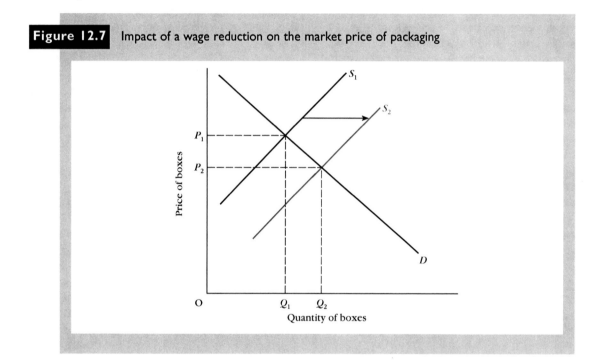

Figure 12.7 Impact of a wage reduction on the market price of packaging

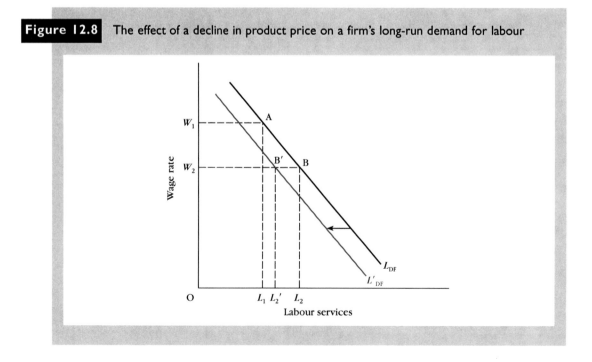

Figure 12.8 The effect of a decline in product price on a firm's long-run demand for labour

long-run labour demand curve shifts to the left, from L_{DF} to L'_{DF} on Figure 12.8. The fall in the wage rate from W_1 to W_2 increases the labour demanded only from L_1 to L'_2, once there has been full market adjustment and the price of the product has fallen to a new equilibrium.

Once market adjustment is completed and the price of the product has fallen to its new equilibrium, output of the packaging industry will be higher than before and labour demand will have increased. However, because of the effects of the decline in product price on labour demand, the long-run industry demand for labour curve including the effects of full market adjustment will be steeper than the curve that would be produced by aggregating individual firms' L_{DF} curves.

Figure 12.9 shows two alternative long-run labour demand curves for the packaging industry, L_{D1} and L_{D2}. The horizontal axis now shows labour in the industry as a whole. The industry's *own-wage elasticity of labour demand* is greater if the labour demand curve is L_{D1} than if it is L_{D2}. The own-wage elasticity of labour demand is measured as:

$$\epsilon_{LD} = \frac{\textit{proportionate change in labour demanded}}{\textit{proportionate change in the wage}}$$

Own-wage elasticity of labour demand ϵ_{LD}

The elasticity of labour demand in response to changes in the wage rate.

A high own-wage elasticity of labour demand means that a change in the wage has a strong impact on the demand for labour. If the elasticity is low, labour demand is much less responsive to a change in the wage. Thus, on Figure 12.9, the fall in the wage rate from W_1 to W_2 as a result of the abolition of the minimum wage is associated with a larger increase in labour demand along L_{D1} (the move from A to B_1) than along L_{D2} (A to B_2). With L_{D1}, labour demand increases to L_1. With L_{D2}, it rises only to L_2.

Measuring the elasticity of labour demand

Figure 12.10 shows how the elasticity of labour demand is measured at a point on a labour demand

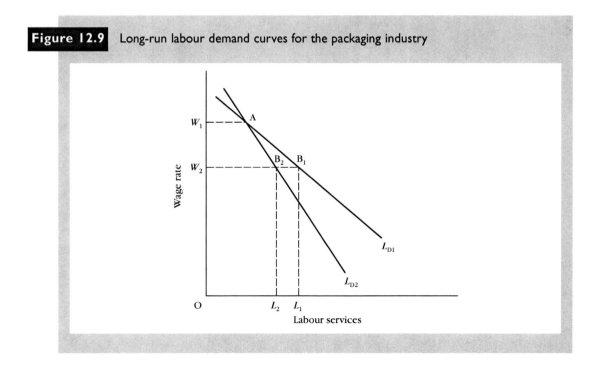

Figure 12.9   Long-run labour demand curves for the packaging industry

curve. Figure 12.10(a) shows a straight line labour demand curve, and Figure 12.10(b) a labour demand curve with a changing slope.

The formula above for the elasticity can be written as:

$$\epsilon_{LD} = \frac{\dfrac{\Delta L}{L}}{\dfrac{\Delta W}{W}}$$

On Figure 12.10(a), W and L are the wage rate and demand for labour at point A on L_D. The term ΔL is the change in labour demand associated with the change in the wage rate ΔW (which is negative). If we have data for W, L, ΔW and ΔL, then we can calculate the elasticity.

The formula for the elasticity can be rewritten with a little manipulation as follows:

Figure 12.10   Measuring the elasticity of labour demand at a point on a labour demand curve

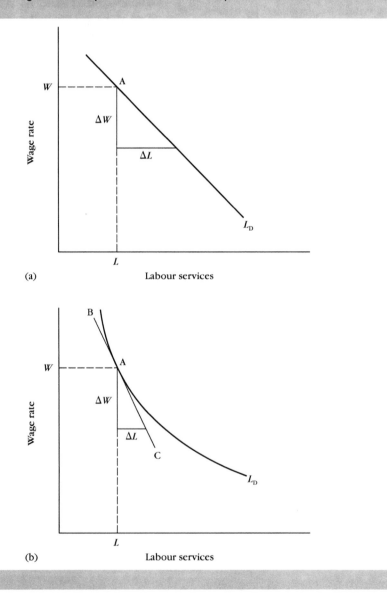

(a)   Labour services

(b)   Labour services

$$\epsilon_{LD} = \frac{\frac{\Delta L}{L}}{\frac{\Delta W}{W}} = \frac{\Delta L}{\Delta W} \cdot \frac{W}{L} = \frac{\frac{W}{L}}{\frac{\Delta W}{\Delta L}}$$

Reflection

Try this yourself. Start by multiplying top and bottom of the first expression by $\frac{W}{\Delta W}$. If you get stuck, *Changing Economies*, Chapter 6, Section 4.2 will help.

The final expression tells us that the elasticity of labour demand is measured as $\frac{W}{L}$ divided by $\frac{\Delta W}{\Delta L}$ which is the slope of the labour demand curve. Figure 12.10(b) therefore shows how the elasticity of the curved labour demand function at point A can be measured:

$$\epsilon_{LD} = \frac{\frac{W}{L}}{\text{slope of } L_D}$$

The slope of L_D at point A in Figure 12.10(b) is $\frac{\Delta W}{\Delta L}$, the slope of the straight line BC tangent to L_D at A.

In practice, economists generally have data for employment rather than for units of labour services such as labour hours. Statistics show numbers of people employed in an industry, perhaps divided up into full-timers and part-timers and men and women. Economists therefore estimate the *employment elasticity*: the responsiveness of employment to a change in wage rates.

If we had data on wage changes and employment changes in the packaging industry along with information about other influences on labour demand, we could calculate the industry elasticity of employment with respect to the wage (see technical box above). Knowing this elasticity and the expected fall in the industry wage following the abolition of the minimum wage, we could calculate the impact of the policy. This would help to assess whether the benefits of the policy, in terms of employment generation, would outweigh the possible costs of the policy (including reduced incomes for existing workers).

Question

The abolition of the minimum wage should increase labour demand. Look back now at Figure 12.9. What does my analysis so far suggest about the main influences on the elasticity of the long-run industry demand curve and therefore on the size of the employment increase?

At the level of the firm, the greater the substitution effect – the more easily labour can be substituted for capital – the greater the rise in labour demand as wages fall. Similarly, at the firm level, the greater the share of labour in total costs the sharper the fall in costs as a result of a decline in wages, and hence the larger the scale and profit-maximizing effects on labour demand. Large scale effects and profit-maximizing effects drive up industry output, and a large decline in firms' costs attracts new entry, further boosting output. The larger these output effects, the more labour demand at the industry level rises when wages fall. At the industry level, furthermore, the more elastic is consumer demand for packaging, the less the product price falls as output rises. Hence, given firms' technology and costs, the L_D curve will be more elastic, the more elastic is demand for the product.

Question

Are there any other market adjustments you can think of associated with the abolition of the minimum wage in the packaging industry?

There are potentially many knock-on effects in other markets. For example, if the output of packaging increases, the output of card and plastic required to make it will also increase. Similarly, a reduction in wages means that workers have less money available to purchase consumer goods. The wage reduction will have an impact on the market for food and clothing. Once you think through all of these interactions and recognize the interdependence between markets, the case for general equilibrium analysis becomes evident (see Chapter 18). The derivation of the labour demand curve in this section uses partial equilibrium analysis for one industry, and therefore only tells part of the story.

From industry to market labour demand

So far this section has analysed the labour demand function for a single industry. If we remain with the assumption of homogeneous labour we can derive the market labour demand curve by summing horizontally the labour demand curve for each industry. The elasticity of the market labour demand curve will therefore depend on the elasticity of each industry's labour demand, which will depend in turn on the different technology, costs and product market conditions in each industry.

I now go on to apply this model of labour demand (still with homogeneous labour) to analyse the employment implications of observed wage rigidity, and the scope for one possible policy response, employment subsidies.

2.3 Employment and wage rigidity

In Section 1, I noted the impact on employment of macroeconomic shocks. Here I begin to consider why this impact is so pronounced. Suppose that the economy enters a cyclical downturn so that, at existing wage levels, the demand for labour falls. This could come about because product prices fall. Or it could come about because firms find that they cannot sell their output at existing prices, their stockpiles

increase, and so they reduce production with a corresponding reduction in the demand for labour. The demand shock is thus transmitted strongly to the labour market. If, in response, wages fall, this will allow firms to limit their reduction in output, and will therefore temper both the reduction in employment and the rise in unemployment arising from the macroeconomic shock. In Figure 12.11, the demand curve for labour L_{D1} has shifted leftwards to L_{D2} as a result of the macroeconomic downturn. The horizontal axis now shows labour demand measured as employment in the employing industries. If the wage rate fell from W_1 to W_2, employment would fall by only a small amount (L_1-L_3).

Suppose, however, that wages remain at the initial level W_1. Then the fall in employment by L_1-L_2 and the resulting rise in unemployment will be much greater than with wage flexibility. *Wage rigidity*, that is wages that do not respond (fall) in the face of significant unemployment, makes the unemployment effect of a fall in aggregate demand worse than it would be with more flexible wages. For the purposes of the present exposition, however, because I want to focus on the impact of a demand shock on employment, I am simply going to accept that wage rigidity exists and examine the behaviour of the labour market under such conditions.

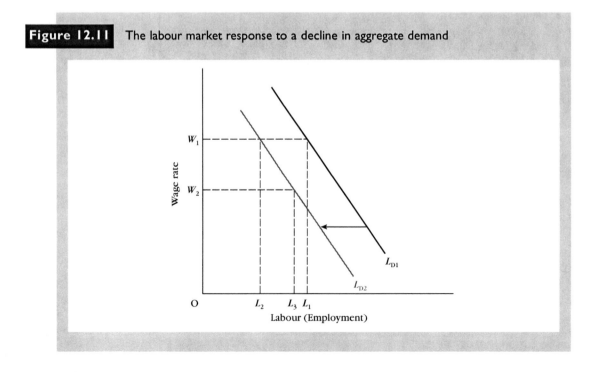

Figure 12.11   The labour market response to a decline in aggregate demand

2.4   A marginal employment subsidy (MES)

In Section 1 I noted that rising unemployment has generated considerable debate around interventionist labour market policies. One such debate has been about a marginal employment subsidy. I can use my analysis so far to consider how firms would respond during a cyclical recession, in circumstances of wage rigidity, to a subsidy intended to raise labour demand by lowering employers' costs.

The basic principle behind a marginal employment subsidy (MES) is that all firms would receive a subsidy payment from the government for each additional job they created above some baseline level of employment. It would come into effect during any severe downturn in the economy and would be phased out as the economy recovered. The focus of the subsidy on *additional* jobs reduces the tax burden for the government. For a given tax outlay it maximizes the reduction in labour costs at the margin for firms (see Layard and Nickell, 1980).

Suppose that, as a result of a demand shock, labour demand falls while wages remain rigid. Then, on Figure 12.12, the labour demand curve shifts left from L_{D1} to L_{D2}, as on Figure 12.11. Wages remain at W_1 and employment falls to L_2 workers at point F.

An employment subsidy will reduce the cost of labour to firms, even if wages remain at W_1. A given subsidy of SB_1 per worker, if paid to all workers in employment, will reduce the wage cost to firms of each employee to $(W_1 - B_1)$. A total of L_3 workers on Figure 12.12 would then be employed. The total subsidy cost to the government would be SB_1 multiplied by L_3, or the area ABCE on Figure 12.12.

However, this is an expensive method of subsidizing employment, since employers benefit from a subsidy on the wages of L_2 workers whom they would have employed at wage W_1 in the absence of the subsidy. A marginal employment subsidy, paid only on the wage costs of additional labour employed above L_2 should use the same subsidy budget more effectively. Figure 12.12 illustrates this argument (Hamermesh, 1996, p.149). The government can afford a larger subsidy SB_2 per worker by concentrating it on additional employees hired above L_2. The firms' wage costs for these marginal employees only is $(W_1 - SB_2)$. The area FGHK on Figure 12.12 represents the total subsidy to these employees, and is equal to area ABCE; that is, it represents the same total subsidy spread over fewer employees. Faced with the lower marginal labour costs, the firms in the labour market will increase employment to L_4 which will be greater than L_3. The size of the employment increase

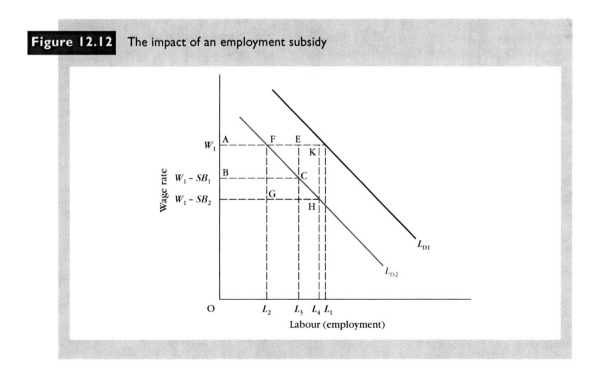

Figure 12.12   The impact of an employment subsidy

resulting from the marginal employment subsidy will depend on the elasticity of the labour demand curve.

There are a number of problems with this analysis. It implies that a marginal subsidy can generate the same increase in employment as the same subsidy per worker applied to all workers in employment. However, the substitution, scale and profit-maximizing effects are most unlikely to be as great for a marginal as for a general subsidy, and therefore the quantitative impact of the marginal subsidy is likely to be smaller. The employment response to a percentage fall in the cost of *all* workers, which is what most estimated elasticity measures capture, will be greater than the response to the same percentage fall in the cost of just the *marginal* workers.

There is some evidence on this issue from empirical studies. In the USA, a MES was operated in 1977–8 and various studies of its impact were carried out. One study concluded that one-third of the expansion of employment in retail and construction could be attributed to the policy. Another study estimated that employment expansion in firms who used the subsidy was 3 per cent greater than for those who did not (Bishop, 1981; Perloff and Wachter, 1979).

In the UK in 1977, a general subsidy of £20 per worker for 26 weeks was introduced under the Small Firms' Employment Subsidy scheme, for manufacturing firms in the worst hit areas of the country. Research revealed that in firms not receiving the subsidy employment expanded by 12 per cent whilst in firms receiving the subsidy it expanded by 20 per cent (Layard, 1979). Modelling of the possible impact of MES for the UK produces a range of estimates. An optimistic estimate for the employment response is equivalent to an elasticity of ó-ó0.08 (Whitley and Wilson, 1983).

generated considerable debate. It is argued that it is hard to identify marginal workers, so some of those for whom the subsidy would be paid would have been employed by the recipient firm anyway. This policy inefficiency raises the subsidy costs to the government. There is considerable scope for cheating, with consequent heavy administrative and policing costs. Moreover, to the extent that a MES has the desired positive effect on employment, commentators argue that government funds may be better used for other employment-generating measures.

There are further doubts about how the policy works in practice. In the short term, capital input is fixed so firms will not substitute labour for existing capital services. They will use their available capital to the full. If there is to be a strong employment effect, it must be because firms substitute additional labour for additional capital as output expands again. In times of depressed demand, however, will the subsidy induce firms to reduce prices and raise output? It seems possible that it may simply raise profits, so the effective incidence of the subsidy benefits shareholders not unemployed workers.

Given the commitment of the Conservative Government in the 1980s and early 1990s to low inflation and to reducing government expenditure, and given its opposition to direct intervention by the state in market processes, no MES scheme was introduced in the UK in the recessions of those years. More recently, Gordon Brown, the UK Chancellor of the Exchequer in the Labour Government that came into power in 1997, implemented the Workstart programme in which a temporary subsidy is available if firms employ the long-term unemployed. This has yet to be fully evaluated in the labour economics literature.

Exercise 12.2

Suppose that a firm employs 500 workers at a wage of £200 per week and that the employment elasticity of a marginal employment subsidy is –0.08. If the government introduces a MES of £50 per week, what would be the impact on employment?

One might therefore anticipate a favourable response to new proposals to bring in a marginal employment subsidy. In fact, such proposals have

3 LABOUR MARKET EQUILIBRIUM

In this section, I bring together the model of labour demand developed in Section 2 with a model of labour supply to generate an analytical framework that will allow me to analyse labour market equilibrium. I then go on in Section 4 to investigate some of the causes of slow labour market adjustment to shocks and the consequent persistence of high unemployment.

3.1   *The market supply of labour*

The New Household Economics suggests that households, composed of one or more potential workers, consume goods which Becker called Z-goods (see Chapter 5, Section 2.4). These Z-goods are the sources of utility a household produces and consumes, using a combination of time spent by family members at home ('home time') and cash income spent on purchased inputs. Z-goods can be produced by different combinations of home time and income from market work. Meals, for example, may be produced by methods intensive in bought inputs (e.g. restaurant meals) or intensive in home time (home-cooked meals).

Households choose how to divide their time between home time and time for market work. If the wage rate household members can earn in the labour market rises, this increases the opportunity cost of consuming Z-goods produced by an intensive use of home time. Households will then move towards less home-time intensive production methods, releasing more time for market work and buying more purchased inputs. And they will reduce their consumption of relatively home-time intensive Z-goods. Both shifts suggest that when the wage rises, the supply of labour to the market increases. Note,

however, that with a higher wage rate the household can also reach a higher level of utility, because with higher income, and the same time available, it can consume more Z-goods in total. So long as this income effect does not outweigh the substitution effect of the wage rise on the household's choice between market work and home time, the supply curve of labour will be positively related to the wage rate. Figure 12.13 shows short- and long-run upward-sloping labour supply curves for a household.

A household's labour supply curve shows the amount of labour (for example, hours of labour) supplied by a household to the labour market at each level of the wage rate. The elasticity of a household's labour supply response to a wage rise in the short run may be smaller than the long-run elasticity. If the wage that can be earned by household members rises from W_1 to W_2 on Figure 12.13, then in addition to the short-run increase in market work from L_1 to L_2, the household may reorganize its production of Z-goods to release further time for market work (for example, by buying childcare). Furthermore, in the long run household members may respond to higher potential income streams by retraining in order to enter the labour markets where earnings are rising. In the long run, labour supply may therefore increase further to L_3 on Figure 12.13.

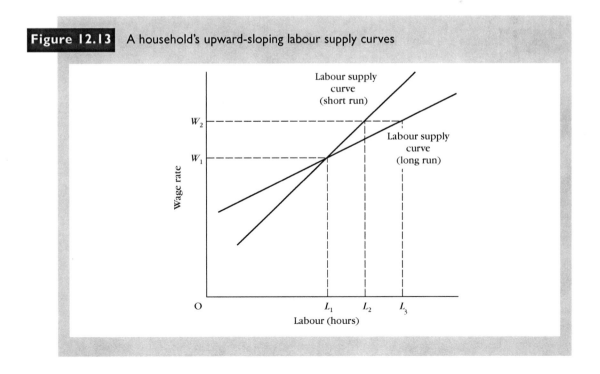

Figure 12.13   A household's upward-sloping labour supply curves

3.2 *Labour markets and demand shocks*

I can now bring together labour demand and labour supply to create the model of a single labour market shown in Figure 12.14. But at this point I want to introduce different types of labour, each with its own labour market. So let me identify Figure 12.14 as a market for a particular type of skilled workers, computer programmers. The labour demand curve $L_{D(P)}$ is the demand curve for programmers, derived from the demand for this type of labour by all the industries employing them. Each employing industry will have a demand curve for programmers. If the wages of programmers fell, each employing industry would go through the kind of market adjustment described for the packaging industry in Section 2.2. After full market adjustment in each industry's product market, the aggregate of the industry demands forms the market demand for programmers at the new wage.

The market supply curve $L_{S(P)}$ is the horizontal sum of individual households' supply curves for this type of labour. The market supply curve too will therefore be more elastic in the long run than in the short run.

In Figure 12.14, the equilibrium market wage is W^*, and the total labour employed by firms in equilibrium is L^*. Given the wage W^*, households that are able actually or potentially to supply programmers decide the extent and form of their participation in the market: the number and composition of the hours offered, and their education/training activities. As a result they supply labour L^* to the market. So at W^* there is an equilibrium in the market for programming labour; there is neither excess demand nor excess supply of labour services.

The central feature of the neoclassical approach is that, with profit- or utility-maximizing agents, labour markets will adjust towards the equilibrium position in the labour market. On Figure 12.14, if the wage were W_1 labour market demand would be L_2 but labour supply would be smaller at L_1. Firms would therefore increase the wage they offer to programmers. This would increase applications, and induce more participation, hours and training, but in the process would temper labour demand. The wage would be bid up until the labour market returned to equilibrium at W^* and L^*.

This labour market model can be used to analyse the consequences of demand shocks. If the demand for the products of all firms using programmers decreases as a result of a demand shock, the market demand curve for the labour services of programmers will shift to the left. In the short run the market supply

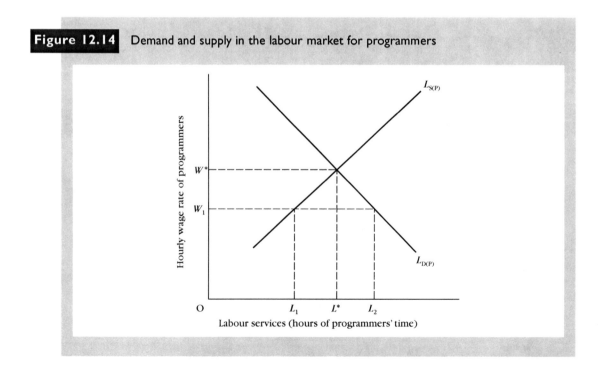

Figure 12.14 Demand and supply in the labour market for programmers

curve – the aggregate of households' short-run supply curves – will be steeper than the long-run market supply curve after people reorganize and retrain. So if wages are flexible the initial fall in programmers' wages may be steep, with wages rising back somewhat later as household members retrain in alternative skills. There will be fewer programmers' jobs, fewer programmers, and less output requiring programming skills.

If the demand for all products falls, market demand curves for labour will shift to the left in all labour markets. Wages will fall, jobs will decrease and firms will reduce output. In the long run, real market wages will be lower than previously, and households will adjust their balance of market work and home time to reflect the lower opportunity cost of home time.

Exercise 12.3

Show on a diagram of a single (representative) labour market with flexible wages the consequences of a change in households' behaviour that implied an increase in labour supply to all labour markets.

3.3 Labour markets and unemployment

At any given level of aggregate demand and supply, preferences and costs are continuously changing through time. Some firms are growing whilst others are contracting. Workers are leaving one job for another. People are retiring and others joining the working population. In this model, the market clearing outcome is therefore a *dynamic equilibrium*. A dynamic equilibrium exists in the labour market when the levels of labour services demanded and supplied are in balance, but their *composition* is continually changing. Individual labour markets are therefore constantly moving out of and back to equilibrium.

Dynamic equilibrium

The levels of demand and supply are in balance in a market, but the composition of demand and supply is changing.

If we relabel Figure 12.14 to show employment rather than labour hours on the horizontal axis, then the wage rate W^* emerges as the wage which balances the desired number of jobs slots firms want

to operate in a given labour market with the desired labour market involvement of households, despite changes in the particular job slots and the individuals wishing to work.

As the economy changes, however, market frictions impede transition. So at any moment not all the jobs offered at the equilibrium wage W^* in each labour market are filled. There are vacancies, V. Nor are all the household members who are offering to work at the wage W^* in employment. There is unemployment, U, across labour markets.

Once we shift to the level of the economy as a whole, it is useful to think of total labour demand, L_D, at a given moment as the total of job slots filled (or employment, E), plus those not filled V. So $L_D = E + V$. The total labour supply, L_S, then becomes the number of household members wanting jobs, equal to those in work plus those unemployed. So $L_S = E + U$. It follows that, in dynamic equilibrium, unemployment equals vacancies, $U = V$. The continuing level of unemployment here is known as *equilibrium unemployment*, which I will call U^*. The level of U^* may be constant in amount, but because labour markets are in dynamic equilibrium, the identity of the workers unemployed is continually changing.

Unemployment includes all those household members who are willing to work at the going wage but do not have a job, those who are looking for work, those who are ready to take up work, and those who are not placing unreasonable preconditions on the job offers they will consider. There are four points to make about equilibrium unemployment. First, it is unemployment and not inactivity. The unemployed are searching and would accept a job offer if one were offered at the current wage rate, and indeed at a lower rate. The inactive, on the other hand, are not searching and would turn down a job offer at the going rate. They are making a rational decision given their circumstances, not to participate. The evidence is that, for men, when labour markets are in balance, inactivity is very low though it has been rising. For female workers, market inactivity is higher, but has been falling rapidly in recent times.

Second, equilibrium unemployment is involuntary. The evidence is that very few workers quit into unemployment. If they want to change jobs, they search in post, or failing that they move and continue to search. So most people become unemployed because of redundancy, dismissal or market entry. Equilibrium unemployment therefore primarily reflects changes in the fortunes of individual firms forcing workers to move jobs (resulting in *frictional unemployment*) and changes in the pattern of demand and costs across industries forcing workers to move skills and location as well as jobs (resulting in *structural unemployment*) (see *Changing Economies*, Chapter 21, Section 4).

To see the distinction between frictional and structural unemployment, consider the South Wales labour markets. If a retail firm starts to do poorly, and reduces its labour force, those of its workers who experience unemployment while looking for another retail job are frictionally unemployed. But when coal mining throughout the UK, including South Wales, made most of its miners redundant, the miners who needed to retrain while unemployed, in order to gain work in a different occupation or industry, were structurally unemployed.

Increased aggregate demand simultaneously raises vacancies and reduces unemployment. There is therefore a negative relationship between U and V, known as the *UV curve*. Such a *UV* curve is illustrated in Figure 12.15. Its shape suggests that neither unemployment nor vacancies will fall to zero under changing labour demand conditions. But vacancies fall as unemployment rises and vice versa.

Researchers have estimated this relationship, and used the equilibrium condition $U = V$ at A to identify the value of U^*. An early example is Pencavel (1975). He estimated the *UV* curve for the UK using time series data for U and V through the 1960s. His method was to use regression analysis to estimate the *UV* curve in the functional form:

$$U = \beta \frac{1}{V}$$

which can be rewritten as:

$$UV = \beta$$

His estimate for β was 2.87. Since in equilibrium $U = V$, it followed that in equilibrium, at point A on Figure 12.15, if:

$$U \cdot V = 2.87$$
$$\text{then} \quad U^* = \sqrt{2.87} = 1.7$$

Other researchers went on to use the *UV* curve in modelling changes in equilibrium unemployment over time.

Given disaggregated data for U and V for various labour markets within the economy, it is possible to use the *UV* method to estimate the amount of frictional and structural unemployment. If in aggregate U is roughly equal to V, then if we add together the unemployment in markets where $V > U$ and the vacancies in markets where $V < U$ we derive an estimate of frictional unemployment. Subtracting this from U gives structural unemployment. Armstrong

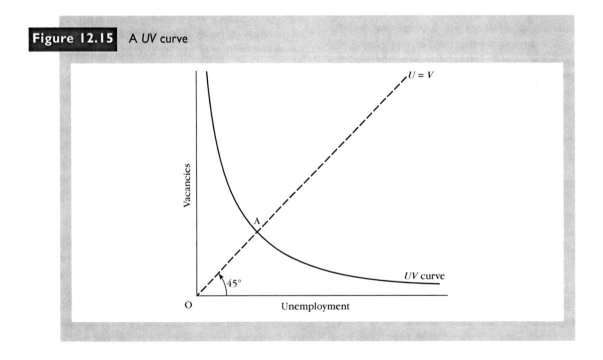

Figure 12.15 A *UV* curve

and Taylor (1981), using this method for the UK, found that for men 45 per cent of U^* was frictional whereas for women it was 77 per cent.

This method of separating frictional from structural unemployment can be explained with an example. Suppose there are just two labour markets in the UK, A and B. In market A there are 100 vacancies and 200 unemployed. In market B there are 150 vacancies and 50 unemployed. So $U = V = 250$ and the UK labour market as a whole is in dynamic equilibrium.

In A, there are more people searching than vacancies, so all vacancies will be filled in time. The vacancies represent frictional unemployment. In B, there are more vacant jobs than searchers, so the unemployed will all get jobs in due course. The unemployment is frictional. So adding together the 100 vacancies in A and the 50 unemployed in B, we have 150 as the figure for frictional unemployment. Structural unemployment is therefore 250 – 150 = 100.

Third, whilst unemployment is wasteful, market transitions are socially worthwhile. In the market model, unemployment arises because workers are having to shift to produce a new mix of goods now preferred by consumers, in the light of changed tastes and cost conditions.

Finally, whilst the private costs of unemployment are far from insignificant, the costs are ameliorated by the limited duration of much unemployment. The identity of the unemployed is changing all the time, so the costs of market frictions are shared around. Unemployment insurance and benefits play a role in providing incomes for households hit by the continuous shifts in labour demand. Through the benefit system the state is subsidizing labour market search, and facilitating more and better search by workers. Reasonable benefit levels for a limited duration can therefore be justified as increasing the chances of workers finding good jobs, to their personal benefit but also to the benefit of society.

Competitive labour markets which function in the way described in this section are productively and allocatively efficient. Competition in product and labour markets ensures that inputs, including labour, are so allocated within each firm and across the economy that a redistribution of those resources could not increase net output. Such static efficiency, however, is of overriding importance only if economic change is best understood as limited to exogenous changes in product demand and production technology. The comparative static analysis used in this chapter models the impact of such changes in competitive labour markets. If labour market behaviour and institutions influence firms' decision on technology and organization, then more complex models are required, such as those introduced in Chapters 13 and 14.

 ## 4 LABOUR MARKET ADJUSTMENT

4.1 Wage rigidity and labour market adjustment

In Section 2.3 I considered labour market response to a demand shock in conditions of rigid wages. Here I consider differential adjustment patterns across different labour markets. Let us first assume that the demand for labour falls in one labour market – say, the market for programmers once again. Figure 12.16 overleaf shows the labour market for programmers, but this time the horizontal axis shows the number of programming jobs. $L_{S(P)}$ is the labour supply curve of programmers, and $L_{D(P)}$ the demand in terms of job slots for programmers.

As product demand falls, $L_{D(P)}$ shifts left to $L'_{D(P)}$. If programmers' wages were to fall, the unemployment impact of the recession on programmers would be reduced. However, with wage rigidity, wages remain at W^*. Job slots are cut back to L' while the number of jobs required by households does not change. Vacancies fall because more workers are searching for work. Employment falls and unemployment increases. Unemployment in the recession is equal to $L^* - L'$, *plus* the kind of frictional unemployment resulting from search and turnover that we find in dynamic equilibrium. Unemployment is now greater than vacancies: the labour market is seriously out of equilibrium.

If similar processes are at work across all labour markets, a reduction in aggregate demand will produce significant unemployment in aggregate.

Question

If there are markets where wages are not rigid, does this mean that aggregate unemployment will not rise above the equilibrium unemployment level when demand falls, whatever happens in markets such as the market for programmers in Figure 12.16?

Labour markets vary in the extent to which wages are rigid in recessions. Labour markets where wages are rigid are sometimes called the 'primary' sector of the economy, while flexible wage labour markets are called the 'secondary' sector. Chapter 13 explores this dual labour market analysis in detail. Here I will simply consider its implications for unemployment in a recession.

As demand falls in labour markets where wages are rigid (the primary sector) workers will switch to markets where wages are not rigid (the secondary sector). The model predicts that wages in the latter will fall until the increase in demand generated thereby is sufficient to absorb workers displaced from the primary sector who remain active. The demand reduction will produce some fall in total employment, some rise in inactivity (as workers react rationally to the low wages on offer in the secondary sector, and opt for more non-market activities), and some additional unemployment (as workers queue for jobs in the primary sector). However, falling secondary sector wages will move the economy back towards equilibrium unemployment.

In practice, however, wages in the secondary sector do not fall enough to prevent significant aggregate unemployment. This may be because of differences in skills, geographical location, or because of the characteristics of jobs across sectors. It may be because notions of fairness in wage payments slow down the fall in wages (see Chapter 14). It could be because of the influence of unions, legislation or local agreements. It could be because of state transfers. All these create a wage floor above market clearing levels in the secondary sector.

The additional unemployment resulting from a demand shock, like equilibrium unemployment, is involuntary. Unemployment far exceeds vacancies, so there are not the jobs to go round. Unemployment duration (that is, the time people spend unemployed) rises. Workers continue to be unemployed, not because they turn jobs down, but because they fail to get offers. In due course, many workers will find the search process so unproductive that they will stop looking for a job. They will enter the murky area of *discouraged unemployment*, somewhere between unemployment and inactivity (although rather more towards the latter in terms of unemployment insurance entitlement, and therefore in UK unemployment statistics). The increased duration imposes heavy private costs of unemployment on a relatively small group of people and households. Furthermore, the costs of unemployment to society are dead-weight losses, with few offsetting gains. Workers' time

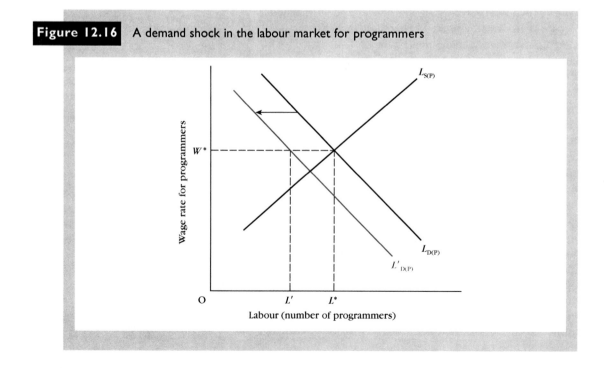

Figure 12.16   A demand shock in the labour market for programmers

spent searching for employment is of little value to themselves or to society.

Measured unemployment rises with demand shocks, but because of discouraged employment official unemployment figures tend seriously to understate the jobless problem. In the UK in 1975, 8 per cent of the population of working age was not in work, including 2 per cent inactive. In 1985, 20 per cent were not in work; 10 per cent unemployed and 10 per cent inactive. One third of those who left unemployment in the mid 1980s went into inactivity, dropping out of the unemployment figures (Wadsworth, 1994)

Unemployment, furthermore, is concentrated not only geographically but by household. Whilst 60 per cent of employed men live with working partners, only 20 per cent of the inactive do. The bulk of increased inactivity is concentrated on the unskilled and those with low education (Wadsworth, 1994).

What happens if demand expands again? According to the neoclassical comparative static model, unemployment should fall back towards equilibrium unemployment as output expands in both the primary and secondary sectors. But as shown in Figure 12.1, this did not happen for the UK economy through the 1980s. The dual labour market model adds a useful insight, but does not explain the persistence of disequilibrium. I now go on to consider explanations of labour market adjustment problems that draw on the concepts of non-wage labour costs, hysteresis and insider power.

4.2   Non-wage labour costs and labour market adjustment

So far I have assumed that the wage is the sole cost of employing labour. It follows that firms in my model adjust to changes in product demand instantaneously and continuously by hiring and firing workers. In reality, there are important fixed non-wage costs associated with changing the labour input, and these have considerable bearing upon the adjustment process. Recruitment costs arise from advertising, screening and selection procedures, initial training and supervision. Severance costs arise from obligatory redundancy payments, penalty clauses in contracts, and dislocation to production. These are non-wage fixed labour costs, in that they do not vary with labour hours but with labour turnover.

To understand the importance of non-wage labour costs consider a firm experiencing a very rapid decline in product demand. The firm will not in fact reduce its workforce immediately because the faster its response to the shock the greater are likely to be its severance costs. The firm will reduce employment gradually, largely through natural wastage. This will of course mean that it will have more labour than is strictly required. The cost of the resulting *labour hoarding* is the difference between the actual wage bill and the wage bill required at the going wage to purchase the minimum labour services needed for the output produced.

Labour hoarding

Labour hoarding occurs when firms purchase more labour services than the minimum they require for the output produced.

To the extent that output can be stored for sale later, or labour can be used to reduce non-labour costs (by capital maintenance for example), the costs of hoarding are reduced. The firm will choose an efficient rate of wastage, given the additional costs of rapid retrenchment. However, if the shock is prolonged, the firm will at some point be driven to adjust downwards very rapidly in order to survive. There will then be major labour shakeouts or 'downsizing' as the recession reaches this critical threshold level. This helps to explain why UK unemployment increased so rapidly during the early 1980s.

When demand expands out of a severe recession, firms know that hiring more workers will involve significant recruitment costs. Since these are likely to be positively related to the speed at which the firm adjusts, the firm will similarly spread the increase in employment over time. In the short term it uses significant amounts of overtime, and makes great demands for effort from its workforce, some of which will be paid for by piece-rates. Capital utilization increases. Firms run down stocks, allow order books to lengthen, buy in output, contract out work, use more overtime and so on. As a consequence, the effects of rising demand may not be seen for some time in the form of rising employment.

The empirical literature suggests that such labour market adjustments costs differ considerably between countries, resulting in very different adjustment behaviour (Emerson, 1988). It has been calculated that in 1981 fixed non-wage labour costs as a proportion of total labour costs in UK manufacturing were about 12 per cent, an increase of one-third over the 1973 figure, and also higher than in other European countries (Hart and Kawasaki, 1988). Evidence suggests that hiring and firing costs in the USA amount to five weeks wages for non-manual workers and one week for manual workers. But legislation in Europe makes the equivalent costs much higher, encouraging labour hoarding (Bentolila and Bertola, 1990). We also observe that employment adjusts more slowly in some OECD countries than in others, and this variation is related to levels of labour adjustment costs (Alogoskoufis and Manning, 1988).

The significance of adjustment costs in explaining UK unemployment persistence through the 1980s has however, I would suggest, as much to do with the general economic climate of the times as with the level of those costs. The decision of a firm to expand and take on additional labour depends upon adjustment costs but also crucially upon the firm's expectations about future demand. Firms will not hire workers, even if the immediate profits from doing so are high enough to justify the hiring costs, if there is uncertainty as to how long the expansion of demand will last (and therefore a strong possibility that severance costs will be incurred). Given the adverse effects of the very severe recession during the early 1980s, the associated uncertainty about the world economy, uncertainty about firms' chances in increasingly competitive international markets and uncertainty as to future government policy, it is not surprising that UK firms in the 1980s reacted cautiously to expanding demand.

4.3 Long-term unemployment and labour market adjustment

With falling aggregate demand, unemployment rises because more people enter the unemployment pool during each period. But fewer leave too, so the average duration of unemployment per person rises. As the downturn continues, the unemployment stock will therefore include more and more people who are long-term unemployed; that is, unemployed for more than 12 months. As the effects of the shock reach their peak, average duration of unemployment, and the proportion of workers in the total number who are long-term

unemployed, reach a very high level. The individuals involved will not remain the same of course, since some do leave long-term unemployment and others join. But the weight of long-term unemployment in the unemployment pool increases. It would appear that for the UK, and indeed for many countries, negative demand shocks affect unemployment primarily as increased duration (reduced outflows from the unemployment pool) rather than as increased inflows to the pool. Figure 12.17 shows the changing composition of the UK unemployment stock, 1979–1996, in terms of the proportion of the unemployed who had been unemployed for at least 52 weeks.

The fact that demand shocks generate significant long-term unemployment has important implications for private costs, for equity and for social costs. A large amount of long-term unemployment means that many of the unemployed will be ineligible for unemployment insurance and will have exhausted their savings. Their income levels will therefore be very low. There are heavy non-financial personal costs involved too, such as ill-health. Unemployment is extremely wasteful of society's scarce human capital resources, but long-term unemployment is particularly wasteful in that it leads to a deterioration in skills, labour quality and market knowledge. This impact of short-term adjustments on the economy's long-term capacity is called *hysteresis* (see *Changing Economies*, Chapter 18, Section 5).

What significance does long-term unemployment have for labour market adjustment during recovery? The labour market model suggests that when demand rises, firms will expand the number of job slots they operate. Firms enter the appropriate labour markets to hire workers, advertising for and screening applicants, some of whom will, at the time that they apply, be unemployed. The resulting hiring reduces unemployment.

But consider now a firm receiving applications from the long-term unemployed. It is likely that the quality of labour services of unemployed workers decreases with the duration of their unemployment. This could be because of the deterioration in their skills, or because their skills have become obsolete. It could be because their self-confidence and drive is undermined. Labour quality, and therefore the probability that an unemployed worker is hired, is thus *duration dependent*.

Duration-dependent unemployment

Unemployment is duration-dependent if the probability that an unemployed worker will obtain a job declines with the length of his or her unemployment.

This problem is made worse by firms' imperfect screening systems (see Chapter 13). Firms find it hard to determine whether a particular long-term unemployed person applying to them is worth employing or not. We can therefore expect that firms will prefer to hire unemployed workers who have experienced only short durations of unemployment.

It follows that when the short-term unemployed become scarce as aggregate demand rises, then rather than hire from the long-term unemployed, firms may decide to leave their vacancies open, or, more significantly, turn to alternative inputs. The anticipated characteristics of unemployed applicants are then not only influencing firms' hiring decisions but also their demand for labour. If firms respond in this way, the problems for the long-term unemployed and for the economy become self-perpetuating, in that if firms restrict hiring, unemployment durations are lengthened and labour

quality falls, which feeds back into the demand for labour decision.

Exercise 12.4

Not all workers who are long-term unemployed offer low quality labour services. So if demand increases, why can firms not expand employment by attracting and hiring only unemployed workers providing high quality labour services?

Even if the quality of skills is not affected by duration, it is possible that workers' search activities and motivation are negatively related to the length of their unemployment. If workers lose heart because of a prolonged spell of unemployment and search less intensively, their chances of getting back into work when demand starts to rise are limited, simply because they are not active in the labour market. If workers' motivation declines with duration, this will adversely affect their chances in interviews and even their responses to job offers. Statistical evidence from time series data suggests that unemployed workers' re-employment probabilities do fall with duration, holding other influences constant (Jackman and Layard, 1991).

Figure 12.17 Percentage of UK unemployed (male and female) out of work for more than 52 weeks

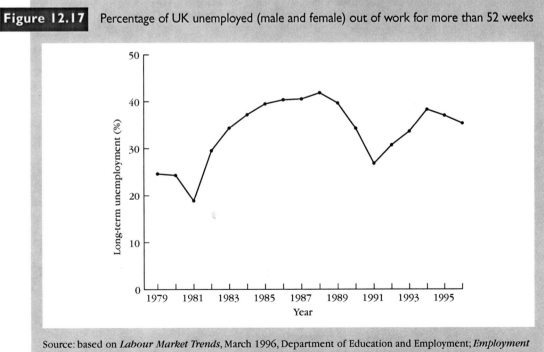

Source: based on *Labour Market Trends*, March 1996, Department of Education and Employment; *Employment Gazette*, various issues

Unemployment history matters when it comes to explaining current unemployment. Given duration dependence and hysteresis, the existence of long-term unemployment can explain the failure of the labour market to adjust to recovery and therefore the persistence of unemployment in many European countries through the late 1980s. The strong and prolonged increase in unemployment generated significant numbers of long-term unemployed. When demand increased, short-term unemployment fell, but for some considerable time long-term unemployment remained virtually unchanged. Once firms had hired the short-term unemployed they reduced their demand for labour.

Evidence to support this argument is provided by empirical work based on the *UV* curve.

Question

Look back at Figure 12.15. A recession moves the economy down and to the right along the *UV* curve. If individuals' chances of employment in the recovery are duration-dependent, how will this affect the position of the *UV* curve?

Hysteresis implies that short-term unemployment rates influence long-term equilibrium unemployment.

In these circumstances, you would expect the *UV* curve to shift outwards as a result of recession, with more unemployment at each vacancy level, as shown on Figure 12.18. The *UV* curve before the recession UV_1 shifts outwards during the recession to UV_2. When the recession ends in renewed growth, and unemployment and vacancies come back into balance, the point where $U = V$ will no longer be at A, but at B with a higher rate of both U and V.

Figure 12.19 graphs the data for vacancy rates and male unemployment rates for Great Britain over the period 1959–87. The data have been used by Jackman *et al.* (1989) to argue that the *UV* curve shifted to the right over this period. After 1980, higher male unemployment rates are found for the same vacancy rates, and they attribute this to the higher proportion of unemployed who are long-term unemployed.

Another set of researchers concluded that: 'Statistical analysis of the *UV* curve has indicated the importance of long-term unemployment in producing such shifts' (Budd *et al.*, 1987). Meager and Metcalf (1987) found that more than one-third of the firms in a sample used a history of long-term unemployment as a criterion in drawing up short lists for vacancies. The number of interviews achieved by applicants very clearly declined with duration.

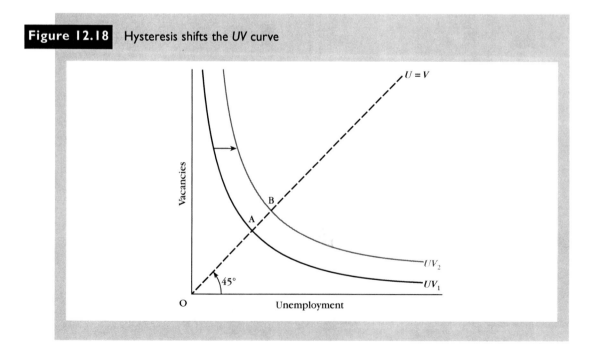

Figure 12.18 Hysteresis shifts the *UV* curve

Daniels (1990) and others have not found in survey work that dislike of unemployment falls, or that hiring conditions and wage demands increase with duration. There is some evidence that workers' search intensity declines with duration but not markedly. However, Hughes (1986) found, in his sample of workers, that the number of firms approached did decrease after unemployment of one year. Another researcher found, '… evidence that workers' motivation suffers seriously during long-term unemployment as money worries, boredom and declining self-respect take hold' (White, 1991).

Finally, consider Table 12.1. The estimates of equilibrium unemployment (U^*) are derived from an estimated labour market model. The figures for U^* here are estimates, for different periods, of the NAIRU (non-accelerating inflation rate of unemployment) (see *Changing Economies*, Chapter 18, Section 5.2). Through the mid 1980s, while demand expanded, actual unemployment (U) remained greater than U^*. By the late 1980s however, the labour market appears to have adjusted to a higher level of equilibrium unemployment, with U close to U^*.

Table 12.1   UK actual and equilibrium unemployment, 1969–95

	1969–73	1974–80	1981–7	1988–90	1991–5
Actual unemployment %	3.4	5.2	11.1	7.3	9.3
Equilibrium unemployment %	3.6	7.3	8.7	8.7	8.9

Source: Nickell, 1996, Table 3.1

Figure 12.19   Unemployment and vacancies in Great Britain, 1959–87

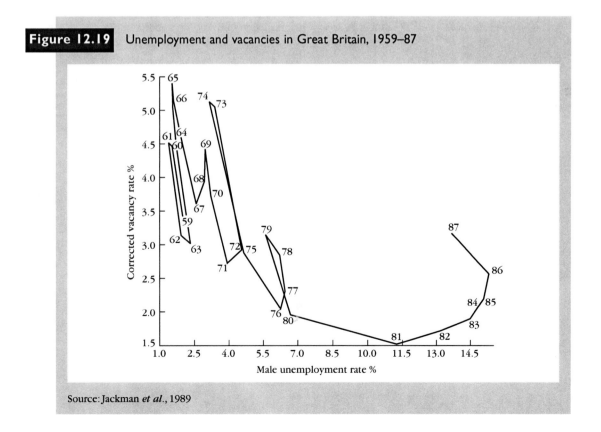

Source: Jackman *et al.*, 1989

4.4 Insiders and wage determination

In Section 4.1, I argued that as aggregate demand expands after a negative shock, firms increase their job slots and therefore hire additional labour, and so unemployment falls. But this overlooks an important point. If, as demand expands, wages rise in some labour markets, then the expansion of demand will have a limited effect upon employment and therefore on unemployment. Consider Figure 12.20, which is based on Figure 12.16. W^* is the (rigid) wage rate maintained from the pre-recession equilibrium. If wages remain fixed as recovery starts, and the recession labour demand curve $L'_{D(P)}$ shifts out to $L''_{D(P)}$, then unemployment will fall rapidly from $L^* - L'$ to $L^* - L''$, plus in each case some frictional unemployment. Suppose, however, that as recovery starts, firms scramble to hire programmers, fearing a shortage of these skills. Then wages rise to W_1, increasing supply but choking off the rise in demand. Unemployment among programmers is then $L_1 - L'''$ plus some frictional unemployment. Total unemployment among programmers has actually risen as recovery gets underway.

Perhaps in due course the expansion of demand in firms located in the secondary sector will take up the unemployed. But this will take some time, especially if the size of that sector is small, its share of any demand expansion is limited, and/or wages there also begin to rise before unemployment reaches equilibrium unemployment U^*. So wage increases in the primary sector prolong the process of labour market adjustment.

Why do wages respond differently in different markets? In contrast to the labour market model in Section 3.2, wages in actual labour markets are often determined not by firms alone but through local collective negotiations between firms and workers. The existence of local wage negotiations implies on the one hand that wages will increase most sharply in firms where the growth of productivity is highest. This will result in substantial earnings differentials if the scope for measured productivity gains varies significantly across sectors. It provides an incentive for local efficiency, and for productivity deals which in turn lead to higher output and growth. On the other hand, local bargaining implies that wages across firms will increase most where firms and workers have most market power. Workers will seek to maximize the return to their bargaining strength. The result is likely to be that wages would be higher and employment in the primary sector lower, and therefore unemployment in the economy as a whole

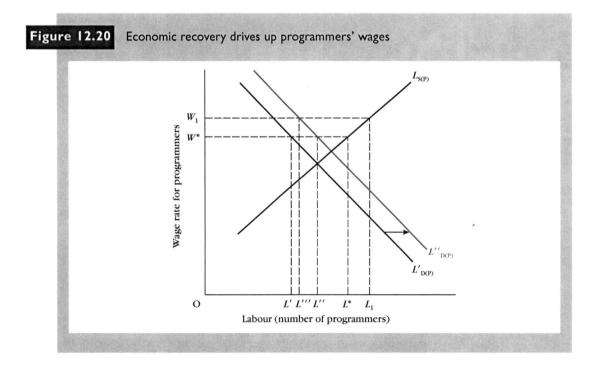

Figure 12.20 Economic recovery drives up programmers' wages

higher, than would otherwise be the case. The external unemployment effects, that might be avoided by market competition or restricted by national bargaining, will be strong.

What significance does local wage determination have for labour market adjustment? One model that suggests it is significant is the *insider-outsider* approach. In all insider-outsider models, there is an inequitable division of power in economic decision making, with the insiders holding more power, for example, over wage determination. Insiders are defined as the core workers in the primary sector; people who have been in their firms for some time. Such insider workers, with low chances of being unemployed, take no account of the impact of their actions on unemployed outsiders. Outsider workers include workers in the secondary sector and marginal workers in the primary sector with limited job durations and work experience, some of whom at any given point in time might be displaced to the secondary sector or to unemployment. Insiders have a strong influence on negotiations due to their experience and long attachment to their firms, and have some status in firms' decision-making processes due to seniority and leverage. Insiders have bargaining power in relation to outsiders because of the recruitment, severance and training costs that would arise in replacing them with outsiders. Insiders can also increase their costs if they refuse to co-operate with and to train new workers. There is now considerable statistical evidence that wages set by firms are influenced by factors internal to individual firms as well as by labour market conditions (Blanchflower and Oswald, 1988; Krueger and Summers, 1988; Gregory *et al.*, 1987).

Suppose then that as a result of a demand shock, employment falls. Insiders retain their jobs because of redundancy rules (such as last in, first out) or because of their greater experience and replacement costs. Unemployment rises amongst marginal workers who fail to find work elsewhere. As demand recovers and firms look to increase job slots, insiders use their leverage to raise the wages. To win employers over, insiders might have to agree to changes in production processes that generate additional output and productivity gains. This will increase the firms' profits, but will also finance insiders' wage gains. The insiders' wage increase will limit the employment effects of the demand increase, and indeed the productivity effect could actually lead to further job losses for marginal workers in the primary sector. Such a process will lead

to increased inequality in the earnings distribution as well as to the persistence of high unemployment.

There is some evidence consistent with this explanation of persistent market imbalances. Through the mid 1980s, UK real wages in manufacturing increased very rapidly despite high levels of unemployment. Productivity growth was very high but nevertheless the growth in output and employment was muted. Those in work clearly did well, whilst others did very badly (Glyn, 1995). However no strong corroborative evidence has yet emerged from statistical analysis (Nickell and Wadhwani, 1990; Nickell *et al.*, 1992).

Question

Can you think of any reasons why the power of insiders should have increased in the UK during the 1980s and why their responsiveness to unemployment might have decreased?

There has been a process in the UK of decentralization of wage bargaining, which has strengthened local insider workers' leverage over the wage determination process. National union leaders have found themselves with reduced power to negotiate national settlements. Furthermore, a wider normalization of attitudes that promote self-interest and an increased tolerance of unemployment and inequality seems to have reduced the sensitivity of those in work to the fortunes of those out of work.

 ## INFLUENCES ON EQUILIBRIUM UNEMPLOYMENT

Table 12.1 in Section 4.3 suggested that the equilibrium rate of unemployment rose through the 1980s. This section considers two influences on U^*: labour market inflexibility and structural change.

5.1 *Labour market inflexibility and equilibrium unemployment*

Labour market inflexibility arises when the result of the actions of agents, pursuing their own private interests, distorts labour market processes. It also arises out of the activities of the state pursuing wider economic, political or social objectives. Economists are generally agreed that UK labour markets were more inflexible until the 1980s than other countries' labour markets, but there is less agreement about the relative importance of the different forms of inflexibility. You are no doubt aware that most debate surrounds the role of organized labour and the impact of legislation on firms.

It has been argued that until the 1980s workers exerted considerable power largely through trade unions, both within the work unit, using strikes and other forms of industrial action, and within society through corporatist pluralism. This severely reduced managers' ability to manage. Firms' employment decisions were strongly influenced by established work practices, employment agreements and the need to obtain labour's co-operation. At the same time legislation, relating to minimum wages, employment protection, regulation of hours, hiring and redundancy reduced firms' options further. This resulted in many firms having too much labour, using it inefficiently and being unable to make the most of product market opportunities.

These pressures, so the argument goes, had negative effects on firms' investment and training decisions, resulting in low productivity growth and declining competitiveness. As UK firms lost market shares abroad and suffered from import penetration, they had to cut output and employment. As in Figure 12.11, the demand curve for labour shifted to the left in many labour markets as UK output fell at constant world prices. With rigid wages in many labour markets, unemployment rose. The shift was not a temporary one. Agents, including the government, adjusted to the new constraints they faced, and the economy settled to a position with a permanently higher level of equilibrium unemployment.

This is a line of argument that found favour with the UK government in the 1980s. It has clear policy implications. In the 1980s the UK, along with a number of OECD countries sought to introduce greater labour market flexibility. Policies in the UK included anti-union legislation banning closed shops, restricting industrial action, and making union membership and representation more difficult. Wages councils setting minimum wages were abolished and employment protection was weakened. Subsequently, David Hunt, then Employment Secretary, claimed that Britain's 'flexible and deregulated labour market is delivering economic growth and jobs'. (House of Commons, 18.11.93).

Does empirical research support David Hunt's position? During the period of the 1980s supply-side economic policies productivity levels and growth certainly increased markedly (Oulton, 1990). Empirical work using regression analysis indicates that, holding other influences constant, unionized firms were likely to have somewhat lower investment levels (Denny and Nickell, 1992) and lower rates of growth of productivity (Nickell *et al.*, 1992). Labour market flexibility did increase, with more employment changes, and greater use of part time work, short term and temporary work, contracting out and flexi-time. Firms reorganized their labour force much more rapidly (Beatson, 1995b). Furthermore, the level of unemployment fell faster than previously when an upturn occurred. Figure 12.21 shows the response of UK unemployment to the expansion of the economy following the troughs in 1980 and 1990. Line A confirms what we have seen in Figure 12.1, that following the trough in 1980, it was a few years before unemployment started to fall. Unemployment continued to rise through the early stages of the recovery. In contrast when we look at line B we see that unemployment began to fall much earlier, much more quickly and to a lower level after the trough of 1990 (Morgan, 1996).

The causal interdependencies here are very strong, so coming to a conclusion is difficult. My own views are (at the moment) as follows. I am persuaded that labour market inflexibility in the 1970s cannot be attributed to labour alone. It was the product of an economic culture in which managers, shareholders and government, as well as workers, exploited the relative lack of product market and global competition to their advantage. Unionized firms with low investment and productivity growth in the 1970s and high employment changes in the 1980s were usually firms with market power (see Wadhwani, 1990). Furthermore, it is not clear that in the UK the impact of the inflexibilities that the government attacked was ever very significant, nor that the changes in these areas have been sufficiently radical to have much impact on labour's position (Robinson, 1995; Nickell, 1996). The 1980s saw a very considerable increase in domestic and international competition, accentuated by some change in UK government macroeconomic policy. Greater market flexibility came as firms and shareholders responded to company failures and declining profits, and workers and unions responded to increased unemployment and job insecurity (Brown *et al.*, 1997).

Flexibility was born of very pressing necessity, that has had very serious economic and social costs in terms of incomes, job security, job quality and less effective employment relationships (Mayhew, 1994; Brown and Read, 1995). Inflexibility was one important source of equilibrium unemployment through the 1970s, and there will be some economic benefits from more flexible labour markets (Oulton, 1994). But I am not convinced that the 'British disease' was just or even mostly a labour problem.

Reflection

From your experiences do you consider that the labour market is now more flexible? If so, in what sense, and why do you think this has happened?

5.2   Labour markets and structural change

To complete the chapter I want to look briefly at the way in which the structure of the economy influences the operation of labour markets within it. In

particular, I want to consider the possibility that high levels of equilibrium unemployment arise because of structural change in the economy and the resulting mismatch between jobs and workers. We hear a lot about the pressure of international competition. Is this why significant labour market imbalance appears to be the norm today?

As incomes rise, consumer spending shifts towards income-elastic, high quality commodities. And as the structure of product demand changes, so too does the structure of labour demand. Over the last thirty years, the most striking aspect of structural change in OECD countries has been the falling share of total spending on manufactured goods and the rising share of total spending on services. The demand for labour in manufacturing has consequently fallen relative to that in services. Moreover, *within* manufacturing the number of jobs has declined markedly in traditional industries, as consumers have switched towards more sophisticated, high-tech products.

This process is sometimes called *positive deindustrialization*. For countries like the UK it has an important international dimension. With 25 per cent

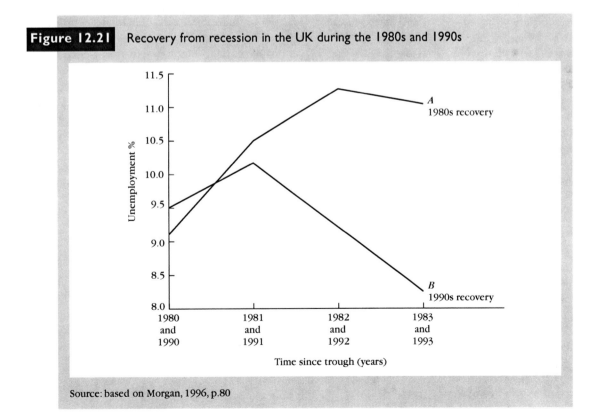

Figure 12.21   Recovery from recession in the UK during the 1980s and 1990s

Source: based on Morgan, 1996, p.80

of GDP traded, and with manufactured goods being an essential part of that trade, the UK economy is very sensitive to structural change in the world economy. Consumers in developed countries are switching their spending towards more sophisticated imported manufactured goods and tradable services, and producers in developed countries are moving towards more sophisticated manufactured goods, attracting UK consumers. Furthermore, developing countries are now producing the less sophisticated manufactures they previously imported, and indeed are exporting them at competitive prices. Positive deindustrialization for the UK therefore requires a shift towards more specialist products and tradable services, both to maintain UK share in world manu-factured exports and to limit import penetration.

Evidence that significant structural change has occurred is to be found in the changing employment composition of OECD countries. Table 12.2 captures both the switch from agriculture to manufacturing of the more recently industrialized economies, and the switch from manufacturing to services of the mature developed economies.

The labour market transitions associated with positive deindustrialization involve not only *indus-trial* redistribution of labour but also changes in the skill composition of the workforce and therefore the *occupational* redistribution of labour. As a result, during deindustrialization the level of structural and therefore equilibrium unemployment will increase. To explain how this works, I need to expand the basic labour market model set out in Section 3.2 to include multiple skills.

Conceptually, it is possible to identify a number of broad categories of skill, or productive potential, each associated with a different type of knowledge and physical application. It is also possible to identify,

within each category, levels of skill according to the amount of knowledge and physical application involved. For each skill, there is an occupational labour market. Each occupational labour market involves a market demand curve from firms and a market supply curve from households. Since workers can move across skills, and firms can substitute across the services of different labour skills as well between labour and capital, occupational labour markets are interdependent.

The formal economic analysis of the demand for and supply of labour in Sections 2 and 3 can be developed readily enough to incorporate multiple skills. This produces a series of market labour demand curves, one for each skill, where labour demand now depends not only upon the degree of substitutability with capital services but also upon the degree of substitutability with other skills. The supply of the labour services of any particular skill increases with the wage as hours and activity rates increase and, in the longer term, as new and estab-lished workers undertake the training necessary to enter the market.

However, identifying the skill structure *in practice* can be difficult. We want to specify skills in a way that is true to the distinction between labour markets in the real economy. There are people who are engineers, lorry drivers, lawyers. The skills here are distinct enough. But these are too broad to reflect working labour markets. What about civil engineers, electrical engineers and mechanical engineers? Despite problems of meaning and definition, here I am going to presume that there are distinct skills, and that we can differentiate between them in theory and in practice.

At a given point in time, with stable aggregate demand, there will be a particular skills composition

Table 12.2 Distribution of GDP and employment: OECD, 1960–94

	1960		1970		1980		1994	
Agriculture: % GDP (% employment)	6.0	(17.3)	4.2	(9.7)	3.1	(6.5)	2.1	(4.0)
Industry: % GDP (% employment)	41.0	(36.7)	39.9	(37.8)	36.5	(34.5)	31.5	(27.8)
Manufacturing: % GDP (% employment)	30.4	(27.2)	30.1	(28.2)	24.7	(25.0)	21.5	(20.2)
Services: % GDP (% employment)	53.0	(46.0)	56.8	(52.3)	60.4	(62.8)	66.4	(68.2)

Sources: *OECD Economic Outlook: Historical Statistics 1960–1990* and 'OECD in Figures', *OECD Observer*, June/July 1997
Note: Figures are for the US, Japan, Germany, France, UK, Italy and Canada.

to the labour force, reflecting the distribution of consumer preferences for commodities and the nature of the production technology governing different commodities. Associated with the occupational labour force structure will be an occupational wage structure. Wage differentials between skills will broadly reflect the costs of training to move from one skill to another, allowing for the non-pecuniary costs and benefits associated with different occupations, and for any scarcity premia associated with ability differences.

To analyse labour market equilibrium, let us focus upon just two skills and two skills markets. Skill M is used primarily by firms in manufacturing, while N is a skill used primarily in services. Figure 12.22 shows the labour markets for the two skills. At the initial equilibrium in Figure 12.22(a), L_{M1} units of skill M are employed at a wage rate W_{M1}. In the market for skill N in Figure 12.22(b), L_{N1} units are employed at a wage rate W_{N1}. The wage rates W_{M1} and W_{N1} are determined by the interaction of demand and supply in their respective markets, but because workers can move between markets the two demand and supply curves, and therefore the two wages, are interdependent. The curves L_{D1}^{M} and L_{S1}^{M} on Figure 12.22(a) are the demand and supply curves for labour services of skill M when the wage of labour services of skill N is W_{N1} on Figure 12.22(b). In Figure 12.22(b), the curves L_{D1}^{N} and L_{S1}^{N} are the demand and supply curves for labour services of skill N when the

wage of labour services of skill M is W_{M1} on Figure 12.22(a). In overall labour market equilibrium, the position of the demand and supply curves generates a wage differential, $W_{M1} - W_{N1}$ on Figure 12.22, such that, given the preferences of the labour force and the costs of training and job change, there is no further movement between labour markets and the market for each skill is in equilibrium.

What happens if we now introduce structural change in the form of positive deindustrialization? As consumers switch their spending towards services, the relative price of services to manufactured goods rises inducing firms in services to increase their output. In Figure 12.22(b), the demand for labour services of skill N therefore rises. The labour demand curve shifts from L_{D1}^{N} to L_{D2}^{N}. Manufacturing firms contract and the demand curve for skill M shifts from L_{D1}^{M} to L_{D2}^{M}. As a result there is a skills mismatch, with unemployed workers in the M market (largely in manufacturing) and vacancies in the N market (largely in services). If wages are flexible, the relative price of labour services of skill N will therefore increase, and the observed wage differential will fall. Employment will contract in the M market and rise in the N market. Figure 12.22(b) shows the narrower wage differential produced by the demand shifts. This will not, however, be the end of the adjustments. As Section 3.1 argued, if the wage for skill N rises, workers with that skill will increase their labour market participation.

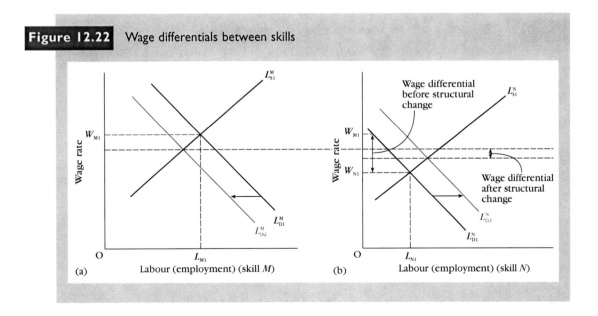

Figure 12.22   Wage differentials between skills

(a) Labour (employment) (skill M)

(b) Labour (employment) (skill N)

More significantly, workers and firms will alter their training decisions. This will lead workers inside and outside the services sector to acquire skill N and to enter the labour market for skill N. The supply curve for skill N moves to the right and that for skill M to the left. These shifts are shown on Figure 12.23 which is based on Figure 12.22. If training costs and preferences stay the same, the two markets will move to the point where the wage differential is once again equal to the initial differential between W_{M1} and W_{N1} in Figure 12.22. Therefore $(W_{M2} - W_{N2})$ on Figure 12.23 is equal to $(W_{M1} - W_{N1})$ on Figure 12.22. At that point, there will again be no incentive for workers to enter the labour market or move between markets. Labour market equilibrium is re-established with higher employment L_{N2} in the N market and lower employment L_{M2} in the M market. Once the structural adjustment is completed, the skills composition of the labour force, as well as its industrial distribution, has therefore altered considerably.

The process described above is one in which workers are *drawn* from manufacturing to services by the wage signals/incentives. This puts pressure on manufacturing to compete for their labour. But services have consumers on their side. Fortunately for manufacturing, however, it has technology on its side. Most of the processes used in manufacturing can generate considerable productivity gains, meaning that they can be adapted and developed so as to produce less output with much less labour.

Consequently, manufacturing is today in a position to facilitate the expansion of services in the same way that agriculture facilitated the expansion of manufacturing in the first Industrial Revolution.

There is, however, a downside to deindustrialization. Demand changes and technical change in manufacturing will result in consistently higher levels of unemployment. First, there is a rise in frictional unemployment. Section 3.3 identified the importance in a dynamic economy of the market frictions which impede the movement of labour *between jobs*. With greater movement there will be more unemployment. Second, and more important, there will be a rise in structural unemployment, because increased movement between industries is impeded by market frictions in the movement *between skills and locations*. The greater the pace of deindustrialization, even if the economy remains in balance in the sense that in aggregate $U=V$, the higher the level of equilibrium unemployment.

If skills mismatch and therefore structural unemployment are to be contained during positive deindustrialization, the crucial facilitating factor must be occupational mobility: the change and improvement of skills. This in turn requires the labour market to signal and reward mobility, and to provide the opportunities to train and retrain. In the 1990s, the UK labour market was characterized by flexible *relative* wages, which moved in favour of labour skills in expanding areas.

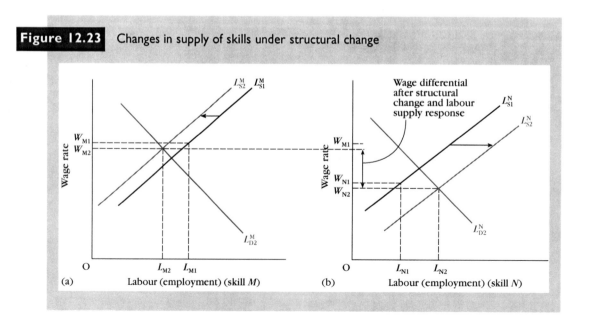

Figure 12.23 Changes in supply of skills under structural change

On the other hand, the evidence is that occupational mobility has been inadequate. Between 1979 and 1991, 5 per cent of firms in the EU reported skill shortages. The figure for the UK was 14 per cent (see Haskel and Martin, 1994). During the 1980s the number of adult workers who received training increased, but over half of all workers still receive no training at all. Training opportunities decline rapidly with age, and they are concentrated in the public, non-traded sector (Mayhew, 1991). And Prais (1994) noted that 'occupational mobility requires that workers have the basic skills to take on additional training. Comparing the UK with Germany again the percentage of the workforce with intermediate vocational qualifications are 25 and 63 respectively.'

So does deindustrialization offer an explanation of the significant rise in equilibrium unemployment that was identified in Table 12.1? Empirical evidence on the extent of structural unemployment confirms that mismatch is an important determinant of the level of equilibrium unemployment. Jackman *et al.* (1990), using methods including summing the absolute differences between unemployment and vacancies across sectors, reach the conclusion that skills mismatch explains one third of equilibrium unemployment. But they find no evidence that its importance increased between the 1970s and the 1980s, except with regard to certain skills specific to traditional manufacturing technologies.

I want to make two final points on this topic. The first is that there is strong evidence of increasing structural unemployment in the 1990s, due to continuing deindustrialization and technical change in the 1990s. This takes the form of a substantial shift in demand away from unskilled workers to skilled workers. With insufficient occupational mobility, this has resulted in very significant inequalities of earnings, skill shortages and unemployment. One cause of the demand shift is that certain low-tech, low-skills manufacturing sectors in the UK, and in other developed economies, have come under considerable pressure from the emerging nations (Wood, 1995). A more important reason, I think, is that in recent years technology has shifted very rapidly towards capital inputs at the expense of labour in virtually *all* industries, a process driven by competitiveness and enabled by technical change. Empirical work confirms that capital and skilled labour are complements in production, whilst capital and unskilled labour are strong substitutes (Hamermesh, 1993). So, especially if it is labour saving, a rapid change in technology will significantly reduce labour demand.

There is evidence that the growth in the use of computer technology has been important here (Machin, 1995).

What appears to have happened in the 1990s is that while the other contributory factors said to determine equilibrium unemployment, that is, high taxes, high benefits, high import prices and strong unions, were becoming less important, structural unemployment in the form of the skilled jobs/unskilled workers mismatch was becoming more important. Consequently equilibrium unemployment has remained high.

The final point relates back to deindustrialization. Whilst the high equilibrium unemployment that results is obviously undesirable, the situation will become very much worse if the rigidities in the economy, including labour markets, mean that structural change results in lower rates of growth of productivity and therefore falling international competitiveness. In the 1980s this is what appears to have happened for the UK. The failure to train and retrain left the economy with a skills gap compared to the UK's main competitors. This, and inherent weaknesses in investment and innovation meant that UK firms experienced a decline, as well as a shift, in demand. These demand changes in turn further limited training, investment, productivity and competitiveness. Consequently, employment as a whole fell and unemployment rose significantly above the equilibrium level.

6   CONCLUSION

The objectives of this chapter have been to investigate the functioning of labour markets, and, in particular, to understand firms' employment decisions. I have used neoclassical analysis to model one view of how labour markets work, and to analyse the sensitivity of labour markets to demand shocks, including imperfect adjustment mechanisms, and the large and persistent imbalances between the number of workers seeking jobs and the number of jobs firms want to fill.

I have considered a number of possible explanations for such labour market behaviour, and the available empirical evidence. I do not believe that it is possible to identify one single overriding source of labour market failure. However, at present it seems clear that the mismatch between unskilled workers and skilled jobs in the UK, associated with structural change within work units due to technical change, is generating considerable structural unemployment because of insufficient training and inadequate occupational mobility.

FURTHER READING

The technical material covered in Sections 2 and 3 can be found in: Elliott, R. (1990) *Labor Economics: A Comparative Text*, New York, McGraw-Hill.

Some of the issues raised in Sections 4 and 5 can be found in: Layard, R., Nickell, S. and Jackman, R. (1994) *The Unemployment Crisis*, Oxford, Oxford University Press.

A discussion of the various policy issues is to be found in: Layard, R. (1986) *How to Beat Unemployment*, Oxford, Oxford University Press.

ANSWERS TO EXERCISES

Exercise 12.1

The effects of an increase in the wage rate are shown on Figure 12.24. The initial factor price ratio is shown by the slope of the isocost line CD. The firm initially produces output Q_3 with factor inputs K_3 and L_3. When the wage rate rises, CD pivots to CE. The wage effect is shown by the change in inputs to L_2 and K_2 as the firm moves from X to Y. The profit-maximizing effect is shown as the move from Y to Z on isocost line $C'E'$ parallel to CE, reducing input use to L_1 and K_1 at output Q_1.

Figure 12.25 shows the scale and substitution effects. $C''E''$ is parallel to CE, and tangential to Q_3 at X'. The substitution effect is represented by the move from X to X', and the scale effect by the movement from X' to Y.

Exercise 12.2

A MES of £50 per week means an effective wage reduction to the firm of 25 per cent at the margin. With an elasticity of labour demand of –0.08 we can expect an increase in labour demand of 2 per cent i.e. $0.08 \times 25 = 2$. Since 2 per cent of the original 500 workers is 10, the MES is estimated to induce additional employment for 10 workers.

Exercise 12.3

Figure 12.26, based on Figure 12.14, shows the results in a labour market for a particular type of labour, computer programmers. You can think of this as a representative labour market: similar shifts will

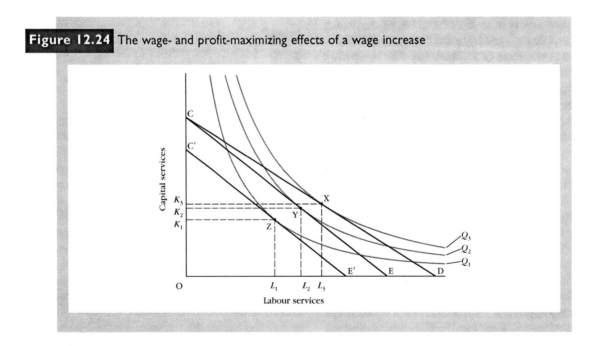

Figure 12.24 The wage- and profit-maximizing effects of a wage increase

occur in each labour market. There is an initial equilibrium at A where L^* hours of programmers' time are purchased at an hourly wage of W^*. An increase in labour supply moves the supply curve to the right from $L_{S(P)1}$ to $L_{S(P)2}$ so supply at point B is greater than demand. Finding that they are getting lots of applications for their jobs, firms realize that they can increase profits by paying a lower wage. The fall in the wage encourages firms to increase the use of programmers' labour services. But it also leads some

Figure 12.25   The substitution and scale effects of a wage increase

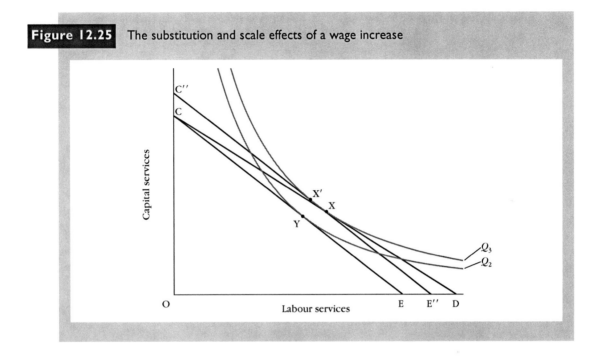

Figure 12.26   An increase in labour supply in the market for programmers

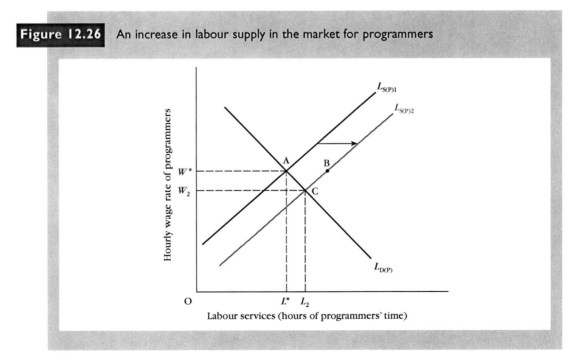

households to change their labour supply. The new market equilibrium is at C, where labour supply is L_2 at a new equilibrium wage W_2.

Exercise 12.4

Firms find it hard to identify good workers, because of imperfections in their screening mechanism, and/or cannot pay similarly skilled workers different wages, because of precedent. Therefore, the fact that not all workers who are long-term unemployed provide poor quality labour services will not have much effect. Firms will screen in terms of the average long-term unemployed worker and therefore screen out long-term unemployed workers. As far as the good long-term unemployed workers are concerned, this amounts to statistical discrimination (see Chapter 13).

DISCRIMINATION AND SEGMENTATION

Robert McNabb

13

LINKS

- In Becker's neoclassical analysis of discrimination the marginal revenue product curve derived in Chapter 12 is employed. Under perfectly clearing markets Becker argues that employers will find it difficult to exercise their individual prejudices against a particular group of workers.

- The neoclassical model of statistical discrimination makes use of the concept of human capital introduced in Chapter 5. Here the source of discrimination is identified with the choices individuals make with respect to their investment in human capital.

- The theory of segmentation is based on the institutional divide, incorporating differences of job security, opportunities for training and trade union organization, between primary and secondary labour markets. This involves relaxing the typical neoclassical assumption of a fully competitive labour market which quickly achieves equilibrium (Chapter 12).

- Positive and negative feedback effects are considered in relation to the labour market. This builds upon the institutional analysis of how children are cared for in Chapter 7.

1 INTRODUCTION

Discrimination can manifest itself in all aspects of life. It may be evident in the type and location of housing available to certain groups, in their access to quality education and health care or how they are treated in the labour market. This chapter focuses on the last of these considerations and, in particular, why the labour market status of some groups of workers is significantly worse than that for the population at large. This does not mean that discrimination in the labour market is a more relevant consideration than other forms of discrimination, nor should it imply that labour market discrimination is independent from other forms of discrimination. Indeed, some economists would argue that a satisfactory explanation of labour market discrimination can only be developed when it is recognized that all forms of discrimination are related.

The fact that some people do better or worse than others in the labour market does not, in itself, signify the presence of discrimination. It would be more surprising if such differences were not observed. What is harder to explain, however, is why particular groups of workers are disadvantaged in the labour market. Why do women and members of ethnic minorities, for example, face significantly lower wages and poorer employment opportunities *as a group*? In this chapter we focus on the general observation that certain characteristics – gender, race, religion, age – actually matter in the labour market when there is no apparent reason why they should.

In the next section we outline the extent to which disadvantage in the labour market varies. There are, of course, many different dimensions to labour market disadvantage. The most obvious is differences in average earnings which may arise either because people from disadvantaged groups are paid less for doing a particular job or because they end up in (or are 'crowded' into) low paying jobs. A second dimension of labour market disadvantage is that the level of unemployment is higher for certain groups of workers than for others. Linked to this is the observation that disadvantaged groups are concentrated in jobs with higher turnover rates and greater job insecurity. Finally, some groups may be disadvantaged in terms of the type of work they

have access to, with an emphasis on menial and repetitive tasks.

Since there are many different ways in which labour market disadvantage can be measured, it is perhaps not surprising that there are also different types of discrimination. The two main types are considered in Section 3.

The theories proposed to explain discrimination in the labour market are equally diverse. Differences are reflected not simply in terms of the underlying theoretical framework adopted but also in the particular aspects of labour market behaviour which are focused upon. Explanations which can be grouped under the heading of neoclassical theories focus mainly on the supply side of the labour market, such as the relationship between labour market disadvantage, low productivity and low levels of investment in human capital. We look in detail at such explanations in Section 4. Other, non-neoclassical theories, such as segmented labour market theory, concentrate on the limited access certain groups of workers have to 'good' jobs (independent of their human capital) and upon why there is segregation in access. We look at these alternative, institutional theories and related features in Section 5. Finally, in Section 6, a formal comparison of the neoclassical and institutional approaches is developed using the simple demand and supply diagram.

2 LABOUR MARKET DISADVANTAGE

2.1 Gender-based disadvantage

The post-war period has seen a significant increase in the participation of women in the labour market, with women now making up around 45 per cent of the UK workforce. Although women still undertake the major share of family responsibilities and domestic activities, an increasing number of women are entering the labour market (see Chapter 5). This increase is evident in many countries and has been associated with an improvement in the relative earnings of women. This trend towards greater equality is evident in Table 13.1, which shows the ratio of female to male earnings in a number of countries over the period 1960–1980.

Question

For the period 1960–80, identify:

● the country with the largest reduction in inequality
● the smallest reduction (or no reduction at all).

Sweden underwent the biggest reduction in inequality with the ratio of female to male wages increasing from 0.72 to 0.90. Both the USA and the USSR had no change in relative wages.

The labour market is complex and the two observations that more women now participate in the labour market and that there has been a narrowing of relative wage differentials reflect a number of possible relationships. On the one hand, it may be the case that more women participate because female wages have increased over time. On the other hand, the stronger commitment of women to the labour market could, in itself, increase female wages and narrow the earnings differential. Thus, if higher wages and higher participation are statistically associated, there are various views on causation which the labour economist must disentangle.

Despite the improvements that have taken place over time, however, it would be misleading to overemphasize the advances that have occurred in the relative position of women in the labour market. Nearly 45 per cent of working women in the UK, for example, are employed part-time, at pro-rata wages well below those of full-time workers. According to *People Management*, 'Women working on a part-time basis earn only 58% of male full-time workers' pay rates' (6 February 1997, p.8).

Data from the *New Earnings Survey* (1995) reveal that the earnings of women working full-time are also significantly below those of men in comparable jobs. As Table 13.2 shows, the average weekly earnings of women managers in 1995 was 68 per cent that of men. This ratio, earnings of women to men, of about two-thirds, was reported in six out of nine occupational groups.

Women may have to wait many years before they achieve equal pay with men. *People Management* state that, '… the average earning discrepancy between men and women remains at around 20 per cent. At the current rate of improvement, women will have to wait until 2040 before they achieve parity' (6 February 1997, p.16). Also, according to *People Management*, '… surprisingly, the gap remains widest of all in professional occupations. For example, women bank and building society managers earn 36 per cent less than men in similar posts' (*ibid*).

That women are paid less within even narrow occupational categories can arise for a number of reasons and does not necessarily involve women being paid less than men for doing the same job. It may reflect the nature of the organizations that employ women or the fact that women are typically

Table 13.1   The ratio of female to male hourly earnings in selected countries, 1960–1980

	1960	1970	1980
Australia	0.59	0.59	0.75
France	0.64	0.67	0.71
Germany	0.65	0.69	0.72
Italy	0.73	0.74	0.83
Japan	0.46	0.54	0.54
Netherlands	0.60	–	0.71
Sweden	0.72	0.84	0.90
UK	0.61	0.59	0.75
USA	0.66	0.65	0.66
USSR	0.70	0.70	0.70

– data not available
Source: Mincer, 1985

employed at lower grades within occupational categories. For example, there is evidence that women academics are appointed at lower points on the university lecturer scale than comparable men and that they are less likely to become senior lecturers, readers and professors (McNabb and Wass, 1997). The failure of women to make significant progress in the professions and in senior management and administrative posts has led to the idea that there is a 'glass ceiling' which means that women are under-represented in positions of responsibility and influence.

In addition to this disparity in pay across all occupations, women tend to be heavily concentrated in occupations and industries that are characteristically low paying. The *1991 Population Census* (OPCS, 1992) recorded that just over 28 per cent of women were employed in clerical and secretarial jobs, 13 per cent in personal service occupations and 10.5 per cent in sales occupations (Table 13.3). The corresponding figures for men in these areas are much lower. In contrast, nearly 30 per cent of male workers are managers and professionals. These occupations employ only just over 19 per cent of women. Moreover, within broad occupational groups we find further concentrations. For example, two thirds of women in professional occupations are teachers whereas teaching accounts for only a quarter of professional males. Similarly, more than half the women in associate professional jobs are nurses.

Table 13.2   Average weekly earnings by occupation 1995 (£)

	Men (£)	Women (£)	Ratio: women/men %
Managers	537.00	367.80	0.68
Professionals	499.70	407.90	0.82
Associate professionals	442.90	333.30	0.75
Clerical and secretarial	269.90	230.40	0.85
Skilled manual	318.30	191.20	0.60
Personal services	296.10	198.70	0.67
Sales	310.30	199.90	0.64
Plant and machine operators	293.70	201.50	0.69
Other	250.50	170.80	0.68

Source: *New Earnings Survey*, 1995

Table 13.3   Distribution of employment by occupation (%)

	Men	Women
Managers	19.3	11.6
Professionals	9.5	7.6
Associate professionals	7.8	9.9
Clerical and secretarial	6.7	28.1
Skilled manual	23.1	3.5
Personal services	6.1	13.0
Sales	4.5	10.5
Plant and machine operators	14.3	5.1
Other	7.5	9.9
Not adequately described	1.1	0.8

Source: *1991 Population Census*, 1992, OPCS

2.2 Ethnicity and disadvantage

Detailed information on other disadvantaged groups in the UK is more limited. Recent studies of the labour market disadvantage faced by Britain's ethnic minorities indicate not only that they fare badly relative to white employees, but also that their relative position deteriorated throughout the 1980s and early 1990s. According to the *General Household Survey*, non-white employees in the UK earned 7.3 per cent less, on average, than white employees over the period 1973–9: this deteriorated to 12.1 per cent through the period 1983–9. The Campaign for Racial Equality reports an even larger disparity in earnings: using the *Labour Force Survey* (Eurostat, 1994) they found that the average hourly rate of pay for ethnic minority workers in Inner London was £5.62 compared with a figure of £9.82 for white workers.

A similar picture both of relative disadvantage and deterioration since the 1970s emerges in unemployment rates. Table 13.4 shows unemployment rates for different ethnic groups since 1979.

What is interesting about this table is that the information is also broken down by ethnic group. This enables us to highlight not just the differences that exist between white and non-white workers but also those that exist between ethnic minorities. Several points are worth noting. First, unemployment in all the years shown is lower for whites than for non-whites: in 1994 the unemployment rate among non-whites was more than twice that for white workers. Second, although the 1980s was a period of rising unemployment for all workers, the increase was much larger for non-whites than for white workers. Finally, there are significant differences within the non-white population. Workers of Indian descent fared significantly better than workers of Pakistani/Bangladeshi descent; workers of West Indian origin have faced the greatest deterioration in their chances of being in work.

Unemployment among young workers paints an even bleaker picture with 37 per cent of those from ethnic minorities unemployed in 1994: amongst young black workers the figure is 51 per cent (Blackaby *et al.*, 1995).

2.3 Other disadvantaged groups

Information on other disadvantaged groups, such as older workers or people with disabilities, is even harder to come by. The problems faced by older workers in the labour market have become an increasing cause for concern in recent years. The nature of the disadvantage faced by older workers is, however, much harder to uncover and the evidence is often anecdotal. One trend that has become evident during the past 15 years is the difficulty older workers have in obtaining any work and, in many cases, the jobs that are available often pay older workers significantly lower wages than they previously received. Job adverts can specify age limits (in contrast to race and gender) in the UK, though such

Table 13.4 Unemployment rates for UK males in selected years

Year(s)	White (total %)	Non-white (total %)	Indian (%)	Pakistani or Bangladeshi (%)	West Indian (%)
1979	4.0	6.0	4.8	8.1	7.3
1981	9.7	17.2	15.4	20.4	20.6
1983	12.0	22.0	17.0	32.0	28.0
1984	11.0	21.0	13.0	38.0	28.0
1985	11.0	21.0	18.0	28.0	23.0
1984–6	11.0	21.0	15.0	30.0	25.0
1985–87	11.0	20.0	15.0	29.0	24.0
1987–89	8.0	15.0	10.0	25.0	18.0
1989–91	7.0	13.0	10.0	21.0	16.0
1994	11.0	25.0	16.0	29.0	33.0

Source: Blackaby et al., 1995

practices have been made illegal in some countries, such as the US, Canada and France.

High general unemployment in the 1980s and 1990s had a significant impact on the employment opportunities for people with disabilities as they had to compete with large numbers of 'able-bodied' workers. The double discrimination facing people with disabilities from ethnic minority places them at even more of a disadvantage than white people with disabilities (Baxter *et al.*, 1990).

3 FORMS OF DISCRIMINATION

We have already seen that labour market disadvantage can take various forms. Equally, discrimination in the labour market itself can manifest itself in different guises.

The most obvious form of discrimination involves women being paid less than men for doing the same or a similar job. This is what labour economists call *wage discrimination*, which has been addressed and formally eliminated in many countries through the introduction of equal pay legislation. Wright and Ermisch (1991) for example, report that 'the *Equal Pay Act* (1970), *Sex Discrimination Act* (1975), and *Employment Protection Act* (1975), contributed significantly to reducing discrimination in the British labour market' (p.508).

Wage discrimination

Under wage discrimination an individual is paid less than another individual working at the same job.

However, the ability of such legislation to improve the relative position of those workers facing discrimination is the subject of much debate. The following case study of performance-related pay shows how discrimination can be difficult to legislate for.

Discrimination can also exist even where earnings are the same for all workers in a particular job.

Employment discrimination

Under employment discrimination an individual has potentially the same level of productivity as those working at a job from which he or she is excluded.

Merit pay scheme 'was discriminatory'

London Underground is changing the way its performance-related pay system is implemented after conceding a £60,000 racial discrimination case last month.

Consultants, Psychometric Research Development, will meet with London Underground in future to discuss any performance-related pay scheme as part of a settlement reached with 20 black station managers. The managers claimed that the scheme, in place for the three years between 1989 and 1992, indirectly discriminated against them.

Fatima Patwa, a solicitor for Brent Community Law Centre, which supported three of the 20 managers, told *Personnel Management* that the performance assessments left too much to the discretion of the senior staff carrying out the appraisals.

She said research found black managers were being awarded lower performance pay than their white colleagues. Some managers were failing to use the appraisal procedure correctly, making the same remarks on all forms while awarding different levels of pay, or ignoring the assessment entirely and simply making a judgement on salary.

In a statement agreed with the black managers, London Underground said that the indirect discrimination had been 'wholly unintentional'. It went on to say that it 'regrets the fact that its performance-related pay exercises for the three years from 1989 to 1992 were not carried out fully in conformity with its laid down procedures'.

The Commission for Racial Equality, which supported 17 of the managers, said the case was the biggest it had ever put to an industrial tribunal.

The case was initially supported by the Transport Workers Legal Action Committee, which was formed by black workers within London Underground to deal with discrimination.

Each of the managers will be paid £1,000 for financial loss plus £1,500 for injury to feelings and £650 for adjustment to voluntary severance payments.

Source: *Personnel Management*, May 1993

Employment discrimination occurs when workers from disadvantaged groups are employed in jobs for which they are over-qualified in the sense that they have higher levels of productivity compared with other workers doing the same job, and with the overall level of ability needed to undertake the tasks involved. This will arise either because members of particular groups face discrimination in recruitment, and so cannot gain access to better paid jobs, or because opportunities for promotion and selection for training are denied.

The definition of discrimination which underlies both wage and employment discrimination is the same. It involves the unequal treatment of individuals who are equally productive (sometimes described as 'of comparable worth') on the basis of characteristics, such as gender, race, age, religion, etc., that are not related to productivity and so should not affect earnings.

While wage and employment discrimination have been the focus of empirical and theoretical research, this should not be taken to imply that other forms of discrimination are less important nor that their impact is of less significance. Harassment at work, for example, is a form of discrimination which, although it has not received the empirical scrutiny of labour economists, is nevertheless an increasing cause for concern. It can affect an individual's performance at work and consequently his or her earnings and employment opportunities. To give one example: in a large-scale survey of junior barristers, 40 per cent of female respondents reported that they had faced some sort of sexual harassment at work (*Equal Opportunities Review*, 1995).

4 NEOCLASSICAL MODELS OF DISCRIMINATION

Our earlier discussion suggested that to understand labour market discrimination we need to answer two principal questions. First, to what extent does the observation that, on average, some groups in society fare worse than others in the labour market actually reflect differences in productivity arising from differences in such things as education and training, and how much represents the unequal treatment of equally productive workers (i.e. discrimination)? Secondly, if discrimination in the labour market

exists, what explanations are proposed to explain why it takes place? These two questions are, of course, not unrelated. The educational and training opportunities available to some groups in society may themselves reflect discrimination. As a result, labour market outcomes, which may or may not be discriminatory, may arise from discrimination that exists outside the labour market.

In this section we consider those explanations usually grouped under the neoclassical label, which build upon human capital theory (see Chapter 5). No attempt is made here to provide an exhaustive coverage of all the neoclassical models and their variations, rather, we present two examples of neoclassically-based explanations. The first, Becker's 'employer taste' model, is based on the standard utility maximizing model and emphasizes the importance of market forces and competition; the second focuses on how imperfect information in the labour market can give rise to wage differentials even among comparable workers.

4.1 Becker's 'employer taste' model

The most prominent neoclassical explanation of discrimination is based on the work of Gary Becker and develops the idea that some workers, employers or customers do not want to work with or come into contact with members of other racial groups or with women (Becker, 1971). No explanation is given as to why this prejudice exists, rather it is simply assumed that there is a 'taste' or preference against people from disadvantaged groups and that this taste can be treated in exactly the same way that economists would analyse individual preferences between goods and services.

Suppose that an employer does not want to employ members of a particular group even though these workers are as productive as any others. If the firm has to pay all workers the same wage it will simply not employ members of the disadvantaged group. However, if it is possible to pay these workers less than those from other groups the firm then faces a trade-off: it can employ members of the disadvantaged group at lower wages and thus increase its profitability, or it can discriminate and employ only workers from the high wage group even though this will mean lower profits. Discrimination in the latter case therefore imposes a cost on the firm.

Figure 13.1 can be used to show what happens in these circumstances. Let us assume for the sake of simplicity that there are no differences in productivity between different groups of workers. Since all workers have the same level of productivity, the marginal revenue product curve faced by the firm is the same, irrespective of which workers they employ. This is shown as MRP_L, the demand for labour curve (see Chapter 12). In a competitive labour market, a firm will employ labour up to the point where the wage equals the marginal revenue product of labour (which is why the MRP_L curve is also the firm's demand curve for labour). So, if the wage rate is W_1 the firm will employ L_1 workers. If the firm discriminates against members of a particular group, no workers from this group will be employed at W_1. This employer will simply exercise prejudice against them and, if this is a common practice amongst firms, the disadvantaged group will face unemployment.

What would happen if these workers were prepared to work at wages below W_1? Clearly, this will depend upon the extent to which the firm is prepared to discriminate since by employing disadvantaged workers at lower wages, the firm can lower its costs and thus increase its profits. Suppose that the firm is prepared to pay W_4 to L_1 workers from the disadvantaged group.

Question

Use Figure 13.1 to identify the volume of total profits which the firm would make from this discrimination.

For each unit of labour employed, the firm makes profits equal to the difference between revenue (MRP_L) and cost (W_4). At L_1 units of labour employed, total profits consist of the sum of differences between MRP_L and W_4 for each unit of labour employed between O and L_1. These total profits are represented by the area AGEC.

Now, if the firm only employed workers towards whom it is not prejudiced at a wage W_1, then total profits would be represented by AGH. Figure 13.1 shows that the firm gains additional profits from its discriminatory behaviour. By charging a discriminating wage of W_4 to disadvantaged workers, additional profits of ACEH are made by the firm. These additional profits compensate the employer for the prejudice held for disadvantaged workers.

This difference in wage rates paid to the two groups of workers results in a different demand curve for the disadvantaged group. This is represented by

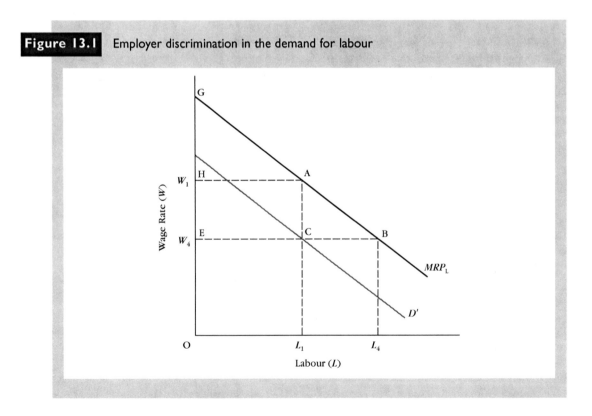

Figure 13.1 Employer discrimination in the demand for labour

the line D' in Figure 13.1. For each level of employment the firm pays a lower wage rate to compensate for its prejudice against disadvantaged workers. This means that the demand curve for these workers is parallel but to the left of MRP_L (the demand curve for advantaged workers). Another way of looking at D' is to say that, at each wage rate, the firm is prepared to employ fewer disadvantaged workers than it will advantaged workers.

The problem, however, is that other firms may not hold the same prejudices. There could be another firm which has only one demand curve for all workers, as represented by MRP_L.

Question

Assume that a non-prejudiced employer hires labour at a wage rate of W_4. Using Figure 13.1, identify the following:

1 the total profits made by this firm
2 any additional profits made in comparison to the prejudiced firm.

The non-prejudiced employer, paying a wage rate of W_4, would employ L_4 workers regardless of their colour or creed. It would make total profits of BGE. By not being prejudiced this firm gains additional profits of BCA in comparison to the profits of AGEC made by the prejudiced firm. The problem, therefore, is that it is difficult for any one firm to indulge in prejudices without losing out to more profit-hungry non-discriminatory firms. Moreover, the additional amount of labour employed by these other firms would enable them to produce more output, thereby forcing down the prices of goods sold in the product market. This fall in product prices would drive the discriminatory firm out of business.

Although we have only considered a simple variant of the Becker approach to labour market discrimination, it is sufficient to highlight the most important conclusion. This is that discrimination can persist only if there are factors which limit the amount of competition in the labour market or in the product market. If these markets are competitive, the increased profitability of non-discriminating firms compared to discriminating ones will encourage non-discriminators to enter the market. This will put downward pressure on the price level and eventually force the higher-cost discriminating firms out of business. The extent of the inefficiency faced by discriminating

firms is shown by the fact that, at wage W_4, discriminating firms employ L_1 workers, whereas a non-discriminating firm would employ L_4 workers and produce more output as a result. If, however, there are substantial barriers to entry which make it difficult for new firms to enter the market, competition will not erode discrimination.

The 'employer taste' model predicts that discrimination exists because employers do not want to employ certain groups of workers and will only do so if these workers are paid lower wages than those paid to workers in general. It thus provides an explanation of wage discrimination – equally productive workers being paid different wages. Other variations on this theme involve discrimination by workers and customers. The case study that follows provides an example of perceived customer discrimination by the Ford Motor Company.

Think global, act prejudiced?

Ford is better known for spraying its cars than re-spraying its employees. Indeed, in the bad old days when the company seemed to specialise in producing tinny boxes, the joke was that Ford's profits came from its skill in spraying metal onto paint rather than the other way around. But when an advertisement featuring line workers from its Dagenham plant in England was used in Poland, the black and brown faces of five employees were replaced with white faces (and hands).

The reason, according to Ford, was that the Poles are not used to seeing non-white faces, and it wanted to adapt its advertisement to suit local tastes. Unfortunately, when the original picture was reused back in Britain, the Polish version was used by mistake.

When they noticed what had happened, the line workers at Dagenham all walked out for three hours – a rare event in a British factory nowadays. Ford, which has apologised to the victims of the retouching and sent them a cheque for £1,500 ($2,320), blamed a mistake by its advertising agency, Ogilvy & Mather. The agency cannot say who was responsible for the mistake, because it happened 18 months ago, and institutional memories in creative organisations clearly do not stretch back that far.

In some ways the Ford saga, which immediately provoked cheap jibes along the lines of 'Any colour you want as long as it's not black', unveils yet another problem of globalisation. In America and Europe, Ford is abolishing many of its regional fiefs and setting up transnational product groups. On the other hand, it has told its managers to demonstrate sensitivity to local peculiarities – particularly on the marketing side. Nobody at Ford seems to be apologising for what happened in Poland.

Source: *Economist*, February 1996

4.2   Statistical discrimination

Investment in education and training

Human capital theory has been used to show how investments in education and training lead to higher levels of earnings (see Chapter 5). One reason why education and training are referred to as investments is because their benefits accrue over time and because training early in a career leads to higher earnings over the rest of an individual's working life. An important consideration, therefore, in the decision about whether to invest in additional human capital is the potential length of working life over which the benefits will be received. This would suggest that if certain groups of workers - most

notably married women with family responsibilities – expect to have interruptions in their careers they will invest less time and energy in acquiring human capital. They thus face lower earnings as a result of having less training and lower skills. Because women themselves choose not to invest in skills and training, their lower earnings would not represent discrimination according to the definition used in this chapter. Of course, it could be argued that some women decide to focus on their family and domestic activities precisely because they perceive poor career prospects for women, prospects which are themselves a reflection of discrimination. This is an example of reverse causation.

The impact that career interruptions can have on the earnings profile of women can be shown using Figure 13.2. We shall initially assume that men come to the labour market with a certain amount of human capital and this determines their initial earnings. Subsequent training and promotion then result in their earnings increasing each year which is reflected in an upward sloping *age-earnings profile*. On the other hand, we shall also initially assume that all women expect to drop out of the labour force because of family responsibilities and, as a result, undertake less education and training before entering the labour market. Hence, their age-earnings profile is lower than that for men. For example, women may choose education and training courses, such as those providing clerical, secretarial

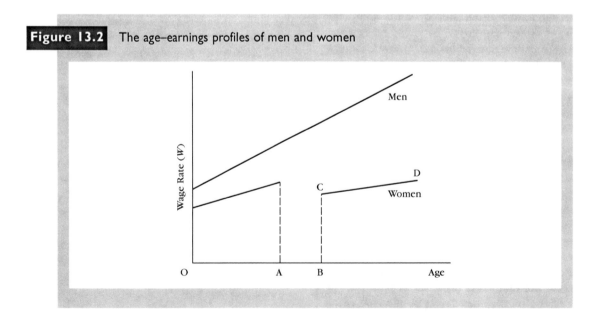

Figure 13.2   The age–earnings profiles of men and women

or nursing skills, that enable them to enter occupations in which breaks from work incur the smallest penalty. Once they enter these occupations they receive less training than men because expected career interruptions reduce the returns from such investments and consequently their earnings profile rises at a lower rate than that for men. This is shown by the segment of the age–earnings profile up to age A. At age A, we assume that women drop out of the labour force and that when they enter the labour market again at age B, depreciation of their skills has resulted in a reduction in their potential earnings. In addition, the interruption has also resulted in a loss of seniority which has depressed their scope for earnings growth even further. This is shown by the segment CD.

Age–earnings profile

This shows how an individual's or group of individuals' earnings change over time.

Human capital theory therefore predicts that women will earn less than men because they do not expect to spend as long in the labour force. Intermittent work histories will also influence career choice. Fewer women will pursue skilled occupations and the professions, and more will be attracted to those jobs that enable them to more easily combine family responsibilities and labour market activity. Women are less likely to be promoted to higher level grades where these involve additional training since the monetary gains to the firm will, on average, be lower for women.

The result is that promotions will be biased in favour of men.

We have, of course, made some very strong assumptions in painting the above picture of participation and occupational choice. Women now account for about half the total UK workforce (though women as a whole work shorter hours in employed labour and a larger proportion are part-time) and many women have as strong a commitment to their careers as men. The ability to combine family responsibilities and a career depends upon a number of different factors, not least of which will be the nature of the job and the availability and cost of such things as crèche and childcare facilities.

Productivity difference

The preceding discussion has only considered what would happen if all women undertake less investment in human capital than men. If men and women invest to the same extent, human capital theory suggests that no wage differences would be observed. What happens, however, if there are differences in skill levels both between genders and within gender groups? To consider this we will also make the additional assumption that firms do not know when recruiting workers who are the most productive. However, employers do know that, on average, women spend less time in the labour market than men because of career interruptions.

Figure 13.3 can be used to describe what will result. Since firms do not know each individual's potential productivity when hiring – both men and women may leave or may not be very productive once trained – they will set wages on the basis of

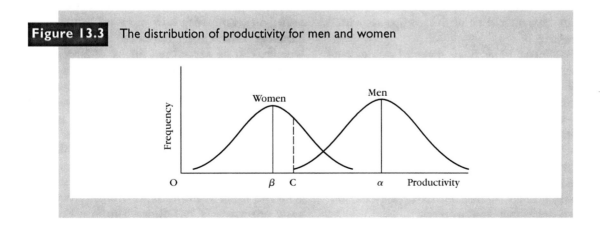

Figure 13.3   The distribution of productivity for men and women

what they do know, and that is the average level of productivity of each group. Since women have less training and work experience, their average level of productivity will be lower than men's. The two distributions show that there are variations in productivity among men and women. The fact that they overlap indicates that some women are more productive than some men. Let α be the *average* productivity of men and β the *average* productivity of women ($\alpha > \beta$).

For a man, individual productivity is equal to:

$$\alpha_i = \alpha + u_i$$

where u_i represents the differences in actual productivity above and below the average for all men.

Individual productivity for a woman is represented by:

$$\beta_i = \beta + u_i$$

The *average* level of human capital investment, and thus productivity, differs between men and women and this is reflected in the *average* earnings differential. On these assumptions, there is no discrimination, on average, against women. However, there is discrimination against *individual* women. Specifically, those women who have a productivity level to the right of the line above point C are being paid less than comparable men. It is also evident that the greater the variation in productivity within the female group, the more women will be underpaid compared with men who may be less productive. The curve showing the distribution of productivity would be wider, and, hence, there would be more overlap with the distribution curve for men. Discrimination here involves the unequal treatment of *individuals* on the basis of actual or perceived differences in the *average* characteristics of the groups to which they belong.

An additional point about potential productivity concerns the methods used by firms to try and identify which applicants are potentially the best employees. Firms use a variety of 'screening devices' when recruiting in order to establish the best potential employees. One such device is psychometric testing which many firms are now using to test applicants. However, it is possible that the very nature of these tests may be biased against women or ethnic minorities, adding further to the discrimination faced by individual workers.

Bringing selection procedures back on track

In early 1991 several ethnic minority guards at Paddington Station took British Rail to an industrial tribunal, alleging that the selection process for train drivers discriminated against applicants from ethnic minorities. In a settlement, BR agreed to work with the CRE to make the selection process fairer.

One element of this was a workshop with the Paddington guards to explore their test-taking behaviour. It became apparent that they were not, as the Americans say, test-wise. As a result, British Rail commissioned an open-learning pack which the guards could work on in their own time before retaking the test in September 1992.

The pack gave advice and tips on how to develop successful test-taking behaviour, as well as extensive practice materials to develop language proficiency. Six weeks were allowed, and the pack was supported with workshops at the beginning and at the end. The result? Five of the seven guards passed the tests and have gone forward for training.

Source: *Personnel Management*, December 1992

4.3 Empirical evidence

The neoclassical approach to discrimination produces a number of different explanations for why discrimination may exist in the labour market. Empirical analysis has tended, however, to focus not so much on testing these explanations but rather on establishing how much of an observed earnings differential between, say, men and women, can be accounted for by differences in their relative skill and education levels, their different work histories and differences in hours of work. That part of the actual differential that remains after allowing for these factors is usually attributed to labour market discrimination – it is the difference in earnings that cannot be explained by the productivity-related characteristics of the two groups. This decomposition is achieved using multiple regression analysis. The basic approach is as follows. Suppose that the earnings of men and women be determined by the following equations:

$$W_M = a_0 + a_1 E_M$$

$$W_F = b_0 + b_1 E_F$$

where W represents average earnings and E represents an education variable which determines earnings. In the first equation W_M represents the earnings of men, while E_M represents, say, the average number of 'A' levels held by men. In the second equation W_F is the average earnings of women, while E_F is the average number of 'A' levels held by women. The terms a_0 and b_0 are the intercepts of the two equations. The observed average gender earnings differential – the difference in earnings between the two groups – can then be broken down by subtracting one equation from the other:

$$(W_M - W_F) = (a_0 - b_0) + a_1 E_M - b_1 E_F + (b_1 E_M - b_1 E_M)$$

The term $(b_1 E_M - b_1 E_M)$ has been artificially added to this equation. The equation can, as a result, be re-arranged to give us the expression:

$$(W_M - W_F) = (a_0 - b_0) + b_1 (E_M - E_F) + (a_1 - b_1) E_M$$

The equation shows that the average wage differential – the difference in average earnings between men and women – is made up of three components.

The first term:

$$(a_0 - b_0)$$

is the part of the gender differential that is due to differences in earnings that take place on entry to the labour market. This will reflect differences in pre-entry human capital investments and/or pre-entry discrimination.

The second term:

$$b_1 (E_M - E_F)$$

shows the contribution that differences in productivity-related characteristics between men and women make to the gender earnings differential. In other words, it shows the effect that gender differences in the average level of education have on the average earnings differential. This component represents that part of the earnings differential that does not reflect discrimination.

The final term:

$$(a_1 - b_1) E_M$$

measures the impact that unequal treatment has on the average wage differential. This is measured by the difference between the coefficients in the two equations on the variable measuring education. These coefficients show how education affects an individual's earnings. This term measures what happens when the labour market rewards productivity-related characteristics in different ways. It is this term, therefore, that is used as a measure of discrimination – women's productivity-related characteristics are treated differently from those of men for reasons that have nothing to do with the characteristics themselves. So, for example, suppose that women with 4 'A' levels earn less than men with 4 'A' levels (assuming all other things equal). This approach says that this can only come about because of discrimination. The extent of this discrimination is captured by the amount that the woman is paid less than her male comparator, which, in a model like the one above, is reflected in a smaller coefficient on the education variable in the female earnings equation compared with the earnings equation estimated for men.

The following example provides a demonstration of how the model can be estimated. Wright and Ermisch (1991) conducted an analysis of discrimination against women in the UK using data from the 1980 *Women and Employment Survey*. A total of 2094 employed women aged between 16 and 59 were interviewed in a nationally representative sample. Alongside this survey of women, husbands of those 1868 women who were married at the time were also interviewed.

Everyone was asked, among other things, their wage per hour, their place of residence, and any educational qualifications they had. Using a statistical procedure developed in a previous study (Wright and Ermisch, 1990), a variable for the potential experience of individuals was calculated. Since, unfortunately, information on the work experience of individuals was not collected in the survey, this was estimated using other information. Variables for education were specified to model the impact on wages of individuals holding CSEs, 'O' levels, 'A' levels, degrees or any other qualifications.

Unlike the model which was introduced at the start of Section 4.2, wages in this model are assumed to depend upon more than one variable. The method of multiple regression (see Curwin and Slater, 2001) is used by Wright and Ermisch to regress wages on a number of variables. It should also be noted that in this study, the logarithms of wages is taken as the dependent variable. The wage equations for males and females are reported in Table 13.5. Note that for ease of exposition, a number of the additional variables used in the study, such as those representing the regions in which individuals reside, are not reported here.

On examining the two wage equations we need to check a number of features. First, we need to check the sign of the coefficients for each variable. In the wage equations for both males and females all the variables shown have a positive sign. This means that all these variables have a positive influence on wages. For example, the positive sign for potential experience means that potential experience is positively correlated with wages – there is a positive premium on experience. As potential experience increases, then, on average, both males and females should get a higher wage. The coefficients for all of the education variables are also positive for both genders. For example, the coefficient on the variable for males with 'O' levels is 0.203; this means that there is a premium in terms of higher wages for male workers obtaining 'O' levels compared to someone with no qualifications. The comparable value for females is 0.116.

Second, we need to check the statistical significance of the coefficients. To do this the t-statistics associated with each coefficient can be examined. A t-statistic greater than 1.96 for a particular coefficient means that we can have 95 per cent confidence in the statistical importance of that coefficient. In Table 13.5, with the exception of a t-statistic of 1.60 for 'Other' qualifications, all the reported t-statistics for males are higher than 1.96. A t-statistic of 0.58 for

'Other' qualifications and a t-statistic of 1.52 for potential experience are reported for females. Econometricians often estimate equations in which some coefficients have low t-statistics, but this reduces their confidence in the results obtained. We might also be somewhat cautious about the two wage equations in Table 13.5 since the R^2s are 0.249 and 0.224 for males and females respectively. This means that over 70 per cent of the variation in wages is not explained by these equations.

The key thing to note about these equations is that, in all cases, the coefficients for males are larger than the coefficients for females. Take, for example, the wage premium for 'A' levels. In the equation for males the premium on 'A' levels (the size of the coefficient) is 0.316, but in the equation for females it is only 0.210. The premium on potential experience shows an even wider disparity with a coefficient value of 0.246 for males and only 0.044 for females.

A formal measure of these differences in the size of coefficients is calculated by using the method of decomposition explained earlier in this section. Look back and make sure you have grasped that the differential between male and female earnings can be explained in terms of two main components:

1 the part of the earnings differential which is due to differences in productivity

2 the part of the earnings differential which is due to male and female workers of equal productivity being rewarded differently.

Table 13.5 Wage equations for males and females, Great Britain, 1980

| | Males (sample size 1868) | | Females (sample size 2094) | |
	Variable	t-statistic	Variable	t-statistic
Intercept	0.595	11.70	0.521	14.43
Potential experience	0.246	6.56	0.044	1.52
Education:				
CSE(s)	0.101	3.84	0.083	3.66
'O' level(s)	0.203	8.23	0.116	5.28
'A' level(s)	0.316	7.96	0.210	4.74
Degree	0.509	21.01	0.508	21.63
Other	0.099	1.60	0.062	0.58
R^2	0.249		0.224	

Source: Wright and Ermisch, 1991, p.516

For the wage equations reported in Table 13.5 and the additional variables not reported in the table, Wright and Ermisch derive the estimate that 11.8 per cent of the wage differential is attributed to (1) and 88.2 per cent to (2). This means that unequal rewards for the same productivity are found to be more important when explaining wage differentials than differences in productivity. It should be noted, of course, that these results are qualified by the small R^2s of their wage equations. It should also be noted that Wright and Ermisch estimate a number of other wage equations with different specifications, which give less weight to the importance of discrimination. Nevertheless, even taking these cautious notes into account, the results reported in Table 13.5 provide a revealing insight into the extent to which discrimination takes place against women in the labour market.

It is more difficult to obtain empirical evidence about racial discrimination than for sex discrimination. Substantial earnings differentials have been found to exist between white and ethnic minority workers, with the latter earning about 10 per cent less than whites (Blackaby *et al.*, 1994). A significant part of this differential reflects the occupational and industrial segregation of ethnic minorities. Indeed, while there is evidence that ethnic minorities face wage discrimination and, in particular, face lower rates of return to education and general training, it is discrimination in terms of occupational access which is found to be of most significance (McNabb and Psacharopoulos, 1981).

However, this type of analysis only compares the earnings of people in work and, as we mentioned in Section 2.2, ethnic minorities are significantly more likely to be unemployed than white workers. This raises two issues.

1 Why do workers from ethnic minorities face worse employment prospects than white workers?

2 What impact does this have on the earnings differential between the two groups?

A study of unemployment among Britain's ethnic minorities (Blackaby *et al.*, 1995) found that although employees from minority groups had less favourable characteristics (in terms of the attributes that affect the likelihood of employment, such as age, education and so on), the main reason for their different unemployment experiences was discrimination. However,

significant differences were found between the ethnic groups considered. For example, relatively high unemployment among workers of West Indian origin reflected their unfavourable characteristics rather than discrimination. In contrast, unemployment among workers of Indian descent was primarily the result of discrimination. They experienced relatively more unemployment even though their characteristics were, in fact, more favourable in terms of the likelihood of finding employment than those of white workers. Finally, the analysis indicated that discrimination against workers of Pakistani and Bangladeshi origin was greater than against those of Indian descent. The authors attribute the latter finding to the fact that workers of Pakistani and Bangladeshi descent, 'have reacted to discrimination in a different way by choosing to be more isolated and have adopted an economic structure which is more autarchic compared to other groups. Greater economic disadvantage is the consequence of this' (Blackaby *et al.*, 1995, p.25).

The same authors also examine the interaction between unemployment and wage discrimination among ethnic minority workers. They find that the limited employment prospects faced by ethnic minority workers is significantly more severe than the earnings disadvantage they face. As unemployment in Britain increased in the 1980s and early 1990s, ethnic minorities suffered disproportionately. Even ethnic minority employees with favourable productivity-related characteristics (those with better earnings potential than white workers) have become unemployed, thereby increasing the wage gap between white and non-white employees.

5 SEGMENTED LABOUR MARKETS

In recent years different explanations of how labour markets operate have been proposed by a number of economists dissatisfied with neoclassical theory in general and its explanation for labour market disadvantage in particular. Some of these alternatives simply extend neoclassical models to include the effects of various institutional factors. Others, however, have sought to develop a new theoretical approach. All reject a predominantly competitive analysis and emphasize instead the fragmented nature of labour markets and the importance of institutional and social influences upon pay and employment. A common label for these alternative approaches is segmented labour market theory. The underlying theme of these approaches is that the labour market should be viewed as a collection of parts or segments. One segment may consist of high-waged, male, white workers, for example, and another of low-waged, female, non-white workers.

The concept of a segmented labour market has been applied in a variety of ways. Analyses differ in the outcomes of interest (pay, employment stability or mobility), in the delineation of segments (by job, industry, gender, race or age) and in the methodology of investigation, whether qualitative or econometric (McNabb and Ryan, 1990). There is, however, a consensus among segmentation economists about the way the labour market can be conceptualized and about how segments function. This convergence of views is primarily encapsulated in one particular variant of the segmentation approach, the dual labour market theory.

5.1 Dual labour market theory

According to this theory, the labour market is composed of self-contained sub-markets or segments. Segmentation economists argue that ignoring the different identities of these segments and the constraints they place on the workers makes it impossible to understand the nature of labour market disadvantage. Basically, the dual approach hypothesises that a dichotomy has developed over time between a high-wage primary segment and a low-wage secondary segment. Working conditions in the primary segment are generally favourable; there is steady employment and job security, and the rules that govern the organization of employment are well defined and equitable. The characteristics of secondary employment, on the other hand, are less favourable. Work here has little job security and there are high turnover rates. There are few opportunities for training or advancement and the work tends to be menial and repetitive.

Corresponding to this duality in the characteristics of jobs is a further distinction between primary (core) and secondary (periphery) industrial sectors. In the core sectors, firms have monopoly power, production is on a large scale, extensive use is made of capital-intensive methods of production and there is strong trade union representation. These establishments operate in national and international product markets. In contrast, employment in the periphery is located in small firms that employ labour-intensive methods of production, operate in competitive local product markets and have low levels of unionization. Although they are not entirely coincidental, there is a considerable overlap between primary jobs and core industries, on the one hand, and secondary jobs and periphery industries on the other.

In contrast to the supply side and individual factors which dominate neoclassical models of the labour market, segmentation theory emphasizes demand side and institutional factors. Specifically, segmentation in the labour market arises because of the characteristics of jobs rather than differences in worker attributes, such as education and training. Secondary jobs, however, are filled largely by groups whose attachment to paid employment has traditionally been weak, notably non-whites, females and youths. Primary segment jobs, on the other hand, tend to be the preserve of 'prime age' white males.

The segmentation that exists in the labour market primarily reflects the nature of *internal labour markets* within which primary and secondary jobs are found.

Internal labour market

This is the labour market that exists within a firm. It determines how wages are set and labour is allocated within the firm.

Internal labour markets can best be thought of as the type of labour market that exists within an organization. At one extreme, the internal and external markets may be very similar: the structure of wages and the allocation of workers within the organization will be determined simply by external market conditions. In this case, the internal market is similar to what is happening outside the organization. At the other extreme are organizations (usually large employers) in which wage structures and employment policies are set apart from external labour market conditions. Such internal labour markets will often be highly structured and regulated, and have employment systems that confer significant advantages to those already employed in the organization – 'insiders' – compared to outsiders. This is because access to jobs within the firm is granted preferentially, even exclusively, to existing members of the organization via promotion along well defined 'job ladders', often on the basis of seniority rather than productivity. Outsiders, on the other hand, have access to only a limited number of low level positions.

Pay rates within structured internal labour markets do not respond to demand or supply conditions in the external market but rather to the specific requirements and needs of the organization. Imbalances that develop over time in the supply and demand of particular types of labour *vis-à-vis* the external labour market are dealt with through a variety of non-wage adjustments, including recruitment and training, job redesign and subcontracting. Crucially, emphasis is on the institutional and social nature of internal labour markets rather than on any efficiency or economic considerations that may be proposed for their emergence. In order to provide an explanation of labour market disadvantage it is clearly important to understand why some organizations adopt employment systems that are protected from external market forces and why workers from disadvantaged groups have only limited access to the favourable conditions of work they provide.

Three features of the segmented labour market theory clearly differentiate it from neoclassical labour economics.

Job rewards

Segmented labour market theory views the labour market as systematically differentiating the job rewards achieved by comparable individuals. The high pay of primary workers cannot be explained simply in terms of their higher quality of labour since many secondary workers are capable of performing well, given the opportunity to do so. The labour market is thus seen as a key ingredient in the generation of economic inequality and not a passive mirror of the inequalities which people bring to it. Wage structures are differentiated by employer characteristics rather than worker attributes.

This is not to argue that all secondary workers are as good as all primary workers. Labour quality will, in general, be higher in primary jobs. The important point, however, is that differences in labour quality across jobs is less than that in pay and the direction of causality between pay and labour quality is reversed. Wage structures are taken as given, differentiated by employer characteristics rather than worker attributes. Under such conditions high-paying employers can take their pick from the applicant queue and rationally hire labour of high

quality. The compensation, however, is only partial, with the differences in job rewards exceeding that in worker quality.

Labour quality and labour productivity must, therefore, be carefully distinguished. Productivity is an attribute of the job rather than the worker and depends upon the equipment available at the workplace and the product market served. Primary workers have higher productivity than secondary segment workers because of the jobs in which they work rather than because of who they are. Were they confined to secondary employment, with its labour-intensive techniques and unfavourable product markets, their productivity would be correspondingly lower. Worker quality, in contrast, is defined in terms of attitudes, behaviour and values.

In many instances, the skills that exist at the workplace involve learning by doing and are characterized by their informality in contrast to the more formal investment framework proposed by human capital theory. Acquisition of these skills involves being 'shown the ropes' by fellow workers and is not a distinct process within the firm. It is more a process of socialization that involves being accepted by existing workers, as well as the internalization of particular sets of norms and values, than a formal training programme. Certain groups of workers are thus segregated from better jobs because they are less acceptable socially rather than because they lack ability. Employers may also believe that particular characteristics, such as gender and race, correlate with those values and norms which characterize primary segment employment.

A similar divergence of interpretation also exists for employment stability. It is argued that the role in the family (for example youths and married females) or in society (for example inner-city, non-whites) of many secondary segment workers may mean lower intrinsic job stability than that displayed by primary workers. The segmentation approach, however, emphasizes the instability of jobs not workers. Many secondary workers, particularly married females, may be interested in and available for steady work but are denied access to it. Thus while the supply side does exert an influence, it is seen as less important than the demand side and social institutions in explaining the differentiation of outcomes in the labour market.

The role of market forces

The second distinguishing feature of the segmented labour market theory concerns the role of market forces in affecting labour outcomes. Although the impact of market forces is not denied, their role is seen to be in the product market rather than the labour market. The part played by labour market influences, particularly excess demand but also trade unions, is seen as subsidiary to such features of the product market as demand variability, employer power and production technology. Similarly, internal labour markets are thought to develop not so much as the result of the type of technology and the skills employed by the firm, as of the power relationships and control strategies that are required within the organization.

A key distinction employed in the segmentation literature is that between those jobs and workers in firms with structured internal labour markets and those in firms which are open to external labour market conditions. What, then, are the consequences of this distinction for the structure of wages? As we discussed earlier, jobs in the primary segment are generated by employers in core sectors whose ability to pay is boosted by large size, high capital intensity and high profitability, as well as a degree of monopoly power in their product markets. Secondary jobs are provided by firms located in the periphery, where firms are smaller and capital intensity is lower, and product markets are highly competitive on price. According to the theory, wages in the periphery will, as a result, be set at competitive levels which, since the secondary segment is characterized by an abundant supply of labour, will be low.

The advantages enjoyed by core firms do not, however, automatically result in favourable employment conditions for workers. Powerful employers can use their substantial resources to deny special advantages to employees through actions such as union busting and the relocation of production to low-wage, low-unionized regions. Conversely, even highly competitive product markets may yield core rather than periphery jobs if employees are well organized and able to fend off competition from home and abroad – as in parts of the coal, trucking and construction sectors in the US.

In any event, core employers need not extend primary jobs to all their employees. As a range of functions, particularly services such as cleaning and catering, is generally limited to secondary status either within the firm or in subcontractors, the contours of segmentation run through individual firms, not simply between sectors. Similarly, small firms may not offer just the low pay and job instability of the classic sweatshop, they may be the source of jobs with the high rewards offered by producers of speciality and high technology goods.

The differentiation of pay within internal labour markets is explained in neoclassical theories in terms of firm-specific skills which can only be developed through on-the-job training. The senior workers who possess such skills must be sufficiently well paid and secure in their jobs to ensure their willingness to train others. A sharper differentiation from neoclassical analysis, however, is achieved by elaborating a further factor, namely custom. The stability of work groups within internal labour markets is a favourable environment for the generation of norms or accepted ways of doing things. Employers must accommodate such norms if production is to continue without constant interruptions. Custom can be seen as both the accumulated total of norms which develop often quite informally as well as a norm in itself – the requirement that established practices be respected. Thus two groups of workers for whom the accepted practice is that they should be paid the same will often be paid the same, even if the presence of excess demand for one and excess supply for the other calls for different pay rates. Similarly, the job evaluation techniques that determine pay in many internal labour markets reward skill and responsibility in proportions which vary not with the relative availability of workers in the external market but with their relative position within the organization.

Tastes and attitudes

In contrast to the neoclassical assumptions of given tastes and attitudes, the segmented labour market theory treats both of these as endogenous. In other words, the prejudices that some groups hold against others, the attitudes that some disadvantaged groups have about work and so on are not taken as given. There are reasons why these prejudices and attitudes develop as they do and understanding these is essential in order to understand how the labour market operates to the detriment of these groups. Thus, on the one hand, unstable inner-city employment can be attributed to an adverse interaction between individual attitudes to work and to wider issues, while on the other hand, it may be attributable to the type of work which may be repetitive, menial and low paid. The experience of secondary jobs cumulatively leads to disadvantaged workers developing high quit rates and other bad work habits.

Workers employed in bad jobs become bad workers. Similarly, the confinement of married women to secondary segment jobs reflects preferences that are moulded by their subordinate positions within both family and society. Finally, our understanding of discrimination can only be achieved once we recognize that some groups in society actually benefit from it.

5.2   The roots of segmentation

Why does segmentation occur? One approach to this question focuses upon the evolution of the product markets, from the competitive and the localized to the producer dominated, and from the national to an international market. Technological change makes capital-intensive methods of production possible. Employers, however, are unwilling to undertake large-scale investment unless the product demand is stable and predictable; when demand is variable, labour-intensive techniques are preferred. A growing division is found between firms which cater for stable markets and those in unstable markets. Firms with stable product demand create primary conditions of employment, including, notably, job security. Firms which face unstable demand operate in the secondary segment of the labour market.

The contours of segmentation, defined according to stability, fluctuate depending on the state of the economy. When labour markets are tight and product markets favourable, employers seek to tie workers to the firm by expanding the number of primary jobs. However, when there is a downturn, particularly one that proves longer and deeper than anticipated, employers seek to increase the share of secondary jobs, emphasizing the virtues of functional flexibility, in terms of workers being able to undertake a number of different tasks (multi-skilling) and numerical flexibility – varying the number of workers through lay-offs and short-time working.

The theory of segmentation advanced by radical economists (for example, Rebitzer, 1993) takes a different tack and focuses upon changing systems of organization within capitalist firms. The key to segmentation, they believe, is the strategy employers use for the control and motivation of their workforces. They argue that systems of labour control that had been developed prior to the 1950s, notably the personalized discipline of 'simple control' and the impersonal machine-pacing of 'technical control', proved increasingly ineffective as some firms turned

into large corporations and worker organization became stronger and more influential. These large employers turned instead to 'bureaucratic control'. As well as providing job security and career prospects in order to win the loyalty of employees, they developed impersonal discipline and monitoring procedures. Internal labour markets emerged and with them the differences between the job rewards of primary employers and those of employers who lacked the incentive to abandon the secondary segment.

The forces which led some employers to create primary jobs thus began with the emergence of the large corporation. Simple control, the open, highly visible, direct command rule by supervisors over subordinates, proved less viable in large plants; the interdependence between workers in mass production systems made it difficult to measure the output of individual workers. Additionally, the power wielded by large firms over product markets permitted them to take a longer view of the market and its likely level of stability. As a result they could offer superior job rewards. At the same time, worker solidarity was undermined by the introduction of job ladders to achieve status differentiation between workers. The rationale for the job ladders was to motivate workers and generate commitment rather than develop skills. The internal labour markets of primary employers represents a sophisticated version of the traditional capitalist strategy of 'divide and rule'.

Within the radical approach, the position of disadvantaged groups is seen as reinforcing the tendency toward segmentation. Segmentation limits the opportunities available to women and minority groups while the forces which support discrimination also help promote segmentation. The differentiation that exists between jobs is easier to maintain when it is associated with differences in workers' characteristics rather than the job itself.

In recent years there have been a number of changes in both product and labour markets in the UK which have led some researchers to rethink the nature of segmentation. Product markets have become more competitive, not simply in terms of increased pressure for lower prices but also in terms of demands for higher quality products and more frequent changes in product specification. In order to achieve and maintain a competitive advantage in these changing conditions, some firms have adopted employment policies which seek to motivate and promote commitment from workers. At the same time, there has been considerable deregulation in the labour market in Britain. This has allowed firms to be more flexible in determining the conditions under which they employ workers and some firms have taken the opportunity to directly reduce their labour costs thereby moving towards secondary segment employment. Other organizations, however, have used the opportunity to introduce innovations such as team-working, multi-skilling and quality circles. Attempts to promote motivation and commitment are based on the philosophy of human resource management, thus moving the organizations into (or further into) the primary segment. However, the types of organizations which benefit from employment practices that foster stability and commitment are not only those traditionally found in the core sector and the simplistic dichotomies that have traditionally underpinned the segmentation approach have given way to differences that are a matter of degree rather than of kind.

The following case study examines the consequences of deregulating the UK docks industry. This is an industry that has used deregulation in the labour market as a way to directly reduce its labour costs. In the process, however, it has moved from the organized, primary sector into the secondary sector.

Docks: The payback

Docks deregulation has led to more millionaire managers, more redundancies, and most alarmingly, more accidents at work. Recent events at Tilbury demonstrate this dramatically. Chief executive John McNab has just pocketed £5 million from the sale of the port to Forth Port Authority. The authority, incidentally, paid nearly four times for the shares than the price paid to the dockers who were made redundant. Forth paid £81.01 for each share whereas at Tilbury the dockers were forced to sell their share for a maximum of £22.72.

To make the sale of the port an attractive proposition, the number of dockers – or cargo handlers as they are now called – has been slashed from nearly 800 to about 300 since deregulation five years ago. And the accident rate among those left has more than doubled. Before deregulation, the national dock accident rate was 3.1 per cent.

Since then it has risen to 7.2 per cent. And this figure probably understates the real rate because of the increased use of casual workers, who are less inclined to report accidents.

At Tilbury, the accident rate is even higher – it stands at 7.8 per cent. This figure comes from statistics compiled by the Port Safety Organisation, to which the employers are affiliated.

Stress and fatigue are obvious factors in this increase. And that is hardly surprising when more arduous conditions of employment have been introduced at Tilbury, including compulsory overtime and double shift working. A recent Health and Safety Executive information sheet on dock work fatigue stated:

'The causes of fatigue can include not only severe physical effort but also the effect of working at times that are contrary to the body's natural inclinations, e.g. at night or on some systems of shift work, intense concentration and working continuously for long periods ... This can lead to stevedores failing to ensure that they are in a safe position with the result that they are hit by a falling object or struck by a swinging load.'

John Connolly, national docks and waterways secretary of the T&G, commented on the similarities of what has happened at Medway:

'Tilbury was sold to the management and employees buy-out group for just £34 million and they have now sold it for £130 million ... The position is very similar to what happened in Medway where shares were sold to staff but were soon followed by an exercise of cutting staff numbers and reducing their terms and conditions of employment. When the men refused to accept these proposals they were made redundant and were paid just £2.50 for each of their shares. Six months later these same shares were sold for £38.50 each in a takeover.

At Tilbury the signs have been evident for two years that the port has been consistently reducing the number of people employed and imposing more arduous conditions of employment, while bringing in casual labour.

Earlier this year tenders to buy the port were asked for and the successful tender came from Forth Ports Authority who bought it as a low cost base, with a low workforce with reduced conditions of employment. This had been done on the back of casual labour and imposed conditions.

At the same time there has been a significant increase in industrial injuries in the ports generally, despite the efforts of the Port Safety Organisation.'

Tug workers are also suffering from attacks on their working conditions. 'There has been reduced manning on tugs combined with increased working hours,' said John. 'The Health and Safety Executive has stated that the longer hours, use of casual workers, and worsening conditions has led to an increase in stress and fatigue in the industry.'

Source: Pentelow, 1996

5.3   *Empirical analysis*

Three key hypotheses have been the focus of empirical evaluation of the segmented labour market theory. First, that the labour market can be represented as comprising at least two well-defined and self-contained segments. Second, that the labour market behaviour of workers and firms in each segment requires a different set of behavioural hypotheses. Finally, that there is limited mobility between the segments reflecting institutional and social barriers in the labour market rather than a lack of productive ability among lower segment workers.

The proposition that there is a clear and evident separation between a primary and secondary segment of the labour market represents a principal hypothesis of the dual approach. It is one, however, that receives only modest support in the empirical literature (see McNabb and Ryan, 1990). In general, there is little evidence of clusters of firms into core and periphery groups on the basis of the various characteristics that supposedly define the two segments. Recent work for the UK, however, has found that while firms do not cluster into distinct groups or sectors, there is clear evidence that some characteristics, in particular characteristics such as monopoly power, size of establishment and union density (variables that are associated with the core sector) are strongly correlated, and that the correlations identify features of the underlying industrial structure that are consistent with a segmented labour market approach (McNabb and Whitfield, 1996). Similarly, the employment of women and casual workers, and the use of part-time labour are also correlated, highlighting the importance of gender in identifying differences between firms. Moreover, the pattern of correlations that emerges from this work is also found to affect labour market outcomes such as the incidence of low pay, employment stability, and so on. Thus, while there is little evidence to support the notion of duality or even of identifiable segments, the industrial structure, the product market and its link with the labour market are consistent with a segmentation approach.

Much of the empirical work on the segmentation approach has, however, dealt with the unequal treatment of comparable workers between segments. Initial attempts to test this hypothesis focused upon whether incremental changes in labour quality are more highly rewarded in the primary segment than in the secondary segment. The basic empirical approach adopted to test this hypothesis involves two steps. First, a sample of workers is divided into two groups to represent the primary and secondary segments. Second, multiple regression techniques are used to estimate wage equations (similar to the ones considered earlier) so that the basic hypothesis can be tested. In general, the proposition that education is rewarded more for primary workers than for employees in the secondary segment is supported by the results of a number of studies (McNabb and Ryan, 1990). Typically, these find negligible gains in annual earnings among (variously classified) secondary segment workers from increases in years of schooling and work experience. This contrasts with the marked benefits recorded for both in the primary segment. Some contradictory evidence may, however, also be found in the literature. Several studies report that the returns to schooling and age, while lower in the secondary than in primary segment, are nevertheless economically strong and statistically significant.

The example detailed below, based on work by McNabb (1987), tests for segmentation using earnings functions estimated for core and periphery industry groups. The basis for this division is two variables typically associated with disadvantaged employment: the proportion of women employed and the proportion of employees not covered by a collective agreement. On the basis of these two variables, industries are defined as either being core or periphery.

The data in the example came from the 1975 *General Household Survey* in which male employees of ages 16 to 64 were interviewed. The key variables were:

Annual earnings	the dependent variable
Schooling	years of schooling
Experience	years of work experience
Experience^2	the experience variable squared
Weeks	weeks worked per year

The schooling and experience variables provide an indicator of the human capital of each worker. The more experience and education an individual has, the higher the quality of his labour. It should be noted that if the employee has worked for only a few weeks this will adversely affect his annual earnings, thereby giving a false picture of the relationship between these earnings and human capital. The weeks variable has been included to control for this.

Two of the wage equations reported in McNabb (1987) are shown in Table 13.6; the first is for the periphery segment, the second is for the core segment. The dependent variable is the logarithm of annual earnings. Note also that the weeks variable is expressed in logarithms (log Weeks).

For both segments of the labour market, the human capital characteristics of workers are positively correlated with earnings. In the periphery segment, for example, a coefficient of 0.67 shows the positive relationship between years of schooling and earnings.

Note that there is a negative sign on the Experience^2 term. This is a standard result in labour economics showing that beyond middle age, as workers get older, the effect of their experience has a diminishing impact on their earnings. Since a square of 50 years experience is much higher than the square of, say, 5 years experience, the squared term puts a greater weight on many years experience, thereby picking up the declining productivity of older workers.

It should be noted that all of the variables, apart from intercepts, are reported to be significant at the 1 per cent level, which means that we can have 99 per cent confidence in their statistical significance. In addition, the R^2s for both equations are just under 0.5, which means that nearly 50 per cent of the variation in wages is summarized by each regression equation.

We can now turn to a comparison of the coefficients for each equation. The dual labour market approach predicts that the return on human capital characteristics should be less in the periphery segment than in the core segment. In fact, Table 13.6 shows that the return on human capital is slightly higher in the periphery segment. The return on schooling is 0.67 in the periphery segment compared to 0.63 in the core segment. Similarly, the return on experience is 0.65 in the periphery segment and 0.55 in the core segment. In this example, however, the coefficients are, in fact, very small, and it cannot be concluded that there is any significant difference between the return on human

Table 13.6 Industry earnings functions

	Periphery segment	Core segment
Intercept	1.39	2.12
Schooling	0.67*	0.63*
Experience	0.65*	0.55*
Experience^2	−0.0009*	−0.0008*
log Weeks	1.21*	1.10*
R^2	0.4707	0.4517
Sample size	1641	3373

Note: * denotes that a coefficient is significant to the 1 per cent level or better (we can have 99 per cent confidence in its statistical significance)
Source: McNabb, 1987, p.262, Table 1

capital in the two segments. This particular evidence shows that a dual labour market does not exist for segments defined according to the proportion of women employed and the proportion of employees not covered by a collective agreement.

Evidence of segmentation can, however, be found if we look at the earnings of particular occupations. Table 13.7, again based on the analysis of the 1975 *General Household Survey* data by McNabb (1987), reports wage equations for professional and semi-skilled manual workers.

Exercise 13.1

Comparing the two wage equations in Table 13.7, examine the evidence that professional workers enjoy a higher return to their human capital than semi-skilled manual workers.

From Exercise 13.1 you can see that Table 13.7 provides some evidence for the existence of occupational segments. Workers in semi-skilled manual occupations are treated differently from professional workers. As they gain more human capital, in the form of schooling and experience, semi-skilled workers are not reimbursed, for each unit of human capital, to the same extent as professional workers. This confirms the insight of segmentation theorists, as discussed in Section 5.1, that workers are rewarded differently according to the jobs they do. Even if workers have the same human cognition characteristics, the amount

they are paid depends on the job they do. This conflicts with neoclassical theory which predicts that workers will be rewarded proportionately according to their level of human capital

The final hypothesis that has received attention in the literature concerns the alleged lack of mobility between primary and secondary segments. This issue has received some attention in recent years as longitudinal data has become available. Concerning the rate of movement between segments, studies which impose clear frontiers between primary and secondary segments have generally found rates of upward movement in excess of the low levels suggested by the descriptive dual labour literature. Moreover, a considerable proportion of this upward mobility can be associated with the possession of increased labour quality.

6 FEEDBACK EFFECTS IN THE LABOUR MARKET

I have considered two main types of labour market model. One is the neoclassical market model which is typically termed the wage competition or price–auction model. At its centre is the adjustment of prices (wages) to reconcile differences in labour supply and demand, and the high responsiveness of economic agents to the signals that are thereby given out. The second model is based on the concept of the segmented labour market. It suggests

Table 13.7 Occupational wage equations

	Professional	Semi-skilled manual
Intercept	−0.054	2.89
Schooling	0.047*	0.007
Experience	0.077*	0.034*
Experience^2	−0.011*	−0.0006*
log Weeks	1.79*	1.10*
R^2	0.556	0.500
Sample size	254	796

Note: * denotes that a coefficient is significant to the 1 per cent level or better (we can have 99 per cent confidence in its statistical significance)
Source: McNabb, 1987, p.264, Table 3

that many of the processes emphasized in the neoclassical model do not operate in reality and that distinct segments, which operate according to different rules, can be identified in the labour market. In contrast to the wage competition model, the reconciliation of supply and demand in this second model is, at best, slow. Adjustment of quantities supplied and demanded is important in addition to, rather than instead of, price adjustment, and some markets might stay in disequilibrium for long periods. Consequently, there is much scope for other factors, such as custom and practice and administrative rules, to influence adjustment other than those central to the wage competition model.

These models differ in a number of crucial respects: the importance of wage flexibility in the adjustment process, the responsiveness of economic agents to changing incentives, the importance of institutional structures in directing change. The main consequence is that some models suggest that market processes will produce equilibrium between labour supply and demand in a reasonably short period of time, whereas others do not.

The key (but not the only) difference between the models from the standpoint of intervention to improve labour market performance is the process by which markets adjust to change. Vietorisz and Harrison (1973) introduced the notion of feedback effects. For example, an increase in wages has an impact upon the labour market such that, eventually, this change feeds back to influence wages once again. In markets that resemble the neoclassical model, the feedback is negative; an increase in wages has a negative feedback effect – the initial increase in wages results in an induced fall in wages. Conversely, in markets which resemble the segmentation model, there is positive feedback: the initial increase in wages has a positive impact which reinforces the initial wage increase. (Feedback effects were discussed in Chapter 7, Section 4.2.)

The differences between the two models can be illustrated by reference to Figure 13.4, which is based on Vietorisz and Harrison (1973). It shows the effect of an increase in wages in labour markets with tendencies to either positive or negative feedback. In part (a) where there is negative feedback, increased wages lead to the adoption of capital intensive techniques. This substitution of capital for labour leads to reduced labour demand and consequently there is a fall in wages. Thus the outcome is in the opposite direction to the initial change – there is negative

feedback. Conversely, where there is positive feedback, increased wages lead to the adoption of more advanced technology, investment in higher skills, higher productivity and increased wages. In this case, the outcome is in the same direction as the initial change – there is positive feedback.

How, then, can negative feedback be generated by a neoclassical view of the labour market and positive feedback by the segmentation approach? This can be explained by looking at the market supply and demand for labour. Figure 13.5 shows an upward sloping market supply of labour curve (L_S) and a downward sloping market demand for labour curve (L_D). This market labour demand curve represents the summation of the individual long-run labour demand curves for each firm in the labour market (see Chapter 12, Section 2). For firms to adopt labour-saving innovations requires a long-run analysis in which both labour and capital can be varied.

The labour market starts at a position of initial equilibrium at A where L_1 units of labour are employed at a wage rate of W_1. Assume that this wage rate increases from W_1 to W_2.

In Figure 13.5, the initial impact of the increase in the wage is a movement from A to B. Firms cannot afford to employ the same number of workers at the higher wage rate so the amount of labour demanded is cut from L_1 to L_2. They replace workers with machines or, in the language of neoclassical economics, they substitute out of labour and into capital.

Eventually, however, this initial impact on the demand for labour is reversed. At point B in Figure 13.5 there is an excess supply of labour as there are not enough jobs to meet the amount of work which employees want to take. This means that in the labour market the wage rate will be bid down until demand and supply are in equilibrium. The wage rate falls from W_2 back to its initial W_1. Having moved from A to B, the market returns back to the initial equilibrium at C (the same point as the original point A). The initial increase in the wage rate has an induced effect which results in the eventual fall in the wage rate – there is a negative feedback from the initial increase to the eventual fall. Having substituted out of labour and into capital, the eventual reduction of the wage rate forces firms to reverse their substitution back to the more labour-intensive techniques of production.

For Vietorisz and Harrison this negative feedback scenario is decidedly neoclassical. First, the smooth substitution between labour and capital by firms is a

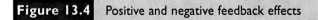

Figure 13.4 Positive and negative feedback effects

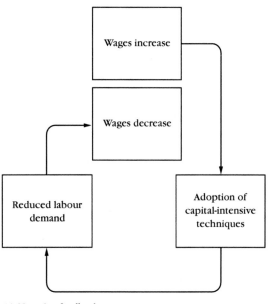

(a) Negative feedback

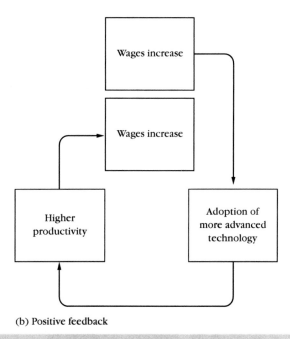

(b) Positive feedback

Source: Adapted from Vietorisz and Harrison, 1971, Figures 4 and 6, p.368

feature of the neoclassical model. Neoclassical econ-omists model this substitution by using isoquant analysis (see Chapter 12). Second, this view of the economy is static. The labour market must return to the static equilibrium at C after the wage increase. There is only one wage rate, W_1, which can clear the labour market, and hence only one equilibrium level of employment, L_1. Although there is a temporary movement from A to B and then back to C, in the long run the economy rests at the static equilibrium.

These characteristics of the neoclassical model are relaxed if the labour market is segmented. As you have seen, in a segmented labour market there are typically primary and secondary segments. Firms in primary segments employ workers at high wages and at a high level of productivity. Firms are typically large and enjoy some degree of monopoly power. Secondary segments, on the other hand, are charac-terized by low wages, low productivity and a large number of small firms.

To illustrate the positive feedback effects of a wage increase in the segmentation model, the demand and supply diagram can be further developed. In Figure 13.6, the initial wage increase is shown as before by the movement from A to B. As before, firms respond to this wage increase by adopting labour-saving tech-niques, substituting out of labour and into capital. Assume, however, that Figure 13.6 relates only to workers in the primary segment. Vietorisz and

Harrison (1973) argue that firms in the primary segment will also react to the wage increase by implementing an innovation in technology: 'When the need to shift to a more mechanized or automated technology becomes pressing for the entrepreneur, he will exchange his existing productive structure – some years out-of-date – for one that is not only less labor-intensive but also more up-to-date' (Vietorisz and Harrison, 1973, p.369). As well as adopting new labour-saving techniques, in which existing tech-nology is used to substitute capital for labour, firms also adopt labour-saving innovations in which the technology is changed. (This is discussed further in Chapter 15, Section 3.2.)

This is a decidedly non-neoclassical view of the economy. Firms do not smoothly substitute between capital and labour as new techniques are adopted. They make decisions in fits and jolts when they move to improved technologies, that raise overall productivity in the primary segment. In Figure 13.6 this means that firms make higher profits since more output is produced for each unit of labour employed. At a given wage rate, more units of labour will be employed by firms and hence the labour demand curve shifts to the right. Firms still pay workers the wage rate W_2, but they now employ L_3 workers at C. After the initial increase in wages, from A to B, the induced effect sustains this increase at C. As was shown in Figure 13.4(b), there is

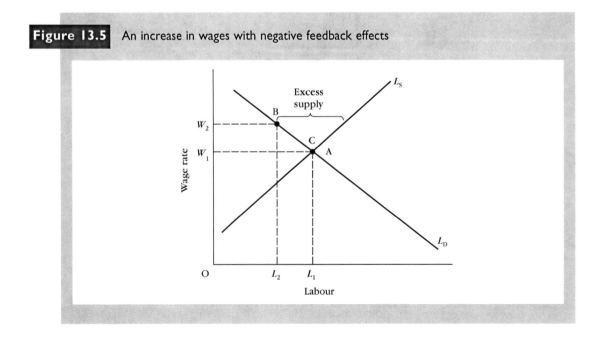

Figure 13.5 An increase in wages with negative feedback effects

positive feedback from the initial wage increase via an increase in productivity. This enables primary segment firms to continue paying this wage at the higher level of output.

This change in technology is possible because of the type of firm that operates in the primary segment. These firms are able to use their monopoly profits to invest in research and development. In response to a wage increase, they are able to change their technology to improve productivity. This contrasts with the neoclassical model in which many firms are assumed to have the same homogeneous technology which is given exogenously to all firms.

In allowing firms to change their technology in this way, the segmentation model is based on a dynamic view of the economy. Technology changes are not reversible as in the neoclassical model: a firm cannot adopt a less labour-intensive technique and then move back to its original technique. The change is historical in that a firm moves into a different stage of its development.

This dynamic change will not take place in the secondary segment. Wages in this segment will remain low, and the technology used by the small firms will remain unproductive compared with the primary segment.

Thus a crucial difference between the negative and positive feedback models lies in the way they treat the decision-making process within the firm and hence in the notion of time that they embody. The negative feedback model can be analysed within a neoclassical framework that constrains firms to varying capital and labour in response to a wage change on the basis of an unchanging isoquant map (Figure 13.5). Once wages return to their original level, the firm's labour-use decision will also revert to its previous position. The concept of time in this model is the formal, reversible concept of time found in comparative static analysis (Chapter 8).

The positive feedback model can be presented within the neoclassical framework, where a change in wage rates induces an innovation which shifts the labour demand curve to the right (as shown in Figure 13.6). But this is unsatisfactory. To understand the positive feedback process, we need to assume that firms can influence their own technology in response to wage changes. In the segmentation framework, the firms' influence over their own technology implies a more historical, non-reversible concept of time, where technological change becomes endogenous. (This view of technical change is explored in more depth in Chapter 16.)

Whether a labour market exhibits negative or positive feedback depends crucially on the behaviour of the economic agents within it. This is related to the institutional environments in which they are located

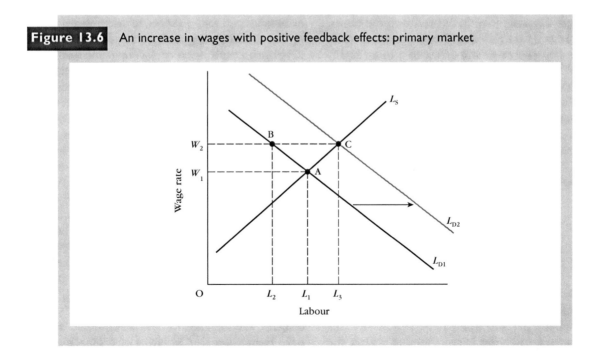

Figure 13.6   An increase in wages with positive feedback effects: primary market

and the incentives on offer. Thus the same agents faced with the same change will react differently in different institutional contexts. It is, therefore, imperative to understand how such structures vary and how they influence economic behaviour.

These two different ways of analysing the labour market each generate different recommendations for policy. In the first approach, a market which resembles the neoclassical model displays negative feedback effects. If, for example, there is an increase in the wage rate, this will initially result in reduced employment and eventually, because of excess supply of labour, the wage rate falls back to its original level. The upshot, if you take this view, is that there should be minimal intervention or regulation by institutions in the labour market. An increase in the minimum wage set by the government, for example, would increase costs to employers and have an adverse effect on employment and wages, as would the intervention of trade unions in forcing up the wage rate. Similarly, legislation which commits employers to spend money on training will also adversely increase the costs of employing workers. In this view, interfering governments and trade unions only suppress market activity.

In the second approach, a market which resembles the segmented model displays positive feedback effects. An increase in the costs to firms of employing workers may be a good thing. Say, for example, an increase in the minimum wage is imposed. Firms are then forced to substitute capital for labour. To do this they have to revamp their production processes and invest in a more highly skilled workforce. As a result, their production processes become more productive and they can afford to employ more workers at the higher wages. The increase in wages is reinforced by the positive feedback effect. Intervention by trade unions in pushing for higher wages or by government forcing firms to pay for training can all have positive feedback effects on employment and wages.

7   CONCLUSION

In this chapter we have examined a number of explanations for why labour market disadvantage, such as low pay, unemployment, and so on, falls disproportionately on certain groups within the labour market. We have shown that these explanations basically fall into two broad schools of thought, the orthodox or neoclassical approach and institutional models of labour market segmentation. The former attempts to explain the distribution of disadvantage in terms of the standard tools of economic analysis with which you are already familiar, namely human capital theory and utility maximization. Human capital theory simply says that some people earn less than others and fare worse in the labour market because they invest less in education and skills and because they show less commitment to the labour market. In a sense, we are explaining labour market inequality in terms of factors found to be closely linked to labour market outcomes.

The neoclassical approach also recognizes that discrimination exists in the labour market. Indeed, the approach adopted by orthodox economists (based upon the early work of Gary Becker) has been used to estimate how much discrimination does exist. These estimates show how much of, say, the earnings differential between men and women reflects differences in productivity-related characteristics and how much is due to discrimination. The problem that proponents of this approach face is why does discrimination take place in the first place? Or, using the concepts employed by these economists, where does the 'taste' for discrimination come from? This is especially puzzling when, as you have seen, to discriminate actually imposes a cost on the economic agents who choose to discriminate.

The alternative approach, the segmentation theory, develops an explanation of discrimination and labour market disadvantage based on the premise that the labour market comprises non-competing groups of workers, some of whom have access to 'good' jobs and others who only have access to 'bad' jobs. The allocation to the low wage, secondary segment is not based on education or training but on the self-interest of dominant groups within the labour market. This institutional approach, which seems to provide an analysis that derives more closely from the actual experiences of those who are discriminated against and marginalized in the labour market, does not perform well when subject to empirical scrutiny. Whether this reflects the nature of the tests employed to date by labour economists is an important question beyond the scope of this chapter.

Finally, using the simple demand and supply diagram, the neoclassical and institutional models have been compared in terms of feedback effects associated with changes in the wage rate. While an increase, for example, in the minimum wage set by the government would have a negative impact on employment in the neoclassical model, the institutional model predicts a positive outcome. These different approaches provide a theoretical basis for discussing and developing labour market policy.

 FURTHER READING

Rosenberg, S. (1989) 'From segmentation to flexibility', *Labour and Society*, 14, pp. 363–407: provides a useful survey of US literature on segmentation.

Rubery, J. and Wilkinson, F. (eds) (1994) *Employer Strategy and the Labour Market*, Oxford University Press, Oxford: describes recent developments in segmentation literature.

Polachek, S. and Siebert, S. (1993) *The Economics of Earning*, Cambridge University Press,

Cambridge: a good analysis of orthodox models of discrimination.

 ANSWERS TO EXERCISES

Exercise 13.1

For professional workers, the estimated coefficient for the return on schooling in Table 13.7 is 0.047, compared to the coefficient of only 0.007 for semi-skilled manual workers. Similarly, the return on experience is 0.077 for professional workers compared to only 0.034 for semi-skilled manual workers. Note that these coefficients are significant to the 1 per cent level, apart from the return for schooling for semi-skilled workers. While this latter finding limits our statistical confidence in this particular coefficient, overall we can state that, according to the data presented in Table 13.7, professional workers enjoy a higher return to their human capital than semi-skilled manual workers.

TRUST AND CONTROL: LABOUR USE WITHIN THE FIRM

Keith Whitfield

CONCEPTS AND TECHNIQUES

Worker motivation
Incentive payments systems
Trust
Idiosyncratic exchange

Implicit contracts
Efficiency wages
The worker discipline model
Partial gift exchange
Hierarchical control systems
Numerical and functional flexibility

LINKS

- This chapter applies new institutionalist methods introduced in Chapter 8 to labour use within the firm. Jobs are argued to be idiosyncratic which means that employers do not have full information about the specific skills required for each job. Employers are forced to exercise bounded rationality in the absence of full information.

- Further use is also made of the new institutionalist type material considered in Chapter 9 in relation to implicit and incomplete contracts.

- More of an 'old' institutionalist approach (Chapters 8 and 13) is used in relation to partial gift exchange where social norms are established as to what is the fair wage and the fair amount of effort expected from workers as a group.

1 INTRODUCTION

One of the most discussed phenomena of the 1990s has been the intense search for competitive advantage by business organizations. The financial press has had constant features on employers' attempts to cut costs, improve productivity or enhance product quality. A consequence has been the introduction into popular discussion of new terms such as flexible production, downsizing, and business process re-engineering. As the following commentary from *The Economist* suggests, however, there is still continuing debate about the nature and implications of these work practices.

New work order

If the second half of the eighteenth century saw the birth of the age of industry, then the second half of the twentieth is bearing witness to the dawn of a less euphonious era: the age of the high-performance workplace. The idea has already spread rapidly, from manufacturing to services and from the private sector to the public.

- The most familiar model is the Japanese one of lean production, spread by car makers like Toyota, which whittled down stocks and used teams of workers to eliminate bottlenecks, guarantee quality and institutionalize continuous improvement. The result was a dramatic fall in how long it took to make things.
- The (northern) Italians excel at 'flexible specialization' – using industrial networks to combine the virtues of small firms (timeliness, customization) with the advantages of giant organizations (economies of scale, global reach). Benetton, a clothes firm, uses its fluid relationship with a myriad of suppliers, some specializing in design, others in manufacturing, to pander to the public's whims.
- The Germans specialize in 'diversified quality' – producing short batches of luxury goods such as cars and machine tools. German managers insist that their traditional advantage in this area – their highly skilled workforce – is being reinforced by information technology, which is making it easier to combine the virtues of craft and mass production.

- The Swedish approach centres on autonomous teams of highly skilled craftsmen. In Volvo's much-discussed Uddevalla plant, for example, teams were responsible for assembling entire cars, and had direct contact with customers.
- The American approach aims to pick out the best from all of the above. It borrows quality circles from Japan, for example, and apprenticeships from Germany.

However, high-performance workplaces do not always live up to the claims made on their behalf ... Indeed, many of the trendiest workplaces are old-fashioned factories in disguise. Italian clothes firms rely on cheap part-timers in southern Italy and Turkey. Nearly half of all workers in high-tech companies in Silicon Valley are unskilled or semi-skilled. The likes of Hitachi, Toshiba, NEC and Fujitsu are even trying to apply mass-production techniques to that quintessentially brainy activity, producing computer software. The high-performance workplace may sound good in academic seminars. To many managers, struggling to control costs and beat the competition, flexible mass production may sound even better.

(Source: *Economist*, 9 April, 1994)

Whether high performance workplace or flexible mass production, the new forms of work organization have profound implications for the way firms use their workforce, and consequently, for the lives of the workers themselves. This chapter explores the economic analysis of the employment relation, and then applies it to understanding these new organizational forms. Models of the employment relation focus on the differences between labour and other factors of production (Section 2). People are not machines and employers are frequently torn, as the above quotation suggests, between ever-increasing attempts at control of the production process, and redesigning work to use the human intelligence of its workforce. Section 3 explores this choice between trust and control in conditions of imperfect information, drawing on the principal-agent model introduced in Chapter 9.

The employment relationship is often a lasting one. Even employment contracts that are in principle short term - such as hourly-paid domestic work obtained through a cleaning agency or daily labouring on construction sites by the supposedly self-employed - can disguise stable, though insecure, working relationships. The use of self-employed labourers is frequently an attempt by employers to gain the benefits of a workforce familiar with the job without the costs to the employer of formal employment. Despite a rise in short and fixed term contracts, the average length of time that workers have spent with their present employer is still 4.9 years in the UK, down from 5.8 years in 1975 (see Table 14.1). For men, furthermore, it is 6.4 years, down from 7.9 years.

As Robert McNabb notes in Chapter 13, Section 5.1, many firms do not hire and fire workers rapidly as market conditions change. Instead, they may run *internal labour markets*, with wage and career structures sharply differentiated from external labour market conditions. Such internal labour markets are still particularly marked within large manufacturing and service employers. Employees are hired only at specific entry ports, with higher level posts being filled by promotion from within. Labour economists have sought to explain these highly structured 'markets' and their associated patterns of hiring, training, promotion and payment.

This chapter draws on both new institutionalist models of contractual relations, and on broader institutionalist approaches to the firm to analyse employment relations within internal labour markets and within less structured, but still stable, employment situations. The chapter examines and compares a number of influential economic approaches to analysing the employment relation. Section 4 outlines new institutionalist models of employment contracts within the firm; it begins with Williamson's theory of idiosyncratic exchange, which draws on the transactions cost analysis introduced in Section 4 of Chapter 8. Section 5, on efficiency wages, explores alternative models that

attempt to explain why wage levels may be positively correlated with labour productivity, including a model of employment relations as a 'gift relationship'. Section 6 considers the concept of control systems, mainly developed by economists in the radical tradition of thought. The chapter then returns in Section 7 to consider further recent changes in employers' use of their workforces, including a case study of changes in work practices in the motor industry.

 2 THE DISTINCTIVE CHARACTERISTICS OF LABOUR

Much economic analysis assumes that the contribution of labour to the production process can be adequately summarized as the number of hours worked by the workforce adjusted for differences in the skills held by the workers concerned (see Chapter 12). That is, the relationship between labour input and the output of goods and services is viewed as a fixed technological relationship, described by the production function, independent of the environment within the firm where that work is performed. This working assumption is problematic, however, since it diverts attention from organizational factors that influence the relative performance of firms (Jacoby, 1990). Employers, and increasingly economists, recognize that the input made by labour depends crucially on the nature of the relationships between managers and workers, and on the structures that mediate their exchange (sometimes termed the social relations of production) (Nolan, 1983; Creedy and Whitfield, 1992).

Table 14.1 Median length of time in present employment (employees aged 16–59/64), 1975–93

	1975	1984	1989	1993
All	5.8	5.0	4.6	4.9
Men	7.9	7.1	6.4	6.4
Women	3.9	4.1	3.6	4.3

Source: Gregg and Wadsworth, 1995, p.75

Interest in employers' attempts to increase the supply of effort from their workforce has long been strong in the radical tradition of economic thought. Radical economists understand the firm in capitalist society as a structure for exploiting workers. By contrast, the expanding literature by more orthodox economists focuses on the extent to which institutional structures generate efficient use of labour within the firm, reflecting such economists' increasing attention to incentive contracts and institutional design (see Chapter 9).

There are three closely related characteristics of labour that make it distinctive in economic terms among factors of production, and that make efficient labour use a difficult issue for employers. The characteristics are:

- the productivity of labour depends greatly on the motivation of the workers concerned
- the skills of the workers cannot be separated from the owners of those skills
- the worker has discretion over how his or her work is done.

The importance of *worker motivation* for labour productivity varies greatly between jobs, but there are few jobs, if any, for which there is no such link. Furthermore, workers are not always highly motivated. The standard economic explanation of low motivation is that work creates disutility. Work is only endured to secure an income and therefore access to the utility that derives from consumption. Being rational decision makers, workers therefore attempt to minimize the imposition of work on their well-being, and try to maximize the economic return from a given level of work effort. In contrast, employers view workers as a resource which must be used as effectively as possible to secure as high a flow of outputs, and therefore income, as possible at a given level of costs. Consequently, employers have developed mechanisms for obtaining greater work effort from employees. Examples include performance-related pay (PRP) schemes, a wide variety of supervision systems, and methods designed to encourage company loyalty and commitment.

The fact that *the skills of workers* cannot be separated from their owners is of far-reaching importance for the way labour is contracted and managed. The main implication is that investment in human capital is more risky for both firms and individuals than investment in physical and financial capital. Firms investing in specific physical assets own those assets, but a firm investing in workers' specific skills has to find incentives to retain those skilled workers. Individuals who invest in financial assets can diversify their portfolios to spread risk widely but individuals who invest in their own training bear the whole risk attached to selling those skills on the market. If the skills are specific to a single firm, the employee will risk 'hold up' once trained and so may not invest (see Chapter 9 for the concept of hold up). Even investment in general skills, that is, skills that command the same price in different firms, runs the risk of a downturn in the demand for the skills or a technological change that makes the skills obsolete. Unless structures such as internal labour markets develop to mitigate these risks, there may be underinvestment in human capital by firms and individuals.

The *discretion* that most workers have over how their jobs are performed underpins the importance of motivation and offers potential for the exercise of power *vis-à-vis* the employer. Given the inherent conflicts of interests between employers and employees, the potential power struggle between the two is bound to be important in shaping the employment relationship.

The combined effect of these three distinctive characteristics of labour as a factor of production is that the relation of inputs to outputs in the production process is far from being the fixed technological relationship assumed in the models in Chapter 10. Rather, it is an elastic phenomenon, heavily dependent on the organizational structures, incentives and understandings that influence the way labour is employed. Hence workers with the same skills may produce different levels of output in different organizational environments, a phenomenon well documented in manufacturing, notably in the automotive industry (Womack, Jones and Roos, 1990).

Furthermore, the employment relationship is asymmetrical. The obligations of the employers are reasonably well-defined, involving the payment of remuneration according to criteria laid down in a contract and undertaking to provide working conditions that conform to certain rules, such as health and safety legislation. In contrast, employees' obligations are much more vague and uncertain, involving the surrender of their time to the employer and, within that time, undertaking those duties that the employer requires. This imbalance offers considerable scope for employers to increase the contribution of employees to the production process, and it is the central concern of economists studying labour use within the firm.

3   TRUST AND CONTROL

Much economic analysis of the employment relation is a variant of the principal-agent problem introduced in Chapter 9. Employers (the principals) employ workers (the agents) to use their capital to make goods or services which yield revenue, from which the firm's various stakeholders can be remunerated. Workers can use their discretion about how they undertake their work to enhance their own self-interest rather than that of their employers. Employers have incomplete information about their employees' level of effort. The employers, therefore, have to develop structures and procedures which prevent or discourage workers from acting in ways which are antithetical to the employers' own interests, or they have to provide positive incentives to employees to act as the employers require.

This section analyses, in a principal-agent framework, the employers' problem of trust and control in employment relations. Section 3.1 outlines the problem in designing an efficient incentive payments system when the firm knows a good deal about the market and production risks facing the company. Section 3.2 analyses the choice between trust and control in conditions of greater uncertainty.

3.1   The principal-agent problem and incentive payments systems

An employer's problem in devising an incentive payments system can be analysed using a model similar to the model of Japanese supplier-customer relationships discussed in Chapter 9. The analysis makes the standard neoclassical assumptions that the worker is self-interested and gets disutility from work. Her interests, therefore, conflict with those of an employer seeking high levels of effort. The worker has substantial discretion, and has hidden information about how hard she is working. We assume that the employer can measure the worker's output, but not the effort put in.

Suppose that the worker can choose between high and low levels of effort. If those levels of effort were straightforwardly associated with high and low output, there would be no problem with devising an incentive scheme. The employer would simply pay for output, say on a piece-rate basis, and the worker would choose the output that suited him or her best. However, life in a company's personnel department is rarely that simple. There are likely to be influences on a worker's output that are not under his or her control.

> **Question**
>
> Try to think of some examples of such influences, perhaps from your own experience, before reading on.

Examples of production and market risks outside the worker's control include successes and failings of the wider organization, such as problems with the timely delivery of supplies, the level of effort of other workers in the company and the effective maintenance of equipment. They also include the health of the individual worker, and his or her relations with supervisors and workmates.

If these risks are known to be substantial, it is likely to be inefficient to inflict them upon the individual worker via an incentive contract such as a piece-rate payment system. A worker is much less able to bear risk than a large company, since individual workers can do little to insure against those risks or diversify sources of income. Hence workers are likely to be risk averse, and will resist and resent a payment system that transfers all the risk to them. In these circumstances, if there are no incentive problems, efficient risk bearing requires the risk to be left with the employer, especially if the employer is large and diversified. This implies paying the employee a fixed wage, whatever the effort. However, the employee would then have no incentive to high effort, and, on the assumptions of the model, would shirk (put in low effort).

Efficient incentive contracts in these circumstances therefore trade off risk sharing and incentives. Incentive payment systems only work if the employee bears some cost of shirking, but the incentives must not transfer unreasonably large risks to the employee. What should the balance be? Suppose that the firm knows what are the expected influences on production that are outside the employees' control. The employer then has two pieces of information on which to base a payment system.

- An indicator of effort, Z. This might be, for example, output. Z must be known to be strongly influenced by effort, though it can also be affected by other influences.

- An indicator of the 'state of the world', X, that is, an indicator of influences other than effort on the firm's results. Such an indicator might be, for example, comparisons with the sales figures of competitors, the stage in the business cycle or production line downtime.

A common payments system intended to balance risk-bearing and incentives is then a compensation formula in which the wage W depends on both Z and X:

$$W = \alpha + \beta (Z + \gamma X)$$

This payments scheme combines a fixed payment, α, with a payment which varies with both output and the state of the world. The greater is α, the larger the part of income that is not influenced by effort or the state of the world. The higher is β, the more of a worker's income depends on output (related to effort but dependent also on the state of the world). The higher is γ, the greater the impact on wages of the indicator of the state of the world. For example, sales representatives are almost always paid part – often a substantial part – of their incomes through commission on sales, but commissions might have to be adjusted if the company fails to provide samples on time, or bad weather makes the roads in some areas impassable. (This kind of compensation formula is discussed in detail in Milgrom and Roberts, 1992, Chapter 7.)

Exercise 14.1

How might this principal-agent model explain why sales representatives are generally paid through a compensation formula that depends heavily on sales, while nurses are generally paid a salary?

All the principal-agent models see a firm as characterized by a large number of internal contracts. The model therefore has a close affinity with the transactions costs theories of the firm (Chapter 8), since it sees the firm's internal working relations as transactions. In the model just discussed, the contracts are both explicit and fairly complete. Although they assume asymmetric information between principal and agent, with the agent having hidden information and the capacity for hidden action, the contracts state what will occur in a wide range of expected states of the world. Firms and

employees may, however, face more uncertainty about future states of the world than this model suggests. The next section discusses the implication of such uncertainty.

3.2 Trust and the employment relation

Incentive contracting can be seen as a search for control. The principal has clear objectives and tries to design contracts that give the best chance of achieving them through the efforts of the agents. However, given asymmetric information, the employer is always at some point required to trust the worker to get on with the job. Furthermore, employers and employees generally face uncertainty. To a differing extent across workplaces, they are unable to foresee all the contingencies that may arise.

Employment contracts therefore tend to be rather vague on the activities required of the employee. While they specify remuneration carefully, and may be highly specific on issues such as confidentiality, they rarely specify the job in great detail. Indeed, even where the job is specified, the specifications may be generally ignored: this is so common that 'working to rule' is an effective form of industrial action and doing things 'by the book' indicates passive resistance. Employment contracts thus leave a good deal implicit, expecting much to be resolved through custom, practice and day-to-day goodwill. The employment relationship is therefore generally a good example of a *relational contract* (Chapter 11, Section 4.1). A central feature of such contracts is the implicit shared objective of sustaining the relationship over time.

All relational contracts involve, as Chapter 11, Section 6.3, argued, some elements of trust. Relational contracts emerge when there is scope for mutual benefit from mutual commitment. Such contracts inevitably allow for opportunistic behaviour, and work best where the parties can trust each other to resist such opportunism in their common interest.

Fox (1974) suggests that employers can respond to the need to trust their workers in one of two main ways. The first is to reduce the workers' scope for discretion, either by designing jobs which allow little scope for discretion or by developing monitoring systems that check whether the worker is shirking. This is known as the 'low trust approach'. Employers may continually redesign jobs so as to make their elements more explicit, via time-and-motion studies, for example. This can result in a tight link between output and the worker's pay through a piece-work system, ignoring the impact of the changing state of the world and raising some of the incentive problems just discussed. Another low trust strategy is to pay workers above market-clearing wages so that they fear the loss of their jobs (since this would bring a drop in income) and, therefore, are less likely to shirk (see Section 5). Which strategy employers choose depends on a variety of factors, including the nature of the product markets in which they compete and the characteristics of their workforces.

The major problem with such low trust schemes is that they minimize the contribution of workers to the process of designing jobs to increase efficiency. This effect can severely constrain productivity, since the worker typically has more knowledge of how the job is best done than someone who is supervising him or viewing his work from a distance. Moreover, developing a low trust employment relationship can emphasize the conflictual elements within the relationship and thereby exacerbate the tendency for workers to think and behave instrumentally in their own interests (Ouchi, 1980). The consequence is that a potentially positive-sum game, in which employers and employees both benefit from jointly developed productivity improvements, can easily degenerate into a zero-sum game in which each party views a gain for the other as a loss for themselves.

In order to avoid generating such a zero-sum game, employers can attempt to encourage employees to align perceptions of their interests more closely with those of the employer. The aim is not to check whether the worker is acting in the best interests of the firm but to encourage such behaviour – the 'high trust approach'. While such an approach is typically costly, involving not only high wages but also job security guarantees and a liberal supervisory system, it does have the advantage of economising on monitoring and supervision. Its aim is to attenuate the propensity of workers to behave opportunistically, and to generate shared productivity benefits. Sections 4.2 and 5.3 look more closely at the problem of sustaining high trust employment relationships.

With both the high and low trust strategies the employer is responding to the need to trust workers by attempting to influence the way in which they work. The two approaches can be seen as being at opposite ends of a continuum which has high trust at one end and close control at the other. A number of attempts

have been made to integrate trust and control concepts into an economic framework. The next section looks more closely at new institutionalist theories of the employment contract, beginning with Williamson's influential concept of idiosyncratic change.

 ## NEW INSTITUTIONALIST THEORIES OF THE EMPLOYMENT CONTRACT

4.1   *The theory of idiosyncratic exchange*

The theory of idiosyncratic exchange was developed by three US economists, Williamson, Wachter and Harris (1975), to explain why the employment relationship has become more highly structured than other exchange relationships in the economy. They argued that three key features of the employment relationship in many industries needed to be explained: the attachment of wages to jobs rather than workers: the restriction of recruitment to lower-level positions; and an emphasis on internal promotion in filling higher-level positions. The authors went on to propose that all of these features are an efficient response to what they term labour idiosyncrasy.

Their argument draws on some of the concepts that you have already studied in Chapter 8, notably Williamson's notion of opportunism and the idea of bounded rationality. Chapter 8 also introduced Williamson's argument that the number of parties involved in a repeated exchange will influence the governance structures of that exchange. Williamson *et al.* (1975) apply this transactions costs framework to the analysis of employment relations.

The authors begin by defining the concept of *job* or *task idiosyncrasy*. This phrase refers to the specific skills or knowledge that can attach to even the simplest task. Practically any job has something about it that is specific, meaning that the job is potentially done better by the experienced. The idiosyncrasy may relate to the peculiarities a machine develops as it wears, so that an experienced machine minder may know when it is going to break down. Or it may be the mutual adaptations by which groups of workers get along together, or informal working routines that lead to reduced performance when a newcomer does not grasp them. This kind of specific skill is acquired on the job, by learning-by-doing. It offers the employee a potential monopoly position in their job, which they can exploit strategically in their own self-interests and against those of the organization. For example, a worker might suggest that it takes longer to undertake a given task than is really the case.

Job idiosyncrasy co-exists with other problematic features of the employment contract. One is its incompleteness: the parties to the contract have to agree procedures for handling unforeseen and unforeseeable circumstances. Given the complexity of the employment relationship, employers and employees adopt a form of rational behaviour which responds to limited knowledge by routinized behaviour. In other words, the employment relationship displays bounded rationality (see Chapter 8). The existence of job idiosyncrasy, furthermore, means that the employment relation is characterized by small numbers exchange: the same small group of people have constantly to readjust their working relationship. Finally, job idiosyncrasy contributes to asymmetry in information, and provides scope for the strategic use of information. Williamson (1975) calls this set of information problems 'information impactedness'.

This combination of features of the employment relationship can lead to costly and mutually destructive haggling over every change in the relationship, where the parties behave opportunistically, exploiting every small advantage in their positions for their own gain. Employers, therefore, set up employment structures which aim to prevent such costly haggling. This could involve 'stick' mechanisms, such as the threat of dismissal for opportunistic behaviour, or 'carrot' mechanisms, such as welfare benefits or promotion prospects, that encourage employees to behave in a more co-operative manner.

The attachment of wages to jobs rather than to workers provides a mechanism to prevent the development of costly bargaining over every change in the nature of the tasks undertaken in every job. This is especially important where there is much on-the-job learning and adaptation. The restriction of recruitment to lower-level positions and an emphasis on internal promotion reflect both the need to develop efficient screening procedures for the filling of upper-level jobs (in which productivity depends crucially on the characteristics of the worker concerned) and the need to develop a motivation structure within the firm.

The theory of idiosyncratic exchange, like Williamson's transactions cost theory more broadly, explores employment contracting as an efficient response to market failure. Williamson *et al.* thus propose that the hierarchical structures of internal labour markets can be explained as a response to job idiosyncrasy. Such structures, they argue, detach wages from marginal products lower down the employment hierarchy, but, over time, knowledge of individuals' productivity brings higher level wages into a 'more perfect correspondence' with marginal products.

Question

How common do you think the three key characteristics identified by Williamson *et al.* of the employment relation really are within firms: attachment of wages to jobs, recruitment mainly at lower levels and high levels of internal promotion?

There are many firms where the employment relations do not fit Williamson's model. Furthermore, recent changes in employer strategies have made it even less accurate (Rubery and Wilkinson, 1994). Examples of such changes are widespread efforts to increase the link between pay and performance via profit-related pay schemes, merit awards and performance-related pay (PRP) schemes; attempts to 'enlarge' jobs via multi-skilling and employee involvement in decision making; and schemes to increase the amount of team work in production.

An unsatisfactory feature of idiosyncratic exchange models of employment is the asymmetric treatment accorded to employees and employers. It is employees alone that are deemed uniquely opportunistic, and employers operating within bounded rationality seek to attenuate this. There seems to be a pro-employer bias in the models that obscures the mutual relations and perceptions of fairness which affect how employment structures develop and are sustained (Willman, 1983). Section 4.2 discusses a rather more even-handed treatment of the two sides.

Radical critics of Williamson have argued that his approach omits the role of power in labour markets. They propose, instead, that the hierarchical nature of the employment relationship emerges not from the quest for efficiency, but because it allows one party (the employers) to dominate the other (the workers). This alternative is explored in Section 6.

4.2   Implicit contracts

As Section 3.2 noted, employment contracts are best seen as relational contracts. They are incomplete, and leave implicit large areas of the working relationship they frame. In this section I consider more carefully the content of the implicit contract between employer and employee, with particular reference to the mutual gains to be had from relational contracting.

Since employees are generally less able than employers to bear risk, a central concern of employees is the stability of jobs and wages through the economic cycle and over time. Firms, therefore, have scope for strategy. As principals, employers can offer implicit insurance to employees against job loss and decline in income in return for behaviour in line with the firm's objectives.

A common implicit contract is one in which the firm offers an implicit guarantee of rising wages over time in return for less opportunistic behaviour by employees. The prospect of rising wages can provide an incentive for employees to invest in learning specific skills, since they will not suffer 'hold up' by an opportunistic employer once skilled. However, there is nothing in such a contract to prevent employees from shirking. So the commitment on the part of the firm to raise wages over time has to be associated with some form of monitoring of work effort: it must be possible to be caught shirking and sanctioned. The rising wages over time reinforce the sanction, because they raise the cost to the employee of being sacked.

This argument would hold for any specific skill. Williamson's analysis in the previous section adds an additional perspective to this analysis, since it suggests that each job is different, risking lots of localized opportunism by employees. Hence, when Williamson and colleagues talk of wages being attached to 'jobs not workers', they mean large categories of jobs, not individual jobs. The payment structure of rising wages over time for categories of jobs seeks to reduce the scope for 'self seeking with guile' by individual

employees, since individual bargaining is ruled out by the structure of the employment contract. If this framework is associated with an internal promotions ladder that is believed to reward merit, Williamson suggests that it will elicit 'consummate' rather than 'perfunctory' co-operation by the employee.

However, there is still one puzzle about these implicit contracts. By definition, they are not written down. Okun (1981) calls them the 'invisible handshake'. So why should the worker trust the firm to fulfil its side of the bargain, as all the deals based on job guarantees and/or rising wages require?

In the new institutionalist framework that underlies the models in this section, the answer must provide a self-interested rationale for the firm's behaviour. Why should a firm not renege the moment the economy goes into a downturn, and sack most of its workers? What prevents a firm reducing wages when a recession arrives? The answers all hinge on the future costs to the firm of a loss of reputation for fair dealing with its labour force.

The basis of the implicit contract is a benefit (an economic rent) from co-operative behaviour that is shared between employer and employee. This shared benefit emerges over time, as the employee learns and her productivity increases. Expectations of fair dealing on both sides are therefore important to sustain the shared benefit. Since the firm contracts with many employees, and may well face trade unions that are in the business of documenting its behaviour, a firm can quickly lose a reputation for fair dealing with employees. Once it loses its reputation, the firm will find it much harder to make mutually beneficial implicit contracts in the future.

Exercise 14.2

You have seen a 'reputation game' before. Look back at the reputation game described in Chapter 9, Section 3.2 and Figure 9.4 in that section. Suppose that instead of consumers, there are many workers, all considering whether to work for the firm or not. An employee E_1 moves first, deciding either to work in a committed way or to shirk. The firm F then decides whether to sustain the implicit job guarantee or to renege. All subsequent employees know the outcome. Construct a 'reputation game' along these lines to show how the firm may benefit from building a reputation for commitment to its workers.

The kind of trust employees have in a firm as a result of the calculations made in a reputation game is called *calculative* trust (Chapter 11, Section 6.3). Employees calculate that committed behaviour is in the firm's interest. A slightly different approach is suggested by the game theorist, David Kreps (1986), who argues that we can think of a firm's organizational culture as a form of reputation. This is more like the notion of *institutional* trust in Chapter 11, based on the establishment of shared norms and behaviour. Corporate culture, according to Kreps, involves the shared experience of 'how things are done' in a particular organization. In long-lived relationships, such as between long-term employees and a corporation, such shared experience 'gives hierarchical inferiors an idea *ex ante* how the organization will react to circumstances as they arise; in a strong sense it gives identity to the organization' (Kreps, 1986, p.257).

Reputations are hard to build up and costly to lose. Clearly, however, in the real world, firms do risk losing them. The early 1990s recession saw large-scale layoffs by firms that had previously appeared to sustain a commitment to workers. Some of this may have been because firms had no option, but no doubt others took the opportunity to cut costs and blame the state of the economy. In such recessions, firms and unions that set great store by stability and commitment, induced by the terms of their implicit contracts, have started to negotiate those terms more explicitly. The case study below offers an example of explicit renegotiation of elements of a relational contract, with firms trying to gain greater flexibility from their workers in return for continuing commitment.

Employment contracts in the German motor industry

In 1995, industrial relations in German metal manufacturing industries were widely seen as facing a crisis. German labour costs had become the highest in the world, and German motor manufacturers risked losing big future contracts to competing countries. Several firms, including Volkswagen, were in serious trouble by 1994. IG Metall, the powerful German engineering workers' union, had been shrewdly exploiting divisions between more and less profitable employers, and the employers' federation for engineering was threatening to pull out of industry-wide collective bargaining.

However, both unions and employers were reluctant to destroy the long-term framework of industrial relations, and both sides understood the mix of high unemployment (fuelled by German reunification) and pressure for productivity gains that was making agreement difficult. The employers' main demand was for productivity gains from more flexible working. The unions' central worry was jobs. In 1995, Mr Klaus Zwickel, president of IG Metall, made clear that the union was willing to consider deals that increased labour flexibility in times of low demand.

A number of innovative agreements were made at company and plant level in the mid-1990s. The key to the agreements was an exchange of explicit job security for workers in the face of recession in return for the workforce bearing some of the costs of recession and restructuring through changed working practices and payment systems. For example, at Adam Opel, the German subsidiary of General Motors, the working week was set at 30–40 hours, rather than 35 hours a week as previously agreed, giving management the right to decide on actual working hours in response to production cycles. Volkswagen did a similar deal whereby, in times of high demand workers would work at the top end of a working week 'window', being paid for part of the time in employment 'vouchers', to be cashed-in at times when demand was low. In each case, the mix of reduced overtime payments and more employer control over scheduling was expected to reduce unit labour costs sharply. Neither firm, however, succeeded in achieving extensive Saturday working. IG Metall said a free Saturday was a 'cornerstone of our social contract ... Our whole living culture is oriented to the free weekend'. At Volkswagen, there was a bitter company-wide dispute, and working time concessions by the unions were made in return for a two year job guarantee to its existing staff.

In 1996, Mercedes Benz followed suit at plant level, with a works council agreeing to the company's right to vary daily working hours between 7.5 and 9, with two years to balance individuals' working hours accounts to an agreed average. In return, Mercedes gave guarantees of no compulsory redundancies.

Source: *Financial Times*, 28 July 1995; 13 September 1995; 23 October 1995; 13 September 1996

5 EFFICIENCY WAGES: DISCIPLINE, SUPERVISION AND COMMITMENT

Firms are frequently observed, as Section 3.2 noted, to pay wages above the minimum necessary in a given market. Furthermore, firms display a reluctance to cut wages in recessions, as Chapter 12 discussed. Why should this be so? Why do firms not hire labour by repeated spot contracts at the market-clearing wage? This section examines a class of economic models, efficiency wage models, that try to answer these questions, drawing on the concept of employment as a relationship.

The *efficiency wage hypothesis* proposes that there is a positive relationship between wages (or, more generally, worker remuneration) and worker productivity (Akerlof and Yellen, 1986; Drago and Perlman, 1989; see also *Changing Economies*, Chapter 21, Section 3). The implication is that wage/remuneration cuts could result in an increase in unit labour costs (the labour cost of each unit of output) because any reduction in costs resulting from the wage cut could be offset by a fall in productivity. Therefore firms may be unwilling to impose such cuts even where they are feasible given external labour market conditions.

Akerlof and Yellen (1986) suggest that such a link between high wages and high productivity could result from one (or more) of four sources. The first is reduced shirking by workers due to a higher cost of job loss. Any worker who is paid more than could be obtained in another job will value the current job more highly. Workers will therefore be more careful not to be caught putting in a low level of effort and dismissed. The second explanation is that the firm may experience lower turnover as a result of raising wages and may thereby be able to reduce the resources that it puts into hiring and selection. The third possible benefit is an improvement in the quality of job applicants, so that the firm needs to spend less on advertising

vacant positions or obtains a better workforce. A fourth explanation could be that the connection between higher wages and higher productivity might work via improved morale within the workforce: the workers will feel better in themselves and more inclined to do their best for their employers. We can add a fifth: in low income countries particularly, the causal mechanism may also involve the improved physical well-being of higher paid workers, who are able to afford a better standard of living.

More formal modelling of such links between wage levels and productivity have focused on two distinct causal mechanisms within the firm. The first type of models, the worker discipline models, suggest that high wages reduce the need for firms to develop close supervisory systems to attain a given level of effort. The other type of models, high commitment models, suggest that high wages yield a higher level of commitment from workers which translates into higher effort (see Sections 5.2 and 5.3).

5.1 The worker discipline model

The worker discipline model assumes that the employment contract is open-ended, in the sense that work intensity is not specified. Employers therefore need to exercise some authority over the employee. This could involve close supervision and the dismissal of employees found to be shirking. However, dismissal is only an effective strategy if it is costly to the employee. It therefore requires a wage that is set above market-clearing levels. Moreover, the higher the cost of dismissal to the employee, the more effective is the threat and the less the need for the close monitoring of the employee's activities. Wages and supervision can thus be seen as substitutes, and firms can be expected to trade one against another.

This trade-off between wages and supervision can be illustrated by drawing isocost lines and isoeffort curves for the firm. On Figure 14.1, the vertical axis shows the firm's wages bill, and the horizontal axis the cost of supervision. The diagram assumes a fixed workforce and a given unit cost of supervision. The isocost line, *IC*, links all points where the total cost of wages plus supervision for a given workforce is equal. A firm can choose between higher wages and smaller numbers of supervisors, or more intensive supervision with lower wages, while keeping total costs constant.

We could draw a set of these isocost lines for different levels of total costs. The isoeffort line *IE* links all the points where the workforce's effort level is equal. The shape of the *IE* curves is difficult to predict, but the standard worker discipline model suggests that they are likely to be convex to the origin. This convexity results from a diminishing marginal rate of substitution of supervision for wages. As the level of supervision increases, adding additional supervisors achieves smaller and smaller savings in the wages bill if the firm wishes to keep effort levels constant.

Figure 14.1 therefore shows the basic worker discipline model of efficiency wages. If the firm wishes to elicit effort level *IE* from its workforce, it will need to spend, at a minimum, the cost level represented by *IC* paying W_1 wages and providing S_1 in supervision at point A. A firm that lowers wages without raising

supervision, will elicit lower effort from its workforce, and so see its output and profits fall.

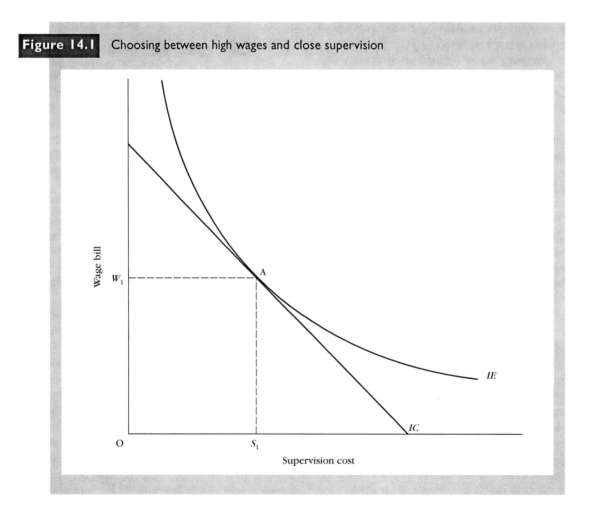

Figure 14.1 Choosing between high wages and close supervision

5.2 A model with competing incentives

The worker discipline model is based on the hypothesis of a trade-off between wage levels and intensity of supervision. Drago and Perlman (1989) suggest, however, that there may be workplaces where, on the contrary, wages and supervision are incompatible modes of obtaining effort. They argue that in a situation of low supervision and high wages, increases in wages and increases in supervision may provide *competing incentives* for effort. This implies that an increase in supervision with given wages will actually cause a *drop* in effort.

The reason for this effect, the authors suggest, is that in a range of workplaces low supervision is associated by employees with an understanding that they are trusted by their employer. High wages reinforce this presumption, but the behaviour of the workforce is not wholly instrumental. Rather, employees have a notion of a fair level of effort for their wage. In those circumstances, a rise in supervision is regarded as an indicator of a decrease in trust; the employees resent this, and turn to more instrumental patterns of behaviour. In other words, they are more inclined to shirk. These assumptions imply isoeffort curves such as those shown in Figure 14.2.

On Figure 14.2, the isoeffort curve *IE* is concave rather than convex to the origin at high wage levels, that is, between A and C. B is at the highest point of *IE* and C is the point at which *IE* turns from concave to convex. Between A and B, any increase in supervision with given wages decreases the employees' sense of being trusted, and hence reduces effort, the resentment effect greatly outweighs any increased effort that might result from extra supervision. Hence, if supervision is increased in this area of the isoeffort curve, wages must rise too to compensate: the firm is simply obtaining the same effort at higher cost. Beyond B, greater supervision at the same wage begins to elicit more effort, and an increase in supervision allows a decline in wages at the same effort level. But there is no minimum cost equilibrium mix of supervision and wages between A and C.

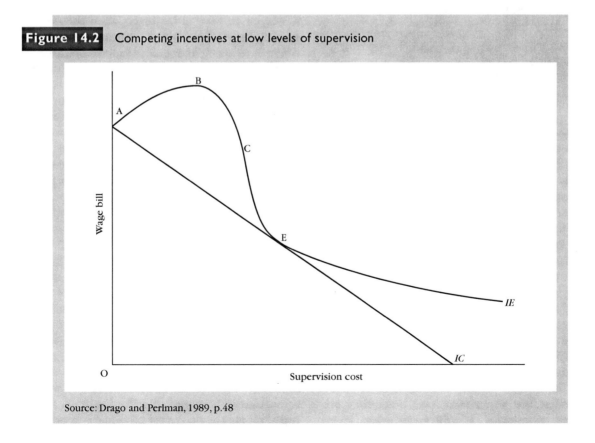

Figure 14.2   Competing incentives at low levels of supervision

Source: Drago and Perlman, 1989, p.48

To the right of C, *IE* turns convex to the origin and the worker discipline model reappears.

The firm will choose the mix of wage and supervision costs at the point at which the isocost line for its chosen level of costs touches the highest isoeffort curve attainable, or conversely, the lowest isocost is tangent to its chosen effort level. If this occurs on the convex section of the isoeffort curve, the low trust worker discipline model will be appropriate. As drawn on Figure 14.2, there are two equilibria. One occurs at A and represents a high trust equilibrium with no supervision. The other occurs at E with much lower wages and substantial amounts of supervision. Point E is a low trust equilibrium.

Drago and Perlman use their model of competing incentives to offer an explanation of segmentation and internal labour markets (Chapter 13). They suggest that concave isoeffort curves may hold in workplaces where monitoring of workers is difficult because of the nature of the workplace technology. So they suggest a general image of the economy as divided into firms with two quite different behavioural models of workplace behaviour: high wage, high trust, low supervision workplaces (primary sector) and low wage, low trust, high supervision workplaces (secondary sector).

There are, however, reasons to think that the competing incentives situation might be – at least potentially – more widespread than the above conclusions suggest. Note that, for any given effort level, the workers' welfare is always greater in the high wage/low supervision case, since they are earning more. Also, at any given wage level,

workers' welfare is likely to be higher in low supervision jobs since they are hassled less. Thus, while it may be rational for individual workers to behave opportunistically by shirking in a low supervision regime, it is irrational for workers as a whole to do so. Such behaviour could provoke the employer to increase supervision by imposing a low trust worker discipline system.

5.3 A high commitment model: partial gift exchange

Look back to the quotation in Section 1 containing examples of the 'new work order'. These suggest that the search for competitive advantage in diversified markets has led firms to explore ways of giving teams of employees much more responsibility for quality and innovation. Such responsibility implies some form of increased trust, if only because team production makes it impossible to identify the contribution of individual team members.

High commitment models of efficiency wages look for ways of overcoming the conflict expressed by the competing incentives model. If close supervision reduces the level of perceived trust and hence employees' effort levels, then the cost to employers of increasing monitoring exceeds the direct costs of employing more supervisors, because it encourages employees to become more opportunistic in making decisions on effort levels. High commitment models explore alternatives to close supervision, for example developing organizations based on shared values, where workers eschew their narrow self-interest in favour of a broader, more 'public spirited' form of behaviour. Once workers accept the high trust model as the appropriate form for employer/employee interactions, the point of equilibrium on Figure 14.2 moves leftwards to the point where the isocost line crosses the vertical axis (point A, the point of no supervision).

A major difference between the discipline and commitment versions of efficiency wage models lies in the type of factors that influence work intensity. In the former, worker opportunism is treated as exogenous to the organization. Even in the competing incentives model discussed in Section 5.2, workers preferences were unexplained. However, in the fully theorized versions of high commitment models, the degree of worker opportunism is modelled as endogenous to the organization. The behaviour of workers is assumed to reflect social or group incentives and pressures in addition to private or individualistic ones.

One of the most innovative commitment models views efficiency wages as one element of a partial gift exchange (Akerlof, 1982). Akerlof's model was innovative in that it modelled explicitly the role of norms of 'fairness' in the determination of work effort. His analysis begins from a well documented example of workers' behaviour that is hard to explain in the neoclassical worker discipline framework. The workers in the example were a group of 'cash posters': young women in a US firm entering cash payments into ledgers. The women were all paid the same wage for a day's work, and were set a minimum rate of work. Each worker's work rate was closely monitored.

A model that assumes workers are self-interested and see work solely as providing disutility would predict that no worker would work more than the minimum work rate. A model that saw the firm as focused on control would predict that if the workers did work at different rates, the firm would use the fact to drive up the minimum rate, or go over to piece-rates.

In fact, neither phenomenon occurred. All the workers exceeded the minimum rate, and occasions when an individual fell below it were met with a 'mild rebuke'. The average work rate was almost 18 per cent above the minimum required. The job had virtually no promotion opportunities, so that was not an incentive for higher than minimum effort. So how is the non-neoclassical behaviour of this group of workers to be explained? Akerlof suggests that a convincing explanation requires the concepts of group norms of a fair day's effort, and a concept of 'gift exchange' between the group of workers and the company.

A group norm depends on the notion that a group of workers develop a 'sentiment' for each other, and use each other as their reference group. So each is concerned with the welfare of others in the group as well as their own, and, furthermore, they judge their own well-being partly with reference to their position in relation to the group. So, for example, a

worker who finds she can easily exceed the group average may be concerned that a worker in the same group who finds it hard to keep up should be treated fairly if she is making a good effort. And the faster worker may be happy with her work rate if she feels it involves much the same effort for her as a slower rate does for others. The group shares a conception of a fair day's work.

Such a group of workers can be modelled, Akerlof argues, as giving a partial 'gift' to the firm. The gift element of the output is the extent to which the average output of the group exceeds the minimum specified for each worker. The firm also provides a partial gift: in the firm's case this 'gift' is the lack of pressure on the slower workers for harder work through raising standards for all towards those of the fastest workers. The 'fair wage' is the wage seen as fair to all the workers in the group, and is the return for the group concept of the fair day's work.

That chapter argues, drawing on the anthropological literature, that gifts create both relationships and obligations. Furthermore, the nature of gifts is determined by norms: only certain gifts are appropriate to given situations. These ideas seem to fit the situation described here quite well. The key idea in Akerlof's model is that the norms of gift giving are influenced by – and influence – the terms of monetary exchange. If the firm went over to piece-rates, the workers would be likely to reduce effort in reaction to the perceived unfairness of the resulting payments.

In this gift exchange, therefore, the firm is willing to pay more than the minimum necessary and to keep supervision light because, in return, they gain higher effort from employees. The employees are willing to work above the minimum required because, in return, they are treated fairly. Both sides perceive the payment system as part of a broader employment relationship, and would react negatively to a unilateral alteration in the gift exchange.

We can now compare the terms of a pure market exchange with a partial gift exchange. In a pure market exchange, the maximum price a buyer is willing to pay is the minimum at which the service is obtainable. Similarly, the minimum price the seller will accept is the maximum at which her services can be sold. In a gift exchange, buyers may be willing to pay more than the minimum, and sellers to accept less than the maximum in order to maintain the norms underlying the exchange. Thus firms may not reduce wages because this might be deemed unfair by the workers, who respond by reducing their notion of fair work effort. Similarly, workers might not allow members of their group to reduce their work effort unilaterally because this might cause their employers to reconsider what they felt was a fair wage.

This partial gift exchange model therefore generates an efficiency wage effect. It offers an explanation of efficiency wages that is rooted in norms and reference groups rather than individual self-interest and the disutility of work.

5.4 Commitment within the large Japanese firm

Akerlof notes that his model applies to primary sector firms, outside market-clearing wage systems, despite the lack of promotion opportunities for the 'cash posters'. An alternative model of high commitment work organization is Ouchi's concept of a 'clan' (Ouchi, 1980). The 'clan' model offers an alternative explanation of workers' commitment.

In Ouchi's model, workers are encouraged by both incentives and exhortation to think in terms of the effects of their actions on the organization as a whole and to pursue those with positive benefits for the organization. Ouchi's model is based on an analysis of large Japanese firms and assumes strong internal promotion systems. It has been suggested that many of the strengths of the Japanese manufacturing system stem from the fact that they developed out of a social system of clan organization and incorporated many of its incentives to transcend the personal. Key elements are the absence of status differences between workers in different functional areas, the importance ascribed to seniority in the selection of team leaders, and the implicit guarantee of continued membership for a long period.

The following case study of the internal employment organization of large Japanese firms enables us to look more closely at how commitment has been generated within them.

Employment relations in the large Japanese firm

The Japanese economist Masahiko Aoki has been analysing the internal organization of large Japanese corporations, and their relations with their suppliers, for many years. He has developed a model of what he calls a 'J' mode of co-ordination, to contrast with the 'H' model of hierarchical control often seen as characteristic of western industrial firms. I look here chiefly at the employment aspects of his 'J' model.

Aoki argues that a striking feature of large Japanese corporations is the combination of a horizontal, relatively non-hierarchical, mode of co-ordination of production activity with a hierarchical incentive system. The internal production co-ordination system, Aoki proposes, is based on knowledge sharing and mutual learning between operating units. The productivity benefits of specialization between units are to some extent sacrificed to this process of learning. Both design and operation involve feedback loops between different teams, and resources are expended on communication and information-sharing. Aoki suggests that these processes of learning, horizontal co-ordination and adaptation at the operational level are particularly effective in rapidly changing but not violently unstable markets, where the benefits of effective co-ordination of many different production steps outweigh the costs of lower levels of specialization.

Horizontal co-ordination requires a production workforce capable of integrating operating skills with autonomous problem solving capability. Assembly line problems, quality defects and production adaptations are dealt with at the operational level. This implies rotation of both blue and white collar workers between jobs, and shared understanding of the process as a whole. This requirement in turn has several implications for payment and incentive systems. It requires incentives which motivate the acquisition of wide-ranging experience. Hence, the firm's personnel department must be able to operate job rotations in the long-term interests of the firm. Aoki suggests that the solution has been found in attaching pay to rank in a hierarchy, rather than to a job. Employees compete for promotion through the ranks on merit, especially at the later stages in their working lives, and employees who do not perform face a credible threat of discharge. The promotion criteria are designed to appear as fair as possible, with multiple supervisors' reports and attention to the representations of the enterprise unions on behalf of particular employees.

Finally, Aoki proposes that this hierarchical incentive system can be seen as having an element of mutuality between workers and management, since organizational goals must adapt to the employees' voice if horizontal production co-ordination is to be elicited: 'This amounts to a set of mutual vertical commitments in which management recognizes the interests of employees and, in return, employees exert greater effort' (p.17). Employees as a group are seen implicitly by the firm as 'assets specific and internal to the firm'; as such, they can withdraw co-operation in horizontal co-ordination if not treated 'fairly' in terms of financial rewards and corporate decision making. However, Aoki argues, this mixture of horizontal co-ordination and a rank hierarchy of incentives, when functioning well, can deliver, in appropriate market circumstances, higher growth and more stable (but lower) employment than is possible in large firms using systems of hierarchical production control and market-based incentives linked to jobs.

Source: based on Aoki, 1990

Question

Before reading on, make some notes on the ways in which Aoki's analysis of the Japanese employment system in large firms could be expressed in terms of the gift relationship framework.

There are a number of features that are common to Aoki's analysis and Akerlof's model of the partial gift exchange. They include the emphasis on group norms in generating a concept of fair treatment of workers by management. Aoki's concept of 'mutual vertical commitments' is also a clear parallel with partial gift exchange, since it specifies fair treatment in terms of both promotion chances and responsiveness of management to shop floor production

initiatives in return for commitment by workers to high effort levels and the responsibility for outcomes. Thus Aoki's model can be characterized as a high commitment model of employment relations.

Analysts of the Japanese firm, such as Ouchi, have often suggested that firms' characteristic employment relations stem from Japanese cultural and social history. Aoki accepts elements of such an explanation: for example, he suggests that the high level of respect long accorded to differentiated status by age, seniority, family background and training levels may in fact make it easier than in other countries for managers to delegate real decision making to subordinates: they do not thereby lose status. However, Aoki also notes that Japanese employment systems act to prevent, by rotation, the formation of small stable work groups whose interests may oppose those of the corporation, and constantly to realign people's allegiance to the organization as a whole.

Finally, a danger in the 'gift relationship' model is that it can give an over-collaborative image of what are still hierarchical working relations. Section 6, on hierarchical control systems, presents a much less consensual image of the employment relation. As a transition to a more conflictual model, Exercise 14.5 addresses the highly competitive element of Japanese employment relationships emphasized in the case study: the competition for promotion. Such a competition can be modelled as a 'rank order tournament' (Ricketts, 1994). That is, people compete, through monitored effort and performance, for a limited number of prizes. The competitors know by how much their efforts will improve their chances of winning, and so they balance effort against the likelihood of reward.

Exercise 14.5

Here is an example of a rank order tournament. Two players compete for a single prize (promotion). They have two choices, work hard (effort) or shirk. They know that the probability that they will gain the promotion depends on two factors, their effort level and the effort level of the other person. If both work hard or both shirk, the probabilities are 0.5/0.5: the outcome will depend on the chance outcome of the monitoring process. If one shirks and the other does not, the other will certainly get promoted. Figure 14.3 shows the *probabilities* that each will get the promotion, given their choice of effort level and that of the other. Assume that the *only* pay-off each player is interested in is promotion, so each prefers a better to a worse chance of getting promoted, and each is indifferent between working hard and shirking except insofar as it influences promotion chances.

1 What is the dominant strategy of each player and why?
2 What, therefore, is the equilibrium outcome?
3 What does the game suggest about employers' benefits from rank order tournaments?
4 Could the employees do better by colluding?

6 THE THEORY OF HIERARCHICAL CONTROL SYSTEMS

Thus far, the analysis of the employment relation has seen conflicts of interest between employers and their workers as partly resolvable, through changes in the rules governing the relationships and in employers' behaviour. A much less benign perspective on this conflict has been provided by radical economists.

The starting point of most radical analyses of the labour market is the notion of conflict in capitalist economies over the rate of return on capital. Such economies are analysed as divided into two classes with conflicting interests: the owners of capital and the suppliers of labour power. The owners of capital desire a high rate of return, and this demands downward pressure on wages and upward pressure on work effort. The suppliers of labour power, however, seek an advantageous effort bargain, that is,

high wages for low work effort. By 'labour power' radical labour economists mean the capacity to perform useful work, while labour is the actual human effort expended in production. Radical labour economists such as Richard Edwards (1979) argue that employers introduce systems of control designed to maximize the translation of labour power into labour (or in non-Marxian terminology, to maximize work effort or motivation).

In these conflictual employment relations, employers possess greater power than workers. Employers can live off their financial capital if physical investment becomes too unrewarding, and can redeploy such capital to activities showing a higher return. So, if workers strike a favourable wage bargain, firms can consider locating to a lower-cost setting. In recent years the scope for this strategy has increased markedly and there has been much shifting of production from industrialized to developing countries. In addition, capital owners exercise substantial leverage over the institutions of the media and hence over public opinion about what is 'fair and reasonable'. They also influence the various organs of the state.

By contrast, workers appear to have very little power in the labour market. They have little choice but to sell their labour power at whatever rate it can fetch and they are thereby forced to surrender their capacity to work under conditions laid down largely by employers. Their major recourse against such an inequality of power is the development of collective organizations, such as trade unions, which concentrate their individually limited leverage into an organizational form that can counteract at least part of the power advantage of employers. Radical theorists therefore argue for the development of such countervailing power.

Figure 14.3 Probabilities of promotion for two players in a rank order tournament

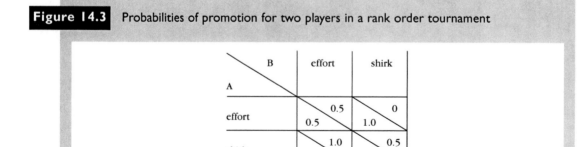

Given the fundamental conflict of interest within the employment relation just identified, in the absence of a system of control the employee would define his work role in his own interests and against those of the employer. Edwards (1979) suggests that employers develop hierarchical control systems to gain the necessary compliance, and in his book, *Contested Terrain,* he traces the historical experimentation and conflict that led to the emergence of several different types of control. He argues that mass production or 'Fordism' sought to impose on the workforce a 'technical control' system embodied in the production line itself. Employees became 'lost' within an automated system, driven by the machines and separated from each other. Firms allied this, furthermore, with welfare programmes designed to tie workers to the firms. However, this system, intended to divide the workforce, instead turned out to be fertile ground for union organizing, and led to a deeply oppositional culture between workers and management.

Firms therefore turned, Edwards argues – drawing his examples from the United States – to different forms of 'bureaucratic control', designed to overcome these patterns of resistance. The key was to 'bureaucratize' the workplace, to tie up work processes in rules and procedures. The aim was to build hierarchy into the very 'social and organizational structure of the firm', embedding it into '… job categories, work rules, promotion procedures, discipline, wage scales, definitions of responsibilities and the like. Bureaucratic control establishes the impersonal force of "company rules" or "company policy" as the basis for control' (Edwards, 1979, p.131).

The key word here is 'impersonal'. The aim of elaborated control systems is to detach control from individual commands and embed it in a system that seems semi-natural, an expression of the organization, making resistance much harder.

Edwards identifies three levels of such impersonal bureaucratic control. The first can be called *rules orientation.* Rules, such as punctuality and basic work routine, are established, and the employee is encouraged to follow them to the letter. A more sophisticated control system develops *habits of predictability and dependability.* The employee is expected to perform his tasks according to the spirit of the work rules, adapting behaviour as conditions change. This behaviour transcends the particular rules to carry out their intent. Finally, the most sophisticated level of control occurs when the employee is

encouraged to *internalize the goals and values of the enterprise* to become loyal and committed and therefore self-controlled and self-directed. These three levels of control correspond to forms of behaviour rewarded by firms' incentive systems, and Edwards notes that large US corporations in the 1970s tended to see the rules orientation as the appropriate system for the lowest paid workers, with the emphasis moving to dependability and then commitment as one moved up the organization.

This concept of control systems has been used as a building block for a different perspective on labour market segmentation. The three systems of control may have segmented the labour market into three distinct types of job. The first is composed of jobs in which a simple rules orientation is dominant, such as assembly line work. The second type of job requires predictability and dependability, and includes those involving technical skills, acquired in an apprenticeship. The third type is jobs which require self-direction, such as professional or managerial jobs. Segmentation theorists argue that workers are encouraged to develop the appropriate behavioural characteristics for each type of job, reducing the potential for workers to move between sectors, and dividing the labour market into a series of non-competing groups.

 # NEW EMPLOYER STRATEGIES TOWARDS LABOUR

Question

Look back once more at the examples of a 'new work order' at the beginning of this chapter. In what ways would these new models pose problems for the bureaucratic control systems just described?

As the examples in Section 1 illustrate, in the 1980s and 1990s many employers have acknowledged that good performance requires the adoption of new models of work organization. These new models involve, among other things, broad job definitions, flexibility in assignment of people and tasks, team working, the continuous training of employees, and employee participation in decision-making. The new models have been accorded a variety of labels, such as 'transformed systems', 'high commitment organizations' and 'flexible specialization workplaces' (Brown, Stern and Reich, 1993; Appelbaum and Batt, 1994; Osterman, 1994).

The primary motivation behind such transformations has been the perception that competitive advantage in contemporary product markets requires that more attention is paid to product quality and that firms become better positioned to respond to frequent changes in consumer demands (Piore and Sabel, 1984; Kochan, Katz and McKersie, 1986). This requires organizational systems which differ markedly from those used during the heyday of mass-production economics, which relied on the extensive division of labour and 'top-down' decision-making structures, a problem acknowledged by Robert Reich (Reich, 1984) who was President Clinton's first Secretary for Labour. The old control structures were argued to downgrade the input of workers into the production process, thereby imposing efficiency losses and a lack of adaptability to changing product market conditions.

New employer strategies try to address these inefficiencies. Commentators and researchers argue that the new practices of 'human resource management', the adoption of 'lean' production techniques (Chapter 9) and the explicit concern with how different parts of the production process interact add up to a qualitative break from the past.

Four arguments drive this thesis of a qualitative break. The first is that the new product markets and more competitive conditions generate a need for more flexibility in the use of labour. Second, good organizational performance in these conditions depends more than ever on the commitment offered by the workforce. Third, the success of employment practices and organizational structures depends fundamentally on their internal consistency. And fourth, such practices and structures must also be compatible with the overall strategy of the organization.

Flexibility is regarded as important for a variety of reasons. It allows firms to reduce the fixed costs of employment, that is, the costs which need to be borne irrespective of whether any output is produced (see, for example, the case study of the German motor industry negotiations in Section 4.2). It also makes it easier for firms to respond to continual changes in the nature of demand for their products.

Labour market flexibility can take a number of forms. Beatson (1995b) distinguishes between *flexibility on the extensive margin* and *flexibility on the intensive margin*. The former refers to the ability of employers to change the number of people they employ, and is sometimes called *numerical flexibility*. It involves the use of part-time, temporary and self-employed workers and the active use of engagements and dismissals to reduce fixed costs. Flexibility on the intensive margin refers to changes in the internal labour market: either changes in working time or in the range of tasks that employees perform, involving shift-working, employment contingent on demand (such as annual hours contracts) and flexitime (in which workers vary their working hours and leave in a flexible manner). The ability of firms to switch from task to task as circumstances dictate is often termed *functional flexibility* and is the antithesis of rigid job demarcation, in which workers are assigned to just one set of tasks. In the 1980s, a number of firms attempted to increase functional flexibility via practices such as multi-skilling (in which workers bring the skills of two or more jobs into a single job) and job rotation (in which workers are moved between jobs in different functional areas to gain all-round experience of the production process).

Numerical flexibility

The ability of firms to change readily the number of people.

Functional flexibility

The ability of firms to switch workers readily between tasks.

Such efforts have been associated with a wide range of new personnel practices, including schemes to encourage workers to take a financial interest in the firms for which they work, in-house newsletters promoting a company spirit and meetings between senior managers and employees. Managers have realized, furthermore, that, human resource innovations need to be introduced in mutually-consistent packages rather than as isolated initiatives (MacDuffie, 1995). A prime example is the need to link changes based on the greater involvement of workers in decision making to mechanisms that offer the promise of greater reward for the extra responsibility taken on as a consequence (Levine and Tyson, 1990). If introduced in isolation, employee involvement schemes can have a negative impact on organizational performance (McNabb and Whitfield, 1998).

Introducing such mutually-consistent packages of practices has been termed 'bundling' (MacDuffie, 1995). There is growing evidence that without such bundling, the introduction of innovative work practices has a negligible effect on performance (Dyer and Reeves, 1995). Furthermore, such bundles of human resource practices must match the overall strategy of the organization. For example, long-term employment commitments are unlikely to be believed by employees who work for an organization that is known to operate a ruthless cost-cutting strategy in its search for competitive advantage. In manufacturing industry, new work practices have been introduced in pursuit of 'lean production' techniques. These involve economising on costs by reducing inventory and repair buffers. Studies of lean production indicate that it needs a high degree of functional flexibility and human resource practices that encourage commitment among the workforce. Also important is a high level of training by the employers concerned (MacDuffie and Kochan, 1995).

There is thus a widespread and growing belief that understanding the nature of labour as a unique factor of production and the development of institutional structures that influence positively its contribution to the production process are of major importance. The key problem from the employers' point of view is that the new systems try to combine control of employees with what we might term employee 'entrepreneurship' (Ricketts, 1994): employees are seen as a source of innovation and adaption. The Japanese model described by Aoki is an attempt to create a set of incentives, not for passive co-operative behaviour but for Williamsons's 'consummate co-operation'. The problem is to convince employees that they will share in the rents generated by their initiatives, and to deliver on that conviction. The case study below illustrates some of the difficulties.

The search for competitive advantage in motor manufacture

By the end of the 1980s, Japanese car producers accounted for 30 per cent of the world output of cars. This reflected substantial differences in productivity and output quality between Japanese and other producers. For example, the average time to assemble a medium-sized car was 16.8 hours in Japan and 36.7 hours in Europe; the defect rate in Japan was 60 per 100 vehicles and in Europe, 105 per 100 vehicles. Furthermore, Japanese car producers were beginning to set up car plants overseas and achieve similar standards of output as at home. Non-Japanese firms therefore felt compelled to 'adapt or die'.

Influential studies of motor manufacture (such as Womack, Jones and Roos, 1990) suggested that there were four main aspects to the Japanese success. The first is total quality control. This involves a strong customer orientation, responsibility for quality at the point of production and an ethos of continuous improvement (*kaizen*). Second is just-in-time (JIT) production. This is based on the principle that all parts of a production process should produce products and components in the correct quantity just as they are needed in the next stage of production. The third element is a new method of work organization involving devolution of responsibility to the shop floor, flexibility in the assignment of workers to tasks and high levels of employee involvement in decision making. Fourth, there are paternalistic personnel practices, which include job security guarantees, selective recruitment and seniority-based payment and promotion systems.

Oliver and Wilkinson contrast the experience of two major manufacturing firms attempting to introduce such practices in the UK. The first is Nissan, which began manufacturing in Sunderland in 1986. They introduced a set of Japanese practices involving teamwork, quality and flexibility. Everyone on the production line was offered common conditions of employment and facilities such as car parking and the canteen. Production staff were divided into teams comprising a supervisor and twenty manufacturing staff. Each shift begins with a work-area meeting focusing on quality issues. At the end of the assembly process, a vehicle evaluation system was instigated which traced faults back to individual operators. Nissan set up 'hands-on' networks of suppliers (often buying shares in them) and developed a JIT system of supply. The recruitment and selection of workers was thorough and those taken on were typically young. A single union agreement was made with the Amalgamated Engineering Union prior to production commencing. Nissan also established a 'Company Council' which is a combined consultative body, the ultimate authority in grievance matters and a pay negotiation forum.

The Nissan plant at Sunderland has been highly successful, producing first the Bluebird model and latterly the Primera and Micra models. Production has expanded steadily and extra shifts have been gradually introduced into the production process. However, not all commentators feel that the Nissan experience is a 'good thing'. For example, Garrahan and Stewart (1991) have suggested that the workers' experience is one of a gruelling work pace which is reluctantly accepted in return for 'good' material benefits in an area of the country with high unemployment.

Oliver and Wilkinson draw a contrast with the experience of Ford in introducing new work practices. Unlike Nissan, Ford has a long history of production in the UK and Continental Europe. Ford's production systems have typically resembled the low trust mass-production model, with top-down hierarchical decision-making structures and an extensive division of labour. Indeed, this model of production is often termed the Fordist model. Little responsibility is devolved to the shop floor, jobs are rigidly defined and production, quality-control and maintenance workers operate in separate functional areas. This has promoted the development of multi-unionism and tensions between different types of workers.

In the late 1970s Ford attempted to move away from this system and towards the Japanese model. In particular, they introduced quality circles, with the aim of improving communication and responsibility on the shop floor. This was largely unsuccessful. The company blamed union bloody-mindedness. Others saw the problem as being the threat that quality circles posed to supervisors and middle management and the failure of the poorly educated workforce to take on the new responsibilities.

During the mid 1980s Ford attempted to introduce a more wide-ranging set of Japanese-style initiatives, including JIT, Total Quality Management, flexible assignment and team working. The result was an all-out strike of manual workers in 1988. It was settled only when the company watered down the proposals. This pattern of attempts to introduce change, resulting industrial unrest and partial retraction have continued since then. Consequently, the changes to Ford's production system have been far less than

management had hoped. The result is that the performance of Ford's UK plants lags well behind many of its European counterparts.

Source: Oliver and Wilkinson, 1993

The comparative experiences of Nissan and Ford in implementing high performance work systems suggests a number of conclusions. First, such work systems are far easier to introduce in a greenfield than in a brownfield (or existing) site. The ghosts of past conflicts tend to haunt the latter. Second, such systems are by no means accepted by all as positive. The workers at Nissan's Sunderland plant seem to accept that, on balance, they are better off than they would be elsewhere, but would they be as accepting if they lived in a region of more opportunity? And third, it seems that only well-educated and motivated workers can function effectively within such a system. This may mean that such systems are never likely to involve more than a minority of the workforce, or that countries with a well-educated workforce have a strong advantage.

8 CONCLUSION

An important component in the attainment of productive efficiency by firms is the manner in which they employ and manage their workers. Labour use within the firm is a complex process and raises a number of fundamental issues for economists. A basic divide can be seen between economists who attempt to extend the concepts of neoclassical economics to cover the special issues raised by labour utilization, and those who attempt to import concepts from other disciplinary areas concerned with the same issues. Thus those coming from the neoclassical economic position use individualistic economic concepts and take an instrumental approach to human behaviour. Others adopting a broader institutional approach use concepts such as fairness and the gift exchange, which are more common in social science disciplines outside economics. They also have a more social view of human nature, emphasizing that economic agents are heavily influenced by the environment in which they operate.

Notwithstanding these differences, the literature on the employment relation does have common themes. The theme that has structured this chapter is that employers have developed two main types of strategy for organizing their workforces. The first involves overt control over the activities of workers by their employers; whereas a second attempts to encourage and to trust workers to undertake their tasks in a manner which is congruent with their employer's interests. These strategies have different implications for the organizational form adopted by firms in the evolution of market systems.

Appelbaum, E. and Batt, R. (1994) *The New American Workplace* (ILR Press) contains a lot of information on how firms have tried to get more from their workers in recent years.

Farkas, G. and England, D. (eds) (1988) *Industries, Firms and Jobs: Sociological and Economic Approaches* (Plenum) contains a variety of perspectives on how the employment relationship can be analysed, and an informed debate between those holding different positions on the matter.

FURTHER READING

Rubery, J. and Wilkinson, F. (eds) (1994) *Employer Strategy and the Labour Market* (Oxford University Press) is a readable collection of essays closely related to this chapter.

ANSWERS TO EXERCISES

Exercise 14.1

Sales representatives' efforts cannot be observed – they are away in cars and planes much of the time – and their sales are likely to be quite closely related to

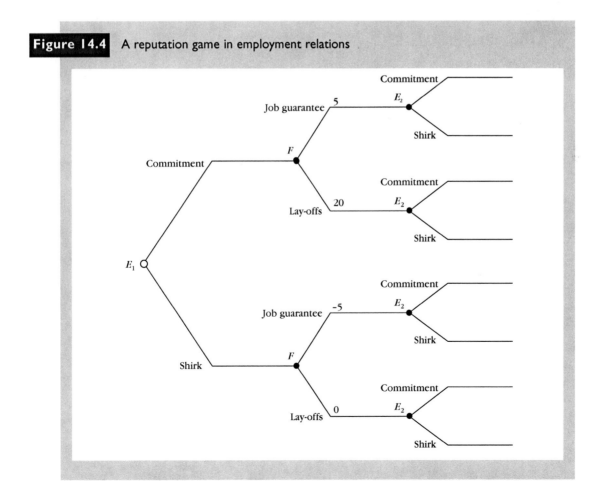

Figure 14.4   A reputation game in employment relations

effort. There is therefore a strong argument for output-related incentives. Furthermore it may be quite feasible to construct indicators of the 'state of the world': examples include the average sales of all representatives, and the weather.

Nurses' efforts may be easier to observe, since they often work in the hierarchical environment of hospitals. So supervision may influence effort, reducing the need for incentives. But more important, it is hard to construct a relevant measure of 'output', and the outcomes of nursing for the patient are deeply influenced by factors outside the nurse's control, including the nature of the illness and the quality of the surgeon's work. It would be unreasonable to expect the nurse to bear the risk associated with an incentive contract based on output or outcomes, hence such a contract would be unlikely to improve a nurse's work.

Exercise 14.2

Figure 14.4 shows a reputation game in extensive form based on Figure 9.4 in Chapter 9. We can assume, as for the washing machine consumers in Chapter 9, that employees, as a group, prefer to work committedly and retain their jobs, but that once they see one of their number cheated by a firm, they never offer commitment to that firm again. The employees only find out whether the implicit job guarantee is genuine after they have made their decision about effort levels. The employee E_1 chooses between committed work and shirking. If she shirks, we assume that the best the firm can do is break even by laying her off in the first downturn. That is, 0 is better than –5 from keeping on a worker who shirks in a recession. If E_1 works committedly, then using similar pay-offs to Figure 9.4, the firm can make a once-off profit of 20 by laying her off in a recession, or keep her on and make profits of 5. The

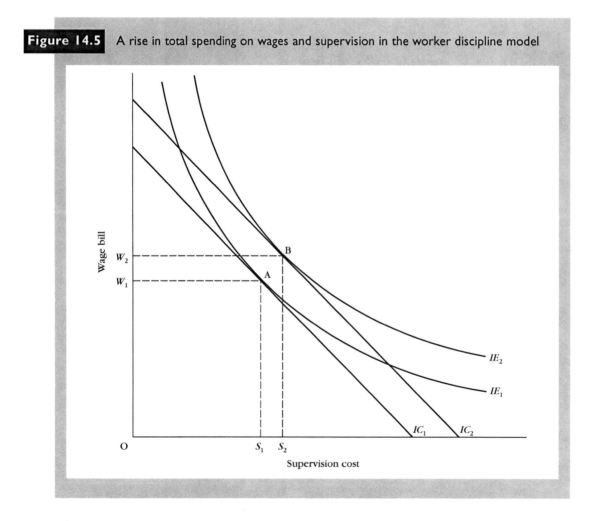

Figure 14.5 A rise in total spending on wages and supervision in the worker discipline model

next employee to move, E_2, knows what has happened to E_1. If E_1 has worked committedly and been laid off, E_2 will shirk and so will all subsequent employees. So long as the firm cares about its future as well as its present returns – so long as it does not discount its future returns too heavily – it will prefer to retain committed employees: a stream of future profits of 5 outweighs a one-off profit of 20 at discount rates below one third (see Chapter 9, Exercise 9.4).

Exercise 14.3

1 The effect of a rise in total spending by a firm on wages plus supervision is to move the firm from the previous isocost line IC_1 out to IC_2 as in Figure 14.5. The firm will gain higher effort levels from its workforce, reaching a new isoeffort curve IE_2. Both wages and supervision levels are likely to increase; the new mix of wage and supervision costs, W_2 and S_2, will depend upon the slopes of the isocost lines and isoeffort curves. The new equilibrium is point B on Figure 14.5.

2 A fall in the unit cost of supervision, with constant total cost, will pivot the isocost line to a position such as IC_2 on Figure 14.6. This will also allow the firm to reach a higher isoeffort line such as IE_2 on Figure 14.6. The change in the slope of the isocost line will also change the equilibrium ratio of wages and supervision: as drawn, the firm will choose point C, with slightly higher wages W_2, and considerably more supervision, S_2.

3 The new technical process will move each isoeffort line inwards towards the origin. Consequently, a given level of effort can be obtained by the firm at a lower cost in terms of wages and supervision. In Figure 14.7, $IE_{(t)}$ before the technical change moves to $IE_{(t+1)}$ after the

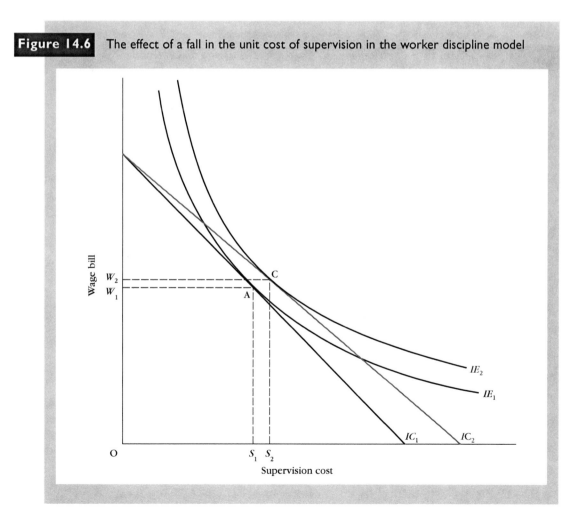

Figure 14.6 The effect of a fall in the unit cost of supervision in the worker discipline model

speed up. The equilibrium point moves from A to E on the lower isocost line IC_2, with lower wages W_2 and less supervision S_2.

Exercise 14.4

See Figure 14.8. The previous isocost line IC_1, rotates to IC_2 and the firm now has a single equilibrium effort level at F on IE_2. A is no longer an equilibrium because it produces a lower level of effort than that attainable at F.

Exercise 14.5

1 If *A* decides to make an effort, *B* will also want to work hard (a pay-off of 0.5 rather than 0). If *A*

shirks, *B* prefers to work hard for certainty of promotion (pay-off of 1.0 as compared to 0.5). So *B*'s dominant strategy is effort. The same argument can be made for *A*.

2 The equilibrium outcome (effort, effort) is in the top left quadrant.

3 Employers can use such a rank order tournament to persuade both workers to work hard, even though their chances of promotion would be exactly the same if they both shirked.

4 No, on these assumptions, colluding to shirk has no effect on the players' promotion chances. This is not a prisoners' dilemma game.

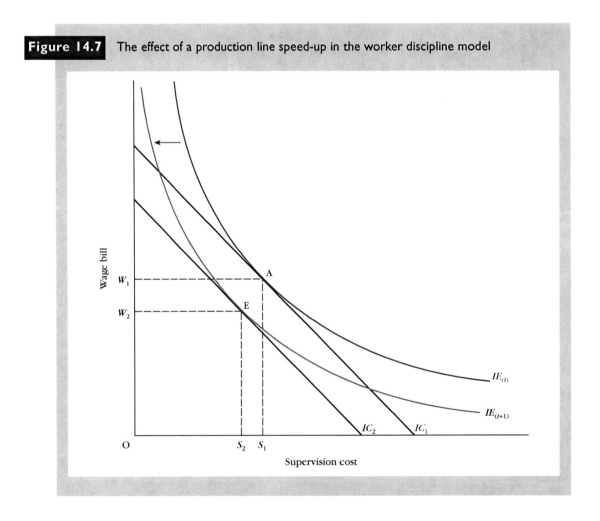

Figure 14.7   The effect of a production line speed-up in the worker discipline model

Figure 14.8   The effect of lower supervision costs on the firm's equilibrium with competing incentives

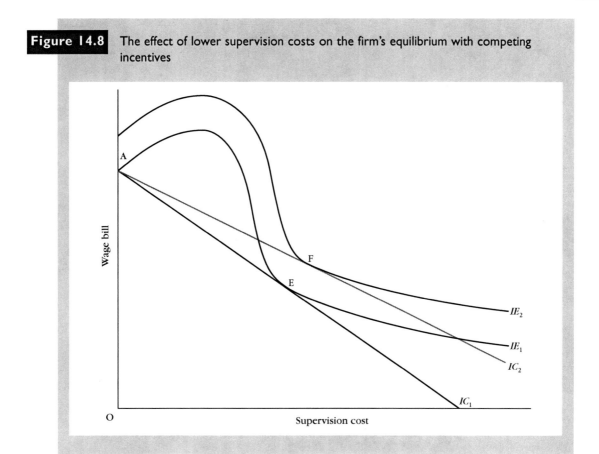

TECHNOLOGY AND FINANCE

TECHNOLOGICAL CHANGE

Roberto Simonetti

15

CONCEPTS AND TECHNIQUES

The neoclassical production function and isoquant maps

Growth accounting

Product and process innovation

Neutral, labour-saving and capital saving technological change

Total factor productivity (TFP) and the Solow 'residual'

Diminishing returns to capital intensity

Technology and competitive general equilibrium: Indivisibilities, appropriability and uncertainty

Public goods and externalities

Patents and property rights

Technology-push and demand-pull models of innovation

Trial and error, failure and tacit knowledge in the innovation process

Technology as a system and systems of innovation

Technological trajectories and paradigms

Path dependence and lock-in

LINKS

- Chapter 10 introduces the neoclassical analysis of technical change, which is based on the production function and isoquant maps, and is the basis for growth accounting in this chapter.

- Competitive general equilibrium and its welfare effects are introduced in Chapter 1 and developed further in Chapter 18. The notions of indivisibilities and the problems of appropriability and uncertainty threaten the achievements of competitive general equilibrium theory.

- Theories of the evolution of technologies are further developed in the next chapter using an evolutionary approach.

1 INTRODUCTION

The economic historian, Maddison, has pointed out that in the 180 years or so since 1820 the total world production of goods and services has increased by a factor of 60, while in the preceding 320 years it expanded by a factor of about 3 (Maddison, 1995). This astonishing performance of industrial capitalism has led many scholars to investigate the determinants of economic growth. This chapter concentrates on the analysis of just one characteristic of capitalist systems that many believe to be a key determinant of economic growth, namely technological change.

Industrial capitalism has been associated with a very rapid rate of technological change and an unprecedented number of innovations. New technology plays an important role in many aspects of our lives, from technically advanced goods, such as telecommunications systems, to food that is often processed and preserved using methods unknown few years ago; from drugs and scientific instruments, that have helped to increase life expectancy significantly in industrialized countries, to new means of transport.

In spite of broad agreement that technological change is of paramount importance for growth in industrialized countries, mainstream economic analysis has long paid inadequate attention to the determinants and effects of new technology, focusing rather on the quantitative accumulation of capital. Things started to change in the 1950s, when economists tried to measure the relative importance of various factors in explaining economic growth. In 1962, Kenneth Arrow wrote:

'It is by now incontrovertible that increases in per capita income cannot be explained simply by increases in the capital-labor ratio. Though doubtless no economist would ever have denied the role of technological change in economic growth, its overwhelming importance relative to capital formation has perhaps only been fully realized with the important studies of Abramowitz (1956) and Solow (1957).'

(ARROW, 1962A, P.155)

This statement is particularly significant given that Kenneth Arrow is one of the founders of modern general equilibrium (GE) theory, the cornerstone of neoclassical economic theory. The key economic problem addressed by the GE framework is how to achieve the optimal allocation of existing resources *given* available technological knowledge and existing consumers' tastes (Chapters 1 and 18). In the traditional formulation of GE theory, the creation of new technology is omitted, technological change is an exogenous variable, and welfare gains and losses relate to resource allocation in a static framework.

However, if our wealth is mainly dependent upon improvements in technology then economic theory that treats technical change as exogenous can say little about economic growth. Such economic theory cannot answer questions such as 'Which organization of economic activity is more conducive to innovation, and why?' Historically, we can see that industrial capitalism has been the most innovative economic system, but why? If this is not just coincidence, then why are some forms of economic organization more conducive than others to innovation? To answer this, we have to assess the performance of economic systems not so much in terms of static allocative efficiency as in terms of the dynamic efficiency of their innovative performance (Chapter 10, Section 4). The relevant question, then, becomes, 'How can we achieve fast technological progress?', rather than, 'Given the technology available, how can we allocate resources in the most efficient way?' Capitalist economies are also different across space and time, which leads us to ask whether some types of capitalism are more dynamically efficient, and whether policy makers can improve the innovative performance of their economies.

These issues are addressed in this chapter and the next. I will start, in this chapter, by analysing the sources of new technology. The next section looks at how it all started: by studying the role of technical change in the Industrial Revolution. In his book *The Unbound Prometheus* (1969), the historian David Landes investigates the origins of the Industrial Revolution and points out a number of features of technical change that can help us understand its sources and effects. Historical statistics also give us some clues to the impressive performance of industrial capitalism. Section 3 explains a method of measuring the relative contributions of capital accumulation and technological change to productivity growth using the production function (see Chapter 10) as a tool. This methodology, known as *growth accounting,* is extensively used to analyse the process of economic growth at the country level.

However, growth accounting analysis does not investigate the sources of technical change. So in Section 4, I explore the implications of conceiving of technology as information, and explore some of the ways in which the production of information differs from that of other goods. Then Section 5 introduces two linear models of innovation: the 'technology-push' model, which has informed the traditional approach to science and technology policy, and an alternative 'demand-pull' model.

In Section 6 I review the history of the steam engine, in order to identify some qualitative aspects of the innovation process missed by such linear models and by the quantitative analysis in Section 3. This case study is used for two reasons. Historically the steam engine revolutionized industrial production in the nineteenth century, and from its history we can understand a great deal about the innovation process more generally.

Section 7 turns to recent work that acknowledges a more complex relationship between economic activity and technological change than that described by the linear models of Section 5. This section argues that an understanding of the sources of technological change requires a systems approach that takes account of the process of learning associated with economic activity and the institutional environment. This economic approach is then developed more fully in Chapter 16.

2 TECHNOLOGICAL CHANGE IN THE INDUSTRIAL REVOLUTION

2.1 *Unbound Prometheus*

In *The Unbound Prometheus*, the historian David Landes explores the role of technological change in Western European industrialization, starting from the Industrial Revolution. Landes sees technology as embedded in a country's social and economic structure. The economy, society and technology co-evolve with each sphere constraining and enabling the others. Landes' emphasis, however, is on technology:

'The heart of the Industrial Revolution was an interrelated succession of technological changes. The material advance took place in three areas: (1) there was a substitution of mechanical devices for human skills;

(2) inanimate power – in particular, steam – took the place of human and animal strength; (3) there was a marked improvement in the getting and working of raw materials, especially in what are now known as the metallurgical and chemical industries.'

(LANDES, 1969, P.I)

It was the diffusion of machines throughout the economy, rather than their initial introduction, that made the Industrial Revolution. Diffusion can take some time from the initial introduction of the innovation, and it occurs through new investment, in which old capital goods are replaced with new. The diffusion of machines particularly in cotton manufacturing provoked an unprecedented increase in production in Britain, which was also associated with dramatic quality improvements.

The advances in cotton technology had two main characteristics that are common to virtually all types of innovation. First, innovations: '… came in a sequence of challenge and response, in which the speed-up of one stage of the manufacturing process placed a heavy strain on the factors of production of one or more other stages and called forth innovations to correct the imbalance' (p.84). When innovations are introduced in particular stages of a production process, they often create bottlenecks and new opportunities elsewhere. Innovative efforts, therefore, are directed towards overcoming the bottlenecks and exploiting the new opportunities.

Second: '… the many small gains were just as important as the more spectacular initial advances. None of the inventions came to industry in full-blown perfection. Aside from the trial and error of creation, there were innumerable adjustments and improvements […] before these primitive contrivances would work commercially' (p.87).

The incremental and interrelated nature of technological advance, furthermore, crosses industry boundaries. Technological advance in certain industries plays a particularly important role in improvements in the whole economy. Innovations that made it possible to exploit the energy provided by inanimate power, especially the introduction of the steam engine, were an essential ingredient of the whole Industrial Revolution. And other industries, besides energy, have pervasive effects on the whole economy.

Question

Can you think of examples of innovation in one economic activity that have repercussions on the whole economy and society?

One good example is the light bulb. Another recent and dramatic example is the microprocessor, which has revolutionized the way in which many goods are produced. Microprocessors are used in a vast range of goods, including aeroplanes, machine tools and telephone exchanges.

At the time of the Industrial Revolution, chemical innovations played a very important role in industrialization by facilitating improvements in many industries, such as textiles, soap and glass. Even more central to the story is the production of metal, since, '... the growing supply of ever-cheaper metal did facilitate enormously the mechanization of other industries, the shift from water to steam power, and, eventually, the transformation of the means of transportation' (*ibid.*, p.89). Figure 15.1 shows the dramatic growth of iron production.

An important factor in the production of iron was the quality of coal used to heat the raw metal. Improvements in iron production and the growth in the scale of the furnaces meant that the demand for coal, especially more efficient types of coal such as coke, grew very fast. The large demand for coal stimulated the growth of mining: 'The more coal man used, the deeper he dug; until, by the end of the seventeenth century, the pits in many areas had penetrated beneath the water table and flooding threatened to put an end to further extraction. (The same difficulties were beginning to afflict the tin, lead and copper mines of Cornwall.) Ingenious systems were devised to lead off the water, when possible, or to pump or raise it out of the pits by animal power. But the task was fast getting out of hand: in one colliery in Warwickshire, five hundred horses were employed to hoist the water, bucket by bucket' (*ibid.*, p.96).

There was an apparent need for a machine that could solve the problem in a more efficient and less expensive way. Many people tried to use steam power, and already at the beginning of the eighteenth century some rudimentary and inefficient engines

Figure 15.1 Pig-iron output of Great Britain, 1740–1860 (long tons)

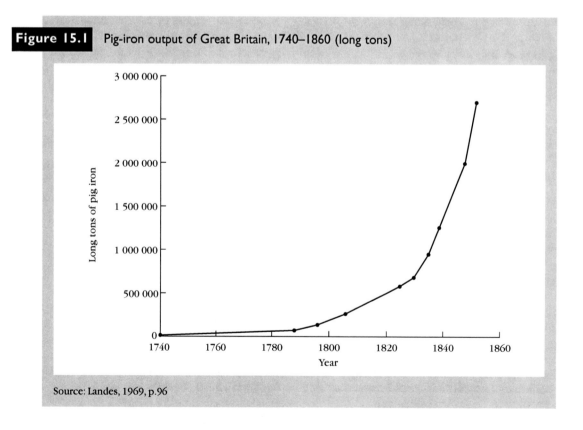

Source: Landes, 1969, p.96

were found in mining. The real step forward, however, happened with the steam engines introduced by Watt and Boulton at the end of the eighteenth century (see Section 6).

Although Landes emphasizes technical change, he does not quantify its impact on economic growth. The growth of output is not all due to the introduction of innovations. So, how can we quantify the relative importance of capital accumulation, population and therefore labour-force growth, and technical change for economic growth?

3 THE PRODUCTION FUNCTION, TECHNOLOGICAL CHANGE AND ECONOMIC GROWTH

3.1 The neoclassical approach: the production function

This section will use the neoclassical production function, which you met in Chapter 10, to measure the contribution of technical change to economic growth. The use of the production function in this way was pioneered by the US economist Robert Solow (1957) in a famous article that redirected the attention of the economics profession towards the importance of technological change.

Solow's study was an empirical investigation of the determinants of economic growth in the USA from 1909 to 1949. He set out to measure the relative importance of capital accumulation and technological change to economic growth by a method known as 'growth accounting'. He used a production function to represent the state of technology at each point in time and estimated the aggregate production function *for the whole economy* from 1909 to 1949. The aggregate production function takes the same form as a production function for a single firm, with the difference that the output produced and the capital and labour employed refer to the whole economy.

Such an exercise immediately raises serious theoretical and methodological questions. Is it legitimate to add up the whole output of the nation into a single output total (Solow used the Gross National Product)? And what about the lack of homogeneity of the inputs? Even within a firm the labour force can be very heterogeneous; this is even more true for the

economy as a whole. The same applies to capital, which can be qualitatively different across industries, and even within the same industry. Solow was well aware of this issue, but he thought that '...one can at least hope that the aggregate analysis gives some notion of the way a detailed analysis would lead' (Solow, 1957, p.312).

Section 3.3 explains how he obtained his estimates. If we want to understand his methodology, however, we have to consider first how we can use the production function to study technical change.

3.2 Process innovation and the production function

Process and product innovation

So, how is technological change represented in neoclassical economics? In neoclassical theory the technology available to a firm can be represented by a production function. Technological *change* can then be defined as a change in the production function (Chapter 10, Sections 2 and 4.2).

Within this framework, technological change can be represented in two ways, depending on whether the innovation is a new product or a new process of production. *Product innovation* is equivalent to the creation of a new good represented by a completely new production function. *Process innovation*, however, is represented by a change in the relationship between quantities of inputs and output in an existing production function; after a process innovation is adopted the firm will need fewer inputs to produce the same output, or will be able to produce more output with the same quantity of inputs (assuming that a new process of production will be adopted by a firm only if it is more efficient than the existing one).

> **Product innovation**
>
> The introduction of a new good or service.

> **Process innovation**
>
> The introduction of a new way of producing an existing good or service.

Thus, process innovation allows existing goods to be produced with fewer inputs while product innovation increases the number of goods available in the economy. Historically, neoclassical economists have focused on process innovations: on measuring gains in productivity they bring about and their effects on the distribution of income between capital and labour.

Neutral and biased process innovation

The general expression for a production function, introduced in Chapter 10, Section 2.3, is:

$$Q = f(L, K)$$

One way discussed in that section to represent the production function is by an isoquant map.

Question

What does an isoquant represent?

Each isoquant connects the different combinations of capital and labour that a firm can use at a given point in time to produce a given quantity of a good but no more than that quantity (Chapter 10, Section 2.1). In the case of smooth but less than perfect substitutability between factors, the shape of the isoquants is convex (Chapter 10, Section 2.2, Figure 10.3).

Process innovation can be represented on such an isoquant map as a shift of the isoquants towards the origin (Chapter 10, Section 4.2, Figures 10.17 and 10.18). Figure 15.2 shows such a shift for a single isoquant, showing the factor combinations that can produce an output level of 10 000 before and after a process innovation. At time t, before the innovation, L_1 units of labour and K_1 units of capital are needed. At time $t + 1$, after the process innovation, only L_2 units of labour and K_2 units of capital are needed to produce the same output. On Figure 15.2, after technological change, the firm, using the same technique A, can produce the same output with less labour and capital, saving $L_1 - L_2$ labour and $K_1 - K_2$ capital. (In Chapter 10, Section 2.1, a firm's technique is defined by its capital/labour ratio.)

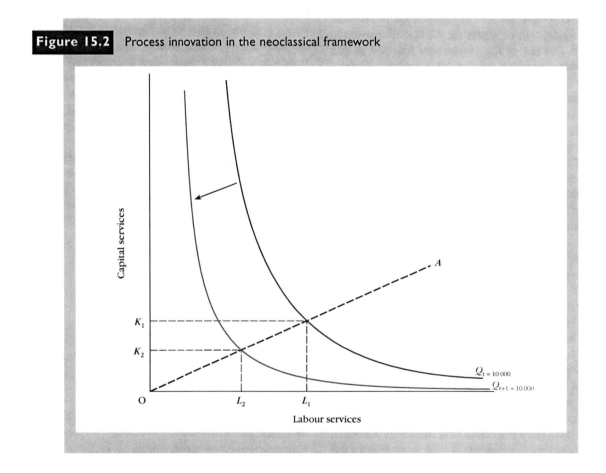

Figure 15.2 Process innovation in the neoclassical framework

It is, however, by no means certain that the firm will use the same technique before and after the process innovation. As Chapter 10, Section 4.2 showed, the firm's choice of technique after a technological change depends on the shape of the new production function (the shifted isoquant map), and on the factor price ratio, that is, on the slope of the isocost line. If we assume that factor prices do not change (therefore isocost lines are parallel, as in Figure 15.3) and the firm produces the same output as before, then we can classify process innovations into capital-saving, labour-saving and neutral technological change according to the firm's choice of technique after the innovation.

Techniques of production in the neoclassical framework can be defined as more or less capital-intensive. The higher is the K/L ratio, the more capital-intensive the technique (Chapter 10, Section 2.1). So a labour-saving innovation will imply that the firm will choose a more capital-intensive technique for a given factor price ratio after the innovation; conversely a capital-saving innovation will lead to a choice of a more labour-intensive technique.

Exercise 15.1

Consider Figure 15.3. Is the process innovation illustrated by the shift of the isoquant a capital-saving, labour-saving or neutral technical change? Look back at Chapter 10, Section 4.2 for help with this exercise.

Exercise 15.2

In Figure 15.3, the absolute quantities employed of both capital and labour diminish after the innovation. Draw a diagram, based on Figure 15.3, showing a case where the use of capital actually increases, while labour use falls, after a technological change.

One can imagine an example of a shift such as that in Exercise 15.2, where mechanization replaces large amounts of labour but requires a sharp increase in expenditure on capital. Mechanization of craft-style production will generally be 'capital-increasing' in this way.

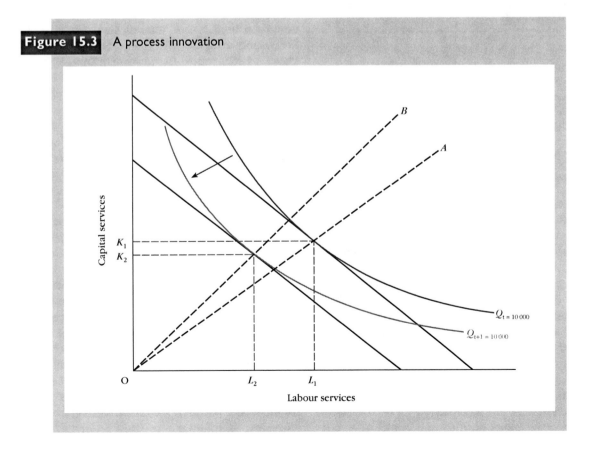

Figure 15.3 A process innovation

Suppose we now remove the assumption that the output is fixed. How then does the firm decide how much to produce after a process innovation?

The firm will have to decide on its profit-maximizing output. Since costs have fallen (the firm can produce the same output on an isocost line closer to the origin), the firm is making higher profits at the same price, and is likely to find it profitable to expand output. However, suppose that the other firms imitate the innovation? If the firms are operating in a perfectly competitive market, the market supply curve will shift rightwards, and the market price will fall. The innovating firm will then find that its profit-maximizing output falls back again. Note that in this neoclassical framework, where the product does not change, the benefits of the process innovation to the *consumer* emerge only when the innovation diffuses through the industry and the market price is pushed down as a result.

Reflection

The analysis in the last paragraph of the feedback through the market of a fall in costs associated with technological change is rather similar to the analysis of the response of firms to a fall in the price of labour in Chapter 12. Look back now at Chapter 12, Section 2, and compare the two arguments.

3.3 Solow's analysis of economic growth

Section 3.2 suggests that analysing technical change should not be too difficult. If we could draw the isoquant map, then using data on the prices of labour and capital we would be able to draw isocost lines to assess the effect of innovations. Unfortunately, statistics such as firms' accounts don't tell us the shape of the isoquants. Each isoquant identifies all efficient available combinations of labour and capital that yield a certain quantity of output, but *only one* combination of capital and labour is actually chosen by the firm at prevailing prices. Therefore, only one point on the diagram is recorded in the statistics, not the whole isoquant. The combinations that have not been chosen are not recorded. So we do not know where other points on the same isoquant lie, nor

about the location of other isoquants that correspond to different levels of output. If we cannot draw any isoquants, we do not know whether or not the isoquant map has moved over time. Things are further complicated if we remove the usual assumption that all firms are technically efficient and therefore are operating *on* an isoquant, a problem we return to later.

Consider the shift from A_1 to A_2 on both Figures 15.4(a) and 15.4(b). Suppose that, from available data, we know that in period 1 the firm produces output Q_1 using inputs L_1 and K_1, while in period 2 it uses L_2 and K_2 to produce Q_2. Let us assume also that input prices have not changed, to keep the analysis simpler. Has there been technical change, or is the increase in output from Q_1 to Q_2 entirely due to the increase in inputs? Possibly there has been technical change, without which it would have been necessary to use more labour and capital (L_2' and K_2' in Figure 15.4(a)) in order to produce Q_2. Without technical change we would then have observed the firm at point A_2' rather than A_2 as in Figure 15.4(a). In this diagram, the movement from A_1 to A_2 involves a shift in the isoquant map as well as a change in inputs. On the other hand, it is possible that there was no technical change and the movement from A_1 to A_2 was only due to increases in the quantity of inputs used. This case is represented in Figure 15.4(b), where the movement from A_1 to A_2 involves no shift in the isoquant map, just a change in inputs. Even if we know (from other sources of information) that a process innovation has been introduced, how can we tell how far the isoquant map has shifted? In other words, how is it possible to identify and measure the contribution of shifts *of* the isoquant map, corresponding to technical change, and shifts to a different point on the same isoquant map, corresponding to changes in inputs.

This is exactly the problem that Solow faced with his aggregate production function for the whole economy and overcame by using *growth accounting*. Solow began by assuming constant returns to scale in order to transform the aggregate production function into a form more manageable for empirical analysis. The aim of the transformation is to reduce the production function to two variables and hence allow us to illustrate it in two dimensions.

Beginning from the general expression for a production function $Q = f(L, K)$, where Q, L and K are the aggregate values of output, labour and capital for the whole economy, we divide both inputs by L. Assuming, as Solow did, constant returns to scale,

Figure 15.4 An increase in production and technical change

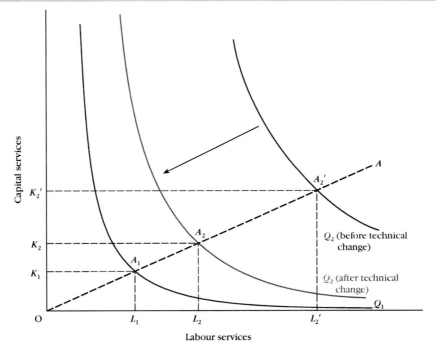

(a) Increase in production with technical change

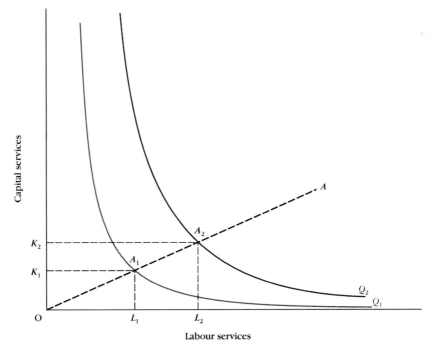

(b) Increase in production without technical change

this divides output by L too. So the production function becomes:

$$\frac{Q}{L} = f\left(1, \frac{K}{L}\right) \text{ since } \frac{L}{L} = 1$$

If we then write output per labour unit, $\frac{Q}{L}$, as q, and capital per labour unit, $\frac{K}{L}$, as k, we can transform this into a new production function:

$$q = g(k), \text{ where } g(k) = f(k, 1),$$

showing how output per unit of labour depends on capital per unit of labour. In this equation, q, output per unit of labour (say, per hour of labour) is the productivity of labour in the whole economy. The variable k, the quantity of capital per hour worked, is the capital intensity. An advantage of this specification of the production function is that it enables us to concentrate the analysis on the relationship between the accumulation of capital and output growth.

Figure 15.5 shows the aggregate production function in this form. Its shape displays diminishing marginal returns to increases in capital intensity; that is, to increases in the capital/labour ratio. The shape

of the curve indicates that each additional increment in k produces a diminishing increment in q. The successive increments in capital intensity from k_1 to k_2, k_2 to k_3 … up to k_4 to k_5 are all equal, but they produce diminishing increments q_2 to q_1, q_3 to q_2, … q_5 to q_4 in output per labour unit. So this production function displays diminishing returns to capital intensity as well as constant returns to scale, the assumption we needed in order to express output per labour unit as a function of capital intensity (see Chapter 10, Section 2.2). Let us now look at how Solow used this sort of transformed production function in his growth accounting model.

An isoquant map is just a representation of a production function. So, just as on Figure 15.4 we could not distinguish between shifts of the isoquant map and shifts to a different point on the same isoquant map (for a firm), Solow faced the problem of how to measure the relative contribution to growth (for the economy) of a shift *of* the aggregate production function, corresponding to technological progress, and of shifts *along* the aggregate production function, corresponding to changes in the quantities of inputs used. On Figure 15.6, in period 1, the economy is at A,

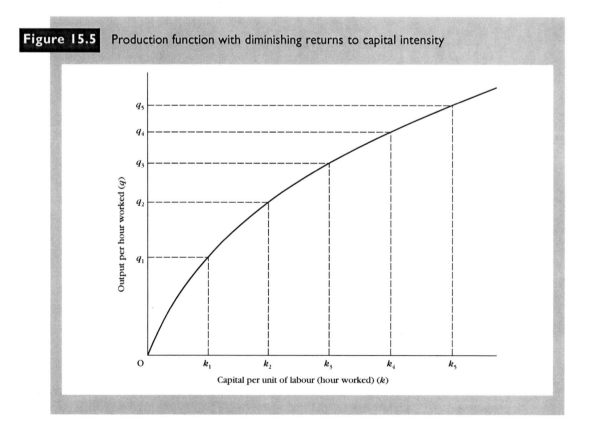

Figure 15.5 Production function with diminishing returns to capital intensity

output per labour unit is q_1 and capital intensity is k_1. In period 2, the economy is at B, output per labour unit is q_2 and capital intensity k_2. The problem is to analyse the relative contributions of increasing capital intensity and technological change that have taken us from A to B. One possibility is that the production function is the line labelled g_0. In this case, the movement from q_1 to q_2 is wholly caused by the increase in capital intensity from k_1 to k_2. However, if the production function in period 1 is g_1 then the movement from k_1 to k_2 only causes output per labour unit to increase from q_1 to q_2' while the remaining increase from q_2' to q_2 is due to *shift* of the production function from g_1 to g_2.

Solow's method of *growth accounting* was designed to discriminate between these alternatives. It enabled him to work out the contribution of any change in capital intensity to the growth output per labour unit, in order to consider how much remaining growth of output per labour unit needed to be explained by other factors, such as changes in technology.

If current output per labour unit is q and we represent its change by Δq, then the growth rate of output per labour unit is $\frac{\Delta q}{q}$. This will be made up of changes due to changes in capital intensity

(movement along the production function) and of changes due to changes in the production function. If we call the change in output per labour unit due to changes in capital intensity $\left(\frac{\Delta q}{q}\right)_k$, and $\frac{\Delta a}{a}$ is whatever the contribution to labour productivity, growth *cannot* be explained by changes in capital intensity and therefore must be due to changes in the production function, then:

$$\frac{\Delta q}{q} = \left(\frac{\Delta q}{q}\right)_k + \frac{\Delta a}{a}$$

Solow called $\frac{\Delta a}{a}$ the rate of change of total factor productivity (TFP), and identified it as the rate of technological change. If $\frac{\Delta q}{q}$ and $\left(\frac{\Delta q}{q}\right)_k$ could both be calculated from existing data, the rate of change of total factor productivity could then be worked out as the *residual* by the equation:

$$\frac{\Delta a}{a} = \frac{\Delta q}{q} - \left(\frac{\Delta q}{q}\right)_k$$

$\frac{\Delta q}{q}$ is just the overall rate of growth of output per labour unit (hours); this can easily be found, but what about $\left(\frac{\Delta q}{q}\right)_k$, the contribution of changes in capital intensity to growth?

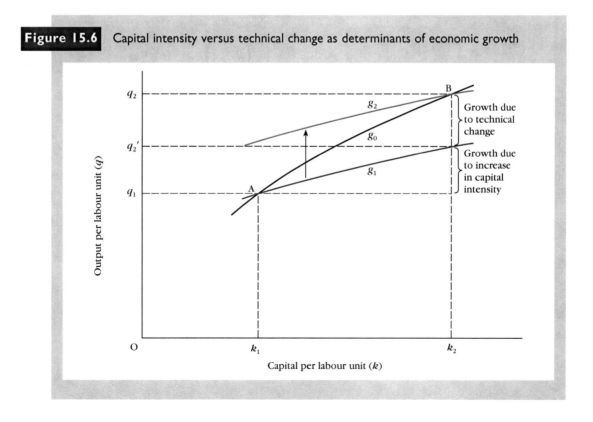

Figure 15.6   Capital intensity versus technical change as determinants of economic growth

The Appendix to this chapter shows you how to work this out and takes you through both the method of growth accounting and Solow's original application of it. Although it is optional because it is rather technical, I recommend that you do work through the Appendix at some time to explore an important moment in economic research on technical change.

Solow's results were startling. He estimated that about 90 per cent of the growth in output per labour hour in the United States over the period 1909-49 was accounted for by the residual (that is, TFP). (His estimate in his original article is 87.5 per cent; the difference from the results in the Appendix to this chapter is due to rounding up and a small arithmetical error, as reported in Nelson and Winter, 1982.) Look now at Figure 15.7.

You can understand this figure even if you have not yet worked through the Appendix. Figure 15.7 is very similar to Figure 15.6, but is drawn using Solow's results. It shows that about 10 per cent of the growth in q, from \$0.623 to \$0.686 per hour, was attributed to a move along the 1909 production function, that is g^{1909}, the production function for the level of TFP in 1909 (in other words, the production function for the economy if there had not been technical change since 1909). The rest of the total rise in output per labour hour to \$1.275 per hour in 1949 was attributed to an upwards shift in the production function from g^{1909} to g^{1949}.

The growth of US output per labour unit was therefore apparently due largely to factors that were not considered explicitly (that is, were not modelled as endogenous variables) by standard economic theory. Suddenly, it became clear to economists that an economic theory that neglected the causes of technological change would have problems of credibility.

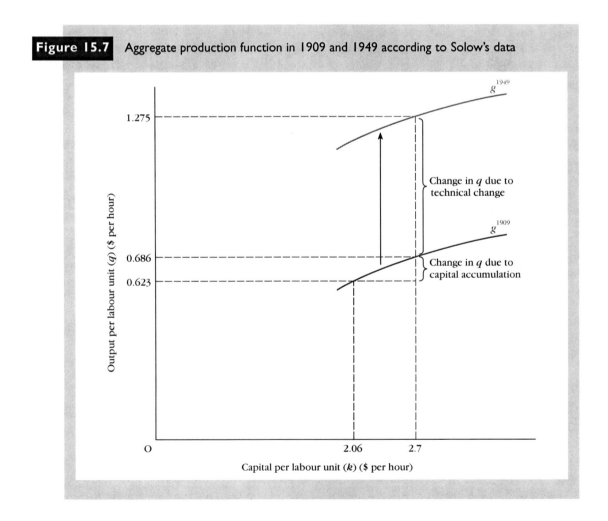

Figure 15.7 Aggregate production function in 1909 and 1949 according to Solow's data

Other studies broadly confirmed the importance of technical change for economic growth (Fagerberg, 1994). Solow's work had two major consequences for the evolution of economic research. First, his methodology was, and still is, extensively used and refined in the study of economic growth. Second, a number of economists became more interested in the process of technological change.

3.4 Technology as a 'black box'

At this stage we should analyse more explicitly some of the assumptions that are implicit in Solow's analysis. The first observation is that technological change is not clearly defined. In fact, it is just a label applied to the residual, the growth that cannot be accounted for in other ways. This residual Solow called the growth in total factor productivity. In other words, the change in TFP is the change in output that we cannot explain by changes in other factors, capital and labour, which are explicitly included in the analysis.

Some refinements to this methodology have been introduced over time. Solow himself noted that increases in the quality of the labour force can account for some of the increase in TFP, and that the quality of the capital stock can also improve as more productive industries expand their shares of GDP. Therefore, one possible way to reduce the residual is to include further explanatory variables, such as education and training, to account for improvements in the quality of labour. Economies of scale also may account for improved efficiency since firms usually become bigger as the economy expands. Solow's method assumed constant returns to scale, so any economies of scale would end up in the residual.

Even if we accept that the growth in TFP is a measure of technical change, fundamental issues still arise when we use the production function to analyse technical change. A major problem is that there is no analysis of the *sources* of new technology. The shift in the isoquants is exogenous, and there is no analysis of the processes that generate the gains in productivity.

Further, the entire theoretical structure focuses on the allocation of resources in a static context. Look back at Figure 15.3. All the analysis is geared towards the determination of the effects of technical change on the amounts of the two factors used to produce each good in the two *equilibria*, before and after the shift of the production function. In other words, as a piece of neoclassical economics it is concerned with how labour and capital are allocated in the two equilibrium situations.

As the economic historian Nathan Rosenberg puts it (1982), the production function works like a 'black box' which transforms inputs of production into output. It only tells us that certain quantities of capital and labour are used to produce a quantity of output, given the prices of K, L and Q. In order to make the analysis of resource allocation more manageable, the important role of the knowledge required to make the transformation is ignored. Solow's results begged the question of whether the price paid for this tractability was too high.

Solow's analysis also neglects the relationships that exist between the three sources of output growth, namely labour, capital and technical change, and possible feedback effects from output growth to investment and technical change. In order to understand how technical change occurs, we must recognize that capital accumulation and technical change are not independent and take into account the links that run from the expansion of output to the increase in productivity. Solow's model only considers the effects of capital accumulation and technical change on output. These are represented by the thick lines on Figure 15.8 overleaf; other links which need to be considered are represented by dashed lines. New technology is diffused through the economy only when firms adopt it by investing in new capital goods, so investment and technical change are interrelated.

Investment also stimulates technical change through the adaptation of existing technology to firm-specific needs. Furthermore, the production process itself generates technical change through learning-by-doing (Chapter 11, Section 2.2). These and other forms of economies of scale can only be reaped by investing. In this way growth generates further growth through positive feedbacks, as in Figure 15.8. Investment furthers technical change through the increase in production that it stimulates.

Growth accounting therefore provides a simple framework that gives us a rough idea of the importance of the various elements in the process of economic growth, but it neglects the processes behind the changes. It simply compares two equilibrium states. Even assuming that the economy is in equilibrium, the process of *how* we move from one equilibrium to the other, and the reasons why (i.e. the sources of technical change) are ignored. This is a consequence of the comparative static methodology adopted.

As Chapter 8 noted, historical time does not enter into comparative static analysis. The analysis compares equilibria associated with different values of exogenous variables and parameters; it says nothing about any process of movement from one equilibrium to another. The method is quite different from *dynamics*: methodologies that try to explain how a process works over time, not the characteristics of a system in states of rest. The explicit introduction of historical time into the analysis has the important consequence that it can generate irreversibility. Since time flows only in one direction, changes cannot necessarily be reversed and the future options open to economic agents may be constrained by past events; that is, by the history of the economic system. History matters.

Finally, the production function analysis assumes that production takes place *on* the production function – that is, on the technological frontier. The isoquant map implies that there is a range of possible best-practice techniques, known to all firms. All firms can operate on the technological frontier because they can all tap into the stock of technological knowledge, and can produce using whichever existing technology they choose. The acquisition of

technology is just like the acquisition of another piece of *information*, and the analysis assumes perfect knowledge.

This conceptualization of technology has two important implications. First, since firms are rational and technology is accessible to all, all firms should be adopting the same best-practice techniques. However, much empirical evidence contradicts this. There are significant and persistent differences in the levels of productivity of firms within most industries. This implies that many firms are not producing on the current isoquant. It is difficult, therefore, to interpret Solow's result since it might be due either to an improvement in best-practice technology (a shift of the isoquants), as in Figure 15.3, or to a movement towards the technological frontier by firms that were not using best practice technology. Figure 15.9 shows a situation in which some firms which had been using sub-optimal technology move towards the technological frontier represented by one isoquant. Even though the isoquant has not shifted, a growth accounting exercise would show an increase in TFP. However, this is only due to the diffusion of existing technology rather than to a shift of the isoquant map and the production function it represents.

The second implication of the production function representation of technology as information is that choosing a technique of production, or

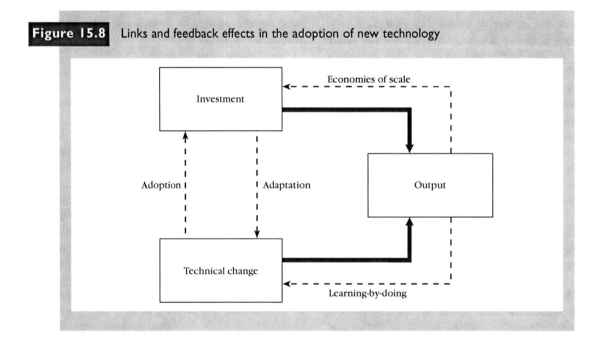

Figure 15.8 Links and feedback effects in the adoption of new technology

changing it by moving along the isoquants, becomes a matter of *choice*. The stock of knowledge is a bit like a recipe book. I can read the recipe and cook a meal. In fact, I would not advise you to come to dinner at my home if I have cooked something for the first time from a recipe book. Some experienced cooks can do it, and they also will probably improve their dishes by adding a 'personal touch' to the recipe. This is because it takes time and a process of learning to do things well, even more so if you lack accumulated experience in the area concerned. Technology requires learning, and its application requires knowledge that may be tacit – that is, unwritten and inexplicit and therefore not easy to acquire. In practice, in many cases changing technique involves a significant investment of time and resources because the firm (or the cook) has not experimented with the new technique (recipe). Therefore, the distinction between movements along and shifts of the isoquant becomes meaningless for

firms, as they have to invest *time* and *money* to change technique of production (see, for example, the Ford example at the beginning of Chapter 10). To a firm a change of technique is like an innovation, since it involves a change in its routines (Chapter 8, Section 5 introduces routines). While some R&D increases the overall stock of knowledge, much R&D undertaken by private firms is directed at assimilating publicly available knowledge (Cohen and Levinthal, 1989).

  # TECHNOLOGICAL CHANGE AND GENERAL EQUILIBRIUM ANALYSIS

If technical change is treated as exogenous, as it is in standard neoclassical theory, then any investigation of the sources of innovation lies outside the boundaries

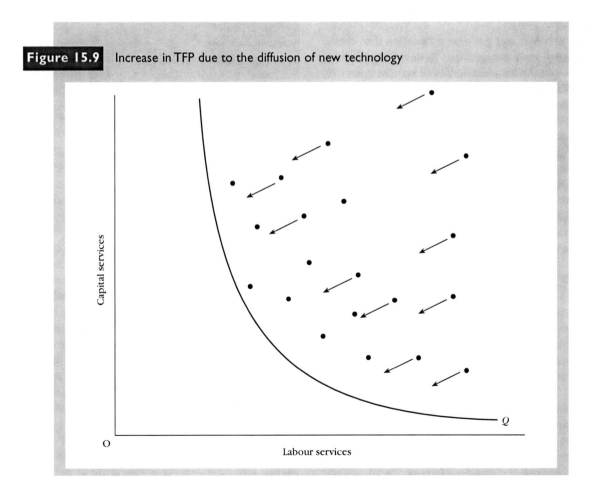

Figure 15.9 Increase in TFP due to the diffusion of new technology

of economics. Solow's results, which demonstrated the significance of technical change, made it clear how unsatisfactory this omission was.

The Nobel prize winner Kenneth Arrow sought to rectify this and addressed technical change explicitly by focusing on how resources are allocated to innovative activities in a competitive economy. In this he retained the neoclassical assumption that technology is like a recipe, a set of instructions that firms use to transform inputs into outputs. However, instead of treating it as exogenously given, Arrow saw the set of instructions itself as the output of a production process, to which resources needed to be allocated.

One of the cornerstones of neoclassical theory is the idea that in a competitive general equilibrium framework the market allocates resources in a Pareto-optimal way (see Chapters 1 and 18). Arrow showed how this was not true of resources for producing new ideas and that the market would underinvest in innovative activity. This was because some of the restrictive assumptions necessary to achieve Pareto efficiency did not hold in the case of innovative activity.

Information has peculiar properties that create problems in a competitive general equilibrium framework. Arrow identified three main reasons why the allocation of resources to innovative activity is likely to be non-optimal. The first is the presence of *indivisibilities*, which means that that the costs of producing innovations are 'lumpy' rather than infinitely divisible. This happens because fixed costs represent a high share of the costs of producing new technology. Second, innovators may not *appropriate* all the benefits from innovations, and so may underinvest. And third, innovation introduces *uncertainty* in a framework, competitive general equilibrium, that assumes perfect knowledge.

Indivisibilities

A large quantity of resources is usually required to produce the information necessary to introduce a new product or process. Once the innovation is introduced, however, the marginal cost of reproducing the information is very low. The bulk of the costs are therefore fixed. A firm can invest years and a lot of money in writing a new piece of software, but the code that makes up the software can be copied very easily and cheaply. The marginal cost of the new information, therefore, is much lower than the average cost, and the innovative firm will have to set price above marginal cost in order to recoup the initial fixed

costs (Arrow, 1962b). The smaller the market and the greater the fixed costs, the greater the difference between price and marginal costs. Thus, one of the conditions for competitive general equilibrium theory, that price is equal to marginal cost, is violated (see Chapter 18). Because of the presence of indivisibilities, a perfectly competitive market structure is incompatible with the production of new information. Since customers have to pay more than marginal cost, they demand less of the good than they would under competitive conditions, and this good, new information, is underproduced.

Appropriability

An even greater problem for the production of new technology arises because in many cases the innovator cannot appropriate all the returns from an innovative investment. This is because information displays some of the characteristics of a *public good*; that is, a good that is non-rival and non-excludable (see *Changing Economies*, Chapter 10).

> ### Public good
>
> A pure public good is non-rival, in that consumption of it does not reduce the total available, and non-excludable, in that no-one can be prevented from consuming it once it is provided.

If technology is just information, then the information available to each firm is not reduced if other firms use it (non-rivalry), and firms that produce information may not be able to prevent others from using it (non-excludability). In practice, there are access costs to information, the costs of copying, but, as noted above, these marginal costs are likely to be well below average production costs. Technology as information is therefore not a pure public good, but it has some public good characteristics. As a result, the innovating firm may not be able to recoup all the costs of innovation and, knowing that, it may not innovate in the first place. The partial lack of appropriability of the benefits of innovation means that there will be a sub-optimal level of innovative activity.

Another way to characterize the same problem is to say that innovation creates positive *externalities*. When a firm innovates, some of the knowledge produced spills over to other firms, through common suppliers, employees who change jobs, and reverse engineering of products (that is, examining the products to determine how they were produced). The innovating firm does not take these external benefits into account when it decides whether to innovate. The private benefits will be below the social benefits and therefore the quantity of knowledge produced will be below the optimum level.

Note that although the public good nature of technology creates negative incentives to innovate, it is also a socially attractive feature of technology. If all technological knowledge remained *tacit* for a significant length of time in the heads of innovators, then innovators could appropriate the returns. However, if knowledge could not be transferred, it would not be available to society and would die with the innovator. In these circumstances, the innovator could charge producers and consumers a very high price. Fortunately, this is not the case. A great part of the knowledge that is embodied in innovations is codifiable and transferrable, and therefore can be used by many other economic agents. In other words, a part of technological knowledge is composed of *ideas* that can be articulated and therefore used again and again.

Tacit knowledge

Tacit knowledge is knowledge acquired by experience that cannot be codified.

Is it possible, then, to combine reasonable incentives for investors and innovators with an assurance that knowledge will not remain permanently in the private domain? The easier it is to copy a technology – the more public its nature – the greater the disincentive to an individual to produce it but the greater the social benefit of its production. This problem has been long recognized, and many governments offer incentives to would-be innovators by granting them a temporary monopoly on innovations through the patent system. Patents provide the inventors with *property rights* over the commercial exploitation of the patented technology; the monopoly is the reward for innovative effort. However, a monopolistic market structure also leads to an inefficient allocation of resources, since the monopolist restricts output and raises price above marginal cost. The economy has to achieve allocative efficiency (see Chapter 10, Section 4.1).

Property rights

A property right in a good confers some degree of control over its use.

If firms are able to restrict output in order to maintain price (P) above marginal costs (MC), as in Figure 15.10, this leads to a misallocation of resources and loss of economic welfare. The inventor holding a patent can maximize total profits by behaving like a single monopolistic firm – that is, by restricting the output produced. This situation can be compared with the benchmark case of perfect competition where firms are price takers and cannot sell any unit of goods produced at a price that is higher than their marginal cost, and therefore they cannot gain any supernormal profits (see *Changing Economies*, Chapters 6–8).

Figure 15.10 compares the welfare effects (or performance) of perfect competition and monopoly. To simplify the presentation, constant returns to scale are assumed; that is, marginal costs are equal to average costs ($MC = AC$) for all levels of output. Note that, in the case of monopoly, the expansion of the industry's output corresponds to the expansion of the monopolist, while in the case of perfect competition expansion of output will be due to entry of new small firms, and the individual firms will experience diseconomies of scale.

The monopolist produces the quantity Q_m at which marginal cost and marginal revenue are equal ($MC = MR$). The monopolist sets price greater than marginal cost, $P_m > MC$, and sells the quantity Q_m, and the firm gains supernormal profits equal to $P_m BG P_c$. If the industry is competitive, by contrast, the firms cannot set price above marginal cost ($P = MC$), and the quantity produced is Q_c. The amount of supernormal profits in the industry is then zero (see also *Changing Economies*, Chapter 12).

To measure the loss of consumer welfare due to monopoly, we employ the concept of *consumer surplus* (consumer surplus is explained in *Changing Economies*, Chapter 8). To understand this concept, refer to the market demand curve ($AR = D$) in Figure 15.10. The demand curve shows the amount consumers are willing to pay for each additional unit of the product. While consumers pay the market price P_c for all units of the good purchased in a competitive market environment, some consumers would be willing to pay more than P_c for units up to

Q_c (the demand curve is above P_c). For each unit of output below Q_c, the difference between the price the consumer is willing to pay and the price actually paid is the consumer surplus. The triangular area AEP_c represents total consumer surplus when an industry is perfectly competitive.

Consumer surplus

Consumer surplus is the difference between what a consumer is willing to pay for a good and the amount actually paid for it. It is a measure of the benefits to a consumer of trading in the market.

Questions

- What area of Figure 15.10 represents consumer surplus under a monopoly?
- What area of the figure represents the decrease in consumer surplus when a competitive industry becomes a monopoly?

The area ABP_m represents consumer surplus under monopoly. The decrease in consumer surplus when a competitive industry becomes a monopoly is therefore the area P_mBEP_c. This decrease can be split into two parts. The area P_mBGP_c is a redistribution of the surplus from consumers to the owners of the firm in the form of supernormal profits. The triangle BEG is called the dead-weight welfare loss resulting from monopoly power. The source of the dead-weight welfare loss is the withdrawal from the market by consumers reacting to the distorted price signal sent by the producer P_m which is above the opportunity cost MC of producing the output foregone $Q_c - Q_m$. The increase of price above marginal cost due to monopoly creates a misallocation of resources among industries. Too little of the good is produced and purchased so consumers spend their money on other goods and services, although they would have preferred the original good at price P_c.

One compromise between the static welfare loss of allocative efficiency and the long-term benefits of

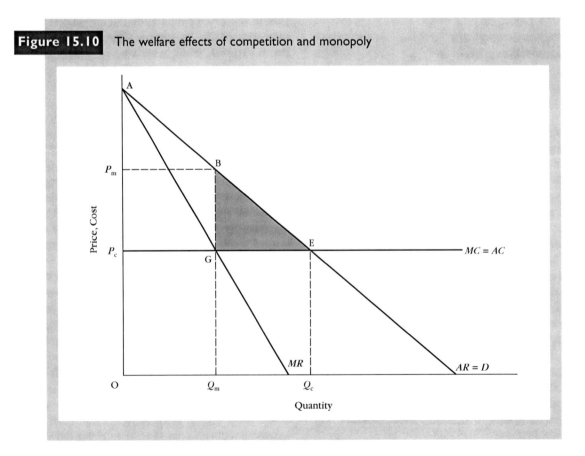

Figure 15.10 The welfare effects of competition and monopoly

innovation is to make patent rights temporary. Then society enjoys the full benefits of the new technology after the patent rights run out, and the patent system facilitates the transfer of knowledge from the patentee to the wider community since the patentee must disclose information about the invention that he wants to patent. In this way, other researchers can start becoming familiar with the technology, and the accumulation of technological knowledge is speeded up.

The patent system, therefore, is aimed at managing the trade-off between static monopoly costs arising from the property rights granted to the patentees and the costs arising from the lack of incentive to innovate in the absence of patents. The system is a clear example of the importance of institutional design for the efficiency of an economy. Short-term static inefficiency is introduced in order to gain dynamic efficiency. Innovation is thus a case in which perfect competition does not yield the best outcome (Arrow, 1962b).

Uncertainty

Innovation is full of uncertainty and this may discourage investment in innovative activities. In process innovation the uncertainty is mainly technical. For new products, however, there is also uncertainty about the response of the market to the new product. Uncertainty, in conditions of limited financial resources, makes it likely that investors will underinvest in risky enterprises (Arrow, 1962a). Some of the risk of innovating is diversifiable through the stock market or financial intermediaries such as banks or unit trusts (Chapter 17), but innovative enterprises remain risky. Insurance cannot eliminate the risk because it introduces moral hazard (Chapter 9, Section 3.1). The insurer would not be able to tell whether any failure to innovate is due to bad luck (a state of nature), or to lack of effort from the insured who knows that the insurer will pay in case of failure.

Increasing returns to use

In addition to Arrow's three problems of innovation, another characteristic of technology further complicates the analysis. The new technology produced in the innovative process is also an input for successive innovations. Consequently, the greater the use of the new technology, the greater the chances of more innovations within a short time horizon. There are thus increasing returns to

the use of new technology. The more it is adopted by other firms, the faster the rate of innovation in the future and the more rapid the increase in efficiency. This effect compounds the problems caused by insufficient appropriability of and uncertainty about the returns to innovative activities, making them even more damaging in the long run. In addition to the patent system, technology policy has sought to raise the social returns to new technology by subsidizing research activity, especially scientific research whose output is both very difficult to appropriate and at the same time crucial for innovation.

 ## 5 LINEAR MODELS OF INNOVATION

5.1 The 'technology-push' model of innovation

Scientific research has long been considered one of the main sources of new technology. Although science and technology are both conceptualized as bodies of knowledge and are often interrelated, it is possible to make some distinctions between them. First, their goals and outputs are different. While scientists try to formulate general theories, engineers are mainly concerned with making products and processes that work. Second, scientists try to promote the diffusion of their theories through publications, and indeed the results of scientific research must be replicable for a theory to be accepted. It is therefore codified knowledge which can be easily transferred to others. Technological knowledge, on the other hand, is more tacit, less general, more specific to the artifacts produced, and therefore less easy to copy and transfer. Further, it is usually kept as private as possible, to provide producers with a competitive advantage in the market.

So scientific and technological knowledge differ in the extent to which the economic returns they generate can be appropriated by the persons or the institutions that carry out innovative investment in knowledge. The high costs and the low degree of appropriability of the returns to scientific research mean that it is frequently publicly funded, while new technology is generally developed by private firms. There are, of course, important exceptions to this distinction, as in the case of the researchers developing the transistor in the R&D department of Bell Laboratories, who were awarded the Nobel prize for their discoveries in physics (Nelson, 1962).

Most of the R&D performed in large industrial corporations is aimed at the introduction of new products and processes. Official statistics on R&D usually distinguish between three types of activity. *Basic research* is directed towards the pure advancement of knowledge, without a specific application in mind. *Applied research* is also directed towards the advancement of knowledge, but with direct commercial applications in mind. *Development research* is directed towards the refinement and improvement of new products and processes. Scientific research is generally classified as basic, while industrial R&D carried out by private firms is usually more applied in nature.

These three types of research activity have been seen as stages of a *linear* innovation process, which runs from basic science to the introduction of an innovation on to the market (as in Figure 15.11). The model in Figure 15.11 is commonly known as the 'technology-push' or 'production line' model of innovation, because advances in the scientific and technological knowledge base are the engines of innovation. Science and technology are the prime movers of economic growth as they increase the publicly available stock of knowledge, which some firms then translate into innovations.

An important feature of this model is that it sees innovation as a process not a single act. After the initial *invention*, a long and costly process is needed before the new product or process is introduced into the economy. Only when this whole process is carried out can we talk about *innovation*.

Figure 15.11 The 'technology-push' linear process of innovation

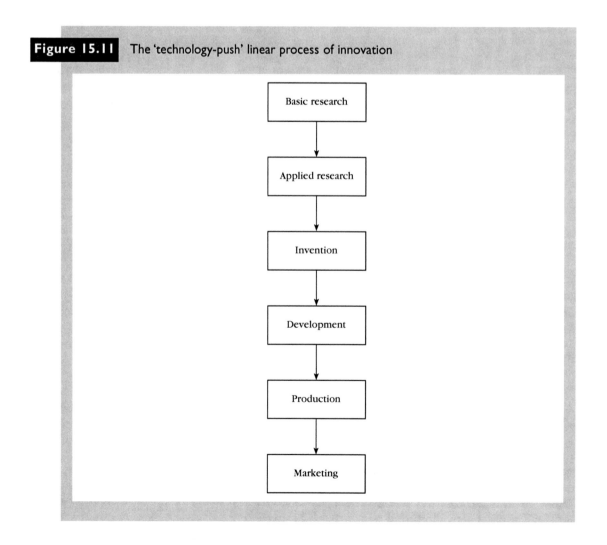

> ### Invention
>
> Invention involves discovery and creation, and denotes the generation of a new idea for a product or a process of production.

> ### Innovation
>
> Innovation is the introduction of a new product or a new process of production into the economy, usually on to the market.

The distinction between invention and innovation goes back to the Austrian economist Joseph Schumpeter, who considered technical change to be the salient feature of capitalism. He argued that entrepreneurs in private enterprise were the key actors in economic development because they were innovators:

> *'As long as they are not carried into practice, inventions are economically irrelevant. And to carry any improvement into effect is a task entirely different from the inventing of it, and a task, moreover, requiring entirely different kinds of aptitudes. Although entrepreneurs of course* may *be inventors just as they may be capitalists, they are inventors not by nature of their function but by coincidence and vice versa. Besides, the innovations which it is the function of entrepreneurs to carry out need not necessarily be inventions at all.'*
>
> (SCHUMPETER, 1926; 1961 EDN, PP.88–9)

The technology-push model of innovation has been highly influential in economic policy. Many arguments for government support for public sector scientific research and private firms' R&D are based on this model, according to which the way to increase the rate of innovation, and therefore economic efficiency, is to increase the pool of scientific knowledge.

5.2   The 'demand-pull' model of innovation

In the technology-push linear model of innovation, market demand does not significantly shape the rate or the direction of technological change. The role for market demand comes at a later stage, when the technological menu is already determined. Demand contributes to determining the point chosen on the isoquant, but does not generate a shift of the isoquant.

Schmookler's book, *Invention and Economic Growth* (1966), introduced the demand-pull theory of technical change. His argument was that:

> *'... since inventions, important and otherwise, generally represent creative responses to felt wants, the means for satisfying these wants in some measure are usually found through one channel if not through another; so that, if a particular important invention had never appeared on the scene, something approximating a functionally equivalent invention would probably have been made and used, or taken off the shelf if it had already been made.'*
>
> (SCHMOOKLER, 1966, P.136)

He backed his conclusions with empirical evidence from two main sources: histories of more than 900 inventions, and data on patents granted in the Untied States. The use of patent statistics in the study of technical change, now common, was an innovation in itself.

Schmookler classified each patent by sector in which the innovation would be used (for example, a patent on textile machinery is used in the textile industry). The analysis of patent statistics across industries showed quite clearly that the larger the industry in which the patented innovation was used, the greater the number of patents. The analysis of patenting over time showed that trends in output, investment and patenting in some industries were very similar, but changes in patenting occurred *after* changes in production, as is suggested by Figure 15.12.

Schmookler's conclusion was that economic activity influences inventive effort. Since firms introduce innovations for economic gains, they tend to put their innovative investment into areas where demand is growing so that they can reap greater returns. Schmookler's theory and findings, however, relate to the inventive *effort* rather than its *output* since patents cannot be interpreted as real innovations. Indeed, only a small percentage of patents are actually used to produce real goods.

Other empirical studies confirmed the role of demand in the introduction of innovations. However, in a comprehensive review of the empirical evidence,

Mowery and Rosenberg (1979) showed that in many important innovations the input of science remained significant, and that in many cases an increase in demand often followed from a reduction in costs due to process innovation. Other case studies have shown that many uses of innovations were unforeseen by the innovator (see, for instance, the history of the transistor in Nelson, 1962), and therefore could not have been generated by demand. This is particularly true for innovations that are technological breakthroughs, rather than being only improvements.

The main problem with both the technology-push and the demand-pull models of innovation is that their linear structure neglects important aspects of the innovative process. The common view, nowadays, is that understanding innovation as a linear process, either from technology to demand or vice versa, is too simplified. Demand influences innovative effort, but the state of technology constrains the output of innovative activities. Technological opportunities also contribute significantly to innovation. If both influences play a significant role, we must understand how they interact with each other and with the institutions that form part of the innovative process. In order to explore such interactions, we turn now to a case study: the history of the steam engine.

 # 6 THE STEAM ENGINE

6.1 Introduction

Researchers in the management of technology and historians have long been interested in the process of technological change, and economists can learn by tapping into their work. I will review here the story of the evolution of steam technology, one of the most important technologies in the history of the modern world. In particular, I will take a closer look at one important step in the development of

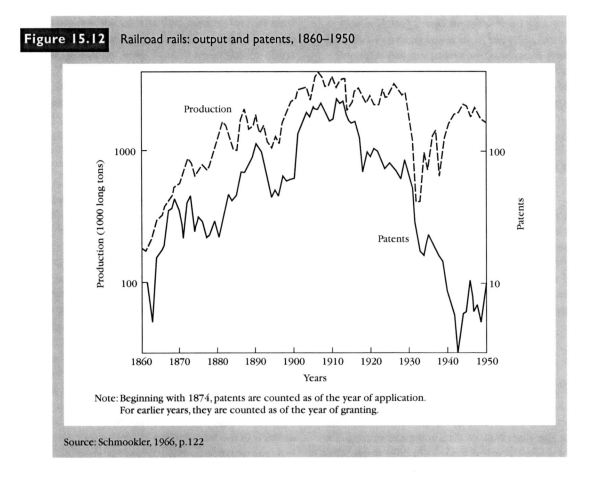

Figure 15.12 Railroad rails: output and patents, 1860–1950

Note: Beginning with 1874, patents are counted as of the year of application. For earlier years, they are counted as of the year of granting.

Source: Schmookler, 1966, p.122

steam technology, the introduction of the steam engine by Watt and Boulton. In this exposition of the history of the steam engine (based on Scherer, 1984), I am going to derive some propositions that highlight features of this technological change that are generalizable to the evolution of other technologies. This method illustrates the way economic researchers can use case studies to develop tentative generalizations that can then be refined or rejected through consideration of further case material. All my propositions are well supported by work on other innovations.

6.2 A short history of steam technology before Watt

The steam engine is a machine that transforms energy from one form (heat) to another (mechanical work) by exploiting the physical property that water expands in volume as it passes from the liquid to the gas state, called steam, and reduces in volume during condensation, thereby creating a vacuum in a sealed container. In the steam engine, water is heated in a boiler, usually using coal, to become steam. The increase in heat and the transformation from water to steam generates an increase in pressure within the boiler, and the steam is transferred to a cylinder, where the pressure generated by the expansion of the steam and the vacuum generated by its expulsion into a condenser are then used to move a piston.

The introduction of efficient steam engines by James Watt and Matthew Boulton enabled the owners of mines to deal with flooding and to dig deeper. More importantly, the steam engine made it possible to take full advantage of the mechanization of production, since it provided a flexible source of power that enabled machines to work for long periods using a large amount of energy. Previously, the major source of power, besides animal energy, was water power. This, however, meant that the choice of location for machines and factories was highly constrained, and not in line with the geographical distribution of labour. The introduction of the steam engine made it possible to overcome geographical constraints on the production of large amounts of energy.

James Watt is widely credited with the invention of the steam engine. In fact, the application of the principle of the expansion of water vapour was well-known long before Watt's time. From ancient Greek times, there are records of machines that exploited the pressure generated by the transformation of water into steam. Leonardo da Vinci wrote that Archimedes invented a cannon that could throw projectiles using steam power. In the seventeenth century, Giambattista Porta is also reported to have built a pump that used steam power, and Denis Papin published a treatise on the *Description and use of the new machine for raising water*, in 1687.

The machine described by Papin is an 'atmospheric engine', and it used the vacuum generated by the condensation of steam only to lift a piston leaving atmospheric pressure to bring it down in the second stage. In 1698 Thomas Savery filed the first patent on an atmospheric engine. This was an atmospheric pump used to extract water from mines. Savery's machine was subsequently improved in 1705 by Thomas Newcomen, whose atmospheric engine became very popular both in Great Britain and in continental Europe.

Newcomen's engine, however, was still very wasteful in terms of energy because the water was both heated and cooled in one place, the cylinder, so the heat used to produce the vapour was lost each time. The great contribution of Watt to steam technology was to work out how the heat used to transform water into steam could be saved and reused.

Proposition 1

The introduction of innovations is rarely an isolated episode. Innovations are best understood as episodes within the evolution of a broadly defined technology.

6.3 Watt and Boulton's enterprise

James Watt became interested in steam engines in 1764, when he was asked to repair one of Newcomen's engines. While he was working at it, Watt was struck by the inefficiency of the engine and started thinking how it could be improved. The answer came to him in the summer 1765, during a famous stroll in Glasgow. That day he realized that it would be more efficient if the process of condensation occurred outside the cylinder so that the temperature of the cylinder would always stay high and the energy necessary to reheat it would be saved. In addition, the engine would work more efficiently without water condensed around the piston.

However, the transition from Watt's original thought to the first commercially viable steam engine was neither easy nor costless. After the initial idea, Watt built a small prototype of the engine in a short time. Having checked the consistency of his intuition, he borrowed some money and started building a larger engine. However, he faced many technical difficulties, and in order to raise the funds necessary to overcome them, Watt had to enter a partnership in 1768 with John Roebuck, an entrepreneur who owned a coalmine that had been flooded and could not be saved by the existing atmospheric engines.

Proposition 2

The process of introducing an innovation is expensive, requires time, and is surrounded by uncertainty. Although intuition is an important moment of innovation, the bulk of the innovative process is represented by a painstaking search for a specification of the original idea that can satisfy economic criteria. This development stage is crucial to the overall innovation process.

Roebuck and Watt's first move was to apply for a patent in order to appropriate the returns from the commercialization of the engine, which could otherwise go to other manufacturers who would copy the idea. The patent was granted in 1769. In 1773, however, Roebuck became bankrupt and had to sell the patent rights to Matthew Boulton in 1774. Boulton was initially interested in the engine because it could provide energy to his manufacturing plant in Soho, which was powered by water and had problems of water scarcity in summer. However, he quickly realized the potential value of an efficient steam engine and planned to supply engines to the world.

One of Boulton's first moves, in February 1775, was to apply for an extension of the patent's life, on the grounds that the expenditure needed to make the engine commercially viable would be far greater than the returns to be gained in the remaining life of the patent (less than 10 years), and therefore the investment would not be worthwhile. The knowledge that most of the improvements to Newcomen's engine until that time had been commercial failures also increased the uncertainty of the venture. Without adequate incentives, therefore, there was a danger that the engine would never come to life, a loss for the whole nation. In May 1775, parliament

approved the extension of the patent for an extra 25 years.

By 1768 Watt had already produced models of the engine that performed satisfactorily (Scherer, 1984). But many problems remained unsolved and Watt had been experimenting with a variety of solutions to the bottlenecks that were limiting the efficiency of his engine. A particular problem was how to fit the piston into the cylinder in such a way that the vacuum could be preserved during the stroke while limiting the extent of friction between the two. Watt tried a number of different materials and shapes for the cylinder and the piston (leather, copper, wood, tin and cast iron), and different types of seals (lead, cork, leather, pasteboard, cloth, oakum, hemp, etc.). Dickinson describes his quest for constant improvements:

> *'Of a number of alternatives he does not seem to have had the flair of knowing which was the most practicable, hence he expended his energies on many avenues that led to dead ends. [...] Still, unless he had explored these avenues, he could not be certain that they led nowhere.'*
>
> (DICKINSON, 1936, QUOTED IN SCHERER, 1984, P.17)

Other problems requiring trial and error experimentation were the design and size of the separate condenser, valves and boiler.

Proposition 3

Innovative activity is a process of trial and error, of which failure is an essential part. Temporary setbacks are part of a process in which firms learn which avenues are feasible and which are not, and why. This learning process produces knowledge that is mostly *tacit*; that is, difficult to articulate and therefore to transfer. Expert judgement, developed through a trial and error process, and intuition are crucial in the innovation process.

The solution to the important problem of the fit between cylinder and piston was in the end not found by Watt, but was a by-product of an innovation introduced by a customer of Boulton's, John Wilkinson, who patented a machine which made it possible to build cylinders and pistons very accurately, so that they adhered well to each other without creating too much friction.

Proposition 4

The successful introduction of an innovation in one industry often depends on technological advance in other industries. The flow of new technology between firms in different industries is a very important source of innovation in the economy. This means that both the sources and the effects of an innovation cannot fully be understood by looking only at the industry in which the innovation has been introduced.

In 1776, Watt and Boulton started the commercialization of their engine. Because of their technical characteristics and huge size, the engines were not built in a factory and then shipped, but were built where they were needed mainly using local labour. Watt and Boulton acted more like consulting engineers than manufacturers, supplying drawings, expertise and a few components (Nahulm, 1981).

However, the instructions and components were not enough. In many instances Watt travelled personally to the sites in which the engines were built. In 1778 he spent most of his time supervising the construction of new engines, especially in Cornwall where the owners of metal mines had to import coal from outside the county and where any saving of the fuel was therefore economically very important.

After a few years, many Cornish engineers trained by Watt had learnt a great deal about the construction of steam engines and started building engines themselves. After tolerating the imitators for some years, Watt and Boulton eventually challenged them and after 1790 spent their time mainly in litigation. In the end, Watt and Boulton succeeded in their legal actions and gained a substantial sum of royalties. In fact, the payment of royalties was the main source of income of the Watt and Boulton enterprise because their engines were more expensive than those of their competitors due to Watt's emphasis on quality.

Question

Does the notion of technology as blueprints – information – fit with the need for Watt's presence in Cornwall? And with the challenge from the Cornish engineers? (Look back at Proposition 3 before you answer. Does the notion of tacit knowledge help explain what happened?)

The need for Watt's presence emphasizes the importance of tacit knowledge in the development of new technology. Watt's blueprints were not enough to replicate the new technology, even for the expert Cornish engineers, and they needed Watt's presence in order to build efficient engines. Only once they acquired tacit knowledge through learning-by-doing and trial-and-error activity during the construction of the first engines could they effectively replicate and even improve Watt's technology.

6.4   Improvements and diffusion of the steam engine

In the years between 1775 and 1780, Watt mainly worked on improving the design of the commercial engine, but from 1780 onwards the process of constant improvement carried on alongside the exploration of new designs. Watt discovered how to generate rotary motion from the engine's reciprocating motion, and introduced the double-acting engine, virtually doubling the engine's power. In addition, Watt and Boulton started producing engines for use in mills and factories.

Watt was not the only one who improved the engine. Other improvements were introduced by imitators even before the patent expired. Jonathan Hornblower introduced an engine that worked with two cylinders and exploited the expansive power of steam as well as the creation of vacuum, but had to pay huge royalties and ended up in prison. Trevithick, one of the Cornish engineers trained by Watt, was never challenged and built engines that worked at higher pressure. These engines were more efficient and smaller, so they were also more portable, and after the patent expired they did well because of their superior efficiency and their lower weight and size.

Hence the development of steam technology was characterized by:

'... [a] multitude of small and often anonymous gains: better materials, closer tolerances, the introduction of safety valves and gauges, the recognition and adoption of coal specially suited to the production of steam, the collection of accurate information on the performance of the engines under different conditions. But it was also punctuated by some great leaps forward, each marked by a critical innovation that

*widened substantially the commercial
application of steam.'*

(LANDES, 1969, P.100)

The effects of the *accumulation of knowledge* over time are clear when the efficiency of the various engines is compared. While Newcomen's engine needed about 30 pounds of coal per horse-power-hour, Watt's engine needed 7.5 pounds, and a compound high-pressure engine in 1850 only 2.5.

This story illustrates the point that the benefits associated with the use of a new and more efficient technology become widespread when it is adopted by many agents in a range of activities. The application of steam engines in activities other than mining, for instance, represented a significant increase in the importance of steam technology in the economy. It also provides my final proposition.

Proposition 5

The diffusion of an innovation in the economy can be seen as a process of accumulation of knowledge in which individuals, firms and other organizations, such as universities, learn about the new technology and improve it. For this reason, the diffusion of an innovation is very often associated with substantial improvements in it.

The performance of the steam engine was significantly improved by many of its adopters, such as the Cornish engineers. Landes stresses the fact that technology is cumulative and it constantly improves through small, almost insignificant advances. If this is the case, is it useful to distinguish between innovation and diffusion? Some authors have developed a new way of looking at technical change, as we shall see in Section 7, using concepts such as trajectories and paradigms that avoid this sharp distinction.

> **Question**
>
> From the history of Watt and Boulton's venture, can you identify the acts of invention and innovation? And who do you think was the innovator?

In the case of the steam engine the difference between invention and innovation is quite substantial. Watt invented the separate condenser in 1765. The act of invention was the intuition one

Sunday afternoon in Glasgow, and the initial idea did not change substantially.

It is not easy, however, to pinpoint an act of innovation. If we have to assign a date to the innovation, probably the best choice is 1776, the year in which Watt and Boulton started to market their engines. But the story shows that innovation is really a process that unfolds in various stages over time, starting from the initial intuition, and in which different actors are involved. The entrepreneurs Boulton and Roebuck were important at different stages of the innovation process. Watt's technical input on the innovation was also decisive, as was Wilkinson's innovation. All of them contributed to the introduction of the innovation in different ways.

6.5 Science and technology in the history of the steam engine

It took more than half century after Watt's first intuition for it to become clear how the steam engine worked. In 1824, five years after Watt's death, Sadi Carnot published his *Report on the driving force of heat and the correct machines to develop this power*, in which he proposed a theory of how the steam engine worked. Carnot's report is generally considered to mark the birth of thermodynamics, which is the science that studies the relationship between heat and other forms of energy such as mechanical energy. After Carnot's death, his contribution was acknowledged and his theory was subsequently modified and improved with the discovery of particle energy. Nowadays, the functioning of the steam engine can be understood using the laws of thermodynamics.

> **Question**
>
> Consider whether the history of the steam engine supports the 'technology-push' linear model of innovation, with a causal relationship running from science to technology, and the idea of technology as the application of scientific principles for a practical use. Think about the ways in which the introduction of the separate condenser in the steam engine fits this model, and the aspects of the story that do not fit it.

The answer is not straightforward. Some elements of the account suggest that advances in science contributed to Watt's breakthrough. James Watt knew the science of the day, and used his knowledge to improve Newcomen's engine. At the time, there was already some understanding of the properties of fluids, and steam in particular. So we can say that scientific knowledge contributed to the introduction of the steam engine with a separate condenser.

However, Carnot's *Report* was published more than 50 years after the introduction of Watt's steam engine. Furthermore, Carnot was explicitly trying to understand how the steam engine worked in order to build more efficient engines. In this case, the technological breakthrough preceded the advancement of science. In fact, the scientific breakthrough was motivated by the wish to understand why a technology was working.

Moreover, the view that innovations are just the application of scientific principles does not fit well with the account of Watt's method of research by trial and error. A substantial element of his research was a *search* for new solutions that would make the engine work, most of which did not work. This is a pattern that appears in the empirical analysis of other technologies, where the process of innovation can be seen as a search by trial and error rather than the application of scientific principles, and the causal link runs more from technological change to scientific discovery than vice versa. Significant inputs from technology to science can be found in flight and aerodynamics, and in steel and metallurgy.

Watt's search by trial and error, however, was not completely blind. The scientific knowledge of the time allowed him to focus his search by ruling out some options that he knew a priori would be unsuccessful. Although science is considered to be a different body of knowledge from technology, the two can interact so closely in economic activities that Derek de Solla Price compared them to two dancers who need each other to perform (de Solla Price, 1984).

7 AN EVOLUTIONARY VIEW OF TECHNICAL CHANGE

7.1 Knowledge and information

The history of the steam engine has shown that technological change is a very complex phenomenon, which suggests that it is necessary to look beyond the notion of technology as just information. Further,

we have seen that viewing innovation as a linear process neglects some important dimensions of the innovative process.

We can start by thinking about technology in two main ways: as a body of knowledge, or as an artifact. These two definitions are linked, since an artifact embodies the knowledge needed to produce it. We have therefore to consider the nature of the knowledge required to produce artifacts. Information, the instructions necessary to transform raw materials, is only one side of technology. Technological knowledge also requires skills that are not codifiable and can only be acquired through experience – for example, learning-by-doing. Those tacit skills are necessary to use codified information effectively. The 'newer' the technology, the more significant its tacit element.

Tacit knowledge is embodied in individuals and organizations. Like individuals, organizations acquire skills that relate to the organization as a whole. Such skills include the way in which people interact – such as, the organizational setting and corporate culture – as well as employees' skills, and are specific to each firm as they are learned through experience. In the management literature, these skills are called capabilities or competencies.

7.2 Appropriability revisited

The tacit aspect of technology affects its appropriability. The disincentive to innovate that arises from the difficulty of appropriating the returns from innovative investment should be reduced when the output is tacit knowledge, which cannot easily be copied. So the balance between tacit and codified knowledge, which varies across industries, affects the extent to which firms can appropriate the returns to investment in innovative activities. We would therefore expect to observe differences in the effectiveness of patents across industries.

Question

Can you think of any mechanism, besides patents, by which firms can appropriate the returns to the innovations that they introduce?

In Chapter 11, Section 2.2, you saw that firms in some semiconductor industries move quickly down the learning curve to reap monopoly profits. In other industries, such as the aircraft industry, learning is also associated with gaining lead time over the competitors since imitation is costly and requires time. Other innovations, especially new processes, can be exploited by keeping them secret. The existence of complementary assets, such as marketing and customer services, also facilitates the extraction of rents from new products.

Information on appropriability is not available in official statistics and it is very difficult to measure. In the 1980s, researchers at Yale University carried out in-depth interviews with 650 high-level R&D managers in American companies and computed scores for various mechanisms of appropriability (Levin *et al.*, 1987). Figure 15.13 shows that patents are not very effective in either discouraging imitation or securing royalty income. They have the lowest score for process innovation, and only secrecy ranks lower than patents for new products (not surprisingly, as the technology embodied in new products can be copied through 'reverse engineering'). Advancing along the learning curve and lead time are the most common ways of protecting revenues from innovations, although secrecy is also important for new processes and sales or service efforts for new products.

The effectiveness of each mechanism varies across industries and depends on the technological base; that is, the characteristics of the technology in the industry.

As Figure 15.14 shows, patents are effective in industries which are based on chemical technology, where it is usually easy to specify the innovation (say a molecule). In cases where the output of the innovation process is a complex system with thousands of components, such as a car or an aeroplane: '... it is more difficult to determine whether comparable components of two complex systems "do the same work in substantially the same way"' (Levin *et al.*, 1987, p.798). In the latter case, it is easy to find different ways of achieving the same results. This practice, called 'inventing around' was quoted in the Yale survey as the most important reason why patents in some industries are often ineffective. Nevertheless, even in industries where patents do not protect from imitation, they still may be taken out for other reasons. They may be used as a reward to, or as a measure of performance of, R&D personnel. Patents are also taken for strategic reasons. In the semiconductor industry, for instance, cross-licensing is very common, and the need for a portfolio of patents acts as a barrier against new entrants.

Although patents are often ineffective, there are rather strikingly only a few industries, mainly in the food and metal-working sectors, in which firms feel that it is difficult to protect the returns from innovation. These findings question the need for

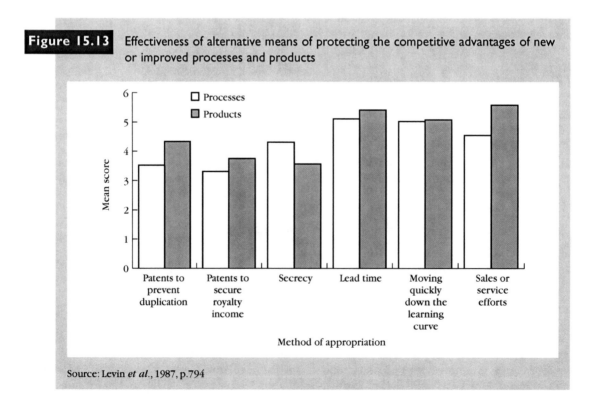

Figure 15.13 Effectiveness of alternative means of protecting the competitive advantages of new or improved processes and products

Source: Levin *et al.*, 1987, p.794

tight property rights and suggest that they may even be damaging, as they limit the diffusion of new technology.

7.3   Technology as a system

One important characteristic of technology is that it is *systemic*; that is, it can be represented as a system. This applies whether we think of technology as an artifact or as knowledge. A system is made of parts that are linked together in some way. Artifacts, even those that seem very simple, such as a ball-point pen, are usually made of components that can be very different in terms of the knowledge and skills required to produce them. Watt's steam engine was made of many components, and he struggled to find the right shape and material for the separate condenser, to improve the efficiency of the boiler and to find the best way to keep the cylinder and the piston parallel during the stroke. All these improvements contributed to the better functioning of the engine, and were interdependent. A breakthrough in

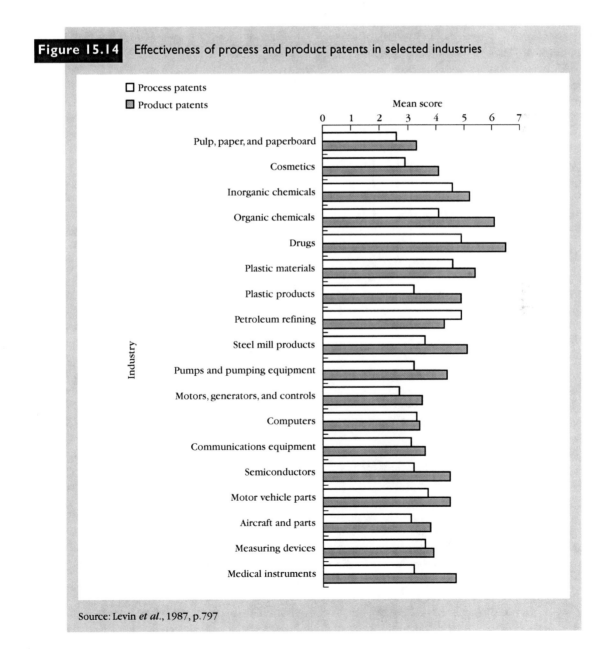

Figure 15.14   Effectiveness of process and product patents in selected industries

Source: Levin *et al.*, 1987, p.797

a part of the system creates imbalances (bottlenecks or opportunities) in other parts of the system.

When the number of components grows, the ways of relating the parts of the system to each other increase exponentially. The sheer number of possible alternatives makes it impossible to try them all out and the solutions that emerge depend on the experience and skills of the engineer. Therefore, complex technologies usually have a high level of tacit knowledge and are more difficult to codify.

One important consequence of conceiving technology as a system is that we have to look beyond the firm that ultimately introduces the innovation to identify the sources of new technology. Innovative firms often do not have all the necessary knowledge to introduce new products and processes and need to interact with other institutions such as suppliers and universities. De Liso and Metcalfe (1996) distinguish between the application of the term system to technologies (that is, bodies of knowledge needed to produce artifacts) and to a set of institutions (which they call a 'technology support system'). The two concepts of system are obviously very closely related, since institutions embody technological knowledge. Many different types of institutions are included in 'technology support system'. In many cases, the role of reliable suppliers in the introduction of innovations is crucial. Watt's own attempts to find a way to preserve the vacuum in the cylinder during the stroke of the piston failed; the breakthrough came from the precision engineering of a supplier, Wilkinson.

Besides suppliers, customers also provide valuable inputs in the innovation process. For instance, the Italian company Bassano Grimeca, a world leader in the production of wheels and brakes for motorcycles, develops its new products in close collaboration with its customers, large companies such as Honda and Aprilia.

The list of institutions involved in the introduction of new technology does not only include profit-seeking firms. Scientific institutions such as universities and government laboratories are also important actors in the innovation process. Besides being the repository of scientific knowledge, they provide essential training for scientists and engineers employed by firms, and play an important role in the development of scientific instrumentation.

Since innovative investments are often substantial, uncertain and usually pay off only after a long time, well-developed financial institutions that support innovation are essential actors in the development of new technology (Chapter 17 discusses the role of finance in innovation). The patent system also suggests that, besides funding R&D activities and ensuring a sufficient level of education, governments can do much to influence innovative activities by designing appropriate institutions. The list of institutions involved in the innovation process can also include trade associations, trade unions and so on.

Figure 15.15 illustrates how innovation, although usually introduced by a private firm, is ultimately the product of a system of institutions that are closely linked together by economic and social relationships. If some of the relevant institutions are missing or cannot communicate properly, then the whole innovation process is jeopardized.

Furthermore, the way in which institutions interact during the innovation process is far from linear. Innovative activities are constantly carried out to improve existing products and generate new ones, and feedbacks occur between the stages of the innovation process. Technical change can be seen as an ongoing process of *accumulation of knowledge* by all the institutions included in the system of innovation. Each innovation is just a small step in the continuous advance of a technology, which co-evolves with the institutions that are part of the system.

The importance of different activities and institutions in the innovation system varies across industries according to how knowledge is generated. In some industries, scientific discoveries are important. In other industries, however, the learning generated in the interaction between the innovators and the users of new technology is more important, while in others suppliers of capital goods are a vital source of innovation (Pavitt, 1984). Within the firm, besides institutional R&D activities, learning also takes place in other activities, such as production, marketing, design and engineering, and informal contacts of technical staff with the staff of other institutions, including competing firms (Freeman, 1982).

Technological systems have been defined in different ways. Christopher Freeman (1988), Bengt-Åke Lundvall (1992) and Richard Nelson (1992), for instance, explore the importance of national systems of innovation for technology policy. Carlsson and Stankiewicz (1991), on the other hand, define technological systems by dimensions such as the type of product, the actors that are part of the system and its institutional structure. The boundaries of such technological systems do not coincide with a country's boundaries, and in general they are more narrowly defined than national systems of innovation; however, the inclusion of multinational companies gives them an international dimension.

7.4   *The evolution of technologies*

The idea of technical change as a process of accumulation of knowledge in a system of institutions brings a new way of looking at technical change. The distinction between invention, innovation and diffusion becomes blurred, and instead of focusing on innovations as isolated acts which introduce discontinuity with the past, economists have recognized that much technical change is cumulative and

have tried to identify regularities in the way various technologies evolve.

Trajectories and paradigms

In the evolution of many technologies, technical considerations, such as bottlenecks or opportunities in one part of the technology system, indicate the 'natural' way for the next advance – Watt's idea of the separate condenser, for instance, was certainly inspired by technical considerations. Researchers and engineers usually focus on the gradual improvements of parts of the system; and improvements that require a major change in the architecture of the technology system are not usually considered, until the possibilities for gradual advance become technically infeasible

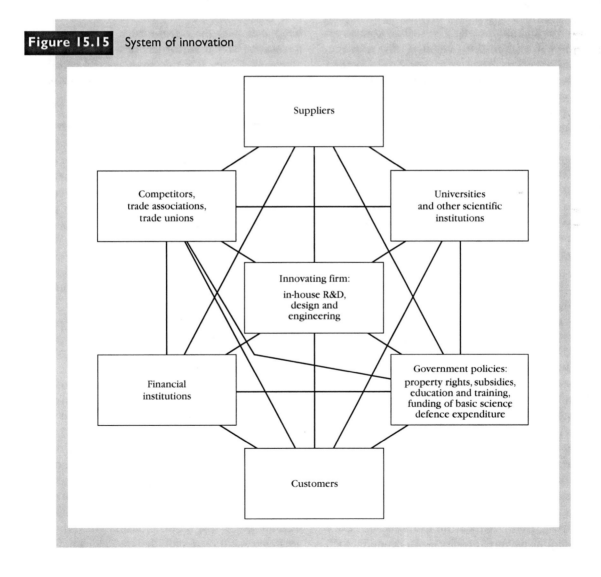

Figure 15.15   System of innovation

and too expensive. Nelson and Winter describe this phenomenon by saying that technologies follow a *natural trajectory* (1982).

This concept has been extended by the economist Giovanni Dosi, who argues that progress along a trajectory occurs within a *technological paradigm* (Dosi, 1982). In his view, individuals and institutions that improve a technology gradually develop a shared understanding of what the core problems are, how they are specified, which scientific principles are relevant and how solutions are to be searched for and applied. Technical change within a paradigm thus focuses on the improvement of some characteristics and does not take place in completely unexpected directions.

Occasionally, however, changes in parts of a system alter its balance to such an extent that established ways of doing things become obsolete and new opportunities open up. The change from steam to internal combustion engines, for instance, switched emphasis from coal to petrol and affected a substantial number of components. Similarly, the emergence of the transistor has deeply transformed telecommunications. In these cases, a change of paradigm occurs:

> '*Together with different knowledge bases and different prototypes of artefacts, the technoeconomic dimensions of innovation also vary. Some characteristics may become easier to achieve, new desirable characteristics may emerge, some others may lose importance.*'
>
> (DOSI, 1988, P.1129)

While the incremental accumulation of knowledge within a paradigm enhances the performance of the whole system, a change in technological paradigm involves the destruction of many skills and competencies that have been accumulated in the past as radically new ways of doing things become established. As Schumpeter pointed out, many horse-drawn carriages put together do not make a train.

Christopher Freeman and Carlota Perez, two economists interested in the relationship between technical change and economic development, use the terms 'incremental' and 'radical' innovations to emphasize the difference between cumulative and discontinuous aspects of technical change (Freeman and Perez, 1988). Radical innovations introduce significant elements of novelty in the economy, such

as the development of a new market, while each incremental innovation has no dramatic effect on its own. However, the combined outcome of many incremental innovations is often responsible for significant advances in productivity.

They also point out that technical change can have a major impact when a widely used technology undergoes a paradigmatic change. In those cases, a change in paradigm is associated with a cluster of radical and incremental innovations that affect various branches of the economy. In some extreme cases, it is possible to observe the emergence of new generic and pervasive technologies whose diffusion affects almost nearly the entire economy. This phenomenon, called a *change of techno-economic paradigm*, is associated with the rapid diffusion of a widely used new input of production based on a new technology. Freeman and Perez argue that this happened with the steam engine in the Industrial Revolution and it is happening today with microelectronics. They link this phenomenon with long-term economic cycles, known as Kondratiev waves (*Changing Economies*, Chapter 25).

Path dependency, lock-in and technological specialization

When a paradigm eventually exhausts its potential for improvement and engineers look for solutions to its problems outside the existing shared culture, a number of new paradigms may appear, but only a few of them – or even only one – become established. Car makers, for example, had to decide between internal combustion and steam engines. The elimination of some possibilities makes search by trial and error cheaper in terms of time and resources as it reduces the alternatives to be considered. This, in turn, facilitates the accumulation of knowledge and the development of a shared vision. Some authors, for instance, talk about the emergence of a *dominant design*.

So the accumulation of knowledge advances in certain directions, and other possible avenues that are feasible in principle are neglected. In other words, the evolution of technological paradigms is *path dependent*; that is, it depends on the previous history of technological development. Once the engineering community is committed to one technology, other paradigms become less attractive. A consequence of the path dependent evolution of technologies is that the accumulation of knowledge creates institutional rigidities that can hinder the creation and diffusion of radically new technologies. Systems can be *locked into* some technological paradigms, and some promising technologies are developed with great delays or not at all (I shall investigate the concept of lock-in in more detail in the next chapter). For example, Carlsson and Jacobsson (1996) found that the development of computer and electronics technology in Sweden was significantly hindered by the success of Swedish companies in mechanical engineering. It is difficult to change things when everything works well just because an emerging technology seems to be promising.

Quantitative studies based on patent statistics have systematically found that areas of technological strength are extremely persistent over time both for countries and firms (Patel and Pavitt, 1994; Archibugi and Pianta, 1992; Cantwell, 1989). German companies, for instance, were strong in chemicals both at the end of the last century and now. The globalization of the world economy also seems to have increased the 'technological division of labour'; that is, the degree in which countries specialize in few technologies (Archibugi and Pianta, 1992).

A characterization of technology as information would suggest a convergence across countries and firms as laggards catch up by copying the leaders' technology. If technology is partly tacit and embedded in systems of institutions, however, this finding is not surprising. Some institutional systems are simply more 'competent' in some technological fields, so that their recent innovative success builds on past achievements.

8 CONCLUSION

This chapter has explored the role of technical change in modern industrial economies. We have seen that both historical studies, such as Landes' account of the Industrial Revolution, and growth accounting models based on the neoclassical theory of production suggest that technical change is of paramount importance in modern capitalist economies.

We then examined some theories that, unlike standard neoclassical economics, do not take technology as given and try to explain the sources of technology. We examined Arrow's analysis of the ways in which the production of new knowledge

differs from that of other goods, and considered two linear models, technology-push and demand-pull, of how innovations are generated.

Using the history of the steam engine, we then explored the nature of technology and found that representing technology as information neglects the important role of tacit knowledge and the complex links between various institutions in the economy. The results from historical studies of technologies and quantitative analysis of technological indicators suggest that using a system perspective is essential to understanding the generation of new technology. This perspective is taken further by exploring evolutionary theories of technical change in the next chapter.

 ## FURTHER READING

Dosi, G., Freeman, C., Nelson, R.R., Soete, L. and Silverberg, G. (1988) *Technical Change and Economic Theory*, London, Frances Pinter: a very comprehensive book that covers many aspects of the evolutionary approach to technological change.

Freeman, C. (1982) *The Economics of Industrial Innovation* (2nd edn), Cambridge, MA; MIT Press: a classic on innovation which also deals with policy issues related to technical change.

Nordhaus, W.D. (1969) *Invention, Growth and Welfare: A Theoretical Treatment of Technological Change*, Cambridge, MA; MIT Press: an orthodox analysis of technical change in economics.

The historical approach is an important source of understanding on the nature and economic impact of technical change:

Dosi, G. (1988) 'Sources, procedures, and microeconomic effects of innovation', *Journal of Economic Literature*, Vol. 26, pp. 1120–71.

Pavitt, K. (1993) 'What do firms learn from basic research?', in Foray, D. and Freeman, C. (eds) *Technology and the Wealth of Nations*, London, Pinter.

Rosenberg, N. (1994) *Exploring the Black Box: Technology, Economics, and History*, Cambridge, Cambridge University Press.

Von Tunzelmann, G.N. (1995) *Technology and Industrial Progress: The Foundations of Economic Growth*, Cheltenham, Edward Elgar.

APPENDIX: SOLOW'S GROWTH ACCOUNTING MODEL

The problem that Solow set out to solve, represented in Figure 15.6, was to distinguish how much of the growth of output per labour unit (which is also the average productivity of labour) was explained by an increase in capital intensity, and how much was due to the residual, which he labelled 'technical change' (or total factor productivity, TFP). Output per unit of labour $q = \frac{Q}{L}$, is average labour productivity, and capital per unit of labour, $k = \frac{K}{L}$ is what we have called capital intensity.

You saw in Section 3 that he derived the growth accounting equation:

$$\frac{\Delta a}{a} = \frac{\Delta q}{q} - \left(\frac{\Delta q}{q}\right)_k$$

Since we can calculate $\frac{\Delta q}{q}$ from available official data on output, Q, and labour, L, we only have to estimate $\left(\frac{\Delta q}{q}\right)_k$ to calculate $\frac{\Delta a}{a}$. I will now show you how Solow estimated $\left(\frac{\Delta q}{q}\right)_k$

The marginal product of capital, MP_K, tells us how much output changes if the capital input is changed by one unit. Expressing output and capital per unit of labour, MP_K tells us how much output per unit of labour, q, changes when capital intensity (capital input per unit of labour), k, changes by one unit. If capital intensity changes by the amount Δk, the change in output per unit of labour due to changes in capital intensity alone, is given by:

$$(\Delta q)_k = MP_K \cdot \Delta k$$

To look at the *growth rate* of output per unit of labour, we have to divide both sides through by q to give an expression for the growth rate of output per labour unit due to changes in capital intensity alone:

$$\left(\frac{\Delta q}{q}\right)_k = \frac{MP_K}{q} \cdot \Delta k$$

Multiplying top and bottom of the right hand side of this by k to leave it unchanged gives:

$$\left(\frac{\Delta q}{q}\right)_k = \left(\frac{MP_K \cdot k}{q}\right) \cdot \left(\frac{\Delta k}{k}\right)$$

$\frac{\Delta k}{k}$ is just the growth rate of capital intensity, which can be easily calculated from published data on K and L. But what about the term $\left(\frac{MP_K \cdot k}{q}\right)$?

It's easier to see what this is if we multiply top and bottom through by L to give $\frac{MP_K \cdot K}{Q}$, where K is total capital input used in the economy and Q is the economy's total output. Under perfect competition, which Solow assumed, the price of capital R equals its marginal product, MP_K. So $MP_K \cdot K$ is the total cost of capital and

$$\frac{MP_K \cdot k}{q} = \frac{MP_K \cdot K}{Q} = \frac{R \cdot K}{Q}$$

is the share of total output appropriated by capital, which we can call r. This too can be found from published data.

By this process Solow could calculate:

$$\left(\frac{\Delta q}{q}\right)_k = \left(\frac{MP_K \cdot k}{q}\right) \cdot \left(\frac{\Delta k}{k}\right) = r \cdot \frac{\Delta k}{k}$$

This expression, the component of productivity growth due to the change in capital intensity alone, gives the contribution to growth provided by movement *along* the production function. To calculate the rate of change of total factor productivity $\frac{\Delta a}{a}$ we just need to take $\left(\frac{\Delta q}{q}\right)_k$ away from $\frac{\Delta q}{q}$ the total rate of change of productivity to leave $\frac{\Delta a}{a}$ as the residual:

$$\frac{\Delta a}{a} = \frac{\Delta q}{q} - \left(\frac{\Delta q}{q}\right)_k$$

In order to calculate this residual, Solow needed only four data series, Q, K, L and r. Table A.1 shows Solow's data for the years 1909–13 and 1946–49.

Columns 2 and 3 contain the series for q and k, obtained by dividing Q and K by L. Column 4 shows the rate of change of national income calculated from column 2. The formula used is:

$$\frac{\Delta q}{q} = \frac{q_{t+1} - q_t}{q_t}$$

For the year 1910, for instance, $\frac{\Delta q}{q}$ is:

$$\frac{q_{1911} - q_{1910}}{q_{1910}} = \frac{0.647 - 0.616}{0.616} = 0.05$$

Similarly, in column 5, $\frac{\Delta k}{k}$ is calculated using the data series for k in column 3. (Note that because data is needed for the following year, Solow could not calculate values for $\frac{\Delta q}{q}$ or $\frac{\Delta k}{k}$ for 1949.) Column 6 reports the yearly data series for r, the share of total output appropriated by capital. That gives us all the elements needed to calculate $\frac{\Delta a}{a}$. All we need to do is to apply the growth accounting equation in the following form:

$$\frac{\Delta a}{a} = \frac{\Delta q}{q} - r \cdot \frac{\Delta k}{k}$$

We can do it in two steps. First, in column 7, we calculate, $r \cdot \frac{\Delta k}{k}$ this is $\left(\frac{\Delta q}{q}\right)_k$, the change of q due only to the increase in k.

For 1910, for instance, we have:

$$r \cdot \frac{\Delta k}{k} = 0.330 \times 0.033 = 0.011 = \left(\frac{\Delta q}{q}\right)_k$$

We can then find the rate of technical change $\frac{\Delta a}{a}$ simply by subtracting the figures in columns 7 from those in column 4. This gives us column 8. So, for year 1910, we have:

$$0.050 - 0.011 = 0.039.$$

Exercise 15.3

Show how the rate of technical change $\frac{\Delta a}{a}$ for years 1947 and 1948 were calculated from the data for q, k and r in Table A.1.

Column 7 gives us $\left(\frac{\Delta q}{q}\right)_k$ for each year. This series is important since it allows us to plot a portion of the production function for the level of total factor productivity for each year. For example, the production

function labelled g^{1909} on Figure 15.7 in Section 3.3 shows how much, in the absence of technical change, q would have increased due to the rise in capital intensity k from 2.06 to 2.7 in 1909.

Column 9 of Table A.1 represents the values of this production function and gives what the level of output per labour unit would have been for each year if there had been no technical change since 1909. The values in column 9 are calculated as follows:

1 The value for the initial year 1909, $q_{1909}^{1909} = 0.623$ is the same as q^{1909}.

2 For every subsequent year, q^{1909} is calculated by multiplying q^{1909} for the previous year by the factor $\left(1 + r \cdot \frac{\Delta k}{k}\right)$ also for the previous year. (Remember $r \cdot \frac{\Delta k}{k}$ gives the rate of change of output per labour unit due only to changes in capital intensity.) So for 1910, for example:

$$q_{1910}^{1909} = q_{1909}^{1909}\left(1 + r_{1909} \cdot \left(\frac{\Delta k}{k}\right)_{1909}\right)$$
$$= 0.623 \times (1 + 0.006)$$
$$= 0.627$$

And for 1911:

$$q_{1911}^{1909} = q_{1910}^{1909}\left(1 + r_{1910} \cdot \left(\frac{\Delta k}{k}\right)_{1910}\right)$$
$$= 0.627 \times (1 + 0.011)$$
$$= 0.634$$

Table A.1   Solow's data

t	q	k	$\frac{\Delta q}{q}$	$\frac{\Delta k}{k}$	r	$r \cdot \frac{\Delta k}{k}$	$\frac{\Delta a}{a}$	q^{1909}
(1)	(2)	(3)	(4)	(5)	(6)	(7)	(8)	(9)
1909	0.623	2.060	−0.011	0.019	0.335	0.006	−0.017	0.623
1910	0.616	2.100	0.050	0.033	0.330	0.011	0.039	0.627
1911	0.647	2.170	0.008	0.018	0.335	0.006	0.002	0.634
1912	0.652	2.210	0.043	0.009	0.330	0.003	0.040	0.638
1913	0.680	2.230	0.003	−0.013	0.334	−0.004	0.007	0.640
1946	1.215	2.500	−0.017	0.000	0.312	0.000	−0.017	0.669
1947	1.194	2.500	0.023	0.020	0.327	0.007	0.016	0.669
1948	1.221	2.550	0.044	0.059	0.332	0.020	0.024	0.673
1949	1.275	2.700	n.a.	n.a.	0.326.	n.a	n.a	0.686

q, k and q^{1909} are expressed in 1939 US dollars per hour of labour.
Source: Solow, 1957

By calculating all the values in column 9 in this way, we can find the shape of the production function, g^{1909}, corresponding to the level of total factor productivity in 1909, depicted in Figure 15.7.

At this stage we are ready to calculate what percentage of the increase in output per labour unit is attributed to technical change and what percentage to capital accumulation. Consider the values of q and q^{1909} for 1909 and 1949. $q^{1909}_{1949} - q^{1909}_{1909}$ is the increase in output per labour unit that we would have observed without technical change. That is, it represents movement along the production function g^{1909}; due to an increase in capital intensity. The value $q_{1949} - q_{1909}$, on the other hand, is the actual increase in output per labour unit. The percentage of the actual increase in output per labour unit due to capital accumulation is therefore calculated from Table A.1 as follows:

contribution of capital accumulation

$$= 100 \cdot \left[\frac{\left(q^{1909}_{1949} - q^{1909}_{1909} \right)}{q^{1949} - q^{1909}} \right] \%$$

$$= 100 \cdot \left[\frac{(0.686 - 0.623)}{1.275 - 0.623} \right] \%$$

$$= 9.7\%$$

In order to calculate the contribution of technical change to the actual increase in output per labour unit, we subtract the percentage contribution of capital accumulation from 100 to give:

contribution of technical change
$$= 100\% - 9.7\% = 90.3\%$$

ANSWERS TO EXERCISES

Exercise 15.1

The shift illustrates a labour-saving innovation. Before the innovation, the firm is producing output $Q = 10\,000$ using technique A, with inputs of L_1 labour and K_1 capital. After the technological change, the firm uses less labour *relative* to capital than before; that is, at the same factor price ratio (shown by the parallel isocost lines), the firm chooses a more capital-intensive technique, B, using L_2 labour and K_2 capital.

This is true even though, as a result of the innovation, the firm uses smaller *absolute* amounts of both capital and labour to produce the same output.

Exercise 15.2

See Figure 15.16. With the same factor price ratio, the firm shifts from technique A to technique C. Capital use increases from K_1 to K_2, while labour use drops sharply. This kind of very labour-saving technological change which actually raises the use of capital is known as 'capital augmenting'.

Exercise 15.3

First you have to calculate $\dfrac{\Delta q}{q}$. For 1947 we have
$$\frac{q^{1948} - q^{1947}}{q^{1947}} = \frac{1.221 - 1.194}{1.194} = 0.023 \text{ as in column 4.}$$

Second, calculate $\dfrac{\Delta k}{k}$:
$$\frac{k^{1948} - k^{1947}}{k^{1947}} = \frac{2.550 - 2.500}{2.500} = 0.020 \text{ as in column 5.}$$

Third, multiply this by the value of r for 1947 (in column 6) to give $r \cdot \dfrac{\Delta k}{k}$:
$$r \cdot \frac{\Delta k}{k} = 0.327 \times 0.020 = 0.007 \text{ as in column 7.}$$

This is the growth of productivity due to the change in capital intensity. The last stage is to subtract this value from the actual growth in productivity:
$$\frac{\Delta a}{a} = \frac{\Delta q}{q} - r \cdot \frac{\Delta k}{k} = 0.023 - 0.007 = 0.016$$

Note: in this answer as in Table A.1, all calculations are rounded to three decimal places.

For 1948, we can repeat the same four steps:

$$\frac{\Delta q}{q} = \frac{1.275 - 1.221}{1.221} = 0.044$$

$$\frac{\Delta k}{k} = \frac{2.700 - 2.550}{2.550} = 0.059$$

$$r \cdot \frac{\Delta k}{k} = 0.332 \times 0.059 = 0.020$$

$$\frac{\Delta a}{a} = 0.044 - 0.020 = 0.024$$

Figure 15.16   A capital-augmenting process innovation

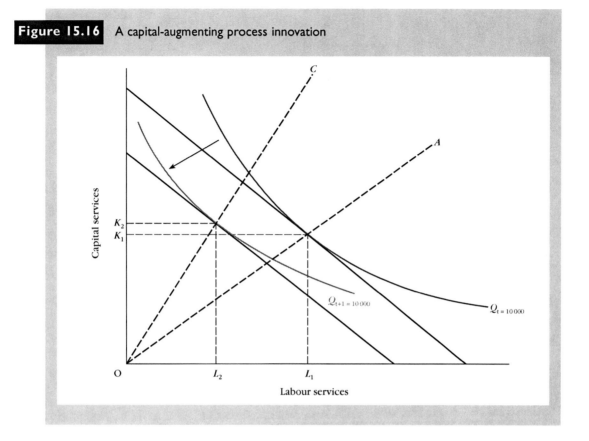

EVOLUTIONARY THEORIES OF TECHNOLOGICAL AND ECONOMIC CHANGE

Roberto Simonetti

CONCEPTS AND TECHNIQUES

Dynamics versus static efficiency

Endogenous change

Creative destruction

Mutation, selection and variety: population perspective

Genes, routines and satisficing

Numerical simulations: Variables, parameters and initial conditions

Selection and imitation: Effects on efficiency and market structure

Fitness, selection and optimization: Panglossian arguments and critique

Increasing returns to the use of a technology: firm (learning) and system (spillovers) level

Network effects

Positive feedback, path-dependency and irreversibility

Stylized facts

LINKS

● The evolutionary theory considered here can be seen as part of institutionalist economics, first considered in relation to one of its pioneers, Thorstein Veblen (Chapter 3)

● Routines, bounded rationality, satisficing behaviour and path-dependency were introduced in Chapter 8. The difference between static and dynamic efficiency was discussed in Chapter 10. Tacit knowledge was introduced in the previous chapter.

● Learning-by-doing and increasing returns to the use of a technology were introduced in Chapters 11 and 15, respectively.

1 INTRODUCTION

You saw in the previous chapter that an increasing number of economists and policy makers have been paying attention to technical change as a central feature of capitalist economies and a main determinant of economic growth. Many of these scholars are also dissatisfied with the neoclassical theory of production, which focuses on static allocative efficiency and neglects the sources of new technology. In particular, the assumption of *rational behaviour* and the focus on *equilibrium* adopted in the neoclassical theory of production do not seem appropriate to the study of technical change, which is characterized by severe uncertainty and is dynamic by definition. Some economists, therefore, have felt the need to incorporate a more realistic representation of how firms behave in order to investigate the dynamic processes that characterize technical change.

Two economists interested in innovation and economic dynamics, Richard Nelson and Sidney Winter, reached the conclusion that technological and economic change is best understood within an evolutionary framework (Nelson and Winter, 1977). Their book *An Evolutionary Theory of Economic Change* (1982) is a source of inspiration for an increasing number of economists. Evolutionary theories, although relatively still in their infancy, have offered interesting insights into the relationship between innovation and economic change.

Although evolutionary theories of economic change have only become accepted in recent years, they build on the work of some institutionalist economists, such as Thorstein Veblen (Veblen's theory of consumption is outlined in Chapter 3). In addition, almost a century ago, an Austrian, Joseph Schumpeter, set out a theory of economic development that is a source of inspiration and a reference point for modern evolutionary economists, including Nelson and Winter.

Evolutionary theories in economics are interesting for several reasons. First, they put dynamics at the forefront of their agenda, thereby filling an important gap in economic theory. Second, they raise methodological issues about theoretical and empirical economic analysis. Third, since their view of the economy is radically different from that provided by general equilibrium theory, evolutionary theories provide a new approach to economic policy.

Section 2 lays out the building blocks of evolutionary theories and Section 3 explores the notions of dynamics and path-dependency. You have already met these concepts in the previous chapter; Section 3 introduces economic models that make them explicit. Section 4 briefly reviews some applications of evolutionary theories, while Section 5 discusses the methodological and policy implications of an evolutionary perspective on economic change.

2 EVOLUTIONARY THEORIES OF ECONOMIC CHANGE

2.1 The Schumpeterian legacy

'The essential point to grasp is that with capitalism we are dealing with an evolutionary process. [...] Capitalism, then, is by nature a form or method of change and not only never is but never can be stationary. And this evolutionary character of the capitalist process is not merely due to the fact that economic life goes on in a social and natural environment which changes and by its change alters the data of economic action; this fact is important and these changes (wars, revolutions and so on) often condition industrial change, but they are not its prime movers. Nor is this evolutionary character due to a quasi-automatic increase in population and capital or to the varieties of monetary systems of which exactly the same thing holds true. The fundamental impulse that acts and keeps the capitalist engine in motion comes from the new consumers' goods, the new methods of production or transportation, the new markets, the new forms of industrial organization that capitalist enterprise creates.'

(SCHUMPETER, 1987 EDN., PP.82–3; ORIGINALLY PUBLISHED 1943)

This statement contains the main theoretical standpoint of the Austrian economist Joseph Schumpeter who was an important source of inspiration for Nelson and Winter.

Question

How do you think Schumpeter (who died shortly before Solow published his analysis of economic growth) would have commented on Solow's results presented in Section 3 of the previous chapter?

It is fair to say that he would not have been surprised. Solow's results showed that innovation was more important than capital accumulation for GNP growth, and in the above quotation, Schumpeter attributes the dynamism of capitalism to 'new consumers' goods' and 'new methods of production' rather than to 'quasi-automatic increase in population and capital'. He therefore stresses that the *qualitative* change that the economy undergoes with economic development is much more important than the quantitative increase in income per capita: '… the contents of labourers' budgets, say from 1760 to 1940, did not simply grow on unchanging lines but they underwent a process of qualitative change' (Schumpeter, 1987 edn., p.83).

Already by the beginning of the twentieth century, Schumpeter had developed a theory of economic development that shared many similarities with modern evolutionary models. He emphasized the importance of *dynamics* and *disequilibrium*, and noted that the main characteristic of capitalism is change from within the system, i.e. *endogenous* change, and the main source of such change is *innovation*. The institution that mainly drives the innovation process is the private firm. In Schumpeter's world, firms do not have access to a public pool of knowledge. They usually follow routinized behaviour while also striving to introduce innovations in order to reap the associated monopoly profits. Like Hayek, another key Austrian economist, Schumpeter embraced the notion of the market as a discovery procedure and creative process (Hayek, 1945). There is no perfect competition, no equilibrium; competition is seen as a process of 'creative destruction' in which successful innovators and some imitators survive, while many other firms disappear (*Changing Economies*, Chapter 6, Section 3). Profits are the reward that entrepreneurs earn for the introduction of innovations, until imitators erode their temporary monopoly. The role of entrepreneurial profit in Schumpeter's theory is very important because entrepreneurs are pushed to innovate by the hope of earning monopoly profits.

In the Schumpeterian theory profits are not seen as a sign of economic inefficiency (see Chapter 15, Section 4) but as the reward that entrepreneurs can earn for successfully introducing innovations. The lure of profits drives the increase in efficiency that stems from the introduction of innovations, and therefore is a major determinant of dynamic efficiency. The price to pay for this dynamism is the static inefficiency that is associated with the temporary monopolies enjoyed by innovators, but it is a price well worth paying in the long run.

The Schumpeterian view of the economy is very different from the picture of an economy in general equilibrium. There are no 'normal profits' nor optimizing agents, and the process of 'creative destruction', in which firms, technologies and industries appear and die, has many similarities with the struggle for survival described in modern evolutionary biology. It comes as no surprise then, that many evolutionary models of 'Schumpeterian competition' have appeared in the literature, and that these models adopt some concepts and mechanisms, such as mutation, selection and fitness, that were originally developed in biology.

Using biological models is not, in fact, a new idea in economics. Alfred Marshall, one of the best known contributors to neoclassical theory, thought that:

> *'The Mecca of economics lies in economic biology rather than in economic mechanics. But biological conceptions are more complex than those in mechanics; a volume on foundations must therefore give a relatively large place to mechanical analogies; and frequent use is made of the term equilibrium, which suggests something of a static analogy.'*
>
> (MARSHALL, 1948; QUOTED IN NELSON, 1995)

The use of equilibrium as an analytical tool was to Marshall only a first step, dictated by the complexity of dynamic analysis. He believed theories that drew on biology would eventually be better at analysing 'the forces that cause movement' (*ibid.*).

2.2   Building blocks of evolutionary theories

Evolutionary theories try to make sense of the evolution of a system, that is, changes in a set of variables that are linked with each other. The approach is necessarily dynamic, as in the Schumpeterian approach. So evolutionary theory is not interested in studying the equilibrium state of a system at a particular point in time, but with understanding the processes by which the variables in a system change. Change and time must, therefore, be explicitly included in the theory.

'Evolutionary', therefore, is not a mere synonym of dynamics. As the British institutionalist Geoff Hodgson points out, evolution in a broad sense can be found in the work of almost all economists, including Walras, the father of the general equilibrium approach (see Chapters 1 and 18; Hodgson, 1993). The types of evolutionary theories that will be considered here study more complex types of dynamics which have two further characteristics. First, they include a mechanism, *mutation*, that generates variety among the units of analysis. Second, they specify another mechanism, *selection*, which, in a systematic way, allows only some units to survive and therefore reduces variety. The existence of variety means that evolutionary theories study populations, groups of heterogeneous units. The explicit adoption of a *population perspective*, therefore, differentiates evolutionary theories from simpler types of dynamic analysis. The existence of selection implies that the individual units in the populations studied interact, for instance, they compete in the same market; some survive and expand their share in the population. It should be clear, therefore, that the concept of a representative agent, a concept commonly used in neoclassical economics, is at odds with an evolutionary approach as it is the existence of differences between units that drives evolution. If all units are the same, there is no selection, no evolution.

Drawing from evolutionary biology, Dosi and Nelson (1994) propose four building blocks of evolutionary theories.

1 An evolutionary theory must define some stable units of analysis – like genes in biology.

2 The units of analysis are 'carried' by some individuals or organizations – like organisms in biology – which are the objects of selection.

3 A mechanism of mutation, which includes some random elements, generates new units of analysis, and renews the variety that is destroyed in the selection process.

4 The organisms that carry the 'genes' interact and some are selected at the expense of others – the fittest survive.

An evolutionary view of the economy requires the presence of these four building blocks. Many specific evolutionary models, however, just focus on particular mechanisms and do not specify all four blocks. I now examine each of these building blocks in more detail.

2.3 Firms, routines and genes

Following the Schumpeterian approach, Nelson and Winter (1982) place the firm at the centre of their evolutionary theory. They reject the neoclassical assumption of rational behaviour as maximization, use Simon's concept of bounded rationality and claim that firms cannot maximize and therefore they have to adopt simple procedures – rules of thumb or *routines* – to determine their behaviour (Chapter 8, Section 5). Routines do not themselves change, they are simply adapted or dropped. Routines that yield satisfactory results, for example a minimum level of profits, are followed until changes in the external environment make them unsatisfactory, or until the firm itself innovates, in which case the firm adopts new routines.

Routines determine what firms can and cannot do. Like individuals, organizations learn through experience and acquire tacit knowledge, skills that are embodied in their routines. Firms' skills include the skills of their employees and managers, but also the way individuals interact, the organizational setting (remember the Ford case study in Chapter 10), corporate culture, patents, brands, and so on. Since each organization has a different history, the combination of routines that embodies its knowledge is different from that of other organizations. Therefore, every firm is unique and possesses unique skills; this is what in Chapter 15, Section 7, I call a firm's *capabilities* or *competencies*.

Routines are important not only because they provide an alternative behavioural assumption to the neoclassical rationality, but also because they provide the basic unit of analysis in Nelson and Winter's evolutionary theory. Routines are the equivalent of genes in evolutionary biology, the stable unit of analysis, since, by definition, they cannot change. Further, since firms do not usually try to substitute new routines if the existing performance is satisfactory, firms tend to behave in the same manner over time. Therefore, the economy is characterized by a significant amount of institutional inertia and any hypothetical convergence towards an equilibrium, in which all firms adopt the most efficient routines, is slow and difficult, or may never happen at all.

The concept of routine is necessarily vague at this general level, and mainly means that firms cannot promptly and constantly adjust their behaviour to ensure that their performance is always optimal. In formal models, however, routines are identified more clearly. They have been defined as 'technologies, policies, behavioural patterns, cultural traits' (Dosi and Nelson, 1994, p.155), depending on what the theory seeks to explain. In the models considered in this chapter, routines are usually defined as technologies and firms as organisms that 'carry' such technologies, which they cannot costlessly or easily change.

It is important to understand that there are two levels of analysis, which correspond to two different populations: genes/routines and organisms/organizations. In Nelson and Winter's theory, routines are the equivalent of genes, whilst the variables that describe the performance of firms, such as profitability, investment and R&D expenditure, are characteristics of organisms.

The second building block in evolutionary modelling is the relationship between these two levels of analysis. In Darwinian biology, organisms cannot change the genes with which they are born during their lifetime. In economies, routines are mostly stable, but this does not necessarily mean that organizations are stuck with their routines in the same way that organisms are stuck with their genes. In most evolutionary models, firms can 'adapt', that is, innovate and/or imitate the routines of successful innovators, although this is not easy and requires expenditure on innovative activities, such as R&D. This is a marked difference between evolutionary theories in biology and economics.

However, imitative efforts are not necessarily successful, just as innovative activities may prove unfruitful. The ease of imitation (and innovation) varies in different theories. If you think of a spectrum, at one end of it you have theories which assume organizations always behave in the same way, and at the other end there are theories which assume organizations immediately adapt their behaviour and quickly adopt the best practice technology. The latter assumption leads towards the neoclassical theory of production, while the former leads to a Darwinian-based economy in which successful routines only increase their share in the population through a Schumpeterian process of 'creative destruction', that is, through the survival and growth of the firms that are lucky enough to have good routines, and the elimination and decline of inefficient firms.

Assuming that firms change routines only rarely (or not at all) might seem quite odd, especially to economists used to the traditional model of the maximizing firm. Nelson, however, points out that 'a number of students of firm behaviour have been impressed that the set of things a firm can do well at any time is quite limited, and that, while firms certainly can learn to do new things, these learning capabilities also are limited' (Nelson, 1995, p.79). Moreover, many empirical studies of firms, technologies and industries regularly show that firms *persistently* differ in a number of features, such as profitability, productivity and innovativeness, and that 'successful firms are often difficult to imitate effectively, because to do so requires that a competitor adopt a number of different practices at once' (*ibid.*).

Some models use just the Darwinian assumption, but the general case allows for situations somewhere along the spectrum. Firms can change their routines, but rarely and slowly. Indeed, you will see that some models include a parameter that specifies the 'ease of imitation', and can study how the results change when the value of that parameter changes.

2.4 Innovation, mutation and variety

Innovation and search routines

Mutation is the mechanism that generates variety, that is, new routines in the population studied – the economy or an industry. The existence of mutation ensures that there is always variety in the pool of routines and in the population of organizations. Indeed, the continued existence of variety is necessary for evolution, so the appearance of new varieties drives the system and gives a meaning to the process of selection. The emphasis on variety, that is, on qualitative differences between technologies and organizations, captures the Schumpeterian emphasis on the qualitative nature of economic change. Not only do productivity and income increase, but also new technologies, firms and industries appear in the economy and compete with existing technologies.

While in biology the creation of variety is achieved through random genetic mutation and sexual reproduction, in the economic models considered here variety is usually created via the innovation process, which, as in the Schumpeterian framework, is influenced by endogenous mechanisms within the model. In some of Nelson and Winter's models the total amount of expenditure on R&D in an industry, which influences the rate of innovation, is not fixed but is determined endogenously from the interaction of competing firms.

Because of the importance of the generation of variety for the theory, evolutionary economists have paid great attention to the innovation process, and have drawn on the literature in various fields in order to identify realistic features of technical change. The works you saw in the previous chapter, historical case studies of technologies, statistical indicators of technical change and studies on the management of innovation, have all contributed to the way in which innovation is conceived and modelled in evolutionary theories. Evolutionary theories stress the importance of tacit knowledge, uncertainty, learning-by-doing and search by trial and error. All regard technology as embodied in a system of institutions, such as firms, universities and government agencies. Indeed, the terms 'national system of innovation' and 'technology system', that you met in the previous chapter, have been developed within an evolutionary framework.

Nelson and Winter embrace the Schumpeterian idea that in capitalist economies the firm is the main source of innovation. However, while Schumpeter, especially in his early writings, mainly attributed the introduction of innovations to the action of the entrepreneur, Nelson and Winter argue that firms have special *search routines* dedicated to the introduction of innovations, that is, of new routines.

You saw in the previous chapter that innovative activity is characterized by severe uncertainty and innovators frequently search by trial and error. The results of the search are partially unforeseeable, and in formal models search can be represented as a random process, as though the outcome was given by, say, the toss of a coin. If firms are lucky they manage to innovate and the greater the resources devoted to innovation, the more likely (but never certain) they are to succeed in innovation. The search, however, is not completely random. Firms employ a set of procedures that involve 'proximate targets, special attention to certain cues and clues, and various rules of thumb' (Nelson and Winter, 1977, p.53). Firms select a small number of projects

following certain criteria that include market considerations, cost, and technical feasibility. The last of these, technical feasibility, is influenced by knowledge previously accumulated by the firm and by the network of institutions with which the firm interacts. As with the case of the steam engine, the innovations introduced will not, in general, be complete breaks with the past but changes in one part of what we called in Section 7.7 of the previous chapter, a technology 'system'. Evolutionary theories are, therefore, particularly applicable to situations in which, instead of distinguishing between innovation and diffusion, it is appropriate to talk about the evolution of technological paradigms (Chapter 15, Section 7.4).

2.5 Economic selection

Selection, variety and efficiency

The picture of the economy that has been built up so far from an evolutionary perspective shows many heterogeneous organizations that have different, fairly stable patterns of behaviour and different competencies which influence their performance. Private firms seek entrepreneurial profits through the introduction of innovations. Only some firms are successful; the others lose out in the competitive race to sell goods and services. The interaction between firms in the economy generates a process of selection in which the fit firms survive and the unfit ones are eliminated.

Selection operates in the opposite direction to mutation by reducing the variety of organizations existing in the economy through the elimination of organizations and routines that are not fit enough to survive. It is important to note that, although the selection mechanism has an ultimate effect on routines, these are not selected directly in the competitive process. Competition on the market acts directly on the organisms (the firms) which undergo selection according to a measure of their performance, for example profitability. Because a firm's performance depends on a combination of factors, the selection of a particular routine will depend not only on the efficiency that it provides, but also on the other factors that contribute to the firm's performance, including the contribution of other routines.

Selection can assume various forms and can operate on different characteristics of firms. The specification of the mechanism of selection is at the core of any evolutionary theory in economics; different selection mechanisms produce different evolutionary theories. In particular, it is important to define which variables affect the performance of firms, and therefore their fitness. In the models we shall be looking at, I start by assuming that the performance of firms depends just on their technology; I relax this assumption later.

The selection environment in many evolutionary models is the market. Firms compete in order to sell more of their products and expand, but only the most efficient firms expand their output. Note that, in this context, efficiency is a *relative* notion; a firm is efficient if it produces at lower unit costs than its competitors. Evolutionary economists do not assume the existence of a known set of best practices. Firms continually search to improve their efficiency, but their search builds incrementally on their specific knowledge. By contrast, neoclassical economists assume the existence of a known set of best practices, hence a known *absolute* level of technical efficiency that firms may or may not attain. In many evolutionary models, efficiency is achieved through successful innovation or imitation. Efficient firms have lower unit costs and therefore, assuming all firms face the same price, higher profits. These additional profits allow them to finance more investment and, through investment, to grow. The ultimate effect of this process is that the use of successful, that is, productive, technology in the economy grows and the use of less efficient technologies shrinks as the less efficient firms who use them contract or disappear. The average efficiency of the whole economy improves with the increase in the share of efficient technology. Selection, therefore, increases economic efficiency by eliminating inefficient technologies.

I shall now clarify how selection works with some numerical examples. These examples will also introduce you to the *simulation* of economic systems, a technique that is widely used in evolutionary modelling. A formal evolutionary model is a system of equations that describe the economic process under study. For our purposes, we can classify the terms in each equation in two types: variables – the terms which evolve over time – and parameters – the terms that are held constant throughout the simulation run. In simple cases, economists can infer the unfolding of evolution, that is, how the variables change over time, by solving the equations algebraically. In many cases, however, the links between the variables in the system are very complex,

and the only way to understand how the economic model 'behaves' is to assign arbitrary values to the variables in the first period (the so-called *initial conditions*) and to the *parameters*, and then to calculate the values of the variables in the following periods using the equations. In this way, economists see how the system evolves, i.e. how the values of the variables change for particular values of the parameters and the initial conditions. By repeating the simulation with different values for parameters and initial conditions, it is possible to have an idea of how the system behaves in a range of situations.

This explanation is rather abstract because the idea of a simulation is not easy to explain in words, the best way is to run one. The following examples should give you an idea of how simulation can be used to help us follow models of how the economy evolves. Models can be very complex, in which case economists have to use computers to simulate the evolution of the economic system under different assumptions. The model we shall examine is simplified, however, so you can 'run' this economic simulation with a calculator, pen and paper.

Although each step of the simulation requires only simple calculations, you may find the density of the formulae and calculations in the next few pages hard going. If you do, carry on reading up to the end of this section only concentrating on the text and the figures in order to understand the basic points illustrated by the simulations. Then, go back through the calculations to gain a deeper understanding of how selection and imitation shape economic competition.

Simulation Run 1: Selection, no imitation

In order to isolate the effect of selection on efficiency, I assume that adaptation, that is, learning or imitation, does not take place; firms are stuck with their technology. I start, therefore, from the Darwinian end of the spectrum that identifies the various types of firm behaviour. In addition, I keep the assumption that the efficiency of the firm, that is, its fitness, depends only on its technology.

Selection dynamics can be very complex. Nelson and Winter use many equations to describe the evolution of an industry. In the simulations that will follow in this section, however, I shall summarize the selection process in a simple equation. Similar selection equations have been used in a variety of dynamic models (see Silverberg, 1998) and the general mathematical structure can be traced back to the biologist R.A. Fisher.

If you consider the population of firms in an industry, the selection equation simply states that the rate of change of the market share of a firm is a function of its *relative fitness* compared with the average fitness of other firms in the industry. The mathematical expression of the law is:

$$G_t^i = \alpha \cdot \left(E_t^i - E_t^{AV} \right)$$

where G_t^i is rate of change of the market share of the *i*th firm at time t, α is a parameter that measures the intensity (and therefore the speed) of selection, E_t^i is a measure of the fitness of the *i*th firm at time t, and E_t^{AV} is the average fitness in the industry at time t. Hence, the expression in brackets, $(E_t^i - E_t^{AV})$ is the relative fitness; that is, the difference between the fitness of the firm and the average fitness of the industry. This equation simply states that those firms that are fitter than average at time t, $E_t^i - E_t^{AV} > 0$, grow, while the others lose market share. The greater the selection parameter α, the greater the effect of a difference in fitness on the changes in market share and therefore the faster the selection. Note that the suffix i in G_t^i (and E_t^i) refers to the ith firm, so for firm A, at time $t=1$, we have $G_{t=1}^A$ and $E_{t=1}^A$.

The next step is to define what is meant by fitness. In this case, I define fitness as the firm's profit margin – the difference between price (the revenue per unit sold) and unit costs. The greater the profit margin made by the firm compared to the industry's average, the greater the rate of change of its market share as it can finance more investment per unit sold than its competitors. If you assume that all firms sell at the same price, the fitness (profit margin) of each firm depends on its costs, that is, on its technology. Firms with better technology have lower costs and earn more profits; therefore they expand their market share. The greater the differential in efficiency, the greater the difference between rates of change in market share and, in turn, the faster the selection – inefficient firms lose market share more quickly.

We are now ready to run our simulation. First, we have to decide on the number of firms in the industry. For our simulation, I have decided that there will be three firms, A, B and C in the industry and each of them has a different technology and therefore different unit costs, C^i. I now have to assign values to the parameters (the terms held constant), which are each firm's costs, C^i, the values of the selection parameter, α, and the output price P, and the initial conditions (the values of the variables in

the first period of the run), which are the market shares of each firm in the first period, $S_{t=1}^i$.

Let us suppose the firms' unit costs are: $C^A = 9$, $C^B = 10$ and $C^C = 11$ and all firms sell at the same price, $P = 15$. Hence, the profit margin of each firm, $\Pi^i = P - C^i$, will be:

$$\Pi^A = 15 - 9 = 6$$

$$\Pi^B = 15 - 10 = 5$$

$$\Pi^C = 15 - 11 = 4$$

Assume that all firms start with the same market share (one third of the market), that is:

$$S_{t=1}^A = S_{t=1}^B = S_{t=1}^C = 0.333$$

and the value of the parameter α is arbitrarily set at 0.5.

Second, the equations that describe the dynamic process we are studying have to be written explicitly. We start from the selection dynamics, which is described by the selection equation, using each firm's profit margin as its measure of fitness. For the ith firm at time t, we have:

$$G_t^i = \alpha \cdot (\Pi_t^i - \Pi_t^{AV}) = 0.5 \, (\Pi_t^i - \Pi_t^{AV})$$

where G_t^i is the rate of change of market share at time t, Π_t^i is the profit margin (fitness) of the *i*th firm at time t, and Π_t^{AV} is the average profit margin (average fitness) of the industry (that is of the three firms) at time t.

We can then use the values of G_t^i to calculate the firm's market shares in the following period, $t+1$, using the formula:

$$S_{t+1}^i = S_t^i \cdot \left(1 + G_t^i\right)$$

where S_{t+1}^i is the market share of the *i*th firm at time $t+1$, and S_t^i is the market share at time t. Thus, the market share of each firm at time $t+1$ is equal to its market share in the previous period multiplied by the factor $\left(1 + G_t^i\right)$.

Finally, we need a formula for the average profit margin in the industry, Π_t^{AV}. To work this out we need to weight the profit margin of each firm by its market share because firms influence average profitability according to their market share. The formula is:

$$\Pi_t^{AV} = \sum_{i=A}^{C} (\Pi_t^i \cdot S_t^i) = (\Pi_t^A \cdot S_t^A) + (\Pi_t^B \cdot S_t^B) + (\Pi_t^C \cdot S_t^C)$$

Thus, in order to calculate the average profit margin in the industry we have to multiply each firm's profit margin by its market share and add the results together. So in the first period, the value of the average profit rate is:

$$\Pi^{AV}_{t=1} = (\Pi^{A}_{t=1} \cdot S^{A}_{t=1}) + (\Pi^{B}_{t=1} \cdot S^{B}_{t=1}) + (\Pi^{C}_{t=1} \cdot S^{C}_{t=1})$$
$$= (6 \times 0.333) + (5 \times 0.333) + (4 \times 0.333) = 5$$

All the values of the parameters (apart from $\alpha = 0.5$) and the initial conditions are reported in Table 16.1.

We can now calculate the growth rate of each firm at t=1. For firm A, we have:

$$G^{A}_{t=1} = 0.5 \cdot (\Pi^{A}_{t=1} - \Pi^{AV}_{t=1}) = 0.5 \times (6 - 5)$$
$$= 0.5 \times 1 = 0.5$$

Question

Calculate the rate of change of the market share of firms B and C at t=1, keeping in mind that:

$$G^{i}_{t=1} = 0.5 \cdot (\Pi^{i}_{t=1} - \Pi^{AV}_{t=1})$$

For firm B, we have:

$$G^{B}_{t=1} = 0.5 \cdot (\Pi^{B}_{t=1} - \Pi^{AV}_{t=1}) = 0.5 \times (5 - 5)$$
$$= 0.5 \times 0 = 0$$

and for firm C:

$$G^{C}_{t=1} = 0.5 \cdot (\Pi^{C}_{t=1} - \Pi^{AV}_{t=1}) = 0.5 \times (4 - 5)$$
$$= 0.5 \times (-1) = -0.5$$

Firm B holds on to its market share because its profits are exactly the same as the average profits of the industry. Firm *C*, however, makes less than average profits so its market share declines in the

following period. The market share of firm *A* in period t=2 becomes:

$$S^{A}_{t=2} = S^{A}_{t=1} \cdot (1 + G^{A}_{t=1}) = 0.333 \times (1 + 0.5)$$
$$= 0.333 \times 1.5 = 0.5$$

Question

Calculate the market shares of firms B and C at time t=2, keeping in mind that:

$$S^{i}_{t=2} = S^{i}_{t=1} \cdot (1 + G^{i}_{t=1})$$

For firm B, we have:

$$S^{B}_{t=2} = S^{B}_{t=1} \cdot (1 + G^{B}_{t=1}) = 0.333 \times (1 + 0)$$
$$= 0.333 \times 1 = 0.333$$

For firm C, we have:

$$S^{C}_{t=2} = S^{C}_{t=1} \cdot (1 + G^{C}_{t=1}) = 0.333 \times (1 - 0.5)$$
$$= 0.333 \times 0.5 = 0.167$$

Since the market shares have changed, we have to calculate the average fitness (profit margin) in period t=2 (the profits are always the same because the price and each firm's costs are fixed for the whole run):

$$\Pi^{AV}_{t=2} = (\Pi^{A}_{t=2} \cdot S^{A}_{t=2}) + (\Pi^{B}_{t=2} \cdot S^{B}_{t=2}) + (\Pi^{C}_{t=2} \cdot S^{C}_{t=2})$$
$$= (6 \times 0.5) + (5 \times 0.333) + (4 \times 0.167) = 5.333$$

Exercise 16.1

Calculate the rates of change of market share for each firm at t=2, their market shares at t=3, and the average industry profit margin at t=3.

Table 16.1 Parameters and initial conditions of the simulation run

	Price	Unit cost	Profit margin	Initial share
Firm A	15	9	6	0.333
Firm B	15	10	5	0.333
Firm C	15	11	4	0.333
Average	15	10	5	–

We can carry on calculating values for many periods, but the dynamics of this simple system are quite clear from the beginning. Firm A, the fittest firm, is gaining market share while the others are declining. Table 16.2 shows the values calculated for the variables up to period 13. The results of the run are summarized in Figures 16.1 and 16.2.

Since all firms sell at the same price, the average unit cost for the industry is the price (unit revenue) less the average profit margin as shown in the final column of Table 16.2. This, and Figure 16.1, clearly show the technical gains that result from selection. As A, the most efficient firm, gains market share, average unit costs for the industry decrease because the best technology is used to produce a greater share of the output of the industry.

Two other features of the model are also worth mentioning. First, Table 16.2 and Figure 16.2 show that, after 13 runs, the fittest firm has become a virtual monopoly, with a market share of 99.9 per

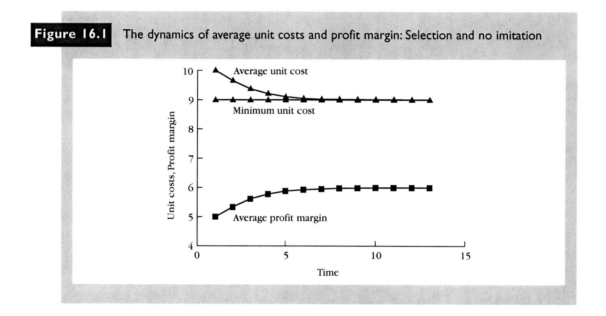

Figure 16.1   The dynamics of average unit costs and profit margin: Selection and no imitation

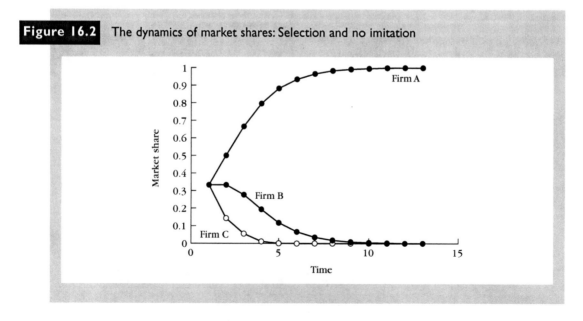

Figure 16.2   The dynamics of market shares: Selection and no imitation

cent, and the other firms have virtually disappeared. Second, since the price is fixed, all the gains in efficiency go to the efficient firm as profit; consumers do not benefit. This result, however, is a necessary consequence of the simple nature of the model, and it is quite easy to set up selection dynamics that do generate benefits to consumers.

Figure 16.2 illustrates well the Schumpeterian process of creative destruction, in which successful firms are rewarded in the market while competitors that do not imitate them in time disappear.

Simulation Run 2: No selection, no imitation

Question

What happens in a second simulation where $\alpha = 0$?

The parameter α quantifies the effect that the difference between the firm's and industry's profitability has on the change in each firm's market share. If $\alpha = 0$, differences in profitability do not affect changes in market share, that is:

$$G_t^i = 0 \cdot (\Pi_t^i - \Pi_t^{AV}) = 0$$

and therefore all market shares remain unchanged and the same at one third, as Figure 16.3 shows. Hence, since firms that use inefficient technologies hold on to their market share, average unit cost remains at the initial level of 10, and does not converge towards the minimum level, 9, achieved by the firm with the best technology (see Figure 16.4). Without selection, the average efficiency of the industry does not improve.

Simulation Run 3: Imitation, no selection

Imitation was explicitly ruled out in our model in the first run, so the fate of firms with inferior technologies was sealed from the start. It is possible, however, to build imitation into the model just by adding an equation. We can assume, for instance, that in every period, firms with inferior technologies catch up with the technological leader by reducing their efficiency gap. This process can be modelled by introducing an equation that describes the dynamics of unit costs for each firm. In the previous model, unit costs for each firm were a parameter, that is, fixed over time. This is equivalent to writing $C_{t+1}^i = C_t^i$, where C_t^i are the unit costs of the ith firm at time t.

Table 16.2 Results of the simulation run 1: Selection and no imitation

Time (t)	Market share (S^i)			Average profit margin (in £)	Rates of change of market shares (G^i)			Average unit costs (in £)
	Firm A	Firm B	Firm C	Π^{AV}	Firm A	Firm B	Firm C	Π^{AV}
1	0.333	0.333	0.333	5.000	0.500	0.000	−0.500	10.000
2	0.500	0.333	0.167	5.333	0.333	−0.167	−0.667	9.667
3	0.667	0.278	0.056	5.611	0.194	−0.306	−0.806	9.389
4	0.796	0.193	0.011	5.785	0.107	−0.393	−0.893	9.215
5	0.882	0.117	0.001	5.881	0.060	−0.440	−0.940	9.119
6	0.934	0.066	0.000	5.934	0.033	−0.467	−0.967	9.066
7	0.965	0.035	0.000	5.965	0.017	−0.483	−0.983	9.035
8	0.982	0.018	0.000	5.982	0.009	−0.491	−0.991	9.018
9	0.991	0.009	0.000	5.991	0.005	−0.495	−0.995	9.009
10	0.995	0.005	0.000	5.995	0.002	−0.498	−0.998	9.005
11	0.998	0.002	0.000	5.998	0.001	−0.499	−0.999	9.002
12	0.999	0.001	0.000	5.999	0.001	−0.499	−0.999	9.001
13	0.999	0.001	0.000	5.999	0.000	−0.500	−1.000	9.001

If we allow for the gradual imitation by firms of best practice technology, unit costs become a variable whose dynamics is described by the equation:

$$C^i_{t+1} = C^i_t - \beta \cdot (C^i_t - C^{MIN}_t)$$

where C^{MIN}_t are the best practice (minimum) unit costs at time t. The value in brackets, $(C^i_t - C^{MIN}_t)$, is the efficiency gap of the ith firm, i.e. the difference in the unit costs of the ith firm and the firm that has the best practice technology. This is what all other firms are trying to reduce by imitation. β is a parameter that measures the ease (speed) of imitation; its value varies between 0 and 1.

If $\beta = 0$, there is no imitation:

$$C^i_{t+1} = C^i_t - 0 \cdot (C^i_t - C^{MIN}_t) = C^i_t$$

Figure 16.3   The dynamics of market shares. Simulation run 2: No selection and no imitation

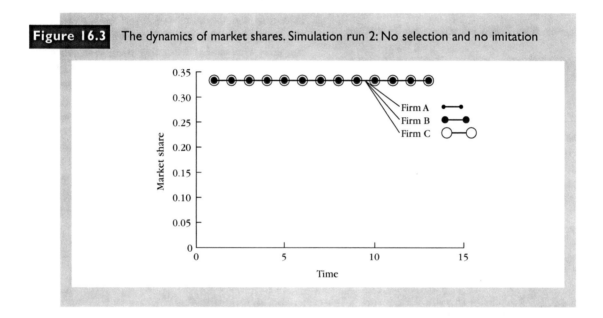

Figure 16.4   The dynamics of unit costs and profit margin. Simulation run 2: No selection and no imitation

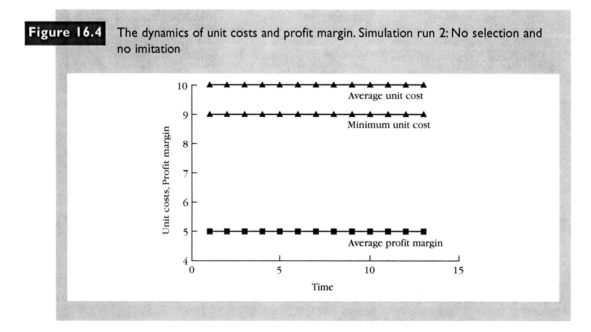

If $\beta = 1$, complete imitation occurs in just one period:

$$C_{t+1}^i = C_t^i - 1 \cdot (C_t^i - C_t^{MIN}) = C_t^i - C_t^i + C_t^{MIN} = C_t^{MIN}$$

If $\beta = 0.5$, in each period the ith firm will halve its efficiency gap. For firm C in the first period, for instance, $C_{t+1}^C = 11$ whereas $C_t^{MIN} = C_{t=1}^A = 9$. Firm C's efficiency gap in the first period is $11 - 9 = 2$. So:

$$C_{t=2}^C = C_{t=1}^C - \beta \cdot (C_{t=1}^C - C_{t=1}^{MIN})$$

$$= 11 - 0.5 \times (11 - 9)$$

$$= 11 - 0.5 \times 2 = 11 - 1 = 10$$

We start by setting $\alpha = 0$ (as in run 2), so that there is no selection and market shares do not change – the chart of the dynamics of market shares is therefore exactly the same as in Figure 16.3. However, unit costs change each period as less efficient firms catch up with the technological leader, firm A. As you can see in Figure 16.5(a), by the time we get to period 10 all firms have virtually the same unit costs, which also correspond to the best practice. For the sake of clarity, average and minimum unit costs are reproduced in Figure 16.5(b). As happened in the first run, the industry average profit margin converges towards 6.

However, there are two interesting differences. First, while in the 'selection and no imitation' model

---

Figure 16.5 The dynamics of unit costs. Simulation run 3: Imitation and no selection

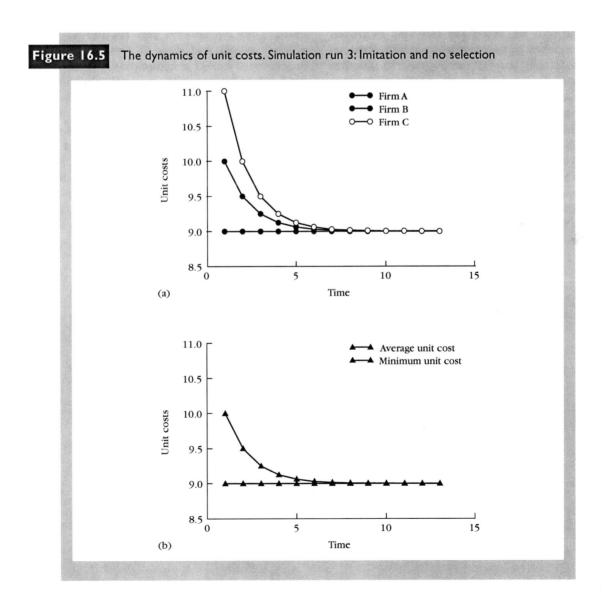

(a)

(b)

we ended up with a monopoly, in this 'imitation and no selection' model, market shares have not changed and industry concentration has not increased. Second, while in the first model technological variety was destroyed by selection *through the elimination of firms* (firms could not change their technology), this time technological variety has been eliminated by the *adaptation of the existing firms*. The 'destruction' of inefficient technologies has occurred inside the firms, not between firms. All firms have become exactly the same in terms of technology. We are now at the neoclassical end of the spectrum, and since all firms are identical it even makes sense to talk about a representative firm that is technically efficient.

Simulation Run 4: Imitation and selection

We can now see in Figures 16.6 and 16.7 what happens when the two mechanisms coexist if we run the model with $\alpha = 0.5$ and $\beta = 0.5$. The imitation process is the same as in Figure 16.5(a) and therefore results in the same fall in unit costs *for each firm*. However, in the early periods, while there are still significant technological differences between firms, selection favours *A*, the most efficient firm. This brings *average* unit costs down faster in Figure 16.6 than in Figure 16.5(b). In Figure 16.6, the dynamics of average unit costs is now clearly visible as they lie below the unit costs of firm *B* in the early periods. Minimum unit costs (best practice technology) still coincide with firm *A*'s unit costs, as in the previous runs.

When imitators manage to catch up with best practice unit costs (in Figure 16.6 it happens around $t = 10$), the market shares of the three firms stabilize (see Figure 16.7). Imitators do not regain the lost market shares, but neither are they driven out of the market. The initial cost advantage has given a permanent advantage to firm *A* before market shares become stable again.

Selection, learning and maximization

The mechanisms behind the results of these simulations are quite intuitive. Either selection or imitation can drive improvements in economic efficiency. You have seen, however, that which assumption we make about firms' behaviour changes the evolution of industry structure quite dramatically. If firms cannot change their behavioural traits (in this case technology) quickly and there is a strong selection, concentrated market structures result. On the other hand, fast imitation tends to generate firms that all behave essentially in the same way.

The models just presented are very simple and focus on the importance of selection and imitation. I have completely neglected innovation and other processes that interact with selection and imitation, such as learning-by-doing and other types of first mover advantages. I have also made some assumptions that may be very unrealistic. For instance, I have assumed that one type of routine – technology – is the only determinant of firm performance, and that

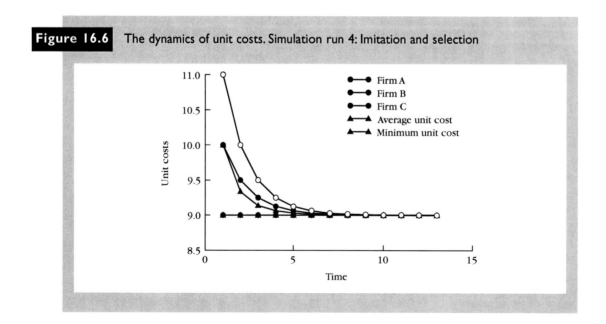

Figure 16.6 The dynamics of unit costs. Simulation run 4: Imitation and selection

imitation is costless. These assumptions can be relaxed and other mechanisms can be taken into account by including more equations in the model. In some cases, the interaction between different mechanisms can generate surprising results, some of which are mentioned later. It is therefore dangerous to interpret these results as a faithful description of what goes on in the economy; reality is more complex.

Because of their intuitive appeal, however, the notions of learning and 'survival of the fittest' are often mentioned in economic arguments in support of the neoclassical assumption that firms optimize their behaviour. Imitation is a form of learning, and you saw in run 3 (imitation and no selection) that if firms learn quickly and selection is weak then all firms end up behaving in the best possible way, i.e. adopting the best practice technology. The neoclassical concept of technology as public information is also associated with the idea that firms can quickly imitate technological leaders. When adaptation fails, selection comes to the rescue. If some firms do not manage to imitate in time, economic selection eliminates them. A standard neoclassical response to the evidence from case studies that firms follow stable patterns of behaviour rather than maximizing is that it is still correct to model firms 'as if' they maximize because the end result is the same (Friedman, 1953). If they do not learn to behave as if maximizing, firms do not survive – as happened in simulation run 1 of our model, although, unlike in that model, the 'as if'

argument assumes that the number of surviving firms is sufficiently large to maintain competition.

Despite its intuitive appeal, however, the 'as if' argument hides some controversial assumptions. First, it implies that selection is faster than mutation, i.e. that competition eliminates inefficient firms faster than it spurs the appearance of new firms and innovations. If variety is generated at least as quickly as it is eliminated, there will always be a significant number of firms that are not using the best technology. This debate can only be solved empirically, and the available evidence offers little support to the 'as if' argument. Evidence that firms are very different, and persistently so, both in terms of behaviour and performance, does not fit with the idea of an economy with strong processes of selection and imitation (Nelson, 1995). On the other hand, many statistical studies of entry and exit of firms strongly support the idea of an economy that continuously eliminates a great number of firms, especially recent entrants (Audretsch, 1995).

The observation that many firms disappear, however, does not necessarily mean that remaining firms behave optimally. In fact, they can even be inefficient in many respects. Our model has reached the conclusion that the firms with the most efficient technology survive and the others are eliminated – either through selection or imitation – only because of the simple assumptions built in it. We have assumed, for instance, that fitness, i.e. profitability,

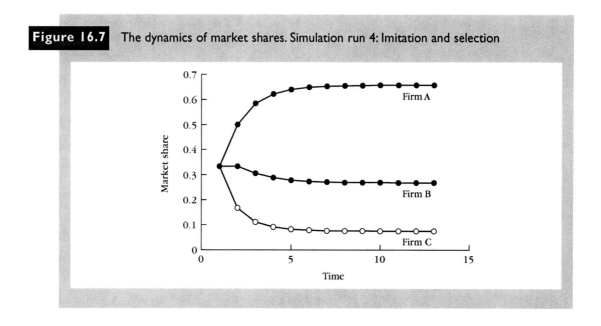

Figure 16.7 The dynamics of market shares. Simulation run 4: Imitation and selection

depends on one single variable, technological efficiency expressed in unit costs, because the price is the same for every firm. Fitness/profitability, however, often depends on non-technological factors, such as marketing strategies, location, ease of access to customers, luck and special privileges. It is quite reasonable, therefore, to assume that firms may be able to sell products at different prices because of product differentiation. In this case, the final result can be different.

Simulation Run 5: Selection, no imitation and product differentiation

Let us assume, for instance, that firm C, which employs the least efficient technology, has a very successful marketing strategy, and creates a brand name that allows it to sell its product at a higher price, $P = 18$. Firm C is now the fittest; it earns a bigger profit $\Pi_t^C = 18 - 11 = 7$ than the other two, $\Pi_t^A = 15 - 9 = 6$ and $\Pi_t^B = 15 - 10 = 5$, although firm C uses the worst technology. If we run our model setting the parameters as in the first run, $\alpha = 0.5$ and $\beta = 0$, that is, with selection working and without imitation, we find out that firm C expands and dominates the industry, as you can see in Figure 16.8.

As in the first run, selection generates a concentrated market structure, but this time it is not the firm with the best technology that dominates. The weight of the best technology in the industry shrinks as the market share of the firm which uses it declines. In fact, Figure 16.9 shows that now the worst technology dominates, and industry unit costs increase, as do average price and profits. As a result of selection, average unit costs in the industry have actually increased.

This example shows that firms selected for growth are not necessarily those that behave in an optimal way in all respects. It also sheds light on the meaning of the phrase 'survival of the fittest'. As in the previous cases, the fittest firm survives; firm C is the most profitable. However, the meaning of 'fittest' is open to interpretation as firm C has the worst efficiency. In evolutionary models the fittest firms survive by definition, because we specify it in the model, but this does not entail optimization. In the last run, firm C had the best selling price, but it is quite possible to build a model in which a firm which is not optimal in any feature becomes the market leader.

The message of this example is that you must not confuse fitness and survival with optimization. Economic selection is often (sometimes implicitly) used to support the argument that firms – or, more generally, institutions – that have survived are the best possible. This position is usually called Panglossian, after the philosopher Pangloss in Voltaire's *Candide* who always claimed that we live in the best of all possible worlds, and that anything that happened was for the best.

The Panglossian argument has two main flaws. First, better institutions that are possible might not

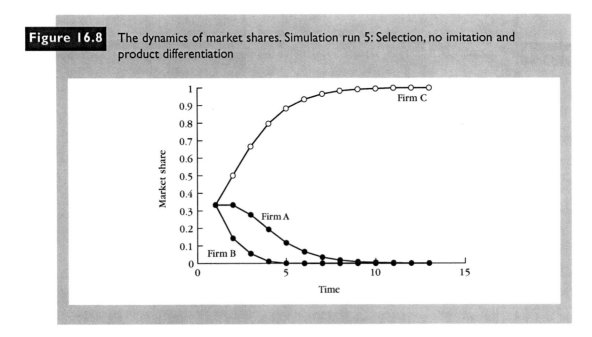

Figure 16.8 The dynamics of market shares. Simulation run 5: Selection, no imitation and product differentiation

have actually appeared. If the creation of variety happens rarely then better institutions are not very likely to appear although they are possible. Second, selection is a complex mechanism that does not guarantee optimization. We have seen a 'perverse' result, from a technological perspective, which occurred because fitness also depends on variables other than technological efficiency. Since selection works on fitness, which may depend on attributes of the organism that are not genetically determined, selection does not always ensure that the best genetic material, the best technologies, survive. In other words, when imitation is weak, the fate of the technologies is strictly linked to that of the organizations which 'carry' them.

3   PATH DEPENDENCY AND ECONOMIC EVOLUTION

3.1   *Modelling innovation*

Now that you have explored the building blocks of evolutionary theories, we can think how simple models of selection and adaption could be extended. We could start by adding innovation to our model of economic selection.

Question

How would you include innovation in the models of economic selection seen in the previous sections?

To capture the unpredictability of the outcome of innovative activities, innovation is often represented in formal models as the output of a random process, such as the toss of a die. In our model, unit costs could be made to depend on such a random variable. If the result of the toss is, say, 6, the lucky firm innovates and becomes the technological leader, otherwise costs follow their usual dynamics.

Modelling innovation in this way, however, conforms to the traditional ideas of exogenous technical change; innovation just 'falls from the sky'. In fact, the output of innovative activity is influenced by economic factors, such as the amount of resources devoted to innovation and the ease with which firms can appropriate the returns to innovation. The fact that the same technology can have different effects on profitability across firms should also be taken into account. Some firms might be able to exploit the opportunities offered by a technology more fully if they have complementary assets, or might use the technology with increasing efficiency as they learn more about them over time. Representing technical change as just a one-off shift in unit costs neglects

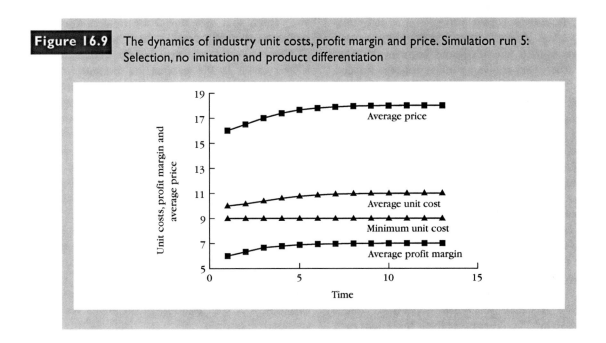

Figure 16.9   The dynamics of industry unit costs, profit margin and price. Simulation run 5: Selection, no imitation and product differentiation

phenomena which generate dynamic increasing returns to use such as learning-by-doing (see Chapter 11, Section 2.2; Jovanovich and Nyarko, 1995).

Further, it should be possible to distinguish, for instance, between discontinuities due to changes of paradigm and incremental technical change within a paradigm (Chapter 15, Section 7). This distinction is useful as it takes into account the fact that technical change is characterized by increasing returns to use for the economy as a whole and overcomes the somewhat artificial distinction between innovation and diffusion (Dosi, 1988). Since the knowledge produced in the innovative process is also used as an input for future innovations, the more a technology (a paradigm) is adopted in the economy, the better it becomes, as firms and other institutions (suppliers, customers, universities) learn about it; many adoptions are therefore also incremental innovations that improve the technology. The time of adoption of a technology, therefore, becomes an important variable. More developed evolutionary models have provided a useful framework for analysing the economic effects of such increasing returns to use in a variety of contexts at the individual firm, industry and economy level.

3.2 Increasing returns and competition between technologies

Increasing returns to use of a technology operate both at the firm level, as each firm uses a technology more efficiently, and at the system level, as many institutions adopt the technology and therefore improve it. Some models have explored both mechanisms while others have concentrated on just one of them.

Variety, selection and diffusion: Silverberg, Dosi and Orsenigo's model Silverberg *et al.* (1988) have built a model of the diffusion of two competing technologies, which includes many of the features of technical change just mentioned. In their model, the existing dominant technology (paradigm) has exhausted its potential for improvement, and a new technology, which has a large *potential* for improvement, becomes available for all firms to adopt. The *actual* efficiency of the new technology, however, is low at the start, and only adoption by pioneers can improve it. Firms that adopt the technology develop it and learn to use it more efficiently with time, and therefore they gain first mover advantages against later adopters. This favours the firms that adopt early

– as in Scherer's study of learning-by-doing in the semiconductor industry that was discussed in Chapter 11, Section 2.2. Some of the improvements, however, spill over into the system, and some competitors can start learning about the new paradigm from a higher level of efficiency (for instance, they might share some suppliers). Since these 'early followers' have not borne the expenditure to develop the technology, they can be more profitable than the pioneers and expand faster.

The authors run the model under different conditions. The outcome of the simulations is influenced by the relative strength of two factors, learning by an adopting firm and spillover effects to other firms. If learning is fast and early adoption generates high efficiency advantages, pioneers gain a substantial lead on competitors who will not be able to catch up, and will go on to dominate the market – this is Scherer's case. However, if appropriability is weak, that is, there are significant spillovers and competitors benefit without spending, pioneers pay for the substantial expenditure incurred to develop a technology which also becomes accessible to competitors for free (this is the problem identified by Arrow, see Chapter 15, Section 4). Pioneers will, therefore, lose market share. When the run starts, firms do not know how fast they will learn and how much knowledge will spill over to other firms, and therefore form different expectations about the relative strength of the two processes. Depending on their expectations, they adopt the next technology at different times. If they think that first mover advantages outweigh spillovers, they adopt early, otherwise they wait.

Various results are possible depending on the values given to the parameters for learning and appropriability. If learning is fast and appropriability strong, the first adopter dominates the industry. For a wide range of values of the two parameters, however, firms that adopt just after the earliest pioneers – early followers – end up dominating the industry, as they exploit the spillovers generated by the pioneers but also start learning early enough. Firms that adopt only when the new technology has overtaken the old technology in productivity, cannot catch up.

This result is very interesting for a number of reasons. First, you can see that there are increasing returns to the adoption of the technology at both the firm and the industry level. Each firm enjoys increasing returns due to learning-by-doing, and the efficiency of the technology improves with the number of adopters.

Second, and more interestingly, when early followers dominate against pioneers and late adopters, the technology would not have come to dominate the industry without the existence of pioneers. At the beginning of the run, the actual efficiency of the new technology is so low that most firms are not ready to invest in it. The early followers adopt the new technology only after its actual efficiency has risen because of prior investment in it by over-optimistic pioneers, who wrongly thought that first mover advantages would outweigh spillovers. Quick followers would not have adopted the technology if nobody else had started the development first, and therefore the actual efficiency of the new technology would not have grown enough to overtake the old dominant technology. The unlucky pioneers, who unwillingly end up paying for their excessive optimism, are necessary for the final success of the new technology. However, they would not have invested in it had they known the real balance between first mover advantages and spillovers.

The intriguing conclusion of Silverberg *et al.*, therefore, is that a potentially better technology might not be developed – or might be developed much later – without the presence of over-optimistic pioneers. Two factors contribute to the success of the new technology. First, firms lack information about the future efficiency of new technology and about the extent of learning and spillovers; they guess. Second, firms are heterogeneous so they have different expectations about the technology and make different guesses. But heterogeneity implies that some over-optimistic firms can exist. If all firms guess correctly, nobody would adopt the new technology, knowing that the first adopters would fail.

The results are certainly not Panglossian, and the mechanism is not neoclassical. A potentially better technology may not come to dominate, and, even if it does, it may have been initially adopted only because firms are different and some get it wrong. Instead of perfect foresight and perfect knowledge about new technology we have a variety of expectations and firms that get it wrong are destroyed. Adaptation is slow, and selection is a driving force in the evolution of the new technology.

Random events, network externalities, irreversibility and path-dependency: Arthur's model

Another very influential model that puts increasing returns to use at its core has been developed by Brian Arthur, an economist interested in the evolution of complex systems (Arthur, 1989). In his model, two new technologies compete, and the returns to the adoption of each technology increase with the number of agents (firms or customers) that adopt it. There is positive feedback to the adoption of either technology. Arthur's model shows how increasing returns affect competition between technologies, and, more importantly, provides a very clear example of path-dependency at work. Since path-dependency has been mentioned in several parts of the course, it is worth looking at it more closely here, using a numerical example. In order to do so, I shall develop a very simplified version of Arthur's model and carry out a simple simulation.

Let us consider a model with two types of agents, H and T, who have to choose between two technologies, A and B. You can think of them as customers that have to choose between two computer operating systems, for instance, Mac and Windows, or as firms that have to choose between two new process technologies. The decision as to which technology to adopt depends on the returns to the adoption of each of the competing technologies, which are, in turn, influenced by two factors. First, agents naturally prefer one of the two technologies because they gain higher returns from the adoption of one technology; in particular, H-agents naturally prefer technology A, and T-agents naturally prefer B. Second, the returns to adoption of each technology also depend on the number of agents that have adopted the technology at the moment of the agent's decision. If most of the agents have chosen a particular technology, it is sensible to make the same choice for a number of reasons; more resources are devoted to the improvement of widely-adopted technology, and the uncertainty that surrounds its effectiveness declines as its familiarity increases; there are more users of the same technology with whom (as in the case with computer systems) to share information (this mechanism is called the *network effect*, or sometimes *network externalities*, as the returns to the adoption of a technology depend on the decision of a network of users); there are *economies of scale*, both static and dynamic, to exploit as producers can sell to a large market; as a technology becomes more common a *complementary infrastructure* appears (as with petrol stations with the diffusion of cars driven by internal combustion engines).

Network effect

This occurs when an agent's returns to the adoption of a technology changes with the number of agents that adopt that technology.

It is reasonable to assume that the difference in the number of adopters only matters when the lead of one technology is large enough. In the model we are considering, I have arbitrarily decided that a lead of ten adopters is the threshold. If neither technology leads by more than ten adoptions, agents choose their naturally favourite technology (H-agents choose A, T-agents choose B). However, if one technology leads by more than ten adoptions, there is positive feedback and *all* agents choose the leading technology, that is, the agents that naturally prefer the other technology switch their allegiances.

Table 16.4 Competition between technologies: Simulation results

Total adoptions (1)	Agent drawn (2)	No. of H-agents (3)	No. of T-agents (4)	Adoptions of A (5)	Adoptions of B (6)	Lead of A (7)
1	H	1	0	1	0	1
2	H	2	0	2	0	2
3	T	2	1	2	1	1
4	T	2	2	2	2	0
5	H	3	2	3	2	1
6	T	3	3	3	3	0
7	H	4	3	4	3	1
8	H	5	3	5	3	2
9	H	6	3	6	3	3
10	H	7	3	7	3	4
11	T	7	4	7	4	3
12	H	8	4	8	4	4
13	H	9	4	9	4	5
14	H	10	4	10	4	6
15	T	10	5	10	5	5
16	H	11	5	11	5	6
17	H	12	5	12	5	7
18	H	13	5	13	5	8
19	T	13	6	13	6	7
20	H	14	6	14	6	8
21	T	14	7	14	7	7
22	T	14	8	14	8	6
23	H	15	8	15	8	7
24	H	16	8	16	8	8
25	T	16	9	16	9	7
26	H	17	9	17	9	8
27	H	18	9	18	9	9
28	H	19	9	19	9	10
29	H	20	9	20	9	11
30	T	20	10	21	9	12
31	T	20	11	22	9	13
32	H	21	10	23	9	14

There is one adoption each round and in each there is an equal probability that the adopting agent is of type H or of type T ($p = 0.5$).

I can now run the simulation using a coin to determine which type of agent makes the decision each round: an H-agent (T-agent) is selected when a head (tail) is shown. You can run your own simulation by simply tossing a coin and recording the results in a table. My results are recorded in Table 16.4:

● column 1 shows the number of rounds (adoptions of either technology)

● column 2 reports the result of each toss H (head) or T (tail)

● columns 3 and 4 indicate the total number of H-agents (T-agents) drawn up to that round

● columns 5 and 6 report the total number of adoptions of each technology; these are the same as columns 3 and 4 until one of the two technologies leads the other by more than ten adoptions; after that the leading technology is always chosen, and so just increases its lead

● column 7 shows the lead of technology A; it is calculated by subtracting the figure in column 5 from that in column 6. When B leads, the figure is negative.

In the simulation presented in Table 16.4, the first toss of the coin (H) indicates that the first adopter is an H-agent. So technology A leads by one adoption. The process is repeated until the 29th round, when the 20th adoption of technology A gives it a lead of 11 adoptions with a total of 20 against the 9 adoptions of B. From this round onwards, all T-agents switch their preference to technology A, as in rounds 30 and 31, and therefore the lead of A increases with every round. Nobody chooses B anymore, and the industry is 'locked into' technology A.

The results of the run are shown in Figure 16.10, which shows the lead of technology A. The thresholds beyond which each technology is always adopted are represented by horizontal 'absorbing barriers'. Once one of the barriers is crossed, there is no return. One technology, in this case A, wins and the other is subsequently never adopted again.

Note that we could have easily had the opposite result: the system could have been locked into technology B if more T-agents had adopted early. The decision of a few firms to be early adopters, which is modelled as a random variable in this model, has determined which technology succeeds. Either technology could have been selected; the success of one depended on a *sequence* of small random events which determined the *path* that the process followed. History – the sequence of events – matters. For this reason, the process is said to be *path-dependent*. Taken to the limit, one can imagine a situation in which the decision of a single agent makes a dramatic difference.

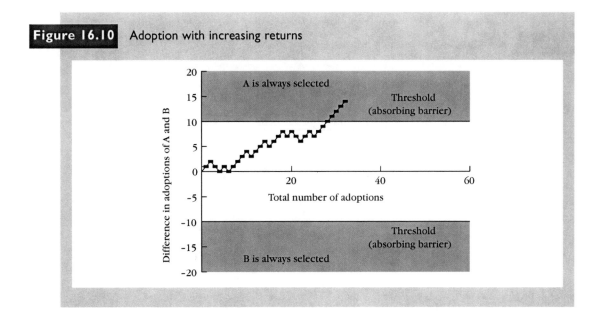

Figure 16.10   Adoption with increasing returns

Imagine a run similar to the one described in Table 16.4, but with the sequence of adoption in rounds 29 and 30 inverted. As shown in Table 16.5, technology A does not reach the threshold after which increasing returns make all firms choose to adopt it, and the system is not locked in. By round 34, if T-agents continue to be the next to adopt, as in Table 16.5, A's lead drops to six and the competition becomes wide open again.

Figure 16.11 shows a run in which technology B ends up winning the 'race'. The switch between an H-agent and a T-agent in rounds 29 and 30 has changed the whole picture. Note that the total number of agents adopting each technology in the first 32 rounds has not changed; only the *order* in which they appear. The action of one agent deciding to adopt the technology one round later, can, unknowingly, change the destiny of the whole system.

Table 16.5 Competition between technologies: Simulation results with a new sequence

Total Adoptions (1)	Agent drawn (2)	No. of H-agents (3)	No. of T-agents (4)	Adoptions of A (5)	Adoptions of B (6)	Lead of A (7)
1	H	1	0	1	0	1
...	...	...	...	...	...	...
27	H	18	9	18	9	9
28	H	19	9	19	9	10
29	T	19	10	19	10	9
30	H	20	10	20	10	10
31	T	20	11	20	11	9
32	T	20	12	20	12	8
33	T	20	13	20	13	7
34	T	20	14	20	14	6
...	...	...	...	...	...	...

Figure 16.11 Adoption with increasing returns: a new sequence

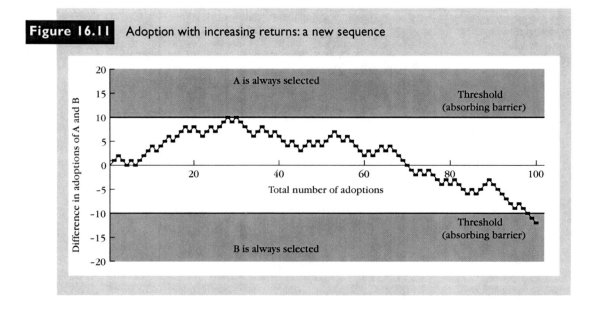

Reflection

If you are deciding between cable or satellite TV, the fate of broadcasting technology may depend on your decision!

A consequence of path-dependency is *non-predictability*. It is impossible to know in advance which technology will succeed because the sequence of values that the random variable will assume cannot be predicted – by definition, they are random.

More importantly, in the presence of increasing returns, processes that are path dependent can generate inefficiency in the long run. Let us assume, for instance, that technology B is better than technology A in the long run, but its superiority is only revealed after at least 30 agents have adopted it. Until the 30th adoption of B, agents base their decision only on their natural preferences and on the number of adopters. In our original run, B never gets the chance to be adopted 30 times because the system is locked-in to A by the time B has been adopted only nine times. Technology B, which is *potentially* better, never diffuses far enough to show it.

Increasing returns also make the *timing* of the introduction of a technology very important. In the model, I assumed that both technologies started at the same time. A technology that has an early start, however, could corner the market straightaway even if another technology is potentially better in the long run.

Note that without increasing returns to use such inefficiency could not occur in this model. If there are constant returns, the returns to the adoption of a technology do not change with the number of adopters, and agents always choose according to their natural preference. There are no absorbing barriers. Sooner or later, technology B will be adopted by 30 agents and its superiority will be revealed. Technology B will also end up dominating in the case of diminishing returns to use, which are represented by 'reflecting barriers'. If a technology leads by more than ten agents, all agents adopt the other, so no technology corners the system until technology B proves superior. Diminishing returns to use occur when scarce resources are needed to use a technology. Arthur (1989), for instance, mentions the case of hydro-electric technology which required a scarce resource, suitable dam sites, to work effectively.

4 METHODOLOGICAL ISSUES: THEORY AND EVIDENCE

The models you saw in the previous section are interesting because they show that market selection does not necessarily produce optimal results. So a question comes to mind: How frequently do these 'mistakes' happen? How many 'inferior' technologies have been adopted just because of historical accident?

A number of studies have argued that these 'mistakes' are more frequent than you might think. The history of the QWERTY keyboard (*Changing Economies*, Chapter 15) is one of the first examples of inferior technology locked in by positive feedback, but some other examples include the competition between VHS and Betamax in VCR technology, between four technologies – light-water, gas-cooled, heavy-water and sodium-cooled reactors – in nuclear energy, between chemicals and integrated pest management in pest control, and, believe it or not, between internal combustion (petrol) and steam technology in automobile engines.

Many of these case studies are very convincing, but the issues often remain unresolved as it is often possible to argue that the successful technology was, in fact, the best one. The problem is that it is impossible to find irrefutable evidence of what 'could have happened' if a few small events had been different. You can run a simulation many times and find out the average behaviour of a complex system, but real history occurs only once.

The possibility that small historical events can dramatically shape history also means that a theoretical model of economic and technical change might require more detailed knowledge of all the events that might have affected the evolution of the process and of their timing, than we can possibly have in such circumstances. There is the danger of giving too much importance to anecdotal evidence that is, in fact, irrelevant. Some technologies might be so much better than the competition that they would end up being successful in any case. It is important, however, to look with suspicion on Panglossian positions that argue the superiority of a technology, a firm or, more generally, of an institution just because it has survived against the competition. Survival alone is not a proof of optimality.

That they warn us that better worlds might be possible is not the only merit of evolutionary theories.

Richard Nelson (1995) argues that evolutionary theories are preferable to those based on equilibrium theorizing because they frequently provide a better explanation of the phenomena studied.

But what does 'better' mean? Nelson specifies that better does not mean that the predictive power of evolutionary theories is greater than that of neoclassical theories, or the statistical fit of regression analyses based on evolutionary models is systematically higher. The complexity of evolutionary theories, which tackle out-of-equilibrium dynamics of complex systems and confer a crucial role on small historical events, can actually reduce their predictive power relative to explanations based on equilibrium. However, 'the advocate of an evolutionary theory might reply that the apparent power of the simpler theory in fact is an illusion' (Nelson, 1995, p.85) when reality is, in fact, complex.

> *'Instead, by 'better explanation' one means that it is consistent with informed judgements as to what really is going on ... [and] ... those informed judgements reflect inferences drawn from a broad and diversified body of data. [...] This said, it is clear that one of the appeals of evolutionary theorizing about economic change is that that mode of theorizing does seem better to correspond to the actual processes, as these are described by the scholars who have studied them in detail.'*

> (*ibid.*)

Nelson's reference to the need to support theory with a 'broad and diversified body of data' is particularly interesting, and leads to two important considerations. First, economic processes are complex, and a single research methodology cannot fully capture this complexity. Economic theories must be evaluated using different types of 'data', by which I do not only mean the statistics used in traditional econometric work, but also evidence from historical research, case studies, interviews, ethnographic research and other research methods. The importance of qualitative differences in evolutionary theories means that quantitative research methods might miss some important aspects of the phenomena studied. Indeed, historical work and case studies have been important sources of knowledge about innovation, and new data sets have been generated in order to carry out quantitative analyses of phenomena that have been originally investigated with qualitative research techniques. For instance, the measurement of appropriability in the Yale survey on innovation, which has been used in econometric studies (Levine *et al.*, 1985), has its roots in qualitative and theoretical research.

Second, Nelson claims that theories should be evaluated by how well they explain a variety of *stylised facts* that have been identified by empirical studies. The notion of a set of stylised facts was originally put forward by Nicholas Kaldor (1978). He argued that the first step in the construction of a theory is the identification of some facts that the theory seeks to explain. However, since facts, as they are recorded in actual data, reflect historical contingencies, the economist should first identify some 'broad tendencies' that the theory should explain. Stylised facts are, therefore, recorded facts filtered from historical contingencies. The theorists should then formulate a hypothesis to account for these stylised facts. Kaldor, for instance, built a theory of capital accumulation and economic growth in industrialized countries that tried to explain some stylised facts; the continued increase of capital per worker, the roughly steady rate of profit on capital, steady capital-output ratios, and the absence of a falling rate of productivity growth.

However, the definition of stylised facts can be a source of controversy because the distinction between broad tendencies and historical contingencies is always debatable. Dosi *et al.* (1995), for instance, seem to identify stylised facts with empirical regularities, results that have been found in a number of studies, and argue that, for a model, 'accounting for a multitude of regularities *together* is certainly a point of analytical strength' (Dosi *et al.*, 1995, p.22, emphasis in the original).

Although evolutionary theories have been quite capable of explaining large sets of stylised facts, currently their use is still largely restricted to explaining technical change in circumstances in which the market operates selection. The evolution of science, and of technologies in sectors where market forces are weak, such as for military and medical technologies, has not been tackled. Evolutionary theories are also less useful in situations in which agents have all the relevant information they need and change is slow; then equilibrium theorizing can produce an acceptable approximation to reality. In these cases, neoclassical theory and game theory may provide the researcher with more useful tools of analysis.

5 CONCLUSION: ECONOMIC EXPERIMENTS AND ECONOMIC GROWTH

This chapter has introduced you to evolutionary theories, which adopt a dynamic view of the economy, emphasize the importance of technical change, and treat uncertainty as a central feature of economic life. In a world full of uncertainty, agents cannot maximize and do not possess perfect foresight. Instead, they make mistakes and stick to satisfactory behavioural patterns, while, at the same time, they learn slowly and attempt to innovate in order to survive in the Schumpeterian gales of creative destruction.

Creation and destruction dominate the evolution of the economy. The innovation mechanism generates new technologies, firms and institutions, while selection and adaptation eliminate institutions that are clearly unfit, and favour those that are good enough; failure at the micro level is widespread but necessary for progress at the system level. Pioneer losers are also sometimes necessary for the successful development and diffusion of superior new technologies.

An evolutionary view of the economy implies a notion of economic progress, although progress is achieved at the high price of a number of individual tragedies and we do not live in the best of all possible worlds. The ultimate source of this progress is the creative development of new technologies and new organizational forms that replace those eliminated by selection. The stunning performance of capitalism described at the start of Chapter 15 is ultimately due to its ability to create organizational diversity, by what Nathan Rosenberg (1992) calls 'economic experiments'. He argues that:

> *'... the history of capitalism involved the progressive introduction of a number of institutional devices that facilitated the commitment of resources to the innovation process by reducing or placing limitations upon risk while, at the same time, holding out the prospect of large financial rewards to the successful innovator. [...] Technological achievements were thus based upon capitalist legal institutions, especially with respect to contracts and property rights, that legitimized the right to experiment with the new organizational forms as well as with new technologies.'*
>
> (ROSENBERG, 1992, PP.190–1)

The emergence of financial institutions has been crucial to the success of capitalism and continues to influence the efficiency of the economy (Chapter 17). Institutions such as limited liability, insurance and the stock market favour the accumulation of capital for investment and innovation, and limit the risks associated with experiments.

Drawing on Marx, Rosenberg also stresses the importance of the rise of the bourgeoisie, which 'is the first ruling class whose economic interest are inseparably tied to change and not to the maintenance of the status quo' (Rosenberg, 1992, p.184). In capitalist societies, authority is decentralized and economic agents have the incentive and are free to chase what Schumpeter called 'entrepreneurial profit' from innovation. The knowledge accumulated by the institutions in the economy through the outcomes of economic experiments has contributed to the success of capitalism. Even failures are important in the long run as they indicate which avenues should not be pursued, thereby limiting the waste of future resources. Indeed, Rosenberg even argues that the failure of socialism in the twentieth century is a consequence of an institutional structure that did not promote, and even hindered, the emergence of new organizational forms.

After so much praise of innovation, evolution and capitalist progress, a warning now is necessary. Although economic growth is not the same as improving welfare and the quality of life, we can reasonably say that the standard of living in capitalist economies has never been so high. However, evolutionary theories teach us that evolution is myopic, and technologies that are more environmentally sustainable might be locked out of the economy while irreversible damage is done (Cowan, 1996). Environmental criteria, after all, rarely determine the selection mechanisms. Industrialization is rapidly increasing in the world, and the levels of pollution and population are reaching levels that worry an increasing number of scientists. Global warming is just one example of a by-product that has been generated, or at least accelerated, by capitalism's economic success. As a final note of caution, when we praise the achievements of capitalism, it is worth keeping in mind what the palaeontologist Stephen Gould wrote about dinosaurs' stupidity:

'The remarkable thing about dinosaurs is not that they became extinct, but that they dominated the earth for so long. Dinosaurs held sway for 100 million years while [...] people, on this criterion, are scarcely worth mentioning [...] a mere 50,000 years for our own species, Homo Sapiens. *[...] Try the ultimate test within our system of values: Do you know anyone who would wager a substantial sum, even at favourable odds, on the proposition that* Homo Sapiens *will last longer than* Brontosaurus?'*

(GOULD, 1980, PP.220–1).

FURTHER READING

Background reading on evolutionary theories and technical change include:

Dosi, G., Freeman, C., Nelson, R., Silverberg, G. and Soete, L. (eds) (1988) *Technical Change and Economic Theory*, London, Pinter.

Schumpeter is constantly quoted by evolutionary economists:

Schumpeter, J.A. (1961) *The Theory of Economic Development* (first edition 1911, second edition 1926), New York, Oxford University Press.

Schumpeter, J.A. (1987) *Capitalism, Socialism and Democracy* (first British edition 1943), London, Unwin Paperbacks.

The following articles discuss path dependency and locked-in inferior technologies:

Arthur, W.B. (1988) 'Competing technologies: an overview', in Dosi *et al.*, pp.590–607.

Cowan, R. (1996) 'Sprayed to death: path dependence, lock-in and pest control strategies', *Economic Journal*, 106, pp.521–42.

The mathematically minded might be interested in two formal evolutionary models of the evolution of technology and market structure:

Winter, S.G. (1984) 'Schumpeterian competition in alternative technological regimes', *Journal of Economic Behavior and Organization*, vol.5, pp.287–320.

Dosi, G., Marsili, O., Orsenigo, L. and Salvatore, R. (1995) 'Learning, market selection and the evolution of industrial structures', *Small Business Economics*, vol.7, pp.1–26.

For those who don't mind trespassing into biology, Gould's work provides a good critique of the Panglossian perspective in biology:

Gould, S.J. and Lewontin, R.C. (1979) 'The spandrels of San Marco and the Panglossian paradigm: a critique of the adaptionist programme', *Proceedings of the Royal Society*, vol.205, pp.581–98.

Gould, S.J. (1980) *The Panda's Thumb*, Harmondsworth, Penguin.

ANSWERS TO EXERCISES

Exercise 16.1

Rates of growth at $t = 2$

Firm A:

$$G^A_{t=2} = 0.5 \cdot (\Pi^A_{t=2} - \Pi^{AV}_{t=2}) = 0.5 \times (6 - 5.333)$$
$$= 0.5 \times (0.667) = 0.334$$

Firm B:

$$G^B_{t=2} = 0.5 \cdot (\Pi^A_{t=2} - \Pi^{AV}_{t=2}) = 0.5 \times (5 - 5.333)$$
$$= 0.5 \times (-0.333) = -0.167$$

Firm C:

$$G^C_{t=2} = 0.5 \cdot (\Pi^A_{t=2} - \Pi^{AV}_{t=2}) = 0.5 \times (4 - 5.333)$$
$$= 0.5 \times (-1.333) = -0.667$$

Market shares at $t = 3$

Firm A:

$$S^A_{t=3} = S^A_{t=2} \cdot (1 + G^A_{t=2}) = 0.5 \times (1 + 0.3334)$$
$$= 0.5 \times (1.334) = 0.667$$

Firm B:

$$S^B_{t=3} = S^B_{t=2} \cdot (1 + G^B_{t=2}) = 0.333 \times (1 - 0.167)$$
$$= 0.333 \times (0.833) = 0.277$$

Firm C:

$$S^C_{t=3} = S^C_{t=2} \cdot (1 + G^C_{t=2}) = 0.167 \times (1 - 0.667)$$
$$= 0.167 \times (0.333) = 0.056$$

The average fitness (profit margin) in period 3 becomes:

$$\Pi^{AV}_{t=3} = (\Pi^A_{t=3} \cdot S^A_{t=3}) + (\Pi^B_{t=3} \cdot S^B_{t=3}) + (\Pi^C_{t=3} \cdot S^C_{t=3})$$
$$= (6 \times 0.667) + (5 \times 0.277) + (4 \times 0.056) = 5.611$$

FINANCIAL SYSTEMS AND INNOVATION

17

Andrew Tylecote

CONCEPTS AND TECHNIQUES

Capital markets, financial investment and capital goods

Auction markets, uncertainty and the price mechanism

Asymmetric information, adverse selection and moral hazard

Formal and organized capital markets

Limited liability

Expected returns

Credit rationing, asymmetric information and control

Principal-agent theory, bonding costs and the market for corporate control

Liquidity, marketability and securitization

Short-termism

Intermediary markets: Size-related advantages and quality of information

Internal capital markets

Stock market-based and Bank-based financial systems: Information and corporate control

Outsiders and insiders

Transactional and relational lending

Shareholders and stakeholders

German financial system: co-determination laws, stakeholders and cultural features

Path-dependency in the reduction of uncertainty in financial systems

Visibility, appropriability and novelty of innovation

Venture capital

LINKS

- The analysis of capital markets carried out in this chapter adopts a mix of old and new institutional approaches. The emphasis on the role of history and culture in the explanation of the institutional structure of financial systems in various countries gives an old institutional flavour to the chapter. The influence of the new institutional perspective can be identified with imperfect (and asymmetric) information and corporate control.

- Various concepts mentioned in the chapter within the new institutional framework, such as principal-agent theory and asymmetric information, were introduced in Chapter 9.

- Chapter 15 introduced the idea that the market tends to fail where externalities are significant, as in the case of the production of new public knowledge.

- The concept of path-dependence, which is a key notion in evolutionary/institutionalist theories, was introduced in Chapter 8 and developed in depth in Chapter 16.

- The existence of variety in the sources of innovation across industries is introduced and explained in Chapter 15.

1 INTRODUCTION

Finance is all-pervasive in the modern market economy. It is virtually impossible to carry out any transaction without using the financial system several times. If, for example, someone decides to buy a new car, they will have to make use of the payments system (cheque or credit card), and may very well have to borrow money to buy a car (use credit markets). Having made the purchase they are likely to need a third branch of the financial system to insure the car. So economic agents have frequent recourse to the financial system as part of other transactions, but inadequacies and imperfections in the financial system may prevent individuals from carrying out transactions. For example, the inability to borrow may prevent the purchase of a car at all. Hence, one is not only interested in the quality of financial services *per se* but also in their impact upon other industries and economic activities. Among the institutions in an economy, the financial system is central and can be considered the infrastructure of the infrastructure.

The importance of finance in facilitating transactions is not limited to capitalist societies. Indeed, money and credit pre-date capitalism by many centuries. They are institutions that are thousands of years old and have been important in almost all civilizations. However, finance plays an especially important role in a capitalist society. First, financial institutions facilitate physical investment and therefore the accumulation of capital (a central feature of the capitalist system). Second, well-functioning financial systems direct investment towards its most productive uses. It will only be by coincidence that a saver is the best person to make an investment and have the most productive opportunities for investing in the economy. Well-functioning financial markets, however, will permit the saver to lend physical resources to other individuals who are proposing productive investments. As a result of a financial transaction, both parties can gain from this exchange. The saver should receive a higher rate of return than would have been available from investing the capital in a project available to him, or holding capital in a sterile form, such as money. The investor may not be able to proceed with this project without access to finance.

This chapter examines how, in different countries, financial systems deal with a particular category of investment projects, namely investment in innovation. Innovation is crucial to the competitive success of capitalist economies (Chapter 15), and an ongoing debate exists on which types of financial system are more successful in funding innovation. In this chapter, I set out a theory of how the institutional structure of financial systems affects innovation, and I present some empirical evidence that is consistent with this theory. I start, in the next section, by classifying financial systems into two main types, bank-based and stock market-based, according to their institutional characteristics. In Section 2, I analyse the different ways in which these systems perform their two functions of providing capital and exercising corporate governance, and how they have developed over time.

Section 3 joins in the debate on which type of system is better for innovation, and looks at how innovation can be funded. Funding innovation is a challenge for any financial system because it requires a special type of investment – investing in intangible capital. Knowledge is a very specific asset: it does not have much of a 'carcass value'. In addition, innovating firms may well not manage to *appropriate* all the benefits from their innovations.

Any general theory suggests a *research programme* – a programme of generating and testing rather specific hypotheses. Some of the hypotheses that I derive from the theory outlined in this chapter in order to answer the question about funding innovation also help us to shed light in Section 4 on some 'stylized facts' that have been identified in studies on the national pattern of technological advantage.

Why, for example, is the UK strong in pharmaceuticals and weak in machine tools, while for Japan it is the other way round? Do these industries make different demands on the financial system? Industries vary in how appropriable innovation is, and in the main sources of uncertainty about it. Some sources of uncertainty can be reduced by tried and tested methods in bank-based economies, others cannot. Uncertainty that cannot be reduced is best tackled by what is called venture capital. I argue that, in principle, both types of system can provide venture capital, although the stock market-based economy of the US is way ahead at the moment.

2 STOCK MARKET-BASED AND BANK-BASED FINANCIAL SYSTEMS

2.1. The main features of the systems

In capitalist economies, various financial institutions have emerged over time to facilitate the transfer of funds from savers to investors. These institutions differ from country to country as the structure of financial systems is influenced by the historical development of a country in various ways.

A big problem is that providers of funds have to be confident that borrowers will invest wisely, otherwise they may be deterred from lending. In addition, lenders face problems generated by the existence of uncertainty and asymmetric information, and their lack of control over investors' behaviour. The relationship between the provider and the user of capital, therefore, involves two elements: information and control.

Financial systems across countries show considerable differences in the way information asymmetries and control over the use of capital are dealt with. In this chapter, I distinguish between two types of financial systems, taking two examples of each: bank-based (Germany and Japan) and stock market-based (the UK and the US). This classification, although it is by no means the only one possible, has already been used in the literature, though with different labels (Berglof, 1990; Corbett and Mayer, 1991; Corbett and Jenkinson, 1994). In fact, every country has its own institutional characteristics, and important differences exist between the UK and the US and between Germany and Japan. However, I shall concentrate on the common features of the two systems in order to show how different financial structures can influence the performance of the economy.

Stock market-based and bank-based systems differ along three main dimensions. The first is the relative importance of long-term bank lending versus equity finance. The second is the nature of the relationship between banks and firms. This is *transactional* or arm's-length in stock market-based systems and *relational* in bank-based systems. In transactional lending each loan is seen as a one-off and is secured against collateral (the carcass value of the firm). In relational lending, by contrast, each loan is seen as being part of an ongoing relationship, in which the bank's risk is

reduced by the bank having thorough knowledge of the firm's prospects. The third major difference is the nature of corporate control. In stock market-based systems there is a pronounced separation between ownership and control in large firms, which leaves greater scope for managerial discretion. In bank-based systems, various *stakeholders*, beside legal owners and managers, control the actions of the firm to a much greater extent than in stock-market based systems.

Stakeholders

Individuals and groups with a stake in the success of the firm.

These dimensions are inter-related and evolve over time. Since the late 1980s, for instance, financial markets around the world have witnessed a great many reforms (partly due to the globalization of finance) and there is a lively debate about whether the institutional structures are converging and, if so, towards which system.

Table 17.1 overleaf summarizes the characteristics of the two systems.

In stock market-based systems, the economy is dominated by large firms that look to the stock market as a major source of equity and other finance, and also as a market for corporate control. Firms must seek to establish a good reputation and a correspondingly high share price so that they are not taken over. Banks are not used as a major source of risk capital, since their lending is transactional rather than relational.

In bank-based systems only a small number of large firms are public companies quoted on the stock exchange (see, for instance, the contrast between Germany and the UK in Figure 17.1 and they do not concern themselves with it as a market for corporate control – they do not fear takeover bids or seek to make them. Instead they and, *a fortiori*, other private companies look to banks as their main source of external long-term funding.

Firms' relationships with banks are accordingly close and lending is relational. This means that each loan is seen as part of a long-term relationship in which the firm is bound to inform the bank fully as to its position and prospects. The bank is committed to support the firm through bad times, in return for influence over its policy and personnel. Where a large firm borrows from more than one bank, one of them is normally recognized as the 'lead' or 'house' bank and this bank will maintain oversight of the firm's financial position (Henderson, 1993).

The relative importance of the stock market in stock market-based economies is illustrated by Figure 17.2 which shows that the total value of all firms quoted on the stock exchange (the market

Table 17.1 Properties of the two systems

Stock market-based (US and UK)	Bank-based (Germany and Japan)
A large number of firms are quoted in the stock exchange	A small number of firms are quoted in the stock exchange
Dispersed ownership	Concentrated ownership and control
Separation of ownership and control	Association of ownership and control
Takeovers are often hostile and antagonistic (market for corporate control is active)	Absence of hostile takeovers (market for corporate control is not active)
Little incentive for outside investors to participate in corporate control	Control by stakeholders (banks, related firms, and employees)
Banks do not hold corporate equity and do not sit on boards of firms	Banks hold corporate equity and sit on the boards of firms
No cross-shareholdings between companies	Cross-shareholdings exist between companies
Low commitment of outside investors to long-term strategies of the firm	High commitment of the various stakeholders to the long-term strategies of the firm
Takeovers may create monopolies	Insider systems may encourage collusion

Source: Adapted from Corbett and Mayer, 1991, pp.63 and 65, Tables 3 and 4

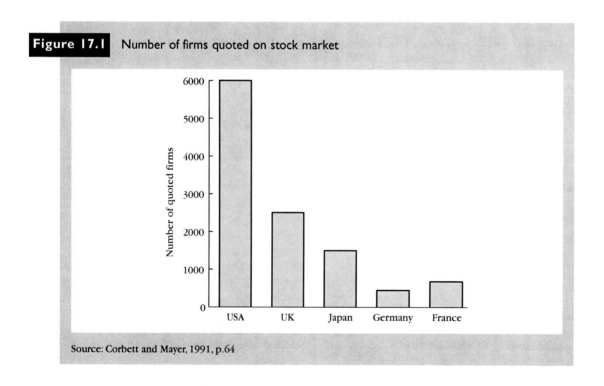

Figure 17.1 Number of firms quoted on stock market

Source: Corbett and Mayer, 1991, p.64

capitalization) is highest in the US and UK, once the size of the economy (GDP) is taken into account.

The differing role of banks and stock markets is only part of the story. The key distinction between the two systems is in their mechanisms of corporate control. While in the UK and US ownership is dispersed among a large number of shareholders and, therefore, ownership and control are separated, in countries with bank-based systems, such as Germany and Japan, stock ownership is concentrated, although in different ways. For example, Table 17.2 shows that in Germany 59 per cent of large firms have a single owner holding over 50 per cent of the equity.

In the continental European countries, founding families have a tendency to insist on retaining control; a tendency which seems to have cultural roots. There is a corresponding insistence on the

obligations of ownership, including the exercise of control (Schneider-Lenne, 1992; Kester, 1992). In Germany, for example, few owners of middle-sized companies seek stock market flotation:

'They are not particularly interested in money ... They are more concerned not to lose their special position within their local community ... If they sell, they become merely rich – as the proprietor of a company they really are somebody. Even when a family decides to list, it rarely abandons control to the vagaries of the stock market. Thus the BMW group – majority-owned by the Quandt family – can enjoy the benefits of the stock market without changing its essential character as a (very large) family business.'

(Waller, 1994, p.21)

Table 17.2   Ownership concentration in large firms: percentage by share of largest owner

Largest owner's share	France	United States	Japan	United Kingdom	Germany
>50%	55	9	17	2	59
10-50%	42	39	42	14	} 41
<10%	2	52	25	84	

For each country, the table shows the percentage of large firms in each ownership category
Source: Berglof, 1990

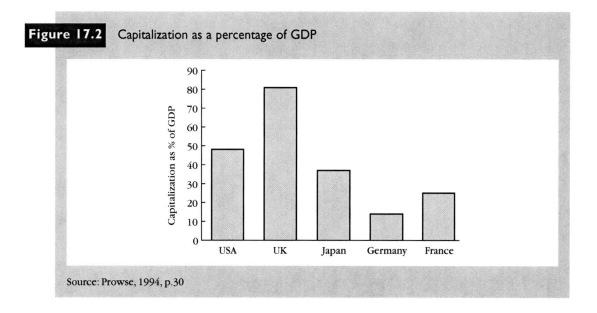

Figure 17.2   Capitalization as a percentage of GDP

Source: Prowse, 1994, p.30

To retain control, owners must avoid diluting their share stake too much by mergers or by raising new voting share capital. If that means staying small, then banks are likely to be the best external source of capital.

The main problem is that banks do not have complete information about the extent of the risk associated with lending to a firm; there are information asymmetries. Not only does the firm know more than the bank, it also has control over the use of assets.

Banks respond in two ways: by screening borrowers and by rationing their funds. If you have borrowed money from a bank you have probably noticed that transactions are not impersonal. In general, in both the UK and the US, banks ask customers to fill in a form known as a scorecard. The bank then allocates points to the potential borrower, for example, for being in regular employment, owing a home, etc. Through this screening process, the bank collects information about the borrower and therefore reduces information asymmetries. The anonymity of standard commodity markets disappears.

On the basis of the total number of points scored, the bank offers the customer a loan of a certain amount at a rate determined by the bank. In some, but not all cases, this will be as large or larger than the borrower requests. Often, however, the prospective borrower cannot borrow as much as he or she wants and no expression of willingness to pay more will increase the amount available. The bank offers a fixed price–quantity package on a take-it or leave-it basis and borrowers can choose neither the quantity nor the price. This behaviour is called credit rationing; borrowers are allowed only a certain quantity of the good they desire – hence they are rationed.

These arguments suggest that companies in Germany and Japan might face financial constraints on investments. However, this does not seem to be the case since the level of investment per unit of output is higher than in the Anglo-Saxon countries (see Figure 17.3).

Relational lending partially overcomes the problem of asymmetric information as banks get to know firms and industries in more depth over time. The development of a close relationship and the

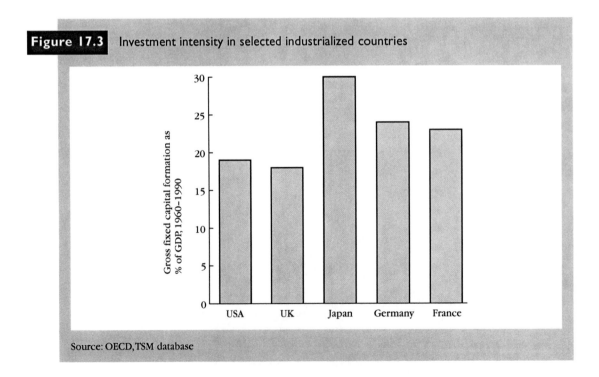

Figure 17.3 Investment intensity in selected industrialized countries

Source: OECD, TSM database

acquisition of reliable information from banks, in turn, depend on the fact that in Japan and Germany banks also hold equity of non-financial firms and exert corporate control in various ways.

For example, since the 1870s German company law has insisted on two-tier boards. The upper, supervisory board is expected to keep a close eye on the lower board which runs the firm. The members of the supervisory board are elected by the shareholders and, under recent co-determination legislation, by the employees. Nonetheless, in large companies with heavy bank borrowing, the chairman of the supervisory board has traditionally been a bank official. The bank's power on this board might arise simply from 'loan leverage', but there is another source. From the beginning, small shareholders have usually deposited their shares with the bank, which has the right (with their agreement) to use their votes at shareholders' meetings. Over time, the banks have built up substantial industrial shareholdings of their own. As long as their survival depended upon the health of the companies to which they had lent, the banks appear to have done a good job of 'corporate governance' in the large companies which were no longer controlled by their founding families.

The role of family shareholders in Japanese industry has been less influential, first because, culturally, there is a tendency to regard firms as communities over which control by outsiders is illegitimate, and second because the great *zaibatsu* holding companies were split up and largely purged of family ownership after the Second World War. From the early 1950s, precisely because of the distrust of outside control, a network of cross-shareholdings grew up among companies with banks and other financial institutions participating so that stable shareholdings became dominant and hostile takeovers impossible (Kester, 1992; Prowse, 1992).

Although in Japan a single bank can only own up to 5 per cent of a firm, the influence of the 'main bank' (the bank that both holds equity and manages the company's cash flow and loans) on corporate control is substantial. 'In 1980 listed firms with bank borrowing had main banks as largest or second largest shareholders in 39 per cent of cases and in the top five shareholders in 79 per cent of cases' (Sheard, 1985, quoted in Corbett and Mayer, 1991, p.63).

Officials of the main bank gain detailed information about the firm through the management of the firm's financial activities and through direct contact with top management and business

partners. This enables them to act early when the existing managers are under-performing and to replace them, usually by other existing employees (Aoki, 1990).

As well as the banks' influence, trade associations, suppliers, customers, competitors and employees also have some say as to how companies are run in Germany and in Japan. In these two countries, industrial managers can put pressure on their fellow managers in related firms. As for the workers, in Japan the life-time employment system for managers and other core workers of large firms helps to ensure that top managers feel an obligation to their fellow employees. In Germany, the co-determination system, in which employees are given a share of control by law, has the same effect. Pressure may also be informal as firms are usually embedded in local communities. In short, the parties that have a stake in the firm – the stakeholders – effectively contribute to corporate governance in bank-based economies. As you will see later in Section 3.2, the existence of such enfranchised stakeholders can make a difference in the innovation process.

In the organization of corporate control, bank-based systems contrast sharply with stock market-based systems. In the Anglo-Saxon economies, with their liberal traditions, wealth has been seen essentially as a commodity rather than enmeshed with rights and obligations, and, accordingly, family shareholders have been more ready than elsewhere to give up control. This is particularly true in the UK, where according to one influential economic journalist: '… successful British capitalists, politicians and officials have always been driven by the social goal of becoming gentlemen, apeing the lifestyle of the English aristocrat, and aiming to have the same kind of effortless, invisible income' (Hutton, 1995, p.114).

Stock exchange flotation has provided a means of exit from owner control. This led first to fragmented individual shareholdings and, more recently, to increasing concentration in the hands of financial institutions, now (especially in the UK) mainly pension funds. These institutions, however, do not behave like the banks of Germany and Japan, rather they have deliberately avoided any control relationship with management, acting as traders rather than investors, with highly diversified portfolios (Tylecote and Demirag, 1992; Porter, 1992).

Because of the widely dispersed shareholding, corporate control rests with management in stock market-based systems, and shareholders rely on the market for corporate control, i.e. *outsiders* are expected to discipline managers. Hence, in the UK and US hostile takeovers are more common.

2.2. Corporate governance and economic efficiency

The differences in corporate governance affect the ways in which the interests of the providers of funds are protected in the system. While the stock market-based system relies on *outsiders* to crack down on the sources of inefficiency, the bank-based system relies on *insiders*. The outsiders are the institutional investors (investment trusts, pension funds etc.) who dominate the US/UK system and are the main actors in the market for corporate control. It can be argued, however, that a stock market which does not value shares properly can give rise to *short-termism*. Keynes (1936, p.155) and his successors associated this with the 'fetish of liquidity', that is, excessive concern with returns in the short term and ignoring longer-term development.

Short-termism

Investment projects with higher expected returns may be rejected because the returns are deferred.

One way in which financial systems that promote liquidity and marketability can generate short-termism is through an excessively competitive market for corporate control. The argument runs as follows. While in many cases the intervention of shareholders is desirable and leads to an increase not only in the profits of the company but also in its efficiency measured from a social point of view, in other cases it can push corporate management to be too anxious to please shareholders by pursuing strategies that generate high profits in the short-run but inhibit long-term planning. Again, the root of the problem lies in the existence of information asymmetries between managers and shareholders. Shareholders will lack the information necessary to decide if expensive investments that do not generate rewards in the short-term are wise or merely managerial aggrandisement (putting growth and size before profits). Furthermore, shareholders know that the board knows more than they do and that the board might use this extra information to put their interests before those of the shareholders. Hence,

shareholders may rationally decide not to fund such long-term uncertain investment (for a version of Akerlof's market for lemons, see Chapter 9).

In the bank-based system, the insiders (family owners, bankers and other industrial managers) are the disciplinarians. They are much less likely than outsiders to generate myopic (short-termist) behaviour because they are much less likely to be ignorant about the firm's activities. Where, however, the key problem is to overcome conservatism, that is, an attachment to old products, processes and ways of doing things, a stock market-based system has an edge. In the bank-based system it is up to a specific group of insiders to crack down on bad management; if they fail the situation can slumber on until the firm runs out of cash. Anglo-Saxon capitalism, with its market for corporate control, means that managers of large firms are never safe to go on with out-of-date routines, because they are never safe from a hostile takeover. If the prospect of such a fate does not keep them on their toes, then the changes needed may take place through a takeover.

2.3 A historical perspective on the systems

You may have noticed that the stock market-based system is characteristic of the economies that developed earlier, the UK and the US, while Germany and Japan are 'younger' advanced economies. Does this mean that 'mature' economies present the others with the image of their own future? When they 'grow up' will they look more or less like the Anglo-Saxon systems? If you create the same circumstances (in this case economic maturity, in some sense) will you produce broadly the same result? Or is it that economies are path-dependent: does their history count?

So far as financial systems go, there seems to be something in both views. Perhaps the most important reason why history does count is the speeded-up nature of late development. Economies like Germany's in the early nineteenth century and Japan's in the late nineteenth century did not simply grow as Britain's had a century previously. They tried to strike out towards where Britain (and other leaders) then were, and close the gap as rapidly as possible. That meant that they needed massive infusions of capital, particularly into their heavy industries, and that key firms had to grow very quickly. The process involved a great deal of risk for the firms involved. The equity markets in these countries were as underdeveloped as the rest of their economies. The only way to get the capital together that was needed for industry was to 'hoover up' the savings of the landowners and the middle class, who would most certainly not entrust them to the stock market as it then existed. With luck and good regulation, however, banks might be trusted. In Japan the tradition was to fear all private financial institutions and stock markets equally. This led people to save in the government-backed institutions such as post offices: the public sector then acted as banker to the rest, including the privately owned banks. But how, then, could the banking system be protected from the riskiness of its investments?

There were broadly two solutions to the fragility of the bank-based system. The first solution was to devise arrangements that gave the major banks such good information about industry, so good an understanding of it, and so much control over it that the risk was drastically reduced. The central bank would back up smaller banks as the lender of last resort in a real crisis. The second solution was for the state, in some way, to take over the risk of lending to industry. In Germany there was a particularly successful example of the first solution, devised mostly in the 1870s. Since 1945 this has been supplemented by a strong system of public-sector banks built up by regional and local government to lend to small and medium enterprises. In Japan, too, the state broadly prefers to support privately-owned banks rather than replace them, but state finance has also played a more direct role, particularly in the aftermath of the Second World War. In addition, the existence of keiretsu, that is, diversified industrial groups, helps to bring providers and users of funds closer. Italy and France, on the other hand, have preferred the second type of solution. Over the last half century in these two countries, the state has borne most of the risk of industrial finance, mostly through public sector banks. In any event, in all these cases, the financial systems that developed were essentially bank-based, rather than stock market-based, and to a large extent they have stayed that way.

It is interesting to note that both the UK and the US used to rely much more heavily on banks than they do today, and in both countries there was an apparently conscious decision to change the system. Will Hutton (1995) shows how provincial banks in the industrial areas of Britain were developing a system of 'relational lending' up to the late 1870s.

The crucial moment came in 1878 when the City of Glasgow Bank and the West of England and South Wales District Bank both faced liquidity problems. They appealed to the Bank of England for support to tide them over, were refused and collapsed. After that, the main British banks withdrew from lending to industry. In the US, however, as in Germany, industry went on being able to depend heavily on bank finance, which helps to explain why they succeeded where Britain failed in the new, capital-hungry electrical, chemical and motor industries that grew up in the first part of the twentieth century. In the US, the crucial turn away from bank finance came in the 1930s, when Congress imposed restrictions on it in the aftermath of the Wall Street Crash (Roe, 1994). What these Anglo-Saxon retreats from bank finance had in common is that they were decided by central institutions – the Bank of England in one case, Congress in the other. Both institutions prioritized financial stability over fast industrial development.

Whether the central institutions in bank-based systems will follow in the footsteps of the US and UK is still a matter for debate. The increasing integration of financial markets in the global economy opens many possibilities as large multinational firms can seek funds from wherever they want in the world.

3 FINANCIAL SYSTEMS AND INNOVATION

3.1 Gains and losses from reducing uncertainty

Now that we have seen how financial systems may differ it is time to ask how we might judge which type works best. Because technological progress is so important in the modern economy (see Chapter 15), we shall focus on what works best for one particular area, technological innovation. Innovation requires investment, and financial systems provide capital for investment, so we will compare the efficiency of the two systems in this role.

In order to make things simpler, we shall start by assuming that the outcome of the project reflects the benefits to the economic system as a whole. We shall then go on to see what happens when we relax this assumption.

In the case of new products and processes, both lenders and borrowers have to live with a lot of unquantifiable uncertainty about the outcomes of investment projects; so one great challenge to the financial system is to reduce that uncertainty as far as possible. A well-organized and expert financial institution may be able, using its expertise, to reduce the uncertainty that surrounds, say, a thousand projects or firms which appear, at first glance, to have a high level of 'downside' risk and choose, perhaps, a hundred or so that seem to have the best chance of success. The remaining risk attached to the chosen projects can then be substantially reduced through diversification.

Expertise requires specialization of some kind and not all financial institutions will be able to assess the prospects of all types of innovative projects. Instead of having many different banks competing to lend to it, all of whom use some neat, quick and cheap way of reckoning its creditworthiness, a firm may find only one or two prospective lenders available. These may be lenders who know the firm already, or know its industry, or know its locality. This situation is more typical of the bank-based system and it suggests an advantage this system may have. Where innovation is concerned it will be a particularly telling advantage over a stock market dominated by outsiders because it takes a great deal of knowledge of the firm, the industry and the technology involved to judge the prospects of any project.

However, there is a price which may have to be paid for this specialization: the economy may suffer from monopoly power as banks do not have to compete for funds. Monopoly power allows monopoly profits and other abuses – for example, finance given or refused on one person's whim, slackness and conservatism.

The Anglo-Saxon financial system allows each large firm access to capital on the same basis as every other, but it does this by having the shares of each firm held by a large number of individuals and institutions. In the bank-based countries, the concentration of ownership, even in large companies, means that shareholders have an opportunity, and the incentive, to become familiar with the company and its industry. However, there is a flip side: there are no large pools of 'impartial' capital slopping about. This means that a cash-rich firm which is on good terms with its major shareholders will, in effect, have a lot of cheap capital available to it. Firms that are short of cash and do not have major shareholders with a lot of cheap capital available to them will probably find equity funding hard to come by.

3.2 Tackling the problem of appropriation

The difficulty of *appropriating* advances in knowledge is a problem that often inhibits innovation (see Chapter 15). The first firm to introduce a new product or pioneer a new process can expect to benefit from it, but others almost certainly will too – its customers particularly, but also its suppliers, its competitors perhaps, and firms in other industries and countries to which its innovation is relevant. And when we say the firm itself will benefit, we don't usually mean only the shareholders via higher profits; its employees, for instance, can expect higher pay, better job security, better chances of promotion. Even the state and local government share in the benefits, through higher tax revenues and lower needs for unemployment benefits. The upshot of all these *spillovers* is that the social return on investment in innovation is likely to be substantially higher than the private return to the shareholders of the innovating firm. If investment is only motivated by that private return, there will be less investment than there should be.

There is one way, however, in which the gap may be narrowed. Those gainers who are close to the firm, or within it, may have an influence over it, and they may make a contribution of some kind to the finance of the investment. They are the enfranchised stakeholders, and the gain to them will count, in effect, as part of the private return which the firm is trying to achieve. In any large Japanese firm there has been an (implicit) deal between the permanent workers and the firm: work hard, show flexibility and accept relatively low pay in your early years, and we will see to it, if we possibly can, that you will have a well-paid job until you retire. In current world market conditions the only way the firm can hope to deliver on that promise is by continuous innovation. In effect, the programme of innovation is being 'financed' by the junior workers, and when they become senior workers they share in the returns. Business customers and suppliers in Japan are also considered to be 'part of the family': in various ways they contribute to the investment, have influence over the firm, and enjoy the gains later.

German firms have a somewhat similar relationship with their workers, who, unlike Japanese workers, have legal rights (from the co-determination laws) to influence management. In Germany, there are also strong inter-firm links. All the firms in an industry share in certain common activities: they will be members of its employers' association, trade association and research association. Sharing the costs and output of research obviously helps to narrow the appropriability gap. So does co-operation within the employers' association. In order to ensure that training takes place, the 'deal' among employers in Germany is that all companies train; none poach others' trained workers. This increases the incentive to train, which is part of the investment in innovation.

To sum up, if there is some set of formal or informal arrangements for relating what stakeholders get out of innovation to what they put into it, this will narrow the appropriability gap and push the rate of innovation up nearer to what is socially desirable. The institutional arrangements in Germany and Japan appear to have this effect.

 4 INNOVATION: DIFFERENCES AMONG INDUSTRIES

In this section, I take into account the fact that innovative activities differ across industries (Chapter 15). So far as the finance of innovation is concerned there are three sorts of differences which are of vital importance.

- The *visibility* of innovation. How easy is it for someone who is not closely involved in managing the development of a new product or process to judge what resources are being devoted to it and how well they are being spent? This is at the heart of the problem of short-termism that was discussed in Section 2.2.

- The *appropriability* of innovation. Can the firm ensure in a straightforward way (for example by patents) that the bulk of the returns on it do accrue to the shareholders; or does innovation in the industry naturally tend to involve large spillovers to other stakeholders?

- The *novelty* of innovation. How far does a product or process innovation involve or need radically new ways of organizing its development or production, radically new technologies, and/or radically new markets or selling methods?

I will be arguing that the stock market-based system is at a particular disadvantage in industries where visibility and appropriability are low. The balance of advantage in coping with a high degree of novelty is not so clear.

4.1 Visibility, appropriability and firm-specific perceptiveness

Innovation involves a variety of different types of investment – not just the research and development (R&D) spending which is normally associated with it. Physical investment, design and engineering, employees' training and marketing costs are all necessary for the success of an innovation. The different types of expenditure will make a very different impression on an industry analyst. Spending on physical capital appears in the accounts as acquisition of a capital asset, which means that it does not have to be subtracted from profit. The same is true of some elements of R&D, which is obviously an investment of a sort, however risky or unwise the industry analyst may think it. The same may be said of training, though much of it is informal and impossible to account for separately. The least visible expenditure is innovative expenses within production (which is where a lot of engineering is likely to be done, including the sorting out of 'teething troubles' after production starts) and marketing. It is very difficult to show to anyone who does not have detailed knowledge of the firm, that the higher costs resulting from such changes are not due to sheer inefficiency. There are wide variations among industries in the pattern of spending on innovation, as Figure 17.4 overleaf shows.

Visibility also depends on the way the innovation and the firm are organized. The more centralized the process, the more visible it is to the outside. In a divisionalized firm with several tiers of profit centre, it is not easy even for the finance director, let alone outside analysts, to tell the difference between unnecessarily high costs in the operating companies, and a big innovative effort which will pay off in future. Again, industries vary in how far the firms within them tend to control the process of innovation centrally. It is much easier to centralize the process (or most of it) when it largely revolves around basic and applied research, than when it revolves around development. So another indicator of visibility is the fraction of R&D that goes to research, as opposed to development.

Figure 17.5 illustrates the types of research undertaken in different industrial sections of the UK.

The less visible the activity, the more perceptive the observer must be in order to judge whether the firm should be funded, and to monitor progress. In general, this perceptiveness needs to be firm-specific, although a general knowledge of the industry will help too. A bank-based economy with enfranchised stakeholders can be expected to have a lot of insiders with good firm-specific perceptiveness; the outsider-dominated financial systems cannot.

We have already seen that systems with enfranchised stakeholders generally cope better with problems of appropriability. Industries vary in how much stakeholder enfranchisement can help, and how far there is a problem anyway. In the pharmaceutical industry, for example, it is less of a help because the firms involved do not have particularly important suppliers and they do not sell to industrial customers. So in this industry there is little scope for getting strong customer–supplier groupings to share the effort and the returns. Anyway, the problem can be quite well controlled by patenting new drug discoveries. An example of such a patent is that of Glaxo's anti-ulcer drug, Zantac, where the patent turned out to be worth hundreds of millions of pounds.

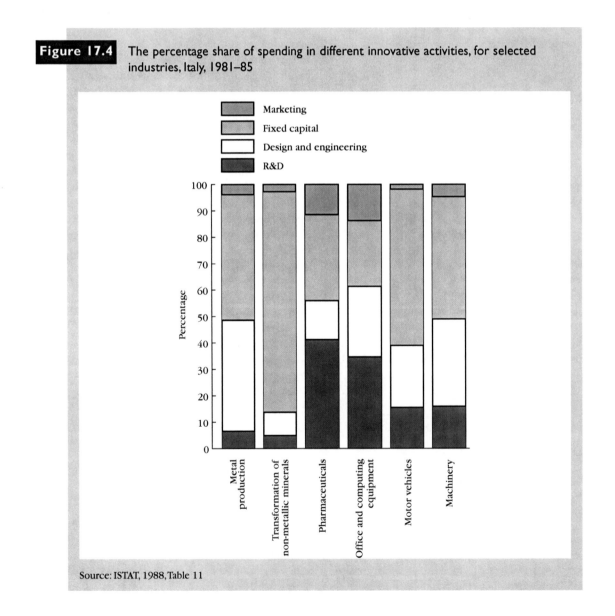

Figure 17.4 The percentage share of spending in different innovative activities, for selected industries, Italy, 1981–85

Source: ISTAT, 1988, Table 11

There is a connection between visibility and appropriability. The easier it is to protect appropriability by patenting, the freer the firm is to explain and publicize its innovations to outsiders. The pharmaceutical industry can and does do that in the UK and the US, by holding regular briefings for stock exchange analysts on the progress and prospects of its drugs. This industry happens to have other advantages in achieving high visibility. An unusually high proportion of its innovative expenditure is on R&D which is conducted in centralized departments and is not devolved to profit centres several tiers down. The mechanical engineering industries, on the other hand, are at the opposite extreme: they are decentralized, their innovations are dependent on low-visibility activities and any innovations are difficult to protect by patent. They tend to have close relationships with their industrial customers and suppliers of components and equipment. This analysis helps explain why, while the US and the UK lead the world in pharmaceuticals, they have become steadily weaker since the 1950s by comparison to Germany and Japan in the main areas of mechanical engineering.

4.2 Dealing with novelty: the stock exchange strikes back?

The advantage of the insiders in the bank-based, stakeholder-enfranchised system arises largely

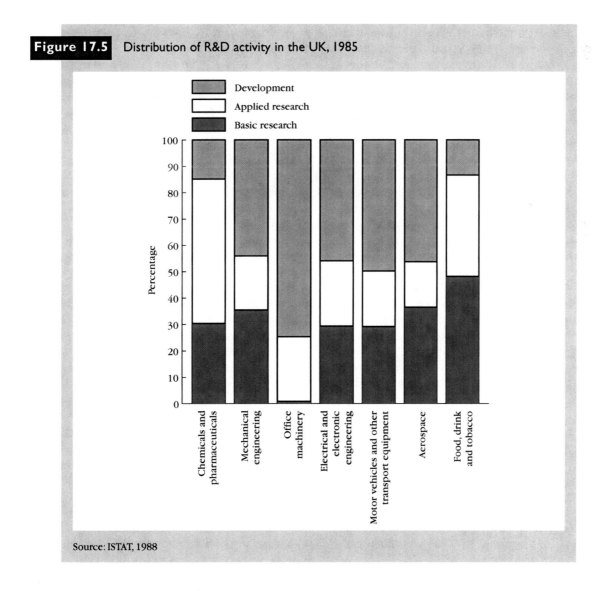

Figure 17.5 Distribution of R&D activity in the UK, 1985

Source: ISTAT, 1988

from a continuity of relationships. For example the firm-specific perceptiveness of a bank may arise through it having known an innovating firm for many years – a specific manager in the bank may even have known the firm's chief executive for a long time. In a new or rapidly-changing industry, however, continuity may be impossible or dangerous. Established firms may be able to succeed only by learning to do things in a radically different way, in terms of organization and technology. Accordingly, new start-up firms may have an advantage as they have nothing to unlearn. Conversely, however, they cannot have knowledgeable insiders to provide finance and corporate governance. The established firms can – but will insiders give the firms the kick they may need to change their ways?

It follows that the sort of industry in which one would expect the Anglo-Saxons to excel is one where visibility and appropriability are not a great problem, but novelty is. The US excels in pharmaceuticals and electronics, the UK in pharmaceuticals. Both these industries are highly technology-based and, thus, likely to be high in novelty. We have already seen that pharmaceuticals have little difficulty with visibility and appropriability. So the facts are reasonably consistent with the theory.

If, in a new industry, firm-specific perceptiveness is hard to come by, how can any financial system do a good job for that industry? The best hope is that someone within the system with access to capital has a high degree of industry-specific expertise. Capital can then be put into selected firms, all or most of it as equity, and the industry-specific expert can take a hand in corporate governance in at least the early stages of the firm's development. When the firm is older and established enough to engage with the ordinary providers of capital – the stock exchange and/or banks, as the case may be – the start-up capital that has been put in can be liberated and put into new start-ups.

The US is one country which seems to have developed an effective way of financing its high-technology industries. In the US, risk finance for the start-up and development of small unquoted companies that have significant growth potential. *Venture capitalists* are now an established part of the financial system, and a large fraction of the capital they provide has gone into high technology industries (65 per cent in 1994, according to the Bank of England, 1996, p.21).

Venture capitalists

A venture capitalist is an organization (or individual) that is prepared to invest long-term risk finance for the start-up and development of small unquoted companies that have significant potential.

The investment is usually in equity and often the venture capitalists expect to share in governance as well as finance. In 1995 the flow of new venture capital in the US was estimated at $3.85bn., but that was only what was called 'formal' venture capital (Authers, 1996). More important, but harder to measure, is 'informal' venture capital provided by 'business angels'. These are rich individuals who use their own personal funds, industrial knowledge and contacts. Estimates of their rate of investment in high-technology sectors have been put as high as $20bn. per year (Coghlan, 1996). Venture capital tends to be concentrated in certain sectors and localities. In the US in 1995, for example, 47 per cent of 'formal' investments went into California, with Massachusetts and Texas receiving another 12 per cent between them (Authers, 1996). High-technology and informal venture capital is even more concentrated – for example, in information and communication technology in northern California – thus enabling venture capitalists to be expert in their industry and to be effective in corporate governance.

Since the US has a stock market-based financial system, venture capital there has grown to be part of that system. After all, a well-functioning stock market is essential for venture capitalists as they reap their reward when the company is either floated or acquired by existing large firms. Formal venture capital institutions are commonly subsidiaries of the financial institutions – mutual funds, pensions funds and insurance companies – which dominate the stock exchange. The UK, having a similar financial system, was the quickest to follow the US lead and by the mid 1990s had the largest venture capital industry in Europe (47.5 per cent of total European new investments in 1995, according to Fazey, 1996). However, the UK, in borrowing the term, has redefined it to include the funding of management buyouts of established firms. By 1995 this use of venture capital absorbed 73 per cent of the total; only 4 per cent was going into 'early-stage' financing.

Technology-based firms in the UK receive a much smaller share of venture capital than in the US, and business angels are also less patient in the UK (Bank of England, 1996).Why is this? On the one hand, ignorance of technology is a particular problem for UK financial institutions; on the other hand, 'many would-be technology entrepreneurs are naïve in areas of financial and other management. This appears to be much less of a problem in the United States, given the more frequent contact between university science departments and their business schools. There appears to be an important cultural difference between the two countries in their attitude towards the commercialisation of research' (Bank of England, 1996, p.26). Bringing the financial, academic and business communities closer together is becoming a priority for UK innovation policy.

Bank-based economies have developed their own versions of venture capital. In Germany in 1994, for example, funds owned by the banks provided most venture capital. The government also contributes significantly. The German venture capital funds are, as you would expect, in less of a hurry to get their capital out. While, on average, US venture capitalists take advantage of stock exchange flotation to get out after five years, and the impatient British do so after only three or four years, in Germany the average period of investment is seven years, and they often continue to hold the firm's shares after the initial public offering (OECD, 1992). However, in Germany, as in Britain, a very low proportion of venture capital (only 7 per cent, according to Deutsche Bank) has gone into early-stage financing in high technology areas (Bank of England, 1996).

5 CONCLUSION

A well-functioning financial system is essential for economic development as it channels savings towards the most productive investment projects. However, financial transactions are fraught with uncertainty and information asymmetries. The level of uncertainty is particularly high in the case of innovative investment as the capital accumulated is mostly intangible (knowledge).

Over the years, countries have developed different institutional structures to facilitate the accumulation of capital. In this chapter, I have classified financial systems in two main categories, stock market-based and bank-based. From the historical discussion it emerges that a key characteristic on which they came to differ is the priority that the state and the central bank have given to industrial development.This priority seems to have been much higher in the bank-based economies.

The two types of financial systems can reduce uncertainty in different ways. The bank-based system has the edge in reducing the uncertainty which arises from low visibility and low appropriability of innovation because these problems can be much alleviated by 'enfranchised stakeholders'.This led us to go back and broaden the notion of financial systems to include all those, including employees, who in some way, cash or kind, might contribute to innovation, and benefit from it: stakeholders in innovation. However, there is another sort of uncertainty which arises from the novelty of an innovation. Here it is open to either system to develop the industry-specific expertise required, but the stock market-based system of the US is currently far ahead. Since industries differ in the degree of appropriability, visibility and novelty, we can deduce that some industries will be favoured by the structure of the financial system in some countries but not in others. In other words, we can explain some patterns of technological specialization by understanding the nature of the financial system.

The main aim of this chapter, then, was to set out a rather general theory of how financial systems affect innovation. Any general theory which is worth having suggests a research programme – a programme of generating and testing rather specific hypotheses. In this case, the hypotheses would be that an economy whose financial system had such and such scores on characteristics a, b and c would tend have such and such a performance in innovation in industries x, y or z. Such a programme requires empirical work to establish what the scores and performances are. When we test our hypotheses, however, we have to take into account that there may be other factors that help to explain the patterns of technological specialization observed, such as the strength of a country's scientific research, the natural resources available and the size of the market.

On this important topic, the programme has only just begun. Many of the empirical statements about financial systems and industries made in this chapter were rather tentative, based on the information available at present. Over the next few years, researchers in this field hope to generate much more cross-country evidence of the impact of financial systems on industrial innovation.

FURTHER READING

There is quite a lot of recent readable work on the differences among financial systems and their implications for corporate governance and management. Some of the best is in the *Oxford Review of Economic Policy (OREP)*. A complete issue of *OREP* in 1992 was devoted to this theme, with articles by Kester on Japan and Schneider-Lenne on Germany, and an overview by Jenkinson and Mayer:

Jenkinson, T. and Mayer, C. (1992) 'The assessment: corporate governance and corporate control', *OREP*, 8 (3), pp. 1-10.

Kester, W.C. (1992) 'Industrial groups as systems of contractual governance', *OREP*, 8 (3), pp. 25-44.

Schneider-Lenne, E. R. (1992) 'Corporate control in Germany', *OREP*, 8 (3), pp. 11-23.

There is also an later overview in *OREP* by Sussman:

Sussman, O. (1994) 'Investment and banking: some international comparisons', *OREP*, 10 (4), pp. 79-93.

Masahiko Aoki offers a more formal analysis of stakeholder enfranchisement (without using that term) in large Japanese firms in 'Toward an economic model of the Japanese firm', *Journal of Economic Literature*, vol. XXVIII, March 1990, pp. 1-27.

Michael Porter criticizes the short-termism of the US financial system in his 'Capital disadvantage: America's failing capital investment system', *Harvard Business Review*, September/October 1992, pp. 65-82.

The British financial system has similar effects on innovation. The impact on innovation in the pharmaceuticals and engineering industries is explored by Tylecote, A. and Demirag, I. (1992) 'Short-termism: culture and structures as factors in technological innovation', pp. 201-25 in Coombs, R., Walsh V. and Saviotti, P. (eds) *Technological Change and Company Strategies*, London, Academic Press.

In case you had written off the US system as hopelessly short-termist, you should read the Bank of England's 'The financing of technology-based small firms', October 1996, which shows how superior the US venture capital system is to all the competition.

Another very readable overview of corporate governance and some of its effects is Charkham, J. (1994) *Keeping Good Company: A Study of Corporate Governance in Five Countries*, Oxford, OUP. (The five countries studied are Germany, Japan, France, the US and UK).

Chapter 5 of Will Hutton's *The State We're In*, London, Jonathan Cape, is a brief but persuasive attack on the effects of the British financial system on the British economy over the last century.

If you find the historical approach to the understanding of the modern economy interesting, there is a whole journal devoted to it. *Industrial and Corporate Change (I&CC)* has carried some excellent articles on the evolution and effects of financial systems, such as:

Lazonick, W. and O'Sullivan, M. (1996) 'Organisation, finance and international competition', *Industrial and Corporate Change*, vol. 5, no. 1, pp. 1-49.

Mowery, D. C. (1992) 'Finance and corporate evolution in five industrial economies, 1900-1950', *Industrial and Corporate Change*, vol. 1, no. 1, pp. 1-36.

Rather out of character for *I&CC*, because it is not historical, is one of the seminal articles for the New Keynesian approach to finance:

Greenwald, B. and Stiglitz, J. E. (1992) 'Information, finance and markets: the architecture of allocative mechanisms', *Industrial and Corporate Change*, vol. 1, no. 1, pp. 37-63.

Markets

COMPETITIVE GENERAL EQUILIBRIUM

Vivienne Brown

CONCEPTS AND TECHNIQUES

Adam Smith's invisible hand and competitive general equilibrium theory

(Own price) excess demand curve

Existence of competitive general equilibrium: system of equations, Walras' Law, numeraire good

Determination of prices: outcome versus process approach

Tatonnement (groping), the auctioneer, the Walrasian rule for price adjustment and false trading

Instability of an equilibrium and multiple equilibria (Giffen goods)

Edgeworth box diagrams

Marginal rate of substitution (MRS)

Marginal rate of transformation (MRT), marginal cost and opportunity cost

Production possibility frontier (PPF)

Edgeworth's recontracting process, decentralization and false trading

Pareto efficiency: First and Second Welfare theorems

Production and consumption externalities

Non-convexities

Economic welfare policy: efficiency versus distribution, the theory of the second best

LINKS

- Competitive general equilibrium theory represents the synthesis of the neoclassical school of thought in its purest form. It embodies all the characteristics of the neoclassical approach. Reflecting the assumptions of methodological individualism and rationality, consumers' preferences and firms' technologies are the exogenous variables which determine the outcome at the level of the economic system through the maximization of consumers' utility and firms' profits. The use of equilibrium modelling and the emphasis on prices are also core assumptions of the neoclassical approach.

- Competitive general equilibrium theory brings together various building blocks that you have met earlier in the book. The theory itself was outlined in Chapter 1, which introduced competitive equilibrium analysis and also examined the concept of Pareto efficiency. Chapter 2 and Chapter 8 illustrated the neoclassical theory of consumption (including technical aspects such as utility functions, indifference maps and the marginal rate of substitution) and production (including technical aspects such as the production function and isoquant maps). Chapter 5 and Chapter 12 examined the role of the labour market, the key factor of production in the economy.

- The discussion of the welfare effects of a decentralized market economy also builds on the discussion of welfare carried out in Chapter 4, which examined in depth the concepts of utility and Pareto efficiency.

- Some assumptions that are necessary for the competitive general equilibrium theory to work have been examined in previous chapters. Chapter 2 introduces the important case of Giffen goods and upward sloping demand curves, while Chapter 15 analyses the problems that commodities with public good qualities such as information pose to the theory.

1 INTRODUCTION

One of the most significant aspects of economic change in the last decades of the twentieth century has been the resurgence of economic liberalism – the belief that decentralized markets promote economic prosperity more effectively than state planning or intervention. This has contributed to the break-up of the Soviet bloc in eastern Europe and also to the many changes seen in mixed economies, such as the UK, where the economic frontiers of the state have been pushed back in a number of ways. These policies have included various combinations of liberalization, deregulation and privatization. In the UK, for example, organizational changes have been introduced within the public sector in an attempt to replicate the market and introduce more commercial practices. Some aspects of such 'social markets' will be discussed in the following chapter. At the same time as these organizational changes have taken place, the traditional legal protections which supported trade union activities have been taken away in order to make the labour market closer to the ideal 'flexible' market which responds to market forces.

These changes are the result of a complex interweaving of many factors, but economic arguments have played their part. In the UK, the apparent failure of Keynesianism in the 1970s to deliver non-inflationary growth contributed to the increasing disenchantment with state intervention in the economy, and provided a new platform for anti-Keynesianism to play an influential role in the shift towards economic liberalism. These liberal economic arguments grew out of a long-running debate about the merits of a decentralized market economy as opposed to state planning, and about the virtues of competition. Neoclassical economics has contributed to this debate.

Chapter 1 sketched in a preliminary way the important result that a competitive general equilibrium is a Pareto-efficient outcome. This result has been used by many economists to argue for the merits of a decentralized market economy and explains why neoclassical economics is generally assumed to represent a free market orientation. On the other hand, the model of the competitive economy that underpins this result is a highly abstract one which is based on very restrictive assumptions. Many economists have questioned whether it does, in practice, provide such a strong case for decentralized market economies. In this chapter we shall investigate this issue. We shall look more deeply into the model of competitive general equilibrium and its links with Pareto efficiency. In the course of this, we shall also find that the model of competitive general equilibrium does not give us any simple or straightforward advice on the extent to which decentralized economic policies should be pursued, and that its actual role in economic debates in the past illustrates the equivocal nature of the policy conclusions that can be drawn from it.

How a decentralized, unplanned competitive market can produce orderly outcomes is a question that has fascinated economists since at least the eighteenth century. As you learnt in Chapter 1, the idea that the unintended consequence of individuals behaving with only their own interests in mind may be an outcome that is orderly – even beneficial – for society as a whole, has been encapsulated by the idea of the 'invisible hand'. The paradoxical nature of the idea that economic outcomes which are unplanned at an economy-wide level may be better than planned ones seems to fly in the face of common sense. The invisible hand becomes even more extraordinary when this beneficial outcome is seen as the result of the pursuit of self-interest on the part of individual economic agents. Somehow the invisible hand transforms private self-interest into overall economic well-being.

HOW MANY ECONOMISTS DOES IT TAKE TO CHANGE A LIGHTBULB?

— NONE, THE INVISIBLE HAND DOES ALL THE WORK!

This apparent paradox has led economists to ask two different sorts of questions. The first question concerns the operation of the invisible hand: just how does a competitive market function? How are prices set in a competitive market, and how is equilibrium restored after a disturbance? The second question concerns the allegedly beneficial outcome of a competitive market: how is it that competitive outcomes promote overall economic well-being? What is meant by 'well-being' and are there different gainers and losers in competitive markets?

These questions are explored in the following sections which together build on and extend the model of the competitive market you first met in Chapter 1. In Section 2 we shall examine the competitive general equilibrium model first put forward by Léon Walras to explain how a decentralized system of

markets can cohere without any overall plan. In Section 3 we shall consider how equilibrium prices are determined in this model. In Section 4 we shall look at a different version of this model, drawing upon neoclassical analysis of consumer and firm behaviour. Section 5 considers what is meant by beneficial outcomes. It looks at the normative or welfare properties of competitive equilibrium outcomes, and the policy conclusions that might be drawn from this.

In addition to addressing the issue of competitive markets, we shall also be reviewing and pulling together different aspects of the neoclassical model that you have met in various parts of the course. We shall be building on the preliminary groundwork of Chapter 1 and linking together the neoclassical analysis of consumer behaviour and household labour supply from Chapters 2 and 5 with the neoclassical theory of the firm and labour demand from Chapters 10 and 12. We shall pull together these different parts of the neoclassical theory so that you can see how they all fit together to form a coherent model of the interrelated way in which markets work. In this way I hope to show you something of the overall theoretical power of the model of competitive equilibrium, while also discussing some of the unresolved issues concerning it that continue to trouble economists.

2   THE WALRASIAN MODEL

2.1   Introduction

When the BSE crisis hit the British beef industry in 1996, in the wake of scientific evidence that beef might not be safe to eat, the price of beef plummeted as consumers lost confidence in beef and cut down their consumption of it. The fall in prices hit retailers, the beef products industry and beef farmers. As their incomes fell, all those involved in the various stages of producing and retailing beef had less money to spend on purchases. Beef farmers in particular were badly hit as it was suddenly not worth taking their animals to market, yet it was costly to keep them until prices increased. The fall in farmers' incomes in turn affected the value of farming land. Many consumers turned to substitute products and increased their demand for other meat, poultry and fish, while others increased their purchases of vegetarian substitutes such as vege-burgers and vegesausages. The increased public awareness of, or misinformation about, farming practices led to an increased demand for organic produce, while food manufacturers who used beef derivatives started looking around for non-beef substitutes. The original crisis in the beef market thus had a number of ramifications throughout other markets.

Some of these effects may have been short-lived, but the BSE crisis was a highly dramatic example of the sorts of changes that are happening all the time in the economy. Fashions come and go, new products are invented as old ones die out and new sources of raw materials are discovered. The economy is like a kaleidoscope of shifting demand and supply, ever restless and changing as shifts in one market have repercussions in many other markets far removed from it. Faced with these intricate interconnections between markets, economists want to explain whether and how order is possible in this kaleidoscope of activity. They want to see whether people operating atomistically as consumers or producers are part of a wider co-ordination of economic activities in which all choices can be realized. Can this complex interplay of different markets cohere as a consistent intermeshing of individual choices, or is the kaleidoscope simply a picture of chaos? Does this kaleidoscope need a visible guiding hand, in the shape of some other kind of institution, to co-ordinate economic activities, or is the invisible hand working efficiently?

2.2 Competitive general equilibrium

The competitive general equilibrium model was first outlined by Léon Walras (1834–1910), who was born in France but became professor of economics at Lausanne in Switzerland where he was a pioneer of the mathematical approach to economics. Walras' interest in economics was part of a methodological desire to apply the methods of the physical sciences to economic theory that resulted from a broad concern with social and political issues. He took a keen interest in social justice and proposed the nationalization of land and natural monopolies. He described himself as a 'scientific socialist' (Walker, 1987).

As we saw in Chapter 1, the Walrasian competitive general equilibrium model is based on the individual choices of economic agents in response to given market prices and the exogenous variables of preferences, resource endowments and technology. The kaleidoscope of economic activity is held fixed for a moment to see whether, given the exogenous variables, the sum of the choices of all individual agents are consistent, so that consumers' plans to purchase coincide with producers' plans to supply. This requires equilibrium in every market, so finding out whether individual choices are consistent implies that we have to find whether there exists a set of equilibrium prices at which demand and supply are in balance everywhere.

Walras' work laid the foundations for an analysis of competitive general equilibrium and his insights have since been developed in advanced mathematical models. We can get some of the flavour of this model by using partial equilibrium analysis of one market in which the prices of other goods are held constant. Figure 18.1(a) shows a demand and supply diagram like the ones you met in Chapter 1, where the prices of all other goods are held constant. Remember that the demand curve derives from utility-maximizing behaviour by households, and the supply curve derives from profit-maximizing behaviour by firms. At the equilibrium price, P_E, quantity demanded equals quantity supplied, Q_E. If price is below the equilibrium price, say at P_a, then the quantity demanded, Q_a^D is greater than the quantity supplied, Q_a^S. If the price is above the equilibrium price at P_b, the quantity demanded, Q_b^D, is less than the quantity supplied, Q_b^S.

As we wish to focus on the determination of the equilibrium price, it is helpful to represent this in terms of an (own-price) excess demand curve which shows the difference between the quantity demanded and the quantity supplied of a good at each level of its own price, again on the assumption that all other prices are held constant. This is shown in Figure 18.1(b). The vertical axis shows price and the horizontal axis shows excess demand which is positive when demand is greater than supply and negative when supply is greater than demand. At the equilibrium price P_E, excess demand is zero because demand and supply are equal; this is the point at which the excess demand curve intersects the price axis. At prices below P_E there is a positive excess demand; this is shown for P_a where the excess demand is Z_a which is equal to the distance

$Q_a^D - Q_a^S$ in Figure 18.1(a). At prices above P_E there is a negative excess demand since demand is less than supply. This is shown for the price P_b by Z_b which is equal to $Q_b^D - Q_b^S$ in Figure 18.1(b).

Figure 18.1 shows just one market with its (own-price) excess demand curve. The exogenous variables here are the prices of all other goods as well as preferences, resource endowments and technology. If any of these changed there would be a shift of the excess demand curve. In a general equilibrium model, however, we are looking at all markets simultaneously and so the excess demand for any good is dependent on all prices, not just on its own price. For example, the excess demand for vegeburgers is dependent not only on the price of vegeburgers, but also on all other prices.

One task for general equilibrium theory is to establish the conditions for the existence of a competitive equilibrium. This requires finding out whether a set of equilibrium prices exists for all markets simultaneously, bearing in mind all the ramifications implied in the notion that all the excess demands depend on all the prices. Certainly, some of these ramifications might turn out to be very small, but finding the total effect of all these interdependencies requires that none is overlooked. Establishing the existence of an equilibrium for the model as a whole involves finding a set of prices where all excess demands are simultaneously equal to zero.

As it is not possible in two dimensions to draw excess demand as a function of many prices, general equilibrium analysis cannot be represented in diagrams in the way that partial equilibrium analysis can. For a mathematical formulation of the problem of the existence of competitive equilibrium, you might like to read the technical box that follows.

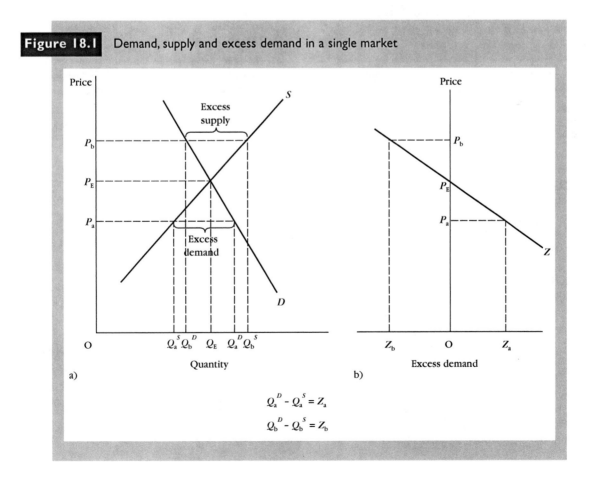

Figure 18.1 Demand, supply and excess demand in a single market

$$Q_a^D - Q_a^S = Z_a$$

$$Q_b^D - Q_b^S = Z_b$$

The existence of competitive equilibrium

The competitive general equilibrium model is composed of n goods and services. The ith good has an excess demand function:

$$Z_i = Q_i^D - Q_i^S$$

where $i = 1, 2, ..., n$

As explained in Chapter 1, the variables which are held constant for this model – the exogenous variables – are the initial endowments of resources owned by households, the preferences of households and the available technology. The variables that are to be determined by the equations of the model – the endogenous variables – are the equilibrium prices.

There is no money in this model, and demand and supply levels depend only on relative prices. An equilibrium set of prices is, therefore, a set of relative prices. If we choose any good, say the nth good, as a *numeraire good* or unit of account in which the prices of all other goods are expressed, then its price $P_n = 1$. This means that the prices of all other goods, $P_1, ... , P_{n-1}$ are just their prices relative to the price of the nth good, because:

$$P_i = \frac{P_i}{1} = \frac{P_i}{P_n}$$

Numeraire good

The numeraire good is the good in terms of which all prices in the model are expressed. All prices are therefore relative prices.

Since P_n is always 1, there are just $n - 1$ relative prices to be found.

How do we write the excess demand function for the ith good? We know that the excess demand for the ith good is a function of all the exogenous and endogenous variables. As it is a general equilibrium – and not a partial equilibrium – model, we must recognize that every excess demand Z_i will depend not only on its own relative price, but on all other relative prices as well. The excess demand for the ith good can, therefore, be written as:

$$Z_i = f_i (U, R, T, P_1, P_2, ..., P_{n-1})$$
U = preferences
R = initial endowments
T = technology

where the excess demand, Z_i for the ith good, is a function of preferences, initial endowments, technology and all $n - 1$ relative prices.

The plans of all economic agents are consistent when all excess demands are zero, that is, all goods and services offered for sale have a purchaser and all potential purchasers are able to find the goods and services they want to buy. To establish whether an equilibrium exists, we therefore need to find the set of prices at which all the excess demands are equal to zero. As it happens, we only need to do this for the excess demands for $n - 1$ goods. This is because each agent spends all their available income (there is no saving) but no more than their income (there is no borrowing either), whether or not the system is in equilibrium. For each individual agent, the total amount planned to be spent on purchasing goods and services equals the total amount expected in income from supplying goods and services. If this holds for each agent, then it must hold for all agents taken together, so that the value (in terms of the numeraire) of the sum of all excess demands must equal zero. This implies that the following expression must always hold, not just for equilibrium prices:

$$P_1 Z_1 + P_2 Z_2 + ... + P_{n-1} Z_{n-1} + Z_n = 0$$

where $P_n = 1$ because n is the numeraire good. This property of excess demand functions is known as *Walras' Law*.

Walras' Law

Walras' Law states that the value of the sum of all excess demands must equal zero whether or not the system is in equilibrium.

As a result of Walras' Law, if the $n-1$ excess demands $Z_1 ... Z_{n-1}$ are zero, then the nth excess demand, Z_n, must also equal zero. This can be seen more clearly by reformulating Walras' Law as follows:

$$P_1 Z_1 + P_2 Z_2 + ... + P_{n-1} Z_{n-1} = - Z_n$$

This implies that we need only find a set of prices such that $n - 1$ excess demands are equal to zero. In other words, in a system where there are n goods, an overall equilibrium exists when $Z_i = 0$ for all $i = 1, 2, \ldots, n - 1$. This implies a system of $n - 1$ equations:

$$Z_1 = f_1(U, R, T, P_1, P_2, \ldots, P_{n-1}) = 0$$

$$Z_2 = f_2(U, R, T, P_1, P_2, \ldots, P_{n-1}) = 0$$

$$\ldots$$

$$\ldots$$

$$Z_{n-1} = f_{n-1}(U, R, T, P_1, P_2, \ldots, P_{n-1}) = 0$$

We have here a model in $n - 1$ equations and $n - 1$ unknown prices. Mathematically, finding the equilibrium prices amounts to solving these equations simultaneously. If these equations can be solved, then equilibrium exists.

Walras' approach to competitive general equilibrium has fundamentally influenced the way that economists now think about it. Mathematical refinements of Walras' insights have deepened economists' understanding of the conditions required for the existence of a competitive general equilibrium, but there is one issue which remains something of a conundrum – and that is the process by which prices are determined. This is the subject of the following section.

3   THE DETERMINATION OF PRICES

3.1   Introduction

When economists talk about the determination of prices, this has (at least) two distinct meanings, although in practice it is hard to keep them apart. One meaning applies to equilibrium models such as the one in the technical box above where equilibrium prices are determined by a system of equations; here 'determined' implies a logical outcome. The other meaning concerns the process by which prices are determined in actual markets; 'determined' now refers to a real process of change through time.

The value of any formal model lies in the insights that it provides into real economic situations, but the model may sometimes be a rather 'idealized' version of real events. A conundrum that has puzzled economists is how the determination of equilibrium prices in the mathematical model relates to the process of price determination in real markets. This conundrum is the subject of this section.

3.2   The Walrasian auctioneer

Because the Walrasian model is an equilibrium model, it does not consider what happens if the system is out of equilibrium. This raises a question as to how equilibrium prices are actually arrived at in real situations where markets are out of equilibrium. This question is made more complicated by the competitive assumption that all agents are price takers, that is, agents accept the going equilibrium prices and make their plans subject to these prices. In the formal model this is straightforward as the equilibrium prices are simply the solution to the system of equations. In the real world, however, this introduces a problem. If all agents are price takers, how do prices ever actually get changed in real markets?

Walras himself tried to show how actual competitive markets could arrive at the equilibrium prices by a process of trial and error, by what he called 'groping' or 'tâtonnement' in his original French. Walras suggested that a competitive market process of price adjustment could be imagined as an auction or a place where prices are openly announced by brokers or criers, and where agents make provisional bids to buy or sell goods on the basis of these prices (Walras, 1954, pp.83–4). This process goes through a number of different rounds; prices are called out and agents make their bids, and then, without any trades taking place, another set of prices is called out and further bids are made, and so on, until a set of prices has been reached at which all the excess demands are equal to zero. Thus agents are able to keep revising their plans with each new price called out until excess demands are eliminated. Only when offers to buy equal offers to sell will trade actually take place at the announced prices. One crucial aspect of this process of groping or tâtonnement is that trades do not take place at disequilibrium prices. It is thus a highly stylized account of price adjustment and it is hard to think of any real world counterpart. Walras recognized that this ideal version of a competitive market was not the norm, but he felt that many markets, such as stock exchanges and trading markets, approximated closely to it. He also argued that it was an acceptable scientific procedure to start off with a theoretical ideal and then work from that, because this was the method used in physics (p.84).

Walrasian rule for price adjustment

The Walrasian rule for price adjustment is that price should be raised if there is positive excess demand and reduced if there is negative excess demand.

Later economists have tried to make sense of the process of tâtonnement as an account of how prices adjust in competitive markets, by adopting the idea of a central 'auctioneer' who calls out prices and who works out, from the bids provided by all agents, the excess demands at each set of prices called out. The *Walrasian rule for price adjustment*, which the auctioneer implements and which competitive markets operationalize, is that price should be increased if there is positive excess demand at that price, and reduced if there is negative excess

demand. This process of price adjustment continues until all excess demands have been eliminated. This notion of a central auctioneer following the Walrasian rule for price adjustment is really a 'fiction', it is not supposed that competitive markets work in this way but it tries to catch the essence of how anonymous markets seem to work. This auctioneer is sometimes referred to as the Walrasian auctioneer.

The Walrasian rule for price adjustment can be illustrated using Figure 18.2, but remember that the auctioneer is not meant to have the information given by the excess demand curve, only the bids to buy and sell at the prices that are called out.

If P_a were called out, the auctioneer would discover that there was positive excess demand at that price equal to Z_a. Following the rule, the auctioneer would then increase the price, maybe to something like P_b. When P_b is called out, the auctioneer discovers that excess demand would now be negative at Z_b which implies that the price change was too great. Now the price needs to be reduced again, but as P_a was too low, the next price should be higher than that. Perhaps now P_c is called out but there would still be excess demand of Z_c, so the price needs to be increased, and

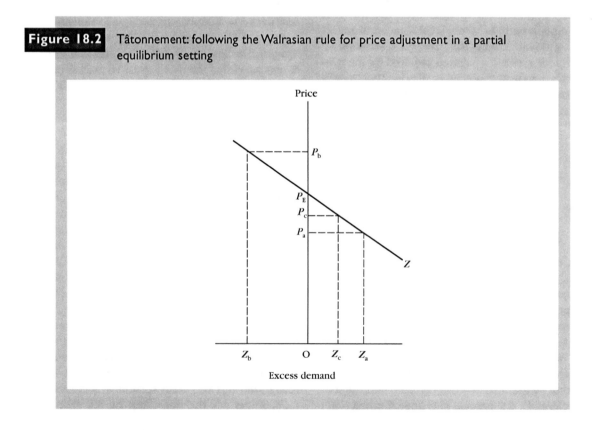

Figure 18.2 Tâtonnement: following the Walrasian rule for price adjustment in a partial equilibrium setting

Exercise 18.1

Try to imagine yourself as the Walrasian auctioneer in a very simple situation – say a single market – just to get a flavour of what is involved. Remember that you are not meant to know what the excess demand curve looks like. Look at the steps below and describe how they follow the Walrasian rule for price adjustment.

1   If a price of 120 were called out, the excess demand would be −100.
2   If a price of 70 were called out, the excess demand would be 50.
3   If a price of 100 were called out, the excess demand would be −40.
4   If a price of 90 were called out, the excess demand would be −10.
5   If a price of 80 were called out, the excess demand would be 20, etc.

What might the next step be?
Where might the equilibrium price lie?

so on. Eventually after groping about in the dark we see that the price should eventually converge on the equilibrium price of P_E.

By examining the properties of excess demand functions such as that illustrated in Figure 18.2, economists have developed mathematical models of the process of Walrasian price adjustment. They have discovered that if an excess demand curve is negatively sloped throughout its range, then the Walrasian rule for price adjustment will result in convergence on a single equilibrium price. If an excess demand curve does not have this shape, the Walrasian rule may not converge on an equilibrium price and/or there may also be more than one equilibrium outcome.

Instability and multiple equilibria

If an excess demand curve is positively sloped throughout its range, the Walrasian rule for price adjustment is unable to converge on the equilibrium price. This is illustrated in Figure 18.3.

Figure 18.3   Unstable equilibrium: an upward-sloping excess demand curve

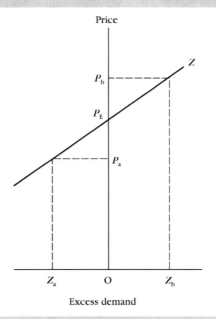

In Figure 18.3 the equilibrium price is P_E but the Walrasian rule for price adjustment would not converge on this price if it started from any other price. If P_a were called out, there would be negative excess demand of Z_a. According to the Walrasian rule, a negative excess demand requires a reduction in price, but if a price below P_a is called out, this would result in an even larger negative excess demand. This in turn would prompt the auctioneer to call out an even lower price, and so the price would diverge further and further away from the equilibrium price. Similarly, if P_b were called out, there would be positive excess demand of Z_b.

According to the Walrasian rule, a positive excess demand requires an increase in price, but if a price above P_b is called out, this would result in an even larger positive excess demand. This would prompt the auctioneer to call out an even higher price, and so again the price would diverge further away from the equilibrium price. Thus, although an equilibrium price exists at P_E, this is an unstable equilibrium because any movement away from it would result in further movements away from it. By contrast, the equilibrium in Figure 18.2 is stable

because any movement away from it results in convergence back on the equilibrium.

If an excess demand curve has a positively sloped section as well as a negatively sloped section, then instability can be combined with more than one equilibrium. This is illustrated in Figure 18.4.

In Figure 18.4 the excess demand curve is negatively sloped at low prices and positively sloped at high prices. There are two equilibrium prices, P_E^1 and P_E^2. An unstable equilibrium price is shown at P_E^1, whereas P_E^2 is a stable one. You can see this by starting from any price below P_E^1 and showing that the Walrasian rule results in convergence on P_E^2. Starting from a price greater than P_E^1 does not lead to a convergence on P_E^1 but results in greater and greater price increases with greater and greater levels of positive excess demand. Figure 18.4 therefore illustrates both an unstable equilibrium, at P_E^1, and multiple equilibria, at P_E^1 and P_E^2, one of which, P_E^2, is stable and one of which, P_E^1, is unstable.

How might excess demand curves have upward-sloping sections? They are caused by the presence of strong income effects which outweigh the substitution effects of a price change, and so

Figure 18.4 Instability and multiple equilibria

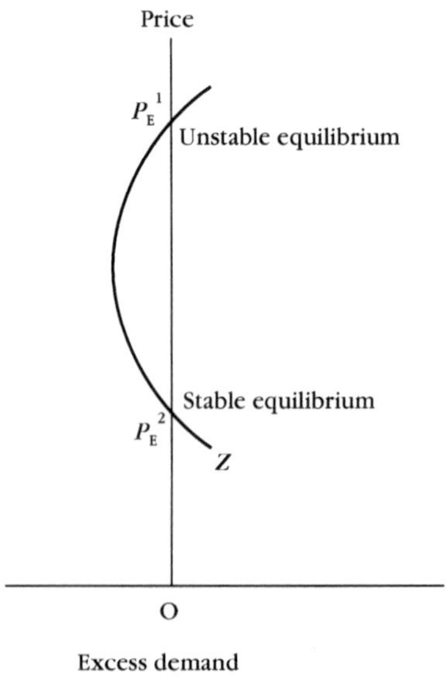

produce demand or supply curves which have the 'wrong' slope for some prices. Chapter 2, Section 3.2, discussed Giffen goods for which demand increases as their price rises, and in Chapter 5, Figure 5.5 showed how the presence of strong income effects in the labour market produces a backward bending supply curve of labour. Either of these cases could result in the excess demand curve shown in Figure 18.4.

Exercise 18.2

Figure 18.5 shows the market demand and supply curves for a good that is a Giffen good at some prices. Derive the excess demand curve for this good. Identify the stable and unstable equilibrium prices for this good. (See Chapter 2, Section 3.2, for the derivation of this diagram.)

I have argued that a competitive process of price adjustment may be thought of in terms of the fiction of the auctioneer, but the auctioneer is really some way from being a good image of the invisible hand. The auctioneer represents a centralization of the process of price adjustment that accords little with the notion of decentralization that is implicit in the invisible hand. In addition, tâtonnement implies that no trades take place until the equilibrium price has been announced by the auctioneer. This, too, is hardly a realistic picture of a decentralized market where equilibrium prices, arising from the give and take of everyday market transactions, emerge gradually out of disequilibrium prices (Hahn, 1987).

3.3   Competitive markets

One of the very few real world instances of tâtonnement is the fixing of the price of gold in London. This occurs at twice daily meetings which are chaired by a representative of N.M.Rothschild & Sons Ltd, and are attended by dealers who are in telephone contact with their dealing rooms who, in turn, keep in touch with customers. At these meetings, the chairman functions as the Walrasian auctioneer by announcing an opening price and then receives bids at that price from the dealers in consultation with their dealing rooms. If the buying and selling bids do not 'balance' the chairman

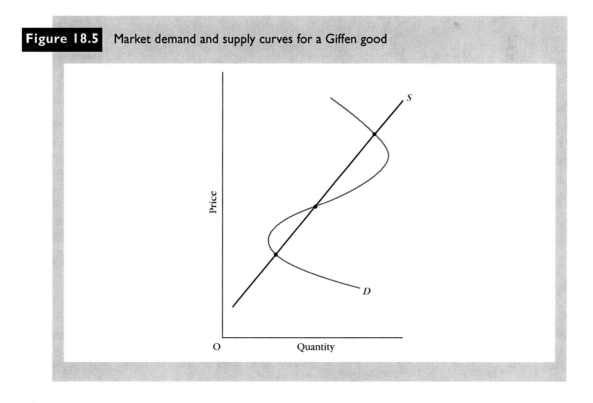

Figure 18.5   Market demand and supply curves for a Giffen good

announces another price and a second round of bids are made. This process continues until a balance is achieved and then the chairman announces that the price is 'fixed'. This 'fixed' price then provides a published benchmark price for gold.

The London Gold Fixing

The fixings are meetings held twice daily at 10.30 and 15.00 hours in the City of London to establish the market price for gold. These meetings provide market users with the opportunity of buying and selling at a single quoted price.

Each member of the fixing sends a representative to the fix meeting who maintains telephone contact throughout the meeting with his dealing room. The chairman of the fixing, traditionally the representative of N.M. Rothschild & Sons Limited, announces an opening price which is reported back to the dealing rooms. They in turn relay this price to their customers, and, on the basis of orders received, instruct their representative to declare as a buyer or seller. Provided both buying and selling interests are declared, members are then asked to state the number of bars in which they wish to trade. If at the opening price there is either no buying or no selling, or if the size for the buying and selling does not balance, the same procedure is followed again at higher or lower prices until a balance is achieved. At this moment the chairman announces that the price is 'fixed' ... The fixing will last as long as is necessary to establish a price which satisfies both buyers and sellers. In general this will be about 10–20 minutes, but in exceptional circumstances may take more than an hour.

A feature of the London fixing is that customers may be kept advised of price changes throughout a fixing meeting, and may alter their instructions at any time until the price is fixed. To ensure that a member can communicate such an alteration, his representative has a small flag on his desk which he raises and, as long as any flag is raised, the Chairman may not declare the price fixed.

The fixing provides a published benchmark price, which is widely used as a pricing medium.

Source: Rothschild pamphlet

The example of fixing the gold price is instructive as it shows the institutional requirements for a tâtonnement process to work in practice; the fixing involves a small group of dealers and their customers within a highly specialized market setting. It is hard to imagine this process working in large markets that involve many buyers and sellers, let alone working across all markets simultaneously in a general equilibrium framework. The gold fixing also shows that any particular institutional setup requires its own resourcing and does not come free; a number of individuals have to give up time in order to attend the gold fixing meetings twice each day. This reminds us that, in practical situations, markets are not simply disembodied forces that cost nothing, but represent particular institutional settings that require their own resources in order to function. Financial markets are a good example of this. These markets are often seen as good approximations of competitive markets, but they are not costless. For example, the size of salaries in major financial centres is legendary – quite apart from the champagne lunches! – and a striking reminder of the resource costs of even highly competitive market institutions.

The gold fixing is also a highly centralized way of determining equilibrium prices, again illustrating the conundrum that the process of tâtonnement seems to require a centralized rather than a decentralized method of fixing prices. This is also illustrated by the argument, originally made in the 1930s, that tâtonnement could be used to carry out a form of socialist central planning! It was suggested by Oskar Lange and Abba Lerner that a central planning board could act like a Walrasian auctioneer in setting the prices of capital goods and state-owned resources and so bypass the need for an actual market in finding equilibrium prices. Against this Hayek argued that the informational assumptions of such planning overlook the way in which information is produced as part of the market process, and that it is precisely the ability of markets to economise on information that enables them to function more efficiently than any plan, making it impractical to try to imitate the Walrasian process of tâtonnement (Vaughn, 1980, summarizes the socialist calculation debate.)

Thus, in trying to operationalize the notion of tâtonnement, some economists saw the Walrasian system as a blueprint for socialist planning rather than decentralized markets. And in arguing against socialist planning, Hayek also argued against Walrasian economics as a theoretical system. A root problem, recognized by neoclassical economists, is that competitive analysis assumes that all agents are price takers, but this leaves unresolved the issue of how prices are changed when the system is out of equilibrium.

Although this problem remains unresolved at a theoretical level, at the practical level of real markets it is clear that the direction in which many prices change does conform to the Walrasian rule for price adjustment, in that positive excess demand leads to a rise in price and negative excess demand leads to a fall in price.

Reflection

As an illustration of this, think about a local market where you do your shopping. Can you think of cases where the goods with a negative excess demand are sold off cheaply at the end of the day? Alternatively, house and flat prices in your area might be a good example of competitive prices. To what extent does the local estate agent perform the role of the Walrasian auctioneer?

In spite of these theoretical difficulties, experiments in economics have also confirmed many times over that there is a rapid convergence on the equilibrium price in various kinds of competitive markets. In particular, there is one trading structure in which the competitive equilibrium price is attained especially fast in experimental situations, and that is the 'oral double auction' (Hey, 1991, p.198). The oral double auction has been described in the following manner:

'This envisages the market participants to be either physically present in the same location or telephonically linked so that they can all communicate with each other. There is an auctioneer who administers the auction process but who otherwise takes a passive role. The active role is taken by the agents themselves, who are free to call out bids (offers to buy) or asks (offers to sell) depending upon whether they are potential buyers or potential sellers ... The process of calling out, and accepting, bids or asks continues until no new bids or asks are forthcoming and trade has ceased.'

(Hey, 1991, p.185)

With oral double auctions, market clearing is a dynamic disequilibrium process in that deals are finalized at going prices rather than waiting until an equilibrium price has been discovered as in the case of the Walrasian auctioneer. And unlike the case of the Walrasian auctioneer, it is a form of competition that is commonly found in real markets, for example the London International Financial Futures Exchange (LIFFE).

Thus, in spite of the theoretical difficulties which have perplexed theoretically-minded economists, for practical purposes many economists accept the usefulness of the insights of the Walrasian model in explaining some real markets. In spite of its strict assumption of price taking and no trading at disequilibrium prices, the Walrasian auctioneer model is regarded as a benchmark illustration of the convergence of competitive markets on the equilibrium price.

4   SOME MORE MODELS OF GENERAL EQUILIBRIUM

4.1   Introduction

We have seen that the question of the existence of general equilibrium comes down to the question whether there is a set of prices at which all excess demands are zero. This is a very complicated question for many goods, but if the idea of a competitive economy is simplified to just two goods and two consumers, it is possible to use Edgeworth box diagrams to represent a competitive general equilibrium and to show that, under certain conditions, equilibrium prices do exist. These diagrams are named after Francis Edgeworth who, like Walras, was one of the founders of general equilibrium analysis. Edgeworth (1845–1926) was born in Ireland and eventually became a professor at Oxford. He was a classicist and linguist, but he also pioneered a mathematical approach to economic analysis, as well as publishing work in ethics and in statistics (Newman, 1978).

In this section I shall use the Edgeworth box diagram first to represent a general equilibrium in a competitive exchange economy in which there is consumption but no production, and then I shall add production to present a general equilibrium of exchange, consumption and production.

4.2 General equilibrium of exchange and consumption

Chapter 2 showed how the behaviour of individual consumers explains the shape of the demand curve. Each consumer's preferences may be represented using an indifference map.

A single indifference curve is shown in Figure 18.6, which is based on Figure 2.6 in Chapter 2. It is assumed that indifference curves are convex to the origin. If the budget constraint is shown by the line BC, then the consumer maximizes utility by consuming the bundle where the budget line is tangent to an indifference curve. This occurs at point A.

The horizontal axis measures the units of good G, and the vertical axis measures the units of good F. At point A, the marginal rate of substitution of good G for good F, $\text{MRS}_{G,F}$, is equal to the relative price of G in terms of F, $\frac{P_G}{P_F}$, that is:

$$\text{MRS}_{G,F} = \frac{P_G}{P_F}$$

In other words, the rate at which a consumer would give up F for G and still remain on the same indifference curve is equal to the price of G in terms of F.

We can use this principle of utility maximization to develop a simple general equilibrium model of exchange and consumption in a competitive economy comprising two individuals and two goods. This model may seem very restrictive, but we shall see that the results generalize to many consumers and many goods. This simple economy can be illustrated using the Edgeworth box diagram in Figure 18.7. There is no production in this economy, but each individual receives a bundle of goods as an initial endowment. The economy's initial endowment of two goods is just the sum of the individuals' initial endowments. Let us say this sum is 50 kilos of figs (good F) and 60 kilos of grapes (good G); this gives the dimensions of the box shown in Figure 18.7. Figs are measured vertically and grapes are measured horizontally on the sides of the box diagram. By reading the axes from the bottom left hand corner for one agent and from the top right hand corner for the other agent, any point in the box can be understood as representing two bundles of goods, one for each agent, such that the two bundles together equal the economy's initial endowment. Such a point is shown as point A in Figure 18.7.

Reading Figure 18.7 from the bottom left-hand corner with the origin at O_x one agent, Xerxes, has 40 kilos of figs and 10 kilos of grapes at point A.

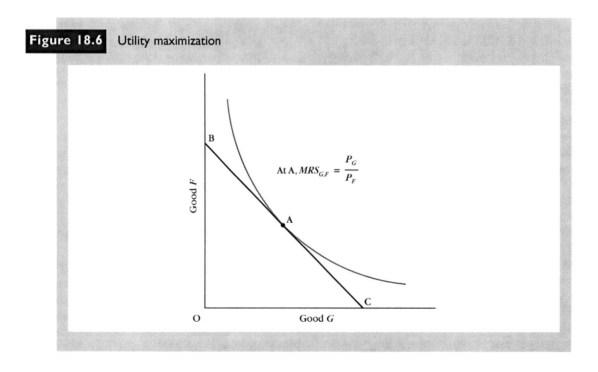

Figure 18.6   Utility maximization

At A, $MRS_{G,F} = \dfrac{P_G}{P_F}$

Good F

Good G

Reading the figure from the top right-hand corner with the origin at O_y the other agent, Yvonne, has 10 kilos of figs and 50 kilos of grapes at point A. (If you find this hard to follow, try turning the page upside down to see Yvonne's quantities. Note that Xerxes' axes are in black and Yvonne's are coloured). The sum of the two bundles of goods comprise the total endowment of the economy. Moving to any other point within the box keeps the same total endowment of the two goods but distributes them differently between the two consumers, Xerxes and Yvonne.

In this exchange economy, the only way for individuals to increase their utility is by exchanging some of their goods with each other. Exchange enables the two individuals to consume different combinations of the commodities that are available in this economy. We can represent the bundles that can be reached by exchange at a particular relative price by drawing a price line in Figure 18.7.

For example, all the bundles on the price line, P, in Figure 18.7 can be reached by exchange from A at the relative price:

$$\frac{P_G}{P_F} = \frac{2}{3}$$

That is, the price of grapes in terms of figs is $\frac{2}{3}$. This implies that, trading along the price line from A to B, 10 kilos of figs would be exchanged for 15 kilo

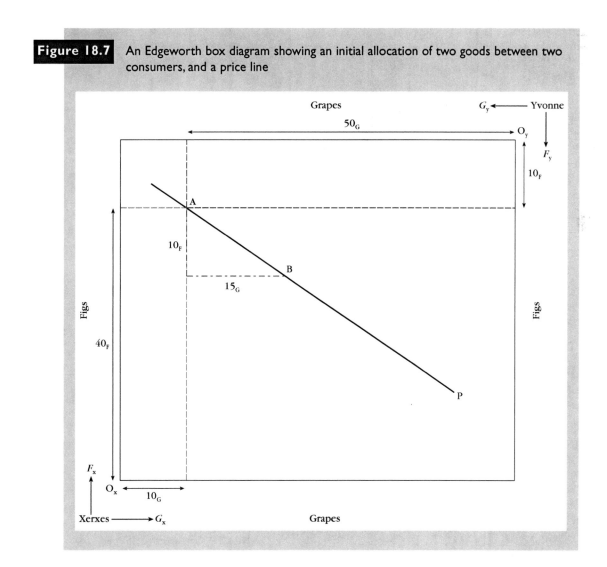

Figure 18.7 An Edgeworth box diagram showing an initial allocation of two goods between two consumers, and a price line

of grapes. Xerxes' consumption bundle at B would contain 15 kilos more of grapes and 10 kilos less of figs than at A; Yvonne's consumption bundle at B would contain 15 kilos less of grapes and 10 kilos more of figs.

The question for general equilibrium analysis is whether, given the agents' preferences, there exists a relative price between the two goods such that, if the individuals were to trade with each other at this price, excess demand for both goods would be zero. (Note: since there are only two goods, there is only one relative price and, by Walras' Law, if there is zero excess demand for one good there must be zero excess demand for the other good too.)

In order to examine the exchange that Xerxes and Yvonne will choose, we need to show their indifference maps in the Edgeworth box diagram. This is shown in Figure 18.8 where the indifference maps are represented by just four indifference curves for each consumer.

The Edgeworth box diagram in Figure 18.8 shows the indifference maps of both individuals, but Yvonne's is turned upside down because her consumption is measured in the opposite direction to Xerxes'. Xerxes' indifference map extends from the bottom left-hand corner up and to the right with the origin at O_x and is shown in black. His indifference curves are labelled U_{x0}, U_{x1}, U_{x2} and U_{x3}. Yvonne's indifference map has been flipped over so that it reads from the top right-hand corner down to the left with the origin at O_y and is coloured. Again you may find turning the page upside down helps

---

Figure 18.8   Simultaneous utility maximization

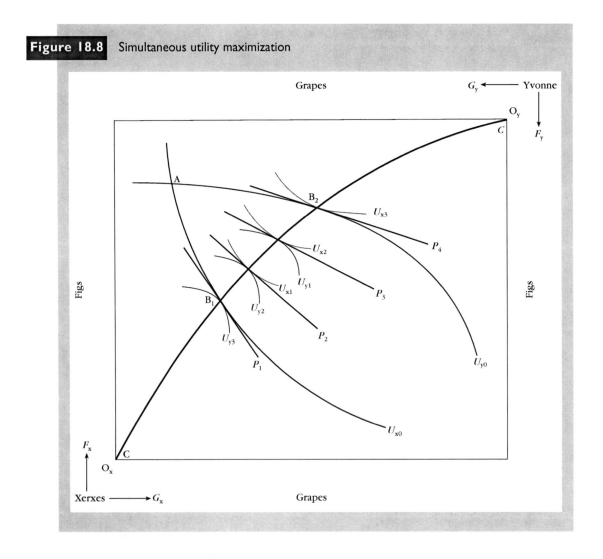

you to see this. Yvonne's indifference curves are labelled U_{y0}, U_{y1}, U_{y2} and U_{y3}. The initial endowment, A, is at the intersection of the indifference curves U_{x0} and U_{y0}.

Looking at the two indifference maps in Figure 18.8, we can see that there are a number of points of common tangency between the two sets of indifference curves. These points represent positions of simultaneous utility maximization by Xerxes and Yvonne, subject to different common prices which are shown by the different price lines, P_1, P_2, P_3 and P_4. For example, with the price line P_2, Xerxes is maximizing utility on indifference curve U_{x1}, and Yvonne is maximizing utility on indifference curve U_{y2}. When all the points of common tangency of all the indifference curves have been joined up, they form a line, *CC*, which is known as the *contract curve*. Note that, as utility maximization for any consumer implies that the MRS equals the ratio of prices, simultaneous utility maximization for both consumers, subject to a common price ratio, implies that Xerxes' MRS is equal to Yvonne's MRS.

Contract curve

The contract curve shows all the points of tangency between the indifference curves of two consumers. These are the points at which simultaneous utility maximization is possible for the two consumers, subject to different prices.

We have seen that simultaneous utility maximization is possible only at points on the contract curve. Given the initial allocation at A, however, not all points on this contract curve represent an improvement for both Xerxes and Yvonne, since there are some points on the contract curve that represent a worse outcome than at A. Xerxes would not want to trade to a point on the contract curve below and to the left of B_1 as this would put him on a lower indifference curve than U_{x0}. Similarly, Yvonne would not want to trade to a point on the contract curve above and to the right of B_2 as this would put her on a lower indifference curve than at U_{y0}. With an initial endowment at A, only points which lie on the portion of the contract curve between points B_1 and B_2 are preferred to A by both Xerxes and Yvonne. This portion of the contract curve, which lies between the two indifference curves corresponding to the initial allocation, is known as the *core*.

The core

The core of a two-person exchange economy is that portion of the contract curve that is preferred by both consumers to the initial endowment.

Starting with an initial allocation at A, the equilibrium outcome must lie within the core, but where within the core? Any point within the core qualifies as such a competitive equilibrium outcome if, at some given price ratio, both consumers would choose to trade to that point from the initial allocation at A. In terms of the Edgeworth box shown in Figure 18.9, such a point must be one at which a price line P drawn to it from A, is tangent to both consumers' indifference curves. Such a point is shown at E in Figure 18.9. In moving from A to E, Xerxes and Yvonne are trading figs and grapes at the price ratio given by the price line, with Xerxes exchanging figs for grapes and Yvonne exchanging grapes for figs.

At E, the amounts demanded and supplied by Xerxes and Yvonne are equal, given the price line, P, and so excess demands are zero. At A, if faced with the price line P, both Xerxes and Yvonne would trade along it until they reached their highest indifference curve at point E, where each would be maximizing utility. Xerxes would be on his highest indifference curve, U_{xE}, and Yvonne would be on her highest indifference curve, U_{yE}, given the price line P. At the equilibrium point E, Xerxes consumes 35 kilos of figs and 25 kilos of grapes, and Yvonne consumes 15 kilos of figs and 35 kilos of grapes. Comparing this consumption with the initial allocation at A, we find that Xerxes has traded 5 kilos of figs for 15 kilos of grapes, and Yvonne has traded 15 kilos of grapes for 5 kilos of figs. Xerxes is now consuming more grapes and fewer figs, and Yvonne is consuming more figs and fewer grapes, but note that Xerxes' offer to sell figs equals Yvonne's offer to buy figs (5 kilos), and Xerxes' offer to buy grapes equals Yvonne's offer to sell grapes (15 kilos). Thus demand equals supply. These trades imply that the price of grapes in terms of figs is:

$$\frac{P_G}{P_F} = \frac{1}{3}$$

Note that at equilibrium both consumers' MRS, as expressed by the slopes of their indifference curves, are equal to relative prices, that is:

$$MRS_{G,F} = \frac{P_G}{P_F} = \frac{1}{3}$$

Exercise 18.3

Consider an economy in which there are two consumers, Brenda and Colin, and two goods. At the initial allocation, Brenda has 30 kilos of figs and 20 kilos of grapes and Colin has 20 kilos of figs and 40 kilos of grapes (Note: in this example the total endowment for the economy is still 50 kilos of figs and 60 kilos of grapes). Brenda and Colin trade until an equilibrium is reached at which Brenda's consumption bundle is 25 kilos of figs and 35 kilos of grapes.

1 What is Colin's equilibrium consumption bundle?
2 What trades have to take place to reach this equilibrium from the initial allocation?

3 What must the price ratio, $\frac{P_G}{P_F}$, be?
4 Draw an Edgeworth box diagram to represent this.

Disequilibrium and multiple equilibria

Disequilibrium

To check whether you understand why Xerxes' and Yvonne's MRS must be equal to the relative price at equilibrium, try thinking through a

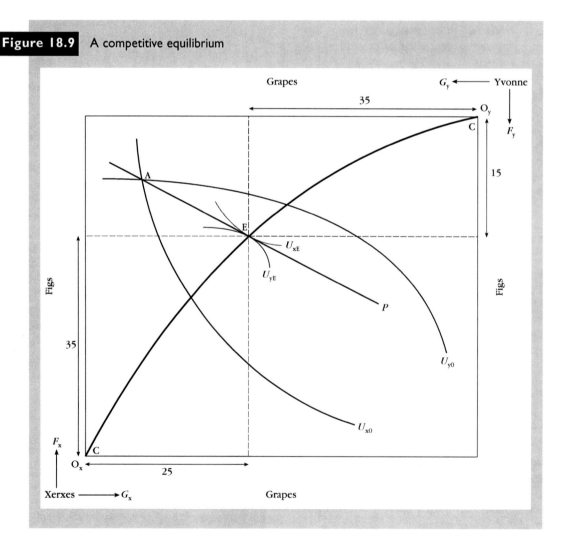

Figure 18.9 A competitive equilibrium

different situation where it does not hold, where their indifference curves are not tangent to the price line and so there is disequilibrium. This possibility is illustrated in Figure 18.10 where the price line cuts the contract curve at point H which is in the core but where the price line is not tangent to an indifference curve of either Xerxes or Yvonne at this point.

In Figure 18.10, at point H, the price line, P, is not tangent to either Xerxes' indifference curve U_{xa} or Yvonne's indifference curve U_{ya}. You can see this because both indifference curves cross P. This implies that at H both Xerxes and Yvonne would prefer to move to a higher indifference curve. Xerxes would prefer to move to H' on indifference

curve U_{xb} and Yvonne would prefer to move to point H'' on indifference curve U_{yb}, but this is not possible because to get from H to H', Xerxes wants to exchange figs to get more grapes but, unfortunately, Yvonne wants to do the same to get to H''. The amounts offered in exchange by Xerxes are not consistent with the amounts offered by Yvonne, and so there is disequilibrium.

Question

Why are the consumption bundles at H' and H'' inconsistent?

At H' Xerxes wishes to consume 13 kilos of figs and 45 kilos of grapes, but at H'' Yvonne

Figure 18.10   Disequilibrium

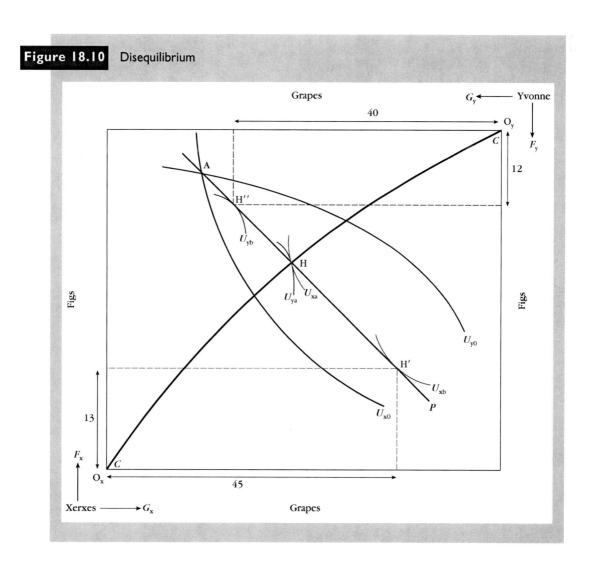

wishes to consume 12 kilos of figs and 40 kilos of grapes. If Xerxes wishes to consume 13 kilos of figs and Yvonne wishes to consume 12 kilos, their total consumption would be 25 kilos. This is less than the total initial endowment of 50 kilos of figs. Similarly, if Xerxes wishes to consume 45 kilos of grapes and Yvonne wishes to consume 40 kilos, this is more than the total initial endowment of 60 kilos of grapes. Given the initial allocation at A where Xerxes has 43 kilos of figs and 15 kilos of grapes, and Yvonne has 7 kilos of figs and 45 kilos of grapes, the amounts offered in exchange are inconsistent and so demand and supply are not equal.

Xerxes wishes to trade 30 kilos of figs for 30 kilos of grapes whereas Yvonne wishes to trade 15 kilos of grapes for 5 kilos of figs. At this relative price of $\frac{P_G}{P_F} = 1$ there is a positive excess demand for grapes of 25 kilos and a negative excess demand for figs of 25 kilos.

So the relative price shown by the price line P cannot be an equilibrium price. If there is positive excess demand for grapes and negative excess demand for figs, the Walrasian rule for price adjustment says that the price of grapes should be raised relative to that of figs.

Exercise 18.4

Should the price line pivot around A in a clockwise or anti-clockwise direction in order to get to an equilibrium from A?

Figure 18.11   Multiple equilibria

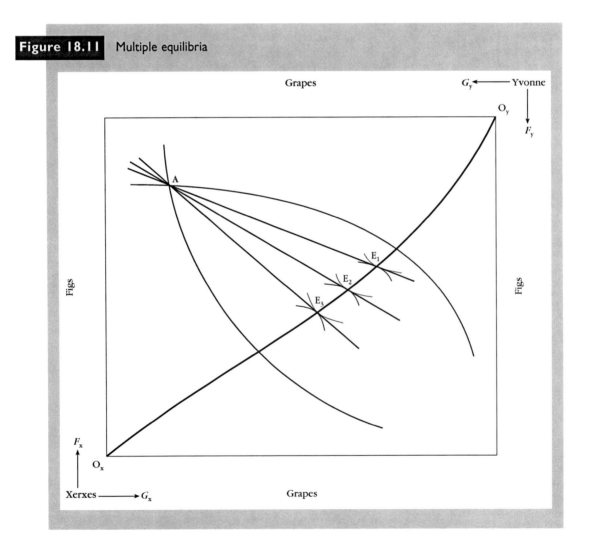

Multiple equilibria

There can be more than one equilibrium point and this can be represented using an Edgeworth box diagram. Multiple equilibria occur when it is possible to draw more than one price line through the initial allocation at A which is tangent to a pair of indifference curves in the core. This possibility is shown in Figure 18.11.

Excess demands are zero at each of the equilibria marked as E_1, E_2 and E_3. Note that at each equilibrium, both consumers' MRS are equal to the relative price:

$$MRS_{G,F} = \frac{P_G}{P_F}$$

but the relative price and corresponding MRS are different for each equilibrium.

Exercise 18.5

On Figure 18.11, is the price of grapes relative to figs higher at E_1 or E_3? What does this imply about the $MRS_{G,F}$ at these two equilibria?

We saw an example of a competitive equilibrium at E in Figure 18.9, but it is important to remember that the equilibrium reached at E depends on the initial endowment of resources between Xerxes and Yvonne as shown at point A. Different initial allocations of resources would result in a different equilibrium. This is shown in Figure 18.12 (overleaf) where the initial endowment at point A′ is more unequal than it was at A in Figure 18.9, as Yvonne has more figs and more grapes than she had at A (and also more at A′ than Xerxes has). The resulting equilibrium at E′ enables her to consume more of both goods than she could at E (and also more at E′ than Xerxes can).

The indifference maps for Yvonne and Xerxes are the same in Figure 18.12 as in Figure 18.9, and the total endowment of 50 kilos of figs and 60 kilos of grapes is also unchanged. The only difference lies in the distribution of this endowment between Yvonne and Xerxes at A′. Yvonne now has 42 kilos of figs and 50 kilos of grapes, and Xerxes now has only 8 kilos of figs and 10 kilos of grapes. With a relative price of $\frac{4}{5}$, the equilibrium is shown at E′. At this point Yvonne consumes 38 kilos of figs and 55 kilos

of grapes and Xerxes consumes 12 kilos of figs and 5 kilos of grapes. Thus we see in this case how a different initial endowment results in a different equilibrium.

This section has presented a very simple model of an exchange economy with only two consumers, two goods and no production. In spite of this, the results using the Edgeworth box diagram illustrate an example of a competitive equilibrium, based on utility maximization by price-taking consumers. The features of a competitive equilibrium which it illustrates hold even when there are many consumers and many goods.

- All excess demands are zero: at equilibrium, Xerxes' offers to buy and sell grapes and figs exactly match Yvonne's offers to sell and buy grapes and figs.

- Until equilibrium is reached, trade between agents can allow all agents to increase their utility, i.e. trade is a positive-sum game: both Xerxes and Yvonne increase their utility by trading with one another. This holds even when the original distribution between the consumers is very unequal.

- The equilibrium outcome depends on the distribution of the initial endowment between the two consumers: the competitive equilibrium at E depends on the initial allocation at A, and a different endowment of goods between Xerxes and Yvonne results in a different equilibrium with different prices and different equilibrium consumption bundles for each of them.

In this section I have focused on a pure exchange economy where there is consumption but no production. In the next section I will look at the production side of an economy, so that in Section 4.4 I can combine the two to give a general equilibrium of exchange, consumption and production.

4.3   Equilibrium in production

To represent the production side of the economy on a diagram, we keep to a simple model of two final goods, but, as with the two-person exchange model, the results generalize to many commodities. Our aim is to find out the amounts of the two goods produced and the price at which they are sold. The first step involves considering all possible combinations of quantities of the two goods that could be produced given existing technology and different techniques of production. The production possibility frontier (PPF), which you met in Chapter 6, shows all the maximum combinations of two goods that are feasible given existing technology. Figure 18.13 shows a production possibility frontier in which kilos of grapes are measured on the horizontal axis and kilos of figs are measured on the vertical axis.

Given the existing technology, every point on the production possibility frontier shows the maximum possible output of one good, given the output level of the other good. For example, point B on the PPF shows that if the quantity of grapes produced is G_B,

the maximum amount of figs that it is possible to produce is F_B.

The slope of the PPF, $\frac{\Delta F}{\Delta G}$, is negative and its magnitude shows the rate at which figs have to be sacrificed (or foregone) in order to produce one more unit of grapes. We have met this idea before too: it is a version of the notion of opportunity cost that you met in Chapter 6 and is called the *marginal rate of transformation* (MRT) as it measures the rate at which one good can be 'transformed' into another by reducing the output of one and increasing the output of the other, assuming that all resources are fully employed:

$$\text{MRT}_{G,F} = -\frac{\Delta F}{\Delta G}$$

Figure 18.12 A general equilibrium where Yvonne is rich and Xerxes is poor

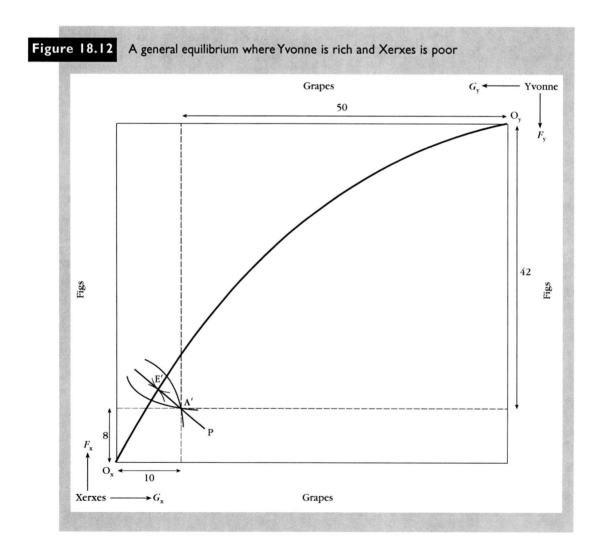

The marginal rate of transformation (MRT)

The marginal rate of transformation of good G for good F measures the rate at which the output of F has to be reduced to obtain an additional unit of G. It is given by the magnitude of the slope of the production possibility frontier $\text{MRT}_{G,F} = -\dfrac{\Delta F}{\Delta G}$

An important feature of the PPF is that its slope is different at each point. The slope of the PPF at any point can be found by measuring the slope of a line which is tangent to it at that point.

On Figure 18.14 compare the slope at point B with that at B′ which is further to the right along the PPF. At point B′, the tangent is shown by the line T′ and is steeper than the tangent T at B. This shows that the slope of the PPF becomes more steeply negative along its length from left to right; that is, the MRT of good G for good F increases as more of good G and less of good F is produced. The MRT of a good increases as more of it is produced because the opportunity cost of producing it increases as more resources are transferred into its production.

We can see that the MRT between two goods measures the rate at which production of one has to be reduced in order to increase production of the other by one unit, and that this is equivalent to the notion of opportunity cost. We can put this in terms of their relative marginal costs (*MC*). The marginal cost of a good is the cost of the last unit produced (*Changing Economies*, Chapter 4, Section 4). In a many-good economy, we think of this as measured in terms of money. In our two-good model, cost can only be measured relative to the other good. So the marginal cost of producing one extra unit of good *G*, is simply the amount of good *F* it costs to produce that unit of good *G*, that is, the opportunity cost of that last unit of *G* in terms of *F*. But this is just the marginal rate of transformation of good *G* for good *F*. In other words:

$$MC_G = \text{MRT}_{G,F}$$

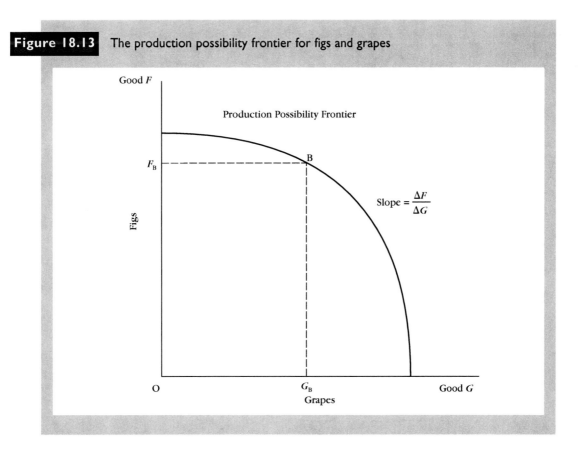

Figure 18.13 The production possibility frontier for figs and grapes

If there were more goods we would have to talk in terms of ratios of marginal costs, and the marginal cost of one good in terms of another would be equal to the ratio of their marginal costs. So in general:

$$\mathrm{MRT}_{G,F} = \frac{MC_G}{MC_F}$$

However, if we are measuring costs in terms of good F, then $MC_F = 1$. For example, if the marginal cost of grapes is twice that of figs, this means that one more kilo of grapes costs two units of figs. In this case also, the $\mathrm{MRT}_{G,F} = 2$, because two kilos of figs have to be given up in order to have one more kilo of grapes.

In a competitive economy, however, profit maximization implies that firms produce at that level at which marginal costs are equal to output prices (Chapter 10 and *Changing Economies*, Chapter 7, Section 4). This means that in equilibrium, the ratio

of the marginal costs of the two goods will be equal to their relative price, that is:

$$\frac{MC_G}{MC_F} = \frac{P_G}{P_F}$$

This implies that the marginal rate of transformation between the two goods is equal to their relative price in a competitive economy, that is:

$$\mathrm{MRT}_{G,F} = \frac{P_G}{P_F}$$

This is an important result because it shows that profit maximizing under competitive conditions results in the relative output price being equal to the magnitude of the slope of the production possibility frontier. This can be illustrated by adding a price line to the production possibility frontier as shown in Figure 18.15. If the relative price of grapes in terms of figs is shown by the price line, P, the

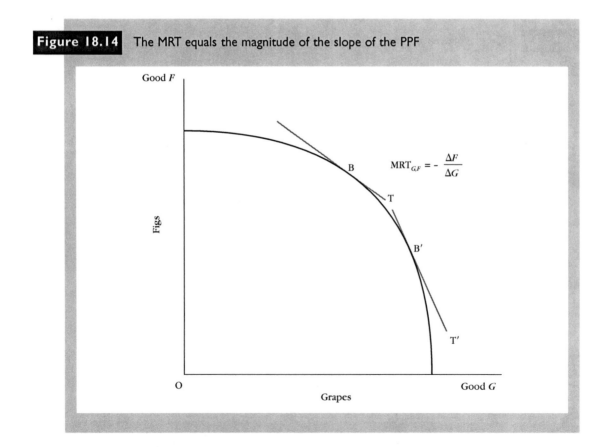

Figure 18.14 The MRT equals the magnitude of the slope of the PPF

profit maximizing output mix under competitive conditions will be at the point E. This is the point at which the price line is tangent to the production possibility curve, making the magnitude of its slope, $\mathrm{MRT}_{G,F}$, equal to the price ratio, $\dfrac{P_G}{P_F}$

We have now derived a production possibility frontier for the economy which shows that, under competitive conditions, the economy's MRT between the two goods is equal to their relative price. We are now ready to expand our model of the exchange economy to include production so that we can find out whether there exists a relative price that will support a general equilibrium of exchange and production simultaneously. This is the subject of the next section.

4.4   General equilibrium with production

We are now ready to examine a simultaneous equilibrium for exchange and production. In this economy, both figs and grapes can be produced. Our task is to find the equilibrium relative price and the output mix of figs and grapes, together with the amounts consumed by Xerxes and Yvonne.

We know that consumer optimization under price taking results in the marginal rate of substitution of grapes for figs being equal to the ratio of prices for both consumers:

$$\mathrm{MRS}_{G,F} = \frac{P_G}{P_F}$$

We have also seen that profit maximization under price taking results in the marginal rate of transformation of grapes for figs being equal to the ratio of prices:

$$\mathrm{MRT}_{G,F} = \frac{P_G}{P_F}$$

This implies that, in equilibrium in a competitive economy, the marginal rate of substitution must be equal to the marginal rate of transformation, that is:

$$\mathrm{MRS}_{G,F} = \frac{P_G}{P_F} = \mathrm{MRT}_{G,F}$$

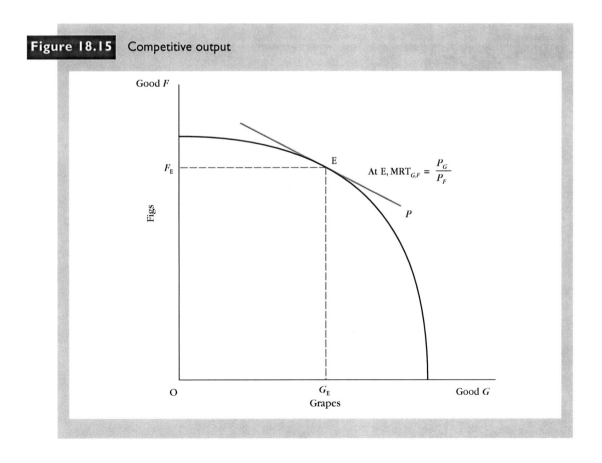

Figure 18.15   Competitive output

At E, $\mathrm{MRT}_{G,F} = \dfrac{P_G}{P_F}$

This can be illustrated by combining the box diagram of exchange and consumption with the production possibility frontier diagram. This is shown in Figure 18.16.

The production possibility frontier shows the competitive profit-maximizing output mix, E, where F_E of figs and G_E of grapes are produced, subject to the price line P. These amounts of figs and grapes then provide the dimensions for an Edgeworth box with the competitive utility-maximizing consumption bundles of figs and grapes at E', subject to the price line P. This is a competitive equilibrium because excess demands for figs and grapes are zero at E', given the price line P. Note that the MRS for each consumer equals the MRT because both equal the relative price. This implies that the MRS and MRT lines are parallel because they have the same slope, that is:

$$\text{MRS}_{G,F} = \frac{P_G}{P_F} = \text{MRT}_{G,F}$$

A complete general equilibrium model also needs to include an analysis of Xerxes' and Yvonne's endowment of the factors of production which are used to produce the final output, and whose sale gives them the income required to buy their respective consumption bundles at E'. Thus the competitive equilibrium in Figure 18.16 depends crucially on the initial endowment of factors of production between Xerxes and Yvonne, although this is not shown on the diagram. With a different distribution of the initial endowment, the relative incomes of Xerxes and Yvonne would be different and so we would expect the output mix and consumption bundles to be different as well. For example, if Yvonne received a greater initial endowment she would be able to consume a larger bundle than before, that is, she would be able to consume more of both figs and grapes. Thus, the output mix at E and the consumption bundles at E' in Figure 18.16 represent just one possible competitive equilibrium. In general, we would expect there to be as many different equilibrium output mixes and consumption bundles as there are different initial endowments of factors of production, assuming that each initial endowment leads to a

Figure 18.16 Competitive equilibrium in exchange, consumption and production

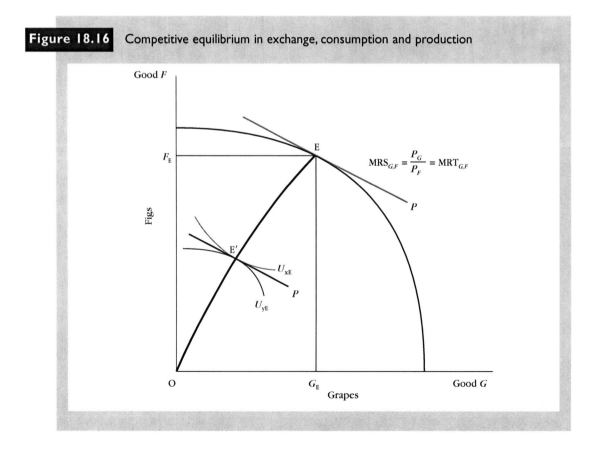

unique equilibrium. Multiple equilibria would, of course, make this more complicated.

Exercise 18.6

If the equilibrium price of grapes in terms of figs were higher than shown in Figure 18.16, what would this imply about the equilibrium output mix of figs and grapes, and the consumers' MRS?

4.5   Conclusion: prices again

This section has examined the existence of competitive general equilibrium in two-person, two-good models which can be illustrated using Edgeworth box diagrams. As with the Walrasian model, we have found that the existence of equilibrium is dependent on there being a relative price that will yield zero excess demands. Note, however, that the issue of how the equilibrium price is actually set is still unresolved. The two agents are price takers, but the process by which the equilibrium price might have been discovered by actual agents falls outside the model.

Edgeworth was aware of this issue and, like Walras, he proposed a way around it. His solution was to think of price setting in terms of a series of contracts made directly between agents which can be renegotiated right up until the moment when the equilibrium outcome is reached. This process of 'recontracting', as Edgeworth called it, ensures that contracts that do not result in the equilibrium outcome are not adhered to, that is, that there is no 'false trading'. It is the equivalent of Walras' idea that no actual trades take place until the process of tâtonnement has finished and the equilibrium prices have been called out. If there are two agents negotiating a price, then the final equilibrium can be anywhere in the core. As we have seen, the core is the part of the contract curve that is preferred by both agents to the original endowment, but the actual point reached within the core depends on the negotiations between the two agents. Edgeworth showed mathematically that the equilibrium outcome negotiated by agents will converge on the competitive outcome of a Walrasian model as the number of agents becomes very large. In this large numbers case, the core of the contract curve shrinks to a single point representing the competitive outcome. (This cannot be illustrated

using a box diagram for the same reason that excess demand curves in a general equilibrium setting can not be illustrated diagramatically: a two-dimensional surface is incapable of representing the multi-good, multi-person case.) The process of recontracting thus attempts to solve the problem of how the equilibrium outcome is actually discovered in real markets without a Walrasian auctioneer. Recontracting means that contracts are made directly between maximizing agents, but to explain how the equilibrium is arrived at we still need to rely on the device that no false trades are concluded. It therefore does not solve the theoretical conundrum of how equilibrium prices in real world markets can be determined as the outcome of ordinary trading relations where 'false', that is disequilibrium, trades are the norm.

5 | COMPETITIVE EQUILIBRIUM AND WELFARE ECONOMICS

5.1   Introduction

In the Introduction to this chapter we saw how arguments for economic liberalism have been linked with the neoclassical analysis of competitive markets. In this section we come to consider the argument that a competitive equilibrium promotes economic well-being, by which I mean Pareto efficiency. This was presented intuitively in Chapter 1, but we will now trace this argument more rigorously. (See Chapter 4 for a discussion of different notions of well-being.)

5.2   Efficiency and competitive equilibrium

The notion that a competitive equilibrium promotes economic well-being is based on the argument that a competitive equilibrium is Pareto efficient, in that it is impossible to improve any agent's situation without making someone else worse off. We can examine this argument by looking back at Figure 18.16 which showed how, in the general equilibrium of exchange and production, the same price line P is tangent to both the economy's production possibility frontier at E and the consumers' indifference curves at E′. This means that the relative price represented by P is equal to both the economy's MRT and consumers' MRS at these points, and therefore that:

$$MRT = MRS$$

This implies that the opportunity cost of grapes in terms of figs in production is equal to consumers' preference for grapes relative to figs. To demonstrate that this competitive equilibrium is Pareto efficient, we now need to show that it is impossible to reallocate production or consumption to make either Xerxes or Yvonne better off without making the other worse off. We do this by showing that MRT = MRS is also the condition for Pareto efficiency.

First consider whether in Figure 18.16 there is any other consumption bundle on the contract curve that is more preferred than E′ by either Xerxes or Yvonne, which does not make the other worse off. Any other consumption bundle on the contract curve will be more preferred than E′ by either Xerxes or Yvonne, but less preferred by the other. Points to the right of E′ on the contract curve would be more preferred by Xerxes as lying on a higher indifference curve than U_{xE}, but less preferred by Yvonne as lying on an indifference curve below U_{yE}. Similarly, points to the left of E′ would be more preferred by Yvonne but less preferred by Xerxes. Thus, all points on the contract curve are Pareto efficient in an exchange economy. This may be contrasted with all those consumption bundles that are off the contract curve and which are not Pareto efficient because moving from them to some point on the contract curve would increase utility for one agent (without reducing it for the other) or for both agents. For example, looking back to Figure 18.9, a point such as A is less preferred by both Xerxes and Yvonne to any point in the core. Another way of saying this, as we have seen, is that it is only on the contract curve that both consumers are maximizing utility, given their preferences and the relative price ratio, and where they have the same MRS of one good for the other.

All points on the contract curve are Pareto efficient in an exchange economy, but in a production and exchange economy, only point E′ is a Pareto-efficient consumption bundle when output is at E. This is because consumers' MRS at E′ equals the MRT at E. If the rate which consumers would give up units of F for an additional unit of G equals the rate at which the output of F has to be reduced to obtain an additional

unit of G, then it is impossible to reallocate production or consumption to make either Xerxes or Yvonne better off without making the other worse off. Consider the case where the MRT of good G for good F is greater than the MRS of good G for good F. In this case, the amount of F given up to produce the last unit of G is greater than the amount of F which a consumer would give up for that unit of G and still remain on the same indifference curve. This implies that reducing the output of G by one unit would increase the output of F by an amount that would place one or both consumers on a higher indifference curve. Changing the output mix by reducing G by one unit and increasing F would, therefore, be a Pareto improvement. Similarly if the MRT of good G for good F were smaller than the MRS of good G for good F, then increasing the output of G would put consumers on a higher indifference curve and so would also be a Pareto improvement. It is only when the MRS = MRT for every pair of goods and for every consumer, that it is impossible to reallocate production or consumption in such a way as to make any consumer better off without making some other consumer worse off. The equality between MRS and MRT for all goods and all consumers is, therefore, the condition for Pareto efficiency.

The reason a competitive equilibrium is Pareto efficient is that, in the absence of externalities, the Pareto condition MRS = MRT always holds. Firms set marginal costs equal to prices and this implies that the economy's MRT equals relative prices; consumers adjust their consumption so that their MRS equals relative prices. The outcome is that MRS = MRT. This result, that, in the absence of externalities, a competitive equilibrium is Pareto efficient, is known as the *First Welfare Theorem*.

First Welfare Theorem

The First Welfare Theorem states that, in the absence of externalities, any competitive equilibrium is Pareto efficient.

There are two points to notice about the First Welfare Theorem. The first is that it is silent about the issue of distribution. When we considered the exchange economy above, we saw that a competitive equilibrium depends on the initial endowment, and so there is a different equilibrium for each initial endowment. This is also true when we include production – there will be many competitive equilibria depending on the initial endowments of productive resources. Each of these equilibria is Pareto efficient but the final allocation of consumption is different in each. The second point is that the First Welfare Theorem contains a proviso that there are no externalities. Externalities occur where private costs/benefits differ from social costs/benefits (*Changing Economies*, Chapter 10, Section 3.1). If there are externalities, then firms and consumers are setting their private costs and benefits equal to prices, and this means that competitive prices will not reflect social costs and benefits. If there are externalities, this means that competitive prices fail to equate the true social MRT with the true social MRS, and so the competitive outcome is not Pareto efficient.

Externalities mean that a competitive equilibrium is not Pareto efficient

Production externalities

In the case of pollution from a factory, for example, the social costs of production exceed the firm's private costs as the latter do not take into account the effects of the pollution on the environment or on people's health. Competitive firms will carry on producing until the private marginal cost equals the market price. If the marginal social cost exceeds the marginal private cost, this means that the social cost at the margin exceeds the market price, and so the true social MRT exceeds consumers' MRS in a competitive equilibrium. This implies that consumers are not paying the full cost of the activity and that there is more than a Pareto-efficient quantity of the polluting activity being produced.

Consumption externalities

In the case of contagious diseases, for example, other people benefit from a person's inoculation against the diseases in addition to the immediate consumer of the inoculation, and so the marginal social benefit is greater than the marginal private benefit. In this case, the true social MRS is greater than the MRT in a competitive equilibrium, and so the quantity consumed is smaller than the Pareto-efficient quantity.

We have seen that the First Welfare Theorem shows that any competitive equilibrium is Pareto efficient, under certain conditions. Is the converse also true, that any Pareto-efficient allocation can be achieved as a competitive equilibrium? The answer to this question is complicated by the problem of nonconvexity. So far in this chapter I have assumed that the production possibility frontier bows outwards and that consumers have convex indifference curves, so I have avoided the problems posed by nonconvexities (see Chapters 2 and 8). The presence of nonconvexities means that a competitive equilibrium may not exist. I will trace through the implications of this for the case of nonconvexity in production, that is, in increasing returns to scale.

A technology is nonconvex if there are increasing returns to scale. These increasing returns to scale are associated with imperfectly competitive firms, not competitive firms (Chapter 8; *Changing Economies*, Chapters 6 and 7). This is because, under increasing returns to scale, large firms may out-compete small firms until the number of firms becomes so small that other strategic considerations will start to apply (see Chapter 11). The presence of increasing returns therefore means that a competitive equilibrium may not exist. For this reason, it is not the case that every Pareto-efficient allocation is also a competitive equilibrium because the competitive equilibrium might not exist. Pareto efficiency is possible even in the presence of increasing returns, but the increasing returns may prevent that outcome from being a competitive equilibrium. This brings us to the *Second Welfare Theorem* which states that, if there are no nonconvexities, every Pareto-efficient allocation can be achieved as a competitive equilibrium.

Second Welfare Theorem

The Second Welfare Theorem states that, in the absence of nonconvexities, every Pareto-efficient allocation can be achieved as a competitive equilibrium.

The Second Welfare Theorem shows that, if there are no nonconvexities, any Pareto-efficient allocation can be achieved by competitive markets from some initial allocation of resources. Note the importance of the initial endowment again. We have seen that every Pareto-efficient competitive outcome is based on an initial endowment of resources distributed among the economic agents. The converse is that any Pareto-efficient outcome is feasible as a competitive outcome but the initial distribution has to be the appropriate one. This result is significant as it shows that, theoretically, the issues of efficiency and distribution are separate. Competitive prices secure an efficient outcome (in the absence of externalities and nonconvexities) from any initial endowment, but an appropriate initial endowment is needed to secure any particular distributional outcome. Thus, the competitive market itself can be said to be distributionally neutral. The policy implication is that issues of efficiency and distribution are better kept separate. Policies to promote competition can be used to secure efficiency, unhindered by distributional considerations, because these can be looked after by adjusting people's initial endowments – preferably by lump sum taxes or benefits that do not distort relative prices or choices at the margin.

How does this result affect the case we considered in Section 4.2 for the exchange economy where Yvonne is rich and Xerxes poor, as was illustrated by the initial endowment A′ in Figure 18.12? If it were decided that Xerxes should have a larger consumption bundle than that shown at E′ what would be the best policy?

Question

Look again at Figure 18.12. If you were to introduce a policy to increase Xerxes' final consumption bundle so that he could consume more of both figs and grapes than at E′, how might you do it?

The implication of the Second Welfare Theorem is that distributional issues should be resolved by changing the initial endowments, and not by changing the competitive pricing mechanism. The solution would be to change the initial endowment at A′, by giving Xerxes more and Yvonne less, and then letting the market mechanism work to produce an equilibrium price at which both Xerxes and Yvonne maximize their utility by trading until their MRS equals that price.

This separation between efficiency and distribution is clear-cut in theory, but it is not so easy to make in practice as we shall see in the following section. The policy implications of the two welfare theorems are considered in the next section.

5.3   Welfare policies

We have seen that, at a theoretical level, there is a strong link between competitive outcomes and Pareto efficiency. This has been used to suggest that a decentralized economy with competitive markets and an absence of government intervention is the one that works most efficiently. According to this argument, government intervention in the form of taxes, subsidies, regulations and the direct provision of services, distorts the role of prices in allocating resources and so introduces inefficiencies into a market economy. The policy issues are, however, more complicated than this would suggest.

Improving efficiency

If the world we live in corresponded to the assumptions required for the two welfare theorems, there would be little need for government economic policy. As, however, the assumptions do not, in general, hold in the real world, it has been argued that the welfare theorems provide a rationale for certain types of government intervention to improve efficiency.

It is clear that many externalities exist in real economies. The problem with externalities is that market prices do not reflect the true social costs or benefits of an economic activity because economic agents set their private MRS or marginal costs to market prices. By doing this they leave out of account the additional external social implications of their actions. One policy response is to introduce a tax or subsidy which reflects the additional social costs or benefits of the economic activity. In this way, it is argued, the market price (including the tax/subsidy) will convey the true social cost/benefit of the activity. This is the economic rationale behind the calls for polluting activities to be taxed, for example. Such taxes are known as 'green taxes'. If the tax reflects the amount of pollution caused, then polluters have an incentive to find ways of reducing the polluting side-effects of their economic activity. This should result in levels of pollution that are Pareto efficient in that the social costs of the products of a polluting activity are made equal to the private costs faced by producers, and the prices consumers pay for the products also reflect these costs (*Changing Economies*, Chapter 10, Sections 3 and 5).

As we have seen, the notion of 'competition' in competitive general equilibrium theory is a highly specific notion that is hard to operationalize given the requirement that all agents are price takers. In many real world markets, it is clear that firms do have a degree of control over prices. Thus, in many real markets, the kind of competition that is relevant may be a far cry from the one needed by the Walrasian model and may be closer to the disequilibrium process emphasized by evolutionary economists (see Chapter 16) or strategic behaviour in oligopoly markets (see Chapter 11). Policies to encourage competition may, therefore, be encouraging not so much Walrasian price taking but other market forms in which prices diverge from marginal costs, especially in markets where there are significant returns to scale.

Furthermore, competitive models of markets tend to see 'market forces' in abstraction from the institutional settings within which these markets actually operate. We had a glimpse of this in the example of the London Gold Fixing in which the benchmark price of gold emerges not from the interplay of impersonal market forces, but as a result of twice daily meetings of a group of dealers with a chairman who acts as a Walrasian auctioneer. This example reminds us that, unlike the model of price-taking competition, information is not a free good. In the real world without a Walrasian auctioneer, both transaction costs and information costs may be considerable.

Thus, in terms of practical policies, the choice is not whether to make markets work so that agents take prices as given, but whether markets can be made to work more competitively in a broad and pragmatic way. This, however, may not bear a close relation to the Walrasian model taken strictly, especially in a world of imperfect competition and increasing returns.

Second-best policies

The policy problems we have considered derive from the fact that a real economy does not meet the strict conditions required for the welfare theorems. This suggests that we live in a 'second-best' world. What should be the guidelines for policy in a second-best world? It has been argued by some economists that the satisfaction of some marginal conditions for Pareto efficiency in the presence of the continued failure of others, will not necessarily improve consumer well-being. For example, if an economy is composed of many monopolists and prices, in general, are greater than marginal costs, then forcing one monopolist to price at marginal cost but leaving the others free to price as they wish may introduce a greater distortion

between the prices of different goods. In these circumstances, the best policy – although it is a *second-best policy* – is to try to ensure that distortions across the economy are kept in balance as much as possible.

The Theory of the Second Best

The Theory of the Second Best states that the satisfaction of some marginal conditions for Pareto efficiency in the presence of the failure of others will not necessarily improve consumer well-being. In cases where the first-best policy is not possible, the second-best policy is to have uniform distortions across the economy, rather than eliminating distortions in only some sectors.

As the real world is a second-best world, this implies that the best policy would involve trying to balance out the various distortions in the marginal conditions for competition and Pareto efficiency. Transport policy offers an example of the difficulties involved. In a price-taking Pareto-efficient world, different methods of transport would compete equally and all market prices would reflect true social costs. The actual mix of bikes, trains, cars, buses and planes would, therefore, reflect consumer preferences in the face of true social costs. But how should transport policy be arranged when some forms of transport have received more subsidies than others? The problem is exacerbated by the problem of defining and measuring social costs. Proponents of rail transport, for example, argue that road users are subsidized by the enormous public expenditure on roads and motorways. In a second-best world where, despite vehicle and petrol taxes, it is politically infeasible to argue that road users should pay the full cost of their road use, rail supporters argue that railways should be subsidized to create more of a 'level playing field' across transport services. The argument that railways should be subsidized to counteract the inadequacy of green taxes on road pollution is an example of a second-best argument. (Cyclists can argue that cycling is the most under-subsidized of all forms of transport, especially in view of the absence of pollution from cycling.)

This approach to a partial improvement in the marginal conditions, however, requires considerable knowledge, skill and a disinterested public spirit on the part of the government. The question of knowledge and skill brings us back to the paradox raised earlier, where the Walrasian tâtonnement seems a far cry from the notion of the invisible hand in a decentralized market economy. We are back to the notion of a more active central agency which uses the Walrasian model as a planning tool to make markets work more effectively than they can unaided. It also brings us to the issue of the 'economics of politics', and whether governments are able to operate – like the auctioneer does – as disinterested players who stand outside the game, uncontaminated either by their own interest in being re-elected or by the special interest groups (such as road and rail users) which lobby the government in support of their own interests (*Changing Economies*, Chapter 10, Section 4).

Distributional policies

The Pareto criterion states that there is a welfare improvement only if someone is made better off (in that person's estimation) without making someone else worse off (in that other person's estimation). This implies that the Pareto criterion is not always relevant when choices have to be made on distributional grounds. For example, the Pareto criterion cannot help in making choices between different initial endowments. Nor can it provide a way of choosing between different Pareto-efficient points on the contract curve, although it may sometimes be helpful in choosing between points off the contract curve compared to a point on the contract curve. This is illustrated in Figure 18.17.

The consumption bundle at J is Pareto efficient and is preferred by both customers to the bundle at K, since both are on a higher indifference curve at J. But what if we want to compare K with L, a very unequal distribution, similar to the distribution we

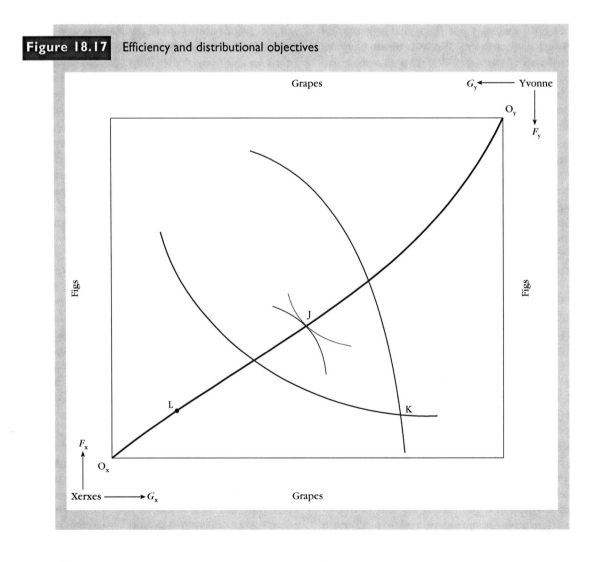

Figure 18.17 Efficiency and distributional objectives

saw in Figure 18.12? L is Pareto efficient because it lies on the contract curve, but it is an unequal distribution compared with K which is not Pareto efficient. Yvonne would prefer to be at L than at K, whereas Xerxes would prefer to be at K than at L. If a society has mechanisms for making collective economic choices, then it might prefer a point such as K to one such as L on distributional grounds, thus choosing to trade-off efficiency for a distributional objective of, say, a more equal society.

Efficiency and distribution

A feature of the Second Welfare Theorem is that it separates efficiency and distributional issues, although, as we have seen, a society may choose to trade efficiency for the sake of distributional objectives. In practical issues of welfare policies, however, it is not easy to keep them separate. The reason for this is that prices perform two functions simultaneously:

- they allocate resources between alternative uses
- they influence agents' budget constraints.

This distinction is sometimes expressed in terms of the allocative and distributional function of prices. Welfare policies that affect prices will therefore have both allocative and distributional implications.

As an example of this connection between the allocative and distributional implications of welfare policies, consider again the case of transport policy. Any transport tax/subsidy, as we have seen, will affect the choices made at the margin by consumers and producers. In this respect it is an allocative policy, but it also has distributional effects because it increases the real incomes of those who use the subsidized service at the expense of those who pay taxes. Or consider health policy. Changes in the prices charged for medical services will have both allocative and distributional effects: demand will fall for a service whose price is increased, and users of this service will experience a fall in their real income, either by having to pay more for it or by failing to benefit from the medical service if they can no longer afford to purchase it.

5.4 Conclusion

This section has examined the First and Second Welfare Theorems which summarize the close connection between competitive equilibrium and Pareto efficiency. In spite of these theoretical results, we have found that there are some welfare arguments

for government intervention in the presence of externalities. In addition, in a second-best world there are arguments for government policy to balance out the various distortions in the marginal conditions for Pareto efficiency and so try to make markets work more efficiently than they can unaided. On the other hand, these welfare arguments raise difficult issues about the knowledge and skill available to governments. We also saw that the separation between efficiency and distribution implied by the Pareto criterion is not always possible in practice and that once distributional objectives are taken into account, an efficient outcome may not always be the most desirable one.

 ## CONCLUSION

This chapter has analysed two different versions of the model of competitive general equilibrium, and has examined the argument that competitive outcomes are Pareto efficient. The chapter has shown that, although the notion of competition as an 'invisible hand' has an intuitive appeal, economic models that analyse the way competition works are complex and highly abstract. These models are useful in showing precisely the assumptions that are required for competition to function, but their significance for contentious policy debates is double-edged. The models have been used both to argue for decentralized policies of non-intervention, as well as for more interventionist policies ranging from socialist central planning in the 1930s to social-democratic tax/subsidy policies that have resurfaced in recent years in connection with 'green' issues, but which have a longer history in connection with welfare policies of income redistribution and the provision of health and education services. The moral, if there is one, is that economic models, by themselves, rarely provide definitive answers to social and political questions, although they are sometimes claimed to do so in public debates.

 ## ANSWERS TO EXERCISES

Exercise 18.1

After the first price of 120, excess demand is negative so the price is reduced to 70. However, a price of 70 leads to positive excess demand, so the price is

Figure 18.18   Excess demand as revealed by a Walrasian process of price adjustment

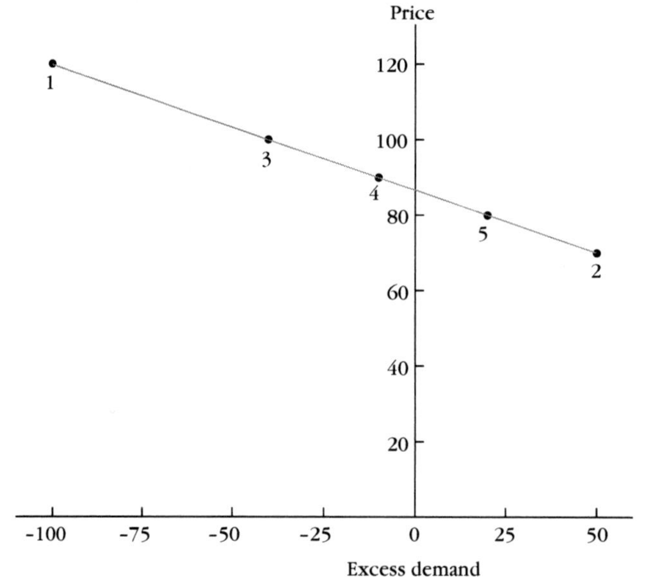

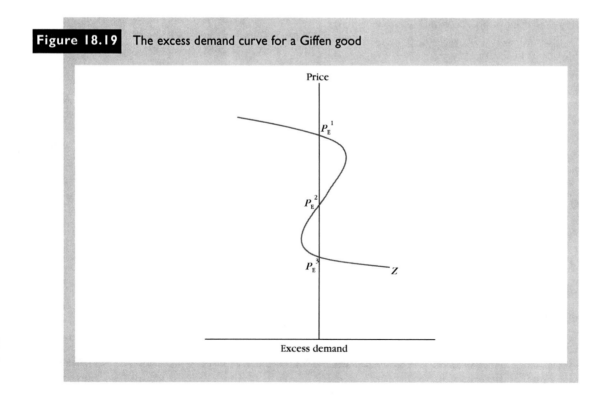

Figure 18.19   The excess demand curve for a Giffen good

raised, though not as high as before, to 100. This still leads to negative excess demand, so the price is reduced to 90. This still leads to negative excess demand, so the price is cut again to 80. Now excess demand is positive, so the price needs to rise to 85 (say). From the information given so far we can plot some points on an excess demand function, as in Figure 18.18.

From Figure 18.18 it can be seen that the equilibrium price should lie between 80 and 90.

Exercise 18.2

Figure 18.19 shows the excess demand curve for this good. There are three equilibrium prices: P_E^1 and P_E^3 are stable and P_E^2 is unstable.

Exercise 18.3

The initial allocation is shown at point A.

1   Colin's equilibrium consumption bundle is 25 kilos of figs and 25 kilos of grapes.

2   Brenda trades 5 kilos of figs for 15 kilos of grapes and Colin trades 15 kilos of grapes for 5 kilos of figs.

3   The price ratio $\dfrac{P_G}{P_F} = \dfrac{1}{3}$

4   The Edgeworth box diagram is shown in Figure 18.20.

Exercise 18.4

If the price of grapes rises relative to that of figs, more figs are traded for each kilo of grapes and the price line pivots in a clockwise direction.

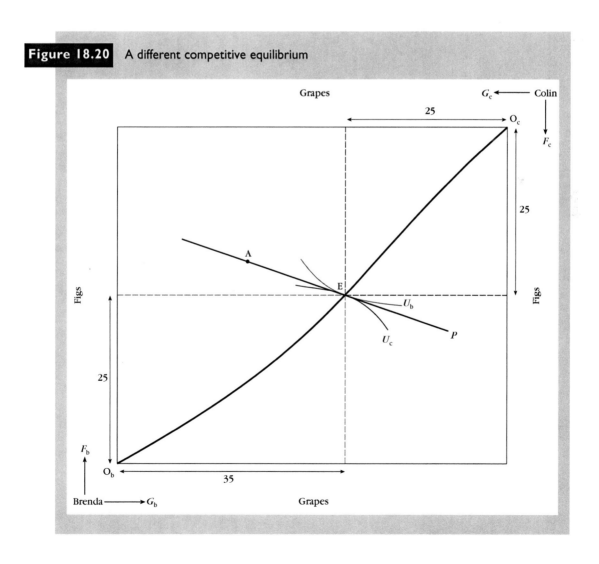

Figure 18.20   A different competitive equilibrium

Exercise 18.5

At E_3 more figs are traded for each kilo of grapes than at E_1. This means that the price of grapes relative to figs is higher at E_3 than at E_1, so $MRS_{G,F}$ is greater at E_3 than E_1.

Exercise 18.6

If the equilibrium price of grapes in terms of figs is higher than shown in Figure 18.16, this implies that the equilibrium output mix is at a point on the PPF which is further to the right since the price line is tangent to a steeper portion of the PPF. This output mix contains fewer figs and more grapes. In this situation, grapes are a more highly valued commodity in relation to figs, and so the consumers' MRS of grapes for figs is also higher.

SOCIAL MARKETS

Maureen Mackintosh

CONCEPTS AND TECHNIQUES

Ethics: Basic human rights
Shared goods
Commodification
Customer markets
Private and public goods: rivalry and excludability
Social goods and social markets
Externalities
Altruism and caring
Efficiency: Static and dynamic
Asymmetric information, moral hazard, and adverse selection
Contacts (price-quality packages) and principal/agent relationships
Clubs and club goods
Ownership, cream skimming and quality shaving
Auctions, franchising, the winner's curse, hold-up, asset specificity and sunk costs
Altruism and the Edgeworth box: Private and social contract curve
Meddlesome preferences, merit goods and Pareto efficiency
Professionalism

LINKS

- The previous chapter has illustrated the importance of the price mechanism in the neoclassical theory of the market. This chapter moves beyond the notion of price in the analysis of markets and analyses how other institutional arrangements are necessary in order for markets to work. It does so by examining examples of social goods, whose commodification is difficult for both technical and cultural reasons.

- The analysis in this chapter draws on all the schools of thought. The neoclassical theory of the market is the benchmark that justifies the attempts to commodify various 'social goods' in order to reap the benefits of market exchange. Moreover, the discussion of externalities, public goods and clubs is based on the neoclassical framework. Finally, the discussion of altruism uses the Edgeworth box diagram to extend the analysis carried out in the previous chapter and examine the impact of the existence of meddlesome preferences on the Pareto efficiency of competitive General Equilibrium theory.

- The technical discussion on which the introduction of social markets is based draws heavily on new institutional theory. It uses concepts introduced in Chapter 9, such as asymmetric information, moral hazard, adverse selection and principal/agent theory, as well as game theory introduced in Chapter 1. Agents are generally assumed to be self-interested maximizers, at least in the sense that in the end what matters is their own self-interest rather than the quality of provision.

- Old institutional theory does not feature much in the chapter, but is central to the underlying notion of social markets as the commodification of 'goods'. This is problematic because of the values that people attach to these goods, and values are a product of culture that changes over time and across countries. The chapter also shows how the effective introduction of social markets may have to rely on the existence of norms and values that support, for example, the maintenance of quality instead of promoting quality shaving. In any social market the structure of incentives would have to give consideration to how the market process affects the participants' values.

1 INTRODUCTION

1.1 The social boundaries of the market

Questions

- Should sex be bought and sold?
- Can love be bought and sold?

The above questions are designed to illustrate some difficult issues about the social boundaries of the market. Make some notes on your answers before you read on. Do not just write 'yes' or 'no'; put down some reasons for and against your answers.

Most of the commonly heard arguments for legalizing brothels and soliciting concentrate on the welfare of the individuals involved. Two chief constables in Northern England restarted a public debate in 1996 when they argued that licensing brothels would help to protect prostitutes from abuse and mistreatment, and help to protect under-age girls from being drawn into the business. Health workers supported them, arguing that it would also mean better treatment for sexually transmitted diseases, including Aids (*Financial Times,* 31.7.96). These views assume that a market for sexual services will always exist, and that illegality merely puts the women and men involved at more severe risk than they experience in legal exchange. Conversely, arguments against legalization generally take a more absolute

ethical position. Opposition in 1996 was particularly sharp from some religious groups, who identified undesirable moral implications of a society's formal acceptance of prostitution (*Guardian*, 30.7.96).

The second question also invites philosophical answers. English common parlance counterpoises 'marrying for love' and 'marrying for money'. The question, as phrased, suggests that there may be a logical or definitional problem about buying and selling love. If it is not freely given, is it love? The same kind of question could be asked of friendship. If we buy our friends' commitment to us, are they friends?

The philosopher Elizabeth Anderson suggests that the problems we have with the sale of friendship and love arise because these are members of a larger category of *shared goods* (Anderson, 1990). A shared good is one which is enhanced by sharing. We cannot, for example, easily experience affection or commitment alone; both are enormously enhanced if they are reciprocated as part of a shared experience. Other personal examples are conviviality, which needs the participation of others; companionship; and sexual relations, which many people feel are enhanced by reciprocated emotion and devalued without it.

These examples suggest that some things should not be or cannot be bought and sold, because the sharing relationship they embody is thereby changed and devalued. The debate on legalizing soliciting illustrates the point. Proponents see their opponents' arguments as irrelevant, arguing that what would be legally advertised, commercial sex between adults, is not a shared good but is a commodity which is already widely traded. It should not be confused with reciprocal emotional relations.

Doubts about buying and selling certain goods extend, furthermore, beyond the category of emotional relationships. Markets in some goods may seem not so much ethically wrong, as plain dangerous. Mercenary armies are a good example, though the word 'mercenary' has a derogatory as well as a cautionary content, carrying the suggestion of a profession of arms devalued by being put to wholly financial ends. Indeed, many activities defined as professions offer services in which we would not wish the motivation of the supplier to be wholly mercenary. We hope that our lawyer has our best interests – and not merely his or her pecuniary interests – at heart when advising us. Doubts on that point about professionals are at the heart of many cautionary tales.

Other doubts about buying and selling certain goods (including services) relate to the exclusionary effects of markets. Consider public green space in cities: a less personal good with some of the characteristics of shared goods. Not everyone enjoys well-used urban parks on sunny days – some prefer solitude – but those who do enjoy these spaces find their pleasure enhanced by the enjoyment of others. Some might not feel quite the same, however, if only those small children whose parents could pay were allowed in. Charging for a public park means that it ceases to *be* a wholly public park. Similar doubts can apply to the market supply of other goods to which access is a strong emotional issue, such as health care.

These examples are sufficient to establish that there is a wide range of goods and services which are problematic market commodities. Buying and selling them seems to risk a loss of worth to society. In the economic and broader social science literature there are two main lines of explanation for why this is so.

1.2 Values and market efficiency

The first sort of explanation of why we might set some social boundaries to the market is based in questions of ethics and values. From her reflections on shared goods, Anderson draws out the general point that there seems to be, entangled with our ideas about these goods, a notion of a hierarchy of values. A characteristic of many shared goods seems to be that the motives of the participants matter to the quality of these goods. Friendship can only be given, it cannot be coerced; and if it is provided instrumentally for a financial purpose, it is suspect. So we seem to have a hierarchy of values here which sets the

motives for participation in shared goods – such as generosity or trust – above the financial motives of market exchange. Some things are above money.

We only have to put it that way to see that it is controversial. The argument depends on assumptions about the values expressed through, and embodied in, market exchange, and on our ranking of those values. Anderson conceives of market exchange as impersonal and self-seeking, a conception defined in contrast to the values of sharing. A suitable commodity is then a good or service, the value of which is not undermined by impersonal and self-seeking exchange. To 'commodify' other goods – to subject them to market exchange – devalues them.

There are two kinds of counterargument to this on the terrain of values. One is to claim that market exchange is misrepresented in this contrast. Markets, it is argued, require such social values as trust and a certain level of honesty to work at all, and they may actively develop such values, for example through the self-reinforcing effects of reputation and repeat business in 'customer markets' (Chapter 1). It would follow that Anderson's assumption that the market undermines such values is at least partly incorrect. The other line of criticism is to argue that market exchange embodies other important values, notably freedom of choice, which are not of lesser worth than values such as generosity and commitment, but are of equal or greater importance in a value hierarchy.

In public debate, competing values or value hierarchies collide, and 'freedom' is a key focus of disagreement. Public space is a good example. Some people in Britain have expressed uneasiness about local developments of US-style fenced and guarded residential areas, on the grounds that it is wrong – a reduction in freedom and community – to close off previously public space in this way. Others see fenced private property as an expression of freedom. A similar debate on the freedom to trade *versus* the freedom of access, in the context of health care, is discussed later in this chapter.

All of these arguments concern values: what kind of society and human relationships do we want? An alternative approach to tackling the difficulties encountered in buying and selling some goods and services is to treat the problem as a *technical* one: what goods can be marketed efficiently, how can efficiency be improved, and does a category of goods exist which cannot be properly commodified in this sense at all?

This is the standard approach of neoclassical economics. In this framework, values are a matter for the individual. The boundaries of the market are a matter of the technical features of goods and services: notably, whether they can be packaged as pure *private goods*.

Private goods

A pure private good is rival and excludable.

Pure private goods in this technical sense are goods which are *rival* and *excludable*. If a good is 'rival', then more for you means less for me. Excludable goods can be supplied to you without also supplying me. The converse, pure *public goods*, are non-rival and non-excludable (see Chapter 15). The predicted problem with public goods is 'free-riding': people will conceal their true willingness to pay, hoping that others will provide a good from which they cannot be excluded. The result will be underprovision (*Changing Economies*, Chapter 10). In theory, therefore, public goods provide one boundary to the market.

Public goods

A pure public good is non-rival and non-excludable.

It is not easy to think of examples of pure public goods. But large numbers of goods have some public good characteristics, including externalities, which make market provision inefficient. Consider the provision of drinking water to households. Drinking water has many characteristics of a private good: it is a rival good (once I have drunk some, it is not available to you) and an excludable good (your water supply may legally be cut off in England and Wales if you do not pay your water bills).

On the other hand, there are a number of public goods aspects of water supply. Clean water has public health benefits, not only to those who drink it, but also to their neighbours by reducing the risk of transmitted infections. For example, the introduction of a clean water supply was the main way in which cholera was eradicated in Western Europe. The water supply process also produces environmental externalities: reservoirs, which may be beneficial (lakes to walk beside), or damaging (farmland drowned); rivers dried out and the depletion of aquifers. The

market price mechanism does not capture either of these types of external effects. So drinking water might be under-supplied because of public health externalities or over-supplied because of negative environmental effects (*Changing Economies*, Chapter 10, Section 3).

The ethical and the technical approaches to explaining the social boundaries of the market are not mutually exclusive. It is quite possible to find the technical arguments illuminating and also to regard the debate on values as relevant. The two lines of thought, however, suggest different explanations for:

● the emergence of regulation and of non-market forms of supply for many goods
● the social resistance to the commodification of some goods and services.

Commodification – the shaping of goods and services into a form approximating private goods and available for market sale and purchase – is a complex historical process. For example, the public goods aspects of the supply of water on tap in houses have led to its public provision in many parts of the world. However in countries such as India, well-off people resort widely to private supply, and water supply in England and Wales was privatized in 1989. It may have struck you that neither of the two theoretical approaches just discussed displayed much sense of this history. Both the technical and the value aspects are typically presented as static, embodied in the goods themselves. But historically, views on what *should* be bought and sold, and the practice of what is, in fact, marketed, have interacted and changed over time. In other words, the social boundaries of the market shift, and are historically and socially constituted.

I will use the term 'social good' in this chapter to refer to the diverse set of goods and services for which, at any historical moment, commodification is regarded as problematic. The central objective of the chapter is to explore some characteristics of markets in social goods: the 'social markets' of the chapter's title. I have chosen examples where ethical and technical issues interact in current debate. Section 2 examines markets in health care, Section 3 uses the example of social care to explore public contracting for the supply of social goods and Section 4 considers how norms of ethical behaviour can improve the operation of social markets. The focus of the chapter is on understanding markets, not on policy formation.

Much of the analysis, however, has an evaluative content. It looks not only at how markets work in specific contexts, but also at how well or how desirably they work, and with what social effects.

2 'MANAGED MARKETS' AND 'QUASI-MARKETS' IN HEALTH CARE

2.1 Health care as a social good

In Section 1, I identified the class of social goods in two ways: goods the commodification of which is felt to be problematic for value reasons, and goods with characteristics which appear to pose technical economic barriers to full commodification. The extent to which health care is a social good by either criterion is a matter of sharp debate, with substantial policy implications. I will begin with the technical arguments.

The World Bank, for example, argues that in low-income countries, governments should fund only primary and preventative health care. This includes diagnosis, pre- and post-natal care, vaccinations and health advice, as well as a small range of medicines for common conditions. Such services, the Bank notes, have strong 'public good qualities'. The Bank contrasts preventative care with curative treatment after diagnosis, by medicines or surgery. It argues that 'individuals can capture the full benefit of curative care interventions so economic efficiency is not reduced by the government not funding this type of care' (World Bank, 1996, p.15). Work through the following exercise, to explore the World Bank's technical argument, and at the same time review some key concepts.

Exercise 19.1

1 What are the public good qualities of primary and preventative health care?

2 Draw a diagram to illustrate the effect of these public good qualities in reducing economic efficiency if primary health care were traded on a competitive market. (*Changing Economies*, Chapter 10 will help here.) Would primary health care be under- or over-supplied?

3 With reference to the diagram, explain the World Bank's reasons for arguing that competitive markets in curative care are fully efficient. Do you agree with their argument?

The exercise established that, in technical terms, health care is neither a pure private good nor a pure public good. Much of it is capable of being sold on a market as a private good, but because of externalities – and for other reasons to which I return below – economists predict that health care markets will tend to be allocatively inefficient.

The World Bank's arguments furthermore focus on efficiency rather than access. But many people see access to health care as a matter of social concern, even as a basic human right. The division is illustrated by a much cited exchange between the philosophers Bernard Williams and Robert Nozick. Williams (1973) argued that the only proper criterion for medical care is medical need. Nozick (1974), in reply asked why then it did not follow that 'the only proper criterion for barbering services is barbering need'?

Question

Stop a moment and think about this for yourself. Are haircuts different from health care? If so, why?

One possible reply is that health care is simply more basic than haircuts: we can do without the latter, but the former is central to the quality of life, one of our basic needs. So we may accept more readily that the rich have better haircuts than that they have better medical care. Michael Walzer (1983, p.87) reflecting on this debate in a book on justice, adds that societies change over time in what they regard as a socially recognized need. He argues that, 'In Europe during the Middle Ages, the cure of souls was public, the cure of bodies private'; hence in the Middle Ages 'eternity was a socially recognized need' and the aim was a church in every parish. As medicine improved, and religious belief declined, the 'socially recognized need' came to be not eternity, but longevity: a new social meaning given to widening access to health care.

Societies differ across space as well as time in the extent to which health care is thought suitable for commodification. Besley and Gouveia (1994) argue that people in the US seem to accept more readily than western Europeans that those with more money to spend should get more health care. John Elster (1992, p.13) puts a US-based point of view clearly: 'I see no reason, for instance, why the rich should not be allowed to buy medical treatments that are not available to others, provided they pay the full social costs. To refuse them the right to do so would be a form of sumptuary legislation, based on barely disguised envy.' This argument treats health care as a consumption good like any other for the purposes of economic analysis.

Conversely, Western European public opinion and opinion-formers are more apt to take the view that access to health care should be determined solely or largely by need, a view likely to be influenced by experience of comprehensive social insurance-based or tax-financed health care systems. In this context it is relevant that Williams was writing in Britain, and Nozick in the US. In some cultures, health care appears to have developed features of a shared good, for which access – publicness – is valued. And for that reason, people may be willing to pay for health care in forms which are redistributive: where those who can pay also pay for those who cannot.

The argument that health care can express social solidarity – and be devalued by exclusivity – was most famously developed by the sociologist Richard Titmuss in a passionate defence of the economic efficiency and ethical desirability of unpaid blood-donning:

> '... the ways in which society structures its social institutions – and particularly its health and welfare systems – can encourage and discourage the altruistic in man; such systems can foster integration or alienation; it can allow the 'theme of the gift' – of generosity towards strangers – to spread among social groups and generations. This ... is an aspect of freedom in the twentieth century which, compared to the emphasis on consumer choice ... is insufficiently recognized.'
>
> (TITMUSS, 1970, P.225)

The reference to 'gifts' suggests one final sense in which health care may have shared goods qualities. Health services rely for their quality, in part, on the relationship between practitioner and patient. The quality of care depends greatly, for example, on the patient conveying clear information (since diagnosis relies very heavily on this), on the ability of the practitioner to listen and interpret, and on the co-operation of the patient in the treatment. Furthermore, the experience of being cared for is part of the service expected; in some areas, such as terminal and long-term chronic care, a very substantial part of it. It is, therefore, an interesting test of Anderson's arguments

to ask if paying for care – and any particular form of payment – threatens the caring relationship. I come back to this issue in Section 4.

2.2 Private market dilemmas in health care

The technical economic problems of health care as a commodity imply that private health care markets will display static inefficiencies. Over time, the markets may also generate dynamic inefficiencies through strategic behaviour by participants. (The distinction between static and dynamic efficiency is explained in Chapter 10.) The sources of static market failure include not only externalities, but also *asymmetric information*. Patients tend to find it very hard to judge the quality of the health care they are receiving because of their lack of medical knowledge, compounded by personal vulnerability at the time when they most need the service. Superior knowledge and control, in turn, create *moral hazard* (or incentives to cheat) for care providers, since they can influence the quality of provision without penalty. (Chapter 9 and *Changing Economies*, Chapter 23 explain these two concepts.)

Potential health care users also cannot predict the care they will need, so the attempt to reduce risk generates a demand for insurance in private markets for health care. If health care is insurance-financed, this implies that the market is characterized by *third party payment*: neither provider nor client is paying at the time the service is received, so neither have an incentive to keep down costs. Taken together, these market failures create some characteristic 'pathologies' of private health care markets.

The first 'pathology' is a tendency to rising costs.

Exercise 19.2

Assume that in a private and imperfectly competitive health care market, doctors are reimbursed on a fee-for-service basis by insurers, that is, they are paid for each separate service they provide. Explain why this may lead to rising unit and total costs of health care.

The US is the only industrialized country where private medical insurance predominates (*Changing Economies*, Chapter 23). Until recently, its health care market was dominated by fee-for-service provision, and its health care system is the most expensive in the world. Studies in a number of countries show that a switch towards fee-for-service payments increases the number of treatments (Donaldson and Gerard, 1993). A telling comparison is between costs in the US and in Canada where there is a universal tax-funded health care system, with far fewer fee-for-service payments. With similar levels of average income, the US had fees around three times higher than Canada in the mid-1980s (Donaldson and Gerard, 1993, p.106). Doctors' incomes were much higher in the US, as was the proportion of spending on administrative costs; and the intensity of treatment was greater (Ham *et al.*, 1990).

Furthermore, the US has a much more hospital-based system than Canada, with poor primary care. This second 'pathology' of private health care markets also raises unit costs, since hospitals and specialists are more expensive than primary practitioners.

Question

In addition to the World Bank's arguments in Section 2.1 about the under-provision of public goods, can you think of other reasons why private health care markets tend to under-provide primary care?

Doctors tend to have market power. This is sustained by their semi-monopoly of information, by the barriers to entry to the profession created by long training and exclusion of the untrained, and by professional collusion. Doctors may use this market power to develop the better paid and more prestigious specialities, relative to primary health care, and may also keep other practitioners, such as nurses, out of primary care, thus biasing the supply of care towards hospitals.

The third main 'pathology' of private health care markets is the exclusion of some of those in need. Some of that exclusion is the result of market failure, since private insurance, like the market for second-hand cars, is subject to *adverse selection* (Chapter 9). This is another result of the asymmetric information in health markets: in this case the *patients'* private information. The health insurance companies know less than each client about that client's likely needs.

Exercise 19.3

Suppose that clients with high expected needs for health care successfully understate their needs to insurance companies, and therefore pay less than their expected costs of treatment. Explain how this may, through a process of adverse selection, lead to some people who would have been prepared to pay the full cost of insuring themselves being excluded from medical insurance. (The 'market for lemons' analysis in Chapter 9 will help with this exercise.)

The response of medical insurance companies to the adverse selection problem is to seek more information: to get better at identifying good risks and charging them low premiums. The better they get at this, the more expensive insurance becomes for high-risk people, because risk pooling is being reduced. (It also further pushes up administration and monitoring costs.)

At this point a nasty interaction sets in between the insurance market and poverty. Poor people will not, in any case, be able to afford average insurance premiums. But the poor also tend to fall into high-risk categories requiring more expensive insurance. They are more likely than the middle classes to be ill and to have chronic and congenital conditions against which one cannot get insurance, or for which insurance cover runs out. Under-consumption in private health care markets is driven by the interaction of income- and risk-based exclusions with rising costs.

2.3 Private 'clubs' in social markets

The development of regulated health care markets

The pathologies of unregulated private health care markets imply a need for regulation and intervention. Most industrialized countries, apart from the US, fall into two groups, those that run most health care as a tax-funded public service – notably the UK and the Scandinavian countries – and those that organize it through some form of compulsory state-subsidized social insurance, such as Germany. All industrialized countries, except the US, achieve virtually universal access to health care through these means (*Changing Economies*, Chapter 23). In recent years, reforms in the organization of health care in some of these countries, for example in Britain and in Finland, have introduced more market-like processes into the tax-funded systems. In the US, the fee-for-service or 'indemnity' insurance system that pays the bills of health care providers who are consulted by those insured, is rapidly being replaced by a health care system dominated by health maintenance organizations (HMOs) which seek to combine insurance and health care provision. It is sometimes argued – controversially – that industrialized countries' health care systems are 'converging' on a model of 'managed markets' or 'managed care' or, sometimes, 'managed competition' (Chernichovsky, 1996).

This section and the next explore some aspects of these highly regulated social markets. An explicit aim of many health care market reforms has been to increase – or in the US case sustain – patients' choice of health care provider, while keeping – or in the US case putting – a lid on costs. The key idea in both the US and the UK reforms, despite the very different contexts, was to ensure that finance (insurance) and provision were in the same set of hands, while allowing potential patients some choice of provider.

The US vehicles for this, the HMOs, are independent commercial or non-profit organizations. The defining feature of the HMO model is that an HMO contracts to provide, for an agreed fee per person, access to a predetermined range of health care over a given period. Unlike fee-for-service insurers, the HMO is also responsible for providing the care. The HMO may contract with groups of doctors to provide the care, or it may employ doctors itself; it will also contract for specialist and hospital care.

The British National Health Service (NHS) has always combined finance and provision in one organization. The 1990 organizational reforms somewhat weakened that link, separating 'purchasers' (funders) from 'providers' (such as hospitals and primary doctors). But they also established 'fundholding' groups of general practitioners (GPs, primary doctors) within the tax-funded service which had some resemblances to HMOs. In this model, a group of GP practices holds a budget, for some or all of the care for their patients, for which they contract as necessary with hospitals. The budget is tax financed, and based on a mix of patient numbers and indicators of need, such as local levels of deprivation. Patients may move between GP practices and GPs may accept or reject patients, but unlike HMOs, patients make no direct payment to the practices.

In both the HMOs and NHS fundholder models, the organizations accept the risk of providing care

within a budget fixed by a 'capitation' charge, that is, a fee per person.

Question

Why should the integration of finance and provision solve the problems identified above of cost escalation and adverse selection?

The providers of care are working to a known budget for a given population of patients in any year. They therefore have a strong incentive to keep costs down, since they retain the benefits for the organization either to spend on their patients or as profits for commercial HMOs. Third-party payment is removed, which should deal with tendencies to over-supply, so long as the organizations face reasonably strong negotiators for those paying. The private buyers of health care in the US are mainly employers, not individuals, and in parts of the US, employers have organized buying groups to negotiate with HMOs over price and the range of provision. The problem of adverse selection is also reduced because employers pay a 'capitation' fee per employee, so HMOs pool risk over quite large groups.

In addition to cost control and widened risk pooling, health care reformers have sought to increase or retain provider competition and patient choice. Economists such as James Buchanan, who are particularly critical of the lack of scope for 'exit' by consumers where the state is a monopoly supplier, have long argued that goods that are neither wholly private nor wholly public goods could be provided by voluntary associations of consumers in 'clubs' (Buchanan, 1965). Models of provision of social goods through clubs are attractive to market-oriented economists and policy makers because they appear to overcome one of the key economic arguments for state provision: the tendency of the market to under-provide public goods. Indeed, on some stringent assumptions which are discussed below, it is possible to reach a Pareto-efficient general equilibrium in which certain types of semi-public goods are provided by voluntary clubs through a market-like mechanism.

These economic arguments for voluntary provision have been developed alongside the growing political attraction in many countries of the idea of social provision through associations outside the state. The political theorist Paul Hirst, for example, argues in an influential book (Hirst, 1994) that,

'Voluntary association is an alternative to top down bureaucracy in the competent provision of services'. And European research documents the rise of 'stakeholder co-operatives' for self-organized provision of welfare (Borzaga, 1996). One way to analyse HMOs is as a set of health care 'clubs' with people shopping around between them. (Fundholders, as we shall see, fit the model rather less well.)

The economics of clubs

In economic theory, *club goods* are goods with partial public goods qualities, being at least partly non-rival, but excludable. The central idea of club goods models is that public goods that are excludable – through distance or institutional exclusion – do not pose the same problems for voluntary provision as pure public goods. In theory, the private provision of public goods leads to under-provision because of 'free riding' (Section 1.2). If the good is excludable, 'free riding' can be prevented, since a club can charge an agreed entry fee to provide a desired level of a good for its members. People reveal their preferences by joining a club that offers the mix of good and cost they prefer. If they change their mind they can 'vote with their feet' and join another club.

Club goods

Club goods are excludable but at least partially non-rival.

The image, then, is of a social market of clubs providing choices of level of consumption of club goods at various entry costs. Shared goods, such as conviviality and sports played with others, are natural 'club' goods. Swimming pools are often used as the example in explaining the models, since (until crowded) they are non-rival, but easily excludable. But the model can also be applied to goods which – although rival in provision (more for me, less for you) – are best financed through insurance of some kind. HMOs provide health care risk pooling, which can be seen as a good which is non-rival in the sense that more risk poolers do not, just by joining, reduce the effectiveness of risk pooling for existing members, often quite the contrary. The HMO may also be providing the non-rival benefit of health care cost-control.

For a social market to work by satisfying preferences, consumers must be able to join a club that maximizes their utility, given their preferences for club goods and other goods. The economic analysis of clubs proceeds in two stages. It first analyses how a voluntary association of consumers can design their preferred club, by making the dual decision about the amount of the club good to be provided and the number of club members to share its consumption. Having shown how the optimum membership and scale of such clubs is determined, from the point of view of the members, the analysis then goes on to consider the conditions under which such voluntary associations can result in economy-wide allocative efficiency.

I will tell the story in terms of a non-profit health club (of the swimming pool and exercise-machines type) and begin by considering the choice of number of members for a particular club.

Optimal membership for a given scale

Assume that the individuals wishing to join this club have identical tastes and incomes. A small group of founder members of the club are considering how many additional members to let in. Suppose the founders have already committed themselves to a given level of services of the club, in terms of the size of pool and range of facilities: I will call this the 'scale' of the club. You will have to think of scale as unidimensional; members can choose a larger or smaller scale but not, for example, more expensive tiles for the same sized pool. All members pay the same fee. This type of club is called a 'homogeneous club' (Cornes and Sandler, 1996).

The decision on the number of members will then take the form shown in Figure 19.1 overleaf. Consider the marginal financial benefits to an existing member of adding one more member. Figure 19.1 shows these marginal financial benefits, *MB*, as large at first and then declining sharply.

For example, if we think of all the club costs as fixed costs then, given the decision on scale, increasing membership from one to two would halve those costs for the first member, a huge financial benefit. Later, the marginal financial benefit to each member of adding one more member becomes smaller, since the cost is already spread over a larger membership. Now consider the marginal cost curve *MC*. This shows the marginal loss in utility to an existing member of adding one more, in terms of crowding in the pool or waiting for machines. *MC* will be zero for the first few members (it might even be negative for those who come for conviviality as well as exercise). But eventually, the crowding effect of new members starts to irritate, and the marginal costs of crowding by new members starts to rise. There will come a point where the extra irritation from an extra member is no longer worth the financial benefits (point M_1), and this is the optimal club membership.

The optimal membership of the club is therefore limited by the costs of crowding. Club goods, unlike pure public goods, are only partially non-rival. As the number of consumers rises, additional consumers start to reduce the utility of others. A pure public good displays no crowding: the *MC* curve would lie along the horizontal axis and the optimal membership of the club would be infinite.

Question

Figure 19.1 is drawn for a club of one scale. How would the *MB* and *MC* curves shift if the founders decided on a larger scale club?

The *MB* curve would move upwards, since the fixed costs would be larger, hence the marginal financial benefit of a new member to an existing member rises. The *MC* curve will shift rightwards: with a larger scale club, crowding will begin at a higher membership. Hence, as we might expect, a larger scale club will have a larger optimal

membership. So we can draw a line such as M_{opt} on Figure 19.2 that shows how optimal membership rises as club scale increases.

Optimal scale for given membership levels

That is one part of the dual decision. Now look at the problem the other way around. Suppose a fixed number of people decide to form a club. They will want to pick a club scale which maximizes their utility (remember I assumed identical tastes and incomes). If they share the financial costs equally between them, they will increase the scale of the club until the extra financial cost to each outweighs their enjoyment of the extra facilities.

Exercise 19.4

Draw a diagram illustrating that last argument.

Exercise 19.4 shows how a given group of members will choose their preferred club scale. If the group of members is enlarged, the marginal cost curve in Figure 19.8 will shift downwards, and the preferred scale of club will increase. We can draw a line, S_{opt}, showing the optimal scale of club for each size of membership group. I have added S_{opt} to Figure 19.2 to give Figure 19.3.

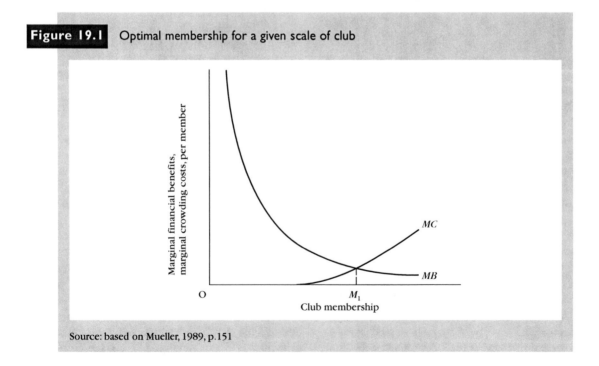

Figure 19.1   Optimal membership for a given scale of club

Source: based on Mueller, 1989, p.151

Figure 19.2 Optimal membership for each scale of club

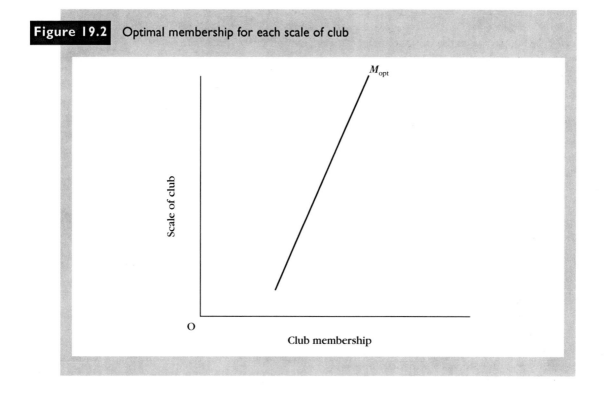

Figure 19.3 The optimal health club

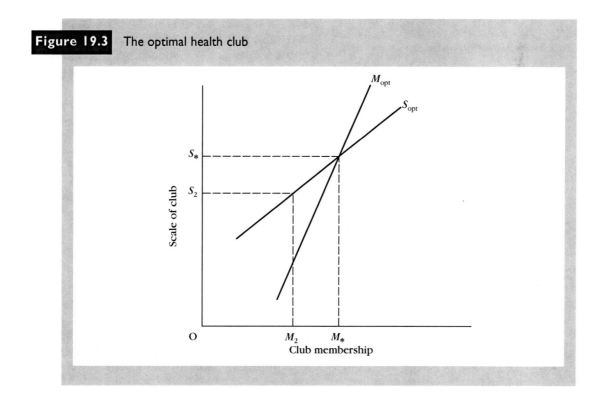

The optimal health club

Figure 19.3 shows the outcome of the dual decision on club scale and membership. The point where M_{opt} and S_{opt} cross defines the optimal club, with scale S_* and membership M_*, given the assumptions about members' tastes and incomes and financial costs of clubs. At this point, the members are each satisfied that no other scale of club would be preferred, nor are there any benefits from adding or ejecting members. This is a welfare maximum *for this club* (not for society as a whole).

Exercise 19.5

To check your understanding, consider a club of scale S_2 with membership M_2 on Figure 19.3. Why is this not the optimum club?

Exercise 19.5 showed that a club of scale S_* and membership M_* on Figure 19.3 forms a stable equilibrium: clubs of different sizes converge towards that optimum size and scale. For such a stable equilibrium to exist, M_{opt} must be steeper than S_{opt} as shown in Figure 19.3.

This model of a homogeneous club shows that such a club can have an optimum size and scale derived from the costs of provision and the tastes of the members, including their dislike of crowding. Club goods can, in principle, be provided by voluntary associations. The expanding club good literature has gone on to consider what happens once we drop the assumption of uniform tastes and allow people of like tastes to form clubs. This allows the voluntary emergence of diverse mixed goods provision to satisfy diverse tastes, potentially raising welfare above that achieved, for example, by uniform public supply.

Charles Tiebout, a US economist, was the first to point out in the 1950s that we could think of local government jurisdictions as clubs – small relative to the national government – and imagine people migrating between them to find the mix of public good provision and cost which suited them best (Tiebout, 1956). He showed that on a set of very stringent assumptions, such a 'voting with the feet' process will produce a Pareto-efficient general equilibrium through voluntary association without the intervention of the state. These conditions include perfect knowledge and the freedom of 'migration'

between clubs. There also have to be enough diverse clubs available to serve all preference patterns and an absence of spillovers or externalities between clubs (Mueller, 1989, p.155). Note particularly the last assumption. The club model assumes that all the benefits and costs of consumption are captured within the club. If not, then such externalities prevent an economy reaching a general equilibrium that is a welfare optimum, just as they do in competitive trading of private goods (Chapter 18, Section 5.2)

Club goods and health care provision

The 'voting with the feet' metaphor is interesting in the context of applying the club goods model to health care. Is this movement between clubs a market process? The model certainly relies on 'exit' as well as 'voice' (Chapter 1) to arrive at an equilibrium, and its political attraction appears to be the element of voluntarism. HMOs and GP fundholding have both been 'sold' politically as offering diversity and choice. In the UK, it was argued that fundholding GPs could offer increasingly diverse types of provision (adding clinics or a range of home nursing care to core primary doctoring, for example). It is also suggested that patients can 'shop around' when choosing a GP, although their choice of GP does not affect the taxes they pay for health care. So the social market of clubs will 'sort' potential patients into 'clubs' of homogeneous tastes, thus raising welfare and increasing freedom.

What, however, of income levels? I smuggled in above, when discussing a single type of good, the assumption that members have identical incomes. If we consider now a diversity of clubs and a diversity of incomes, then these models predict that clubs, as voluntary associations, will tend to become homogeneous as to income levels as well as tastes (Ricketts, 1994, p.321).

Question

Can you explain intuitively why this is likely to be so?

The theory of clubs identifies an optimum which depends on preferences, the characteristics of the good, and willingness to pay. Willingness to pay will tend to differ between income levels since ability to pay varies. Hence a rich person will generally find the facilities in a poor members' club too basic, while a poor person is likely to find a rich members' club too expensive.

With purely social clubs, this result may be seen as just an extension of the private benefits of high income in terms of the private goods it buys. But health care? A health care 'club' which includes members of different income levels provides a common level of service to all. If different health care clubs offer different levels of service and charge different fees, then they will tend to differentiate themselves by income level.

Question

Can GP fundholding avoid this outcome?

In principle it should do so. GP fundholders in the UK do not fit the 'clubs' model to the extent that GP budgets are financed from general taxation. So people can join clubs they could not pay for if the payment were a fee. The budgets are set on the basis of the numbers of patients registered plus various allowances for greater than average predicted need, for example for high numbers of elderly patients or high indicators of local social deprivation. Inner-city GPs have claimed, however, that these supplements are too small to even-out provision, and fundholding spread most rapidly in wealthier areas where the demands on GPs are lower than in the inner cities.

Nevertheless, the principles of GP fundholding, in contrast to HMOs, should largely sustain the redistribution from richer to poorer which occurs when any public good is provided to a community of mixed incomes financed by proportional or progressive taxation. This kind of redistribution through public and semi-public goods is a very important mitigator of private income inequality in many societies, which is no doubt one reason why the highly regressive poll tax was so resented in the UK. Dennis Mueller, an American economist who specializes in 'public choice' issues, puts the point this way:

'A given distribution of private incomes might be considered just when individuals reside in communities of heterogeneous income strata, so that the relatively poor benefit from the higher demands for public goods by the relatively well-to-do. The same distribution of income might be considered unjust if individuals were distributed into communities of similar income and the relatively poor could
consume only those quantities of public goods which they themselves could afford to provide.'

(MUELLER, 1989, P.172)

We can make an analogous point for health insurance. If a shift occurs from central to local or 'club' provision of health care, or if 'voting with the feet' becomes more pronounced in an existing system, then any existing income inequality is likely to be made worse.

2.4   The behaviour of health care 'clubs'

How do health care clubs behave in practice? This discussion draws on experience in the US of HMOs, and also considers GP fundholders in the UK, who do not fit the formal clubs model (since they do not charge patients directly) but offer some interesting comparisons.

Ownership

The clubs model of social markets is associative, based in voluntary agreement and shared ownership, so the model club is a non-profit organization for its members' benefit. But as Martin Ricketts (1994) points out, many 'clubs', including many health clubs of the type I used for my example, are profit-seeking firms, and they do differentiate themselves, as predicted, into high price, high quality provision and more basic, cheaper clubs. Ricketts suggests that where investment funds are a constraint, profit-seeking clubs are more likely to emerge, whereas clubs where the social environment is the product – 'social' clubs where the main product is the shared good of conviviality – are more likely to be, and to remain, non-profit making.

In this context, the evolution of HMO ownership is interesting. Early HMOs in the US tended to be non-profit making organizations. In the 1980s, many non-profit HMOs converted to commercial status and most new HMOs were profit-seeking firms. Langwell (1990) attributes this shift to a search for better access to equity capital and the end of Federal incentives to non-profit HMOs. Most HMOs are now commercial finance organizations who contract with providers. In California, large organized groups of doctors integrate finance and provision, but these HMOs, too, tend to be profit-seeking (Robinson and Casalino, 1996).

In principle, one would expect the behaviour of non-profit making and profit-seeking organizations to differ in response to the same incentives (Chapter 9). I will return to this issue in Section 4.

Cream skimming

Consider the following set of incentives. You are a group of doctors with a known budget with which you provide comprehensive care for a population of patients. You can exert some, but relatively little, influence over the prices you face for the care you buy-in rather than provide yourself. The care any individual will need is uncertain, but some patients are in higher risk categories than others and hence have a high probability of costing more to care for than others. You can make a well-informed estimate of which patients are high risk.

> ### Question
>
> If you can select your patients, how will you be tempted to do it?

You may seek to refuse patients in high-risk categories. This means either that you will keep a larger financial surplus for yourselves, or that you can provide a better service to your remaining patients. If you are an HMO you can also lower premiums and increase your enrolees. Refusing potentially expensive patients in this way is called 'cream skimming' or 'favourable selection', and has a serious exclusionary effect. The behaviour occurs in both HMOs and GP fundholding, but is poorly researched. In the US, HMO premiums tend to rise in a region as HMO coverage increases, because early opportunities for competition through favourable selection are exhausted (Wholey *et al.*, 1995). In the UK there is some relevant anecdotal evidence, for example of seriously mentally ill patients being excluded from lists because of the cost of their drugs, but, as yet, no systematic research is available on the extent of cream skimming.

Quality shaving

Now turn to the following scenario. A government health care purchaser or a financial HMO is seeking to contract for hospital and community services. They have a fixed budget, and genuinely wish to do well by the population for whom they are responsible. They also, however, wish to satisfy their principals' objectives. In the UK, these are the government targets for the health service, notably more services at lower unit costs and shorter waiting lists. In the US this may be the HMO's shareholders' desire for reasonable revenues, and employers' desire to keep premiums down.

Health care providers, such as hospitals, are bidding for contracts to provide the services. The contracts pass some of the risk to the providers, by giving them a fixed budget, though with some scope for renegotiation. The contracts cover both cost and quality; they state how much the service should cost for a particular quality of service. Providers bid a proposed price/quality package, and the contracts must include information on outputs that can be fairly easily monitored.

Finally, this bidding process happens each year, and each year the same mix of objectives is in place. Both sides know this.

> ### Question
>
> Describe the incentive structure in this bidding process. On which issues will each side's sticking points be likely to emerge, and what will be sacrificed?

The purchasers have 'sticking points' set by their principals: notably price control, plus 'throughput' in the government case and profits in the shareholder case. The providers, to win the contracts, therefore need to keep a grip on unit costs. Quality is something everyone genuinely cares about, but it is no one's sticking point. Furthermore, quality of treatment, as opposed to numbers treated and costs, is hard to measure and monitor since it relies heavily on professional judgement.

In the UK before the NHS reforms that divided 'purchasers' from 'providers' came into effect (Section 2.3), there was an experimental simulation of the reforms known as the 'Rubber Windmill'. The report on this simulation noted that the logic of the new system implied that, 'Providers are, to an extent, freed from direct responsibility for health outcomes'. Given the pressures on providers, it went on, '… there exist circumstances in which both purchasers and providers may walk away from quality issues' (East Anglian Regional Health Authority, 1990, p.11).

In other words, the outcomes of contracting will depend on the priorities of the participants under pressure. If the purchasers focus on 'throughput' or profits above quality of care – and that is what they monitor – and if providers have a choice between lower 'throughput' or profits and lower quality, then there are shared incentives to let quality slip. Whether this is happening is hard to know precisely because quality of treatment is so hard to monitor.

3   PRIVATE PROVISION THROUGH PUBLIC CONTRACTING: AUCTION MARKETS IN SOCIAL GOODS

3.1   Auctions and franchising in social goods

It is not only in health care that the incentives embedded in contracting for social goods are becoming a matter of public concern. The 1980s saw the beginning of an international wave of 'privatization' of public monopolies, including both the wholesale transfer of firms to the private sector, and increased contracting-out of government-financed services that had previously been directly supplied. As Ricketts (1994) has noted, goods and services for which competitive markets with large numbers of buyers and sellers are hard to establish include infrastructure networks which display large economies of scale. Power and water supply networks are excludable through connections and charging, but their services are non-rival below capacity output. Other industries, too, display economies of scale and local monopolies. An ambulance service for a medium-sized city, for example, may be most efficiently run through a centralized dispatch system, and such a city may need only one general hospital providing a full range of specialisms. These features tend to create monopoly power for suppliers.

Social polices also create supplier power. Decisions not to exclude people from a service, by providing it free at the point of use – examples include public libraries, parks, primary education, clean water, as well as emergency and primary health care – tend to create local monopolies whether funding is public or voluntary. Such policies add the 'public' quality of free access to goods which would technically be excludable. They also change people's experience of using those services, generating a concept of access to certain services as a right rather than a market choice. This social understanding of certain goods as primary goods from which people should not be excluded – especially in countries where average incomes are

well above subsistence levels – applies to a number of the services provided by the utilities. The classes of goods which have tended to be public monopolies for technical (network) and social (access) reasons therefore overlap. Dieter Helm, an industrial economist who writes on regulation, argues that privatized utilities will always remain under public scrutiny because they 'provide basic social primary goods' (Helm, 1995).

Whether public or private, monopoly power can lead to X-inefficiency and unresponsiveness to consumers: supplier-led rather than user-led services (*Changing Economies*, Chapters 8 and 10). One solution now frequently proposed is to institute competition *for* the monopoly, through a separation of financing and provision, with competition to provide the service. Such attempts to make local monopolies contestable through auctions and franchising are now widespread internationally. Competitive tendering by independent contractors (or indeed by separately constituted public enterprises) for a time-limited licence to operate the monopoly is now used over a wide range of services. In this section we examine the application of this form of market mechanism to social goods.

3.2   Bidding to supply local services

The aim of an auction for monopoly power is to try to achieve the cost benefits of supply by a single firm while avoiding some of the associated problems. Such auctions result in the transfer of some property rights and initiative to the contractor for a fixed period. The competition may be to manage the service, with the assets remaining with the public authority; or it may involve a transfer of assets to a contractor; and it may involve various levels of contractor obligations concerning investment in the service. In the case of Private Finance Initiative (PFI) in the UK, the contractor bids to build and run a facility with some local monopoly power for a fixed number of years, gaining a return on the investment from charges or government revenue payments.

Bidding for public monopoly contracts has many similarities with franchising in the private sector. Franchising is quite common in retailing; McDonald's is the most famous example and many petrol service stations are run in the same way. It is often found where there are different economies of scale at different stages of production and distribution. The franchiser develops the intangible asset of the brand name, since economies of scale in advertising the brand name are considerable, and may also provide wholesaling. The outlets, which have few scale economies, are franchised, and the franchisee uses the brand name subject to conditions on the nature of the product. Would-be franchisees bid for each local franchise.

In Britain, local government has become something of a test-bed for competition for local monopolies. Legislation until mid-1997 enforced competitive tendering within local government for construction, cleaning, catering, roads, building and grounds maintenance, refuse collection and street cleaning, vehicle maintenance, management of housing and leisure facilities, construction-related services, and personnel, legal, information technology and financial services. Financial and policy pressures have also led to extensive contracting-out of social care. Enforced tendering was also instituted in the 1980s for cleaning and catering in the health service, and for many central civil service activities, including prison management (Walsh, 1995).

Bidding for franchises in the public sector is typically done through what is called a Chadwick/Demsetz auction (called after its inventors, Edwin Chadwick, a Victorian social reformer who originally advocated this kind of public auction, later formalized by the American economist, Demsetz). Prospective contractors are invited to bid on price to provide a specified quantity–quality package or to bid a price–quality package. The bids can only be put in when the public authority has decided on the extent of asset transfer to the bidders.

Social care, by which I mean such services as long-term physical care and support for the frail elderly and the disabled, offers an example. Firms (commercial or non-profit) that wish to supply residential or home-based (domiciliary) care tender prices and quality levels in a bid to be included on an 'approved list'. The list will then be used to place those needing care who are supported by public funds. This is, therefore, quite close to the private sector franchising model, since the approved list gives those included a 'marque' of approval by the authority. In this model, suppliers undertake their own investment and own their assets. The same is true in refuse collection, where private contractors normally supply collection vehicles in their own livery, while authorities continue to provide waste treatment, which has much higher scale economies and requires more specific fixed assets. I will use the similarities and contrasts between refuse

collection and social care to illustrate some of the strengths and problems of franchising in social goods.

Refuse collection and social care have some similarities. Both have some economies of scale and both are technically excludable. Both generate demands for open access for those who cannot pay: refuse collection because of the health effects and environmental externalities, and social care for social and ethical reasons.

Reflection

You can probably also think of some other differences! Make a list of these before working through the discussion that follows.

The aim of the auction process is to drive down costs for given quality levels. To achieve this, there must be some X-inefficiency to be exploited, some way of paying less for inputs, or some scope for innovation in working methods which the previous public supplier was not pursuing because of their monopoly position. The effectiveness of auctions is also influenced by the nature of the assets required and the scope for monitoring quality, as the following examples show.

The winner's curse

Competitive auctions have been fruitfully explored by game theorists, and the so-called 'winner's curse' offers a reason why potential competitors may be reluctant to bid against an incumbent firm. Usually presented as an analysis of *over*-bidding for natural monopolies such as North Sea oil drilling concessions (Kreps, 1990, pp.83–5), it can be adapted to explain why outside firms may bid too low in social auction markets.

The game can be conveyed intuitively with an example from social care. Suppose that six firms are bidding for a single contract to provide meals at home to people unable to cook for themselves. All the firms have imperfect information (as does the local authority letting the contract) about the likely costs of providing the service, because neither delivery conditions nor demand can be wholly known in advance. Furthermore, each firm's internal cost structure is different.

On this basis, each firm makes a private estimate of their expected costs of fulfilling the contract. They must then bid a fixed price per meal to the authority, up to a maximum number of meals. The firms' estimates of expected costs will vary, with some being more optimistic than others about their ability to keep costs down. Each firm will bid a sum which represents their expected costs plus a mark-up to provide them with a profit.

Question

Stop here a minute and think about this story. Which firm will win? Why may that firm regret that it bid as it did?

The most optimistic firm will win, that is, the one that makes the lowest estimate of expected costs and bids accordingly. However, each firm has different partial information, so if all the firms shared all the available information, then the best estimate of expected costs would be higher than the most optimistic firm's estimate. Hence, the winning firm is likely to have underestimated its costs. The winner's curse is to win the contract but lose money in those circumstances.

In the case of public auctions, it is likely that the incumbent firm has the best information; and the more uncertain the demand and technical conditions, the more likely that is to be true. In those circumstances, outside firms may be discouraged from bidding: they will think it only too likely that if they win, they will suffer from the winner's curse. Hence, competitive bidding may not occur or, if it does, the winning firm may reduce quality or find it hard to operate profitably.

The hold-up problem

Now consider a situation where several firms are bidding for a welfare meals contract in a situation where a local authority has a run-down and inadequate set of kitchens to produce the meals, and wishes to expand the service. It lacks the funds for investment, hence it seeks tenders to provide an enhanced service, including the provision of the relevant production facilities. The new assets (the kitchens) are highly specific to this activity and there is no incumbent firm (Chapter 8 defines specific assets).

Question

Suppose you are one of the firms bidding. How will the specific nature of the assets affect your bidding behaviour? (The discussion of the 'hold-up' problem in Chapter 8 will help you here.)

A firm acquiring this contract for, say, five years, will incur sunk costs in the form of the new kitchens. When the next tendering round occurs, if it then loses the contract, a dispute will arise about pricing the kitchens to hand over to the next contractor. If the contract offers no guarantee of a reasonable price for the kitchens at the end of the contract, you may decide not to bid at all, or offer only minor refurbishment of the kitchen. You fear being 'held up' when the contract ends.

An authority may try to overcome this problem by specifying the terms of the handover of assets. But if the authority sets the figure too low, the winning firm may still under-invest, or run down the assets towards the end of the contract. If the figure is set too high, however, there will be a deterrent effect on competition in subsequent rounds. Alternatively, the authority could retain ownership of the assets and lease them to the winning firm. This helps with the competition problem – but not with the renovation of the run-down assets which was one of the authority's objectives in holding the auction in the first place.

The authority letting the contract faces the further problem that once an incumbent firm has established itself, that firm will have better information than its competitors next time around. Other firms may then be reluctant to bid, fearing both the winner's curse and the hold-up problem. So the incumbent may bet successfully on being able, as sole bidder, to put in a higher bid and raise profits next time round. A public authority is particularly likely to be held hostage in this way and will be vulnerable to price collusion among contractors when it cannot, itself, put up an alternative bid.

Quality and monitoring

Finally, if quality is hard to measure, auctions for local services also face the danger of 'quality shaving' by the competitors (discussed in Section 2.4) either to reduce the bid price or increase the profit margins of the winning firm. So franchising tends to work best for areas of public services where output is more easily measured. One local government contracts officer with a private sector background whom I interviewed put it like this:

'... cleaning contractors, like building contractors, will cheat, and you know they're going to cheat, and it's a question of how much you let them. The contractors are much

easier to monitor because you know if something's been cleaned or not ... with [manual services] contracts you end up with a statement of fact: it wasn't cleaned, it wasn't cooked, it was cold.'

The contrast the speaker was drawing was with social care contracts where quality is very much harder to monitor.

In general, the best candidates for auctions seem to be easily monitored services that use widely available equipment: for example, grounds maintenance, industrial cleaning and refuse collection. Particularly problematic candidates include those involving large specific investments, such as big IT systems and defence contracting, and those where quality is hard to measure. This last category notably includes services with a care element.

Evidence on the working of local public auctions is still fairly thin, in part because we need a long cycle – ten years perhaps – to pick up some of the dynamic effects of the system. One service, which has been studied in detail, is refuse collection (Symanski and Wilkins, 1993; Symanski, 1996), and this is often cited as *the* example of the benefits of compulsory tendering. While information is poor on quality changes, the service has seen large cost reductions for the same or even improved contract specifications since tendering was introduced.

In labour-intensive services, such as catering and especially cleaning, much of the decline in costs has come from making the pay and conditions of already low-paid staff worse (Walsh, 1995). In catering, where profit margins are narrow, there have been problems of underbidding, and bidders have not been numerous. In the newer auction market for social care, there is evidence of strong competition on price (some of it at the expense of the wages of low-paid staff), some lack of continuity of care and sometimes of refusal by contractors of difficult work (Mackintosh, 1997). The problem of sustaining quality in services which are hard to monitor

depends partly on the working culture, and is a problem I return to in Section 4.

4 MAKING SOCIAL MARKETS WORK: SOCIAL NORMS IN SOCIAL MARKETS

Given the increasing international tendency to create markets in social goods, how can these social markets be made to function as well as possible? This section explores a number of answers to this question using as the main example the newly expanding market for social care: the long-term physical and domestic care of those unable to care for themselves but not acutely (or curably) ill. This market is expanding internationally as a result of the growing number of people who are living longer into old age. The social organization of the market is deeply influenced by the social policies of individual countries, since affordable access depends on wide risk pooling and on state subsidy for those on low incomes.

There are several reasons why social care provides a good case study of the potential and problems of commodifying social goods. Some issues have already been explored: notably the difficulty in monitoring the quality of care, and the public concern with access. Social care has some shared goods characteristics. In particular, the nature of the relationship between the carer and the person cared for forms an important element of the quality of care. Social care is therefore a good test case of Anderson's proposition (Section 1.1) that shared goods are devalued by market trading. I explore also the counter-proposition that the devaluing effect depends on the form in which commodification develops, rather than on the process of exchange itself. And this in turn leads to a consideration of working cultures in social care.

4.1 Altruism and market trading

Let me start with the concern for access. I argued in Section 2.1 that goods to which access is a matter of social concern have some shared goods qualities: the access others have to those goods influences our attitude to using them and paying for them. Bringing those kinds of concerns for others to market implies that competitive markets cannot be relied upon to produce a welfare optimum even in the limited sense of Pareto efficiency (Chapter 18). Concern for the access of others undermines the welfare properties of general equilibrium.

The reason for this is the nature of the concern felt for others. Some formulations of altruism can be incorporated quite easily into neoclassical theory. The most straightforward is the 'altruism' of someone who cares about the welfare of others as well as themselves. Altruism of this kind between people in the same household is often modelled by economists (Chapter 6). Here I will explore the implications of relaxing the assumption that such altruism is confined to the household and consider what happens when those engaged in market trading feel altruistic towards each other.

Altruistic preferences can be incorporated into utility theory by supposing that one person's utility function includes the welfare of others. Suppose that two people, X and Y, get utility V_x and V_y from their own consumption. However X cares not only about her own consumption-related utility, V_x, but also about that of Y, V_y. So her full utility function is of the form:

$$U_x = f(V_x, V_y)$$

If Y has a full utility function of the same type, then the trade between the two individuals can be illustrated on an Edgeworth box diagram of a two-person economy. (Edgeworth box diagrams are explained in Chapter 18).

Figure 19.4 overleaf is an Edgeworth box on which quantities of good G are measured on the horizontal axis and quantities of good F are measured on the vertical axis. X's allocation is measured from the bottom left-hand corner and Y's from the top right-hand corner. The indifference curves on Figure 19.4 correspond to V_x and V_y, the utility that each individual gains from their own consumption alone. The contract curve, CC, connects the points of tangency between the indifference curves, the equilibria corresponding to different price lines if X and Y were simultaneously to maximize the utility each gets from their own consumption (see Chapter 18, Section 4.2). I can call CC the 'private contract curve' since it takes no account of the utility X and Y get from each other's consumption-related utility.

However, once we take into account that X and Y also care about the utility the other gains from consumption, then there are points on the private contract curve that can no longer be considered Pareto efficient. Suppose that X's altruism means that she prefers her allocation of good F and good G at

point A to any allocation between A and O_y that leave Y on a lower utility level from private consumption than V_{ya}. In that case the points along the dotted segment AO_y can no longer be considered Pareto efficient. Similarly, if Y's altruism leads him to prefer his allocation at B to any other allocation between B and O_x that leave X on a lower utility level from her own consumption than V_{xb}, then the points along the dotted segment, O_xB, are no longer Pareto efficient. On Figure 19.4, therefore, X's most preferred point along the contract curve is A and Y's most preferred point is B.

The remaining part of the private contract curve, BA, can be called the 'social contract curve'. It connects the allocations of goods F and G that are Pareto efficient once we take account of the altruism X and Y feel towards each other. Since X and Y care about each other's consumption-related utility – and not about the particular mix of goods F and G that the other prefers – we know that the social contract curve does not include points that do not lie on the private contract curve. This sort of altruism does not make new allocations Pareto efficient.

Now consider what happens in general equilibrium. If one person's initial endowment is so small that the general equilibrium outcome would lie outside the social contract curve, then both X and Y would be made better off by moving to a point between A and B. This could be achieved by the richer person voluntarily transferring some of their initial endowment to the other, with trading then occurring as before (Collard, 1978). So altruistic preferences of this limited kind shrink the contract curve, but otherwise leave the welfare properties of general equilibrium untouched, so long as gifts, as well as trades, can be made between X and Y.

The same is not true, however, as soon as X and Y begin to care what particular mix of goods F and G the other consumes – as they do the moment they take the view that poverty should not constrain people's access to certain social goods. Then X's full utility function will be of the form:

$$U_x = f(C_x, C'_y)$$

where C_x is all of X's consumption, but C'_y is just the consumption of, say education, health and social care by Y.

Such preferences can be described as 'meddlesome' because the weighting that X puts on the components of Y's consumption is different from Y's weighting of those components. From a different political perspective, such preferences can also be described as 'caring'. Goods over which many people hold such preferences for other people's consumption are sometimes called 'merit goods' (*Changing Economies*, Chapter 23). Merit goods have always fitted uneasily into neoclassical discussions of social welfare because they overturn the assumption that individuals are the best judges of their own welfare.

For precisely that reason, this type of altruism undermines the welfare arguments for allowing private contracting. Altruistic preferences can be thought of as one kind of consumption externality: your consumption affects my welfare, and vice versa. Such preferences can operate like other externalities to undermine the welfare properties

of general equilibrium (Chapter 18). If people have non-meddlesome preferences then, as just shown, allowing gifts as well as trades is enough to restore the welfare properties of general equilibrium. However, with meddlesome preferences, the social contract curve is skewed compared with the private contract curve because the individuals care about each other's consumption of the social good, G say, but not of the other good, F. So with meddlesome preferences, the social contract curve does not coincide with the private contract curve, and private trading no longer produces a Pareto-efficient outcome.

In these circumstances, individuals may be willing to make transfers of social goods to others through voluntary redistribution. In the two-person case, it might be possible for the two to reach a Pareto

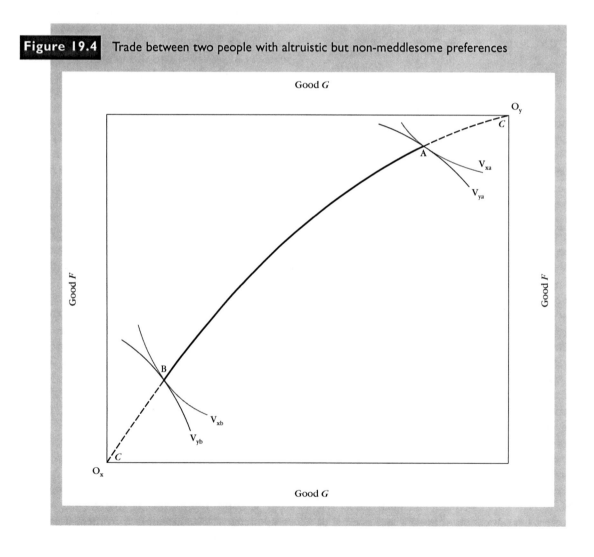

Figure 19.4 Trade between two people with altruistic but non-meddlesome preferences

optimum co-operatively, with one person transferring specific goods to the other (which they must, however, be willing to consume!) In the case of contracting among large numbers, some kind of organized redistribution is needed, bringing with it the potential problems of free riding, since each person donating will, presumably, wish to ensure that others in similar circumstances also contribute, so that the redistribution is effective. Once members of an economy decide that all citizens should have access to at least a minimum level of a given service – such as social care – in response to need, we are back with a role for tax financing, or for large scale co-operative action. Markets for social goods then have to operate with such a redistributive framework and be compatible with it.

4.2   Reputation and commitment in social care markets

In social care provision there are complex three-way relationships among those receiving care, those giving care, and those funding the care giving. State-supported social care does not always involve market relationships, but in industrialized countries it has strong, though varying, market elements. In some European countries, such as France and Italy, the state provides funds to those with disabilities to purchase care. In others, such as Sweden, municipalities employ relatives as care givers on market wages (Ungerson, 1995). In still others, such as the situation in Britain after the Community Care reforms, local government pays care-giving 'provider' firms (public, private and non-profit) to provide care for individuals on the basis of means testing and needs assessments. It is the British model, with state

'purchasers' buying on behalf of those requiring care, which is typically described as a 'quasi-market'.

The sociological literature on these markets focuses on the complex networks of kinship, obligation and affection, which structure both the care given and the payment systems. European countries all have complex and shifting boundaries between unpaid care, 'formal' paid care, and the 'grey' area in-between of small payments to neighbours, volunteers and kin. Most volunteers and informal carers are women, hence, caring is deeply influenced by changing gender roles. The economic literature, by contrast, tends to focus mainly on 'formal' paid care. This section looks at relations between funding bodies and firms supplying formal carers; the next section returns to user-carer relations.

Social care contracting between local government and providing firms suffers from a number of the problems identified for health care: asymmetric information (the providers have most of the information on the quality of care they are providing); vulnerable clients who may find it hard to judge the care and hard to assert themselves, and who may have low expectations; services which, as a result, are difficult and expensive to monitor; and a danger of 'quality shaving'. If we assume profit-seeking firms and self-interested purchasers, then we can model the problem to be solved as a prisoners' dilemma game. Such games inevitably over-simplify complex issues, but they do allow us to explore the problem of how monitoring costs can be kept under control while providing incentives for high quality, on different assumptions about participants' motivations.

Figure 19.5 shows a game between a local government purchaser of social care services and a profit-seeking provider. The provider is assumed to

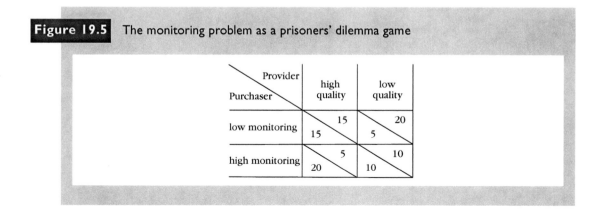

Figure 19.5   The monitoring problem as a prisoners' dilemma game

have a choice between high quality and low quality care. The pay-offs to the provider reflect the fact that quality shaving pays, but when the authority spends a lot on monitoring it has less to spend on care, reducing the provider's profits (and the total care provided). The purchaser has a choice between high (expensive) and low (cheap) monitoring, and is chiefly concerned to meet the government's targets of avoiding financial waste and public complaints. The purchaser's pay-offs, therefore, reflect these concerns: you do not want to be caught funding shoddy care. The worst case scenario for a purchaser is, therefore, to monitor little and find you have (probably) paid for low quality (but you are not sure): this is likely to lose you your job. Next worst is to find out, through high monitoring, that you have paid for low quality. In this situation you can at least claim to have identified the problems. It would be better to be reasonably sure you have paid for high quality. And best of all to be sure that you have done so.

Exercise 19.7

Show that the game in Figure 19.5 is of the pris-oners' dilemma form with a single equilibrium, and explain why.

So what can be done? How can monitoring costs be kept down and quality maintained? Game theory suggests two routes out of the dilemma: reputation and commitment.

Reputation effects can, in theory, rescue con-tracting parties from a prisoners' dilemma in a competitive market where there are repeated inter-actions. Even with low monitoring, a purchaser will get an idea that quality is slipping when complaints start to increase. If the parties contract repeatedly with each other in a 'game' of indefinite length, and if they punish each other for apparent departures from – in this case – the high quality/low monitoring equi-librium by retreating to low quality or high moni-toring, then each will have an incentive to sustain their reputation by not succumbing to the low quality and high monitoring temptations.

Chapter 9 analyses a reputation game and Chapter 11 explains how a 'trigger' strategy of co-operation (in this case high quality/low monitoring) while the other party co-operates, and of punishing default by default, can sustain co-operation in a repeated pris-oners' dilemma game. The trigger strategy works so long as each party cares sufficiently about their future as well as current pay-offs.

The other way out of the prisoners' dilemma is to change the pay-offs by altering the players' motiva-tions. Suppose that instead of the self-interested assumptions underlying Figure 19.5, we assume that the providers and the purchasers both care about the clients as well as their own self interest. In this case the providers will care about both profits and the quality of care to patients; and the purchasers will care about both watching their backs and the quality of care to patients. This, at least in my expe-rience, is a more realistic reflection of the mixed motives and pressures such quasi-markets generate.

In Figure 19.6, the pay-offs represent the mixed motives of the players. The provider prefers high quality and low monitoring, because it gives a mix of respectable profits and good treatment of clients. After that, the provider prefers to offer low quality (keeping up profits) rather than high quality for fewer users because of high monitoring costs. The

Figure 19.6 The monitoring problem as an assurance game

Purchaser \ Provider	high quality	low quality
low monitoring	20 / 20	15 / 5
high monitoring	5 / 15	10 / 10

purchaser prefers low monitoring and high quality too, balancing risk to themselves against the welfare of users. But after that risk aversion takes over. They prefer high monitoring and their worst outcome is low monitoring and poor quality.

Exercise 19.8

There is more than one equilibrium in this game. Identify them, and explain how they arise.

Whether the players end up in the top left or bottom right quadrant depends on their expectations of each other. This is the key characteristic of an *assurance game*: that the outcome depends on how much assurance each party has about the behaviour of the other (note that this is *not* true of a prisoners' dilemma game).

To see this, suppose that in Figure 19.6, the provider believes that there is a 60 per cent chance that the purchaser will pick low monitoring. Then the expected value of the provider's pay-off from choosing high quality is:

$$(0.6 \times 20) + (0.4 \times 5) = 14$$

while the expected value of the pay-off from choosing low quality is:

$$(0.6 \times 15) + (0.4 \times 10) = 13$$

(Chapter 8 explains expected values.)

So a rational provider strategy, based on those expectations, would be to choose high quality. Exactly the same calculation is true for the purchaser, since the pay-offs are symmetrical. A reasonable expectation of goodwill from the other causes the game to settle at the top left equilibrium which best suits them both – and seems likely to be better for the users too, on the story I told about the game.

Exercise 19.9

What happens if the provider expects that the purchaser will pick low monitoring only 40 per cent of the time, and the purchaser expects high quality only 40 per cent of the time also?

The 'assurance' in this game can be treated as a shared commitment to patients and/or to a collaboration in which each has some confidence. Such assurance can be interpreted as a norm of expected behaviour within the market, which overcomes some of the problems generated by self-interested and mutually destructive behaviour based on poor information and narrow motivation. The question remains, however, how can such norms arise and how can they be sustained?

One partial answer to that question is organizational culture. A firm's culture offers staff a way of deciding what to do in a variety of common working situations without constant and impracticable recourse to first principles. Culture, therefore, has considerable bearing on firms' objectives (Chapter 8; Kreps, 1988). Now suppose that the environment of a firm, in the sense of the incentives it faces, changes sharply. For example, a big non-profit organization which had previously supplied, partly from public grant funding, a range of support to the elderly infirm now finds itself contracted by a public authority to supply more extensive services. In place of an earlier situation where the organization's self perception was that of a 'voluntary' specialist organization, independently complementing statutory provision, and being appreciated for it, it is now a public supplier subject to higher levels of formal monitoring.

Look back at Figure 19.6. If an organization that has previously been settled into a low monitoring/high quality equilibrium suddenly finds itself subjected to much more intrusive monitoring, then, this game was designed to suggest, it may resent the intrusion and back off into more instrumental profit-seeking behaviour. Its response depends, presumably, on the strength of commitment to clients, and on whether the organization thinks the new behaviour of the public authority is an aberration from which it will recover. British evidence suggests that in these circumstances the organization's culture can go in two directions: it can take on a quasi-public sector role, accepting the political visibility, or it can settle down as a more instrumental contracted supplier. Where non-profit firms act as contractors in competition with profit-seeking firms, evidence from US social care shows little difference in behaviour between the two in terms of quality and cost (Clark and Estes, 1992).

4.3 Professionalism and legitimacy in social markets

So far in this discussion, game players have been organizations. But organizations are composed of people, and within social markets the people frequently have a lot of autonomy of action. Many social goods are provided by staff who see themselves as professionals. One important way in which social markets are policed is through the development of market-specific concepts of professionalism which respond to the commodification of service activity by setting constraints on behaviour. Professions, according to Matthews (1991), are characterized by:

- qualification-based rules of entry
- professional codes of various sorts which provide non-business objectives
- rules which prohibit certain practices, such as touting for clients, which are thought to undermine the professional codes.

All of this can allow for self-interested restrictive practices to maintain professional incomes, especially in the better paid professions. But professional codes of practice or ethics which become internalized as social norms – indeed, as expressions of self on the part of professionals – can play a role in sustaining high quality equilibria against material incentives which tend to work in the opposite direction. In fields such as health and social care, the autonomy of public service staff and their control of quality is frequently recognized by salary-based payments systems detached from 'results'. Commodification through quasi-markets brings pressure for results-based payments systems, and for clocking in and out, which can have perverse results. If people who saw themselves as professionals trusted to take responsibility suddenly find themselves treated as if their motivation were wholly mercenary, they may react by 'working to rule' and reducing their effectiveness.

In social care, where the extent of developing professionalism remains at issue, the process is contested for a number of interlocking reasons. Professions exhibit hierarchy. The health and social care hierarchy has doctors at the top and carers at the bottom of the health-related activities. Those higher up tend to contest the 'professional' credentials of lower-paid professionals. Among informal carers, ideas about payment are complex. Relatives often resist payment from kin, although research shows that family members will often accept payment if the funds come from the state for the purpose of acquiring care (Baldock and Ungerson, 1994). Neighbours are more willing to be paid. Once paid care becomes prevalent, wage payments – and conditions of service – become matters to be negotiated more openly. A key difficulty with the social care market in Britain is that low and casualized wage payment is developing at the same time as increasing demands are made of care staff for levels of responsibility, autonomy and risk-acceptance which are much more characteristic of salaried professions.

The messages concerning professional culture are therefore mixed. If, as suggested in Section 2 in relation to health care, good quality services of the social goods type require trust and co-operation between users and staff, then these circumstances do not easily generate such assurance. It is not merely that those needing care are often distressed; it is, as two social policy researchers put it, that users and informal carers dealing with the care market are coping with an 'unscripted' process: they lack information, but are also uncertain what *should* be done. They are thinking through the ethics as they search for solutions (Baldock and Ungerson, 1994).

People, furthermore, are not sure of the legitimacy of paying for certain things at all. There is no feeling that home nursing is devalued by nurses being paid – only a resistance to paying cash for what people feel should be tax financed, or an embarrassment or nervousness at a cash transaction. But cash payment to kin for care is more complicated, through fear of behaving improperly or giving offence. The British social care market is still very unstable in terms of what is sold, to whom, for what, and within what relationships.

5 CONCLUSION

Social markets involve goods which are important to people: basic needs, services which respond to vulnerabilities, and goods which are tied up with personal relationships and with ideas about the kind of society we live in. As a result, people attach social meanings to the organizations that supply the goods to the staff who work in them and to the terms of access to the goods. Many of these social goods are also problematic commodities for technical reasons, because of natural monopolies and externalities.

This chapter has explored the operation of markets in these social goods and services. Not all social goods are marketed, and all societies set limits to such social markets by 'blocking' some exchanges (the phrase is from Walzer, 1983). Blockage may be statutory: the chapter began with a current debate on one such legal prohibition, on brothels and soliciting. Or the blocking may be built into our understanding of social relationships, as with the sense of contradiction surrounding the buying of love and friendship. Over time, our willingness to treat or recreate social goods as commodities changes, and recent years have seen a new wave of market creation in social goods. This chapter has analysed different ways of organizing social markets: as 'clubs' and through auction mechanisms. The final section drew on the analysis of Sections 2 and 3 to argue that motivations and incentives matter greatly to the operation of social markets (as in other markets); and that the recognition of ethical as well as material motivations of staff may be key to the tolerable operation of social markets.

FURTHER READING

The article by Elizabeth Anderson (1990) 'The ethical limitations of the market', *Economics and Philosophy*, vol.6, referred to at the start of the chapter, is readable and stimulating.

Keiron Walsh (1995) *Public Services and Market Mechanisms* is a non-technical survey of the UK quasi-market reforms.

An accessible book on the economics of health care is Donaldson, C. and Gerard, K. (1993) *Economics of Health Care Finance: The Visible Hand*.

ANSWERS TO EXERCISES

Exercise 19.1

1   Preventative care has considerable externalities, that is, effects not experienced by the immediate user of the service. Vaccinations and learned improvements in hygiene and maternal and child nutrition, for example, can greatly reduce the spread of disease to others. Primary care includes a mix of such prevention and information, inextricably associated with minor curative care and diagnosis.

2   See Figure 19.7 which shows a competitive market for primary care. The marginal social benefits (*MSB*) of a given number of visits exceed the marginal private benefits (*MPB*). But it is the marginal private benefits which users compare to the price charged for the visit ($MPB = D$). The marginal cost curve, *MC*, is the supply curve for primary care. Hence primary care will tend to be under-supplied in competitive equilibrium: Q_1 will

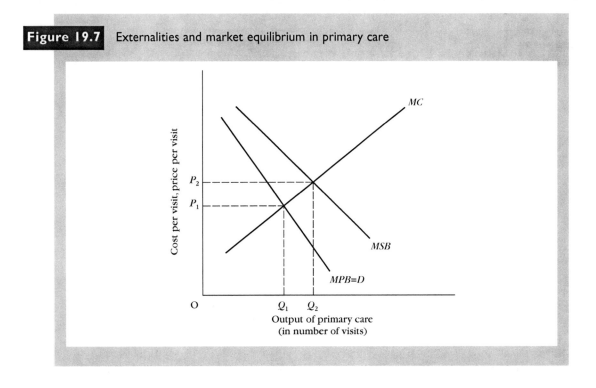

Figure 19.7   Externalities and market equilibrium in primary care

be supplied at price P_1 rather than Q_2 which would be the optimum output at price P_2

3 The World Bank argues that there are no externalities in curative care, hence the *MPB* and *MSB* curves will coincide so the competitive market equilibrium will be a fully efficient one, that is, in equilibrium:

$$MSB = MPB = MC$$

In discussing this issue, it is relevant that a high proportion of curative health care in low income countries deals with infectious diseases such as tuberculosis; curing these may have an external effect in preventing disease spreading, thus casting doubt on the statement that curative care is a wholly private good.

Exercise 19.2

A doctor makes a decision about treatment, faced with an anxious patient. Since the insurer (a 'third party') is paying, the private cost at the moment of decision is zero to the patient (much less than the social cost) so the patient has no financial incentive to resist treatment. The more treatment given, the more the doctor will gain, hence the doctor has a positive incentive to increase treatment. Furthermore, in an imperfect market, the doctor may be able to influence the fee per treatment, and faces no incentive not to attempt this. Collusion among doctors would reinforce both effects.

Exercise 19.3

Suppose clients of insurance companies range between good and bad risks. Clients know more than the insurance companies about their own health and, therefore, have a better idea where they are likely to fall on the spectrum of good to bad risks. Suppose further that a proportion of bad risks succeed in representing themselves as good risks. The insurance company will then find that premiums do not cover the full costs of treatment, because some bad risks are underpaying. They will therefore put up premiums. As premiums rise, some good risks will find the insurance not worth the price, so they will drop out of the market. This just leaves the worse risks, so premiums have to rise again. A vicious circle of rising premiums and declining coverage will set in, the result of which will be that many people who would have been willing to pay an appropriate premium for the risk category into which they fall may fail to find insurance at a premium they are willing to pay.

Exercise 19.4

Figure 19.8 illustrates the idea. I have drawn the *MC* curve as horizontal. The marginal benefit curve, *MB*,

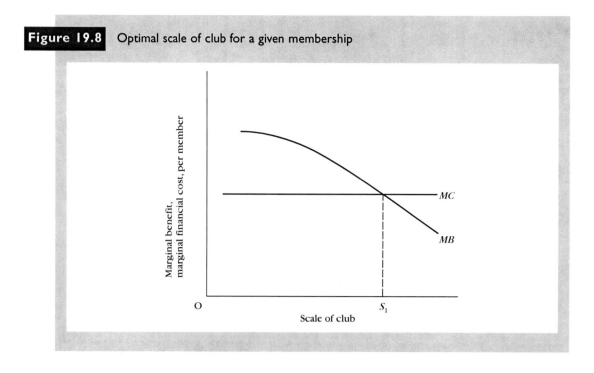

Figure 19.8 Optimal scale of club for a given membership

is the same shape as it would be for a private good: marginal utility falls as more of the club good is consumed. The optimal scale is S_1. Note that these are not the same marginal benefit and marginal cost curves as in Figure 19.1. On Figure 19.8, the marginal costs are financial costs, while the marginal benefits are enjoyment of the club good.

Exercise 19.5

From the line M_{opt}, we can see that at scale S_2, the optimum membership is M_3. However, from the line S_{opt}, it can be seen that a group of size M_3 would prefer a larger scale club, at S_3. However, at scale S_3 the optimum membership is higher than M_3. Only at M_* and S_* is there no incentive to change. This is an equilibrium at the optimum club scale and membership. This is shown in Figure 19.9.

Exercise 19.6

Auctions are most likely to reduce costs without a decline in quality where:

● there are a lot of potential bidders who find it hard to collude

● there are well-established markets with widely available technologies and rather low levels of

uncertainty about future conditions, so that the private information of the incumbent firm does not imply too large an advantage

● there is X-inefficiency to be addressed

● assets are not highly specific and sunk costs are low

● cost of inputs can be reduced

● quality of output is easy and cheap to monitor.

Refuse collection seems to fit more of these criteria than social care. In Britain, tendering for refuse collection was introduced at a time when there was scope for innovation and changing working methods; monitoring of quality is relatively easy; assets are not highly specific (there is quite a wide market for refuse trucks) and technology is not complex. *But* collusion among contractors is not difficult. In social care, there are large numbers of providers at present, though some areas are dominated by a few; the service is highly labour intensive, and some innovations can reduce quality (for example, cook-chill meals). There seem to be few ways to reduce costs except for paying already low-paid staff less, which may also reduce quality of care; and most serious, quality is very hard to specify and monitor, since the relationship with the carer is key to service quality. Refuse collection looks a better bet.

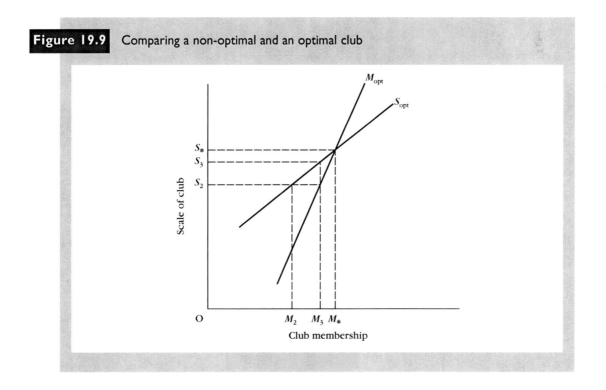

Figure 19.9 Comparing a non-optimal and an optimal club

Exercise 19.7

The purchaser will choose high monitoring over low monitoring whether they believe the company will produce high or low quality: high monitoring is the dominant strategy. Similarly, the provider has a dominant strategy, choosing low quality for each possible decision of the purchaser on monitoring (and therefore also on the level of provision). So the single equilibrium is in the lower right-hand quadrant. However, both would have preferred the upper left to the lower right-hand quadrant, since it produces higher profits for the provider and a better outcome for the purchaser.

Exercise 19.8

There are two equilibria, top left and bottom right. They are both Nash equilibria in that once the game settles on that quadrant, players have no incentive to move. So if the purchaser is engaging in low monitoring, the provider will prefer high quality, and vice versa. But if the purchaser is doing high monitoring, the provider will prefer low quality, and vice versa. The outcome of the game depends on the *expectations* each player holds of the other's behaviour.

Exercise 19.9

The expected value for the provider of choosing high quality is:

$$(0.4 \times 20) + (0.6 \times 5) = 11$$

and from choosing low quality is:

$$(0.4 \times 15) + (0.6 \times 10) = 12$$

So the provider will choose low quality. The purchaser on the same calculation will choose high monitoring. The game will settle at the lower-right equilibrium.

REFERENCES

Abramovitz, M. (1956) 'Resource and output trends in the United States since 1870', *American Economic Review*, vol. 46, no. 2, pp. 5–23.

Akerlof, G.A. (1970) 'The market for "lemons": quality uncertainty and the market mechanism', *Quarterly Journal of Economics,* vol. 84, pp. 488–500; reprinted in Akerlof, G. (1984) *An Economic Theorist's Book of Tales,* Cambridge, Cambridge University Press.

Akerlof, G.A. (1982) 'Labour contracts as a partial gift exchange', *Quarterly Journal of Economics*, vol. 97, pp. 543–69.

Akerlof, G.A. and Yellen, J.L. (1986) *Efficiency Wage Models of the Labor Market*, Cambridge, Cambridge University Press.

Alogoskoufis, A. and Manning, A. (1988) 'Wage setting and unemployment persistence in Europe, Japan and the USA', *European Economic Review*, vol. 32, pp. 698–706.

Amsden, A.M. (ed.) (1980) *The Economics of Women and Work*, Harmondsworth, Penguin.

Anderson, E. (1990) 'The ethical limitations of the market', *Economics and Philosophy,* vol. 6, pp. 179–205.

Aoki, M. (1990) 'Towards an economic model of the Japanese firm', *Journal of Economic Literature*, vol. 28, March, pp. 1–27.

Appelbaum, E. and Batt, R. (1994) *The New American Workplace*, Ithaca; NY, ILR Press.

Archibugi, D. and Pianta, M (1992) *The Technological Specialization of Advanced Countries: A report to the EEC on International Science and Technology Activities*, Dodrecht, Kluwer and Commission of the European Communities.

Armstrong, H. and Taylor, J. (1981) 'The measurement of different types of unemployment', in Creedy, J. (ed.) *The Economics of Unemployment in Britain*, Sevenoaks, Butterworth.

Arrighetti, A., Bachmann, R. and Deakin, S. (1997) 'Contract law, social norms and inter-firm cooperation', *Cambridge Journal of Economics*, vol. 21, pp. 171–95.

Arrow, K. (1962a) 'The economic implications of learning by doing', *Review of Economic Studies*, vol. 29, pp. 155–73.

Arrow, K. (1962b) 'Economic welfare and the allocation of resources for invention', in National Bureau for Economic Research, *The Rate and Direction of Inventive Activity*, Princeton; NJ, Princeton University Press.

Arthur, W.B. (1988) 'Competing technologies: An Overview', in Dosi *et al.* (1988), pp. 590–607.

Arthur, W.B. (1989) 'Competing technologies, increasing returns and lock-in by historical events', *Economic Journal*, vol. 99, pp. 116–31.

Asanuma, B. and Kikutani, T. (1991) 'Risk absorption in Japanese subcontracting: a microeconometric study on the automobile industry', *Journal of Japanese and International Economics,* vol. 6, pp. 1–29.

Audretsch, D.B. (1995) *Innovation and Industry Evolution*, Cambridge; Mass., MIT Press.

Auerbach, P. (1988) *Competition: The Economics of Industrial Change*, Oxford, Blackwell.

Authers, J. (1996) 'The industry in the US: alarm call for the American dream', *Financial Times Survey of Venture and Development Capital*, 20 September, p. 6.

Baines, S., Wheelock, J. and Abrams, A. (1997) 'Micro business owner-managers in social context: household, family and growth or non-growth' in Deakin, D., Jennings, P. and Mason, C. (eds) *Entrepreneurship into the 90s*, London, Paul Chapman.

Baldock, J. and Ungerson, C. (1994) *Becoming Consumers of Community Care*, York, Joseph Rowntree Foundation.

Bank of England (1996) *The Financing of Technology-based Small Firms*, October, London, Bank of England.

Banks, J. and Johnson, P. (1993) *Children and Household Living Standards*, London, Institute for Fiscal Studies.

Barten, A.P. (1964) 'Family composition, prices and expenditure patterns' in Hart *et al.,* (1964).

Barwise, P. and Ehrenberg, A. (1988) *TV and its Audience*, London, Sage.

Baumol, W.J. (1958) 'On the theory of oligopoly', *Economica*, vol. 25, pp. 187–98.

Baumol, W.J. (1967) *Business Behaviour, Value and Growth,* revised edition, New York, Harcourt, Brace and Company.

Baxter, C., Poonia, K., Ward, L. and Nadirshaw, Z. (1990) *Double Discrimination: Issues and Services for People with Learning Difficulties from Black and Ethnic Minority Communities*, London, Kings Fund Centre.

Beatson, M. (1995a) 'Progress towards a flexible labour market economy', *Employment Gazette*

Beatson, M. (1995b) *Labour Market Flexibility*, London, Employment Department, Research Series no. 48.

Becker, G. (1965) 'A theory of the allocation of time', *Economic Journal*, vol. 75, no. 299, pp. 493–517.

Becker, G.A. (1991) *A Treatise on the Family* (enlarged edition), Cambridge; MA, and London, Harvard University Press.

Becker, G.S. (1962) 'Irrational behaviour and economic theory', *Journal of Political Economy*, vol.LXX, pp.1-13.

Becker, G.S. (1996) *Accounting for Tastes*, Cambridge; MA, Harvard University Press.

Becker, G.S. and Stigler, G.J. (1977) 'De gustibus non est disputandum', *American Economic Review*, vol.67, no.2, pp.76-90.

Bentham, J. (1789) *Introduction to the Principles of Morals and Legislation* (Chapters 1-5), in Warnock, M. (ed.).

Bentolila, S. and Bertola, G. (1990) 'Firing costs and labour demand. How bad is Eurosclerosis?', *Review of Economic Studies*, vol.57. pp.318-402.

Berglof, E. (1990) 'Capital structure as a mechanism of control: A comparison of financial systems', Chapter 11, pp.237-62, in Aoki, M., Gustaffson B. and Williamson, O.E. (eds) *The Firm as a Nexus of Treaties*, London, Sage.

Berle, A. and Means, G. (1932) *The Modern Corporations and Private Property*, New York, Commerce Clearing House (republished in 1993 by Legal Classic Library).

Besley, T. and Gouveia, M. (1994) 'Alternative systems of health care provision', *Economic Policy*, no.19, October, pp.200-58.

Bettio, F. and Villa, P. (1998) 'A Mediterranean perspective on the breakdown of the relationship between participation and fertility', *Cambridge Journal of Economics*, vol.2.

Bishop, J. (1981) 'Employment in construction and distribution industries: the impact of the new jobs tax credit', in Rosen, S. (ed.) *Studies in Labour Markets*, Chicago; IL, University of Chicago Press.

Blackaby, D., Clark, K., Leslie, D. and Murphy, P. (1994) 'Black-white earnings and employment prospects in the 1970s and 1980s: evidence for Britain', *Economic Letters*, no.46, pp.273-9.

Blackaby, D., Leslie, D. and Murphy, P. (1995) 'Unemployment among Britain's ethnic minorities', Discussion Paper 95-103, Department of Economics, University of Wales, Swansea.

Blanchflower, D. and Oswald, A. (1988) 'Internal and external influences upon pay settlements', *British Journal of Industrial Relations*, vol.26, pp.363-70.

Bonner, F. and du Gay, P. (1992) '*Thirtysomething* and contemporary consumer culture: distinctiveness and distinction' in Burrows, R. and Marsh, C. (eds) *Consumption and Class*, pp.166-83, London, Macmillan.

Borzaga, C. (1996) 'Stakeholder co-operatives in European welfare', *Soundings*, no.4, pp.203-12.

Bourdieu, P. (1979) *Distinction: a Social Critique of the Judgement of Taste*, London, Routledge. (English translation 1984)

Broadberry, S.N. (1991) 'Unemployment', in Crafts, N. and Woodward, N. (eds) *The British Economy Since 1945*, Oxford, Oxford University Press.

Brown, B., Deakin, S. and Ryan, P. (1997?) 'The effects of industrial relations legislation 1979-97', *National Institute Economic Review*, pp.64-8.

Brown, C., Stern, D. and Reich, M. (1993) 'Becoming a high performance work organization: the role of security, employee involvement and training', *International Journal of Human Resource Management*, vol.4, pp.247-77.

Brown, N. and Read, D. (1995) 'The changing nature of the employment contract', *Scottish Journal of political Economy*, vol.42, pp.363-77.

Brown, V. (1994) *Adam Smith's Discourse: Canonicity, Commerce and Conscience*, London, Routledge.

Buchanan, J. (1965) 'An economic theory of clubs', *Economica*, vol.32, pp.1-14.

Buchanan, J.M. and Vanberg, V.J. (1991) 'The market as a creative process', *Economics and Philosophy*, vol.7, no.2, October, pp.167-86.

Buckley, P.J. and Casson, M. (1996) 'An economic model of international joint venture strategy', *Journal of International Business Studies*, Special Issue, pp.849-76.

Budd, A., Levine, P. and Smith, P. (1987) 'Long term unemployment and the shifting U-V curve. A multi country study', *European Economics Review*, vol.31, pp.296-305.

Cain, M. (1977) 'The economic activities of children in a village in Bangladesh', *Population and Development Review*, no.3.

Campaign for Racial Equality (1994) *Labour Force Survey*, EUROSTAT, Brussels.

Campbell, C. (1995) 'The sociology of consumption' in Miller, D. (ed.) *Acknowledging Consumption*, pp.96-126, London, Routledge.

Cantwell, J. (1989) *Technological Innovation and Multinational Corporation*, Oxford, Blackwell.

Carlsson, B. and Jacobsson, (1996) 'Technological systems and industrial dynamics: implications for firms and governments', in Helmstadter, E. and Perlman, M. (eds) *Behavioral Norms, Technological Progress, and Economic Dynamics*, Ann Arbor; MI, University of Michigan Press.

Carlsson, B. and Stankiewicz, R. (1991) 'On the nature, function and composition of technological systems', *Journal of Evolutionary Economics*, vol.1, no.2, pp.93-118.

Carver, T. (ed.) (1991) *The Cambridge Companion to Marx*, Cambridge, Cambridge University Press.

Cathie, K. (1976) *The Complete Calorie Counter*, London, Pan Books.

Chandler, A.D. (1990) *Scale and Scope: The Dynamics of Industrial Capitalism*, Cambridge; Mass., Belknap Press.

Chernichovsky, D. (1995) 'Health systems reform in industrialised democracies', *Millbank Quarterly,* vol.73, no.3, pp.339-72.

Clark, L. and Estes, C. (1992) 'Sociological and economic theories of markets and non-profits: evidence from home health organizations', *American Journal of Sociology,* vol.97, no.4, pp.945-69.

Coase, R. (1937) 'The nature of the firm', *Economica,* vol.4, pp.386-405.

Coghlan, A. (1996) 'Pennies from heaven', *New Scientist,* 24 August, pp.14-15.

Cohen, W. and Levinthal, D.A. (1989) 'Innovation and learning: the two faces of R&D', *Economic Journal,* vol.99, pp.569-99.

Coleman, J.S. (1990) *Foundations of Social Theory,* Cambridge; MA, Harvard University Press.

Collard, D. (1978) *Altruism and Economy,* Oxford, Martin Robertson.

Corbett, J. and Jenkinson, T. (1994) 'The financing of industry, 1970–89: an international comparison', *CEPR Discussion Papers,* no.948, May.

Corbett, J. and Mayer, C. (1991) 'Financial reform in eastern Europe: progress with the wrong model, *Oxford Review of Economic Policy,* vol.7, no.4, pp.57-75.

Cornes, R. and Sandler, T. (1996) *The Theory of Externalities, Public Goods and Club Goods,* 2nd edition, Cambridge, Cambridge University Press.

Coulter, F.A.E., Cowell, F.A. and Jenkins, S.P. (1992) 'Equivalence scale relativities and the extent of inequality and poverty', *Economic Journal,* vol.102, no.414, September, pp.1067-82.

Cowan, R. (1996) 'Sprayed to death: Path dependence, lock-in and pest control strategies', *Economic Journal,* vol.106, pp.521-42

Crawford, I. (1994) *UK Cost-of-Living Indices, 1979-92,* London, Institute for Fiscal Studies.

Creedy, J. and Whitfield, K. (1992) 'Opening the black box: economic analyses of internal labour markets', *Journal of Industrial Relations,* vol.34, pp.455-71.

Curwin, J. and Slater, R. (2001) *Quantitative Methods for Business Decisions,* London, Thomson Learning.

Daniels, W. (1990) *The Unemployed Flow,* London, Policy Studies Institute.

Davies, H. and Joshi, H. (1990) 'The foregone earnings of Europe's mothers', *Discussion Papers in Economics,* no.24, London, Birkbeck College.

De Liso, N. and Metcalfe, J.S. (1996) 'On technological systems and technological paradigms: some recent developments in the understanding of technical change', in Helmstadter, E. and Perlman, M. (eds) *Behavioral Norms, Technological Progress, and Economic Dynamics,* Ann Arbor; MI, University of Michigan Press.

Deaton, A.S. and Mullbauer, J. (1980) *Economics and Consumer Behaviour,* Cambridge, Cambridge University Press.

Department for Education and Employment (1995) *New Earning Survey,* London, HMSO.

Dickinson, H.W. (1936) *James Watt: Craftsman and Engineer,* Cambridge, Cambridge University Press.

Digital Equipment Corporation (1993) *Annual Report,* Maynard; Mass.

Digital Equipment Corporation (1995) *Brief Guide,* Maynard; Mass.

Dixit, A. (1980) 'The role of investment in entry-deterrence', *Economic Journal,* vol.90, pp.95-106.

Donaldson, C. and Gerard, K. (1993) *Economics of Health Care Finance: The Visible Hand,,* Basingstoke, Macmillan.

Donaldson, P. (1973) *The Economics of the Real World,* Harmondsworth, Penguin.

Dosi, G and Metcalfe, J.S. (1991) 'On some notions of irreversibility in economics', in Saviotti and Metcalfe (1991).

Dosi, G. (1982) 'Technological paradigms and technological trajectories: a suggested interpretation of the determinants and directions of technical change', *Research Policy,* vol.11, no.3, pp.147-62.

Dosi, G. (1988) 'Sources, procedures, and microeconomic effects of innovation', *Journal of Economic Literature,* vol.26, pp.1120-71.

Dosi, G. and Nelson, R. (1994) 'An introduction to evolutionary theories in economics', *Journal of Evolutionary Economics,* vol.4, pp.153-72.

Dosi, G., Freeman, C., Nelson, R.R., Soete, L. and Silverberg, G. (eds) (1988) *Technical Change and Economic Theory,* London, Frances Pinter.

Dosi, G., Marsili, O., Orsenigo, L. and Salvatore, R. (1995) 'Learning, market selection and the evolution of industrial structures', *Small Business Economics,* vol.7, pp.1-26.

Drago, R. and Perlman, R. (1989) 'Supervision and high wages as competing incentives: a basis for labour segmentation theory' in Drago, R. and Perlman, R. (eds), *Microeconomic Issues in Labour Economics: New Approaches,* New York, Harvester Wheatsheaf, pp.41-61.

Dwyer, D. and Bruce, J. (1988) *A Home Divided: Women and Income in the Third World,* Stanford; CA, Stanford University Press.

Dyer and Reeves (1995) 'Human resourse strategies and firm performance: what do we know and where do we need to go?', *International Journal of Human Resource Management,* vol.6, no.3, pp.656-70.

Earl, P. (1995) *Microeconomics for Business and Marketing,* Cheltenham, Edward Elgar.

East Anglian Regional Health Authority (1990) *Contracting for Health Outcomes,* Cambridge, Office of Public Management.

Economist, February 1996.

Edwards, R.C. (1979) *Contested Terrain: The Transformation of the Workplace in the Twentieth Century,* London, Heinemann.

Ehrnberg, E. (1995) 'On the definition and measurement of technological discontinuities', *Technovation,* vol.15, no.7, pp.437-52.

Elster, J. (1992) *Local Justice,* Cambridge, Cambridge University Press.

Emerson, M. (1988) *What Models for Europe?,* Cambridge; MA, MIT Press.

Equal Opportunities Review (1995) 'Junior barristers face sex discrimination', March/April.

Estrin, S. and Laidler, D. (1995) *Introduction to Microeconomics* (4th edn), Hemel Hempstead, Harvester Wheatsheaf.

Eurostat (1992) *Fertility: Measurement and Changes in the European Community,* Luxembourg, Office for Official Publications of the European Communities.

Fagerberg, I. (1994) 'Technology and international differences in growth rates', *Journal of Economic Literature,* vol.32, pp.1147-75.

Fazey, I. H. (1996) 'Funds enjoy vintage years', *Financial Times Survey of Venture and Development Capital,* 20 September, p.1.

Fine, B. and Leopold, E. (1993) *The World of Consumption,* London, Routledge.

Flinn, M. (1984) *The History of the British Coal Industry, vol. 2, 1700-1830; The Industrial Revolution* (with the assistance of D. Stoker), Oxford, Clarendon Press.

Folbre, N. (1984) 'Market opportunities, genetic endowments and intrafamily resource distribution: comment', *American Economic Review,* vol.74, no.3, pp.518-20.

Folbre, N. (1994) *Who Pays for the Kids? Gender and the Structures of Constraint,* London, Routledge.

Folbre, N. (1997) 'Gender coalitions: extra family influences on intrafamily inequality' in Alderman, H., Haddad, L. and Hoddinott, J. (eds) *Intrahousehold Allocation in Developing Countries,* Baltimore; MD, Johns Hopkins University Press.

Folbre, N. and Hartmann, H. (1988) 'The rhetoric of self interest and the ideology of gender' in Klamer, A., McCloskey, D. and Solow, R. (eds) *The Consequences of Economics Rhetoric,* Cambridge, Cambridge University Press.

Folbre, N. and Weisskopf, W. (1997) 'Did father know best? Families, markets and the supply of caring labor', in Ben-Ner, A. and Putterman, L. (eds) *Economics, Values and Organizations,* Cambridge, Cambridge University Press.

Fox, A. (1974) *Beyond Contract: Work, Power and Trust Relations,* London, Faber.

Freeman, C. (1982) *The Economics of Industrial Innovation* (2nd edn), Cambridge; MA, MIT Press.

Freeman, C. (1988) 'Japan: a new national system of innovation?', in Dosi, G., Freeman, C., Nelson, R., Silverberg, G. and Soete, L. (eds) *Technical Change and Economic Theory,* London, Pinter.

Freeman, C. (1994) 'Marching to the sound of a different drum', paper presented at the Eunetic conference, *'Evolutionary Economics of Technological Change: Assessments of Results and New Frontiers',* Strasbourg, 6-8 October, 1994.

Freeman, C. (1994) 'The economics of technical change', *Cambridge Journal of Economics,* vol.18, pp.463-514.

Freeman, C. and Perez, C. (1988) 'Structural crises of adjustment, business cycles and investment behaviour', in Dosi, G., Freeman, C., Nelson, R., Silverberg, G. and Soete, L. (eds) *Technical Change and Economic Theory,* London, Pinter.

Friedman, D. (1978) *The Machinery of Freedom,* New York, Arlington House.

Friedman, M. (1953) 'The methodology of positive economics', in *Essays in Positive Economics,* Chicago, IL. University of Chicago Press.

Fry, F. and Parshades, P. (1986) 'The retail price index and the cost of living', London, *Institute for Fiscal Studies,* Report Series No. 22.

Gabriel, Y. and Lang, T. (1995) *The Unmanageable Consumer,* London, Sage.

Galbraith, J.K. (1958) *The Affluent Society,* Harmondsworth, Penguin.

Galbraith, J.K. (1992) *The Culture of Contentment,* London, Sinclair-Stevenson.

Garnham, N. (1993) 'Bourdieu, the cultural arbitrary and television' in Calhoun, C., LiPuma, E. and Postone, M. (eds) *Bourdieu: Critical Perspectives,* pp.178-92, Cambridge, Polity Press.

Garrahan, P. and Stewart, P. (1991) *The Nissan Enigma: Flexibility at Work in a Local Economy,* London, Mansell.

Gaskins, D.W. (1971) 'Dynamic limit pricing: optimal pricing under threat of entry' *Journal of Economic Theory,* vol.3, pp.306-22.

Gershuny, J., Godwin, M. and Jones, S. (1994) 'The domestic labour revolution: a process of lagged adaptation' in Anderson, M., Bechhofer, F. and Gershuny, J. (eds) *The Social and Political Economy of the Household,* Oxford, Oxford University Press.

Glyn, A. (1995) 'Unemployment inequality', *Oxford Review of Economic Policy,* vol.11, pp.1-25.

Godelier, M. (1973) *Perspectives in Marxist Anthropology,* Cambridge, Cambridge University Press.

Goodman, A. and Webb, S. (1994) *For Richer, For Poorer: The Changing Distribution of Income in the UK, 1961-91*, London, Institute for Fiscal Studies.

Gort, M. and Klepper, S. (1982) 'Time-paths in the diffusion of product innovation', *Economic Journal*, vol.92, pp.630-53.

Gould, S.J. (1980) 'Were dinosaurs dumb?', *The Panda's Thumb*, Harmonsworth, Penguin.

Granovetter, M. (1992) 'Economic institutions as social constructions: a framework for analysis', *Acta Sociologica*, vol.35, pp.3-11.

Gregg, P. and Wadsworth, J. (1995) 'A short history of labour turnover, job tenure and job security, 1975-93', *Oxford Review of Economic Policy*, vol.11, no.1, pp.73-90.

Gregory, C.A. (1982) *Gifts and Commodities*, London, Academic Press.

Gregory, M., Lobben, P. and Thomson, A. (1987) 'Pay settlement in manufacturing, 1979-1984', *Oxford Bulletin of Economists and Statistics*, vol.99, pp.129-50.

Griffin, J. (1986), *Well-Being: its Meaning, Measurement and Moral Importance*, Oxford, Clarendon Press.

Hahn, F. (1973) *On the Notion of Equilibrium in Economics*, Cambridge, Cambridge University Press.

Hahn, F. (1987) 'Auctioneer' pp.136-8 in Eatwell, J., Milgate, M. and Newman, P. (eds) *The New Palgrave: A Dictionary of Economics*, London, Macmillan.

Ham, C., Robinson, R. and Benzeval, M. (1990) *Health Check: Health Care Reforms in an International Context*, London, Kings Fund Institute.

Hamermesh, D. (1993) *Labour Demand*, Princeton; NJ, Princeton University Press.

Hamermesh, D. (1996) *The Economics of Work and Pay* (6th edn), New York, HarperCollins.

Hammer, M. and Champy J. (1993) *Reengineering the Corporation: A Manifesto for Business Revolution*, London, Nicholas Brealey Publishing.

Hansard (1975) House of Commons, 13 May, London, HMSO.

Hansmann, H. (1987) 'Economic theories of nonprofit organization', in Powell, W. (ed.) *The Nonprofit Sector: A Research Handbook*, New Haven; CT, Yale University Press.

Hargreaves-Heap, S. (1988) *Rationality in Economics*, Oxford, Blackwell.

Hargreaves-Heap, S. (1992) 'Bandwagon effects', in Hargreaves-Heap, S., Hollis, M., Sugden, R. and Weale, A. *The Theory of Choice: A Critical Guide*, Oxford, Blackwell.

Hargreaves-Heap, S.P. and Varoufakis, V. (1995) *Game Theory: A Critical Introduction*, London and New York, Routledge.

Harkness, S., Machin, S. and Waldfogel, J. (1996) 'Women's pay and family incomes in Britain, 1979-91' in Hills, J.

(ed.) *New Inequalities*, Cambridge, Cambridge University Press.

Hart, O. (1989) 'An economist's perspective on the theory of the firm', *Columbia Law Review*, No.1757; reprinted in Buckley, P.S. and Michie, S. (eds) (1996) *Firms, Organisations and Contracts*, Oxford, Oxford University Press.

Hart, P.E., Mills, G. and Whitaker, J.K. (eds) (1964) *Econometric Analysis for National Economic Planning*, London, Butterworth.

Hart, R. and Kawasaki, S. (1988) 'Payroll taxes and factor demand', *Research in Labour Economics*, vol.9, pp.257-85.

Hartmann, H. (1981) 'The family as the locus of gender, class and political struggle: the example of housework' *Signs*, vol.6, no.3, Spring, pp.366-94.

Hartwell, R.M. (1971) *The Industrial Revolution and Economic Growth*, London, Methuen.

Haskell, J. and Martin, C. (1994) 'Will low skills kill recovery?', *New Economy*, vol.1, pp.135-9.

Hausman, D.M. and MacPherson, M.S. (1996) *Economic analysis and moral philosophy*, Cambridge, Cambridge University Press.

Hayek, F. (1945) 'The use of knowledge in society', *American Economic Review*, vol. 35, no.4, September, pp.519-30.

Hayek, F. (1982) *Law, Legislation and Liberty: A New Statement of the Liberal Principles of Justice and Political Economy*, London, Routledge and Kegan Paul.

Henderson, D. (1986) *Innocence and Design: The Influence of Economic Ideas on Policy*, Oxford and New York, Basil Blackwell.

Henderson, R. (1993) *European Finance*, London, McGraw-Hill.

Hey, J.D. (1991) *Experiments in Economics*, Oxford, Blackwell.

Hicks, J. (1935) 'Annual survey of economic theory: the theory of monopoly', *Economica*, vol.3, no.8.

Hills, J. (1991) *Unravelling Housing Finance: Subsidies, Benefits and Taxation*, Oxford, Clarendon Press.

Hirschman, A.O. (1970) *Exit, Voice and Loyalty: Responses to Decline in Firms, Organizations and States*, Cambridge, Mass., Harvard University Press.

Hirst, P. (1994) *Associative Democracy*, Cambridge, Polity Press.

Hoddinott, J. and Haddad, L. (1995) 'Does female income share influence household expenditure? Evidence from the Cote d'Ivoire', *Oxford Bulletin of Economics and Statistics*, vol.57, no.6, February, pp.77-96.

Hodgson, G.M. (1988) *Economics and Institutions*, Cambridge, Polity Press.

Hodgson, G.M. (1993) *Economics and Evolution: Bringing Life Back into Economics*, Cambridge, Polity Press.

Hollander, S. (1965) *The Sources of Increased Efficiency: A Study of DuPont Rayon Plants*, Cambridge; Mass., MIT Press.

Hughes, P. (1986) 'The changing picture of male unemployment in Britain', *Oxford Bulletin of Economics & Statistics*, vol.48, pp.309-30.

Humphries, J. and Rubery, J. (1992) 'The legacy for women's employment: integration, differentiation and polarisation' in Mitchie, J. (ed.) *The Economic Legacy 1979-1992*, London, Academic Press.

Hutton, W. (1995) *The State We're In*, London, Jonathan Cape.

ISTAT (1988) 'Indagine statistica sull'innovazione technologica nell'industria italiana', *Notiziario*, vol.4, no.41, Issue 13, December.

Jackman, R. and Layard, R. (1991) 'Does long term unemployment reduce a person's chance of a job?', *Economica*, vol.58, pp.93-106.

Jackman, R., Layard, R. and Pissarides, C. (1989) 'On vacancies', *Oxford Bulletin of Economics and Statistics*, vol.51, no.4, pp.377-94.

Jackman, R., Layard, R. and Sevouri, S. (1990) 'Mismatch: a framework for thought' in Padoa *et al.* (eds) *Mismatch and Labour Mobility*, Cambridge, Cambridge University Press.

Jacoby, S. (1990) 'The new institutionalism: what can it learn from the old?', *Industrial Relations*, vol.29, pp.316-41.

Jenkins, R. (1992) *Pierre Bourdieu*, London, Routledge.

Jevons, S. (1871) *The Theory of Political Economy*, London, Macmillan.

Jordan, B., James, S., Kay, H. and Redley, M. (1991) *Trapped in Poverty? Labour Market Decisions and Low-Income Households*, London, Routledge.

Jorde, T.M. and Teece, D.J. (1990) 'Innovation and cooperation: implications for competition and antitrust', *Journal of Economic Perspectives*, vol.4, pp.75-95.

Joshi, H., Layard, R. and Owen, S. (1985) 'Why are more women working in Britain?', *Journal of Labor Economics*, no.3, Supplement, S147-S176.

Jovanovic, B. (1982) 'Selection and evolution of industry', *Econometrica*, vol.50, no.2, pp.649-70.

Jovanovic, B. and Nyarko, Y. (1995) 'A bayesian learning model fitted to a variety of empirical learning curves', *Brookings Papers on Economic Activity*, pp.247-305.

Jowell, R., Brook, L., Taylor, B. and Prior, G. (1991) *British Social Attitudes: The 18th Report*, Dartmouth, Aldershot

Kabeer, N. (1994) *Reversed Realities: Gender Hierarchies in Development Thought*, London, Verso.

Kabeer, N. (1995) 'Necessary, sufficient or irrelevant: women, wages and intra-household power relations in urban Bangladesh', Institute of Development Studies Working Paper 25, University of Sussex.

Kaldor, N. (1978a) 'Stylized facts as a basis for theory building', in Kaldor, N. (1978) *Economics Without Equilibrium*.

Kaldor, N. (1978b) 'Capital accumulation and economic growth' in Kaldor, N. (1978) *Further Essays on Economic Theory*, London, Duckworth.

Kaplan, A.D.H. (1954) 'Big Enterprise in a Competitive System', Washington DC, The Brookings Institution.

Kawasaki, S. and Macmillan, J. (1987) 'The design of contracts: evidence from Japanese subcontracting', *Journal of Japanese and International Economics*, vol. 1, pp.327-49.

Kay, J. (1993) *Foundations of Corporate Success*, Oxford, Oxford University Press.

Kester, W.C. (1992) 'Industrial groups as systems of contractual governance', *Oxford Review of Economic Policy*, vol.8, no.3, pp.25-44.

Key Note (1996) *KeyNote Plus Market Report: Soft Drinks (Carbonated and Concentrated)* (12th Edition), KeyNote, Hampton, Mddx.

Keynes, J.M. (1936) *The General Theory of Employment, Interest and Money*, London, Macmillan.

Klepper, S. (1992) 'Entry, exit and innovation over the product life cycle: The dynamics of first mover advantages, declining product innovation and market failure', paper presented at the *Conference of the International J.A. Schumpeter Society*, Kyoto, August.

Klepper, S. and Graddy, E. (1992) 'The evolution of new industries and the determination of market structure', *Rand Journal of Economics*, vol.21, pp.27-44.

Kochan, T., Katz, H. and McKersie, R. (1986) *The Transformation of American Industrial Relations*, New York, Basic.

Kotler, P., Armstrong, G., Saunders, J. and Wong, V. (1996) *Principles of Marketing*, Hemel Hempstead, Prentice Hall Europe.

Kreps, D. (1986) 'Corporate culture and economic theory' reprinted in Buckley B. and Michie J. (eds) *Firms, Organizations and Constructs,* Oxford, Oxford University Press.

Kreps, D.M. (1988) 'Corporate culture and economic theory' in Alt, J. and Shepsle, K. (eds), *Positive Perspectives on Political Economy,* Cambridge, Cambridge University Press.

Kreps, D.M. (1990) *Game Theory and Economic Modelling*, Oxford, Clarendon Press.

Krueger, A. and Summers, L. (1988) 'Efficiency wages and the inter-industry wage structure', *Econometrica*, vol.56, pp.259-93.

Lamont, M. and Lareau, A.P. (1988) 'Cultural capital: allusions, gaps, and glissandos in recent theoretical developments', *Sociological Theory*, 6.2, pp.153-68.

Landes, D.S. (1969) *The Unbound Prometheus: Technological Change and Industrial Development in Western Europe from 1750 to the Present*, Cambridge, Cambridge University Press.

Langwell, K.M. (1990) 'Structure and performance of HMOs: a review', *Health Care Financing Review,* vol.12, no.1, pp.71-9.

Lawson, T. (1985) 'Uncertainty and economic analysis', *Economic Journal*, vol.95, December, pp.909-27.

Layard, R. (1979) 'The costs and benefits of selective employment policies: the British case', *British Journal of Industrial Relations*, vol.17, pp.187-204.

Layard, R. and Nickell, S. (1990) 'The case for subsidising extra jobs', *Economic Review,* vol.90, pp.51-73.

Le Grand, J. (1997) 'Knights, knaves or pawns? Human behaviour and social policy' *Journal of Social Policy*, vol.26, no.2, pp.149-69.

Leibenstein, H. (1950) 'Bandwagon, snob and Veblen effects', *Quarterly Journal of Economics,* 64, pp.183-207

Leibenstein, H. (1966) 'Allocative efficiency vs. *X*-efficiency', *American Economic Review*, vol.56 (June), pp.392-415.

Levine, D. and Tyson, L. (1990) 'Participation, productivity and the firm's environment' in Blinder, A. (ed) *Paying for Productivity*, Washington D.C., Brookings Institute.

Levine, R., Cohen, W.M. and Mowery, D.C. (1985) 'R&D, appropriability, opportunity and market structure: New evidence on some Schumpeterian hypotheses, *American Economic Review,* vol.75, no.2, pp.20-4.

Levine, R., Klevorick, A.K., Nelson, R.R. and Winter, S.G. (1987) 'Appropriating the results from industrial research and development', *Brook Papers on Economics Activity*, vol.3, pp.783-820.

Littlechild, S. (1978) *The Fallacy of the Mixed Economy*, London, Institute of Economic Affairs.

Lundberg, S.J. and Pollak, R.A. (1993) 'Separate spheres bargaining and the marriage market' *Journal of Political Economy,* vol.10, no.6, December, pp.988-1010.

Lundberg, S.J., Pollak, R.A. and Wales, T.J. (1995) 'Do husbands and wives pool their resource? Evidence from the UK child benefit' (mimeo), University of Washington, Seattle.

Lundvall, B. (ed.) (1992) *National Systems of Innovation: Towards a Theory of Innovation and Interactive Learning*, London, Pinter.

Lyons, B.R. (1996) 'Empirical relevance of efficient contract theory: inter-firm contracts', *Oxford Review of Economic Policy*, vol. 12, no. 4, pp.27-52.

MacDuffie, J.P. (1995) 'Human resource bundles and manufacturing performance: organizational logic and flexible production systems in the world industry', *Industrial and Labor Relations Review,* vol.48, pp.197-220.

MacDuffie, J.P. and Kochan, T.A. (1995) 'Do US firms invest less in human resources? Training in the world auto industry', *Industrial Relations*, vol.34, pp.147-68.

Machin, S. (1995) 'Changes in the relative demand for skills in the UK labour market' in Booth, A. and Snower, D. (eds) *Acquiring Skills*, Cambridge, Cambridge University Press.

Machlup, F. (1946) 'Marginal analysis and empirical research', *American Economic Review,* vol.57, pp.1-33.

Mackintosh, M. (1997) 'Economic culture and quasi-markets in local government: the case of contracting for social care', *Local Government Studies*, vol.23, no.2, pp.80-102.

Maddison, A. (1995) *Monitoring the World Economy 1820-1992*, Paris, OECD.

Malerba, F. and Orsenigo, L. (1994) 'The dynamics of evolution of industries', paper presented at the Eunetic Conference, *'Evolutionary Economics of Technological Change: Assessments of Results and New Frontiers'*, Strasbourg, 6-8 October, 1994.

Manne, H.G. (1965) 'Mergers and the market for corporate control' *Journal of Political Economy*, no.73, pp.110-20.

Manser, M. and Brown, M. (1980) 'Marriage and household decision making: a bargaining analysis', *International Economic Review,* vol.21, no.1, February, pp.31-44.

Marris, R. (1964) *The Economic Theory of Managerial Capitalism*, London, Macmillan.

Marshall, A. (1907) *Principles of Economics* (5th edn), London, Macmillan.

Marshall, A. (1978) *Principles of Economics* (8th edn), London, Macmillan.

Marx, K. (1867) *Capital*, vol.1, Chicago, Kerr (1912).

Mason, C. (1991) 'Spatial variations in enterprise: the geography of new firm formation' in Burrows, R. (ed.) *Deciphering the Enterprise Culture: Entrepreneurship, Petty Capitalism and the Restructuring of Britain*, London, Routledge.

Mason, R.S. (1981) *Conspicuous Consumption*, Aldershot, Gower.

Matthews, R.C.O. (1991) 'The economics of professional ethics: should the professions be more business-like?', *The Economic Journal*, 10 July.

Mauss, M. (1974) *The Gift,* London, Routledge and Kegan Paul (first published in 1925).

Mayhew, K. (1991) 'Training: the way ahead', in *Improving Britain's Industrial Performance*, Employment Institute.

Mayhew, K. (1994) 'Labour market woes', *New Economy*, vol.1, pp.68-73.

Mayhew, K. and Rosewell, B. (1979) 'Labour market segmentation in Britain', *Oxford Bulletin of Economics and Statistics*, vol.41, no.2, pp.81-116.

McClements, L. (1977) 'Equivalence scales for children', *Journal of Public Economics*, vol.8, pp.191-210.

McCracken, G. (1988) *Culture and Consumption*, Bloomington, Indiana University Press.

McElroy, M.B. and Horney, M.J. (1981) 'Nash bargained household decisions', *International Economic Review*, vol. 22, no. 2, June, pp. 333–49.

McKendrick, N., Brewer, J. and Plumb, J.H. (1982) *The Birth of a Consumer Society, the Commercialization of Eighteenth-century England*, London, Europa.

McNabb, R. (1987) 'Testing for labour market segmentation in Britain', Manchester Business School, no. 3, pp. 257–273.

McNabb, R. and Psacharopoulos, G. (1981) 'Further evidence on the relevance of the dual labour market theory for the UK', *Journal of Human Resources*, vol. 16, no. 3, pp. 442–8.

McNabb, R. and Ryan, P. (1990) 'Segmented labour markets', in Sapsford, D. and Tzannatos, Z. (eds) *Current Issues in Labour Economics*, London, Macmillan.

McNabb, R. and Wass, V. (1996) 'Gender discrimination in salary levels and promotion probabilities', Cardiff Business School Discussion Paper in Economics, 95-021.

McNabb, R. and Wass, V. (1997) 'Male-female salary differential in British universities', *Oxford Economic Papers*.

McNabb, R. and Whitfield, K. (1996) 'Labour market segmentation in Britain: evidence from the Third Workplace Industrial Relations Survey', Cardiff Business School Discussion Paper in Economics, 95-022.

McNabb, R. and Whitfield, K. (1998) 'Financial participation, employee involvement and financial participation', *Scottish Journal of Political Economy*.

Meager, N. and Metcalf, H. (1987) 'Recruitment of the long term unemployed', Report No. 138, *Institute of Manpower Studies*.

Messer, E. (1990) 'Intra-household allocation of resources: perspectives from anthropology' in Rogers, B.L. and Schlossman, N.P. (eds) *Intra-household Resource Allocation*, Tokyo, United Nations University Press.

Metcalfe, J.S. (1993) 'Competition, evolution and the capital market', paper presented for the *Metroeconomica Conference on Alternative approaches to competition*, Venice, Italy, May, 1993.

Metcalfe, J.S. (1994) 'Completion, Fisher's principle and increasing returns in the selection process', *Journal of Evolution Economics*, vol. 4, pp. 327–46.

Mies, M. (1982) *The Lacemakers of Narsapur: Indian Housewives Produce for the World Market*, London, Zed Books.

Milgrom, P. and Roberts, J. (1990 and 1992) *Economics, Organization and Management*, Englewood Cliffs; NJ, Prentice Hall International.

Miller, B.D. (1981) *The Endangered Sex: Neglect of Female Children in Rural North India*, Ithaca; NY, Cornell University Press.

Mincer, J. (1962) 'Labour force participation of married women: a study of labour supply' in *Aspects of Labour Economics: A Report of the National Bureau of Economic Research*, Princeton, Princeton University Press.

Mincer, J. (1985) 'Intercountry comparisons of labor force trends and of related developments', *Journal of Labor Economics*, no. 3, Supplement, S1–S32.

Mirowski, P. (1989) *More Heat than Light*, Cambridge, Cambridge University Press.

Mishan, E. (1982) *Introduction to Political Economy*, London, Hutchinson.

Mishan, E.J. (1961) 'Theories of consumer's behaviour: a cynical view', *Economica*, February, pp. 1–15.

Morgan, J. (1996) 'What do comparisons of the last two economic recessions tell us about the UK labour market?, *National Institute Economic Review*, May.

Morishima, M. (1982) *Why Has Japan 'Succeeded'? Western Technology and the Japanese Ethos*, Cambridge, Cambridge University Press.

Mowery, D. and Rosenberg, N. (1979) 'The influence of market demand upon innovation: a critical review of some recent empirical studies', *Research Policy*, vol. 8, pp. 102–53.

Mueller, D.C. (ed.) (1990) *The Dynamics of Company Profits*, Cambridge, Cambridge University Press.

Nahulm, A. (1981) *James Watt and the Power of Steam*, Hove, Wayland.

Nash, J.F. (1950) 'The bargaining problem', *Econometrica*, vol. 18, no. 1, April, pp. 155–62.

NBER (ed.) (1962) *The Rate and Direction of Inventive Activity*, Princeton; NJ, Princeton University Press.

Neave, E.H. (1989) *The Economic Organization of a Financial System*, London and New York, Routledge.

Nelson, J.A. (1996) *Feminism, Objectivity and Economics*, London, Routledge.

Nelson, R.R. (1962) 'The link between science and invention: the case of the transistor', in National Bureau of Economic Research, *The Rate and Direction of Inventive Activity*, Princeton; NJ, Princeton University Press.

Nelson, R.R. (ed.) (1992) *National Innovation Systems: A Comparative Analysis*, Oxford, Oxford University Press.

Nelson, R.R. (1995) 'Recent evolutionary theorizing about economic change', *Journal of Economic Literature*, vol. 33, pp. 48–90.

Nelson, R.R. and Winter, S.E. (1977) 'In search of useful theory of innovation' *Research Policy*, vol. 6, pp. 36–76.

Nelson, R.R. and Winter, S.E. (1982) *An Evolutionary Theory of Economic Change*, Cambridge; MA, Harvard University Press.

Newman, P. (1978) 'Francis Ysidro Edgeworth', pp. 84–98, in Eatwell J., Milgate M. and Newman P. (eds) *The New Palgrave: A Dictionary of Economics*, London, Macmillan.

Nickell, S. (1996) 'Can unemployment in the UK be reduced?', in Halpen, D., Wood, S., White, S. and Cameron, G. (eds) *Options for Britain*, Aldershot, Dartmouth.

Nickell, S. and Wadhwani, S. (1990) 'Insider forces and wage determination', *Economic Journal*, vol. 100, pp. 496–509.

Nickell, S., Wadhwani, S. and Wall, M. (1992) 'Productivity growth in UK companies 1975-1986', *European Economic Review*, vol. 36, pp. 1055–85.

Nolan, P. (1983) 'The firm and the labour market', in Bain, G.S. (ed.), *Industrial Relations in Britain*, Oxford, Basil Blackwell, pp. 291–310.

Nozick, R. (1974) *Anarchy, State, and Utopia*, Oxford, Basil Blackwell.

Nussbaum, M. (1995) 'Introduction', in Nussbaum, M. and Glover, J. (eds) (1995).

Nussbaum, M. and Glover, J. (eds) (1995) *Women, Culture and Development: a Study of Human Capabilities*, Oxford, Clarendon Press.

Nussbaum, M. and Sen, A. (eds) (1993) *The Quality of Life*, Oxford, Clarendon Press.

OECD (1992) *Technology and the Economy: the Key Relationships*, Paris, OECD.

OECD (1997) 'OECD in Figures', *OECD Observer*, June/July

OECD (1997) *Economic Outlook: Historical Statistics 1960-1990*, Paris, OECD

Office of Population Census and Surveys, Social Survey Division (1976) *General Household Survey 1975*, London, HMSO.

Office of Population Census and Surveys, Social Survey Division (1992) *1991 Census*, London, HMSO.

Okun, A. (1981) *Prices and Quantities: A Macroeconomic Analysis*, Oxford, Basil Blackwell.

Oliver, N. and Wilkinson, B. (1993) 'Japanization in the UK: Experiences from the car industry', in Gowler, D., Legge, K. and Clegg, C. (eds) *Case Studies in Organizational Behaviour and Human Resource Management*, London, Paul Chapman Publishing, pp. 30–41.

Osterman, P. (1994) 'How common is workplace transformation and who adopts it?', *Industrial and Labor Relations Review*, vol. 47, no. 2, pp. 173–88.

Ouchi, W. (1980) 'Markets, bureaucracies and clans', *Administrative Science Quarterly*, pp. 129–41.

Oughton, E.A. (1992) *Vulnerability, Seasonality and the Public Distribution System in Western India: A Micro-level Study*, University of Newcastle upon Tyne, unpublished Ph.D.

Oulton, N. (1990) 'Labour productivity and unit labour costs in manufacturing: the UK and its competitors', *National Institute Economic Review*, May, pp. 49–60.

Oulton, N. (1994) 'Supply side reform and UK economic growth: what happened to the miracle?', *National Institute Economic Review*, November, pp. 53–69.

Pahl, J. (1995) 'His money, her money: recent research on financial organisation in marriage', *Journal of Economic Psychology*, vol. 16, pp. 361–76.

Pareto, V. (1971) *Manual of Political Economy*, London, Macmillan (first published 1909, revised edition 1927).

Patel, P. and Pavitt, K. (1994) 'Technological competencies in the world's largest firms: characteristics, constraints and scope for managerial choice', mimeo, Brighton, Science Policy Research Unit, University of Sussex, March.

Pavitt, K. (1984) 'Sectoral patterns of technical change: towards a taxonomy and a theory', *Research Policy*, vol. 13, no. 6, pp. 343–73.

Pavitt, K. (1991) 'What makes basic research economically useful?', *Research Policy*, vol. 20, pp. 109–19.

Peacock, T.L. (1831) *Crotchet Castle*, London (Penguin edition, 1969).

Pencaval, J. (1975) 'A note on the use of unemployment and vacancy statistics to measure some effects of government legislation', Standard University Working Paper, 94305.

Penrose, E.T. (1959) *The Theory of Growth of the Firm*, Oxford, Blackwell.

Pentelow, M. (1996) 'Docks: the payback', *The Record*, Transport and General Workers Union Publications.

People Management, 6 February 1997, p. 16

Perloff, J. and Wachter, M. (1979) 'The new jobs tax credit: an evaluation of the 1997-78 wage subsidy programe', American Economics Association, *Papers and Proceedings*, vol. 69, pp. 173–9.

Personnel Management, December 1992

Personnel Management, May 1993

Pescatrice, D.R. and Trapani, J.M. (1980) 'The performance and objective of public and private utilities operating in the US', *Journal of Public Economics*, vol. 13, pp. 259–76.

Phipps, S. and Burton, P. (1992) 'What's mine is yours? The influence of male and female incomes on patterns of household expenditure', Working Paper 92-12, Department of Economics, Dalhousie University.

Pigou, A.C. (1920) *The Economics of Welfare*, London, Macmillan.

Piore, M.J. and Sabel, C.F. (1984) *The Second Industrial Divide*, New York, Basic.

Polanyi, K. (1946) *Origins of our Time: The Great Transformation*, London, Victor Gollancz.

Ponting, C. (1994) *Churchill*, London, Sinclair-Stevenson.

Porter, M. (1992) 'Capital disadvantage: America's failing capital investment system', *Harvard Business Review*, September/October, pp. 65–82.

Prais, S. (1994) 'Vocational qualifications of the labour force in Britain and Germany', *National Institute Economic Review*.

Prais, S.J. (1976) *The Evolution of Giant Firms in Britain*, Cambridge, Cambridge University Press.

Price, D. de S. (1984) 'The science/technology relationship, the craft of experimental science an policy for the improvement of high technology innovation', *Research Policy*, vol.13, no.1, pp.3-20.

Prowse, S. (1994) 'Corporate governance in an international perspective: a survey of corporate control mechanisms among large firms in the United States, the United Kingdom, Japan and Germany', Bank of International Settlements, *Economic Papers*, no.41, July.

Putnam, R. (1993) *Making Democracy Work: Civic Traditions in Modern Italy*, Princeton; NJ, Princeton University Press.

Rawls, J. (1972) *A Theory of Justice*, Oxford, Oxford University Press.

Rebitzer, J. (1993) 'Radical political economy and the economics of the labour market', *Journal of Economic Literature*, no.31, pp.1394-1434.

Rees, R. (1993a) 'Tacit collusion', *Oxford Review of Economic Policy*, vol.9, pp.27-40.

Rees, R. (1993b) 'Collusion equilibrium in the great salt duopoly', *Economic Journal*, vol.103, pp.833-48.

Reich, R.B. (1984) *The Next American Frontier: A Provocative Program for Economic Renewal*, New York, Penguin USA.

Reid, M. (1934) *The Economics of Household Production*, New York, John Wiley and Sons.

Reiman, J. (1991) 'Moral philosophy: the critique of capitalism and the problem of ideology', in Carver, T. (1991), pp.143-67.

Reisman, D. (1980) *Galbraith and Market Capitalism*, London, Macmillan.

Ricketts, M. (1994) *The Economics of Business Enterprise*, 2nd edn, Hemel Hempstead, Harvester Wheatsheaf.

Robbins, L. (1935) *An Essay on the Nature and Significance of Economic Science*, 2nd edn, London, Macmillan (first published 1932).

Roberts, P. (1991) 'Anthropological perspectives on the household', *IDS Bulletin*, vol.1, pp.60-4.

Robinson, J.C. and Casalino, L.P. (1996) 'Vertical integration and organizational networks in health care', *Health Affairs*, vol.15, no.1, pp.7-22.

Robinson, P. (1995) 'Evolution not revolution', *New Economy*, vol.2, pp.167-72.

Robinson, W.T. and Chiang, J. (1996) 'Are Sutton's predictions robust?: Empirical insights into advertising, R&D, and concentration', *The Journal of Industrial Economics*, vol.44, pp.389-408.

Roe, M.J. (1994) *Strong Managers, Weak Owners: The Political Roots of American Corporate Finance*, Princeton; NJ, Princeton University Press.

Rosenberg, N. (1976) *Perspectives on Technology*, Cambridge, Cambridge University Press.

Rosenberg, N. (1982) *Inside the Black Box: Technology and Economics*, Cambridge, Cambridge University Press.

Rosenberg, N. (1992) 'Economic experiments' *Industrial and Corporate Change*, vol.1, no.1, pp.181-203.

Rosengren, K.E. (1995) 'Substantive theories and formal models - Bourdieu confronted', *European Journal of Communication*, 10.1, p.7-39.

Rosenzweig, M.R. and Schultz, T.P. (1982) 'Market opportunities, genetic endowment, and the intrafamily resource distribution: child survival in rural India', *American Economic Review*, vol.72, no.4, September, pp.803-15.

Rothschild & Sons, *The London Gold Fixing*, information pamphlet, London, N.M. Rothschild & Sons Limited.

Rothschild, K. (1993) *Ethics and Economic Theory: Ideas - Models - Dilemmas*, Aldershot, Edward Elgar.

Rubery, J. and Wilkinson, F. (eds.) (1994) *Employer Strategy and the Labour Market*, Oxford University Press, Oxford.

Sahal, D. (1985) 'Technology guide-posts and innovation avenues', *Research Policy*, vol.14, no.2, pp.61-82.

Sako, M. (1992) *Prices, Quality and Trust: Inter-firm Relations in Britain and Japan*, Cambridge, Cambridge University Press.

Samuels, W.J. (1987) 'Institutional Economics' in Eatwell J., Milgate M. and Newman P. (eds) *The New Palgrave: A Dictionary of Economics*, London, Macmillan.

Samuelson P.A. (1938) 'A note on the pure theory of consumers' behaviour', *Economica*, vol.5, pp.61-71.

Samuelson, P.A. (1956) 'Social indifference curves', *The Quarterly Journal of Economics*, vol.70, no.1, February, pp.1-21.

Saviotti, P.P. and Metcalfe, J.S. (1991) 'Present developments and trends in evolutionary economics', in Saviotti and Metcalfe (eds).

Saviotti, P.P. and Metcalfe, J.S. (eds) (1991) *Evolutionary Theories of Economic and Technological change: Present Status and Future Prospects*, Chur, Harwood Academic Publishers.

Schelling, T.C. (1956) 'A essay on bargaining', *American Economic Review*, vol.46, pp.281-306.

Scherer, F.M. (1984) *Innovation and Growth: Schumpeterian Perspectives*, Cambridge; MA, MIT Press.

Scherer, F.M. and Perlman, M. (eds) (1990) *Entrepreneurship, Technological Innovation, and Economic Growth Studies in the Schumpeterian Tradition*, Ann Arbor, The University of Michigan Press.

Scherer, F.M. and Ross, D. (1990) *Industrial Market Structure and Economic Performance* (3rd edn), Boston; MA, Houghton Mifflin Co.

Scherer, M. (1996) 'Learning-by-doing and international trade in semiconductors' in Helmstädter, E. and Perlman, M. (eds.), *Behavioral Norms, Technological Progress and Economic Dynamics*, Ann Arbor, The University of Michigan Press.

Schmookler, J. (1966) *Invention and Economic Growth*, Cambridge; MA, Harvard University Press.

Schneider-Lenne, E. R. (1992), 'Corporate control in Germany', *Oxford Review of Economic Policy*, vol.8, no.3, pp.11-23.

Schumpeter, J.A. (1961) *The Theory of Economic Development* (first edition 1911, second edition 1926), New York, Oxford University Press.

Schumpeter, J.A. (1987) *Capitalism, Socialism and Democracy* (first UK edition 1943), London, Unwin Paperbacks.

Sellers, P. (1996) 'How Coke is kicking Pepsi's can', *Fortune*, 28 October, pp.30-8.

Sen, A. (1982) 'Equality of what?', Chapter 16 of *Choice, Welfare and Measurement*, Oxford, Basil Blackwell; originally published in *The Tanner Lectures on Human Values* (1980), vol.1, Cambridge, Cambridge University Press.

Sen, A. (1987) *On Ethics and Economics*, Oxford, Basil Blackwell.

Sen, A. (1990) 'Gender and cooperative conflicts' in Tinker, I. (ed.) *Persistent Inequalities: Women and World Development*, Oxford, Oxford University Press.

Sen, A. (1993) 'Capability and well-being', in Nussbaum and Sen (eds) (1993).

Shackle, G.S. (1972) *Epistemics and Economics*, Cambridge, Cambridge University Press.

Shapiro, C. (1989) 'Theories of oligopoly behavior', in Schmalensee, R. and Willig, R.D. (eds.) *Handbook of Industrial Organization*, vol.1, pp.330-414, Netherlands, North-Holland.

Sharpe, M.E. (1973) *John Kenneth Galbraith and the Lower Economics*, London, Macmillan.

Silverberg, G. (1988) 'Modelling evolutionary change', in Dosi *et al.* (1988).

Silverberg, G., Dosi, G. and Orsenigo, L. (1988) 'Innovation, diversity and diffusion: A self-organising model', *Economic Journal*, vol.98, pp.1032-55.

Simon, H.A, (1957) *Models of Man*, New York, Wiley.

Simon, H.A. (1959) 'Theories of decision making in economics and behavioural science', *American Economic Review*, vol.49, June, pp.253-83.

Singh, S., Utton, M. and Waterson, M. (1997) 'Strategic behaviour of incumbent firms in the UK', *International Journal of Industrial Organization*, pp.1-23.

Sippel, R. (1997) 'An experiment on the pure theory of consumer's behaviour', *Economic Journal*, **107** (444).

Smiley, R. (1988) 'Empirical evidence on strategic entry deterrence', *International Journal of Industrial Organization*, vol.6, pp.167-80.

Smith, A. (1776) *An Inquiry into the Nature and Causes of the Wealth of Nations*, (1971 edn, eds Campbell, R.H. and Skinner, A.S., Oxford, Clarendon Press).

Smith, A. (1853) *The Theory of Moral Sentiments*, London, Henry G. Bohn (first published in 1759).

Snell, M., Glucklich, P. and Povall, M. (1981) *Equal Pay and Opportunity*, Department of Employment, Research Paper no.20.

Solow, R. (1957) 'Technical change and the aggregate production function', *Review of Economics and Statistics*, vol.39, no.3, pp.312-20.

Strawson, P.F. (1959) *Individuals: An Essay in Descriptive Metaphysics*, London, Methuen.

Stubbs, C. and Wheelock, J. (1990) *A Woman's Work in the Changing Local Economy*, Aldershot, Avebury.

Sutton, J. (1991) *Sunk Costs and Market Structure: Price Competition, Advertising, and the Evolution of Concentration*, Cambridge; Mass, MIT Press.

Swann, P. and Gill, J. (1993) *Corporate Vision and Rapid Technological Change: The Evolution of Market Structure*, London and New York, Routledge.

Symanski, S. (1996) 'The impact of compulsory competitive tendering on refuse collection services', *Fiscal Studies*, vol.17, no.3, August.

Symanski, S. and Wilkins, S. (1993) 'Cheap rubbish? Competitive tendering and contracting out in refuse collection, 1981-88', *Fiscal Studies*, vol.14, no.3, August.

Tawney, R.H. (1942) *Religion and the Rise of Capitalism*, Harmondsworth, Penguin.

Teece, D.J. (1986) 'Profiting from technological innovation', *Research Policy*, vol.15, pp.286-305.

Teece, D.J., Pisano, G. and Shuen, A. (1990) 'Firm capabilities, resources and the concept of strategy', *CCC Working Papers*, University of California at Berkeley, No. 90-8.

Teece, D.J., Rumelt, R., Dosi, G. and Winter, S. (1994) 'Understanding corporate coherence: Theory and evidence', *Journal of Economic Behaviour and Organization*, vol.23. pp.1-30.

Thomas, D. (1990) 'Intra-household resource allocation: an inferential approach' *Journal of Human Resources*, vol.25, no.4, Fall, pp.635-64.

Thomas, D. (1994) 'Like father, like son: like mother, like daughter: parental resources and child height' *Journal of Human Resources*, vol.29, no.4, Fall, pp.950-88.

Tiebout, C. (1956) 'A pure theory of local expenditures', *Journal of Political Economy*, vol.65, pp.416-24.

Titmuss, R.M. (1970) *The Gift Relationship*, London, George Allen and Unwin.

Trigg, A.B. (2001) 'Veblen, Bourdieu and Conspicuous Consumption' *Journal of Economic Issues*, March.

Tushman, M. and Anderson, P. (1986) 'Technological discontinuities and organizational environments', *Administrative Science Quarterly*, vol.31, pp.439-65.

Tylecote, A. (1987) 'Time horizons of management decisions: causes and effects', *Journal of Economic Studies*, vol.14, no.4, pp.51-64.

Tylecote, A. and Demirag, I. (1992) 'Short-termism: culture and structures as factors in technological innovation', pp.201-25, in Coombs, R., Walsh, V. and Saviotti, P. (eds) *Technological Change and Company Strategies*, London, Academic Press.

Ungerson, C. (1995) 'Gender, cash and informal care: European perspectives and dilemmas' *Journal of Social Policy*, vol.24-1, pp.31-52.

United Nations (1992) *World Population Monitoring 1991*, New York, United Nations.

United Nations Development Programme (1995) *Human Development Report 1995*, Oxford, UNDP/OUP.

Utterback, J.M. and Abernathy, W.J. (1975) 'A dynamic model of process and product innovation', *OMEGA*, vol.3, no.6.

Varian, H.R. (1982) 'The nonparametric approach to demand analysis', *Econometrica*, vol.50, pp.945-73.

Vaughn, K.I. (1980.) 'Economic calculation under socialism: the Austrian contribution', *Economic Inquiry*, vol.18, pp.535-54.

Veblen, T. (1889) *The Theory of the Leisure Class*, New York, Dover (1994 edn.).

Vickers, J. (1985) 'Strategic competition among the few – some recent developments in the economics of industry', *Oxford Review of Economic Policy*, vol.1, pp.39-62.

Vietorisz, T. and Harrison, B. (1973) 'Labor market segmentation: positive feedback and divergent development', *American Economic Review*, no.63, pp.366-76.

Wacquant, L.J.D. (1993) 'Bourdieu in America: notes on the transatlantic importation of social theory' in Calhoun, C., LiPuma, E. and Postone, M. (eds) *Bourdieu: Critical Perspectives*, pp.235-62, Cambridge, Polity Press.

Wadsworth, J. (1994) 'The terrible waste', *New Economy*, July, pp.25-7.

Wadwani, S. (1990) 'The effects of union on productivity, growth, investment and employment: a report on some recent work', *British Journal of Industrial Relations*, vol.23, pp.371-85.

Wajcman, J. (1983) *Women in Control: The Dilemmas of a Worker's Co-operative*, Milton Keynes, Open University Press.

Walker, D.A. (1987) 'Léon Walras', pp.852-63, in Eatwell J., Milgate M. and Newman P. (eds) *The New Palgrave: A Dictionary of Economics*, London, Macmillan.

Waller, D. (1994) 'German groups reluctant to list', *Financial Times*, 21 February, p.21.

Walras, L. (1954) *Elements of Pure Economics*, George Allen & Unwin, London. (first published 1874).

Walsh, K. (1995) *Public Services and Market Mechanisms: Competition, Contracting and the New Public Management*, London, Macmillan.

Walzer, M. (1983) *Spheres of Justice: a Defence of Pluralism and Equality*, Oxford, Blackwell.

Warnock, M. (ed.) (1962) *Utilitarianism: Selections from the writings of Jeremy Bentham and John Austin*, London, Collins.

Weatherhill, L. (1986) *The Growth of the Pottery Industry in England, 1660-1815*, New York, Garland Publishing.

Weber, M. (1968) *Economy and Society*, New York, Bedminster Press (first published in English translation in 1922).

West, J. (ed.) (1982) *Women and Work in the Labour Market*, London, Routledge & Keegan Paul.

Wheelock, J. (1990) *Husbands at Home: The Domestic Economy in a Postindustrial Society*, London, Routledge.

Wheelock, J. (1994) 'Survival strategies for small business families in a peripheral local economy: a contribution to institutional value theory' in Lustiger-Thaler, H. and Salée, D. (eds) *Artful Practices: the Political Economy of Everyday Life*, Montreal, Black Rose.

Wheelock, J. and Mariussen, (eds) (1997) *Households, Work and Economic Change: A Comparative Institutional Perspective*, Boston; MA, Kluwer Academic Press.

Wheelock, J. and McCarthy, P. (1997) 'Employed mothers and their families in Britain' in Frankel, J. (ed.) *Families of Employed Mothers: An International Perspective*, New York, London, Garland.

Wheelock, J. and Oughton, E. (1996) 'The household as a focus for research' *Journal of Economic Issues*, vol.30, no.1, March, pp.143-59.

White, M. (1991) *Against Unemployment*, London, Policy Studies Institute.

Whitley, J. and Wilson, R. (1993) 'The microeconomic merits of a marginal employment subsidy', *Economics Journal*, vol.93, pp.862-80.

Wholey, D., Feldman, R. and Christianson, J. (1995) 'The effect of market structure on HMO premiums', *Journal of Health Economics*, vol.14, no.1, pp.81-105.

Williams, B. (1973) 'The idea of equality', in *Problems of the Self*, Cambridge, Cambridge University Press.

Williamson, O.E. (1964) *The Economics of Discretionary Behaviour: Management Objectives in a Theory of the Firm*, Englewood Cliffs; NJ, Prentice Hall.

Williamson, O.E. (1975) *Markets and Hierarchies: Analysis and Antitrust Implications*, New York, The Free Press.

Williamson, O.E. (1985) *The Economic Institutions of Capitalism*, New York, The Free Press.

Williamson, O.E. (1988) 'Corporate finance and corporate governance' *Journal of Finance*, no.43, pp.567-91.

Williamson, O.E. (1993) 'Calculativeness, trust, and economic organization', *Journal of Law and Economics*, vol.36, pp.453–86.

Williamson, O.E., Wachter, M. and Harris, J. (1975) 'Understanding the employment relation: the analysis of idiosyncratic exchange', *Bell Journal of Economics,* vol.6, pp.250–78.

Willman, P. (1983) 'The organizational failures framework and industrial sociology' in Francis, A., Turk, J. and Willman, P. (eds) *Power, Efficiency and Institutions,* London, Heinemann.

Winter, S.G. (1984) 'Schumpeterian competition in alternative technological regimes', *Journal of Economic Behavior and Organization*, vol.5, pp.287–320.

Womack, J.P., Jones, D.T. and Roos, D. (1990) *The Machine that Changed the World: The Triumph of Lean Production*, New York, Rawson.

Wood, A. (1995) *North South, Trade, Employment and Inequality*, Oxford, Clarendon Press

World Bank (1996) *Health Policy in Eastern Africa: A Structural Approach to Resource Allocation, Volume I, Main Report*, Eastern Africa Department, Africa Region, Nairobi, April.

Wright, E. and Ermisch, J. F. (1990) 'Male-female wage differentials in Great Britain', Department of Economics, Birkbeck College, Discussion Paper.

Wright, E. and Ermisch, J. F. (1991) 'Gender discrimination in the British labour market: a reassessment', *Economic Journal*, no.101, pp.508–22.

Yeandle, S. (1984) *Working Women's Lives*, London, Tavistock.

Zamagni, S. (1987) *Microeconomic Theory*, Oxford, Basil Blackwell.

INDEX